The CIA & Congress

The CIA & Congress

THE UNTOLD STORY FROM
TRUMAN TO KENNEDY

David M. Barrett

 University Press of Kansas

Portions of chapters 27–29 are replicated from the author's
article, "An Early 'Year of Intelligence': CIA and Congress, 1958."
Journal of Intelligence and Counterintelligence, 2004, 17 (3), with the
permission of Taylor and Francis. © 2004 Taylor and Francis.
http://www.taylorandfrancis.com.

Published by the University Press of Kansas (Lawrence, Kansas
66049), which was organized by the Kansas Board of Regents and is
operated and funded by Emporia State University, Fort Hays State
University, Kansas State University, Pittsburg State University, the
University of Kansas, and Wichita State University

Library of Congress Cataloging-in-Publication Data
Barrett, David M., 1951–
   The CIA and congress : the untold story from Truman to Kennedy / David
M. Barrett.
          p. cm.
     Includes bibliographical references and index.
     ISBN 978-0-7006-1400-4 (cloth : alk. paper)
     ISBN 978-0-7006-2525-3 (paperback : alk. paper)
     1. United States. Central Intelligence Agency—History. 2. United
States—Foreign relations—1945–1989. 3. United States. Congress.
I. Title.
     JK468.I6B38   2005
     327.12'73'009045—dc22   2005008584

British Library Cataloguing-in-Publication Data is available.

Printed in the United States of America

10 9 8 7 6 5 4 3 2 1

The paper used in this publication meets the minimum
requirements of the American National Standard for Permanence
of Paper for Printed Library Materials Z39.48-1984.

Contents

Acronyms

ADD/A	Assistant Deputy Director for Administration
A-DD/A	Assistant to the Deputy Director for Administration
AEC	Atomic Energy Commission
BOB	Bureau of the Budget
CAT	Civil Air Transport
CG	Comptroller General
CIA/DRM	CIA Declassified Reference Materials
CIG	Central Intelligence Group
COMINT	U.S. communications intelligence
CREST	CIA Records Search Tool
DD/A	Deputy Director for Administration
DD/I	Deputy Director for Intelligence
DD/S	Deputy Director for Support
ECA	Economic Cooperation Administration
FOC	first operational capability
FRUS	Department of State, *Foreign Relations of the United States*
GAO	General Accounting Office
GMIC	Guided Missile Intelligence Committee
HUAC	House Committee on Un-American Activities
ICBM	intercontinental ballistic missile
JCAE	Joint Committee on Atomic Energy
NA	National Archives
NIA	National Intelligence Authority
NRA	National Recovery Administration
NSC	National Security Council
OAS	Organization of American States
OCB	Operations Coordinating Board
ONE	Office of National Estimates
ONI	Office of Naval Intelligence
OPC	Office of Policy Coordination
ORR	Office of Research and Reports
OSO	Office of Special Operations
OSS	Office of Staff Secretary
OSS	Office of Strategic Services

PBCFIA	President's Board of Consultants on Foreign Intelligence Activities
PSB	Psychological Strategy Board
RFE	Radio Free Europe
SANSA	Special Assistant for National Security Affairs
SAS	Senate Armed Services Committee

Acknowledgments

I am delighted to thank those who helped me while I researched and wrote this book. My wonderful graduate research assistants in the Political Science Department at Villanova University since 1995 have included Jeannie Matava, Frank Pryor, David Domes, Ron Fleming, Sean Matthews, Jianhua Liu, Amy Sitnick, Surovi Abeyratne, Kelly Woody, and Ray Wasko.

A former student, Patrick Burke, has become at least as skilled and persistent an archival researcher as I am. He did research on my behalf at the Lyndon Johnson and John Kennedy presidential libraries and in the Mike Mansfield papers. Others who assisted me in archival work include Sue Kincaid, Cindy Kolski, Christina Kolski, Lisa Borowski, Kendra Gage, and Patti Woolery-Price. Bill Burr shared useful documents with me.

The staff at Villanova's Falvey Memorial Library, especially those handling interlibrary loans, has been wonderful. (I also benefited from staffers at the University of Delaware Library, who guided me to their rare microfiche holdings.) Three Political Science Department chairs, Jack Schrems, Lowell Gustafson, and Craig Wheeland, have consistently supported my work. So have the Rev. Kail Ellis, O.S.A., Dean of the College of Arts and Sciences, and Dr. Jack Johannes, Vice President for Academic Affairs at Villanova. The Office of Research and Sponsored Projects has helped me obtain external funding and granted me a Summer Research Fellowship. My Political Science Department colleague, Ann Lesch, advised me in this area as well. Margaret King and Gail Hudgins, departmental secretaries, helped me solve many problems, as did Rachel Schaller of the University Information Technologies office.

So many archivists have given me their warm and professional help over the past decade or so that I fear any attempt to mention all of them would fail. To the best of my recollection, out of the fifty or more archivists I have called on for assistance, only two were not responsive. I think that is a remarkable batting average. I called on a few such professionals so often, though, that I must thank them by name. I came to understand why John Taylor at National Archives II in College Park, Maryland, is a living legend. His knowledge, enthusiasm, and skill at putting researchers in touch with others sharing similar interests are amazing. At the Center for Legislative Archives, part of the National Archives in Washington, I have benefited from the professionalism of Richard McCulley and Ed Schamel. In the early 1990s, when I had a mere curiosity about Senator Richard Russell's relationship with the CIA, I first explored the topic at the Russell Library in Athens, Georgia. Ever since, Sheryl Vogt has been especially helpful.

The late Walter Pforzheimer was enormously obliging and entertaining in numerous personal and telephone interviews. John Warner, who later took on congressional liaison duties, was similarly generous in a lengthy personal interview and in phone conversations. I also thank William Darden, John K. Knaus, Richard Helms, Elias Demetracopoulos, and Samuel Halpern for spending time with me.

The Dirksen Congressional Center twice provided assistance to cover my research expenses. The American Political Science Association has assisted me with its Small Research Grant Program. I began writing this book at the Rockefeller Foundation's retreat in Bellagio, Italy, a beautiful and rewarding place to work.

Good friends and colleagues who helped me in a variety of ways include Alan Gibson, Max Holland, Bret Kincaid, John Foster, Michael Bridgeman, Noreen Deane-Moran, Joseph Hernandez-Kolski, Richard Valcourt, Loch Johnson, Susan Silveus, Mike Lattanzi, Marc Gallicchio, Satya Pattnayak, Stephen Knott, Irene Langran, and my siblings Edward Barrett, Stephen Barrett, Mary Louise Barrett, and Frances Coleman.

I have also come to regard the staff at the University Press of Kansas as friends. As well, I thank David Rudgers and Richard Best, who critiqued an earlier draft of this book for the press. Of the advice they offered, I decided what to follow and not follow, so any mistakes or misinterpretations herein are mine alone.

Shortly before the completion of this project, my mother, Frances S. Barrett, died. A few close friends — Cindy Kolski, Bruce Thiel, Kathleen Friesen, Marlene Spletzer, Diane Mozzone, and Bob and Eleanor Langran — saw me through the months of her final illness. My mother often rolled her eyes at Mothers' Day traditions, but she once said to me, "I don't know what I would do if I didn't have children." I knew that she was not referring just to the practical assistance that adult sons and daughters can provide. She meant especially that our relationships with her made life meaningful and pleasurable. Having her in my life was a joy. I dedicate this book to her. I also dedicate it to students I have taught over the past fifteen years. Despite my businesslike demeanor in the classroom, I have respect and great affection for them.

Introduction
First Hidden, Then Lost

"I just get no comfort out of anything that the Admiral has said to us!" The stocky, grim-faced speaker was one of the U.S. senators and representatives making up a joint committee of the U.S. Congress. In October 1949, this committee had summoned the director of central intelligence (a former rear admiral in the navy) to a secret hearing in the Capitol building. Twice-a-year recipients of estimates that the DCI and associates had produced since the Central Intelligence Agency was created two years earlier, the committee members had been stunned by the Soviet Union's first test explosion of an atomic bomb. So were others, including President Harry Truman, since the CIA had not predicted the event. Its director took a pummeling at the hearing from the angry senator and others for not having "the remotest idea" of what the Soviet Union was up to. The chairman excused the DCI after ninety minutes with a warning not to let Soviet progress on a much more powerful hydrogen bomb go similarly undetected: "It might well mean the difference between our existence as a nation and not existing."

The following year, a Democratic leader of the House of Representatives went to CIA heads and then to the president, insisting that the agency rid itself of a flamboyant homosexual who managed covert action projects. Republicans were determined to attack Truman and his agency over this, he said, putting "friends" of the CIA in an impossible situation. By week's end, the man was gone.

In 1951, Congress, which rarely had hinted at American covert operations around the world, debated an amendment that would authorize the president to spend up to $100 million on such interventions against the USSR and its Eastern European satellites. "Aiding the underground organizations that may now exist," using "refugees from behind the Iron Curtain," and "going on the offensive" were the intended results, said the amendment's sponsor. The ultimate goal of the amendment, which passed the House and Senate overwhelmingly, was "liberation" of those living under communism.

Two years later, the House Appropriations Committee's new Republican chairman hired additional staff to investigate executive branch agencies that had proliferated during twenty years of Democratic rule. After the staff examined the CIA's performance, he imposed a personnel ceiling on the agency, provoking the complaining words "arbitrary and capricious" heard at the CIA.

Late in 1958, the Central Intelligence Agency's legislative counsel began counting how often his superiors appeared on Capitol Hill annually. There had been thirty informal sessions, mostly with individual legislators, so far that year, and two dozen hearings held by fifteen committees or subcommittees. Five concerned the CIA's failure to anticipate the overthrow of Iraq's pro-U.S. government, thereby heightening instability in Lebanon and provoking an American military intervention there. "Our intelligence was just plain lousy" about Iraq, said one of the scores of legislators who complained publicly about the CIA's performance. By year's end, the chairmen of the House Appropriations and Armed Services Committees had appointed trusted younger colleagues as chairs to energize their CIA subcommittees' performance.

Early in 1960, following over a year of off-and-on private and sometimes angry interactions with intelligence leaders, a senator charged publicly that intelligence estimates had been "juggled so that the budget books may be balanced." An economy-minded President Dwight Eisenhower had (the senator said) intentionally downplayed grave intelligence estimates about growing Soviet nuclear war fighting capabilities.

Through the rest of the year and into early 1961's new presidency and Congress, some legislators agitated for the overthrow of Cuba's Fidel Castro. The United States "would be committing suicide in allowing any unfriendly regime in Cuba," which would establish "military bases of the Soviet universal empire 90 miles away from our shoreline," said a powerful House member. Privately, a senator stressed to the DCI that there should not "be any appeasement shown to Castro, no softness of any kind." The DCI and four assistants soon went before eight members of a House subcommittee and their staff assistant. After the director's usual warning — "this is very classified"—he described plans for what would later be known as Bay of Pigs. No representative advised against secretly invading Cuba, but some questioned whether "a force of 1,000, however well-trained, would be able to hold … a sizeable enough piece of Cuban real estate."

No history of the Central Intelligence Agency's early Cold War relations with the branch of government substantially responsible for its creation — the U.S. Congress — has ever been published.[1] (In-house CIA historians produced such a volume, but the U.S. government has yet to declassify it, implausibly claiming that it might harm the nation's security. The government still keeps tens of thousands of pages of CIA documents from the 1940s and 1950s secret.) Since the Constitution specifies that Congress must appropriate every dollar that executive branch agencies may spend, the nation's legislature has always asserted the right to monitor those bureaucracies' performance. The first such instance was a House committee's 1792 investigation of the U.S. Army, following a calamitous battle with a Native American nation.

Nonetheless, congressional oversight of agencies has been a "variable phenomenon," as one pair of scholars politely worded it, across American history.[2] Whether legislators monitored the CIA during the Truman and Eisenhower presidencies has been particularly doubted by knowledgeable persons. Some have suggested to me that a history of congressional oversight of the CIA during those years would surely be a thin volume. Their skepticism is perfectly understandable. Stories that circulate about that era's treatment of the CIA by Congress tell only of deference:

- An agency administrator recalled the "story" of securing money in a mid-1950s hearing for a new CIA headquarters. A House committee chairman told DCI Allen Dulles, "You probably are going to ask us for about $25 million." The director responded, "Mr. Chairman, we're going to ask you for $50 million." With a deep southern drawl, the chairman replied, "My, my, that is going to be a nice building."
- In 1956, when the Senate debated a resolution that would create a joint House-Senate intelligence committee, a CIA subcommittee's ranking Republican faced questions about the efficacy of his oversight. He spoke words that have endured in many a history book: "The difficulty in connection with asking questions and obtaining information is that we might obtain information which I personally would rather not have, unless it was essential for me as a Member of Congress to have it."
- In the mid-1970s, a much-publicized Senate committee investigated alleged abuse of powers by the CIA. Convinced that Congress needed to monitor the agency aggressively, it found that in prior decades oversight had been "more perfunctory than rigorous."

Such accounts, though, convey only part of the reality of the struggles of the CIA and Congress with each other and against a widely perceived and feared Soviet threat.[3]

Some authors have described Congress and the CIA in the years since the mid-1970s, when the House and Senate created and sustained large intelligence committees with extensive staffs. But the story of Capitol Hill and the agency during the early Cold War years is a history that was initially hidden and later lost. From the start, heads of congressional subcommittees on the CIA insisted even more strongly than agency leaders that their hearings be shrouded in secrecy. They succeeded. Later, the records that members of Congress created concerning the CIA — limited as they were — became dispersed around the country and effectively lost. Situated in typically large collections, they became proverbial needles in haystacks.

Many records of congressional interactions with the agency were destroyed. The papers of the late Georgia Democrat Carl Vinson, who headed the House Armed Services Committee and was one of the CIA's important early overseers, do not exist. He apparently had them burned. Similarly, at the National Archives, there is nothing approaching a decent accumulation of his committee's papers from those years. And that era's papers of the House Appropriations Committee? Nonexistent.

A related problem is the understandably widespread tendency of legislators and CIA officers in those days not to document critical business. Having spent innumerable days exploring the papers of dead members of Congress and the considerable (if censored) declassified CIA papers, I have found violations of this tradition — a representative's handwritten notes of Dulles's briefings, another's notes about one year's CIA budget (still classified as "Top Secret" a half-century later), a subcommittee's transcript of a discussion of covert action, etc. On such occasions, I have sent heartfelt thanks to those late officials.

The secret and usually informal interactions of the CIA and legislators from 1947 to 1961's Bay of Pigs crisis were the darkest years of intelligence oversight's dark ages. Still, those mostly unchronicled encounters illustrated two dilemmas that confront any democratic nation in a dangerous world: First, if the government is not open about its functioning, citizens cannot know if agencies are performing with competence, incompetence, or even mendacity. Many a member of Congress shared the worry of a colleague who warned in the late 1940s about "the establishment of a Gestapo in the United States by which people may be hounded and harassed." Yet, in a menacing world, even a democratic government must shield information about its military and intelligence capabilities, as well as its knowledge of other countries' secrets.

Second, as George Washington suggested in his Farewell Address, a "novel" U.S. foreign policy guided by "exalted justice" could inspire other nations and someday transform the world. A century and a half later, though, the superpower United States was increasingly vulnerable to annihilation. A commission secretly advised President Eisenhower, "If the United States is to survive, long-standing American concepts of 'fair play' must be reconsidered. We must develop effective espionage and counterespionage services and must learn to subvert, sabotage and destroy our enemies by more clever, more sophisticated, and more effective methods than those used against us."[4]

Unless the world evolves into a collection of peaceable democracies, or at least an arena free of aggression, the two dilemmas will not disappear for the United States. An imperfect solution exists, though: direction and oversight of powerful, secretive bureaucracies by elected officials. The Constitution gives the president such "executive power." Citizens may hope that the president knows the CIA's most important secrets and that only with his approval does it operate in foreign nations. Since Congress passes the laws that create, direct, and fund such organizations, it has a constitutional right and obligation to monitor them, as well.

Part One

The Truman Era: 1947–1952

No "American Gestapo," But "No More Pearl Harbors"

"The proposed agency has all the potentialities of an American Gestapo," thundered Edward Robertson (R-WY) to fellow senators in the summer of 1947. His fears about a proposed Central Intelligence Agency were not unique in Congress and resided even in President Harry Truman's mind. Nonetheless Congress would pass the National Security Act that July and the Central Intelligence Agency Act two years later, designating some CIA roles and purposefully leaving others vague. Robertson's fears would be trumped by five-and-a-half-year-old memories of Pearl Harbor and the potential for future disasters in the new Cold War.

Many legislators believed in the late 1940s that the dispersion of intelligence in scattered military/diplomatic bureaucracies in 1941 had caused a "total lack of knowledge of those forces that were marshaling to destroy American democracy," as Frank Wilson (D-TX) told the House of Representatives. In the Senate's 1947 deliberations, Chan Gurney (R-SD), chair of the Armed Services Committee, warned, "It is not being an alarmist to point out that, with the development of supersonic planes and guided missiles with atomic warheads . . . hostilities will be initiated without prior warning. . . . to procrastinate is to invite disaster." Therefore, most legislators concluded that the United States needed to centralize intelligence obtained by diverse bureaucracies in order to craft the best possible analyses and estimates for the president and his advisers.[1]

Drafts of the National Security Act emerging in the spring and summer of 1947 said little about functions of the CIA but specified that the agency would take on roles previously carried out by the Central Intelligence Group (CIG) — an ineffectual bureaucracy created by Truman after he abolished the powerful World War II–era Office of Strategic Services (OSS). As well, the director of central intelligence (DCI) heading the old CIG would keep the same title and would at the same time head the CIA and be responsible for centralizing intelligence produced by varied bureaucratic sources. In addition, the act's Section 202 specified that the agency would perform "other functions and duties" as directed by those leaders.[2]

The initiative for creating the CIA lay partially in the fact that the Central

Intelligence Group had not been constituted by a legislative process and lacked legal authority for some of its ongoing pursuits. This frustrated CIG leaders, while many at the White House and in venerable foreign policy departments saw the CIG's reputation flounder as world politics grew more menacing. After struggles over possible legislation in 1946, Secretary of State George Marshall and others from the War and Navy Departments making up the National Intelligence Authority (NIA) acted with White House approval in directing the departing DCI, General Hoyt Vandenberg (who was to become air force chief of staff and who would be replaced by Rear Admiral Roscoe Hillenkoetter), to draft revised legislative language early in 1947. In working with his staff on innumerable drafts early in the year, Vandenberg took part in dozens of meetings about or with members of Congress.[3]

Committee Action

The Senate Armed Services Committee and the House Committee on Expenditures in the Executive Departments worked secretly from spring through early summer in crafting the act, which would also create the National Security Council (NSC), the National Military Establishment (renamed the Department of Defense in 1949), and other agencies. On Capitol Hill and in the press, the proposed "unification" of the military far overshadowed intelligence issues. Also, the act was hardly the only important legislation addressed by the committees in 1947. Expenditures dealt with other government reorganization bills, while Armed Services would hold forty-seven open hearings and twenty-three "executive sessions" that year.

Of the questions the committees faced in deliberating creation of a Central Intelligence Agency, some concerned the narrow interests of existing intelligence bureaucracies, but others were troublesome and profound: How could Congress create a powerful foreign intelligence agency that would not meddle in, or be drawn into, domestic affairs? Assuming it spied and otherwise gathered information abroad and then organized its presentation to political leaders at home, what else should the agency do? To what extent should U.S. military intelligence units influence the CIA? What should the DCI's role be? How should Congress fund the agency year to year? Should congressional leaders or other members, representing the public, know the agency's darkest secrets? Could Congress ensure an intelligence bureaucracy's competence?

From the beginning, Walter Pforzheimer, the CIG's (and then the CIA's) legislative liaison, knew that it would not be smooth sailing through the committees. Although the House Expenditures Committee initiated National Security Act hearings in April, a threat loomed from the Rules Committee, which controlled virtually all proposed bills' chances for a floor vote. On May 29, Pforzheimer informed Hillenkoetter that Rules chairman Leo Allen (IL) had said that his fellow Republican leaders viewed the bill as too controversial. "Current thinking is to let the measure ride for this session and not bring it up," Allen had told Pforzheimer. Still, the liaison learned that Expenditures chairman Clare Hoffman (MI) was "perfectly willing to go ahead with the hearings and report out a measure," so the bill was not dead.

From April through June, recurring fears of a dangerously powerful CIA emerged in Hoffman's committee. The chairman, as one writer has noted, "had no previous military service, no seat on any committee dealing with military matters, and no major military installations in his district. In addition, he had been a strong pre-war isolationist, with little apparent interest in foreign or military affairs. . . . The strong civilian orientation of the committee's responsibilities generated concerns ignored in the upper house and overlooked by proponents of the legislation: the question of civil liberties."

> I talked this morning with Congressman James Wadsworth (R-NY) [wrote Pforzheimer in his work diary in late spring]. . . . I told him we were somewhat concerned regarding the feeling of certain members of the Committee and some witnesses appearing before it that we were or might become an incipient Gestapo, or interested in domestic intelligence of any sort. I told him that we were considering addressing a letter to the Chairman, suggesting that a provision be included in the bill . . . prohibiting any police or internal security or law enforcement powers.[4]

Around the same time that Pforzheimer, legal counsel Lawrence Houston, and DCI Vandenberg worked on that, Senate Armed Services chairman Gurney partnered with Pforzheimer to get Section 202 through his committee and to the floor. Pforzheimer had earlier noted in his diary a conference with the senator and Vandenberg on a hearing to be held by the large committee (newly created out of the old Naval Affairs and Military Affairs Committees):

> Gurney requested that the Director place as much material on the record as possible, testifying in this manner for 30 minutes. He agreed to shut off any

embarrassing questions from the floor, and to inform the Committee that there could be an executive session with the Director, if further questioning was desired. Possibility of appointing a subcommittee was considered, in view of the Chairman's statement that at least two of the Committee members were leaks to [newspaper columnist] Drew Pearson. The Chairman assured the Director of all possible support.

This was key, as was that of the Senate Armed Services' ranking Democrat, Millard Tydings (MD). Not every committee member was on board, though. After the session with Gurney, Vandenberg sought out Styles Bridges (NH), chairman of the Appropriations Committee and the second most senior Republican on Armed Services. Bridges, an off-and-on pal of Drew Pearson, had "made some adverse comments" at a recent hearing, Pforzheimer noted. Why, Bridges wondered, had a French newspaper accurately reported that Admiral Hillenkoetter, who had just visited Paris, was about to become director of central intelligence? And why did the French newspaper say that CIG controlled "all secret foreign intelligence"? American newspapers had hardly mentioned this.

Bridges would insist on answers about Hillenkoetter's apparent publicity-seeking. Less shrewd and influential in the Senate than the Appropriations chair was Armed Services' Gurney. A one-time radio pioneer in South Dakota, he had done statewide play-by-play broadcasts of high school basketball tournaments for years. Though from a historically isolationist region, the Republican dared to be internationalist — before, during, and after World War II. Pforzheimer thought Gurney was "priceless" in working to create the CIA, if sometimes oblivious to people around him. On a couple of occasions, Pforzheimer observed Gurney treating General Dwight Eisenhower in too familiar a fashion — backslapping and coming out with "Hi, Ike!" — something the general hated.[5]

Pforzheimer learned of Gurney's limitations again when Armed Services deliberations turned to the CIA section in late May. The liaison recorded in his diary that Gurney "was 'holding his breath' on Section 202 of the National Security Act, which was coming up for discussion and decision this morning. He stated that General Donovan had been very active on the Hill in opposition to Section 202." Despite communicating with the former OSS head, Gurney mistakenly thought William "Wild Bill" Donovan opposed authorizing the new CIA to carry out espionage, counterintelligence, and covert operations. Pforzheimer patiently read with Gurney "several paragraphs from Donovan's memorandum which specifically states that clan-destine operations should be placed in the Central Intelligence Agency, and in no other departments of the government."[6]

DCI Vandenberg's initial committee testimony at this stage of events, only partially released to the press, seems to have been crucial for legislators. He told the House and Senate committees in identical prepared statements, "All intelligence is not sinister, nor is it an invidious type of work." However, he added, "I know you gentlemen understand that the nature of some of the work we are doing makes it undesirable — from the security standpoint — to discuss certain activities with too much freedom. . . . I therefore ask your indulgence — and through you the indulgence of the people — to limit my remarks on the record."

Still, his prepared remarks presciently addressed the problems of unifying American intelligence. "There must be coordination and some centraliza-tion," he warned the committees, "so that no future congressional commit-tee can possibly ask the question asked by the Pearl Harbor Committee: 'Why, with some of the finest intelligence available in our history — why was it pos-sible for a Pearl Harbor to occur?'" In the early days of World War II, "we had to rely blindly and trustingly on the superior intelligence system of the British," but the United States "should never again have to go hat in hand, begging any foreign government for the eyes — the foreign intelligence — with which to see." Nor should the CIA be hostage to the individual military or civilian departments of government: "It must be objective, and it must transcend the exclusive competence of any one department." Since the war had ended, it was no longer easy to recruit "a great number of extremely intel-ligent, widely experienced, able men." It would remain difficult, he told the two committees, until the CIA could offer applicants the chance for solid careers. This could only happen after "the will of Congress is made known."[7]

Only portions of Vandenberg's Senate Armed Services testimony were ever declassified, though it appears that questions went well beyond vague intelligence generalities. On the House side, there were twenty days of open testimony, mostly on other aspects of the National Security Act, but Expen-ditures chairman Hoffman decided in June to hold an additional day of secret testimony featuring Vandenberg, his rivals in military intelligence, and others. Hoffman also planned to have the hearing transcribed, but this wor-ried some members, since (as Ohio Republican Clarence Brown said) "someone" might be interested in getting it. The committee accepted the suggestion of Representative Chet Holifield (D-CA) that a "code name or number" be used in the transcript instead of the actual names of those testifying. With that business agreed upon, "Mr. A" (Vandenberg) presented himself in Room 1501 of the New House Office Building for questions.

Wadsworth asked Vandenberg if there was or soon would be "employment of new groups of agents." He had broached a sensitive topic: committee leaders and executive branch figures had held private discussions about espionage and other covert work to be done by the agency, but committee hearings had barely touched on them. The DCI decided to give a lesson:

> The way it works is that you have an expert in the clandestine field, or as near an expert as the United States has, and who we can hire for the money that we can pay. He goes out. . . . They go to a certain locality and live in that locality and build up an acquaintance and then know the politics and the intrigue that is going on in that nation. They pick a man, after very careful study with records back here . . . and they start him as a nucleus. He then builds a chain of people that he knows.
>
> Then, we have to have another man picked, in whom we have full confidence, who builds a chain alongside, who is just watching him. Then you have to keep these two people and their reports to make sure that this man is not giving you information and receiving pay from a foreign government. Then, this man who has established this is pushed out in front here, and he then has a contact back with what we call the letter box or the place through which we got this information; and the man who originally set up the net ostensibly has no connection with any person or any department of the government. That is what we term a "cut-out."

Hoffman and colleagues wondered if Vandenberg assumed that U.S. intelligence officers could not be deceived in such dealings: "We can be deceived," he responded, "and we can have infiltration within our ranks. . . . however, when it happens to us with this cut-out, this man who is the man who is in contact with this, is told that if he gets into trouble, we wash our hands of it. For that reason, his pay has got to be fairly good, because his throat is cut and we wash our hands of him, and we say we know nothing about him."

Knowing that some military intelligence leaders wanted to ensure the continued usage of a mysterious, semiautonomous intelligence-gathering organization that had served Army Intelligence since World War II, the DCI also warned the committee about the hazards of relying on such an "inefficient . . . commercial concern." Vandenberg and other CIG leaders despised the group, having read its "intelligence reports" produced by supposed "agents" worldwide. About this, John McCormack (D-MA) asked, "Who would the contractee be?" The DCI spared no sarcasm: "Some chap who comes into the office and tells you that he can get some companies lined up . . . and he has already got agents in these companies and he is paying them, and he would be very glad if you would give him $500,000 a year." Of course, Vandenberg said, "many people who were on this gravy train will object," but a "Director of Central Intelligence, who is responsible in the final analysis for good foreign intelligence, has got to get more for his money." (Largely because of pressure from Styles Bridges and others on Capitol Hill, the shadowy no-name agency would have its contract continued for years.)

Clarence Brown — conservative, genial, large, and described in print as "the 1947 Smelt Eating Champion of the House of Representatives" — leaned toward specifying the roles of the CIA. In previous open hearings, the Republican had hectored navy secretary James Forrestal: "I am not interested in setting up here in the United States any particular central policy agency under any President — and I do not care what his name may be — and just allow him to have a Gestapo of his own." Ought not Congress "fix some limitations on what the power of this individual [the DCI] might be," he asked, so that the "rights of the citizen may be protected?" Forrestal mostly evaded the question. In the closed hearing, Vandenberg suggested to Brown that Congress, except for writing language that would prevent the agency from becoming a Gestapo, "let this thing grow in the hands of people who are primarily interested in getting this intelligence." But members of Congress, "as representatives of the people, have a duty and a responsibility to guarantee the protection of . . . their rights and privileges under the Constitution," Brown reminded him, adding: "We are supposed to say what an agency of the government can do." Vandenberg sympathized, but said, "I do not think we can do that today."

One Expenditures member had suggested to colleagues during Vandenberg's appearance that the DCI "be allowed to sit here all day, if he so desires," to hear military intelligence witnesses, but Chairman Hoffman refused: "There are some witnesses who just will not testify as they would if somebody were here."[8] This was an understatement. Some Army Intelligence (G-2) and other leaders preferred that there be no CIA at all; Pforzheimer and others at CIG soon wondered, Did they suggest as much to the Committee? Or did they advocate creating a CIA so weak — not permitted to carry out foreign espionage, for example — as to be no more effective than the CIG? Pforzheimer pondered how he might find out.

The legislative liaison energetically served the exiting DCI Vandenberg and the new director Hillenkoetter with his political antennae in Washington. A Yale graduate and politically shrewd, he knew that some of the legislators he interacted with would eventually go on to greater things, though it was impossible to know which ones. In July 1947, Pforzheimer wrote in his diary, "Received call from Rep. John Kennedy . . . who stated that he was interested in the size of our Personnel Division, and that he was somewhat concerned by the possible lack of qualifications of various people. . . . Told him I would look into the matter." Hillenkoetter, though, "indicated that the information is classified and should not be made available. . . . he will stand behind anyone who has been appointed." For weeks, the young JFK insisted to Pforzheimer on knowing "background information on ten individuals." It was apparent, Pforzheimer wrote, "that the information is being leaked to Congressman Kennedy by a former OSS employee, [name deleted]." Whether the DCI ever agreed to the representative's inquiry is unrecorded.

Similarly, Pforzheimer could not have known what lay ahead when he informed "the office of Rep. Lyndon B. Johnson . . . re application of a [name deleted]" for a CIA job that "there is no vacancy for him." Legislators made scores of such employment requests each year. All were politely handled, but some — like a telephone call from House Appropriations chair John Taber (NY) — received extra attention: the assistant deputy director for administration, L. K. "Red" White, would write in his diary later in the Truman presidency, "I told Mr. Pforzheimer to insure that the applicant received every possible consideration and that he was not to be turned down without my knowledge."

The liaison had generally good relations with members of Congress and their staffs. Sometimes, legislators were desperate for his assistance. When Florida's Democratic senator Claude Pepper would be derided during his 1950 reelection campaign as soft on communism for having spoken favorably about the Soviet government while visiting Moscow in 1945, he would realize that he had little record of his remarks there. Pforzheimer wrote in his diary of a call from an assistant to "Pepper, requesting copy of the Senator's speech made in Moscow in 1945." The liaison informed him that CIA "did not have a copy of it." Whenever possible, though, Pforzheimer served CIG/CIA interests by doing all that he could for legislators. Sometimes it was information ("talked with Senator Gurney, who requested CIA's opinion as to Russian reaction should the Americans try to run a train or armored column to Berlin"); often it was other favors (after "a request from the office of

Congressman Sasscer . . . furnished him with a two-minute text for a radio appearance").

In this and other ways, Pforzheimer made himself valuable to his superiors. Giving them advice about the political landscape of Capitol Hill was almost a daily part of his job, as in spring 1947 when he warned Hillenkoetter "that certain people in the State Department had indicated that they felt that General Vandenberg had knifed the State Department intelligence setup in his testimony before the House Appropriations Committee, and that therefore the Director might . . . receive a knifing in return before the Senate Appropriations Committee."[9]

In July, to learn about the military intelligence testimony, Pforzheimer befriended a bartender at a hotel where two of the testifiers gathered to discuss political strategies vis-à-vis the Expenditures Committee. To protect themselves, they spoke only in French. But so did the bartender, to the delight of Pforzheimer, who picked up useful information. The liaison then used his relationship with Carl Hoffman, a committee staffer and son of the chairman. Only one copy of the closed hearing's transcript existed, and the chairman kept it in his office safe. Pforzheimer found Carl — a fellow bachelor who lived with his father in an environment of no smoking, no drinking, and not much fun — a great bore. For purely political reasons, Pforzheimer had spent some evenings with him. After one rule-breaking night on the town, Pforzheimer recalls, "I finally decided to pull in my chips. I said, 'Carl, the Chairman's got a transcript, and I need to see it!' And Carl produced it for me long enough to run back and make a copy before returning it to him."

Pforzheimer and others at CIG discovered from the transcript that committee members could hold their own against the legislation's critics. Peter Vischer, an aggressive former G-2 leader who had previously advised the old House Military Affairs Committee on intelligence issues, said CIG was getting "clogged up" because its people were "bored with dissemination, and they want to be in this spy business." Vischer envisioned the CIA "correlating" intelligence, but told Congressman W. J. Bryan Dorn (D-SC), "I oppose the collecting." The same official could not "correlate, evaluate, and also engage in operations."

Committee members hit Vischer with critical questions, though. How, Walter Judd (R-MN) asked, could a DCI protect intelligence sources and methods (as the act required) "that are not under his control?" To Vischer's prescriptions for an elaborate intelligence establishment with no strong centralized authority, Judd noted that it would involve "more rival organizations."

Porter Hardy (D-VA) criticized Vischer for promoting "operational" details that the committee "could not possibly write in this bill." And, on one point, Judd told Vischer, "Your report is wrong."

Pforzheimer learned from the transcript that additional witnesses in the closed House Expenditures hearing opposed creating a strong CIA. Colonel John "Frenchy" Grombach, who had been an independent-minded military intelligence leader during World War II, did so on the basis of self-described "horse sense" and on the relative success of the FBI and the War Department in handling intelligence collection. General Hayes Kroner, just retired from G-2, said, "It would be unwise to empower the Central Intelligence Authority to overburden itself with operations, particularly collection operations, which takes our thought and time, is romantic, takes a lot of activity, is the most exciting part of intelligence, takes a lot of running, which would take their eye off their main strategic mission." But Kroner could not clearly articulate that mission.

The military intelligence leaders also warned committee members about the National Security Act's vague language. General Merrit Edson of the Marine Corps noted that "nowhere in the provisions of the bill are the functions of the Agency defined." John McCormack challenged him: "Do you not recognize that the CIA might have a lot of duties to perform in connection with national security that could only be properly covered by a broad delineation of powers as distinguished from a detailed one?" McCormack had faith "that those who are in charge are doing what they ought to do for the country. I would not want to know all about it."[10]

Nonetheless, the military intelligence leaders had highlighted a few important questions, among them, Should the DCI be a military person, and should the military intelligence services and the CIA be protected from dominance by each other? The answers would be "possibly" and "yes," though those answers were not to be easily achieved.

In the closed hearing, Expenditures members also heard a vivid warning on the bureaucratic politics that the CIA might run into. Rear Admiral Thomas Inglis, chief of Naval Intelligence, said, "There is a lot of professional jealousy between one outfit and another. . . . the relations between G-2 and OSS were miserable. You would have thought that one was the enemy, rather than the Germans and the Japanese." But this demonstrated to many committee members the need for a strong CIA, headed by a properly empowered DCI. "I have never seen a hydra-headed organization which functions as well as one headed by a single man," said Judd.

Most importantly, Pforzheimer discovered from the purloined transcript that little damage control was required, since the military intelligence leaders had encountered tough Expenditures members. The "very, very bitter fight" — Pforzheimer's words — for the committee's favor was at an end within days of the closed hearing. (While the Pforzheimer-Hoffman affair set an unfortunate precedent for a new organization that was supposed to be entirely apart from American politics, it was the CIA's copy of the Expenditures transcript that survived. Decades later, when Congress sought evidence of how it had created the CIA, the Expenditures' successor committee learned that its original transcript had been destroyed and had to borrow the CIA's copy.)[11]

Well before the two committees would vote, their members understood that part of the agency's "gathering" function would be done by spies, and that this complicated and dangerous mission would not easily be monitored by Congress. In the Armed Services hearings, none of the twelve members (not even Bridges, who withdrew what he called his "prejudice" against CIG, which denied giving any information about Hillenkoetter to the French press) questioned the necessity of this CIA function. Nor was much concern apparent on the Expenditures Committee.

The committees also approved language that would be open to vastly different interpretations in the future. The CIA was mandated to "perform, for the benefit of the existing intelligence agencies, such additional services of common concern as the National Security Council determines can be more efficiently accomplished centrally" and — more vaguely — to perform "such other functions and duties related to intelligence affecting the national security as the National Security Council may from time to time direct." The earlier language reflected a belief that certain services like foreign broadcasts' interpretation, transcriptions, and dissemination could best be handled by a single agency. The latter language has resisted authoritative interpretation. Defenders of the CIA, including many members of Congress, have interpreted it to mean that the agency can do most anything that the president directs, unless it is specifically forbidden by the Constitution or (possibly) by other laws. Others have found the congressional language dangerously nonspecific, leading to questionable activities — e.g., attempts to overthrow governments, assassinate foreign leaders, or influence domestic organizations.[12]

At the CIA, legal counsel Lawrence Houston would be a central interpreter of congressional will. Houston's understanding of congressional leaders' statements in off-the-record encounters in 1947 led him to suggest that, at a minimum, the Appropriations committees would want to be informed at least in general terms about covert operations. The interpretive difficulties arose partly because the Truman administration decided, with the permission of harried Armed Services and Expenditures committee leaders, to postpone detailed treatment of the CIA's roles and functions to a later bill.[13]

A strong sense emerged during the weeks of the 1947 hearings that only a handful of legislative leaders should know much about secrets gathered, intelligence estimates, covert operations, and funding levels of the CIA. That view derived from legislators' experiences in World War II and with the Central Intelligence Group. During the war, only a very few of them had known of the Manhattan Project, which created the atomic bomb. In fact, for most of the war, Roosevelt administration leaders persuaded them to appropriate over a billion dollars for the purported critically important project while knowing almost nothing about it. Eventually, Clarence Cannon (D-MO), then House Appropriations chair, and others insisted on knowing particulars of the program. Late in the war, he and four other legislators toured Oak Ridge, Tennessee, where the bomb was being created, and asked a number of questions, the most urgent of which had to do with protecting the secrecy of the project. Congressional knowledge of OSS operations were similarly minimal. Senator Harry Truman's own Special Committee to Investigate the National Defense had accepted Roosevelt administration warnings and not investigated OSS's performance.[14]

CIG leaders had found it difficult to secure appropriations without meeting too many members of Congress. Some legislators were equally displeased about this. In winter-spring 1947, even as efforts to create a CIA began, Appropriations heads began crafting a Fiscal Year 1948 CIG budget. One House Appropriations hearing with Vandenberg occurred in February — "2 o'clock Monday, 10th, Full Committee Room, House Wing, across from barber shop," one CIG leader noted. In April, an assistant informed Secretary of State Marshall of another meeting on financing CIG:

> You will be met at the House door of the Capitol Building by a member of Mr. Taber's staff. Those members of Congress who will be present at the hearing will be the Chairmen and ranking minority members of the full Appropriations Committee of the House and of the Navy, War, and State Department Subcommittees. Mr. Taber requests that you bring a very limited number of people with you — one or two was the figure suggested. The . . . meeting is being held in the State Department Subcommittee room rather than in Mr. Taber's office in an attempt to avoid notice by the press.

Months later, Taber told Marshall that he had had to deal with twenty-six people in securing CIG's 1948 appropriation of just under $40 million (which would ultimately fund the CIA's first year of operation). The secretary of state and colleagues on the NIA agreed with the Appropriations chair: regarding all but the administrative part of the CIG/CIA budget, "knowledge of that fund and an accounting of it" should be "confined to a very few congressional leaders."[15]

As leaders grappled with such oversight problems, newspapers reported, not entirely inaccurately, that the CIG had usurped clandestine intelligence functions from the military and was replacing skillful and experienced military spies with amateurish civilian ones. This provoked a chorus of congressional complaints, but navy secretary Forrestal seemed to speak for others on the NIA, indicating "he did not see how answers could be given to unfavorable publicity . . . due to security reasons." Members of the NIA agreed that they should write a detailed joint letter addressed only to Chairman Hoffman stating, "These charges are not true." Further, they authorized Hillenkoetter to contact publishers of the critical newspapers to convey that answer. This response to charges in the press and Congress — contacting a crucial committee chair and a few press elites — foreshadowed the future.[16]

In facing questions of congressional funding and knowledge of secretive CIA activities, Truman administration leaders confronted nearly intractable tensions between democratic practice and concerns for the nation's security. So had the committees working on the National Security Act. A surplus of "experts," some genuine, were ready to offer remedies, though. Allen Dulles, formerly of the OSS, advised Expenditures (as he had Armed Services) that the CIA should have "exclusive jurisdiction to carry out secret intelligence operations," "its own appropriations" supplemented by those from the new Defense Department "in order to carry on certain special operations," and access to "all intelligence information relating to foreign countries . . . including 'Magic,'" as he and others called signals intelligence.

Americans "who have no official connection with the government," meaning business executives, professors, and "Americans of all types and descriptions," would likely furnish "a high percentage of the valuable intelligence" acquired by the new CIA, Dulles said. "I imagine that would not be excluded by the terms of your bill." Carter Manasco, Expenditures' ranking Democrat, responded (and others agreed), "As to collecting information on our own nationals, we do not want that done, but I do not think the Committee has any objection to their going to any source of information that our nationals might have on foreign operations." Dulles — who had misleadingly described himself to the committee as having "no government connections," and was working hard for the creation of a strong CIA, free of military domination — seemingly assented to this. About fears of the agency becoming active in domestic politics or violating American civil liberties, he added, "I do not think there is any real danger of that."

Most committee members suspected, correctly, that Soviet spies were trying to learn about American atomic research, military capabilities, and intelligence operations. The legislators knew, too, that some in government haphazardly kept secrets. Therefore, while committee leaders envisioned having a few legislators monitor the CIA on behalf of Congress, they agreed with Dulles and administration leaders that secrecy took priority over openness.

Without fully realizing it, legislators on the committees in 1947 were crafting not just a CIA, but an elite model of legislative oversight, since most members of Congress would learn almost nothing of agency activities. Critics would later charge that this was a sell-out of democratic governance. Those creating the CIA, however, thought they were preserving a democratic nation with such extreme secrecy.

Ultimately, CIG leaders, backed by the White House, won the overwhelming agreement of the committees that a CIA was necessary. Threats from the House Rules Committee to block floor consideration of the National Security Act evaporated. The Armed Services Committee approved the act on June 12, followed by the Expenditures Committee on July 1.[17]

Floor Debate

On Monday, July 7, 1947, following a national three-day holiday weekend, the act went before the Senate. Important as the legislation was, it hardly dominated national news coverage — newspapers paid far more attention that day and the next to reports of "flying saucer" sightings in Washington, DC, and in thirty-nine states. "Disks Soar over New York," reported the *Times*. Chan Gurney ignored the hysteria and assured colleagues that "every paragraph, every sentence, every phrase" of the National Security Act had been "carefully weighed." Because of much-lobbied controversy over bringing the military services under a single department, the CIA figured little in the debate. However, a familiar concern arose: Senator Robertson charged that the CIA "would be an invaluable asset to militarism." The act, by permitting the appointment of a military leader as DCI, made such a choice almost inevitable, he thought. But few other senators showed an interest in this or other CIA-related issues, thereby accepting Gurney's view of the National Security Act that they ought to "hurry it along into law." It won approval on July 12.[18]

The House, too, quickly took up the legislation. Chairman Hoffman and Manasco agreed on the floor that the committee "did its best" on the bill's CIA language. Still, said Hoffman, "we had a great deal of doubt when we finished whether we were right or not." The most heated debate about the CIA concerned the "American Gestapo" risk. According to one scenario, a future military leader, as DCI, might misuse the agency or might fall under the influence of higher-ranking officers who would force the DCI to violate its charter. Congressman Walter Judd said, "If a one-star general is Director of Intelligence, and a two-star general or a three-star general talks to him, it is wholly unrealistic to imagine that they will not have influence over him, despite the law."

No legislator expressed fear of civilian presidents or DCIs using the agency for improper or illegal activities. Indeed, for half a dozen House debaters on July 19, the model of an ideal DCI was a person who would later personify violations of democratic virtues. Said Judd of a hypothetical future DCI, "He ought to take it as J. Edgar Hoover has taken the FBI job — make it his life's work."[19]

Manasco told the House that Section 202 on the CIA "was the most difficult section to write," and then warned against a proposed amendment which would have required a civilian DCI. "Eventually" some civilian would be qualified, he said. In the meantime, the nation was stuck with Hillenkoetter: "We do not have any man in the United States who has adequate training today to do this kind of work because unfortunately the United States has never gone in for the right kind of intelligence." Manasco also claimed to be handicapped by the dangers of speaking publicly about this: "The things we say here today, the language we change, might endanger the lives of some American citizens in the future."[20]

Across town, the secretary of state agreed. A note-taker recorded on June 26 that "Marshall stated he was still troubled by the debates in Congress over the allotment of money for intelligence activities, and further, it was his opinion that the allotment of funds for intelligence activities should be appropriated in a lump sum and controlled by one person." House Appropriations chair Taber endorsed this idea, he said.

Ultimately, the House bill (approved on July 19 by overwhelming voice vote) required a civilian DCI, thus overturning Expenditures' recommendation, but did not subject the CIA to detailed financial regulations. A characteristic explanation came from Expenditures member Forest Harness (R-IN): "When such an organization was first proposed, I confess I had some fear and doubt about it. Along with other members of the committee, I insisted that the scope and authority of this agency be carefully defined and limited. . . . Now, however, I am convinced that such an agency as we are now considering is essential to our national security." In a conference committee, senators from Armed Services faced counterparts from House Expenditures who had put language in Section 202 to outlaw domestic activities for the CIA. The agency was to have "no police, subpoena, law enforcement powers, or internal security functions." The senators concurred but won agreement from representatives that the DCI could come from civilian or military life.

More broadly, members emphasized their intent to preserve the military services' intelligence units. The CIA's most important tasks, they agreed, would be to gather, coordinate, analyze, and present foreign intelligence to the president and others on the National Security Council. Such estimates ought to be crafted with the nation's security in mind, not the interests of any civilian or military bureaucracy. DCIs should manage the CIA competently, coordinate intelligence affairs with military, the State Department, and the FBI, as necessary, and protect the secrecy surrounding their sources and methods. The two houses passed the fine-tuned act overwhelmingly by voice votes. On July 26, Harry Truman delayed a planned flight from Washington to Missouri, where his mother was dying, to sign the new law.[21]

The act's creation gained little attention from the general public, though Americans regarded foreign affairs as crucial. In July 1947, when pollster George Gallup asked citizens the open-ended question — "What do you think is the most important problem facing this country today?" — almost half named some foreign policy topic. Also, a majority gave the Republican 80th Congress a "good" or "fair" assessment. It had worked with President Truman to create the Central Intelligence Agency and other bureaucracies but would be derided the following year by the president in his reelection campaign as "do nothing."[22]

Initial Oversight: Budgets and Covert Action

From its first days, the CIA was involved in most areas of intelligence: collecting and evaluating raw information for top policymakers, countering other nations' intelligence efforts abroad (while the FBI continued its counterintelligence activities within the United States), and taking on what one administration leader called "specialized extracurricular activity," meaning covert operations.[1] The path would not be smooth for Roscoe Hillenkoetter in presiding over those doing such tasks. Tall, usually unsmiling, with very short, dark hair, the DCI had distinguished himself in the navy. Wounded at Pearl Harbor, he recovered and organized intelligence in the Pacific area for Fleet Admiral Chester Nimitz. As naval attaché at the American embassy in France, he had worked with resistance groups in the Vichy era. Though out of his element in Washington's intrigues, anyone would have struggled in trying to run the new CIA and influence the older intelligence units.

Many State Department leaders wanted to control the CIA but avoid blame if things went wrong. Among the most vigorous was George Kennan, the containment theorist who directed the Policy Planning Staff and answered to Undersecretary of State Robert Lovett and Secretary Marshall. Kennan had an unconcealed low opinion of Hillenkoetter and pushed for a covert action agency wholly or mostly independent from the DCI. Covert operations in the CIA's first year, in Kennan's view, were ineffectual and too limited. With communism seemingly on the move in Europe and elsewhere, the need for aggressive, skillfully managed operations was overwhelming, he thought. Similarly, army intelligence and the FBI barely cooperated with the new CIA. Until the latter's creation, J. Edgar Hoover's Bureau had been in charge of U.S. intelligence activities in Latin America. When CIA officers arrived in the various countries south of the United States to take over American intelligence, they often found that FBI papers had been destroyed and that the FBI's agent in charge had already departed. Nor were U.S. ambassadors and their embassy staffs typically well-disposed toward the new CIA arrivals showing up in "their" countries.[2]

Except for members of Congress closely allied with the new agency or one of its bureaucratic rivals, most legislators knew little about such wrangling.

The center of action in Congress was at the level of committees and sub-committees. Nelson Polsby wrote, "The so-called leadership — Speaker, majority leader, whip" had custody of routines and schedules, but were much-constrained. In the House, for example, "Committee chairmen — always those most senior in committee service in the House majority party — dominated the policy-making process with their respective domains, frequently collaborating with ranking minority members."

So, out of sight to most legislators, patterns of congressional-CIA interactions emerged in 1947–1948. The Appropriations committees of the House and Senate were to have authority over the CIA's budget. The Senate Armed Services Committee's sway over intelligence went unchallenged; in the House, with no apparent opposition from Expenditures, the Armed Services Committee took on responsibility for agency oversight. Only sporadically would Expenditures continue to involve itself in CIA affairs.

There was more to the new pattern, though: the Appropriations and Armed Services committees delegated their oversight authority to tiny, usually unnamed subcommittees. For instance, on December 11, 1947, Pforzheimer wrote in his diary, "J. R. Blandford, General Counsel, House Military Affairs [*sic*] Committee . . . pointed out the fact that Subcommittee # 3 was charged with keeping itself closely informed on the plans and operations of CIA, and that members of the subcommittee felt that they would like to talk with the Director." The delegation of responsibility did not rest there: the small subcommittees were usually dominated by chairs who were also heads of their parent committees. The chair of the House Appropriations Committee, therefore, was the key overseer for that committee and its CIA subcommittee. The ranking minority member was the second most important member. With few exceptions, the same pattern of intelligence oversight would follow in the three other relevant committees of Congress for years to come.[3]

Though there was much bitter partisanship in Congress itself over China and some other foreign affairs issues, very little arose on the CIA subcommittees. This mattered: while Democrats dominated Congress in the early decades that followed World War II, Republicans won majorities in both houses in the 1946 and 1952 elections, in both cases only keeping control for two years. This caused legislators to alternate between the roles of chairman and ranking minority member in the CIA's early years. On House Appropriations, for example, alternating chairs John Taber and Clarence Cannon were not exactly fast friends. But if any important disagreement between the

two of them occurred regarding the CIA, they kept it concealed. This preserved and enhanced the practice of cooperation on the committee between
chair and ranking minority member.[4]

An example of this cooperation between the two barons was keeping the
same chief clerk for the committee — George Harvey — while they switched
in and out of its chairmanship. As much or more than Cannon or Taber,
Harvey knew details of the CIA's budget and its hidden location in the
accounts of other government departments. In one or two of the CIA's first
years, only the chairman and Harvey would know such details. Similarly,
William Darden, chief clerk for the Senate Armed Services Committee in the
1950s and beyond, remained a prominent staffer when parties changed
power. With little partisanship on CIA and other national security matters
among the chairs and ranking minority members of the committee, it was
a "joy" to work there, Darden later said.[5]

How inquisitive congressional leaders were about international counterintelligence efforts of the CIA is unknown, though there was a lively interest,
to say the least, about what the FBI and others were turning up inside the
United States concerning agents of the Soviet Union. The legislative overseers
clearly did want to know about another prime CIA function — intelligence
collection, analysis, and reporting. They began to receive partial or complete
versions of some estimates, on topics ranging widely from Soviet nuclear
capabilities to other nations' civil aviation.[6] But regarding what came to be
widely regarded as the third crucial role of the CIA — covert operations —
the fragmentary records suggest the working out of an arrangement between
the CIA, congressional leaders, the White House, and a few others. Little was
committed to paper and no law on covert action was passed during Hillenkoetter's tenure, though any members of Congress reading newspapers or
attuned to rumors floating around Capitol Hill sensed that the CIA had
begun doing shadowy things worldwide.

In its first year, as the CIA increasingly took on secret interventions
abroad, how did it read congressional intent about this? The reading, such
as it was, took place in a national capital whose most powerful players were
sometimes deeply conflicted about doing "dirty tricks" abroad. At the head
of such a list would be the president, who would approve many covert operations during his last five years in office but deny it long afterward. The man
Truman most admired in his administration, Secretary of State (formerly
General and subsequently Secretary of Defense) Marshall, had equally mixed
views. He would not allow his department to carry out such operations,

believing that — if they were revealed — State's ability to interact effectively with foreign governments could be destroyed. Beyond that, said one close observer, "Secretary Marshall's character was opposed to sinister practices." Still, Marshall thought someone — logically in the CIA or another secret agency — had to do them in support of U.S. foreign policy. Similarly, Admiral William Leahy, adviser to Presidents Roosevelt and Truman, said that he thought guerrilla warfare was "murder."[7]

More surprisingly, neither DCI Hillenkoetter nor his successor, Walter Bedell "Beetle" Smith, were covert action enthusiasts. Besides their distaste for its moral messiness, they worried that covert action might become so high a priority as to harm intelligence gathering and analysis. The DCIs also feared that the State and Defense Departments would burden the CIA with responsibility but not authority to do effective covert action, and that, if operations were revealed, the agency's reputation would be ruined.

Truman administration leaders, convinced that covert operations were necessary in a world menaced by an expansionist Soviet Union, resembled an increasingly worried American public. Seventy-three percent of those polled in March 1948 told the Gallup organization that the United States was "too soft in its policy toward Russia." Even more Americans agreed with a statement that "Russia is trying to build herself up to be the ruling power of the world." Later that spring, Kennan repeatedly beseeched his bosses to formulate a clear, aggressive covert action policy for Europe and elsewhere. On May 19, he wrote Lovett, "If we are to get into operations in this field before the end of summer, Congress must be approached immediately with a request for the necessary funds." Like others, while Kennan employed the word "Congress," he would bring only a few legislators into such meetings.

While Kennan had mixed views about the CIA's proper role in covert action, that problem was less urgent than the sheer necessity of getting officers to work in countries vulnerable to counteractions by the Soviets and their allies in Europe and elsewhere. The virtual crisis meant that State would have to agree to a covert action policy that would take into account the beliefs and interests of others in the administration, including the CIA and military chiefs. On May 25, 1948, Kennan renewed his request for attention to "the political warfare question. If the Executive Branch does not act soon to firm up its ideas as to what should be done along these lines, the possibility of getting secret funds out of Congress for covert operations will be lost." Suddenly, it was not just a problem of getting extensive covert action launched by summer's end: if policy were not clarified and congressional leaders not approached quickly, "it will mean that this Government has given up hope of conducting effective political warfare activities for the duration of this administration."[8] Like many others, Kennan apparently believed that Truman would be out of office the following January.

Kennan, advocating a presidential directive on covert action (ultimately to be designated *NSC 10/2*), disagreed with Hillenkoetter about whether their times, featuring the bitter United States–Soviet rivalry, were best defined as "war" or "peace." That difference was more than semantic. Unlike Kennan, the director thought that covert action was of two types: those to be carried out in the current "peacetime" (including "black propaganda . . . morale subversion, assistance to underground movements, and support of resistance movements") and those "which it is very obvious that the United States would not perform except in relation to war or when war was so close that it was felt it could not be avoided" (including "sabotage, anti-sabotage, demolition, subversion against hostile states, guerrilla support, and evacuation"). The first group should be carried out by the CIA, but the latter by the military. This, Hillenkoetter claimed, would follow "the intent of Congress, as derived from conversations with both Senators and Representatives."[9]

Besides his (barely documented) talks with members of Congress, Hillenkoetter drew on the analysis of congressional intent provided to him the previous September by Lawrence Houston. The legal counsel, too, distinguished between special wartime operations like "commando raids, behind-the-lines sabotage, and support of guerrilla warfare" and the less aggressive operations like propaganda that might naturally go along with carrying out effective espionage. Granting that certain sections of the National Security Act "could bear almost unlimited interpretation" as to what the NSC might have the CIA do, Houston judged that there was no "thought in the minds of Congress that the Central Intelligence Agency under this [NSC] would take positive action for subversion and sabotage. . . . confirmation is found in the brief and off-the-record hearings on appropriations for CIA." However, Houston did not rule out the legality of such operations, instead suggesting that special operations should not be "undertaken by CIA without previously informing Congress and obtaining its approval of the functions and the expenditure of funds for those purposes." (Like Kennan, when Houston said "Congress" he meant a few relevant committee leaders.) Approval solely by the NSC was not enough, he advised Hillenkoetter.[10]

In the crisis-laden years of 1947 and 1948, nine months was a long time, and Houston's analysis, itself open to varying interpretations, may not have influenced many leaders besides Hillenkoetter. Some in the State and Defense Departments who read Congress differently used their interpretations as weapons in debates about handling covert operations. Wishing to weaken the DCI's influence over covert programs, they cited Congress in arguing that, in order for operations to be legal, they had to be controlled by the NSC. This, in practice, meant their agencies.[11]

Available evidence suggests that key congressional leaders were approached for the funding and informed of the CIA's covert plans. In a rare documented case, the DCI appeared before a House Armed Services Committee subcommittee in April 1948, by which time Hillenkoetter had been nudged by the NSC and NIA toward greater enthusiasm for covert operations. It was a typically small gathering, with Pforzheimer and four legislators present, plus a stenographer ("except during those times when the discussion was off-the-record"). The director testified that certain purchases and contracts for "services" would need to be made to support "any possible action in connection with the Italian election." Also, DCI Hillenkoetter spoke of the need to contract for the "employment of individual specialists and professional services" in support of the acquisition and effective use of "special intelligence equipment, such as machine records, communications, and explosives." As in the wartime OSS, contracts had and would be made for weapons not developed in "normal ordnance channels." These might include "explosive pencils, suppository capsules, trick concealed weapons, explosive plastics . . . the baseball grenade, special silencers . . . barometric switch detonators and similar gadgets."[12]

More strikingly, legislators off and on oversight subcommittees sometimes offered unsolicited suggestions that the CIA (or others in government) pursue more aggressively the quiet option with varying names — "psychological warfare," "special operations," "political warfare," and others. Senate Appropriations chair Styles Bridges volunteered to Lovett in spring 1948 — when Kennan worried about funding — that he could guarantee $50 million from Congress for "covert operations . . . to be conducted at the present time." (Some in the press would give exaggerated credit to Bridges the next year for having sponsored "Operation X, a secret program to counter communist influence in Europe, which was reportedly responsible, at least in part, for the defeat of communists in the 1948 Italian elections.")

Almost simultaneously, Representative John Davis Lodge (R-CT) told the House of "a vacuum" in American Cold War strategy. In Eastern Europe, Soviet puppets used "freedom for the purpose of destroying freedom.

Respect for law does not require us to stand supinely by while these laws are perverted and demolished." The United States needed a "peacetime OSS" to learn to "operate in this no-man's land." Others in the coming few years of the Cold War would approach administration leaders asking the sort of question "on the lips of a large number of Congressmen" that one legislator (not on a subcommittee on the CIA) posed privately to Dean Acheson at the beginning of 1950: "Why don't we instigate a large program of stirring up guerrilla activity on the Chinese mainland?"[13]

Similarly, at an executive session of the Senate Foreign Relations Committee, just months after the CIA's creation, discussion moved from foreign aid to recognition that the United States dominated the politics of numerous countries. Senator Henry Cabot Lodge Jr. (R-MA), brother of Representative Lodge, offered words frequently spoken in private on Capitol Hill but rarely transcribed. Referring first to Greece ("one of those important CIA assignments where reputations were won or lost," wrote historian Thomas Powers), Lodge moved on to other nations:

> I sometimes think we get a little bit too sensitive about interfering in the internal affairs of these other countries. I was in Greece last summer, and [Dwight] Griswold [Director of the American Mission for Aid to Greece] had all this money, and he was doing the biggest business of anybody in Greece.... he was just right into the internal affairs of that country up to his neck. He couldn't help it.... I think this whole question of interfering in the internal affairs is going to come up all the time, and God knows this Marshall Plan is going to be the biggest damned interference in internal affairs that there has ever been in history.... It doesn't do any good to say we are not going to interfere when the people in power stay there because of us. The Russians, who have compared our President to Hitler, have gone about as far as they can go in what they say; and whether we interfere or whether we don't, they are going to accuse us of the most dreadful things.... We are in it up to our neck, and almost everybody except a few political leaders will be damned glad to see us interfere!

Some of Lodge's comments were expunged from the transcript, after committee chairman Arthur Vandenberg (R-MI) questioned his need to "spread it all over the record." But no one present disagreed with Lodge's analysis of the new interventionist role of the United States in the post–World War II world. Senator Walter George (D-GA) tried to calm Lodge after the chair attacked his indiscreet on-the-record honesty: "Of course, Cabot, I agree with you. We are going to have to run the whole show."[14]

In mid-June 1948, Kennan regarded *NSC 10/2* as insufficient to meet "the more important needs of this Government for the conduct of political warfare" but grudgingly decided that it was "probably the best arrangement we can get at this time." It was "important that some funds be obtained from Congress this year for minor activities of this nature" and "we will at least know where we stand in these matters."

The president approved the secret directive on June 17. It took "cognizance of the vicious covert activities of the USSR, its satellite countries and Communist groups to discredit and defeat the aims and activities of the United States and other Western powers" and determined that, "in the interests of world peace and U.S. national security, the overt foreign activities of the U.S. government must be supplemented by covert operations." Such activities would be carried out so that,

> if uncovered, the U.S. government can plausibly disclaim any responsibility for them.
>
> Specifically, such operations shall include any covert activities related to propaganda; preventive direct action, including sabotage, anti-sabotage, demolition and evacuation measures; subversion against hostile states, including assistance to underground resistance movements, guerrillas and refugee liberation groups, and support of indigenous anti-communist elements in threatened countries of the free world.[15]

The directive said, "Supplemental funds for the conduct of proposed operations for Fiscal Year 1949 shall be immediately requested." It also created what came to be known as the Office of Policy Coordination (OPC) to run covert action. Its head, "nominated by the Secretary of State" and "acceptable to the Director of Central Intelligence," would answer to the DCI but also to "designated representatives of the Secretary of State and of the Secretary of Defense."

Appropriations heads in the House and Senate probably learned of the directive, since Kennan had stressed the necessity of approaching Congress for funding. In moving more toward such policies, almost all Truman administration leaders believed that they had a quiet mandate from such select legislators. The legal, budgetary, and political arrangements developed between Congress and CIA in 1947–1948 regarding covert action were fragile, as most participants understood, but would be consolidated over the coming few years and would endure for almost three decades.

"A South American Pearl Harbor"

The agency experienced its first highly publicized congressional scrutiny over an intelligence "failure" in 1948. The spring of that year was not short on international activities and challenges for the U.S. government. Besides busily and successfully helping to steer the Italian elections in April away from a triumph by the Communist Party, the United States was initiating the Marshall Plan, and the Soviet Union began railroad-stoppages in Germany that led eventually to a blockade of Berlin. Trouble was flaring in Palestine, meanwhile, with a British withdrawal impending. Amid those and other events, the United States participated in and led the weeks-long Ninth International Conference of American Republics in Bogota, Colombia, which began on March 30.

Secretary of State Marshall attended, determined to move Latin American governments more firmly in an anticommunist direction, while reaffirming trade and other economic relations. Marshall's delegation included Representative Donald Jackson (R-CA), a purveyor of strident anticommunist rhetoric. The opening days were uneventful enough, although Marshall had been warned by an assistant of demonstrations and efforts planned by communists and others to sabotage the conference and embarrass the U.S. government. Marshall dismissed such threats with salty language.

Colombia was a political tinderbox, with severe divisions between its Liberal and Conservative Parties. It also had a Communist Party whose numbers were not impressive but which had influence in the labor movement. Senator Jorge Gaitan, leader of the Liberals and a popular figure with the masses, had withdrawn all of his party members from a coalition government in January. In the ensuing months, there was widespread violence, including assassinations of hundreds of Liberal Party figures.

On April 9, Gaitan was murdered in broad daylight in a busy public section of Bogota. Though it would later become clear that the murderer acted out of personal revenge motives, the crime quickly sparked a wave of demonstrations and riots. Congressman Jackson, lunching at a restaurant with three other U.S. delegates, had just lifted fried chicken to his mouth when he heard a horrific crashing noise. He grumbled to colleagues, "Apparently the waiters down here are just as clumsy as those in the United States." But with the noise continuing and growing, a waiter informed the legislator, "Gaitan has been assassinated. There is revolution." Jackson later recalled:

> Within minutes the mobs were surging through the Plaza. The unarmed police were powerless to cope with the situation and were brushed aside by the rioters as they streamed in the building. Red flags were in profusion and I personally saw hammer-and-sickle flags. Using stones, bricks, machetes, and boards, the mob commenced a methodical tour of destruction which was to render the first floor of the capitol building [the Conference's locale] a shambles within a matter of minutes.[1]

Order was not easily restored, in part because many police officers idolized Gaitan and joined the rioting. After three days, during which hundreds were killed and many more were injured, the Colombian Army enforced a tense peace. Whole sections of Bogota were in ruins, but U.S. delegates escaped harm.

A South American riot would not normally have riveted journalists, politicians, and the public in the United States, but the lives of Marshall and others had been endangered and the conference halted. Colombia's government responded by announcing it would break diplomatic relations with the USSR (then reversed that decision a day later). Among the least flustered by all of this was the secretary, a survivor of far worse crises in the past. The conference should resume its work soon, he decided.

Back in the United States, the not usually hysterical editorial page of the *New York Times* wrote, "The fact that a single shot was able to produce such an uprising . . . can be taken as an indication that there was a well-planned revolutionary strategy behind it all, such as is taught in Russia's schools of revolution." Representative Clarence Brown joined others in pronouncing the event a "South American Pearl Harbor." Congressman Jackson, returning to the United States, told fellow legislators, "What has happened in Bogota can and will happen again in such places as New York City, Chicago, and San Francisco unless we, who still remain free and unfettered, gird ourselves for all-out battle with the enemy." (Jackson's replacement as congressional member of the U.S. delegation still at work in Colombia was Representative Mike Mansfield [D-MT], who would become an energetic advocate years later of vigorous intelligence oversight.)[2]

For the Central Intelligence Agency, the question naturally arose, What is the CIA for, if not to warn national leaders of impending disasters? Undersecretary of State Robert Lovett prompted the question by telling reporters that he knew of no advance predictions of violent upheavals in Colombia.

President Truman blithely admitted that he was as "surprised as anyone else" at what happened, though he did not single out the CIA. Thomas Dewey, campaigning in Republican presidential primaries, said, "Because of the dreadful incompetence of our present Government, we apparently had no idea what was going on in a country just two hours bomber time from the Panama Canal." Seeing that a congressional investigation of the CIA was likely, Hillenkoetter lobbied the Senate's most influential Republican, Robert Taft, at a private lunch with the message that such an inquiry would "backfire" against the Republican Party. Afterward, an aide to the DCI privately estimated that Congress would not investigate the CIA.[3] He was mistaken. Clarence Hoffman suspected that the CIA had failed, since other countries' intelligence services (he claimed) "knew about the pending revolution." On April 12, 1948, Hoffman appointed a special Expenditures investigative subcommittee to be chaired by Representative Brown and including Hoffman plus John McCormack. Brown observed, "I think Congress has a right to know what is going on in this agency," and set a hearing for April 15 with Hillenkoetter as the first witness.

That afternoon at four o'clock, the subcommittee gathered in room 1401 of the House Office Building. Opening the hearing, Brown said, "This subcommittee is authorized to launch an investigation of the Central Intelligence Agency and learn whether the Secretary of State and other high officials were promptly warned that a revolution was impending in Colombia, and that their attendance at the Bogota conference might endanger their lives and bring embarrassment to the United States."

Hillenkoetter began his testimony by asserting that the agency had been the object of many attacks in the press. In response, "I have made it my invariable rule to answer 'no comment.' . . . Public controversy inevitably tends to blow such cover of our personnel as has been painstakingly developed." Worse, he implied, were the comments of Dewey. "No one, however, until your committee was convened, has seemed to want to ask what to us appears to be the $64 question, namely, did the Central Intelligence Agency know of the situation in Colombia and did they inform responsible officials of the State Department?" The answer was, "Yes."

The DCI then illustrated for the subcommittee the chronic tensions between his young agency and the State Department, saying that the CIA had given many warnings to U.S. embassy officials and their superiors in Washington. To back up his claim, Hillenkoetter read from top secret dispatches and reports that had been given to State personnel. One, dated

March 9 and citing Communist sources, described "the initiation of plans to sabotage the Pan American Conference." In reading such raw intelligence reports, Hillenkoetter persuasively made the case that the CIA had been knowledgeable and forthcoming with others in government. However, in naming names and speaking indirectly about sources of intelligence, he only irregularly or barely disguised persons' positions and names: "I would like to use instead of names now just the initials [he said], because we are giving away our people if we use names: 'Mr. I., in charge of drafting the policies of the Communist Party of Colombia, made the following comments . . .'; 'Mr. G., a leading Colombia communist . . .'; 'The president of the chauffeurs union and a well-known agitator stated . . . .'"

Hillenkoetter told the alert subcommittee members that one CIA analysis, written in Colombia, had not been sent to the State Department but had gone to CIA headquarters. It "confirmed information that Communist inspired agitators will attempt to humiliate Secretary of State and other members of U.S. delegation . . . by manifestation and possibly personal molestation." Why, Congressman Brown asked, had that most frightening cable not been sent to the State Department? Hillenkoetter said it was "delivered to the Ambassador in Bogota and to the State Department's advance representative in Bogota, but at their request was not transmitted to the State Department." State personnel in Bogota, he said, did not wish to alarm higher-ups unduly and therefore muzzled the CIA.

Incredulous, and referring to the State Department's advance representative, Brown asked, "He exercised a veto power upon the activities of your agency and of your representatives who would have normally made that report, and you in turn would have made it to the Secretary of State or his department here in Washington, is that correct?" Correct, said Hillenkoetter.

What had been envisioned as a lengthy hearing ended after just an hour, with Brown affirming to the DCI, "I am sure that it was not the intent or the purpose of Congress to give any agency of the government, whether it be the State Department or ambassadors or others, the right of censorship or control over your activities." Brown even apologized to Hillenkoetter, then called in reporters and had Hillenkoetter repeat his testimony for them in detail.[4]

The CIA, barely mentioned in newspapers during its creation nine months earlier, gained its first widespread front-page newspaper coverage the next day. "Intelligence Chief Declares State Department Agent Barred Cautionary Notice," read the *New York Times* headline. Widely noted also was committee chairman Hoffman's verdict on the CIA — "It performed its duty" — and Brown's comment after the hearing that "the Iron Curtain must not come down upon any part of the Western Hemisphere." The truth about the "disaster" had emerged "only through formal congressional inquiry," Brown added. Furthermore, "we have asked for a copy of the official directive which established this arrangement of State Department censorship over CIA." It might take new legislation to free the agency from that control. Otherwise, he said, "we might as well turn the intelligence agency over to the State Department and let those dumb clucks run it."

While most press commentators agreed with Hoffman's evaluation of the CIA's performance, some noted a bad precedent: the hearing was "perhaps the first authorized publication in United States history of top-secret intelligence documents," said the *Times*. The *Washington Post* editorialized that any future committees of Congress examining intelligence controversies should do so out of press and public view. Even a subsequent agency report judged that Hillenkoetter revealed "something of the scope of United States intelligence collecting which should better have remained unsaid."[5]

The hearing "actually violated security," a U.S. embassy official in Bogota told a reporter. "If I were a local Communist and read some of this stuff that's coming down from Washington, I'd feel like heading right for the Embassy and starting another fire." Those running the State Department in Marshall's absence were similarly livid. One told the DCI, "It is inconceivable to me that you personally could have had the information to which your man attached such importance and not have sent it to the Department regardless of your subordinate's instructions from Bogota." Hillenkoetter admitted that he had made a mistake in not getting the cable to Marshall, but had decided not to do so because his top officer in Colombia had to "live" with the U.S. embassy and "could not afford to antagonize the personnel there." Facing derision from the State official, Hillenkoetter countered that the department "deserved whatever heat might now be on it" and poured forth a litany of complaints over State's harassment of the CIA. "If relations with the Department did not improve in the near future," a memorandum of conversation summarized the DCI as saying, "he intended to inform the President and, if necessary, the Congress, that they could not hold him responsible for obtaining the intelligence information that he is charged with at present."

Quickly, the State Department circulated a draft national security directive titled "Protection of Intelligence Sources and Methods from Unauthorized Disclosure." While it no doubt made disgruntled security-conscious officials feel better, stating that "any subpoena, demand or request for such disclosure shall be respectfully declined," it ignored the constitutional prerogatives of Congress and the political reality that when legislators with funding and lawmaking powers were united in wanting to examine the CIA, they could not be resisted easily.[6]

In the midst of all this in spring 1948 came another indication of Congress and the CIA's long-term future, in which legislators would publicize sensational news reports about agency activities. In this case, Vito Marcantonio (American Labor Party–NY), widely regarded in the House as a virtual communist, described a report of the *Boston Herald* on American intervention in Italy. Marcantonio was "a dark, burning, but also humorous little man who held in fief a New York district made up primarily of Negroes and Puerto Ricans," according to journalist William S. White. The representative inserted the story (headlined "United States to Buy Italian Election") into the *Congressional Record*. It accurately reported, "Political methods similar to those once employed by the old Pendergast machine in Kansas City are to be used by the Truman administration in an effort to sway the April 18 elections in Italy." The Italian people would "refuse to be bribed," Marcantonio predicted, but he wondered "just what kind of democracy this is."

The *Herald*'s story and Marcantonio's speech received scant attention in the press and in speeches by other members of Congress. Still, a major covert action program of the United States government was no longer a well-kept secret.

Agency officials feared that such controversies might permit others to hinder the CIA's unsteady path toward acceptance in Washington circles. A former head of Naval Intelligence, for example, aggressively criticized the agency regarding Colombia and other matters in conversations with radio and newspaper reporters, who publicized his comments. He also approached the House Expenditures Committee, offering his services as an investigator into the CIA's functioning — an offer quickly declined.

Another indication of the future emerged in late April. Congressman Edward J. Devitt (R-WI) took thirty minutes on the House of Representatives' floor to offer a resolution to create a joint congressional committee on intelligence. He said that "the most neglected and incompetent of our national security efforts is in the field of intelligence," as aptly demonstrated by "the fiasco in Bogota." The proposed committee, with nine members from the House and nine from the Senate, would be "charged with the responsibility of making a continuing study of the programs and activities of the

Central Intelligence Agency," the shortcomings of which were "manifest." Remarkably, Devitt reported that he had spoken with Hillenkoetter about his "intention to introduce this resolution today, and he has expressed his approbation of it. He told me that while he believes there is much merit to the independent position of his agency in the field of government, he feels somewhat at a loss for the lack of some specific committee of the Congress to whom he can turn for confidential guidance and counsel and to whom he can resort for needed changes in the legislative operations of his agency."[7]

The resolution went nowhere, but the White House noticed Devitt's account of the conversation with the DCI. President Truman was not overtly hostile to congressional oversight of the CIA. While heading a Senate investigative committee during World War II, he had only reluctantly agreed to back off from investigating the OSS, which he considered wasteful, arrogant, and dangerous. Nonetheless, an assistant suggested to the president, "Perhaps someone should have a talk with Admiral Hillenkoetter."

With NSC members agreeing on an increasing need for covert operations, Secretary of Defense Forrestal soon pointedly told Hillenkoetter and others — according to notes passed on to Truman — that "if intelligence activities are to be effective, they must be secret."[8]

"This Is an Espionage Bill"

When Congress opened for business in January 1949, John Taber — demoted to ranking Republican at House Appropriations because the Democrats had won the November elections — learned from a top aide of poor "integration of the intelligence arms of the government." The U.S. Air Force was "building up their own intelligence in further competition with Army, Navy, CIA, FBI, State Department, etc." This and other concerns about CIA missions and performance received significant attention the following spring, when Congress took up the Central Intelligence Agency Act. Historians usually treat the bill as having sailed through Congress without a hitch, saying that the words "national security" and "confidential" imposed silence in what should have been vigorous debates. Such analyses underplay the questions and obstacles faced by the bill's supporters.

The act had made it past committee stage to the Senate floor in 1948, where Armed Services chairman Gurney and CIA lobbyists realized they had not gotten all of their ducks in a row: Gurney had assured Senate majority leader Kenneth Wherry that there would be "no controversy involved" in bringing the bill up for a vote, and so Wherry interrupted previously scheduled Senate business on June 19 to get quick passage of the bill. Gurney spoke for precisely one minute in explaining the CIA Act and then said, "The bill has the unanimous approval of the committee, and I ask for its immediate adoption." To Gurney's surprise and dismay, Brien McMahon (the young chairman of the Joint Committee on Atomic Energy) announced, "It is with great reluctance that I rise to object." McMahon complained that the bill said that "sums made available to the Agency may be expended without regard to the provisions of law and regulations relating to the expenditure of government funds" and authorized the DCI, with no more accounting than a signature on a secret certificate, to spend funds on "objects of a confidential, extraordinary, or emergency nature."

McMahon admitted that other senators told him that the section "is a most necessary provision for the successful operation of this Agency," but he insisted on deleting it. The senator's complaint was not trivial, since the Constitution requires that government agencies' "receipts and expenditures" be "published from time to time." Not having been granted time for an actual debate, a deflated Gurney agreed. No doubt, citizens watching from the gallery would have been surprised to see that just one senator could derail a widely supported bill. Veteran observers, though, would have understood. As one wrote, "Individual senators . . . can, according to the rules and customs of the Senate, play a powerful hand in the disposition of legislation reaching the floor."

Immediately, though, senators and a visibly angry Walter Pforzheimer descended upon McMahon. Whether they employed reason, pressure, or threats is unknown, but he soon took the floor again to announce, "I have resolved that the thing to do is to withdraw the objection." Senators cast a voice vote again, unanimously approving the CIA Act, its unique spending provisions intact.[1]

Before a four-person subcommittee of the House Armed Services Committee in 1948, Hillenkoetter discussed the most sensitive of CIA activities in a 100-page opening statement (which he probably had used earlier with senators). The DCI told members,

> It was thought, when we started back in 1946, that at least we would have time to develop this mature service over a period of years. . . . Unfortunately, the international situation has not allowed us the breathing space we might have liked, and so, as we present this bill, we find ourselves in operations up to our necks, and we need the authorities contained herein as a matter of urgency. . . . It is necessary to use funds for various covert or semi-covert operations and other purposes where it is impossible to conform with existing government procedures and regulations. . . . In many instances, it is necessary to make specific payments or reimbursements on a project basis where the background information is of such a sensitive nature from a security viewpoint that only a general certificate, signed by the Director of the CIA, should be processed through even restricted channels.

At the same hearing, Lyndon Johnson proposed an amendment that would have essentially allowed the president to exempt the agency from *any* "provisions of present law which requirements of security may dictate." The remarkable idea emerged during discussion of the possibility that floor debate might "force out certain classified information." The subcommittee seemed favorably disposed toward Johnson's provision, though its members were later persuaded that it was "too broad" to be effective. Although the full Armed Services Committee approved the CIA Act in summer 1948, its members turned down a key section permitting the fast-track importation of up to fifty foreigners each year. The problematic bill never went before the House. The CIA would have to try again the next year, when there would be new obstacles.

In the meantime, Hillenkoetter and other CIA leaders suffered through a five-part analysis by the *New York Times'* Hanson Baldwin in late July. The reporter seems to have drawn on leaks from his friend Allen Dulles, the former OSS officer (and later DCI) who headed an NSC-sanctioned committee that was investigating the CIA. The articles were replete with criticisms: intelligence was one of the "weakest links in our national security"; the agency had numerous "chair warmers" and "empire builders"; the "full scope" of the Bogota riots had not been anticipated; the need for "secret operations" including "sabotage," "encouragement of anti-communist minorities," and "black radio" was obvious, and though "most of these will be conducted by CIA," it was not yet well situated to do so. In fact, Baldwin wrote, the CIA had already bungled secret operations in Romania, Hungary, and Finland. He had a suggestion: "Because the grants of power given to intelligence agencies must be major and secret, a congressional committee to act as a discreet 'watch-dog' over all our intelligence agencies — particularly CIA — ought to be established."

An aide prepared a response to the articles for Hillenkoetter to use before an unspecified audience. Some of Baldwin's reporting represented a "serious breach of security," it said, whether or not it was "based upon fact." A "watch-dog committee" was "not required and would further complicate a field which is highly sensitive." After all, "CIA is primarily responsible, in so far as the Congress is concerned, to the Armed Services and Appropriations committees."[2]

Committee Action

Senate and House committee members were as determined in 1949 as before to shroud their deliberations of the Central Intelligence Agency Act in secrecy. They did so to such an extent that other legislators would criticize this in floor debates. In the decades since, no Senate Armed Services Committee documents from 1949 relating to the act have surfaced, although some evidence of the CIA's preparation for House committee hearings exists. In gearing up for the DCI's 1948–1949 appearances, Pforzheimer created "a detailed section-by-section brief in support of the proposed CIA legislation. . . . In view of the need for this justification, each section, where applicable, should be carefully supported by specific examples — at least two or three in each instance."

Pforzheimer also asked to be furnished with "examples where we have succeeded in ascertaining details as to the size and scope of foreign intelligence organizations or operations through knowledge of their appropriations or number of personnel employed." This would strengthen committee members who wanted to keep CIA budgets secret. Pforzheimer also suggested that "the Director should be supplied with two or three obsolete gadgets, either in the nature of trick fountain pens, trick cameras, or other toys which would be effective as exhibits indicating the specialized nature of certain of our procurements."

The director of central intelligence lobbying committee members in 1949 was not unpopular on Capitol Hill, despite early setbacks for the CIA. Indeed, when compared to controversial State Department leaders, one historian claims that "Hillenkoetter enjoyed downright popularity." Some Armed Services members apparently renewed questions to him about authorizing the agency (upon certification by the DCI and attorney general) to bring in aliens — this time 100 was the number — who would have permanent residence. Committee members assumed (correctly) that among those aliens entering would be former Nazis and other unpalatables, whatever useful secrets might accompany them. Hillenkoetter was therefore prepared (in the words of a colleague) "to reduce the number to 50 at the first sign of congressional objection to the number of 100." This was prudent, given the problems before the committee the previous year on this issue, but CIA leaders won members' approval of the full number.

The committee's resulting 1949 report was (by its own words) incomplete in its "explanation of all of the provisions of the proposed legislation, in view of the fact that much of such information is of a highly confidential nature." Among the notable provisions of the bill reported by the committees to their full houses was authorization for the CIA to avoid public disclosure of its personnel levels and budgets and (as Chairman Carl Vinson would later explain) "the expenditure of funds for confidential purposes to be solely accounted for by certification of the Director."[3]

Floor Debates

While no one explicitly mentioned covert operations, leaders in both houses would acknowledge in debates open to the public that CIA personnel overseas had begun doing spying and other dangerous activities abroad. Senator

Tydings, chair of the Armed Services Committee and a former combat hero in World War I, would admit with self-described reluctance that "many" agents of the CIA had already died overseas, adding, "I think this debate is unfortunate. I think it ought to be in executive session."

In the House, the question of whether the CIA should be able to import unsavory aliens would receive prime attention, as did the secrecy surrounding the CIA and how that affected congressional deliberations. This became inevitable due to Sunday radio interviews on March 6, when House Republican leader Joseph W. Martin (MA), who had been Speaker when the National Security Act passed two years before, questioned the aura surrounding the proposed new law. In light of the bill's consideration by the two Armed Services committees and executive branch leaders, he found it "difficult to see why it is so secret. . . . in Washington, if three people know anything, everybody does." Still, Martin agreed to consult with Dewey Short and other Republicans on Armed Services. That same day, Short endorsed limiting House debate of the bill because it dealt with "pretty dirty business." Chairman Vinson agreed, telling interviewers, "When you're in the spy business, you can't go shouting about it from the house tops," while Clarence Brown insisted that the CIA Act was "not secret legislation" since it had been "taken up with responsible members of the House in confidence."

House debate began on March 7 under a suspension of normal rules, with debate limited to forty minutes, no amendments permitted, and a two-thirds vote required for passage of the bill. Congressman Lansdale Sasscer (D-MD), the bill's floor manager, explained why the Armed Services Committee had held closed hearings without even making stenographic records: "The members of CIA who appeared before the committee went into the operational background of the Agency [which] . . . go to the very heart of CIA's activities." He reminded and attempted to reassure legislators that "the CIA is prohibited from any internal security functions."

Only a few objected to the committee's mysterious report. Vito Marcantonio ignored a colleague's caution that "this is an espionage bill," and warned, "If, under the wave of hysteria, you want to abdicate your legislative functions to just one committee of the House, that is your privilege, but, as for me, I refuse to do it." Another, far more influential, member flirted with opposing the bill: Judiciary Committee chair Emanuel Cellar (D-NY) noted sourly that the Armed Services Committee had "nothing to do with immigration." That was normally Judiciary's arena. But Armed Services had approved a CIA bill that allowed the DCI and the attorney general to admit "communists, Hitler sadists, morons, moral perverts, syphilitics, or lepers" into the United States. Furthermore, if Armed Services "can hear the detailed information to support this bill, why cannot our entire membership? Are they the Brahmins and we the untouchables?" The Cold War, he said, was "unhinging the nerves" of high-ranking authorities who should not be given "carte blanche" to import aliens.

Other House members vividly defended those who might require such fast-track procedures: "Many of them live in police states," said Carl Durham, (D-NC). If they stayed in their home countries, "their heads may be cut off," said Sasscer. Despite further bitter complaints about the bill, Cellar eventually said, "I shall not oppose it." (Cellar's counterpart in the Senate, Judiciary chairman Pat McCarran [D-NV], sought and would soon receive the agency's assistance in investigating "persons who came to this country under various diplomatic cloaks, but whose primary duties are fundamentally espionage or subversive activities." He readily endorsed the CIA Act.)[4]

All of the CIA budget, Vinson told the House, would be approved by the congressional appropriations committees; the budget would additionally be cleared by the Bureau of the Budget (BOB), except for the "unvouchered" funds designated to the DCI for those "confidential purposes." (Though Vinson did not say so, the latter funds would go predominantly toward covert operations that could not be anticipated, due to the uncertainties of world politics.) The act also allowed the CIA budget to be hidden in other agencies' accounts.

In both houses, floor managers admitted that members of Congress were being asked to trust and delegate power to a small number of colleagues on a few committees. Heartily endorsing this, Dewey Short told Marcantonio, "You are going to have to trust somebody. . . . perhaps the less we say in public about this bill, the better off all of us will be." Chairman Tydings agreed: "Forgive me if I appear a bit vain in what I am about to say — that military and scientific developments have reached such wide ramifications today that it is not always possible to give to the Senate the detailed information." In neither house was covert action explicitly discussed, though one representative noted, "In spite of all our wealth and power and might, we have been extremely weak in psychological warfare, notwithstanding the fact that an idea is perhaps the most powerful weapon on this earth."[5]

The CIA Act passed with only four dissenters in the House on March 7. One of its supporters, Arthur Klein (D-NY), immediately inserted a statement into the *Congressional Record* that attacked the "bad precedent" set by the "secret legislative consideration" on March 7: "I regard this kind of legislative proceeding in the United States as dangerous and subversive to our form and philosophy of government." Such dissents, minuscule in number, received little attention. (Klein's predecessor in his New York district was, by coincidence, Democrat Samuel Dickstein who had sold intelligence secrets to Soviet agents during World War II.)[6]

The road to passage was rockier in the Senate, where, by long tradition of the filibuster, one or more members could extend debate for hours or even days. Of the half-dozen senators who joined the May 27 debate with critical questions, the one who could conceive of filibustering was Republican William Langer of North Dakota — this, despite the fact that Pforzheimer had had the impression two months before that Langer was "extremely receptive" to the legislation. Something changed Langer's mind, though. Tough, flamboyant, and independent-minded, he had dominated his home state's unusually raucous political scene for years. After World War II, Langer was dismissed by some on Capitol Hill and the press as an old-fashioned isolationist. In anticipation of one of Winston Churchill's visits to the United States, Langer sent a telegram to the vicar of Boston's historic Old North Church, requesting a re-enactment of Paul Revere's warning that the British — whose empire he called fascist — were coming. The maverick had criticized many of Truman's internationalist programs, but endorsed him over Dewey in the 1948 presidential election. Some, including Drew Pearson, thought Langer courageous for speaking out against anticommunist hysteria. Few senators would join Langer in supporting Truman's veto of the Internal Security Act in 1950, filibustering against the bill all night long until he literally collapsed on the Senate floor at 5:00 in the morning. He entered the CIA Act's debate with equal gumption.

"I, for one, am not going to take any chances without a protest," said Langer, "even though I vote alone, against the establishment of a Gestapo in the United States by which people may be hounded and harassed by a central bureau, or by anyone else." The "purposes" of the bill enunciated by Tydings were fine, he admitted, "but I totally disagree with him as to two aspects of the bill. . . . I propose to offer amendments in the hope that we may be able to make the bill what it ought to be." It was horrendous that the act had not been formally considered by the Judiciary Committees of Congress, he said. Surely it was dangerous that the bill did "not protect the people of the United States from having a group of communists, or fascists, or whatever they may be, come into this country." He was not comforted by the bill's provision that the DCI and the attorney general would have to agree to the quick entry of useful but unsavory aliens. After all, "if we had another Attorney General like Harry Daugherty, I would not want him to pass on anything, even a dog, coming into this country." Tydings pleaded with Langer not to insist on amending the bill: "This is asylum for military agents who are working for the United States, and who are faced with death if they are caught." Ultimately, Tydings agreed to accept a Langer amendment that added the Commissioner of Immigration to the short list of officials who would have to agree to the quick importation of aliens.

Langer also addressed the danger that agents of the CIA might spy on American citizens. He harkened back to memories of his own supposed harassment by the Roosevelt administration: "As Governor of the state of North Dakota, I had men following me all over the United States, and my telephone was tapped, and my desk in the Governor's office was broken into by men whom Harold Ickes had snooping around, trying to pin something on me." Congress would "do the country a great deal of harm" if it left in the bill wording that said, "While in the continental United States on leave, the service of any officer or employee shall be available for work or duties in the agency or elsewhere." Surely, Congress did not intend to "enable this agency to send its men inside the United States," snooping into the affairs of government officials and breaking up labor unions. Langer's solution: change the bill to read, "While in the continental United States on leave, the service of any officer or employee shall not be available for work or duties, except in the agency for training or for reorientation for work." Tydings insisted that CIA officers would never have done "espionage in the United States" but acceded to Langer's "worthy thought." The North Dakotan, in turn, endorsed the bill.

Tydings faced other skeptics that day. The elderly and often prickly Appropriations chair Kenneth McKellar (TN) announced that, while he supported the bill, he "doubted the wisdom" of the bill's unique language regarding CIA spending and accounting procedures. After all, his committee "appropriates specifically for every department of government. It has been found to work extraordinarily well." An impassioned Tydings, though, called the secretive budgetary practices imperative:

> If there are vouchers containing the names and the circumstances, going through government channels, it might be possible for foreign-espionage agents to check on who the agents are. . . . Strange as it may seem, expert men, skilled

in detecting from little things the probabilities, are quite often able to detect who the agents are. . . . I hate to discuss these matters on the floor, but there is no other way I can make the Senate have confidence in the bill than by discussing these things which I would rather not mention.

This seemed to satisfy McKellar. When Senator Edwin Johnson (D-CO) raised the old refrain, "We are setting up in this country a military Gestapo," Tydings renewed and elaborated his argument that "there is nothing in this bill to permit internal military espionage." Johnson accepted Tydings's "comforting" analysis, and said he, too, would support the act.

Finally, Senate Republican leader Kenneth Wherry expressed fear over the dangerous ways the bill's vague language might be interpreted in the future. This led him into a remarkable dialogue with Tydings on a topic that the *New York Times* had reported—that Congress was giving "protection of law to activities that already were in motion." Wherry read some of the act's language aloud, and then asked, "Are we doing this now?"

> Tydings: Yes.
> Wherry: Then why is it necessary to have the legislation?
> Tydings: I think it is a question whether or not the law is being winked at, unless the bill is written into law. . . . In my opinion, we have not the authority, but nobody is going to raise the question.
> Wherry: But we are actually doing what is provided for in the bill?
> Tydings: Much of it.

Wherry eventually deferred to Tydings's defense of congressional handling of the CIA: "We are throwing every possible democratic safeguard around it." The act passed the Senate without an opposing vote on May 27.[7]

A conference committee quickly resolved the few differences between the two houses' versions of the bill, accepting Langer's amendments, and it came back to the House and Senate in the first week of June. In the House, most members skipped the final, inevitable vote, but Marcantonio protested again, "It substitutes for our constitutional guarantees a Gestapo system." His was the only negative vote. No one dissented in the Senate's voice vote. Truman signed the bill a few days later. In the three months that legislators had spent on the CIA Act that year, floor debaters never mentioned the Democratic or Republican parties, their divided control of government in 1947, or the Democrats' control of the executive and legislative branches in 1949.

To the satisfaction of Hillenkoetter and those legislators who interacted with the CIA, press coverage of the bill's passage had been restrained and generally favorable. Press deference was no surprise, though: the DCI had befriended or won the cooperation of many elite journalists. Early on in his tenure, "Admiral Hillenkoetter" had interacted with "Mr. Joseph Alsop," one of the nation's most influential columnists, but by 1949 it was "Hilly" and "Joe." Also, a CIA memo told the NSC earlier in the year, "By special plea of the Director, various periodicals and newspapers (*Life, Time, Newsweek, U.S. News,* New York *Herald Tribune,* among others) have refrained from publishing articles."[8]

CIA leaders were pleased to obtain the new law's authorization to bring in foreigners who had assisted the agency abroad and to use funds in ways that otherwise would have been illegal. Still, they continued to struggle with those in OPC, the State Department, and elsewhere over the ramifications of the new law and the earlier National Security Act. In a September 1949 legal analysis, Houston and Pforzheimer emphasized to Hillenkoetter that Congress intended the DCI to run the CIA and coordinate all intelligence activities of the government. In principle, at least, Hillenkoetter agreed. In retirement, he would recall, "It was always the Director of Central Intelligence who was called up for any congressional committees on any discussions. It was never the collective chiefs of the other agencies." But controlling all intelligence activities was more easily said than done. With backing from the State and Defense Departments, Allen Dulles (then working for a New York law firm) headed a committee that reviewed the CIA's early performance and had returned a report in January that damned the agency and its leaders with faint praise and distinct criticism.

One of the issues in dispute after the report's secret issuance to executive branch figures was congressional oversight. Dulles and his colleagues judged that the agency had been "favored by adequate Congressional support" and reported approvingly that "both Congress and the Bureau of the Budget have refrained from examining in detail the internal workings of the Central Intelligence Agency." But it noted (in a still-classified section apparently referring to the Washington aftermath of the Bogota riots), "Lest further incidents of this character occur, every effort should be made to prevent the public disclosure of secret information relating to operations of the Central Intelligence Agency." It urged the DCI either to resist "disclosure of secret information" or to ask the NSC to ward off such congressional pressures.[9] The CIA responded: "It is all very well for a group with no responsibilities or authority to state that both Congress and the Bureau of the Budget must understand that the Central Intelligence Agency must be given, in effect, a blank check and a free hand. In practice, the Central Intelligence Agency must justify its demands with some reason and logic and must reassure both of those bodies that the Central Intelligence Agency is, at least, somewhat careful with government funds and does its best to guard against waste and fraud."[10]

Truman's National Security Council considered and approved the Dulles Report (designating it *NSC/50*) in the very months that Congress debated and passed the CIA Act, but tensions between Hillenkoetter and other bureaucratic managers endured. The DCI wanted one of his assistant directors, for example, to preside over the Office of Special Operations (OSO, which did espionage) and the new OPC, energetically headed by Frank Wisner. Of this, one State Department leader told another in September, "The situation has the real makings of a jumble, because it is obviously impossible to get a man big enough to be over Wisner and small enough to be under Hilly." Still, Houston and Pforzheimer argued to the DCI that Congress, through the National Security and CIA Acts, conveyed clear intent that the agency

> look to the National Security Council only for broad direction, and that the day-to-day operations of the Agency were to be in the hands of the Director. Furthermore, there was no question but that if anything went wrong with the Agency, or if any questions arose (as they did at the time of the Bogota riots), the Congress would hold the Director personally responsible. . . . It was the intent of Congress . . . to establish an independent agency which would be the focal point of *all* foreign intelligence information, to correlate and evaluate *all* such information and to disseminate the product to the necessary Government officials.[11]

Only a miserable war a year later would focus Truman's and congressional leaders' attention on unresolved tensions over the CIA. In the meantime, Hillenkoetter faced other problems. Few would burnish his reputation.

The Soviet A-Bomb: "We Apparently Don't Have the Remotest Idea"

Harry Truman rejoiced at being inaugurated in his own right as president in 1949, but worsening relations between the United States and the Soviet Union would cast a cloud over the White House that year. The president would seek and usually win support from legislators to help him assist "free peoples" resisting communist aggression and subversion. One usual supporter was Brien McMahon. Late in the morning of September 22, 1949, with only a dozen members on the Senate floor as others wandered off to lunch, the senator rose to defend a military aid bill supporting the president's policy. One of the Senate's boy wonders since his election in 1944, McMahon chaired the Joint Committee on Atomic Energy (JCAE), of which one author writes, "No other committee, before or since, has been granted such unique and far-reaching powers. The pace and the scale of the nuclear weapons program . . . is in no small measure attributable to the considerable influence of the JCAE and, in particular, to Brien McMahon."

Created by the Atomic Energy Act of 1946, primarily authored by McMahon, JCAE functioned as a near coequal with the executive branch's Atomic Energy Commission (AEC) on nuclear matters, much to the frustration of presidents. Commission chairman David Lilienthal's diary describes Truman, annoyed over what he viewed as the Joint Committee's unconstitutional usurpation of presidential power, referring to its members as "those fellows on the Hill who think they are the board of directors of this thing." When *really* angry, Truman "glared through his thickish glasses" and erupted over "those bastards on the Hill." About McMahon, an unquestioned authority on atomic energy, who had insisted that other JCAE members also become knowledgeable, the president was grateful for his frequent support but repelled by his fervency. The president told Lilienthal, "There's something about McMahon — I don't know. Now I remember a debate in the Senate and McMahon making a speech. When he began, I was for his proposition, but the longer he talked, the more I was against it."[1]

At one point in the early 1950s, McMahon would be the only member of Congress to know the precise size of the U.S. atomic stockpile. Other JCAE members declined to hear such sensitive information from the AEC.

Throughout the Truman and Eisenhower era, though, the Joint Committee would periodically hear from the Central Intelligence Agency on such equally critical matters as friendly and unfriendly countries' attempts to build nuclear capabilities. DCI Hillenkoetter sometimes even discussed the not-very-successful U.S. espionage and covert actions against the USSR.

The legislation promoted by McMahon that September morning seemed shockingly expensive to most legislators, costing almost $1.5 billion. It would give conventional armaments to U.S. allies, even as they and their American partner focused increasingly on the possibility of some future nuclear war. Supporters of the bill had to work hard to secure votes; even many strong anticommunists retained an isolationist streak and hated this "give-away." McMahon described the military aid as necessary, since the USSR sought to "accomplish the mastery of the whole human race." He warned, "We must anticipate war from the Soviet Union as soon as they achieve the where-withal, which consists of a stockpile of atomic bombs." When that day would come, "no man knows, but that it will come is as certain as that I stand on the floor of the Senate today."

Actually, Harry Truman did know: the Soviet Union had exploded its first atomic bomb a few weeks earlier. While the president had decided to inform legislators and the public — denying Joseph Stalin the belief that America could not detect atomic tests — he delayed doing so until after Congress, he hoped, would pass the military aid bill. In Truman's mind, this would avert charges that he exploited the Soviet explosion to gain the arms bill's passage.[2]

When Congress approved the legislation later on September 22, Truman summoned McMahon to hear the news at the White House. The senator was not squeamish on the nuclear topic; a few months before, he had written Secretary of Defense Louis Johnson, "There is a doctrine that we may reach a point when we have 'enough bombs.' To my mind, this doctrine is false." After talking to Truman, McMahon quickly scheduled an emergency JCAE hearing for the next morning. (Records of that session, at which Hillenkoetter and others testified, appear to be nonexistent, although reporters spotted a "very solemn-faced parade" of legislators exiting the meeting.)

With true Hollywood drama, dark clouds that had thickened and reached downward toward Washington during that Friday morning hearing broke into a fierce storm of lightning and hailstones, as eleven o'clock approached. Just then, Truman told his cabinet the atomic news in one part of the White House, while in another (locked) room his old friend and press secretary Charlie Ross watched an assistant pass out copies of the president's statement to reporters. Ross then read it aloud: "We have evidence that within recent weeks an atomic explosion occurred in the USSR." When Secret Service agents unlocked the room's doors, the reporters bolted toward telephones to deliver the news to their organizations. Minutes later, McMahon spoke for the second day in a row to fellow senators, this time with news of "transcendent importance." After reading Truman's statement to a hushed Senate floor, McMahon expressed hope that forthcoming U.S. decisions would be reached "without fear, without hysteria."[3]

The CIA was not the agency to discover the news, but early on as DCI in 1947, Hillenkoetter had urged the U.S. Air Force to employ "suitably equipped planes" to monitor possible Soviet nuclear tests. It started doing so the following year. Using airborne radiological equipment over the Pacific Ocean, the air force had detected reliable evidence of the Soviet's August 29 atomic detonation at the Semipalatinsk test site in Kazakhstan. By contrast, soon after Truman's announcement, Hillenkoetter heard from Willard Machle, the assistant director for scientific intelligence, that the espionage side of the CIA had "failed completely to discharge its responsibility for covert collection of scientific and technical intelligence."

Painful as it was to face such an analysis, Hillenkoetter and associates at the CIA would not be able to deny that the agency had failed to predict the timing of the USSR's transformation into the world's second nuclear power. It was not reassuring to the DCI that a front-page headline in the September 24 *New York Times* read, "Soviet Achievement Ahead of Predictions by 3 Years." Hillenkoetter could only hope that few would ask specifically how the CIA had performed. For the most part, he would be lucky: almost no one in the major newspapers and magazines, not even in the *Times'* story on September 24, raised the question. Nor did the public flood legislators' offices with such inquiries, although ordinary Americans understood the explosion's significance. One Chicago resident asked a *Times* reporter the logical question: "Does Joe Stalin's air force have long range planes capable of carrying A-bombs to Chicago?" The answer, for the time being, was "no," and there was nothing approaching panic among most citizens, who seemed to agree with the logic set forth in *Newsweek*: "It is highly unlikely that Russia would ever consider using the atom bomb to strike a surprise knockout blow. Instead, it probably wanted the bomb primarily as a weapon of retaliation." Further, the magazine (correctly) assured readers, "While the size of our stockpile remains a top secret, it almost certainly numbers more than 100 bombs." In contrast, *U.S. News* predicted, "Skyscrapers no longer will be built, if needs of atomic security are observed. . . . Few persons in such a building will escape, if an atomic bomb is exploded within half a mile."[4]

In Washington, reactions varied wildly. Representative Jacob Javits (R-NY) had the uphill battle of arguing that, despite the successful Soviet test, the United States was winning the Cold War with its "bipartisan foreign policy." He listed major successes: communism had been "nipped in the bud in Italy and Turkey; the blockade of Berlin broken; Trieste pacified; Indonesia on the way to pacification; great progress in Kashmir, Indochina, and Malaya; all countering democracy's very great and very real losses in China." Still, James Reston (in Washington for the *Times*) wrote, "The atomic explosion inside the Soviet Union is already affecting the political atmosphere here very much as the communist coup in Czechoslovakia and the Soviet blockade of Berlin affected it in 1948." Among the most panicked on Capitol Hill was Senator Alexander Wiley (R-WI), who proposed the physical decentralization of the Defense Department, since the Pentagon building was an obvious "suicidal target."[5]

Newsweek wrote, "The news shocked Capitol Hill," but "some members — and this was particularly true of the isolationists — refused to believe it. . . . House Republican leader Joseph W. Martin said it was a 'scare' story and that it meant 'some new Administration request is going to be sent to the Hill.'" At JCAE, though, there was surprise and consternation over the news. Until September 23, its members thought that the Soviet Union would not soon explode an atomic bomb, and for good reason: the CIA had said so.

Agency–Joint Committee relations had developed slowly after the CIA's birth in 1947. Among its occasional reports on Soviet atomic research and development was one conveyed by Hillenkoetter in July 1948 to Truman and Senator Bourke Hickenlooper (R-IA), then JCAE's chair, which said it continued "to be impossible to determine its exact status or to determine the date scheduled by the Soviets for the completion of their first atomic bomb." But it had been "learned" that Stalin was disturbed at his government's lack of progress, and the CIA said that "the earliest date by which it is remotely possible that the USSR may have completed its first atomic bomb is mid-1950, but the most probable date is believed to be mid-1953." How committee members regarded such analyses is unknown, but AEC's Lilienthal had told J. Edgar Hoover a few months earlier that "foreign intelligence on atomic energy" was dreadful and that the president might have to bring about "a drastic change" at CIA.

As CIG's director, Hillenkoetter had appeared at least once before JCAE, but his first documented testimony after the CIA's creation was on March 21,

1949. Then, as in its prior written estimates, the CIA said it had no evidence that the USSR had seriously pursued atomic research before the United States exploded atomic bombs in 1945 and repeated that a Soviet A-bomb was at least a few years from completion. Later in the two-and-a-half-hour hearing, which also featured heads of the different military intelligence services, "Many specific questions were asked Adm. Hillenkoetter by Sen. Tydings as to the relative degree of difficulty in obtaining information from Russia."[6]

Even after the Soviets exploded their first atomic bomb in late August — but before the CIA knew of air force detection of it — the agency produced an "Estimate of Status of Atomic Warfare in the USSR" on September 20. "The current estimate of the Joint Nuclear Intelligence Committee is that the earliest possible date by which the USSR might be expected to produce an atomic bomb is mid-1950 and the most probable date is mid-1953." It was perhaps the most embarrassingly ill-timed and mistaken estimate of the CIA's early years.

On October 14, weeks after the atomic shock, McMahon opened a morning JCAE session by reading (according to meeting notes) that last "report on the Russian stockpile potentialities submitted by a Central Intelligence Authority. The reading of this document evoked considerable discussion." The one thoroughly angry member of the Joint Committee was Senator Eugene Millikin (R-CO). After eight years in Washington, Millikin had become influential among Senate Republicans and showed no reluctance to speak his mind in hearings and on the floor. Earlier in the year, when Dean Acheson waffled on the question of JCAE's authority to shape nuclear policy, including diplomacy, Millikin reproached him sharply — Congress had "pre-empted this field" and would not permit the administration to negotiate with allies over nuclear information sharing without first getting JCAE approval of offers to be made. In the October 14 hearing, when he heard fellow JCAE members first debate whether or not a president would ever really use an A-bomb and then fret over who would have the power to make such a decision in the event of presidential disability, "Senator Millikin commented that he had always assumed that there would be men with guts enough, when the time came, so that the proper decision would be made with regard to the use of the bomb, regardless of the law."

The stout Millikin — considered a bully by Pforzheimer and a juvenile by McMahon — seethed at the hearing over his distinct memory that the JCAE had "been misled by previous assurances of the CIA Director Admiral Hillenkoetter, when it was told . . . that the United States actually had agents in Russia; that it had gotten some of its agents out of Russia with information; that it was screening people leaving and escaping Russia; and the implication that it possessed much factual data upon which the previously estimated date of completion of the first weapon by Russia had been arrived at." The best that Millikin could say about Hillenkoetter was that his distortions were possibly unintentional. Senator Tom Connally (D-TX), who headed the Foreign Relations Committee, "replied that it was a difficult matter to obtain actual information from Russia," but the lengthy discussion ended with a mandate "that the Chairman should summon the CIA people to a meeting as soon as possible."

Before recessing, members heard from General Omar Bradley, the JCS chair, who "stated that he did not anticipate that Russia would attack immediately. He said he felt that they would wait until they had a reasonable stockpile upon which to draw." Another general "stated that the military fears that now that the Russians have a regular atomic weapon, they may be pushing for the super-weapon and conceivably might succeed prior to success in this country." Asked how "super" the hydrogen bomb might be, if actually invented, he said there would be "no limit to its power." The prospect of an American H-bomb no doubt thrilled some JCAE members, but Connally "commented that he would like to resign from the whole damn thing. And when asked what he meant, said that this thing was going beyond all bounds." Bradley responded, "Well, gentlemen, whether it is atomic bombs, machine guns, or gas, in the final analysis my position is that war itself is immoral, and most any weapon might be used under certain circumstances to achieve a military end."[7]

After the Friday morning hearing, McMahon wasted no time in summoning Hillenkoetter. On the following Monday morning at 10:30, again in Room 48-G of the Capitol, the DCI faced the Joint Committee, with some AEC members also there. "I will try to explain how this joint nuclear energy intelligence committee arrived at that estimate," he said, and then claimed that "our estimates were not too far off," in that CIA assumed a passage of "five years from the time they knew about the bomb until it was produced." Unfortunately, "it looks very much now as if the Russians, instead of starting in 1945, certainly started the theoretical side and made perhaps even part of the construction side in 1943." Furthermore, the Soviets apparently had relied on "espionage cases . . . much more than we gave them credit for."

In stating this, the DCI quietly verified some conservative legislators' public claims. Hickenlooper had complained to the Senate on September 26, "I have been repeatedly accused of seeing ghosts around every corner by those who pooh-pooh security," but it was obvious that America's "atomic energy project has been Russia's number one espionage target." Administration officials denied that espionage mattered much in this case, though historians have subsequently claimed that the German-born Soviet agent Klaus Fuchs and others obtained information that (as Richard Aldrich wrote) perhaps "saved the Soviets between a year and eighteen months of scientific work."

If Hillenkoetter had known what critical questions lay ahead in the hearing, he might have also explained in his opening statement that he had urged the air force to monitor atmospheric conditions around the USSR, pushed the military to focus signals intelligence on Soviet nuclear efforts, and led his agency to decide earlier in 1949 that it was "essential that every means be utilized to . . . fix the precise location of the major atomic installations in the USSR." He also could have described a dysfunctional AEC-CIA relationship, with both bureaucracies responsible for the intelligence failure.

Skipping the customary compliments that legislators usually offered high-ranking officials after their opening statements, committee members started questioning the DCI about the CIA's latest nuclear intelligence. Were the Russians researching creation of thermonuclear weapons, McMahon asked, only to be told, "They must be in that, but we have come across nothing to indicate that at all so far, sir." Hearing that the Russians were about to complete construction of a third atomic bomb, meaning they would have an arsenal of two, McMahon inquired, "Are we sure of that, that they have two?" The CIA was sure, Hillenkoetter said. Furthermore, Soviet leaders were uncertain over "how we found out about this atomic bomb explosion." "I would like to believe that," said McMahon, but he did not.

When members took the discussion to the fact that Drew Pearson, Walter Winchell, and others in the press claimed to have known a Soviet explosion was coming, Hillenkoetter was reduced to labeling them "damn poor patriots" who did not "come around and tell us anything about it until after it had been announced." Another member reminded Hillenkoetter that General Walter "Beetle" Smith had predicted the previous June, in an off-the-record speech, that the Soviets would soon do a test explosion. In fact, the JCAE had written Hillenkoetter on June 29, after Smith's speech, seeking a comment. The DCI—unaware that he was evaluating the remarks of his eventual successor—had brushed off the prediction as vague.

Some members wanted a spoken world tour of the sort that would become customary when future DCIs appeared before legislators, discussing conditions and events in various countries. One extended dialogue concerned the odds that the Soviet Union might invade Western Europe. Hillenkoetter told Representative Henry Jackson (D-WA), "There is no indication now under present conditions, sir, and that is certainly good for about six months. It does not mean that it is going to change after six months, but that is as far as we can see ahead." "What about Yugoslavia, against Tito," asked Jackson. "No, sir, they will not," responded the DCI. Senator William Knowland (R-CA) asked, "What is the significance of the reports that the Russians had moved some armored divisions into proximity of the Yugoslavia border? Is that merely sword rattling or is that a fact?" That was "definitely a step in the Cold War," said Hillenkoetter, who continued, "We have had the order of battle there for a long time and it is the 57th Guards Mechanized Division, and it is not an armored division."

How much notice would the CIA get, Jackson asked, if the USSR were "getting ready for a strike?" "You can figure a minimum of a month," was the response. "But aren't they prepared right now with the ground forces they have, and the air forces they have, and by the end of the year what they will have in the atomic weapon field, to move on very short notice?" asked Jackson. "No sir . . . they could start an air raid and put on an air raid over Belgrade or Paris or Berlin on practically no notice, but they could not move their ground forces or their air forces in any numbers without a month's notice," said Hillenkoetter, who added that "assistance" from Eastern European allies to the Soviet Union would be "almost nil." If the USSR did decide on an invasion, "most of their divisions are going to be walking divisions." He reminded Jackson, "They are not preparing for war now."

Jackson was not reassured: "I hope that we don't under-rate them again." To this, Hillenkoetter was firm: "We are not under-rating them. We are giving them every benefit and every assumption in their favor." He cited a multitude of Soviet difficulties, should they foolishly choose war. Among them was that "transportation facilities are very weak in Russia, and they are going to be weak for years there." Still, Hillenkoetter assumed that the Soviets wished to take Western Europe. When Jackson asked about "the Russian mind" in relation to war, the DCI said, "If they knew that they were going to have victory, you would probably have it today."

Hillenkoetter's last moment of placid exchange at the hearing came when McMahon asked, "Has your organization given any thought to methods of detection against bringing bombs in here on ships in our harbors?" "No, sir, not directly," he replied. "There is a committee of internal security which takes in the FBI and all of the military things, and the Navy considered some of that." McMahon then suggested that the bomb-in-a-harbor scenario had once been the subject of "a great deal of concern," but Hillenkoetter only responded, "That has been referred to this committee, and Mr. Hoover is the chairman of that thing to try to work out something."

To this point, JCAE members had treated Hillenkoetter with some deference, but Millikin — having steamed for four days — demanded an explanation of "why we were taken by surprise on the Russian explosion." Hillenkoetter was unprepared for the question: "What do you mean, Senator? I don't think that we were taken by surprise." Millikin then summarized several previous "inquiries" made by the JCAE "as to what our intelligence service consisted of" and described what "we were told" about Soviet nuclear capabilities. While his summary is still classified over a half-century later, Millikin's evaluation of CIA performance is not: "It seems to me that we muffed it at least a year and maybe longer. . . . How did we muff it, and what is wrong with our system?" Hillenkoetter launched a brief defense of the CIA working from "a very great number of fragments of information," but quickly admitted, "I think we made a mistake."

Millikin's next question and Hillenkoetter's response remain completely censored, but it obviously did not satisfy the senator, who acknowledged "the difficulties that you operate under and I know that you have to deal with fragmentary information." He then apparently rephrased the question, to which Hillenkoetter answered, "Well, the only thing that I can give you on this is that we just didn't get enough information out on it." After another (still censored) restatement of the question and an unsatisfactory answer from Hillenkoetter, Millikin was all the more exasperated: "I want to know why we didn't get the information as to what was going on." Hillenkoetter began to equal Millikin in his own exasperation: "I can't answer that 'why?'. We didn't get enough to do it."

Senator Connally attempted his own characterization of the intelligence failure: "We knew that they were working on it, but we didn't know that they had the bomb until it went off?" Hillenkoetter tried again:

> We knew that they were working on it, and we started here, and this organization [CIA] was set up after the war and we started in the middle and we didn't know when they had started and it had to be picked up from what we could get along there. That is what I say: this thing of getting a fact that you definitely have on the exploding of this bomb has helped us in going back and looking over

what we had before, and it will help us in what we get in the future. But you picked up in mid-air on the thing, and we didn't know when they started, sir.

Millikin sourly responded, "That is not quite a victory for intelligence," and then took Hillenkoetter through questions and answers that fill up still-censored transcript pages. Accompanying remarks suggest that one of the topics was the CIA's poor human intelligence capabilities, the enhancement of which Millikin thought Congress would gladly pay for, if only the CIA would better mobilize its spies. Millikin capped off that exchange with a sarcastic question: "Does that begin to commence to start to represent an adequate intelligence organization?"

Again, another JCAE member tried to allow Hillenkoetter to give a better explanation of how the A-test came about so soon. The DCI did so by focusing on the quality of Russian scientists as "number one," but Millikin thought this an evasion: "I am not challenging that. I am challenging the fact that we apparently don't have the remotest idea of what they are doing until after they have done it, and I am not so much interested in what has happened, but I am interested in how bad we are going to muff future developments."

When Jackson and McMahon reviewed with Hillenkoetter the different nuclear estimates provided to the JCAE in 1949, it became clear that the CIA had at least described some progress in the Soviet program. But, as Hillenkoetter admitted to Millikin, the CIA had never suggested any possibility of a test before 1950. The senator saw little difference between two of the estimates — one was "a very erroneous estimate as of January 1, 1949," the other a "very bad mis-estimate as late as July of this year." Summarizing the damage done, Millikin said, "Our diplomatic plans and the whole complexion has been predicated on having enough room to work out solutions, and that is what makes it so serious that we muffed it."

Next the senator turned to the "industrial material" necessary to build an A-bomb:

> I am talking about the equipment, the valves, the filters, and the rest of it. Where have they gotten that stuff?
>
> Admiral Hillenkoetter: Most of it they made themselves, sir.
>
> Senator Millikin: They have built up the industry which we have always estimated that they could not build up for a number of years ahead of this time?
>
> Admiral Hillenkoetter: Yes, sir.

Senator Millikin: They have done that and we didn't know about it. Well, what are we going to do now to keep from getting caught that bad off-base in the future?

Admiral Hillenkoetter: We will do the best we can to get all of the information. We would desire it more than anybody else, to get all of the information.

At this point, McMahon joined other members in voicing concern about "press and magazine articles in great number about the possibilities of a super-weapon" program in the USSR. Convinced that the United States was moving too slowly to build a super-weapon, the chairman secured Hillenkoetter's acknowledgement of press reports, then observed,

I know, because I have talked with you privately, that you agree with me that the detection of progress upon the super-weapon is of the greatest and utmost importance to us. Because, frankly, if they should get it and we should not have it . . . it might well mean the difference between our existence as a nation and not existing.

Admiral Hillenkoetter: That is right.

The Chairman: You are bearing a very, very heavy responsibility.

Admiral Hillenkoetter: I haven't slacked down on trying to get any more information, sir. We have increased as much as we can and given it high priorities and everything else and we are trying to get all we can, sir.

The Chairman: Now, Admiral, that is all I can say to you.

McMahon started to end the hearing, but Millikin blurted out, "I just get no comfort out of anything that the Admiral has said to us. We have not had an organization adequate to know what is going on in the past and he gives me no assurance that we are going to have one in the future." Millikin returned to the CIA's failed utilization of human intelligence toward the USSR. Though most of this discussion remains censored, Millikin's surviving remarks and Hillenkoetter's responses make clear that the "need" for the DCI to bring about a far more robust spying organization was the topic. Hillenkoetter was finally agitated: "There is no way of getting an organization like that. We could put 10,000 people in Russia, and there is no assurance that we would have all of the information that we have, that you would be certain of it. I couldn't take the responsibility of saying that you can give us 100,000, and say that we would definitely know what they were going to do, and when they were going to produce a bomb. This thing doesn't work that way." But Millikin insisted that he had not made so crude an assumption: "I suggest that maybe one qualified observer might be worth 10,000 or 100,000 that you are talking about." On this, Hillenkoetter said, they could agree.

Chet Holifield briefly addressed Millikin in Hillenkoetter's defense: "You can't order a piece of intelligence out of Russia like you order groceries in the morning." Senator Knowland wondered to Hillenkoetter, "Is there anything . . . that the Congress can do in the way of funds or authority that you do not now have that you need, be it the problem of placing the agents and correlating the information?" Not a thing, said Hillenkoetter. What about the CIA Act recently passed, "allowing a certain number of aliens," Henry Jackson asked—had it "been quite a bit of help" and was the quota of aliens permitted adequate? "Yes, more than adequate."[8]

Not for the first or last time had the director lacked the shrewdness to protect himself, politically, in a hearing. With an unsolicited assurance from McMahon that JCAE would leak nothing from the hearing, Hillenkoetter was excused. Records of his probable appearances before other committees about the Soviet test have not surfaced, but news of his unimpressive performance at JCAE would have spread—many of its members led other foreign affairs and defense committees. The Joint Committee would also call Hillenkoetter back to testify again about the intelligence failure the following year. (Hillenkoetter was faithful, though, and often prudent: with his pledge to the committee in mind—of maximum increased intelligence efforts— he urged air force chief of staff Hoyt Vandenberg to expand the charter and funding of the agency that had detected the Soviet blast.)

The CIA reputation among government heads in Washington suffered, too, even though the press hardly picked up on the "intelligence failure" theme. Truman later wrote that the Soviet test "came sooner than the experts had estimated," but claimed that the "direction" of the U.S. nuclear program did not change because of that surprise. Atomic energy commissioner Lilienthal, following talks with "fine minds," conveyed to his diary on October 29 his impression that "the Russian bomb has changed the situation drastically, and that the talk about our having anticipated everything and following the same program we had before is . . . bunk."

Like some others, Brien McMahon became so unnerved by apparent Soviet nuclear progress and America's inability to monitor it that his fears about all-out war deepened for the rest of the year. Lilienthal wrote of the Halloween night during which he and colleagues "spent a couple of hours in my office with Senator McMahon. Pretty discouraging. What he is talking is the inevitability of war with the Russians, and what he says adds up to one thing: blow them off the face of the earth, quick, before they do the same to us." To McMahon's apparent anger, Lilienthal responded, "I don't believe that." A few weeks later, McMahon urgently advised Truman to speed up H-bomb development and stockpiling. "Our first duty consists in doing what is necessary to win," he said, adding that there was no reason to keep those efforts secret: "The people of New York are entitled to know that an innocent-appearing merchant vessel registered under the Dominican flag might introduce a Russian super into their harbor and destroy, not just a few square miles, but their entire metropolis. The people of Chicago are entitled to know that a robot-controlled bomber, located only a few hours away in Kamchatka, might visit their city at night and leave it a wasteland."

Truman did authorize prompt development of an H-bomb, and the United States would have its first successful test explosion in November 1952, shortly before Truman's presidency ended. McMahon, though, would not live to see it. Early in the year, he had announced his candidacy for the Democratic presidential nomination but died quickly after being diagnosed with cancer in the summer. In 1953, the Soviets would also become a thermonuclear power.

As a result of the October 17, 1949, JCAE hearing, the previously noted warning by Hillenkoetter's aides rang all the more true: Congress had placed "on us the burden of correlating and evaluating intelligence relating to the national security." Legislators left no doubt that if "any questions arose . . . the Congress would hold the Director personally responsible and look no further."[9]

Communists and "Perverts" in the CIA

Early in 1950, Wisconsin's Republican senator Joseph McCarthy pounced on an issue that, while not new, was ripe for political exploitation — communist infiltration of the U.S. government. The House Un-American Activities Committee had long highlighted the problem, which gained more public attention on February 2 when the impending arraignment of Klaus Fuchs, the Soviet agent who had worked for Britain as a scientist on the Manhattan project, was announced in London. "The roof fell in today," wrote David Lilienthal. "Tie on your hat," Harry Truman told a national security aide. (The beleaguered Hillenkoetter heard from Pforzheimer on February 7 that JCAE wanted "to question you further in connection with the Russian atomic explosion, and . . . whether we have taken the Fuchs defection into account in our present estimates. They also wish to discuss the background information and our present feeling as to the reliability of certain matters contained in our semi-annual report.")

Even before the Fuchs event, some legislators had worried about the communist infiltration issue or considered how to make hay out of it. Still, no one else on Capitol Hill had developed the rhetorical skill and killer instinct that McCarthy suddenly evidenced in Wheeling, West Virginia, on February 9. Although the State Department was the primary target of the Wisconsin senator when he claimed to possess a "list" of communists working there, the CIA was no uninterested bystander. Its overseers, like Senate Armed Services chair Millard Tydings, would be inclined to protect the agency, although that would hardly be their top priority in so fevered a year. Eleven days after McCarthy's Wheeling speech, he was to detail his supposed findings on the Senate floor. Although he had gained considerable national attention at Wheeling, the establishment press and McCarthy's fellow senators were still unsure whether he deserved sustained attention, much less respect.

With the sun already setting and bitter winter temperatures enveloping Washington on February 20, most senators had left for the day before McCarthy began speaking on the Senate floor. He and Democratic majority leader Scott Lucas (IL) soon quarreled angrily over whether to adjourn or find a quorum's worth of senators from restaurants, theaters, and homes. Those senators present would not adjourn, and so others were rounded up to hear McCarthy's speech, which would last until 11:30 p.m.[1]

Among the 81 persons he mentioned (by case number, rather than name) that evening, McCarthy said all worked for the State Department, except one. That man, "Case Number 11," was "disloyal" to the United States, said McCarthy: "This individual was an analyst in OSS from July 1943 to August 1945, and was employed in the Division of Map Intelligence in the State Department after August 1945. He is a close pal of a known Communist and has stated it would be a good idea if the Communists would take over in this country. He is a regular reader of the Daily Worker. This individual is not in the State Department at this time, but has a job in the CIA as of today."

Two days later, with a huge outcry unfolding in the press, the Senate voted unanimously to investigate the Wisconsin senator's charges. To head the designated special subcommittee of the Foreign Relations Committee, senators chose Tydings, who promised there would be "neither a witch hunt, nor a whitewash." If he sensed that the task at hand might lead to his political doom, the patrician Marylander — described by *Time* magazine as a "thorough and careful" legislator — gave no hint.[2]

In response to the depiction of Case No. 11, Hillenkoetter mobilized Pforzheimer, who wrote in his work diary a few days later, "Delivered letter from Director to Sen. McCarthy regarding Case No. 11. He supplied the name thereof. He stated he was sorry that time had not permitted his informing us of his information prior to making same public, but that he had been rushed into his disclosures prematurely."

Hillenkoetter and Pforzheimer knew that McCarthy was wrong — Case No. 11 had been thoroughly investigated dating back to 1944 and was no communist. The CIA would review those prior investigations, but Pforzheimer recorded that Hillenkoetter "approved my suggestion that an appropriate letter be drafted to Senator McCarthy, first for clearance at the White House, and that this open attack on the Agency must be retracted on the floor of the Senate and the record made clear. If Senator McCarthy is unwilling to do this, then some friendly senator should be requested to do so." As the Wisconsin senator well knew, the CIA had some Republican friends.

If, as weeks passed since his floor speech, McCarthy thought he had Hillenkoetter on the run, he learned otherwise on March 2, 1950, when Pforzheimer hand-delivered the DCI's next letter. It avoided threats but told McCarthy that the charge had been "sufficiently serious to warrant an immediate investigation by the Central Intelligence Agency." Case No. 11 had first been investigated in 1944. After his transfer to the CIA, agency officials had investigated and cleared him. Another investigation, in 1948, had involved a thorough check by the FBI. The CIA "had left no stone unturned" regarding any employees whose loyalty might be in question, Hillenkoetter firmly indicated, and "the charge . . . cannot be sustained." (The DCI sent copies of his communications with McCarthy to Tydings who, besides investigating McCarthy, continued as a CIA overseer.)

Pforzheimer recalls the day he delivered the letter to McCarthy, "The two of us were in his office. Joe read to me all that he wanted me to hear. . . . I said, 'Joe, I know this case from top to bottom. There's nothing to it.' " Additionally, Pforzheimer apparently conveyed the possibility of having a senator publicize McCarthy's error.

The list of supposed communists that McCarthy soon presented to Tydings included eleven State Department employees who had transferred from the old OSS. It would take a few months for Tydings's subcommittee to investigate McCarthy's charges. Quickly, though, the Wisconsin senator, while not offering a public retraction regarding Case No. 11, did suggest a compromise (reported in Pforzheimer's diary): "Sen. McCarthy . . . stated, however, that in view of the fact that the record was satisfied, he would raise no further questions about the case, provided that the Director did not make his letter public or make political issue." Publicizing his letter would have burnished Hillenkoetter's reputation with contemporary and future critics of McCarthy, but the DCI accepted the senator's offer and kept his word.[3]

Years later, Pforzheimer said the DCI's reproach to McCarthy was "an easy call for Hillenkoetter." Not that easy, though. Polls showed that more Americans believed McCarthy's charges than disbelieved them that spring. On Capitol Hill, Drew Pearson had two conversations in March, one with Senator Charles Tobey (R-NH): "He said that every day Republican senators gathered to ask, 'How's Joe doing?' " At the same time, a friend at State's Korean desk told Pearson "that McCarthy has paralyzed almost all the thinking in the State Department, also made it impossible to hire good men." In retrospect, Hillenkoetter's response seems risky and courageous, compared to the widespread trembling by many in front of McCarthy that would continue for four years. Unlike Allen Dulles, celebrated across decades for holding firm against the Wisconsin senator, the Central Intelligence Agency's first director has never been properly credited for standing up to Joe McCarthy.[4]

As March came to a close, Hillenkoetter and Pforzheimer may have expected McCarthy to remain quiet about the CIA. It was not to be. Another issue arose — that numerous homosexuals working in foreign policy bureaucracies endangered national security. Since homosexuality had historically been considered a disgraceful condition in the United States (and elsewhere), the Cold War era was hardly the first time that the American government viewed non-heterosexuals as susceptible to blackmail or simply bad for the "morale" of others in military or intelligence agencies. Thus, the Office of Naval Intelligence (ONI) could reassure a Senate subcommittee in 1950 that, since the beginning of World War II, it had collected files on "7859 known or alleged homosexuals." Though many of those listed were "Naval and Marine Corps personnel — both uniformed and civilian — all of whom have been separated from the service." Others worked "in other branches of government or outside the government."

In Congress, particularly, there was little doubt that homosexuals did not belong in sensitive government positions. Some occasionally argued that homosexuals tended to be communist sympathizers. Joe McCarthy claimed to have asked a top intelligence official about homosexuals, "Is there something about the communist philosophy that attracts them?" He said, "Senator McCarthy, if you had been in this work as long as we have, you would realize that there is something wrong with each one of those individuals. You will find that practically every active communist is twisted mentally or physically in some way."[5]

Still, the Wisconsin senator gave uneven attention to the homosexual "threat." Indeed, McCarthy may have been bisexual. Millard Tydings's files include some lurid letters from men who claimed to have had casual sex with McCarthy and to be outraged by his hypocrisy. "When I was in D.C.," wrote an army lieutenant of McCarthy in December 1951, "he picked me up at the Wardman Bar and took me to his home. While I was half drunk, he performed sodomy on me. So, apparently, the best way to avoid suspicion is to accuse somebody else." McCarthy married, but not until 1953, when he was in his midforties. It may not have been fair for critics to make much of this, but such inferences were common. Drew Pearson claimed, "Many thinking Catholics are dead opposed to McCarthy [and] don't like the fact that he has never married." A memorandum titled "Homosexual Investigations" and circulating at the CIA at roughly the same time said, "The subject's biography furnishes the first indications that he is a homosexual. To detect him, it is vital that the investigator be inquisitive. What is his age? What is his marital status? Is he 35 years old, single, never been married? Why?"

The memo aimed to prevent the employment of homosexuals at the CIA, of course, and did not mention McCarthy. But a few U.S. newspapers wrote of McCarthy's supposed homosexuality. *Las Vegas Sun* publisher Hank Greenspun described McCarthy in print as "the country's leading sex deviate." Most journalists thought it improper to write about politicians' sex lives, however, and only a handful of political figures hinted at their suspicions about the senator.[6]

Some Republican conservatives, mostly allies of McCarthy, raged loudly over evidence that homosexuals held critical government positions. Perhaps most aggressive on the topic was Kenneth Wherry, a Nebraska mortician who led Senate Republicans from 1949 to 1951. The roots of Wherry's considerable fears about homosexuals are unknown. An owner of small businesses back home and a determined moralist, he had become active on the issue by spring 1950, just as McCarthy charged that scores of communists worked in the State Department. In April, having conducted his own "preliminary studies," Wherry told the Senate that homosexuals were as dangerous as the communists. When completed, his study — which would contribute to an Appropriations subcommittee's formal investigation — would be a "revelation," he promised.

Fervent as Wherry was on the issue, his language was not the most extreme on Capitol Hill. In the Senate, speaking on the same April day as Wherry, Karl Mundt (R-SD) described State Department homosexuals as a "ring of sexual perverts." Ralph Owen Brewster (R-ME), saying "a case of this character was brought to my attention by Mr. J. Edgar Hoover" — whose own sexual orientation would be debated by future generations — described homosexuals as "moral degenerates." William Jenner (R-IN), widely viewed by fellow senators as just plain mean, repeatedly used the slur "homos" in urging a reluctant Tydings, already investigating McCarthy's State Department charges, to expand his inquiry. Tydings used Jenner's terminology ("there is a great desire to shift from communists to homos") but reminded the Senate, "The history of spy work has largely been based upon a beautiful woman's extracting secrets from men in government service."[7]

House members' language was no less restrained that spring. Cliff Clevenger (R-WI) asked, "Do we have a cell of these perverts hiding around government?" while Arthur Miller (R-NE) described homosexuals as "pathological cases." Clare Hoffman spoke of "those dirty, nasty people on the Federal payroll" and — when asked by a colleague, "Can you tell me what a homosexual is?" — responded, "I will not dirty my mouth by defining it."

Still, most members of Congress were not so impassioned about the issue, as Miller learned that spring when he introduced an amendment banning the

Economic Cooperation Administration (the ECA, which administered the Marshall Plan) from employing homosexuals. Miller had successfully pushed a bill through the prior Republican-majority Congress criminalizing homosexuals acts in Washington, DC. Now, he wished to "strip the fetid, stinking flesh off this skeleton of homosexuality and tell my colleagues of the House some of the facts of nature." Despite the relatively new law, he said sarcastically, "Washington attracts many lovely folks. The sex crimes in the city are many." He went on to elaborate about "fairy parties" in "one of our prominent restaurants," and explained homosexual terminology — "you will find those people using the words as, 'He is a fish. He is a bull-dicker. He is a mamma, and he is a papa, and punk, and pimp.'" Many, Miller claimed, previously or still worked in the State Department and other agencies. "I sometimes wonder," he said, "how many of these homosexuals have had a part in shaping our foreign policy. How many have been in sensitive positions and subject to blackmail?" Miller later told the House of his education on the topic:

> Within the last ten days, a gentleman from CIA told me that Mr. [Herman] Goering of Germany and others had a complete list of all the homosexuals in the State Department, the Department of Commerce, and the Department of Defense, and that they knew who to contact when they came over here on espionage missions. . . . I do know from very extensive reading the last few weeks that the Russians rather glory in the accomplishments resulting from homosexuality, and they undoubtedly have the same list of homosexuals who were in key positions in government in this country, so they knew who to contact when they came here.

Few wanted to debate his amendment, though. Not even half of the House membership voted, and it lost on a near party-line vote. This led Miller to complain on the floor, "Yesterday a taxicab driver told me that the homosexuals had quite a celebration on Saturday and Sunday nights. . . . I think the Democratic majority in the House who voted on a straight party line would want to know about this celebration, because you like to spread joy and sunshine and, by your vote, did bring joy to the homosexuals now employed in government work."[8]

Those voting against the amendment were hardly friends of homosexuality. Many in and out of government knew just enough about it to convince them that they did not want to know more, much less wage any crusades. General Dwight Eisenhower personified this view after a painful, enlightening experience described by a scholar:

During the postwar occupation of Europe . . . Eisenhower heard rumors of lesbian activity among the WACs. He reportedly asked his staff associate, WAC Sergeant Johnnie Phelps, to conduct an investigation and to obtain a list of suspected lesbians, who would then be separated. Phelps, who greatly respected Eisenhower, recalls that she agreed to conduct the investigation, but told him that discharging all the lesbians would clean out the battalion of its most industrious and decorated personnel and officers. She added, "and the first name on the list will be mine." Eisenhower's secretary corrected her: "If the General pleases, Sergeant Phelps will have to be second on the list. I'm going to type it. My name will be first." By Phelps's later account, a stunned Eisenhower shook his head and said, "Forget the order."

While many in government shared Eisenhower's lack of fervor, the early 1950s was a time of growing hysteria and homophobic government policies. The government had dismissed, on average, about five homosexuals from civilian posts each month in the late 1940s; by 1954, when Eisenhower was president, that number had grown twelvefold. Historian Neil Miller writes, "Dire warnings about perverts in Washington helped create an atmosphere of persecution and purge nationwide. In the nation's capital itself, arrests of gay men numbered one thousand a year in the 1950s, with D.C. police entrapping men in Lafayette Park and downtown movie houses."[9] Mixed in with the hysterics was some logic, though: homosexuals faced condemnation and discrimination, and most of them — wishing to conceal their orientation — were vulnerable to blackmail. The CIA had a most unusual case in 1950, however, of a homosexual who was open about his sexuality.

His name was Carmel Offie. Born to a working-class family in Pennsylvania, a bright, energetic, young Offie joined the State Department as a mere clerk in 1931. On his first assignment abroad, in Honduras, he quickly earned the admiration of the mission chief, Lawrence Higgins. By 1934, he was at the U.S. embassy in Moscow. With big teeth and lips and a double-bar mustache contributing to looks that one author has described as "small" and "oily," Offie devoured information and loved gossip, always doling it out to serve his interests. During a long career, he would endear himself and become indispensable to many powerful patrons in and out of the State Department, including Ambassadors William Bullitt (for whom he worked in Moscow and then Paris) and Joseph Kennedy (who tried to hire Offie away from State as a personal assistant), the foreign service officer Douglas

MacArthur II, and even the Duchess of Windsor. As a sometime-admirer put it, "Everybody used Offie. He was funny as the dickens."

An under-studied figure from CIA history, Offie's astonishing personality has been best captured by Burton Hersh, who writes, for example, of the day in 1940 when Ambassador Bullitt and associates reluctantly left Nazi-dominated Paris:

> On June 30, a five-car caravan directed by military attaché Roscoe Hillenkoetter finally started south. It included Robert Murphy, Offie, and Mr. and Mrs. Dudley Gilroy. Mrs. Gilroy was a childhood friend of the ambassador, and she and her British husband were entered in the documents as Bullitt's butler and maid. "She is not a maid," a Spanish frontier official charged, judging by Mrs. Gilroy's fashionable ensemble.
>
> "Of course not," Offie piped up, never at a loss. "Don't you understand that the ambassador has a mistress?" The group crossed over.

Years later, a still-amazed admirer told Hersh, "Who was it that said about Offie that either he was going to be Secretary of State some day or his body was going to be found floating down the Potomac River?"

One of Offie's appreciative superiors in the late 1940s was Frank Wisner, head of the OPC, which, as noted earlier, was substantially autonomous from Hillenkoetter's control. Not understanding Offie's sheer usefulness to his bosses, some friends thought Wisner had a remarkable blind spot toward his subordinate, whose open homosexuality was only one characteristic that might have disqualified him from high-ranking intelligence service. Another was his cavalier use of government funds and services for personal aggrandizement: once, while working abroad for the State Department, he illegally used the diplomatic mail service to ship jewels, currency, and, on one occasion, hundreds of lobsters. After such practices finally got him thrown out by State in 1948, his mentors persuaded Wisner to take Offie into the new OPC. Soon, Offie was handling such important tasks as overseeing recruitment of refugees from European camps to work in covert efforts against the Soviet Union. Offie also presided over the importation of scores of refugees each year into the United States, as allowed by the Central Intelligence Agency Act of 1949.

"For two largely hell-for-leather break-in years," Hersh writes, "the Office of Policy Coordination functioned in a power warp, largely outside the allotted bureaucratic constrictions of close operation oversight and line accountability." Everyone who worked in Offie's office recalls his "practice of stamping in early every morning to place a round of calls to OPC stations in London, Paris, Rome, Frankfurt. Fortified, he'd summon his staff and pass assignments out with both hands. Discussion was not encouraged." Many at CIA and OPC hated him. "I thought he was just a shit," recalls Pforzheimer. Nonetheless, Hersh writes that, until Offie took over, "most of the planning sessions around the government which dealt with stopping the Soviets, rolling Eastern Europe back, amounted to that entirely—talk. He supplied the spark plug: with Offie on board, suddenly the politically unthinkable became inevitable, what once seemed remote turned into the shortest distance between two policy objectives." Most of the European ventures ultimately failed, but OPC and CIA leaders only acknowledged this with the passage of years. One more-or-less successful venture was Radio Free Europe, which owed its early functioning to Offie's skills. Hersh notes, "Offie scrounged up the first of Radio Free Europe's transmitters, a mobile unit borrowed from the Army, and initiated the Czech broadcasts. Then, calling on his many contacts throughout the occupation command, he secured 'a decent status for the Radio in Munich,' one participant remembers."[10]

Busy as he was at OPC's dowdy Washington headquarters, where he spent millions of dollars each year, the sexually promiscuous Offie also presided over a lively DuPont Circle residence and often branched out from the home front. As a result, Offie's formal employment by OPC/CIA came into question after he propositioned the wrong young men in a public restroom at Lafayette Park and was arrested by District of Columbia police. It happened, apparently, very early in 1950. Some weeks after the event, Senator Wherry—whose investigative subcommittee had established close relations with DC police—learned of Offie's arrest. A portion of one of Wherry's hearings, where he discussed Offie's arrest with an ONI leader, survives:

> Senator Wherry: Let's be frank about this. Do you know a man by the name of Offie?
> Mr. Mullikan: I know him.
> Senator Wherry: Isn't he in CIA at this time?
> Mr. Mullikan: Yes, sir. I know something about him.
> Senator Wherry: Is it a fact he was loaned by the State Department to CIA?
> Mr. Mullikan: I think it is a fact to say that he went from the State Department to CIA. I don't know about the loaning.
> Senator Wherry: Do you know whether that fellow has anything against his record?

Mr. Mullikan: Yes, sir.

Senator Wherry: Well, it is a matter of record, and it is right down here at the Police Department, isn't that true?

Mr. Mullikan: Yes, sir.

Senator Wherry: . . . How could it be possible that that man can hold the post he holds now?

Mr. Mullikan: . . . I couldn't answer, except to say that Offie was never of any direct interest to us as a direct responsibility.

Senator Wherry: . . . Have you seen his record?

Mr. Mullikan: Yes, sir.

Senator Wherry: From the record you have seen, would you think he would be a good employee in intelligence?

Mr. Mullikan: I would say not.

Senator Wherry: . . . The State Department, if they know about that record, and I think they ought to know about it, they should never have loaned or leased or let him go to CIA.[11]

Wherry's hearing was in secret, but word about a "pervert" working in a key covert action position at the CIA spread around Capitol Hill. This process was apparently aided by certain OPC/CIA members who saw an opportunity to oust Offie from government service. Some of these later claimed that Wisner supported their "investigative" efforts. Meanwhile, J. Edgar Hoover authorized agents to spy on Offie. Hersh writes of teams of special agents shadowing Offie "through well-established gay haunts like Mickey's Grill and David's Bar; they submitted a file entry each time some youngster in uniform rebuffed Offie; they logged strangers entering and leaving Offie's residence." Hoover and others even suspected, but certainly never established, that Offie was a spy for the USSR. Paul Nitze, who advised presidents for decades about foreign policy, later observed, "I don't know whether Carmel Offie was a double agent or whether he was not. . . . He didn't scare anybody because everybody knew he was a pansy." CIA's counterintelligence head James Angleton sometimes wondered aloud about Offie but claimed in retirement that no one had ever seriously "questioned his loyalty."

The growing commotion about Offie occurred just weeks after McCarthy began charging that scores of communists worked in the government. Indeed, McCarthy appears to have referred to Offie as Case No. 14 during his initial February floor speech detailing eighty-one cases, when he referred to a flagrant homosexual who had retained a government job a few years earlier following intervention by a "high State Department official." Initially, the case gained little attention, but by March, McCarthy and Republican allies knew more of the Offie story. They would make such frightful noises about it that a leading Democrat, a self-described "friend" of the agency, considered taking decisive action to end the controversy.

Legislative liaison Pforzheimer's work diary, in portions declassified a half century later, conveys the Capitol Hill rumblings: "Friday — 10 March 1950. . . . [CIA security chief Sheffield] Edwards informed me that information had been received that Sen. McCarthy was considering charging an employee of this Agency with homosexual practices in connection with the present investigation of security risks in the Government."

On that day, McCarthy referred to the matter again on the Senate floor, but it was not until a March 14 Tydings subcommittee hearing that he specifically linked the Offie case — his name not mentioned — to the CIA. As the *Post* reported, "In addition to the four persons he named publicly, McCarthy gave the subcommittee one name in private. He said it was a man formerly in the State Department, with a record of homosexual activities. He was allowed to resign from the Department, McCarthy said, and now obtains a $10,000 to $12,000 salary from the Central Intelligence Agency."

At CIA, Pforzheimer noted:

Tuesday — 14 March 1950. . . . Regarding Sen. McCarthy's charges in the Senate subcommittee today, the Director stated that he would handle this case personally, and that Col. Edwards and myself would not step into it at this time.

Thursday — 16 March 1950. . . . Call from Mr. Druckenbrod of the International News Service requesting comment on charges by Senator McCarthy that this Agency was employing a notorious homosexual. Informed him that in view of the fact that we had not been supplied with a name, either by Senator McCarthy or the committee, we could not comment. The same information was given to Mr. Roger Green of the Associated Press.

Friday — 17 March 1950. . . . The secretary to Rep. Nixon called . . . to inquire whether a certain homosexual was presently employed in this Agency and was informed that he was.[12]

Hillenkoetter's and Wisner's actions in the Offie case remain obscure. The director of central intelligence had a long acquaintance with Offie, going back to their work for Bullitt in Moscow and Paris. But Hillenkoetter confided in few subordinates at the CIA and never told his legislative liaison Pforzheimer what — if anything — he was doing either to save or dismiss Offie. Pforzheimer recalled, years later, that Wisner was more likely to protect his protégés. Indeed, Pforzheimer remembers another "case" of "a guy that some of us thought was homosexual and some of us were involved in trying to get him out. He was one of Frank's pets. He was fired from the CIA, but I heard that he was given a job in Latin America and that Frank arranged that."

Early in April, House Democratic majority leader John McCormack stepped in. The Massachusetts representative was a leading member of the Executive Expenditures Committee and had helped create the Central Intelligence Agency. Despite his skeletal, pale face and white head of hair, McCormack was energetic and a quick study. The CIA was a vital asset in the Cold War, he believed. Though a whole-hearted Catholic and probably horrified at the thought of homosexuality, McCormack was not one to lead campaigns against them. Dismayed that McCarthyite House Republicans were beginning to publicize Offie's arrest and criticize the CIA for keeping him on, McCormack summoned Pforzheimer to his office. The liaison's diary reads:

> Monday — 3 April 1950. . . . House Majority Leader requested that I talk with him. The question he wished to discuss was the problem of homosexuals in the CIA, and one case in particular. The congressman pointed out that this Agency could not afford to have any such personnel and that he had been informed of this particular case by the press. It was his further information that the Republican Policy Committee had determined to attack CIA in this connection, and that this Agency's friends would be completely defenseless and would be unable to defend the Agency in this connection. I have discussed the matter with the Director, who has authorized me to take certain additional steps with Rep. McCormack.

By April 14, Pforzheimer learned that "Senator Wherry had in his possession photostatic copies of the police record of the CIA employee engaged in homosexual activities and planned to make use of same on the floor of the Senate at the appropriate time." About the same time, Republican National Chairman Guy Gabrielson asserted that "sexual perverts who have infiltrated our government in recent years" were "perhaps as dangerous as the actual communists." The story was "the talk of Washington," he claimed in a newsletter to party leaders around the nation.

With the reputation of the CIA endangered, McCormack quickly took his message to Hillenkoetter — Offie had to resign. The DCI's response is unknown, but McCormack may have sensed reluctance on Hillenkoetter's part, for (as Pforzheimer noted), "Mr. McCormack informed me that on the 18th of April, he discussed with the President the question of a homosexual in CIA." Harry Truman's calendar for that Tuesday morning indicates that his Oval Office meeting with McCormack included two other top congressional Democrats — Speaker Sam Rayburn and Senate majority leader Scott Lucas. The unrecorded discussion almost certainly solidified powerful Democratic sentiment that the CIA could not continue to have as one of its top covert action managers a homosexual alleged to have solicited sex in public places.[13]

Wherry, meanwhile, was not yet publicly mentioning the CIA in relation to the case but warned on the 24th that if persons dismissed from State are then "employed in any other branch of the government in a high position, he is just as bad a loyalty risk." Wherry and many others were furious but saw political opportunity that night upon learning that President Truman claimed that not a "single person who has been adjudged to be a communist or otherwise disloyal remains on the government payroll today," and that communists in the United States, while "noisy" and "troublesome," were "not a major threat." His remarks came just three months after a jury convicted Alger Hiss, formerly of the State Department, on two counts of lying about past communist associations and activities.

In the meantime, McCarthy surmised that Offie, while technically working at the CIA, received his paycheck from another agency. On April 25, he chided Tydings on the Senate floor, asking if he had forgotten receiving "a complete criminal record of a man getting somewhere between $10,000 and $12,000 a year? This man has now been assigned to the Central Intelligence Agency. . . . The record shows — it is a police record — that he spent his time hanging around the men's room in Lafayette Park. This man is still in an extremely sensitive position." Still more legislators spoke up. Karl Mundt said Tydings must look into the problem of "espionage and sexual perversion." On the defensive, Tydings nonetheless asked: "Suppose a man has an unfortunate disease — I use that term for want of a better one — but has never been charged with being disloyal. What should we do about that?"

Any attempts by Offie to save his job remain unknown. He may well have reflected on the injustice of facing professional demise because of his sex life, but Offie had hardly been innocent of such intrigues himself. He had helped destroy the career of the bisexual Under Secretary of State Sumner Welles seven years earlier by distributing evidence of Welles's indiscreet prowling on a train back in 1940. Offie schemed at the behest of Welles's enemy, Bullitt, who (Hersh writes) "handed Carmel a pile of incriminating railroad documents and directed him to distribute these handbills around Capitol Hill. Then Bullitt pushed in on Roosevelt and told the aghast FDR that he 'could not ignore the scandal any longer, because now every congressman, every senator knows.' " Maine's Senator Ralph Owen Brewster drew on the evidence from Offie and Bullitt to lead an increasingly unquiet crusade against Welles, who resigned in 1943, much to FDR's distress. By 1950, Brewster described himself as "startled" by Tydings's softness on the security threat posed by "moral degenerates" in government and pressed the Truman administration for the removal of his one-time ally, Carmel Offie.[14]

Pforzheimer's diary entry for April 25, 1950, tells of two fires, one literal, the other figurative. "A fire broke out in Central Building," he wrote that day, "and was attended by the General Counsel and myself." Despite Pforzheimer's and Lawrence Houston's dousing the fire, someone had also called the fire department. This immediately raised the question of whether firemen should be let into a CIA building. They were, without apparent harm to national security, but the uncertainty that day called (Pforzheimer wrote), "for a complete overhaul of the Agency disaster plan and all procedures connected with emergencies in CIA building." Though declassified in 2000, another section of the diary entry remains partly censored by the CIA: "Senator McCarthy informed me that he had found out why CIA had been unable to fire its pet homosexual — namely, because he was [words censored] and not by the Agency." On the Senate floor, McCarthy explained that State paid Offie's salary, so he could not be fired by the CIA, but perhaps the Senator conveyed some awareness of OPC in talking to Pforzheimer. Also on the floor that day, Wherry kept up his attacks by posing a question to Jenner: "I wish to ask the Senator whether he can think of a person who could be more dangerous to the United States of America than a pervert who is in the most vulnerable position to be blackmailed into giving information which he would not give for any reason in the world — not even for money — except for the position in which he finds himself." Jenner responded, "Personally, I cannot. I think the American people are utterly disgusted."[15]

Millard Tydings was outraged, too, for a different reason. Even as he attempted to chair his subcommittee hearings to explore McCarthy's charges, staffers frequently informed Tydings of the latest attacks on that investigation.

Tydings would then excuse himself from the subcommittee and go to the floor to defend himself. On the afternoon of the 25th, when Wherry called Tydings's hearings a "pantomime show," the subcommittee chair responded that he was "a little fed up with such stabbing in the back": "I ask my colleagues to stop the continual heckling of the subcommittee about homosexuals and other matters of that kind, and let us get down, first, to the matter of investigating any possible disloyalty. Obviously, a man may have the terrible disease which has been referred to, and yet may not be a party to foreign espionage or may not be a party to deliberately being disloyal to his government."

That senators would have known nothing about McCormack's talks with Pforzheimer, Hillenkoetter, and the president helps explain McCarthy's mistaken thinking that Offie could not be removed from the CIA. In fact, late on the afternoon of the 25th, Wherry announced on the Senate floor,

> I have been informed by the head of a government agency that the man against whom the Senator from Wisconsin made a charge on the Senate floor this afternoon has finally resigned, and his resignation is going to be accepted within the next day or two. It is my belief that had the Senator from Wisconsin accomplished nothing more than that one thing, it would be worth the effort, the chagrin, the embarrassment, the charges, and all the smear to which he has been subjected. I am proud to be associated with a man who is doing his level best to clear this country of communists and moral perverts in the government.

An Associated Press reporter was among those watching as Wherry then shouted his coda, "You're going to get some more resignations!"

For some reason, Hillenkoetter told Pforzheimer that Wherry was mistaken about the resignation. Perhaps the agency "head" that Wherry had talked to was OPC's Wisner, who was not unknown on Capitol Hill. The next day, Hillenkoetter and Pforzheimer met to review the latest statements of McCarthy, Wherry, and others, with no indication that the controversy was over. That afternoon, though, Pforzheimer wrote, "The Director has informed me that, with the express approval of the President, the CIA homosexual will be allowed to resign at the close of business 30 April 1950." On the 27th, he added, "I have informed Mr. McCormack, with the Director's authority, that we now have the necessary resignation."[16]

For better or worse, legislators had not been passive on the issue of homosexuals at the CIA. Nor would they let up any time soon on homosexuals anywhere in government: months later, the *New York Times* had a small story (on yet another newly commissioned investigation) that captured the spirit of the decade: "Pervert Inquiry Ordered." In July, the Investigations Subcommittee of the Senate Expenditures Committee, chaired by Clyde Hoey (D-NC), summoned Hillenkoetter and heads of other intelligence agencies. The subcommittee did not insist on talking about Offie, but genuinely seemed to want the DCI's insights. His testimony was full of references to "homos" and "moral weakness" and a judgment that any government agency imperiled itself by hiring homosexuals: "One pervert brings other perverts."

Perhaps Hillenkoetter's vivid and repeated condemnations of employing homosexuals were intended to prepare the senators for a distasteful exception to the rule: "The use of homosexuals as a control mechanism over individuals recruited for espionage is a generally accepted technique which has been used at least on a limited basis for many years." As soon as the director voiced those words, Walter Pforzheimer spoke up: "This part should be off the record." The stenographer stopped transcribing, but the DCI's prepared notes show what he said next:

> While this Agency will never employ a homosexual on its rolls, it might conceivably be necessary, and in the past has actually been valuable, to use known homosexuals as agents in the field. I am certain that if Joseph Stalin or a member of the Politburo or a high satellite official were known to be a homosexual, no member of this committee or of the Congress would balk against our use of any technique to penetrate their operations, provided that we surrounded our agent with the proper safeguards. After all, intelligence and espionage is, at best, an extremely dirty business.

Hillenkoetter supported this policy with two examples: One, the ongoing use by an "allied embassy in a foreign capitol" of an attaché who "has been seen frequently out alone with a Soviet officer who is suspected of homosexual tendencies. While it is occasionally difficult in these cases to tell who is attempting to subvert whom, it looks in this instance as if the allies were attempting to subvert a Russian officer for intelligence purpose." Second, the CIA had recently "found what I believe to represent a Soviet intelligence operation, and we believe that our task will be made considerably easier by the appearance in the area of a known homosexual who we think will be extremely helpful in this particular case."

When the stenographer began transcribing again, the DCI told the subcommittee that the Soviets had long "directed intensive recruitment efforts against foreign diplomats who have homosexual tendencies," usually by photographing their "homosexual acts, endeavoring to recruit them in this way by blackmail." Only grudgingly, senators agreed that the CIA had to be flexible. Senator John McClellan (D-AR) said, "Except in possibly your agency, your division, and the FBI, for temporary employment only, I cannot see that we could tolerate them anywhere in government."[17]

At the end of 1950, Senator Hoey's subcommittee issued its report titled "Employment of Homosexuals and Other Sex Perverts in Government." He boasted, "I am glad to report that a great many sex perverts have been removed." Indeed, hundreds of homosexuals had been forced out of jobs that year, most of them in the military, but others at the Department of Agriculture, the Library of Congress, and elsewhere. (At the CIA, too, some were "dismissed" in 1950, others were "allowed to resign," and still others were "now under investigation" at year's end. Pforzheimer had furious arguments with committee staff in following Hillenkoetter's directive to share numbers with Hoey's subcommittee but absolutely forbidding their publication. Five decades later, the CIA would still censor those numbers from relevant documents.) The State Department, wrote the *Washington Times-Herald*, "was cited as a glaring example of how homosexuals find their way from one government job to another. . . . Of 90 homos discharged by the State Department between January 1947 and January 1950, some 23 found new federal jobs, the report said."[18]

Finally, in response to McCarthy's eighty-one much-publicized "cases," Tydings's subcommittee reported its main finding on July 14, 1950: McCarthy had perpetrated "a fraud and a hoax." The report provoked enormous news coverage but seemingly did little damage to the Wisconsin senator. Weeks before the Tydings report, a crisis on the Korean peninsula had temporarily moved McCarthy off the front pages but suggested to many that he must have been on to something. Only the Democratic majorities in the subcommittee, the Foreign Relations Committee, and the Senate itself endorsed the Tydings Report. Republicans rejected it. This reflected the reality that GOP leaders, typified by Styles Bridges (a past and future chair of the Appropriations Committee and a CIA overseer), were prepared to work with and defend Joe McCarthy. Jenner accused Tydings of conducting "the most scandalous and brazen whitewash of treasonable conspiracy in history." He also slugged subcommittee counsel, Edward Morgan, calling him an "S.O.B."

After McCarthy campaigned in Maryland against his reelection, Tydings went down to defeat. Suddenly, taking on the Wisconsin senator seemed nearly suicidal. DCIs, future and present, would have to keep McCarthy on their minds. Tydings's defeat had another repercussion for the CIA: Richard

Russell of Georgia prepared to succeed him as head of the Armed Services Committee and its agency subcommittee.

As for Carmel Offie, Hersh writes that, for a few years at least, Wisner kept him on "contract status." Offie served as director of the International Labor Information Service, "in a position to nursemaid Wisner's Eastern European interests." Eventually, though, Wisner acceded to pressure to cut Offie out of government service. The former subordinate turned on Wisner furiously. One piece of revenge spoke volumes: Offie showed up, unannounced, at Frank and Polly Wisner's residence one day, confronted the outstanding cook he had secured to work for the couple, and ordered him to resign immediately. Polly Wisner later recalled, "I walked into the kitchen and the cook was gone."[19]

Korea: "No Better Today Than on December 7, 1941"

Only in retrospect did the calm before the Korean storm seem eerie. Leaders on Capitol Hill and in the administration felt and sounded relaxed in June 1950, after months and years of chronic international tensions. Congress wrestled over a foreign aid bill but had the luxury of doing so during what Styles Bridges called the welcome "quiet period." President Truman pondered the improving chances for world peace in the presence of reporters. Even John Foster Dulles, functioning awkwardly as a prominent Republican assistant to Secretary of State Dean Acheson, had been hopeful in his comments about Asia, despite the young communist government of China.[1]

Those familiar with CIA estimates in the late spring and early summer of 1950 knew that North Korea had the capability to wage war against the South, but few in the agency or elsewhere in Washington seemed to expect it. On the afternoon of Friday, June 23, DCI Hillenkoetter went before a secret hearing of the House Foreign Affairs Committee. Neither that committee nor its Senate counterpart played a leading role in overseeing the CIA, but the agency occasionally testified before them. While the subjects at hand varied widely, James Fulton (R-PA) inquired into prevailing conditions on the Korean peninsula. Hearing nothing from Hillenkoetter to suggest that a crisis was at hand, the representative wondered whether CIA's sources in Korea were (in Fulton's later words) "broad in extent and whether our personnel dependable. I felt assured specifically on Korea that that was the case." The only noticeably unhappy words from Hillenkoetter had to do with continuing conflicts between the CIA and other U.S. agencies.[2]

Harry Truman headed out the next day to his home state of Missouri in hope of an easygoing weekend. On Saturday night (4:00 a.m., Sunday, June 25, in Korea), North Korea invaded the South. Suddenly and painfully, American policymakers confronted anew the distinction between nations' capabilities and intentions and how terribly hard it was to discern the latter, even when the former could be uncovered. Awkwardly for the Truman administration, which had specifically declined in previous months to describe South Korea as strategically important, the government and military of that country were unprepared to deal alone with the invasion, which immediately seemed globally significant.

The possibility of "losing" South Korea to communism, coming so soon after the United States had experienced the "loss" of China, unnerved virtually all of Washington officialdom, the press, and the public. Though ordinary Americans were as surprised as elite policymakers by North Korea's attack, the public had already been persuaded by events in the early Cold War period (and perhaps by the speeches of Truman and others) that involvement in a "big war" was likely in the coming decade. Also, two-thirds of Americans (according to the Gallup organization) thought in spring 1950 that defense spending should be increased.

Hardly anyone in the nation's capital doubted that North Korea's attack occurred at the direction or with the approval of the Soviet Union and China. Within days, Truman decided that the United States would do whatever was necessary to save South Korea. He neither sought nor wanted a formal declaration of war by Congress in support of what he termed a "police action" on the part of the United States and the United Nations. Months later, the public would become restive over the lack of a congressional mandate for the war, but almost no legislators objected to the conflict's irregular constitutionality. Soon it would evolve into a miserable war, with American soldiers enduring severe winters, insufficient supplies, and an aggressive enemy. Tens of thousands of Americans were to be killed and many more wounded.

"There was the making of a great argument in Washington tonight," said the *New York Times* on June 25, "on whether the administration was surprised by the timing of the invasion of South Korea. It was a dispute that Republicans appear likely to follow up and make a national issue." For Hillenkoetter and the CIA, the "argument" posed a major threat. On Capitol Hill and elsewhere, the references to Pearl Harbor and Bogota were frequent, as were questions about what a CIA was for, if not to warn of approaching calamities.

Had the agency been primarily responsible for an American intelligence failure in Korea? No consensus answer would emerge in 1950. (In fact, historians a half century later are split over the issue. Bruce Cummings, a leading American scholar of the Korean War, could not authoritatively answer the question even late in the twentieth century.) While the CIA, itself, was unlikely to be banished from the American government as a result of the debate's results, the same could not be assumed about Hillenkoetter.[3]

Among the most influential to speak on the Senate floor on Monday, June

26, was Styles Bridges. Upon his motion that morning, the Appropriations Committee had requested Hillenkoetter's appearance at 3:00 in the afternoon. In the meantime, Bridges asked his fellow senators, "Will we continue appeasement?" and mocked the State Department for calling on the United Nations to "do something" about Korea. Furthermore, he told the Senate, "Neither the State Department nor the Department of Defense was informed by the Central Intelligence Agency of the impending attack." This the Appropriations Committee would examine "in some detail." Whatever they might uncover about such failures of the immediate past, he said, "Now is the time for decisive action" by the United States.

Bridges's low view of the agency's performance resulted from the nimble trashing it took at the Appropriations hearing that morning from Acheson and Secretary of Defense Louis Johnson. Senator Homer Ferguson (R-MI) asked the two secretaries if they had received any warning of an impending attack. By Bridges's and others' accounts, Acheson and Johnson told the senators that CIA had given them no such warning. "It was a complete surprise," said Johnson. "Why wasn't the Central Intelligence Agency on the job?" asked the incredulous Bridges, who then improperly blurted out the number of dollars the agency got from Congress that year. "What are they doing with it?!" "You'll have to ask Admiral Hillenkoetter," said Johnson. To the Senate, at midday, Bridges pronounced himself "amazed" to learn of the failure by the CIA, "which was supposed to prevent another surprise such as the Pearl Harbor attack."

Following the hearing, Acheson told an unwitting Hillenkoetter that he had tried to pacify the committee on the CIA's behalf, but the DCI soon believed otherwise. Pforzheimer recalls the day vividly: "Hilly was furious" over the secretaries' testimony and met briefly with Truman that afternoon, seeking permission to accept Appropriations' invitation. The DCI had not become influential with the president in the preceding three years, although Truman found the daily and weekly agency reports he received "extremely useful," according to an aide. Now, about his proposed Appropriations appearance, Hillenkoetter told the president, "I think it would do us a lot of good." Obtaining Truman's blessing, the DCI had Pforzheimer, who waited in Hillenkoetter's car, telephone the committee staff that the CIA leader was coming.[4]

The afternoon hearing had its bizarre moments because of the eighty-one-year-old, ill-tempered Kenneth McKellar, the committee chair. "There was nothing sinister about him," observed a staff member who was fond of

McKellar, a senator since 1917, but "withered and flabby, he was a lonely, sick old man . . . and should have retired gracefully." Instead, Richard Russell, Homer Ferguson, Joseph O'Mahoney, Carl Hayden, and others on Appropriations performed many of his duties. At the June 26 hearing, McKellar alternated between aggressively questioning the DCI and nodding off while others quizzed him. Hillenkoetter testified that the agency had warned all relevant leaders in the executive branch for the preceding year that North Korea was capable of mounting an attack on South Korea and might do so.

As in the 1948 hearings on Colombia, the DCI brought a stack of agency intelligence estimates previously passed on to the NSC and read two of them aloud. One, from the previous August, told of North Korean activities along its border with the South; the other, dated June 20, specifically described (according to Drew Pearson, who was close to Bridges) "increasing border incidents, including a concentration of 65,000 to 75,000 communist troops. These troops, according to the report, were well equipped, with artillery, tanks, guns and ammunition of the type which the Japanese army surrendered to Russia. There were also a total of 195 planes, all late Russian models. . . . Skirmishes along the border might have continued another year, he [Hillenkoetter] said, or the invasion might have come the next day."

Senators also questioned the DCI about chances for direct Russian intervention in the war and heard his estimate that it was unlikely, though he described a large Soviet "military training center on the northern side of the border," and said that an attack on Formosa was entirely possible in the near future. In explaining to senators why the CIA had not specifically predicted that the North Koreans *would* attack and *when* they would do so, Hillenkoetter managed to confuse at least some of his listeners who afterward told reporters that the DCI had claimed that it was not the CIA's job to analyze intelligence, but merely to pass it on to high-ranking policymakers. That apparently was not what he said, but some news accounts which emerged on that point embarrassed many at the agency.[5]

Chairman McKellar remained skeptical and insisted on written evidence demonstrating that such reports had been delivered (as Hillenkoetter claimed) to those in the White House and elsewhere. Pforzheimer dutifully returned to the irritable McKellar the next day with such evidence. The senator taunted the aggressive but affable young CIA staffer with the prediction of a new DCI who would find a better legislative liaison than Pforzheimer.

Still, most senators thought Hillenkoetter had ably explained and defended the CIA's performance. Most press analyses took a favorable turn after Hillenkoetter's testimony, too, due to committee members' comments afterward. The *New York Times* said Hillenkoetter had altered Bridges's view of the CIA's performance. Similarly, Richard Russell initially had believed that the U.S. government was completely surprised by the invasion of South Korea but spoke differently after the DCI's appearance.

A few days later, committee member William Knowland reflected the shift of opinion by telling colleagues, "The Central Intelligence Agency was doing its part of the job." He would later claim privately that Hillenkoetter had demonstrated that the CIA had "indicated rather clearly the build-up that was taking place north of the 38th parallel, the clearing of a line north of the 38th parallel of several kilometers of all civilian population, which is certainly a danger signal, the building of roads and bridges, and reinforcing them toward the frontier which, I think, is a major danger signal." Still, in July, Knowland introduced a newspaper article analyzing CIA performance, which, although commending the agency, said its morale was low, that other departments were uncooperative with it, and that Hillenkoetter might soon be replaced by General Walter "Beetle" Smith as DCI. Another legislator placed an article in the *Record* that spoke of "a recent black-out on intelligence from behind the Iron Curtain" and said, "There is no public clamor for scalps in connection with the Korean surprise, although there is word in Washington that that will come, too."[6]

The agency had one advantage in the opening few days of the war: the State Department's blatant unpopularity. Many Republicans and some Democrats in Congress hated Acheson and blamed him and his department for the outbreak of war. The 1950 primary elections had just happened in many states, and the November general elections were four months off, offering Republicans a vision of regaining the Congress lost to Democrats in 1948. Their targets were Truman (whose approval rating in the polls was well under 50 percent for most of the year), the Democratic Party, and government bureaucracies said to be bloated and soft on communism. In that inflamed political environment, the CIA was less of a target. In fact, John Taber turned to the agency for help in determining whether an infamous speech by Dean Acheson the previous January — which had implied that Korea was not of strategic importance to the United States — had helped bring on the war. But Pforzheimer told Taber that the CIA had no intelligence on what North Korea's reaction had been to the speech.

Numerous legislators savaged the secretary of state. Senate Republican leader Wherry said, "The whole thing is the fault of our China policy" and pinned the blame personally on the "fence-sitting" Acheson. Senator Robert Taft grudgingly endorsed Truman's policy of saving South Korea but said "bungling" by the administration had "invited" the North's attack. Acheson ought to resign, Taft said, to the rule-breaking applause of a small huddle of Republican senators, including Joseph McCarthy.

On June 27, though, Truman won many Republicans over to his Korea policy in a White House meeting. Very early the next morning, Senator H. Alexander Smith (R-NJ), who literally saw the hand of God in Truman's decisions, wrote in his diary, "Yesterday will stand out in history as a great day for America and the world. The President invited a group to meet at the White House. . . . It was all very wonderful. . . . we Republicans were elated." Smith and some others thought Truman's determined intervention in Korea also signified a new and greater commitment to Nationalist China. By contrast, Smith would soon view fellow Republican Taft as a "foot dragger."[7]

Meanwhile, the CIA displayed a willingness to do analyses that might alienate Truman. Days after the invasion, an agency report delivered to the president noted that American withdrawal of troops from South Korea in 1949 and "subsequent US policy probably led the Kremlin to believe that the US had abandoned any intention of giving effective military support to South Korea and that North Korean aggression could be undertaken with only a slight risk of US intervention." In other words, the United States had virtually invited the invasion. Truman could take pleasure, though, in reading: "The prompt US reaction in ordering air and naval support of South Korea has probably exceeded Soviet expectations, and the USSR is now faced with a strong possibility of global war if it supports the North Korean invasion sufficiently to overcome combined US and South Korean resistance. It is still estimated that the USSR is not yet prepared to risk full-scale war with the Western powers."

Rumors increased in July that Hillenkoetter would return to naval service. On July 11, Bridges (for reasons he did not explain) again turned on the CIA: "Our ability to detect in advance the antagonistic movements of a potential enemy is no better today than it was on December 7, 1941. . . . Our intelligence was completely unaware of the North Korean tank concentration and all the other preparations indicative of a large-scale offensive."[8]

Urging a "far-reaching" reform of the intelligence establishment, Bridges's speech must have been a bitter surprise for Hillenkoetter. Two days later, on July 13, Representative Fulton delivered his devastating public account of the DCI's June 23 briefing of the House Foreign Affairs Committee, which had not hinted of impending trouble in Korea. Fulton specifically challenged Hillenkoetter's post-invasion claim to Senate Appropriations that CIA knew of and warned administration leaders of a menacing North Korea. How could Hillenkoetter have held such views and not have said any such thing to the House Committee? Fulton wondered. "As a member of the committee, I made a particular point of Korea. . . . Admiral Hillenkoetter should be given the opportunity to explain publicly to the Congress and to the American people why so little was known or communicated to the Foreign Affairs Committee within approximately 30 hours of the North Korean invasion."[9]

Hillenkoetter also testified before some members of the House Armed Services Committee, chaired by Carl Vinson, in the weeks after the invasion, though no substantial account of that testimony exists. Representative James Patterson (R-CT) — who mentioned it in passing a month later — said, "With our present system of intelligence, no proper evaluation of information is possible." The Joint Committee on Atomic Energy also raised the intelligence surprise question with Hillenkoetter on July 12. He asserted that, while the CIA had not been able to predict that the invasion would get "going at five o'clock in the morning," it had issued reports "of a constant daily threat of aggression from North Korea." But those sorts of analyses would have been "true a year ago," said an unimpressed Representative Sterling Cole (R-NY). "Not nearly as much," claimed the DCI. When another committee member assumed that the CIA had underestimated the number of tanks North Korea had ready for its invasion, Hillenkoetter challenged him: "The estimate of tanks they had when they came across was between 100 and 120, and that hasn't changed." The DCI declined to predict whether or not Chinese troops would intervene in Korea but said there were "about 200,000 in Manchuria," which was "fairly close" to North Korea.[10]

The press, having given Hillenkoetter reasonably good reviews immediately after his Senate Appropriations appearance, also became more negative as weeks passed. By late July, *U.S. News* published a detailed analysis of the CIA's "new start on preventing 'another Pearl Harbor' " and reported "much general agreement that Admiral Hillenkoetter's service fell down in Korea." By early August, the *New York Herald-Tribune* published a lengthy account of the CIA's functioning in its first three years, listing five major intelligence "failures." Many newspapers around the country reprinted the article, and a member of Congress placed it in the *Congressional Record*.

Hillenkoetter sent a detailed defense and response to the president on August 3. The "fall" of Czechoslovakia in 1948 had not been an intelligence failure, said the DCI, who quoted three agency estimates foreshadowing the coup that overturned a national unity government. Furthermore, "CIA predicted the elimination of Nationalist China from the mainland time after time," while the agency had functioned respectably in dealing with crises in Colombia, Palestine, and Yugoslavia. The DCI would also appear again before the full Senate Appropriations Committee, but that occurred too late to do him any good, after Truman announced in mid-August that Beetle Smith would replace him as director.[11]

Politically, the question of who within the U.S. government was to blame for the Korean surprise would spill over into the congressional campaigns of the following autumn, leading up to elections on November 7. Missouri's Representative Dewey Short — the senior Republican on Armed Services — told listeners in a radio address on October 9 that the administration "carefully avoided telling you that Admiral Hillenkoetter, chief of our intelligence, had repeatedly warned the White House, the Departments of State and Defense, that mass mobilization was being carried out along the 38th parallel prior to the attack." Senator Wherry, much better known to the nation, traveled into Short's (and the president's) home state and gained headlines with the same claim: Hillenkoetter *had* warned Truman and Acheson the previous June that "the communists were evacuating women and children from along the 38th parallel and massing the Red Army there, [but] no action was taken by the Administration." Wherry further blamed Truman for the fact that the transcript and supporting documents offered in the DCI's testimony before the Senate Appropriations Committee in early July had never been made public: "One word from President Truman and those documents would be immediately made public. I challenge him to give the order before November 7!"

In so tortuous a political environment, Hillenkoetter may have been telling the truth in claiming that he was glad to return to sea as a navy commander. His departure was mostly unlamented on the floors of the House and Senate, except for a speech by Majority Leader McCormack, who spoke a polite fiction that "it was with the greatest reluctance" that the president "permitted" Hillenkoetter to leave. Fortunately, said McCormack, the new DCI would be a person of the "greatest distinction."[12]

A New DCI

As John McCormack suggested, General Walter Bedell Smith *was* extremely capable, having served during World War II as Eisenhower's chief of staff, handling military leaders' egos and other tasks and complexities. His friends called him "Beetle" (so did his subordinates, though not in his presence), and Smith embossed his personal stationery with nothing but an image of that insect. For three years after the war's end, as ambassador to the Soviet Union, Smith had gotten to know Joseph Stalin but could work no diplomatic miracles. Though he had surgery for severe stomach ulcers in 1950, the general eventually acceded to President Truman's insistence that he head the CIA. "It is the most thankless task one can assume," Smith told his British intelligence friend, General Kenneth Strong. He wrote another associate, "The American people expect the incumbent to be able to predict with accuracy just what Stalin is likely to do three months from today at 5:30 a.m." To diplomat Llewellyn Thompson, Smith joked, "I can only hope that you and my other friends will be prepared to identify the body when it finally emerges from the Washington mill."

Despite his foreboding, Smith's nomination received rave reviews. Senator William Benton (D-CT), a former diplomat and one of Joe McCarthy's fiercest enemies, congratulated Truman on the choice: "It is seldom, indeed, that the perfect man can be chosen and can be prevailed upon to accept." Benton advised Smith, "When I left the State Department, I said I would never take another administrative job in Washington unless I had one senator that I could always count on and surely count on. That, I discovered, is the key need of any administrative officer. I want you to know that I am that man, as far as you are concerned. . . . Please send up that man in your office who is responsible for your liaison with Congress." Walter Pforzheimer went to see Benton, hiding his conviction that the senator was one of the least influential legislators to be found.

Emulating Truman's foreign policy bipartisanship, Armed Services chairman Tydings had Oregon's maverick Republican Wayne Morse manage Beetle Smith's confirmation on the Senate floor. Morse would write Smith, "Our country is very fortunate to have you in charge of the Central Intelligence Agency." Not just outsiders liked the nomination: Virginia's veteran Democratic senator Harry F. Byrd, soon to be on Armed Services' CIA subcommittee, wrote Smith, "Other senators and I have felt there should be a thorough reorganization of our Intelligence Service, and I am certain this will result from your appointment."

About the CIA, Dwight Eisenhower wrote Smith, "God knows it needs a firm hand, coupled with some imagination and leadership." Ike would become a political and personal enemy of Truman over the following two years, but Smith would stay loyal to the president. He would work for Eisenhower again in the future, but — having humble military beginnings in the Indiana National Guard — had as much in common with the modestly schooled Truman. Also, more than Eisenhower ever had, Truman would thank Smith for his hard work.[1]

Hillenkoetter accompanied Smith to the Senate Armed Services Committee confirmation hearing on August 24, 1950, only to be damned with faint praise by Tydings: "He was the first head of this agency, and got it organized and got it going." Smith reflected on "some of Hillenkoetter's troubles," and entertained senators with the observation that "to really meet what popular conception there is of the Chief of Intelligence, there are only two personalities that I know of who might do it. One is God, and the other is Stalin, and I do not know that even God can do it, because I do not know whether he is close enough in touch with Uncle Joe to know what he is talking about." Smith emphasized to the committee that he intended to follow the law and congressional intent. (Agency general counsel Lawrence Houston would follow up with a memo to the new DCI, titled "Legal Responsibilities of the Central Intelligence Agency," which stressed adherence to "congressional intent.")

The press, too, mostly lionized Smith. Reaching out to the new DCI was columnist Drew Pearson, whose aide Tristam Coffin dined cordially with Smith and wrote a follow-up note "on specific ways Drew might be helpful," among them: "Assist in organizing psychological warfare behind the Iron Curtain. You said you would designate a contact man in the CIA. In addition, material could be planted with Drew that could be quoted." Pearson could also help by creating a "public awareness of the danger, and a willingness to sacrifice. This cannot be done by preaching, but rather by a sharp, factual item. For example, one line, 'Moscow, exclusive — Russia is now producing every week 100 of those monster tanks that broke through American lines in Korea.' "

About the only caution expressed in Congress or elsewhere was Senator Bourke Hickenlooper's belief that a DCI should serve a long tenure, providing stable leadership for the CIA. More than most legislators knew, this mattered, for the agency was experiencing explosive growth in its budget and its activities — especially in covert operations — due to the war in Korea. If Pearl Harbor left a lasting fear of surprise attacks, World War II left Americans with a liking for unambiguous victories. The "limited war" experience in Korea was different, frustrating and bewildering American soldiers, citizens, and politicians.[2]

Smith's confirmation by Armed Services and the full Senate was swift and unanimous. He would be far more self-confident and shrewd than Hillenkoetter in navigating the shark-infested waters of the executive branch. At CIA, he would exercise a blunt, take-charge manner. The day would come, for example, when one of his underlings noted (in a diary) "a long meeting at which General Smith emphatically advised everybody that he commanded all field organizations; and DD/P, as well as other people in Washington, were mere staff officers acting in his name." Regarding Congress, Smith would make clear to those at the agency that he knew and respected the origins of CIA's budget and legal mandate. With rare exceptions, he would respond shrewdly to House and Senate members. Toward the CIA subcommittee chairs, Smith would show all the deference they wanted: later in 1950, Carl Vinson would summon Smith and aides to a secret hearing, where they would sit through hours of testimony by other national security leaders, then be sent off without ever getting to testify, on an assurance that Vinson would soon beckon Smith again.

One of Smith's innovations would be frequent luncheons at the CIA with small groups of legislators, not all of them on oversight subcommittees. Had he lived long enough, Smith would have been surprised to read the Church Committee's claim in the mid-1970s that he and other early DCIs appeared "only rarely" before members of Congress. While Smith's work calendar has never been declassified, Pforzheimer recalls that Smith was on Capitol Hill much more frequently than Hillenkoetter, who had been no stranger there — the fragmentary, surviving records indicate about ten appearances per year by the CIA's first head. No doubt, other visits remain unrecorded.[3]

One incident toward the end of Hillenkoetter's service as DCI could have poisoned Smith's inclination to testify fairly often on Capitol Hill. Pforzheimer recalls a hearing before Vinson's Armed Services Committee at which Hillenkoetter unintentionally embarrassed Omar Bradley, chairman of the Joint Chiefs of Staff:

> Hillenkoetter was invited one afternoon to come and testify, which he did. Among others there was General Bradley, seventy-three assistants in tow; Hilly had three assistants there. When Hillenkoetter finished testifying, Vinson said,

"Admiral, how does that compare to the U.S. equivalent of those materials?" Admiral Hillenkoetter said, "Mr. Chairman, I am only qualified to testify about the Soviet things; I'm not privy to the American strength in this field. But General Bradley is present, and I'm sure he can testify to this."

Vinson said, "General Bradley, will you please come forward?" General Bradley comes forward with his assistants. He was furious because he was asked a figure he wasn't absolutely sure of.

In the days after the hearing, Bradley and others in the Pentagon grumbled loudly about the CIA testifying too often. These complaints found their way to Smith, just as he was to become director. Weeks later, says Pforzheimer,

> We learned that the House Armed Services Committee wanted us back to testify about some subject. Smith said, "Pforzheimer, I'm told we testify too much on the Hill and that we should cut back!" Well, I took my heart in my hand and I said, "General, I think I know the story that's on your mind and I'd like to explain." And I told the story, because Smith and Bradley hated each other. Bradley resented Smith's presence because he hadn't been at West Point; he treated him like dirt.
>
> A few weeks later, I heard someone say to General Smith that the CIA ought not to testify on the Hill so much, and the General said, "I know all about that, and it's not true."[4]

Though most members of Congress liked what they heard of Smith's initial CIA leadership on Korea-related matters, the war provided him with an early experience of withering skepticism and anger from an individual member. It happened at the White House, in the aftermath of China's intervention on behalf of North Korea late in fall 1950. As Americans, South Koreans, and others fighting under the United Nations mandate retreated from the invading Chinese forces, citizens in the United States fell into deep apprehension. At the Senate, on November 28, Chan Gurney told Millard Tydings, "During the past hour, I have received two telephone calls from South Dakota — both of them telling me that business in these small South Dakota towns has practically stopped today, for everyone is talking about the terrible situation in Korea." A few days later, Dewey Short wrote to friends in Missouri, "I really feel we are facing the greatest crisis in our history. I only hope and pray that we can shorten and strengthen our lines and rescue our men before they are slaughtered by the Communistic hoards."

Contrary to General Douglas MacArthur's military intelligence and his reports back to Washington, the agency told him and the president in October/November that, in light of UN forces pushing their way into northern North Korea, an intervention by China was increasingly likely. After it became clear that such an incursion had begun, the CIA predicted—again correctly, Truman would later acknowledge—that it would not be limited in scope. Even a MacArthur supporter like Short confided to a friend, "It is difficult to understand how 200,000 to 300,000 troops could move in, and MacArthur not know anything about it."

Truman later described the December 1 meeting with his national security advisers and the congressional leadership, where

> Senator [Kenneth] Wherry wanted to know why our intelligence had not seen this attack coming, and he would not be satisfied with any explanation that [General] Bradley would give. He [Wherry] was antagonistic and abrupt in his manner.
>
> General Smith then set up a huge chart that showed the Soviet Union, its satellites and its neighboring area. He showed how the events in Korea tied in with events in Europe. . . . The congressmen were visibly impressed, with the exception of Wherry. The Senator from Nebraska, with doubt and disbelief written all over his face, wanted to know how Smith had gotten his facts. Had he used all sources? What were those sources?

Such questions were usually answered in much smaller meetings, and only if the legislator posing them was on a CIA subcommittee or the Joint Committee on Atomic Energy. Wherry, the Senate Republican leader, was not. Endearing himself to agency personnel was of no interest to him, as he thought the CIA was plagued by incompetents and communists. Pforzheimer, in turn, regarded him as a "loud, aggressive son of a bitch." Truman continued: "Smith side-stepped these questions very smoothly, but when he began to take up Korea and China, Wherry again wanted chapter and verse for everything mentioned. Time went quickly in this exchange of questions and information, and I had to ask General Smith to conclude his presentation so that I could speak to the group."

Beetle Smith had a heroic reputation on Capitol Hill, but this would not be his last encounter with persistent members of Congress who wanted to know about the CIA or influence it. The DCI would usually find shrewd ways to accommodate them.[5]

The "Dirty Business"

The anxieties of the war years brought about widespread yearning in Congress for more innovative attacks against enemies in North Korea, China, and the Soviet Union. DCI Smith, like Hillenkoetter before him, doubted that covert action should be a prime task of the CIA, though. After a couple of years on the job, Smith would tell the NSC of

> a three-fold increase in the clandestine operations of this Agency.... These cold war projects are worldwide in scope (with the effort intensified in the Far East) and they include psychological warfare as well as paramilitary operations; denial programs with respect to strategic materials; stockpiling on a limited scale in strategic areas to assist the military in the event of war; the organization and planning of sabotage teams to support resistance operations; and the planning and organization of escape and evasion networks and stay-behind movements for use in the event of war.

Such activities, Smith continued, were not "essential to the performance by Central Intelligence Agency of its intelligence responsibilities.... Regrettably (from my personal viewpoint) it seems impracticable, for reasons of coordination and security, to divorce these from other covert operations." At one meeting at CIA headquarters, Smith lamented to his staff, "We have almost arrived at a stage where it is necessary to decide whether CIA will remain an intelligence agency or become a 'cold war department.'" At the White House, the DCI detailed for legislators some of the CIA work in south Asia, then added that it was a "dirty business" with "no morals." After hearing this, Dewey Short told a friend, "We have to protect that man against himself."

Congressional inclinations toward covert action were manifested in the words of individuals and informal groups, CIA subcommittees, and other committees. Also, contrary to the later historical wisdom that ignorant legislators bore no responsibility for American covert action, Congress would publicly authorize spending $100 million for such efforts in 1951.[1]

Individuals and Informal Groups

When Senate Appropriations chair Styles Bridges eagerly assured Robert Lovett in spring 1948 that he would see to it that Congress would appropriate $50 million for "covert operations . . . to be conducted at the present time," the Truman administration may have thought such an offer (or pressure to do something innovative about communist advances worldwide) would not happen again. If so, they were wrong. No one in Congress except Vito Marcantonio seems to have urged the Truman administration or the CIA from 1947 onward to forego covert action, but multiple records of legislators urging secret interventions have surfaced:

- In January 1950, the leading Republican on House Appropriations, New York's John Taber, noted, "Off-the-record testimony indicated that we have no real penetration behind Iron Curtain countries." Other legislators were hearing similar things: James Richards (D-SC), chair of the House Foreign Affairs Committee, went to Dean Acheson's office that same month. The secretary of state recorded that Richards "said he just wanted to talk to me, informing me not only about his attitudes, but those he finds reflected in conversation with other members of Congress, and to place before me warning flags." Richards first asked the question which was "on the lips of a large number of congressmen, namely, why don't we instigate a large program of stirring up guerrilla activity on the Chinese mainland?" Acheson explained that "there are covert activities underway which are essentially of a top secret character," but then detailed three different Chinese groups whose "disruptive influence" the United States was trying to assist. Learning that the administration had received "sufficient money" for this, Richards told Acheson he was "confident Congress would give us whatever we needed, both in form and amount for this character of activity."[2]
- In a July 12, 1950, JCAE hearing, Senator John Bricker (R-OH) told Hillenkoetter, "I have often had a thought that there is a possibility of this country stirring up more trouble than we have within Russia, and China is more fertile for that than Russia, of course." What were the possibilities, he asked. Without specifically conveying what the CIA and OPC were then doing, Hillenkoetter began to respond, "I think they can be done, particularly in China, without too much trouble," when Bricker interrupted, "That was my hope and that is the only ray of hope I see."

In Russia, continued the DCI, "it is more difficult to get actual battling going on, because they will get overrun in the end." Bricker obtained Hillenkoetter's prediction that "the greatest hope we have got" of provoking a "break" among Soviet military figures would occur with the death of Stalin. "There would be an excellent chance," he said.[3]

- Senator Estes Kefauver (D-TN), a future presidential candidate, pursued the irregular warfare/CIA question at Armed Services' confirmation hearing for Beetle Smith in August 1950: "Particularly in Asia, we have been needing very badly some way to at least cause some confusion and diversity of opinion . . . in other words, the type of work that General Donovan did during the last war." Smith suggested that Kefauver pursue the topic with Hillenkoetter, still in office, but assured the senator (not on Armed Services' informal CIA subcommittee) that "there is one department of the Central Intelligence Agency which is responsible for that type of work." That same month, Senator Ralph Flanders (R-VT), who described himself as exasperated with the Truman administration's unimaginative, passive foreign policy, continued his private campaign to persuade John Foster Dulles at the State Department (as he had previously approached Allen Dulles in 1949) with ideas for "proposed underground operations in Russia." Foster Dulles claimed to Senator Alex Smith that he would have leaders at the State Department study Flanders's ideas carefully.[4]

- Bourke Hickenlooper — a senior member of Foreign Relations and sometime JCAE chair — typified legislative concerns about world politics and hopes about covert operations. Not on Armed Services/Appropriations CIA subcommittees, Hickenlooper had limited knowledge of the extent to which the United States *was* engaged in secret interventions in south Asia. Like James Richards eleven months earlier, he went to Acheson, privately and somberly seeking a "wholly confidential" bipartisan consultation. As the secretary noted later that day, the senator "asked whether it was not desirable and necessary to have what he called a diversion in Asia. By this he meant fomenting outbreaks against the communists in China and possible use of the army on Formosa to make landings [and] . . . assisting dissension on the mainland. . . . I said that we were not overlooking the possibilities of stirring up trouble in China. I spoke of some of the problems which had to be surmounted and of the fact that this was not a matter which lent itself to public discussion." Though committing nothing to paper that day about the CIA, Acheson directed his staff to arrange for further briefings of the senator "in detail on particular problem areas."[5]

- Three weeks later, Brien McMahon forwarded a long list of carefully formulated questions from JCAE to DCI Smith. The last of nine questions was, "What plans do we have for covert activity against Soviet atomic energy installations, both before a war breaks out and afterward?" Smith's response is unknown. A few months later, on behalf of the DCI, Deputy Director Allen Dulles answered a letter from Senator Henry Cabot Lodge Jr., which suggested unconventional warfare approaches for the CIA. These ideas were "more in the field of work of the Pentagon than here with us," said Dulles, but they would nonetheless be "studied by those interested in closely related matters." (Lodge's brother, Representative John D. Lodge [R-CT], had suggested creation of a "peacetime OSS" to engage in "roll back" as early as 1948.) Shortly thereafter, Senator H. Alexander Smith, one of Dulles's closest friends in Congress, shared with him the latest ideas from former OSS head William Donovan and a Chinese exile on how "America should instigate and help the revolution fermenting in the Chinese mainland. . . . cooperation with Chinese political and military leaders to organize and assist the hundred thousand of guerrillas is absolutely necessary." Donovan had been working with Alex Smith for a year to get Foreign Relations committee members on board to press the Truman administration toward the "centralization of instruments of irregular warfare." Smith had also lobbied Foster Dulles in 1950 to discuss some ideas on operations in Russia with "some of your pals there in the State Department." Later, in March 1952, Senator Smith sent Allen Dulles a *Saturday Evening Post* article: "As it is right in line with the work that you and General Smith are doing, I urge you to read it. . . . The whole story points out the way in which Russia and her satellites are honeycombed with opposition and how the whole scheme of things in Russia might collapse with the proper feeding of this discontent from the outside." Dulles responded that the article was "on the optimistic side, but that does not mean that we are overlooking the opportunities that do exist." Mrs. Dulles, he added, had been in touch with Mrs. Smith to "find an evening when you could join us for dinner."[6]
- Some Washington figures, including legislators not on the CIA subcommittees, banded together to lobby the Truman administration to operate covertly against communist countries. In spring 1950, Drew Pearson invited four senators, Representative Mike Mansfield (D-MT), and a few others to dinner to discuss (according to Pearson's diary) "penetrating the Iron Curtain." Worried and well-intentioned, the group

went about planning to have Chief Justice Fred Vinson approach his friend, the president, on the subject. One senator present described his plan to consult Senate Democratic leader Scott Lucas and others about how to promote covert activities. "The purpose of the meeting . . . to wedge the Iron Curtain, itself . . . must not be allowed to taper off," the dinner guests agreed.[7] The ignorance of Pearson (who lived across the street from Allen Dulles) and the others about what Truman, the CIA, and top legislators on the Appropriations/ Armed Services committees were doing demonstrates that the agency and its superiors had succeeded in keeping such activities mostly secret.

The dinner also illustrates the CIA's compartmentalization of information given to congressional leaders, because one outspoken diner was the powerful Brien McMahon, who often interacted with agency leaders. Pforzheimer notes that McMahon, who knew how the CIA pursued Soviet atomic intelligence, "probably didn't know much about covert action." This fits a Psychological Strategy Board (PSB) leader's summary of what CIA general counsel Lawrence Houston told him about the agency's openness with legislators. Toward some, there "has been complete disclosure of CIA operations. For others, there has been partial disclosure and, for still others, there has been no disclosure whatsoever."[8]

CIA Subcommittees and Other Committees

Only fragmentary records illustrate Armed Services or Appropriations CIA subcommittee members' knowledge of covert operations during the Truman era. Those subcommittees' leaders, at least, knew of the tremendous boost in the number of such activities and other changes in different intelligence activities. By the Beetle Smith era, if not before, those on Appropriations subcommittees specifically approved the big covert action spending increases. Records suggest that anywhere from one to five members of each subcommittee knew budgetary and/or other details about the CIA in a typical year late in Truman's presidency. (Sometimes, other members of Congress asked to be informed by the CIA of its budgetary specifics. Usually, the answer would be "no." If a legislator were sufficiently powerful, like Senator Byrd, a DCI typically would still decline to give him anything in writing; however, as Hillenkoetter wrote Byrd during the agency's first year, "I have no desire to withhold these figures from you personally, and will be pleased to see you at your convenience and to inform you verbally of our actual and contemplated strength.") Overall, perhaps 10 to 12 of the 531 members of Congress were in the business of approving the increasingly extensive covert action programs, though some knew far more than others about them.[9]

No full transcript of a CIA subcommittee hearing devoted to covert action has ever been declassified, forcing historians to rely on other documentation plus the memories of those who attended. One set of CIA notes exists for a planned July 1951 hearing involving three senators — Joseph O'Mahoney, Homer Ferguson, and Richard Russell — and over half a dozen CIA leaders. (Appropriations chairman McKellar had passed on substantial CIA oversight duties to the three senators.) Plans for the hearing came about after O'Mahoney and Ferguson had been briefed by DCI Smith on agency budgetary matters earlier in the summer and had "indicated their desire to come down to CIA for further briefing," noted Pforzheimer. Being joined by Russell meant having a fellow Appropriations member who also chaired Armed Services.

Smith, Dulles, Wisner, and others geared up to brief the senators on the CIA's diverse activities. Part of Smith's presentation was to cover "counterespionage overseas" and "covert operations including [words censored]." Dulles was to go into details, planning to use eight different charts (including an "Operations map") to illustrate the new Directorate of Plans' (which replaced OPC) work in covert action. In reserve, he also had eight foreign-language posters (topics unknown) and three folios of "photos on Ukrainian Resistance," then being supported by the CIA. Another CIA leader was prepared to discuss and show a chart on "1952 budget for Covert Operations [sentences censored]."[10]

The DCI's executive assistant, Lyman Kirkpatrick, who "marveled" at Smith's rapport with congressional overseers, later recalled being asked by his boss to do part of a 1952 briefing of Clarence Cannon's House Appropriations CIA subcommittee that also included George Mahon and John Taber. The topic for Kirkpatrick's presentation would be covert operations. The DCI

> had made the decision that the Agency should describe to the Subcommittee the philosophy of the operational side of the house, where at the time I was one of the assistant directors. His philosophy was that the members of the CIA Subcommittee should have a thorough grasp of everything that the Agency was try-

ing to do, and how it was trying to do it, so that they could better judge the results and the impact on American foreign policy.

General Smith had been quite specific that I should not take more than twenty minutes, and I knew him well enough to be aware that he meant that, to the second. . . . I could just touch the highlights in twenty minutes.

I made my presentation before a very solemn group, and concluded it promptly in twenty minutes. Smith said, "Thank you. You can go now." I went back to my office. My curiosity was too great to restrain until the next time I saw the Director, and later that afternoon I got him on the telephone and asked him how he thought the briefing went. He expressed himself as pleased, and I then asked what the reaction was to my contribution and he commented, "You scared hell out of them."[11]

Pforzheimer recalls another session on a Friday in 1951 or 1952 when he accompanied the DCI and one or two other agency leaders, this time to a Senate Appropriations or Armed Services subcommittee hearing conducted by two or three members. The meeting began with lunch in a hearing room, with the CIA people and senators chatting informally. When it was time for business, one senator inquired broadly about current activities of Smith and the agency. Unbeknownst to the senators or Pforzheimer, Smith had brought along a complete list of covert operations and other secret activities then in progress around the globe. Smith was not "concerned about talking about classified matters to the senators involved," Pforzheimer recalls, and so, "very sure of himself, reached into his pocket and took out a piece of paper, and unfolded it, and said 'This is a list of some of the things we do in the covert action field.' . . . He started going over them from the top of the page to the bottom and on to the next one. It was one page, but with writing on both sides. It ran to nearly 50 or so things going on."

After the three or four hour meeting ended, Smith was in a foul mood. Pforzheimer did not ask why but guessed that his anger was self-directed for having been so forthcoming. An additional explanation is plausible: as Pforzheimer recalls, subcommittee members approved the covert actions, while Smith (privately) regretted that they overshadowed CIA intelligence gathering/analysis mission.

Six months after taking the CIA job, and more directly controlling OPC than Hillenkoetter ever had, Smith spoke wistfully at what was labeled a "where we go from here, and how far" meeting about the CIA being threatened by its own expansion into a "Third Force." His audience was a handful of subordinates, all covert action enthusiasts, including Dulles, Wisner, and deputy director William H. Jackson: "If left to me, I would not take the responsibility. I believe it would be doing a disservice to the Intelligence Agency. The operational tail will wag the intelligence dog. The top people will be forced to take up all their time in the direction of operations and will necessarily neglect intelligence. I think that this would be inconsistent with my responsibilities to the people and the Congress in ensuring a strong intelligence agency to prevent another Pearl Harbor."

The subordinates repeatedly reminded Smith that the question of whether or not the CIA should have the mission was, in the words of Jackson, "rather academic, since we've clearly got it now." Smith argued, though (according to meeting notes), that "he didn't want to make the attempt because he felt it was a disservice to the intelligence function and because he just didn't think we could staff up to do it." The director took the counterarguments calmly that afternoon until one of his staffers "observed that he would like to work for somebody who would make the attempt, and would try to do it. General Smith said that he would see that [name deleted] was transferred to whatever agency was given responsibility for making the attempt." But the DCI was merely exhaling frustrations — CIA/OPC had the covert action job. Later, a report prepared for the president and NSC, but also "for presentation to Congress" — surely just the CIA subcommittee leaders — warned about covert operations that "their size in relation to the intelligence aspect of the CIA budget is such that special methods of presenting it to Congress may have to be developed."[12]

The evidence is overwhelming that spending increases on covert action during the Korean War years were exponential. As Smith told his top staff at the 1951 meeting, the Fiscal Year 1952 OPC budget that he had approved "provided for a 100% increase in both personnel and money, and that's about all we could hope to expand in the near future." By the last year of the Truman presidency, the small coterie of congressional overseers of the CIA was approving budgets in which 75 percent of resources were devoted to covert action. In February 1952, according to a still-classified document found in the papers of George Mahon, the House Appropriations subcommittee on the CIA approved an agency budget of $587 million for Fiscal Year 1953; that would mean about $440 million went to support covert operations. (Other documents suggest that the Senate Appropriations subcommittee initially cut that House-approved budget by at least 20 percent. DCI Smith wrote Senator O'Mahoney that the CIA was "most unhappy" about this. Mahon pledged to Pforzheimer to fight for as much of the $587 million as possible in a Senate-House subcommittees conference meeting. Apparently much of the cut was restored.)

Documentation parallels the memories of CIA figures that such discussions with, and approvals by, congressional leaders of covert action did happen. Reminded of the widespread belief decades later that no one in Congress had known of covert operations in the early Cold War period, Pforzheimer responded: "I remember many occasions in the House Appropriations subcommittee particularly, where we talked about what today you'd call covert action of which we were extremely proud, namely the radios — Radio Liberty and Radio Free Europe. We held nothing back on that sort of thing. And there were other covert actions and I can't recall them all. When we got into the Italian elections, we would always tell the committees and we always told them with great pride if we won the election, which we usually did."[13]

In the view of most agency officials and legislative leaders in the Smith era, such encounters and the resulting appropriations had obvious legal significance. Sidney Souers (who had run the Central Intelligence Group) asserted to historian Arthur Darling that Congress, "for all practical purposes, validated" covert action by "allotting unvouchered funds."[14]

The "Legislative Spy Program"

All of the preceding helps explain one of the most remarkable congressional actions of the early Cold War — House passage of the Kersten Amendment in August 1951 and Senate agreement two months later to authorize expenditure of up to $100 million by the president in support of covert action against the Soviet Union. This event, though since mostly neglected by historians, provoked vigorous Soviet complaints to the United Nations.

The story began in the imagination of Charles Kersten, an energetic Republican representative from Milwaukee, who hated the Truman administration's "passive" containment doctrine. Kersten had first won election to Congress in 1946 from a district that had many Democrats. In 1947, he began chairing a subcommittee authorized to examine education and labor conditions in the USSR. The Soviet government, not surprisingly, denied Kersten and colleagues the necessary visas to travel there. The assertive congressman then asked Secretary of State Marshall to retaliate by requiring the "immediate removal of all excess Russian nationals" from the United States, a request that went unfulfilled. Kersten lost reelection in 1948 but retook the seat two years later. All along, he bristled with anticommunism, investigating Red influence in U.S. labor unions and castigating the Soviet Union.[15]

Not leading any legislative body that interacted regularly with CIA, and not even on the Foreign Affairs Committee, Kersten apparently knew little-to-nothing of agency attempts to roll back Soviet influence in Eastern Europe since 1948. Few did. Wallace Carroll, a consultant to the Defense and State Departments, wrote in a 1949 issue of *Life* magazine, "We must prepare to support guerrilla warfare on such a scale as the world has never seen before." In *Nation's Business* magazine, Paul Linebarger (formerly in military intelligence during World War II) suggested "subversion" as an offensive U.S. weapon against the Soviet Union in 1951 and asked, "Why haven't we done this? Or are we doing it so secretly that the American people themselves don't know it? Take the second question first. I don't think we are doing it, at least not on an effective scale. Subversion is secret, but its consequences are not." Kersten placed the provocative article in the *Congressional Record*.[16]

Like some others, the congressman was horrified by Secretary of State Acheson's remark to newspaper editors in 1950: "We do not propose to subvert the Soviet Union. We shall not attempt to undermine Soviet independence." Following the unnerving "fall" of China and American reverses in Korea, such an analysis seemed remarkably obtuse to Kersten, who began agitating by 1951 among fellow House members and any available forum for the American government to support anticommunist elements within the Soviet Union and its satellites. Based on interactions with figures, including exiled Russian academics at Georgetown University in Washington and elsewhere in the United States, the Catholic Kersten believed that innumerable angry individuals and groups were ready to revolt against Soviet rule. In February, the *Milwaukee Sentinel* reported, "Kersten is going to propose that Congress go on record to express its sympathy with the oppressed people of Russia and satellite countries, to say that the governments that rule them are not legitimate governments, and to offer every possible assistance to the movement for freedom." Although it was not his prime focus, Kersten also estimated (the newspaper said) that a revolt was "brewing in Red China."

In April, a Kersten resolution endorsed assisting "the non-Russian peoples of the Soviet Union, who constitute one-half of the population, to obtain liberation from their present Communist enslavement." Soon, he was introducing more resolutions than anyone could keep up with, specifying different Eastern European nationalities whose liberation struggles should be supported. One concerned the liberation of Czechoslovakia: "The President of the United States is hereby requested . . . to formulate a new and stronger foreign policy which, among other things, recognizes the essentially evil nature of the international Communist regime, bent on the destruction of the United States and of the free world." The president should also find ways to "offer aid and moral support to active fighters now struggling for the liberation of the Czech and Slovak peoples and other Communist-dominated countries."[17]

Kersten saw his big chance in summer 1951, when the Foreign Affairs Committee passed the Mutual Security Act, which ultimately would authorize $7.5 billion in foreign economic and military aid. On August 17, Kersten told the full House that the act would "mean nothing more than an armaments race. So, we must begin to move in the direction of eventual liberation of the eastern nations of Europe." He offered an amendment that would not only pay to create national armies of exiles wishing to liberate their home countries but also contemplated "the possibility of aiding the underground organizations that may now exist and may come into existence in the future." The amendment, Kersten admitted in a brief debate, was "permissive" — the president *could* determine that it was "important in the defense of the North Atlantic area and of the security of the United States" to use persons "residing in or escapees from the Soviet Union" and nearby countries for "other purposes." The latter phrase, whose vagueness bothered some members of Congress, would allow the president (Kersten later explained) to give "positive aid to selected persons residing in Iron Curtain countries. . . . We can begin to infiltrate their regimes, instead of letting them infiltrate our governments."

Nine House members spoke to Kersten's amendment, which put no limit on how much money the president could use out of the billions authorized in the Mutual Security Act. At first, Foreign Affairs chairman James Richards said, "I just cannot see it." Opposition from Richards might have killed the amendment, but after sufficient defense of the amendment by Kersten and a few others, the chairman joined Kersten's ally, Orland "Charlie" Armstrong (R-MO) ("this will be a step forward in the psychological war that we need to wage") and the others who spoke up. John Vorys, perhaps the most influential Republicans on Foreign Affairs, also implied his support, to his subsequent regret. The amendment passed overwhelmingly in a voice vote.

On the Senate side, the combined Foreign Relations and Armed Services committees passed the Mutual Security Act of 1951, Kersten Amendment intact, but with the proviso that the president could spend no more than $100 million for its "purposes." Kersten complimented Richards on the floor for his handling of the requisite conference committee with Senate members and endorsed the revised version just before the House passed it on October 5. The unique Mutual Security Act "might well mean the beginning of the end of communistic aggression throughout the world," he observed. After the Senate gave its final approval, Harry Truman did so, too, on October 10.[18]

What had Kersten wrought? Legally and symbolically, a lot: Though most legislators thought it best to say little publicly about the $100 million it handed President Truman — "whereby the United States can render aid for underground liberation movements in communist countries" (Kersten's words) — the fact remained that Congress had done so overwhelmingly and the president had signed it into law. Journalists eventually paid attention, especially after Soviet foreign minister Andrei Vishinsky (later labeled "the outstanding unpunished criminal of our times" by Kersten's committee) told the United Nations that the amendment "provides for financing of traitors to their native land and of war criminals who have fled from their countries."

Though the Soviet Union had done the same in the opening years of the Cold War, Vishinsky had a point. After all, Kersten had enthusiastically endorsed (and made part of the *Congressional Record*) articles in American newspapers and magazines that advocated unbridled covert war against the USSR. Paul Linebarger in *Nation's Business* had speculated about what could be achieved with $500 million in support of "black" operations: "Three armed rebellions at $50 million each; another good-sized underground just short of rebellion for $50 million. Forty major political conspiracies at $2.5 million. Twenty thousand rumor-mongers, saboteurs, assassins, racketeers, and other revolutionists at an overhead cost of $20,000 per man." Yes, "assassination and similar methods might be needed," he wrote.

Newspaper columnist Bob Considine, endorsing Kersten's advocacy, admitted that encouraging the "downtrodden masses" in communist countries to revolt could "result in great bloodshed." Kersten was "the most unpopular American in the Kremlin circles today," claimed the columnist. Soviet leaders had "attacked this Kersten amendment more savagely than any other program ever instituted by the United States. That should only make us understand that we have hit them on their most vulnerable button." The congressman was delighted by the Soviets' complaints and advised the Truman administration to organize Iron Curtain escapees "promptly" to wage "underground operations."[19]

On the day after the House first passed the Mutual Security Act in August, a *New York Times*' page-one story had an uninformative paragraph on an inside page about Kersten's measure. A few weeks after Congress and Truman completed action on the act, though, a front-page story detailed the pathbreaking, potentially illegal aspects (under international law) of its Kersten Amendment. The UN General Assembly was soon to meet in Paris and, coincidentally, planned to consider a draft code titled "Offenses against the Peace and Security of Mankind." Kersten, the *Times* reported, was worried that the assembly might outlaw as "terroristic" any attempts by one nation to undermine another. When the State Department's Warren Austin advised Kersten that no one could view an "attempt to restore a people's freedom" in such a fashion, the legislator said, "I do not share Mr. Austin's optimism as to how such underground liberation activities would be characterized." The congressman almost seemed to defend terrorism: "To say that terror would play no part in a liberation movement in Eastern Europe is to be utterly unconversant with what constitutes a liberation movement. One of the main objectives of a real liberation movement is to strike terror into the hearts of the communist tyrants." Kersten entered those comments into the *Congressional Record* as an "extension of remarks," meaning that they were not voiced on the House floor, but such language made some Washington insiders wary of Kersten.

In a subsequent story, on November 24, the *Times* turned its attention to the Vishinsky critique of the amendment, but a sidebar story — headlined "Issue Now Out in Open" — was far more interesting. "The Soviet government's protest over the alleged subversion provision of the Mutual Security Act has brought into the open a long-standing debate within United States government circles on policy toward anti-communist movements within communist-controlled countries." After detailing the amendment's intent, as explained by Kersten, the report described how part of the $100 million might, for example, help a struggling anti-Soviet underground in the Ukraine (and its backers in the United States). The story concluded, "Many Washington observers believe that the whole incident illustrates perfectly the great difficulty that democracies have in waging underground warfare. Where a totalitarian regime appropriates resources and goes to work in secret, the Kersten amendment tries to do the same thing in the white glare of public view, exposing the United States to the vigorous Soviet counter-offensive, one whose vigor is undiminished by the very considerable similar activities carried on by the Soviet regime almost from the day of its birth."[20]

In another important sense, though, the Kersten Amendment made no difference: CIA/OPC did not need more money for covert action. How soon Kersten learned this is unknown, but Allen Dulles (successor to William Jackson as deputy director) met with the legislator in the months after the amendment became law. That encounter remains unrecorded, but Kersten surely heard of another secret meeting Dulles had on March 5, 1952, with the Foreign Affairs Committee. (The hearing's transcript, unlike most congressional documents involving CIA testimony that even hinted at covert action, somehow avoided destruction and was declassified decades later.)

Dulles appeared in support of using $4.3 million of the Kersten Amendment money for building more extensive reception facilities to care for escapees from the Soviet Union and Eastern Bloc nations. This "overt" work would be done by the State Department but would serve crucial purposes for the CIA, he said: "We need the machinery for taking care of these people when they come out. Then later we can decide whether they are useful for intelligence, whether they are useful for psychological warfare, whether eventually they could be used for the 'other purposes' of the Kersten Amendment." Abraham Ribicoff (D-CT) pointed out that the amendment's language was decidedly "broad enough to encompass the proposal of Mr. Dulles, legally." Soon, all but one of his colleagues agreed.

More provocative discussions unfolded, especially about the recent attempts by committee members Mike Mansfield and John Vorys to deny the amendment's intent at the United Nations General Assembly meeting in Paris. Within a year, the scholarly Mansfield would move to the Senate and become a covert action critic, but there was little hint of this in his House years. Vorys would become the leading House defender of the Eisenhower administration's foreign policy in coming years. The two had served on the conference committee that worked out House-Senate differences on the Mutual Security Act, before working on the U.S. delegation at the UN session. Responding to Vishinsky's bitter complaint over the Kersten Amendment as "aggression," Mansfield and Vorys lied, telling the assembly on November 27, 1951, "There are in this law no aggressive acts or aggressive threats contemplated against the Soviet Union or against any of the countries it dominates." The Soviet foreign minister was a "skunk," and "up to his old tricks," choosing to "misinterpret this section and to call it an attempt to subvert government in the USSR." The real purpose of the amendment, the legislators said repeatedly, was "defense of the North Atlantic area." Not easily, the U.S. delegation persuaded the assembly not to support the Soviet claim.

At the subsequent Dulles hearing, Mansfield asked how much of "this $100 million" had been spent. "None," said Dulles. Should the expanded refugee reception, and the moneys in support of it, be shifted to the CIA, inquired Mansfield. "We do not want it," the deputy director said. Vorys, who regretted his support of the Kersten Amendment, then initiated a discussion of the Paris struggle: "I want to talk to you about a little psychological warfare that Mike Mansfield and I were in. He was in the frontline. We made all the lemonade that we could make out of this lemon." Vishinsky had confronted them with Kersten's explanation of the amendment's permissive words. Vorys continued, "We had to talk fast and not very clearly." Allies of the United States assumed the Americans did covert action, but asked the legislators, "Why did you write it into the statute?"

Trying to soothe the representative, Dulles said, "I recognized the difficult position and admired the way you and Mr. Mansfield handled the situation in Paris." Vorys, businesslike and mostly humorless that day, was not pacified. When Chairman Richards joked to the committee about Vorys's view of the refugees — "John wants to get them in the uniform and get them across the border and get them shooting" — he sourly denied it. He also doubted that the Kersten funds should be used for the purpose proposed by Dulles, despite the latter's plea that adept refugee handling could have great "psychological effect": "We are now dealing with the escapees from the satellite countries. Those are the countries now where we wish to have an impact." Vorys, though, was vexed by different interpretations of the amendment that were arising and began reading to the committee the entire statement that he and Mansfield had given UN delegates. When he read the phrase, "for the purpose of defense only," Chairman Richards again interrupted Vorys to tease him: "You did not believe all you said there, did you?" Vorys said not a word in response, then read the rest of the statement, which ended with the repeated, specious claim that the amendment's "provisions are limited to 'the defense of the North Atlantic area.'"

Vorys — a tough-minded internationalist but not knowledgeable about the CIA — worried that using Kersten funds to set up reception camps would "make liars out of me and Mike." It would be a hard sell, he claimed, to insist that the camps would be created for the "defense of the North Atlantic area." Nor, he said, could the United States issue a statement saying, "Well, we are just going to train 12,000 spies here." Vorys had no coherent plan for dealing with the Kersten Amendment, whose "stupid words" he hated as "the worst way in the world" to undermine the USSR. Yet, he admitted, "Charlie Kersten is right! Charlie Armstrong is right!" — refugees from the Soviet Union and the Eastern Bloc were "burning to join an army of liberation, an offensive army of liberation, to go in and liberate their country. But, merely to sit in a NATO defense unit, they are not interested." Saying this, Vorys looked at Dulles — who had already assured the committee that the CIA had all the money it needed for what Richards called "your type of work" — and said, "I thought we had some real smart plans going on here, well-financed plans." The deputy director responded dryly, "John, do you want us to advertise them if we have them?" No, said Vorys, but it would be helpful to have "some testimony . . . on what has been done so far."

Without giving specific information that moment, Dulles attempted to explain the CIA dilemmas regarding the use of exiles against Eastern European governments or the USSR:

> The question of creating ethnic forces out of the Poles, Czechs, and others is a very explosive one. We want to keep alive in these countries the desire for liberty, and the hope of liberty. But until we are much better prepared, do we want to do anything as provocative as having legions sitting there, ready to go in, but not able to go in?
>
> It is a very difficult question. And I must admit there are times when I feel we have almost stirred up Czechoslovakia too much, without the military ability to do something.

Vorys agreed that it was a "vast, perplexing question." For all his enthusiasm for rolling back the Soviet Union, he doubted that there was "any way to use these people." Frances Bolton (R-OH), who also had been in Paris with Vorys and Mansfield and would be critical of the CIA in years to come, added her doubts that the amendment would work, but she, too, favored operations against the USSR: "I am all for doing everything we can through the CIA, but I would do it quietly." (Bolton had previously received a tutorial about American covert action from OPC's Frank Wisner, who suffered Beetle Smith's wrath for doing so.) Then Mansfield recalled Congress's original intent: "It was brought up time after time" that covert activities "should be done on the order of the Manhattan Project," meaning there would be "no accounting." That, he said, "would be the way to do it."

Having agreed that the CIA should pursue the quiet option, committee members roundly criticized their own Congress for passing an amendment it could not publicly defend. "I was accused of sitting on a committee that did not know the effect of words," said Bolton of her Paris encounters.

Richards observed, "This committee deals with words. We eat them for breakfast, dinner, and supper." Perhaps there should have been more debate before passing the amendment, said some. Vorys responded, "I discussed it on the floor," but maybe the Senate and State Department were "negligent" in not warning about the complications that could arise. "Is it not a fact," asked James Fulton, "that the Kersten Amendment is probably the first time in all history that there was legislation publicly debated and acted on, without any thought whatever on a whole spy program for a country for one year?" Without answering that awkwardly worded question, Vorys volunteered, "I have a clipping stating that six men were executed in one country on the basis of this Kersten Amendment." Still, Richards noted of the amendment's intent, "It is an awfully appealing thing to Congress, itself."

Nonetheless, most committee members agreed with Richards that the topic should not be broached again on the House and Senate floors; otherwise, once raised, "you have it, regardless of whether you are going to hit it directly as the legislative spy program, as it was in Kersten's amendment, or dissemble it and put it another way." In the future, Richards suggested, maybe "we ought to ask these gentlemen, Mr. Armstrong and Mr. Kersten, on up and maybe we can get the CIA . . . to explain it to them, and I think they will play ball with us." Having agreed on that, and authorizing the State Department's use of the $4.3 million to improve refugee handling, the committee adjourned to the chairman's invitation to members to "stay around and talk informally" with Dulles.[21]

Although Foreign Affairs members had expressed doubt that Congress should ever publicly express itself again as it had with the Kersten Amendment, it is notable that during the months when it was a live topic, from the August 1951 floor discussion to the hearing with Dulles in March 1952, not a single legislator seems to have spoken out against the amendment's purpose — anti-Soviet covert action — but a fair number endorsed that goal. Still, by the end of the Truman presidency, those at the CIA's Directorate of Plans knew that covert action in Eastern Europe and the USSR had peaked because it had mostly failed. One deputy director wrote another in January 1953, "With the knowledge available to us, blown operations indicate lack of success, and there have been a number of these in recent months."

Covert action in Eastern Europe would continue to be reduced in the early Eisenhower years. Kersten would hear from Eisenhower aides in the first week of the new administration of the "undesirability" in the president's view "of Congress undertaking to deal with the subject matter." In March

1953, the CIA analyzed "probable communist reaction" to creation of the sort of military corps envisioned by Kersten, concluding that the Kremlin would regard it "as another indication that the United States is preparing to attack the Bloc," though not in the near future. The Soviet government would "almost certainly give the impression of greater alarm than it actually feels," since it would probably doubt the military effectiveness of such a corps.

When the House Foreign Affairs Committee discussed the amendment again in an early 1953 hearing, one member observed of its language, "It is an open door. . . . You can drive a train right through it." This at a time when the CIA, the Psychological Strategy Board, and the Defense Department would seriously explore creation of the amendment's envisioned "foreign military units." But DCI Dulles told Kersten later in 1953 (according to Lyman Kirkpatrick) "that the numbers of escapees who meet the qualifications are discouragingly few." Nonetheless, the agency went out of its way to cooperate with Kersten; when his committee planned hearings in Europe in 1954 and wished to interview defectors from the communist side, the committee's counsel informed Kersten, "I was in Frankfort on June 17th and 18th for conferences with Lt. Gen. [Lucian] Truscott, head of the CIA, and his staff. General Truscott was most cooperative and assured me of the complete assistance of the CIA. . . . after the conference with him, the wheels started to roll."

Radio Prague would denounce Kersten as "the American organizer of espionage and murder" that same year. Knowing that he was hardly an "organizer," the congressman continued to believe and hope that "even one battalion of escapees would have a broad psychological impact." Little of the money authorized would ever be used, though. Kersten would write to his fellow Wisconsinite, Republican senator and Foreign Relations chairman Alexander Wiley, that "the failure to use this amendment for its primary purpose in the face of Soviet objection has bothered me for some time." Kersten seemingly never understood how his legislation had mattered: Smith, Dulles, Truman, and Eisenhower learned all too well that Congress favored covert action. Still, leaders on Capitol Hill and at the White House would work harder in coming years to keep low-seniority legislators like Kersten away from the topic.[22]

Portraits

Chairmanships of House and Senate Appropriations and Armed Services committees (and their secretive CIA subcommittees) experienced considerable turnover during the Truman era because Democrats and Republicans traded control of the two houses and some key legislators lost reelection battles. Still, a dominant cast of characters emerged by the early 1950s.

Richard Russell's rise to the chairmanship of the Armed Services Committee in January 1951 was an early, if obscure, blow to McCarthyism. The Georgia Democrat was a long-credentialed conservative anticommunist and enormously respected within the Senate. He had observed and worked under two chairs of the committee — Republican Gurney and Democrat Tydings — in the few short years since the CIA and other national security agencies had been created in 1947. Both men were denied reelection in 1950, and so the CIA and the huge Defense Department came under Russell's purview.

Eighteen years had passed since he entered the Senate as its youngest member. On that day — January 12, 1933 — Senator Robert LaFollette Jr. (Progressive-WI) had posed for an uncharacteristically jolly photograph with Russell, passing to him the informal title as "baby" of the Senate. The new senator was shy, serious, and courteous and would remain so his entire life. A long-time smoker, Russell was diagnosed in the 1950s with a "mild" case of emphysema. Still, he would remain reasonably energetic during that decade and, as a socially reclusive bachelor with many evenings alone, read voluminously in his apartment, especially committee reports and history books.

In 1951, the mostly conservative Russell's national fame and his reputation within the Senate and its "inner club" were cemented and enhanced by his handling of an explosive issue: Harry Truman's firing of General Douglas MacArthur, commander of U.S. and UN forces in the Korean War.[1]

As he chaired hearings in May and June, perceptive observers saw that Russell was managing them in such a way as to give all relevant figures in the controversy — MacArthur, his defenders, and his critics — their say, but under the protective secrecy that resulted from keeping the press and public out of the hearings. Russell briefed reporters daily and (after removing sensitive military or intelligence information) provided them with the day's hearings transcripts.

Russell's initial months as Armed Services chair had allowed him to practice extracting documents from civilian and military bureaucracies. In March 1951, Russell wrote Secretary Marshall a scorcher of a letter detailing the inadequacies of a Defense Department response to a committee request for information. The "astonishing" response, Russell wrote, was "completely lacking in responsiveness" and "completely unacceptable." The Defense Department responded again, quickly and in detail.[2]

Russell's committee sought and received a number of documents from the CIA, State, and Defense Departments during the MacArthur controversy that detailed the administration's deliberations. Among them was a transcript of the president's private meeting with MacArthur at Wake Island the previous fall, at which the president asked, "What are the chances for Chinese or Soviet interference?" and the general responded, "Very little." From the CIA, Russell's group seems to have obtained conclusions from "national estimates" just prior to the Chinese intervention. That Russell had Truman's respect and considerable confidence may account for what success the senator had.[3]

When the hearings ended in August, he and a majority of colleagues again chose discretion — avoiding an official committee report, turning hearing records over to the Senate, and issuing a bland statement to the public that emphasized the existence and the importance of American unity against alien aggressors.

Afterward, Washington insiders honored Russell for his leadership, as have historians. CIA leaders were pleased, too, having faced less heat than MacArthur's intelligence apparatus. When, for example, Senator Alex Smith asked JCS chair Omar Bradley if U.S. intelligence "fell down" in not anticipating China's intervention and then added, "Was it MacArthur's intelligence staff, or was it the CIA in Washington?," Bradley responded that MacArthur had relied "primarily" on "field intelligence."[4]

In his opening months as Armed Services chair in 1951, Russell put Republicans Leverett Saltonstall (MA) and William Knowland, plus Democrats Harry Byrd and John Stennis (MS) on the CIA subcommittee for the new congressional session. Saltonstall would be the Armed Services subcommittee's key Republican figure for the next decade and a half. A kindly, patrician figure, he is remembered by Pforzheimer as "supportive and helpful." Friends called him Lev or Salty. "His engaging homely face is his No. 1 political asset," wrote *Time* magazine, "with its drooping eyelids, lean cheeks, long nose, wide-spaced teeth, and the famed cow-catcher chin." Overwhelmingly popular in his home state and moderately liberal, Saltonstall had earned colleagues' sympathy and respect for the dignity he had shown when his son Peter was killed at Guam in World War II.[5]

Joseph C. O'Mahoney (D-WY) and Homer Ferguson (R-MI) handled much of Senate Appropriations' interactions with the CIA during the last couple years of the Truman era. Pforzheimer remembers O'Mahoney as "a first class guy, tough, and able." Massachusetts-born, with an accent to prove it, O'Mahoney had lived in the West since 1908 and had represented Wyoming in the Senate since 1934. A fierce opponent of big business and a former crusading reporter, O'Mahoney was (according to Pforzheimer) "much smarter than Ferguson," a former coal miner and lawyer who, as a Michigan judge, gained fame for jailing crooked politicians. He had a mixed reputation in Washington, though. David Lilienthal wrote in his diary that Ferguson, who presided over secret Appropriations hearings for AEC, was "actually stupid."

Though agency duties were largely delegated to those less senior Appropriations members by the near-senile Chairman McKellar, ranking Republican Styles Bridges continued his lively, critical interest in the CIA. He would soon assert himself and become the Republican on Appropriations to whom agency leaders reported. In many respects, Bridges was everything Salsonstall was not — the thrice-married New Hampshire senator had a capacity for meanness that scared some colleagues. Once an agricultural agent for the government, he won his Senate seat in 1936 and unsuccessfully sought the Republican vice-presidential nomination in 1936 and the presidential nomination in 1940. In subsequent years, he had won the support of the Senate's most hard-core conservatives and could actually deliver votes when critical issues were at hand; no one imagined Saltonstall delivering blocs of votes.[6]

Carl Vinson chaired the House Armed Services Committee and, informally, its CIA subcommittee. A representative since the days of Woodrow Wilson's presidency, Vinson had a way of referring to certain executive branch agencies in personal terms: "my CIA" and "my Pentagon." He had functioned with his Senate counterpart Tydings in shaping the CIA Act of 1949. In future years, he and fellow Georgian Richard Russell would coexist warily as chairs of Armed Services committees. Vinson's Republican counterpart on the committee was Dewey Short of Missouri. Short, too, had helped shepherd the CIA Act through Congress, despite his hostility to Truman's foreign policy. Like Republicans on other committees, he would get the chance to chair Armed Services during the first two years of the Eisenhower administration. In some ways, Short was a rarity: a former Methodist minister and chaplain in World War I. Nonetheless, Short sometimes got spectacularly drunk in public. This, wrote Drew Pearson in his diary, was something few journalists thought "worthy of news comment. I disagree. Dewey is the man who almost publicly, at least in the presence of a thousand dinner guests, shouted foul language at the Chief Justice of the United States when [Fred Vinson, the Chief Justice] was trying to speak at Frank Boykin's [D-AL] dinner last summer."

The other most important House member to oversee the agency was Democrat Clarence Cannon, who chaired the Appropriations Committee. Like his Republican counterpart, John Taber, Cannon was one of the three or four most knowledgeable members of the entire Congress concerning the agency's budget. Intrigued by intelligence history, "Cannon never lost his keen interest in the CIA," recalls Lyman Kirkpatrick. He often reminded CIA leaders of his belief that they had failed miserably in not predicting North Korea's attack on South Korea in 1950. Cannon repeated his criticism for so many years that it became a kind of running joke for CIA leaders, though it could not have been funny to them in the early 1950s.[7]

Taber had chaired Appropriations in 1947/1948 and would do so again for the first two years of the Eisenhower presidency. In the meantime, he tried to get along with the chairman. Like Cannon, he relished having the role and reputation of "watchdog of the Treasury." While the upstate New York Republican was internationalist enough to have supported the Marshall Plan and U.S. entry into NATO, he often tried to cut foreign aid programs throughout the early Cold War years. Also like his Democratic counterpart, Taber was frequently ill-tempered and had no close friends in the House.

On the whole, Cannon's temper was the worse; there is no authoritative count of how many encountered his fists. Once, in the late 1940s, Taber and Cannon turned on each other, after the New Yorker called the Missourian a liar in a private conversation on the House floor. Cannon then invited Taber into his office, just off the floor, where (as the *Saturday Evening Post* later wrote) "without further ado, he belted Taber in the mouth, drawing blood." Soon both men were crashing into the furniture. Representative Everett Dirksen (R-IL), not on the House floor, came from another direction toward the chairman's office. As he later wrote,

> There was John Taber — sober, serious, and well behaved — lying on his back on a divan in Chairman Cannon's office, and there was the Chairman with his

hands on Congressman Taber's throat, trying to choke him. I had to separate them. . . . I have thought of it a great many times. To me it was a spectacle to see two men who were both in their sixties, and who had gone far in public life, become so upset about a public question that they undertook to settle it by main force. Had I not accidentally walked into the Chairman's office, I am not sure what would have happened.

Nonetheless, Cannon and Taber got along most of the time. And, as the *New York Times* noted, "Cannon actually is one of the most scholarly men in the House."

The other House Appropriations member who would become crucial in the early 1950s was Democrat George Mahon. The Texan was gentle, hard-working, and trusted. By 1951, Cannon had Mahon, who headed Appropriations' Defense Department subcommittee, play a more hands-on role in interacting with the agency.[8]

During difficult times, these and a handful of other CIA overseers would sometimes privately criticize and even micromanage the CIA on select issues. In quieter periods, they were usually not so inclined.

CIA Subcommittees, Intelligence Roles, and Budgets

In April 1948, a House Armed Services subcommittee telephoned the CIA with four questions that would be posed in an upcoming hearing. Though only indirectly affecting the agency's funding, its members wanted to know how the CIA had and would obtain "appropriations without disclosing the amount and source." The agency responded that it would "prepare its regular budget for review by certain designated Bureau of the Budget officers. . . . These proposals would then be discussed in Executive Session with the appropriations subcommittees." If approved, the CIA appropriations would be hidden in other bureaucracies' budgets.

While the Armed Services subcommittees had time to work out relations with the CIA, from its first year onward, the agency literally could not function without action by the Appropriations subcommittees. Walter Pforzheimer, CIG/CIA legislative liaison from 1946 to 1956, recalls the roots of one such subcommittee. A committee hearing early in CIA history had proved "too big, too unwieldy, so they set up this subcommittee, selecting senior members. . . . They would call and ask, 'Is the Director available to testify on the budget next Thursday at 10 o'clock?' and I'd say, 'Sure, we'll be there. Where do you want us to be?' They said, 'We'll tell you before the meeting.' And about a half hour before we were to leave headquarters, a staffer would call me and say, 'Go to this door of the capitol. Someone will meet you.' And someone would meet us. Security of the CIA and its budget was a congressional fiat from the very beginning." (Appropriations and Armed Services barons applied the secrecy priority to themselves, too: for years, the subcommittees would not divulge their members' names publicly, and only grudgingly did so to others in Congress.)

Of the Appropriations' process, Pforzheimer adds, "In the House, it would be more detailed than in the Senate because appropriations, by the Constitution, start in the House. We might take several days."[1] DCI Smith's executive assistant, Lyman Kirkpatrick, recalls

accompanying him to a hearing of the House Appropriations Subcommittee on the CIA in 1951. The hearing was held in a small room somewhere under the back steps of the Capitol. We were there more than three hours and the bulk of the time was spent by General Smith giving a brilliant review of the workings of the Agency and an analysis of the world situation. When he had finished, I remember Mr. Clarence Cannon of Missouri, chairman of the Appropriations Committee, saying, "Thank you, Mr. Director. Now it is understood that everything that has been said here today is secret, even the fact that this meeting was held."

(Two decades later, Kirkpatrick judged Cannon's motives "the purest," but regretted that such meetings had not been somewhat publicized, since the agency might have been spared by claims in later years that no oversight system had existed.)[2]

Allen Dulles later described how, when he was Smith's deputy, the agency prepared and supplied to the Appropriations subcommittees a booklet including "requirements for the fiscal year under consideration, as well as our estimate of obligations and expenditures for the current fiscal year, and our actual obligations and expenditures for the year preceding." The annual booklets were accompanied by a "great deal of supplementary information, including explanation of specific programs and projects." They were returned to the agency after they had "served the committees' purposes."

In the House, the chairman (whether Democrat Cannon or Republican Taber) and the committee's chief clerk, George Harvey, knew (as Pforzheimer reported in 1951) "the amount of the CIA budget and its location" in the larger federal government budget. In most years, the ranking minority member — again Cannon or Taber, depending on the year — knew these two facts. From 1952 onward, George Mahon and one or two others also knew the CIA's budget in detail, including expenditures for covert operations. (How much Appropriations leaders knew of some covert officers' financial irresponsibility is unclear, though. The chief of the CIA's Finance Division, upon return from a tour of stations around the world, reported to OPC and other heads in 1952 a "great improvement in the handling of finances abroad," but added that "many individuals evade or avoid any accounting for funds.")[3]

Early in the twenty-first century, the U.S. government continued to treat the declassification of early CIA budgets as dangerous to the security of the nation. Nonetheless, some appropriations documents survive in the papers of deceased CIA subcommittee members. They show that agency budgets approved by the Senate and House appropriations subcommittees grew swiftly across the early Cold War years. For Fiscal Year 1948 (i.e., from the agency's birth through June 30, 1948) the legislators approved a budget of $40 million (technically for the CIA's predecessor, the Central Intelligence Group). Very likely, the appropriations leaders subsequently approved additional funds for covert operations that — as noted earlier — the State Department requested. The funds for the CIA were hidden in the budgets of the State and (especially) Defense Departments. The following year — Fiscal Year 1949 — the congressional leaders authorized a 25 percent growth in the agency's budget, to $50 million. Another $32.5 million was spent that year for intelligence activities of the State Department and military services.[4]

Because of the State Department's unpopularity with McCarthyite members of Congress, its budget proposals were often subject to reductions during the appropriations processes. More than once this led (unintentionally) to cuts in planned CIA budgets. Senator O'Mahoney suggested to Pforzheimer in 1951 that all of the CIA's fast-growing budget be hidden in Defense Department accounts, an idea the Appropriations subcommittees implemented the following year for the Fiscal Year 1953 budget.[5]

Available evidence shows exponential growth of the 1950–1952 agency budgets. In May 1952, a report to the Deputy Director for Administration (DD/A) indicated that, from October 1950 to May 1952, "the dollar volume of expenditure of appropriated funds has more than doubled." For Fiscal Year 1951, the CIA requested and received twice as much for OPC as it had the previous year in support of covert operations in Korea and other locales. (Possibly the other reason the agency needed more for OPC is that an arrangement with the Economic Cooperation Administration [ECA], which administered the Marshall Plan and had funneled unknown millions of dollars to OPC in the years 1948 to 1951, was coming to an end.) In 1949, OPC employed 302 persons fulltime and had seven stations overseas; by 1952, there were 2,812 employees, plus 3,142 contract personnel abroad at 47 stations. For Fiscal Year 1952, OPC's budget was $82 million. Just in sheer numbers, compared to 1949, "Cold War covert activities, including guerrilla warfare," had grown threefold by 1952. In the latter year, 74 percent of the CIA budget was devoted to clandestine activities, including covert action.[6] These were enthusiastically supported by leaders of the Appropriations committees. By Fiscal Year 1953, the last CIA budget requested by the Truman administration approached $587 million — over 1,400 percent larger than 1947's.[7]

At some point in the very early 1950s, the appropriations legislators also began approving a large annual "unvouchered contingency reserve fund." The DCI could draw from the account, subject to "specific approval of the Bureau of the Budget" (BOB), with some level of General Accounting Office (GAO) knowledge, but only for "unforeseen emergencies" around the world. For the regular and unvouchered portions of its budget, the CIA usually received the funds it requested annually, although, in 1952, senators apparently forced modest cuts in the Fiscal Year 1953 budget.

One or more members (typically the chair and the ranking minority member) of the House and Senate Appropriations subcommittees set the annual amount for the unvouchered account, as indeed they did for the whole agency budget. The DCI sought the approval of Appropriations' CIA subcommittee chairs when he wished to authorize large withdrawals from the account.[8]

After Fiscal Year 1949, the CIA attempted to create budgets in which the costs of covert action and other so-called Cold War activities were fully planned for as part of its "normal" budget; the unvouchered accounts were then to be drawn upon only in case of unexpected crises. In 1952, heads of the Appropriations subcommittees approved a $92 million unvouchered fund for Fiscal Year 1953. This followed Beetle Smith's report to the NSC in April: "The presently projected scope of these activities . . . will require next year a budget three times larger than that required for our intelligence activities." George Mahon informally conveyed news of House approval of this huge budget to Allen Dulles (in Smith's absence) in April 1952. Upon his return (a CIA leader wrote in his work diary), the DCI would "talk to two senators in this connection," most likely O'Mahoney and Ferguson. "It is expected that there will be no problem in the Senate."

Surprisingly, with the Korean War raging, the CIA did not touch the reserve fund during Fiscal Year 1953 (July 1, 1952, to June 30, 1953). With permission of Appropriations leaders, the amount would be carried over into the next year's agency budget. The legislators hid the entire half-billion-dollar CIA appropriation that year in the Defense Department's budget.[9]

CIA overseers occasionally rejected budgets for agency projects. In the fall of 1951, many CIA personnel still worked in eight not-so-grand buildings at 2430 E Street in Washington, formerly the home of the OSS. Other CIA (and OPC/OSO) staff were scattered in over a dozen other buildings in the DC area, to the dismay of Beetle Smith. He was convinced that the dispersion endangered the CIA's ability to keep secrets. Smith rode herd on his assistants to come up with a plan for a secure building just across the Potomac River from Washington that would headquarter most, if not all, of those doing the agency's most sensitive work. The building would be expensive, at $38 million.

CIA leaders had been optimistic about getting the money, but in addition to whatever else the agency did that fall of 1951 to irritate Mahon — and it appears that there was something — agency heads were tardy in bringing their request before his Defense Department subcommittee. On October 9, Mahon wrote Pforzheimer, "It is the intention of the House Committee on Appropriations to deny the funds for the project in which you were interested." More sternly, Mahon wrote that same day to Assistant Secretary of Defense W. J. McNeil about the denial of the appropriation and an additional "$6 million project" linked to the CIA request: "Members of my subcommittee and I myself would feel highly incensed if the Department of Defense should secure funds for a project of some consequence without advising the Committee that funds were wrapped up in the bill."

For a while, Smith favored an alternate idea: a smaller, windowless building that would cost less but not hold all CIA personnel. Among those underwhelmed by that plan was Dulles, who insisted to the DCI one day that he could never work in an office without a window. Amused by Dulles's stubbornness, Smith pulled out a blank sheet of paper, drew a large building and penciled in one window, handed the drawing to Dulles, and assured him that the problem was solved.

At Senate Appropriations, Pforzheimer recalls the day that "the building was up for discussion. McKellar's mind was gone. He sort of fell into a little doze. A Republican senator said that it would be a building without windows. McKellar suddenly came to and blurted out, 'What!? A building without any women?!' then fell back to sleep." The Senate approved the building appropriation, but this became a moot point after House Appropriations voted "no."

In 1952, Smith thought he would try again, asking for $42 million. Mahon persuaded him against it — the political atmosphere of Congress during a fiercely fought presidential-congressional election year would be too adverse. A few years would pass before the next DCI, Allen Dulles, would ask Congress for a new headquarters with plenty of windows.[10]

Overall, records from the Truman era suggest that the House and Senate Appropriations subcommittees on the CIA, while hardly systematic in their monitoring of the agency, were sometimes assertive and seemed to shape CIA activities. Their uneven influence over CIA budgets is best judged in light of the extraordinary Section 10 ("Appropriations") of the CIA Act of 1949: "The sums made available to the Agency may be expended without regard to the provisions of law and regulations relating to the expenditure of Government funds; and for objects of a confidential, extraordinary, or emergency nature, such expenditures to be accounted for solely on the certificate of the Director and every such certificate shall be deemed a sufficient voucher for the amount therein certified."

One way to interpret Section 10 is that Congress intended the DCI to have absolute power to spend moneys appropriated to the CIA each year for any purpose. But, notes CIA in-house historian Arthur Darling, "No one, least of all the Director of Central Intelligence, thought so. The understanding in the committees of Congress, the Bureau of the Budget, the Office of Comptroller General [CG], and the Agency was that so great power was overshadowed by the even greater responsibility attendant upon it."

Furthermore, as Darling suggests, congressional appropriators sometimes exercised their power indirectly, through the Comptroller General of the United States. Beetle Smith encountered this various times, including a 1951 confrontation with CG Lindsay C. Warren. The comptroller, though appointed by the president, is subject to Senate confirmation. As head of the General Accounting Office, he "functions as an agent of the Congress in controlling and auditing the budget execution process in the executive branch."[11]

Having once opposed as a "fraud" the unorthodox spending powers granted in 1946 by the Atomic Energy Act to the chairman of the Atomic Energy Commission, Warren had only reluctantly accepted the extraordinary spending provisions being crafted in 1949 for the CIA Act. The subject of the dispute that emerged in 1951 was a seemingly minor question — Smith's attempt to use the unvouchered account to grant a retroactive pay raise to agency employees. When Warren ruled that the CIA had no "specific statutory authority for granting . . . retroactive salary increases," Smith responded that he was authorized to do so under Section 10. On November 21, Warren made a rejoinder: "The extraordinary powers granted to the Central Intelligence Agency by Section 10 and other sections of the 1949 act — and this I am sure you will agree — result solely from the congressional recognition of the extraordinary functions assigned that Agency by the act." Smith's proposed retroactive pay raise "would be subject to legal objection."

The DCI soon acceded to Warren's interpretation of congressional intent, and approved a message to agency employees: unvouchered funds could not "be used to relieve ourselves of administrative problems which are common to Government generally." General Counsel Lawrence Houston thought this politic, since "certain congressmen, jealous of their appropriating powers and antagonistic to the concept of secrecy, would like only too well to discover an abuse of power."[12]

"We Don't Let Just Anybody Look at Our Files"

From the beginning, committees or subcommittees other than Armed Services and Appropriations occasionally interacted with the CIA, despite the inclinations of President Truman. As the Kersten Amendment hearings showed, the House Foreign Affairs Committee sometimes explored sensitive topics with agency leaders; in the early 1950s, Senate Foreign Relations would also begin to do so. Most active was the Joint Committee on Atomic Energy, before which the CIA appeared two to three times each year. Much like the tiny, obscure Appropriations and Armed Services subcommittees on the CIA, the JCAE rarely leaked secrets. One JCAE member barely exaggerated in telling colleagues in 1951, "Compared to the Pentagon, we are an airtight safe."

Joint Committee members wished to have agency heads' analyses of Soviet atomic progress and more. On July 12, 1950, DCI Hillenkoetter gave the JCAE as thorough an analysis of Soviet atomic and thermonuclear weapons programs as the intelligence establishment could come up with. The USSR, he said, would probably have its first hydrogen bomb by mid-1952. The hearing's first hour focused on that topic and then subsequently ranged widely, from the potential for high-altitude photography by the CIA of the Soviet Union to the ongoing "flying saucer" scare. On the first topic, four years before the CIA would begin creating U-2 aircraft, Chairman McMahon asked Hillenkoetter, "Have you given any consideration lately to getting high level photographs?" The DCI assured him, "We are working on that, sir." Abstaining from "any further detail," the senator urged Hillenkoetter to "do it, if you can."

Bourke Hickenlooper brought a moment of levity to the hearing by recommending that the CIA consult Al Capp, the creator of the popular newspaper cartoon strip "L'il Abner": "He has a flying saucer going around." Another member pursued the topic seriously. "When people like [former World War I flying ace] Eddie Rickenbacker say there is such a thing, I begin to wonder. Do you know if there is anything like that?" Hillenkoetter avoided sensationalizing the topic: "We haven't been able to find out, the Air Force hasn't been able to find out, and neither has the Navy." Another member saw potential in the possibility that the unidentified flying objects were real: Earthlings, he speculated, "would get together to fight the invader." About that prediction, Hillenkoetter remained silent.[1]

After one briefing by Smith and others from the CIA at a hearing in the early 1950s, McMahon pushed the DCI for information about the sources and methods underlying CIA information about the Soviet nuclear program. Of that topic, the agency's knowledge had been grossly lacking, but — through secretive means — the CIA had lately become more knowledgeable. This progress was described, at least in general terms, to the Armed Services/ Appropriations subcommittees, but in asking "how we at CIA knew these things that they on Joint Committee knew nothing about" (Pforzheimer's words), the young senator treaded on sensitive ground. Smith understood and accepted the imperative of cooperating with the JCAE and suggested a compromise to McMahon: "If you'll come down alone to my office, I will tell you how we know, but I'll not tell the full committee." McMahon agreed and swore himself to secrecy. At CIA headquarters, Smith, Pforzheimer, and others initiated the briefing. Smith was not above putting on a bit of a show occasionally to make a point, though, and made much of dismissing his staffers for the briefing's conclusion. Alone with McMahon, he explained that U.S. communications intelligence (COMINT) allowed the agency to gain considerable insight into Soviet atomic capabilities.[2]

On another occasion, in February 1951, the JCAE chair stirred up a hornet's nest between the CIA and the Pentagon. He continued to believe that the United States might soon need to engage in a "major atomic offensive" against the USSR and requested CIA analysis of that nation's ability to counter such an attack. (McMahon and some of his Joint Committee colleagues bristled with ideas about launching offensive war. Around the time of their CIA request, they asked Defense Secretary Marshall, "How does the Defense Department view the possibility of a leaflet campaign generally warning all Russians living in industrial areas to evacuate?") In order to do the JCAE's proposed analysis, the CIA would also have to measure the *U.S.* military's offensive nuclear war–fighting capability. The Joint Chiefs of Staff, whose military services would be the subject of such a study, resolutely objected. In a "Dear Smith" letter, Marshall conveyed the news that the Defense Department would not cooperate. The embarrassed DCI wrote the chairman, who told his JCAE colleagues about the CIA, "This amuses me a little bit — we suggested they undertake a study which they had never undertaken, the ability of Russia to absorb this attack. And not only can we not get the results of the study which we initiated, but the Defense Department will not cooperate with the CIA in making the study."

Smith seems to have tried his hardest to please the JCAE, despite pressures from others in the executive branch. The following year, he insisted to committee members that he had shared British atomic intelligence with them "that I really was not authorized to do. But it would have been perfectly silly for me to come down here and try to describe to you a joint project in which the British were participating, at least in an attempt to get your moral approval, without telling you what the devil they were doing."[3]

House and Senate subcommittees on immigration, both part of Congress's Judiciary Committees, also carried out occasional oversight, especially in relation to aliens brought into the United States under the CIA Act. As well, the subcommittees cast a suspicious eye on foreign nationals brought into the country by delegations of communist countries with membership in the United Nations. In 1949, Senator Pat McCarran (D-NV) provided DCI Hillenkoetter a list of one hundred persons "to whom visas have been issued for admission into the United States," asking how many were "subversives" who had participated in "foreign intelligence organizations or active Communist organizational work" prior to assuming duties in the United States. Noting that the agency could not legally deal with those persons' activities within the United States, the DCI reported that thirty-two of them had "reportedly or allegedly been engaged in active work for the intelligence services of their respective countries"; twenty-nine were "high-ranking Communist Party officials." A few were of "high moral standards or idealistic motivation," though.[4]

Counterintelligence Blues

And then there was HUAC — "hew-ack," as everyone called it. In 1952, through bizarre circumstances, the director of central intelligence would find himself unhappily facing the House Committee on Un-American Activities, which dated back to 1938. In its early years, the committee targeted alleged subversives of the political right and left, but its focus shifted heavily leftward in the Cold War. Its most controversial activities included 1947's "Hollywood hearings," exploring the influence of communists in the entertainment industry, as well as 1948 hearings at which alleged traitor Alger Hiss and his accuser Whittaker Chambers testified. Periodically, the CIA was drawn into the committee's orbit, though agency leaders rarely emulated J. Edgar Hoover, whose Federal Bureau of Investigation worked closely with HUAC.

The FBI was charged with handling most counterintelligence problems within U.S. borders, but these were concerns as well (to say the least) of the CIA. Infiltration of the agency by persons working for the Soviet Union was widely understood as a possibility in the early Cold War years. This was all the more true when the Un-American Activities Committee and McCarthyism reigned. One agency report from spring 1952 claimed, "No major penetrations of the Agency have been discovered; rather, a number of possible penetrations have been found in advance by counter-intelligence research. The Agency has not had one case of an alleged subversive brought before Congress, before the public by allegations in the press, or reported by the FBI."[5]

Beetle Smith knew better, though. Perhaps the worst counterintelligence disaster of his era was the agency's close association with Harold "Kim" Philby, former head of counterintelligence for the British Secret Intelligence Service (SIS, also known as MI 6), who came to Washington in September 1949 and worked for two years as a liaison between British intelligence and the CIA. Philby could be charming and held his alcohol better than many CIA leaders, with whom he often had long drinking lunches. Among his luncheon partners were Deputy Director Dulles and James Jesus Angleton, who ran CIA counterintelligence. "His entree was unchallenged, his access to the most sensitive operational details unlimited," given the intimate partnership between U.S. and British intelligence services during and since World War II, writes one historian. Unfortunately, Philby's real "employer" was the Soviet government. This only became evident to Smith and the CIA in May 1951, with the defection of Philby's housemate in Washington to the USSR, at which point the DCI insisted that the British recall Philby immediately. The damage done was huge, though the American public and press at the time knew nothing of it.[6]

The Philby episode helps explain why Beetle Smith would say, for all the world to hear, that the CIA was probably infiltrated by communists. It happened on September 29, 1952, during testimony in a libel suit filed by Senator McCarthy against his Democratic colleague William Benton, who had urged McCarthy's expulsion from the Senate for misconduct in his anti-communist crusade. Two and a half years had passed since the Wisconsin senator had riveted the nation with his Wheeling, West Virginia, speech charging that the State Department, especially, was infiltrated by communists. Truman and Democratic presidential nominee Adlai Stevenson were being pummeled for "softness" toward communism.

In that still overheated domestic political environment, further polarized by thoughts of American boys fighting communist forces in Korea and dying by the thousands, DCI Smith — with Philby a fresh, painful memory — faced Senator Benton's call to testify. Though unenthusiastic about testifying, Smith was Benton's friend and despised McCarthy for, among other things, ruining a covert operation against the USSR and newly communist China. As a *New York Times* article later recounted,

> intelligence operatives remember "Tawny Pipit," code name for a CIA operation which McCarthy and his ally, Senator Pat McCarran, both ruthless witch hunters, helped to break up. John Paton Davies, in 1949 a leading State Department expert on the Far East, devised the plan. It would have created an American study group on China made up of distinguished scholars, including some pro-communists (as well as an unannounced CIA man). The group would inevitably make contact with Red China; the pro-communists would become the Red Chinese–Russian contacts inside the study group. Then the CIA would introduce phony intelligence about Russia to help sow dissension between the two communist allies.
>
> McCarthy, to publicize his attacks on Davies, used this as "evidence" of Davies' "pro-communist" sympathies. When General Smith of the CIA told McCarran's Internal Security Subcommittee the truth, it was too late to save either Davies or "Tawny Pipit."[7]

In his Benton-McCarthy testimony, Smith described Davies as a "very loyal and capable officer." (Unusually, the DCI had previously told subordinates that they "might tactfully suggest" to one or more other congressional committees that he was willing to testify about Davies.)

Then Warren Magee, McCarthy's lawyer, took Smith to a more explosive topic, reminding him that Benton, a former assistant secretary of state, had allowed that there probably had been some communists working somewhere in the State Department in recent times. Did Smith agree? "I do. I believe that there are communists in my own organization." Did the DCI know who those persons were? "I wish I did. I do everything I can to detect them. I believe they are so adroit and adept that they have infiltrated practically every security agency of the government."

Smith did not anticipate the political explosion that would follow. From the unusual vantage point of a hospital bed, Lyman Kirkpatrick recorded that day's events. Hospitalized for months with polio, Kirkpatrick often was visited by his boss, whom he greatly admired. Just hours had passed between the testimony and the hospital visit when Smith stalked in, having "hit the headlines in a most unhappy manner." "When Smith arrived," Kirkpatrick continued, "at Walter Reed that afternoon, he had heard all he wanted to from others about this episode and opened with, 'And I don't want to hear from *you* about it!' He then proceeded to tell me about the calls he had received from the White House, and being greeted when he arrived home that afternoon by some rather pointed comments from his wife, Norie, and from Ruth Briggs, who had been his WAC aide for years."[8]

Benton soon informed Smith, "McCarthy made a big point" at a campaign rally in Connecticut out of the DCI's testimony. "Your old associate Ike is in strange hands these days," he added. Still, those somewhat knowledgeable about espionage and Washington, DC, in a Cold War environment and not inclined toward hysteria thought Smith's testimony was obviously accurate. Columnist Walter Lippmann wrote a few days later, "For anyone . . . who understands the business of secret intelligence, it was inconceivable on its face that General Smith had made any kind of revelation. If the director of the secret service is a competent man — and General Bedell Smith is an exceedingly competent man — then we may take it for granted that even when or if he seems to be making revelations, he will not be revealing anything." Nonetheless, many Americans naively thought that large national security bureaucracies could be absolutely free of infiltrators. Others thought Smith had been foolishly indiscreet. Certainly, spokesmen for other agencies in the capital were not prepared to admit that communists worked in *their* ranks.

In the ongoing and bitter presidential campaign between Dwight Eisenhower and Adlai Stevenson, Smith's testimony threatened to provoke a partisan debate about the CIA's ability to counter Soviet penetration attempts. Truman reprimanded Smith in writing, gently reminding him that loose talk during a political campaign could endanger proper policy making. The president and DCI learned, to their alarm, of the comments of the Republican National Committee's head, Arthur Summerfield, who said that he was shocked by Smith's "revelation." The GOP would soon broadcast by radio "a nation-wide expose" to explore the problem, he promised.

Smith admitted to the president that he provoked "a thoroughly bad discussion" that was "grossly unfair" to Truman. Further complicating the picture, Smith learned through an aide and reported to the president, were suspicions of Democrats on HUAC that "my testimony was the result of disloyal connivance on my part to injure your position or that of the Democratic candidate." This stemmed, he assumed, "from my past close official and personal association with General Eisenhower," but Smith added, "I am sure of your realization that I have only one loyalty and that is to the Chief under whom I am serving." At Truman's direction, Smith moved to eliminate the problem by telephoning Eisenhower and then describing that conversation to reporters: "I said to him that if he had the same confidence in me which he had previously expressed on several occasions, he would accept my previous statement and that, in view of the way this matter had been seized upon politically, only he could put a stop to the thing in the GOP." Eisenhower called Summerfield, who canceled the radio plans.

For Lippmann, it was a case study of the problems facing intelligence agencies in democratic governments: "How then, we must ask ourselves, can a free and democratic nation operate an efficient, which means necessarily a silent and deceptive, secret service? There is only one way. That is to rely on the judgment of someone who is competent to judge the operations of the secret service. It is impossible to have a secret service and to have it investigated publicly. [But it] is impossible in a free society to allow any agency of government to operate without being investigated and held accountable."[9]

Whether the House and Senate subcommittees on the CIA held Smith accountable for his statement is unknown. However, a subcommittee of HUAC called Smith to a hearing on October 13. One aide had advised the director to "defer" such an appearance and wrote cryptically in his diary of a "necessary investigation" by the CIA of subcommittee member Francis Walter (D-PA). Nothing more is known of that inquiry, but the director appeared at a federal courthouse in Philadelphia, where the subcommittee was continuing a series of hearings around the country.

He was a businesslike, unsmiling witness. In terms of secrecy, the hearing was everything that normal interactions between the agency and its Appropriations/Armed Services subcommittees were not: open to nine HUAC staff members, the press, and the public (which filled the courtroom to capacity). The DCI and HUAC members traded few compliments, as the legislators had fretted about Smith's description of communists infiltrating "practically every security organization of Government." Though that sweeping statement had caused him to face the subcommittee, Smith refused to elaborate much on the theme. In trying to allay HUAC members' fears of the CIA being "riddled" with communists, he said that of those few sus-pected communists in the CIA, "none" had been "in the United States."

Perhaps thinking of Philby, he quickly qualified the statement by adding, "No Americans, and none within the scope of interest or responsibility of this committee." Though he did not mention it to the HUAC subcommit-tee, the Philby case obviously involved a foreigner; the only legislative bod-ies whose "scope of interest or responsibility" would relate to the Philby matter would arguably have been the CIA subcommittees. Their chairs prob-ably knew the Philby story. Philby himself later wrote that J. Edgar Hoover, who had known but distrusted him and knew the whole story behind his departure from Washington, "made a great deal" out of it on Capitol Hill. Since Philby essentially failed at penetrating the FBI but succeeded with the bureau's rival, the CIA, his speculation is entirely plausible.

(Certainly, Hoover and the DCI were enemies. Early in his tenure as DCI, Smith concluded that Hoover was arrogant in various refusals to cooperate with the CIA and told him so, suggesting that taxpayers would be outraged if they knew. Smith's reproach of the FBI head had a predictable result. As Congressman James Patterson [R-CT] noted, "divided authority" plagued the government's handling of foreign spies on U.S. soil. An article placed into the *Congressional Record* by Patterson said that liaison between the FBI and the CIA was at a "low ebb.")

Representative Walter, soon to chair HUAC, pushed hard in the hearing. A Democrat who had entered Congress as Franklin Roosevelt's presidency began, his forceful anticommunism — he had once tried to strip American Communist Party members of their citizenship — had alienated Truman and many others in his party. Like Beetle Smith, the tall, lanky Walter was stub-born and willing to be unpopular. Few in Congress would ever speak as dis-paragingly to this CIA director (or the next). Not taking a second to welcome the DCI before the October hearing, Walter reminded him of "the fact that we have given to your organization free access to the files of our committee."

> General Smith: Indeed, you have.
> Mr. Walter: And when you made this statement, it disturbed all of us, because we don't let just anybody look at our files . . . so I think we are entitled to know why you stated under oath, "I believe there are communists in my own organization."

Committee counsel Frank Tavenner joined Walter in the questioning:

Mr. Tavenner: Now, I would like to know what security organization of Government within the United States you had reference to, specifically.

General Smith: None. My responsibilities are all abroad, and my knowledge is restricted to what goes on abroad.

Mr. Tavenner: But that is not what you said in your testimony, and you did not limit it to activities abroad, and so as the testimony stands on the record it is an indictment of every security Government agency in the land. . . .

General Smith: I did not delimit it, Mr. Counsel, and I don't think that it should be taken as an indictment by anybody who is familiar with the law and with the limitations of my own responsibility. Those are very clear.

Mr. Walter: We are familiar with the law, but what we want to know is what you meant when you made this very plain statement.

General Smith: Exactly that.

Mr. Walter: And more than that, I would like to know whether or not you felt that there had been a penetration into this committee.

General Smith: I meant exactly what I said, Congressman.

Mr. Walter: You said that they have infiltrated practically every security organization of the Government in one way or another.

General Smith: That is exactly what I meant. I have made certain exceptions, but remember, please, that when I talk, I talk about the operations with which I am familiar. . . .

Mr. Walter: Well, on the 29th of September, you said one thing, and on the 30th you said something else. What you said on the 29th stirred this committee, for the reasons I have already given you. Now, as I understand your testimony, you base this statement [reading]: "I believe there are Communists in my own organization; there are Communists in the State Department" — on the fact that you know of two Communists in the State Department, and you don't know of one in your organization in the United States, and that is the basis for this statement?

General Smith: Have I allayed your disturbance?

Mr. Walter: You haven't allayed my disturbance. I am disturbed because you happen to be occupying the position you are occupying, General, to be brutally and perfectly frank. . . .

General Smith: You are asking me to go into methods which I would be happy to do in a closed session, but aside from that, all I can say is that I have observed what they have been able to do elsewhere, and I am conscious and I know what they have been able to do in the past, let us say, in Canada, in the United States itself. . . .

Mr. Walter: That is exactly what you meant on the 29th of September, and you assumed and presumed that there had been an infiltration and that was merely an assumption based on nothing more than the history of the past?

General Smith: A little more than that.

Mr. Walter: Plus the two cases that you know of in the State Department?

General Smith: A little more than that.

Though elusive in his responses, the director avoided perjury in the hour-long stand-off. Only at the session's end did the DCI admit that he had not had HUAC in mind when making his infiltration remark. He added, though, "I won't give you absolution; you are responsible for your own internal security."[10]   ·

The McCarthy-Benton-HUAC episode surely reinforced the DCI's wariness toward the press. To colleagues, he admitted in 1951 that the few reporters with specialized knowledge who covered the CIA on occasion were "basically respectful of an institution that talks as little as possible." About the press, at large, though, Smith told his aides (according to meeting notes) "that when news correspondents request information regarding some story that they might have, involving CIA, they should be told nothing. He added that in rare cases, however, it might be necessary to go to the top man of a news organization in order to kill a story." Smith's comments were to subordinates, including assistant directors of the CIA, who recalled the DCI circulating a confidential memorandum to them a year earlier. It had leaked to the press within days.[11]

"There Will Be No Changes"

By the close of the Truman presidency, the CIA had established itself with Congress, the public, and press as an important, if mysterious, agency. In the popular press, articles appeared with titles such as "They Fight the Cold War under Cover" and "Inside CIA." Sometimes, CIA leaders cooperated with reporters in the creation of such articles — despite Smith's views on this — provoking bitter fights. In 1952, a few agency leaders worked with author John Gunther and editors of *Look Magazine,* who were to publish an in-depth portrait of the CIA. Sherman Kent, assistant director of the Office of National Estimates, was appalled at CIA openness with Gunther when he saw the first draft of the article. As he said to Colonel C. B. Hansen, public relations aide to the DCI, "the whole cover" of covert action chief Frank Wisner was "blown" by the article. Further, did Hansen really want *Look* "to mention cryptography?" As to coverage of national estimates of Soviet capabilities, Kent angrily scolded Hansen for a "grisly error." Kent disassociated himself "completely from any hint of permission to print." Hansen responded that the article's "cumulative effect" would be to reassure Americans that "the CIA is good" and that the "policy-making processes of government" were legitimate. But he also persuaded *Look* to remove Wisner's name, not to mention cryptography, and to redo the treatment of estimates.

Americans could be sure that the CIA was doing "a first-class job" and that Congress had "little inclination to go after them," the article said. It treated Beetle Smith favorably and Allen Dulles obsequiously, describing his work in the OSS during World War II as "worth a brace of Allied divisions." Like most other press articles of the day, the essay raised questions about the CIA's effectiveness, but not its missions.

A different and much more critical published account caused Walter Pforzheimer to lose his normally good sense. He recorded on March 5, 1951, "Talked with Solicitor of the Post Office Dept. as to possible action to be taken in connection with the publication of the book 'Washington Confidential.' Book states that CIA is 'full of Commies' at the lower levels. Post Office Dept. can do nothing re: libelous material, if it is not on the wrapper."[1]

Truman, himself, went before an audience of CIA officers toward the end of his presidency, thanked the "gentlemen and ladies" for their work, and judged, "We have an intelligence information service now that I think is not inferior to any in the world." Still, the honest Walter Bedell Smith never pretended that the CIA had substantially achieved its goals during his tenure — he reported to the president and others in 1952, "In view of the efficiency of the Soviet security organization, it is not believed that the present United States intelligence system, or . . . available intelligence assets of other friendly states, can produce strategic intelligence on the Soviet Union with the degree of accuracy and timeliness which the National Security Council would like to have." Nor was the director optimistic about the future of world politics. He and colleagues heading other U.S. intelligence bureaucracies generally agreed in a late 1952 session "that, over the next ten years, the odds were better than even that we would become engaged in war with Russia." Further, "there seemed to be agreement on the following points which were made principally by DCI. . . . (1) Russia is planning war. The only thing we don't know is where or when. (2) Russia is adamantly maintaining a policy directed towards control of the world." Sooner or later, Smith and the others agreed, the United States might have to initiate war, as it "cannot forever maintain a huge counterforce, or afford putting out brush fires."[2]

Smith was generally happy, at least, with the agency's congressional relations. One disappointment was the collapse of his lunches with diverse members of Congress, who were usually too busy, it seemed. At a session with new CIA officers in 1952, one of them asked Smith if the agency should not "do more to win a better understanding of what we do and why we do it, on the part of the press and the American people?" The director responded: "The United States needs one silent service and I think that it would be all to the good if we could so qualify. We can't, of course. Under our laws and under the rights of Congress, there are necessities for discussion. We could not, for instance, get the money that we need if we didn't tell a good deal about our operations." Smith added that the "two or three" members of "appropriate" committees that the agency dealt with were "extremely reluctant to have it known that it is they who look into our little business because they fear, and quite justly, that there would be a demand from others to be permitted to know."[3]

Historians have disagreed on whether Smith wanted to continue as DCI in the next administration. Certainly, he lacked enthusiasm for the job of undersecretary of state, which he knew Eisenhower might want him to accept. Some have written that an unhappy Smith wanted to leave the CIA when the Truman administration ended. He occasionally muttered and wrote such things, but the best evidence suggests the opposite. It emerged in CIA papers declassified half a century later: at the eighth annual orientation course at the CIA on November 21, 1952, an officer asked Smith, "Will the change in administration have any effect on the Agency?" The director expressed certainty that, being "non-political," he would continue as CIA head: "Since this is a statutory agency supported by a career service, there will be no changes. . . . While the Director himself must undoubtedly be a man whom the Chief Executive is willing to accept, and to whom he will give a certain measure of confidence, it is unlikely that you will ever have a Director whose status will change with changes in the administration." Little did Smith know what Eisenhower would tell him on a train that night in Baltimore — he must accept the job at State. A reporter observed the DCI leaving the train "glum and shaken."

Congressman John McCormack, who had such kind words for Hillenkoetter when he retired as DCI, was in the White House when Smith's change in status was imminent. The majority leader learned from the president that Smith, before agreeing to take the new job under Truman's enemy, had a private talk with the outgoing president. Later, with tears in his eyes, Truman told McCormack that Smith had said he would not take the job without the president's blessing, which was given.

Despite his bad temper, Smith earned the enormous affection and respect of many CIA staffers working under him, including Pforzheimer. The legislative liaison would stay on to work under Allen Dulles, but for him "the greatest of all DCIs" was Beetle Smith. The general inspired such loyalty on Pforzheimer's part that the liaison was happy to engage in unusual activities to protect and defend the DCI's reputation at the Capitol. He recalls, "There was an Assistant Secretary of Defense, a woman. . . . there were reports running around town that General Smith's car was seen in front of her house many afternoons. We were coming off the Hill one day, and the General said, 'Walter, are you hearing a lot of gossip about Anna Rosenberg up here on Capitol Hill?' " Stories *were* spreading. A reporter noted privately that J. Edgar Hoover "got the gossip out" about Smith and Rosenberg being "in bed. . . . it was all over D.C." Pforzheimer recalls, "I said, 'Well, General, as long as you ask me, the answer is "yes," ' and the general responded, 'You can tell them, in all honesty, that it is untrue. I wish it were true, but I am too old!' "[4]

Part Two

The Eisenhower Era, 1953–1960

Meddling?

There had been a time when Congress and its committees dominated the functioning of executive branch departments. President Andrew Johnson's refusal to accept this in the late 1860s caused his impeachment and near-conviction. But the growth of the modern presidency and so-called Big Government in the 1930s and 1940s put such deference to Congress well into the ancient past. As Capitol Hill acceded to President Franklin Roosevelt, especially, and created scores of powerful agencies, it barely increased its oversight capabilities. Regarding domestic issues, which directly affected the well-being of their constituents, legislators would remain fairly assertive in the early Cold War era. As Nelson Polsby wrote, "Congress and the presidency existed in a sort of equilibrium described as a 'deadlock of democracy.'"

However, in light of dangers posed in a world with nuclear weapons and menacing ideologies, members of Congress usually saw their branch as being of secondary importance in the foreign and defense policy realm. Lewis Dexter conducted scores of interviews on Capitol Hill in the 1950s and reported that "Congressmen interviewed generally indicate that they have little tendency to raise or consider questions of military policy in terms of its meaning for some national or international political objective or goal." The "most experienced staff man on military matters on the Hill" famously told Dexter, "Our committee is a real estate committee. Don't forget that." By that, he meant that the House Armed Services Committee mainly focused its attention on the "location of installations and related transfer, purchase, and sale of properties." Dexter's explanation for the avoidance of big issues by members of Congress, and thus their deference to the executive branch, was a fear that they lacked "competence." Another scholar from the era wrote that the expectation that presidents should lead Congress was "as widespread on Capitol Hill as anywhere else." In that context, the odds against assertive congressional oversight of the CIA were always long.[1]

Nonetheless, early in his presidency, Dwight D. Eisenhower told subordinates to "make certain of appropriate and timely consultation with congressional leaders." The president's sentiment extended to the CIA. Impressed by outgoing DCI Smith's 43-minute-long "round-up of the world situation" at the January 29, 1953, National Security Council meeting, Ike told Smith he could do "a great deal of good" by presenting it to the foreign affairs committees of

Congress. The president's advisers were cautious, though: surely, said the new Mutual Security Agency director Harold Stassen, the committees should not be told of "our aiding the Italian elections." A note-taker caught Eisenhower's logic: "General Smith had emphasized that one of the communist aims was to split the West. . . . by neglecting to give selected members of Congress what we could, we were promoting the same danger within our own government."

Five weeks later, as NSC members pondered reports that Joseph Stalin had suffered a debilitating stroke, new Director of Central Intelligence Allen Dulles told the president that Senate Foreign Relations chair Alexander Wiley had requested the DCI's presence at a hearing to analyze the repercussions, if Stalin should die. Dulles suggested that complying "would be a fatal mistake. . . . once the precedent had been set," a director would spend most of his time on Capitol Hill. At first, Eisenhower "felt that Mr. Dulles should try to find some way by which he might respond to Senator Wiley's request," but his advisers overwhelmingly recommended otherwise, so the president instead decided to send Smith, in his new capacity as undersecretary of state. (Smith provided the March 4 meeting's moment of color: while NSC members dithered over imperfect evidence emerging from the USSR over Stalin's illness and worried that superpower relations might actually worsen if he died, the former DCI gave Eisenhower a prediction: Stalin was "dead as hell.")[2]

Despite the president's initial inclination to send Dulles before congressional committees, he soon came to hate what seemed aggressive oversight of the CIA by certain members of Congress. Eisenhower would complain increasingly over the years of White House meetings about a legislative "tendency toward supervision" of intelligence, especially by those not on the four CIA subcommittees. He particularly hated the Joint Committee on Atomic Energy, which had already made one of its periodic "demands for detailed information as to intelligence sources." Other thorns in the president's side during the coming years would be Senator Joseph McCarthy and, later, Stuart Symington (D-MO), who would question, investigate, and publicize the agency's alleged failings. The president, Dulles, and congressional allies eventually would prevail over McCarthy but would mostly fail to prevent the ambitious Symington from looking into CIA affairs. And only after considerable struggles would they defeat freshman senator Mike Mansfield's efforts to create a joint congressional committee on intelligence. After a year or two as DCI, Dulles would come to believe that certain legislators, even some not on Armed Services/Appropriations subcommittees on the CIA, should know a good deal about the agency. By his second term, the president would experience chronic tensions with Dulles over his responsiveness to Congress.[3]

While Eisenhower never expressed enthusiasm for the intelligence oversight of the four CIA subcommittees, he respected the judgment and discretion that most of their leaders displayed. When Leverett Saltonstall and Richard Russell worried in 1953 about U.S. ability to defend against a Soviet attack, the president agreed to give a mutually acceptable representative (air defense specialist Robert C. Sprague) access to all CIA and military intelligence resources on the topic. The two senators then received a twelve-hour briefing one Saturday from Sprague, and in turn had him address their Armed Services subcommittee, thus cementing their relations with the president.

Eisenhower's contempt for congressional "meddling" in intelligence matters derived from a belief (exemplified by his two most recent predecessors) in presidential domination of foreign and defense policy. It was rooted also in his knowledgeable enthusiasm for intelligence . . . the ways it was gathered, the importance of making coherent, useful information available to leaders, and the need to surround it in secrecy. He often complained that Congress (and his own subordinates) leaked too much sensitive information. Ike would have been horrified if he knew of the DCI's "not for attribution" appearance before the Overseas Writers Club (made up of leading foreign reporters covering Washington, plus some American correspondents) in April 1953, where he talked about "secret operations" aiding "the forces of democracy throughout the world."

Despite his propensity to talk to such groups, Dulles would complain to *U.S. News and World Report* in 1954, "We tell Russia too much." Perhaps it was due to the president's periodic prodding of Dulles to tell Congress less that the agency's Intelligence Directorate carried out an "analysis of intelligence use and abuse in the 83rd Congress." Whatever the study's results were, Dulles never publicized them.[4]

Leadership Changes

Though reporters and citizens paid more attention to changes at the White House in January 1953, the leadership shifts at Congress were substantial: Republicans gained a narrow majority of seats in the House and Senate, unseating Democratic chairs. Though loathe to give up his command of the

Armed Services Committee in the Senate, Richard Russell wrote to a Democratic friend, "My intention is to cooperate with the new administration whenever I can conscientiously do so, especially on a sound national defense and foreign policy." The conservative Georgian told the new House Speaker Joseph Martin, "We've got to make the Eisenhower administration a success . . . because if it fails, the next administration will be a radical one."

Russell relinquished the chairmanship to the kindly Saltonstall, who spoke affectionately of Russell for guiding "this very important Committee safely and sanely."[5] Saltonstall was not as shrewd nor nearly as influential in the Senate as Russell and did not strike fear into the hearts of executive branch leaders. He unabashedly admired the CIA. L. K. "Red" White, the assistant deputy director for administration, wrote in his work diary on January 8: "Met with Senator Saltonstall at 10:15 a.m., as he requested. He is in search of staff members for the Senate Armed Services Committee, which he expects to head, and has three vacancies for people with military background. . . . I agreed to make every effort to come up with some recommendations for him." When the senator received Dulles and Pforzheimer in his office in February, the legislative liaison noted in his diary, "Senator Saltonstall agreed that it might be best to appoint a special subcommittee for handling CIA matters, as Senator Russell had originally done, and asked that Mr. Pforzheimer 'keep after me to appoint such a group.' "[6]

Styles Bridges took the Appropriations chair. Since he usually supported Joe McCarthy's anticommunist crusade, this made Bridges suspect in administration circles. Though he was a "walking 25 votes in the Senate," as White House legislative liaison Bryce Harlow would tell Eisenhower, he would never meet alone with the president until 1958. The senator had a capacity for meanness that shocked even his sometime friend, the ruthless Drew Pearson, who learned and reported that Bridges and another senator mercilessly pressured Senator Lester Hunt (D-WY) not to seek reelection in 1954, threatening to publicize the "homosexual troubles" of Hunt's son, who had been tried on a "morals" charge. Hunt, seriously ill at the time, committed suicide soon thereafter.[7]

Bridges would send a worrisome signal to Dulles by putting the unscrupulous McCarthyite senator Pat McCarran (D-NV) on the CIA subcommittee in summer 1953. This had severe implications for the agency, but McCarran would drop dead of a heart attack while giving a political speech in 1954. Bridges would often do the real business of monitoring the agency and setting its budget, in private meetings. After conducting necessary business with Dulles in late spring 1954 and then scheduling his CIA subcommittee's hearing with the DCI, he would miss the event, which Senators Hayden, Ferguson, and Saltonstall would attend.[8]

Saltonstall's and Bridges's differences in personality and drive were evident to many in Washington, including Lyndon Johnson. Reporter Russell Baker viewed the "rascal" Bridges as about the most interesting member of the Senate, except for LBJ, with whom he shared "a Florentine subtlety." Throughout the 1950s, as Johnson became a more powerful Senate Democratic leader, he had a warmer relationship with Saltonstall, whose nickname for Johnson was "Lynd." Johnson once told colleagues that Saltonstall was incapable of double-crossing anyone. LBJ, though, was adept at manipulating his Republican colleague. Bridges knew this, and once said to LBJ, "Lyndon, you can pull off that sort of thing with Lev, but not with me!" Johnson laughingly agreed, evidence of his ability to manipulate Bridges, too. About the worst criticism of Saltonstall came from his good friend, Senator Alex Smith, who once confided to his diary, "I am devoted to him, but cannot discover deep conviction."

During the two years that they chaired their respective subcommittees on the CIA and for the many more years that they served as ranking minority members, Saltonstall was a loyalist, and Bridges was not. This was confirmed to Allen Dulles by a March 1, 1954, memo from Matthew Baird, the agency's director of training. Baird had learned from a Washington hostess (whose son worked at the CIA) that

> at a party given in her home recently, Senator Styles Bridges expressed to the people present his disappointment at the type of briefing recently given him by CIA. [Name deleted] quoted him as saying that the briefing was given by young men who did not seem to be fully familiar with their subject and was given in a manner described as "blasé and disinterested." Senator Bridges said that as a result of this briefing, he felt that the whole CIA setup needed looking into. ... [Name deleted] also quoted Bridges as saying, "I have told Allen Dulles just how I felt about the briefing given me by CIA."

Saltonstall, though, would have breakfast, dinner, and drinks with Dulles, sometimes at the CIA and other times at "Highlands," the DCI's wooded, eight-acre estate (featuring a stone house with vine-covered columns, set back from Wisconsin Avenue) in Washington. In turn, Dulles would take pains to keep Saltonstall just as well-informed as he wished to be. Saltonstall would later recall, "The most sensitive discussions were reserved for one-to-one sessions between Dulles and individual committee chairmen."[9]

On the House side, fifty-five-year-old Dewey Short of Missouri took over Armed Services from Carl Vinson. Like many other Republicans, Short would be a thorn in the president's side sometimes, as when he complained, about the July 1953 Korean War truce, that victory had been possible, if only the U.S. Army had not been constrained. The most memorable chapter of Short's long political career, which would end in defeat in 1956, was his presence with a few other legislators to examine German death camps soon after they were discovered by Allied forces late in World War II. Before that, his only claim to national fame had been for labeling the trademark eagle of the National Recovery Administration (NRA) with the epithet, "the blue buzzard." While chairman of Armed Services, Short claimed that the committee gave vigorous attention to the CIA. This may have been true, although documentary evidence of it is lacking.[10]

Days before Allen Dulles became director, he prepared for a visit by two Budget Bureau executives, assuming they wanted to talk about trimming the agency's budget. Instead, a Dulles aide noted, "their primary mission was to encourage him to call on Mr. Taber . . . which Mr. Dulles indicated he would make his first order of business." John Taber, from rural upstate New York, had taken the House Appropriations chairmanship. Like his Democratic counterpart, and sometime friend, sometime foe Clarence Cannon, Taber had entered the House of Representatives on March 4, 1923. Colleagues and executive branch leaders feared Taber, a tough, stubborn budget-cutter and a grouch who enjoyed needling others. After the CIA goofed on March 17, 1953, Dulles received a "Dear Mr. Director" letter from Taber:

> Yesterday, you were going to send a car up for us, and we could not find it. We approached a car that looked like it might be it, license no. DC 1-5073. On calling later, we found that this car was a CIA car. The driver said he was waiting for a lady.
>
> It looks like you have too many cars and too many chauffeurs, and that could be a very simple way of reducing requirements.

Even in relations with constituents, Taber could be combative. Well before the 1950s, legislators had created standardized letters to be mailed to citizens who wrote on issues of the day. Uniquely, though, Taber developed one which said, "You have not the slightest idea of what you are talking about."[11]

In Washington circles of the late 1940s and early 1950s, to "taberize" meant to force budget cuts and/or staff reductions on federal bureaucracies.

Upon taking the chair of Appropriations, Taber would hire over a dozen new staffers and preside over detailed reviews by subcommittees of the budgets of all major executive branch bureaucracies, with an eye toward cuts. To Eisenhower's distress, Taber hated foreign aid, and despite the president's personal lobbying at a White House breakfast in 1953, his committee cut $700 million from Eisenhower's $5.1 billion request. Pforzheimer could not have been surprised to receive a tip that Taber's staff "was seeking to recruit personnel for an investigative look into all overseas governmental activities, including CIA."[12]

Much like Congress, the press would mostly continue to defer to the CIA, but there were to be periodic critiques. Just as Eisenhower and Dulles were about to take on their new jobs, the *Washington Post* editorialized about the agency:

> There are those who insist that such an agency is incompatible with democracy. This is certainly the case so long as the agency retains its operational functions in the field of what is called black propaganda. . . . Let us give a few samples of the extraordinary exploits in the field of "foreign" policy that these freelance irresponsibles have been pursuing in the shadows. . . .
>
> 1. Subsidization by CIA of a neo-Nazi organization which had marked for liquidation the leaders of the Social Democratic Party.
>
> 2. Incarceration for eight months of a Japanese citizen under excuse of cross-examination . . . a job initially undertaken by General Willoughby's Army Intelligence and passed to CIA.
>
> 3. Tapping of the telephone of Jose Figueres, former Costa Rican President, at which a CIA man was caught red-handed.
>
> 4. Abortive effort by CIA cover men to start a revolution in Guatemala and blame it on the United Fruit Co.
>
> 5. Burmese and Siamese and Vietnamese suspicions of CIA activity in promoting guerilla forays from the Burmese border into mainland China.
>
> . . . This type of operation, for which the CIA Huhus carry around a hunting license, may one day get all of us over our heads in hot water.[13]

Nonetheless, Dulles's nomination as DCI sailed through the Senate Armed Services Committee after ten minutes of dialogue between the nominee and senators on February 19. The closest thing to a hitch in the proceedings was a friendly warning from Senator Margaret Chase Smith (R-ME) that she had "a good many questions" about the CIA that she wished to raise privately with the new DCI.

Another measure of congressional sentiment toward the agency would come during an April debate over a bill clarifying the qualifications for holding the position of deputy director of central intelligence (to be filled by General Charles Cabell). Representative Overton Brooks (D-LA) had "heard a lot of condemnation of the failure of our intelligence to properly function" but thought the CIA was "coming along fine." Timothy Sheehan doubted that the CIA had used "sufficient security safeguards" for keeping communists out of the agency, but Dewey Short assured him and a few other critics that certain Armed Services Committee members were "being more fully informed now than we have been during any other time." The bill became law without a dissenting vote in the House or Senate.

Nonetheless, Allen Dulles astutely judged the political environment to be mixed, not simple and secure, and would seek out Taber and other barons as solo luncheon guests at the CIA early in 1953. Staffers would prepare him for topics and questions that might arise in those deceptively casual affairs.[14]

Getting "Taberized"

Letters, diaries, and memoranda from 1953–1954 suggest an under-told story in intelligence history — Congress reducing the CIA's budget in the early years of the Eisenhower administration, with the president's concurrence. In a February 1953 meeting with his agency leaders, Dulles spoke of "economies" that would have to be "effected in personnel, construction, and programs," even though the agency was taking on "increased missions." In Fiscal Year 1953, when the agency and the Eisenhower administration functioned under a budget created by the Truman administration and a Democratic Congress, the agency had a budget of approximately a half-billion dollars. As Eisenhower took office, though, he told Allen Dulles that he expected fiscal conservatism from the CIA. Though the DCI did not say so, that challenge may have seemed unattainable, with the Korean War continuing and the agency performing covert action in approximately fifty countries. Eisenhower also specifically warned the new DCI (according to Dulles's recounting of the conversation to agency leaders on February 9) that "there must be very carefully controlled . . . use of the unvouchered funds." Dulles assured Eisenhower that, while those moneys were "already subject to close scrutiny and accounting," policies on their usage would be made "more stringent."

Dulles soon wrote to all CIA employees that the young agency had won a respected reputation "in the Executive and Legislative branches." But, he added, "great confidence has been shown in our Agency in that we have some unvouchered funds at our disposal. . . . It imposes on us a sacred trust, and I propose to hold each and every person in the Agency personally responsible to see that this trust is faithfully and economically executed."[1]

Eisenhower's and Dulles's warnings reflected Republican orthodoxy of the early 1950s, which demanded reductions in government agencies' budgets but favored aggressive responses to perceived communist aggression. The new vice president Richard Nixon told a large contingent of CIA officers in February 1953 — citing his recent perspective as an "average congressman and senator" — that the Soviets were engaged in "a revolutionary conspiracy to overthrow the free nations," while the United States had lost its "military supremacy." All in Congress would agree, he said, that "the bolstering of our national defense in the development of political and psychological counterattack is essential."

The vice president concluded his talk with characteristically clumsy humor: "So much for analyzing the congressional mind — assuming that any congressman or senator has a mind. That, I admit, is a debatable point!" Still, Nixon knew Capitol Hill sentiment. Few Republicans or Democrats in the new Congress would have objected to the agency secretly intervening in dozens of countries, had they known of it. Those legislative leaders in the know enthusiastically supported covert action. Any questions they might raise concerned the costs, efficiency, and vigor of such operations.[2]

Eisenhower rivaled or exceeded most congressional Republicans in his passion for national defense and governmental thrift. He pointedly reminded them of this at a White House session in February. The invited two dozen legislators of both parties met with him and Allen Dulles, plus General and JCS chair Omar Bradley. Afterward, one Republican told reporters, "We're in a hell of a fix." He and others had heard that the United States was on the defensive around the world and (said *Newsweek*) that "Soviet Russia, in her aggressive foreign policy, was acting from strength, not weakness." Berlin was "the chief friction point," according to Drew Pearson's account of the meeting: "Dulles would not predict whether they would try to choke us off with another blockade or send East Germans into the West Sector to stage serious riots. However, he warned that trouble was coming." Furthermore, "the Kremlin was likely to hit the West in several places at the same time, and one of these, according to Allen Dulles, is French Indo-China." The DCI "urged that American supplies be stepped up to aid the French."

The prime reason for so depressing a briefing was not just global tensions but (*Newsweek* claimed) to condition the leaders "for a brutal prospect: the administration might not be able to reduce expenditures as quickly and as drastically as many Republican leaders had been promising." Rather than take on an apologetic, defensive posture, Eisenhower chided Republican leaders in a smaller meeting days later. As quickly as "extravagances" were weeded out of the Fiscal Year 1954 budget legislation, Eisenhower said, "you fellows try to keep them in." It was true; even Taber did not always resist the temptation to bring pork home to his district.[3]

The significance of the chair of House Appropriations as an overseer of the CIA can be judged by asking two critical questions: was he assertive in shaping budgets and did he know about covert action? The evidence suggests that, more than any other CIA subcommittee chair of his era, Taber believed in monitoring the agency. Since fragmentary records from diverse archives show Taber meeting with CIA heads on five days in the first half of

1953 and ten such meetings in the first half of 1954, it is safe to assume that more occurred. Appropriations carried out a serious review of the agency's proposed Fiscal Year 1954 budget in the spring of 1953 and would do so again the next year. Taber's surviving CIA papers and more voluminous declassified agency records show that CIA leaders traded many messages about preparations for hearings and numerous, less formal meetings with Taber, the subcommittee, and its expanded staff.

Subcommittee records of hearings planned for April 27 and 29, 1953, indicate that a contentious issue arose between the CIA and Taber's staff — how many persons should attend? On April 23, Pforzheimer wrote in his diary of a discussion with committee chief clerk Kenneth Sprankle, who "indicated that there would be six or seven members present, plus himself and Mr. Orescan, and a committee stenographer. I informed Sprankle personally and unofficially that, in my opinion, the presence of a stenographer was unnecessary, and would serve to limit operational details which we were preparing to give the committee. I also informed him that I would consider it preferable if only one staff man were present."[4]

The reason for Pforzheimer's advice is made clear by Deputy Director for Plans Frank Wisner's notes for the hearings. Wisner was among five aides who would testify alongside Dulles. Wisner or the DCI planned to remind the subcommittee of the CIA's "exclusive authority within this government to conduct all organized federal espionage and counter-espionage operations outside the United States." Also, they would inform the subcommittee (not for the first time) that, based on NSC's 1948 directive, the "CIA engages in covert psychological, political, and economic warfare." This included "a very substantial program of covert and 'unconventional' military activities — including guerrilla warfare, counter-guerrilla operations, sabotage and counter-sabotage, and the development of escape and evasion networks in enemy or potentially hostile territory." Such activities were "the most expensive in terms of money, money, and material." The Wisner document, heavily censored by the CIA well after the Cold War's end, included specific examples of ongoing and past operations and the countries where they occurred.[5]

Shortly after the first hearing, and without comment, Pforzheimer listed its congressional attendees: "Messrs. Taber, Cannon, Wigglesworth, Scrivner, and Mahon, together with Messrs. Sprankle, Orescan, and Crosby of the staff, plus Julian Searles — staff stenographer." After the second day's session, the liaison wrote, "the committee desired that certain information be furnished to them, and an agreed upon list was developed." The "list" was preparatory to further hearings to come. As it did with other agencies, Taber's subcommittee staff examined evidence of the CIA's functioning prior to hearings; such discussions were "fairly detailed and technical," wrote L. K. White. On May 4, assistant CIA directors devoted a meeting to "our budget hearings" scheduled before the subcommittee, deciding what should go in a "book" of sensitive information that responded to the subcommittee's "list." On May 5, an agency officer wrote in his diary: "Mr. Dulles agreed to accept the recommendations of Mr. Kirkpatrick and General Cabell as to what should be included in the book. (The book has been prepared accordingly and is ready to go to the staff of the House Appropriations Committee.) Mr. Dulles telephoned Mr. Taber and made arrangements for us to be the custodian of the information at all times. [Name deleted] will take the book to the Hill, remain with the staff while they are working on it, and return it to CIA when they are finished." The arrangement angered Taber's staffers, but the chairman had spoken.[6]

House Appropriations' activity led to some surprising news coverage. Gannet newspapers (including one in Taber's home district) reported that "the super-secret Central Intelligence Agency is going to get its first all-out congressional investigation. Rep. John Taber . . . disclosed yesterday that the House Appropriations Committee . . . has named five of its most senior members to a special subcommittee which will 'go over carefully the budget request and performance of CIA.' The agency has been all but immune to congressional and public scrutiny until now. The Appropriations Committee's action follows mounting complaints in Capitol Hill that CIA is doing an unsatisfactory job." Allen Dulles came across the story in Utica's *Press* with the dramatic headline, "Taber Hones Ax for Cloak, Dagger Probe." The director may have assumed that, as the story implied, the chairman was its source. Still, the new DCI treated all those heading CIA subcommittees with the utmost deference, so he referred to the article's publication as an "amusing" event in passing it on to Taber on May 13.

Once again, the chairman was not amused and fired off a "Dear Allen" response: "I don't know anything about any disclosures that I have made to anybody indicating that I was going into the question of the Central Intelligence Agency at all. I have talked to no one outside of the five members of the subcommittee and the clerk. It is absolutely ridiculous that anything like that should get out and I don't know how it could. We had the hearings down in the basement of the Capitol so that we would be out of sight and out of range, just for the purpose of making sure that nothing was given out."

Taber soon asked to see agency heads again. Red White, the Assistant to the Deputy Director for Administration (A-DD/A) noted on June 9 that "Mr. Pforzheimer called to say that . . . Mr. Taber desired to meet with Mr. Saunders, Mr. Pforzheimer, and me tomorrow afternoon to pursue the discussion of our budget." White feared that

> Mr. Taber has forgotten most of the things that we told him at the hearings. The fact that he has attended so many other hearings in the meantime contributes to this. The 'on again-off again' records made at the hearings are not very help ful, and he is having great difficulty in understanding our budget. He feels, I am sure, that we are holding out on him and we must make every effort to set aside this feeling. He asked no questions that would get at the heart of our budget, but was generally concerned about the buildup, both in personnel and money, for 1952, 1953, and 1954. We are to return on Monday for further conferences with Mr. Taber.[7]

Weeks later, CIA bureaucrats traded memoranda that referred to the challenges of living with the "Taber limitation," which was "for the time being . . . a very firm ceiling" based on "the number of people we had on board as of 30 June." One official charged with building up CIA scientific and technological capabilities complained to Dulles on July 1 that the agency might "lose one of our chief objectives — building up our technical competency." While they faced this pressure from House Appropriations early in the summer, CIA leaders hoped that a forthcoming White House meeting would address "whether or not there is a serious risk to the national security by further reducing expenditures." Deputy Director for Intelligence (DD/I) Robert Amory was less apocalyptic, saying his office would live with the limitation by implementing a "drastic curtailment of collection and evaluation of low-grade sources, such as press, broadcast intercept, and unclassified materials."

In a conversation in his congressional office with Dulles at the end of July, Taber informed the DCI that an Appropriations colleague would soon inspect Radio Free Europe, "as well as certain other CIA installations. Mr. Dulles acceded to this request." When the DCI raised the personnel "limitation," though, Taber denied that he had intended the agency to face an absolute hiring ceiling. He summoned Sprankle to bring in a copy of Taber's "limitation" letter to the Budget Bureau, which apparently had some wiggle room in it. Taber told Dulles to "work out an agreement" with the Bureau, and the CIA obtained "relief" for limited, essential hiring.

The story of retrenchment in spending and number of covert operations

hardly fits with what would come a few years later and is much more prominent in published histories — explosive spending increases on, and expanded
activities by, the CIA and other intelligence agencies. Still, during the first two
years of the Eisenhower-Dulles period, when Taber and Bridges headed the
House and Senate Appropriations subcommittees on the CIA, the agency's
budget fell from around $500 million in Fiscal Year 1953 to approximately $335
million in Fiscal Year 1954 and stayed at that level the next year, the last budget
to be crafted by the Republican Congress in 1954. (We know this not because
the CIA at the turn of the century declassified its early Cold War budgets. It
did not. Agency budget information was not entirely cleared out of the papers
of Bridges, Taber, and George Mahon after their deaths or retirements.)[8]

In Fiscal Year 1952— when the Democrats still controlled the presidency
and Congress, and with a war on in Korea — the agency spent $63 million of
the $150 million available in the contingency reserve fund, according to some
remarkable handwritten notes by Taber. (These were found by his staff on
his desk on February 23, 1954. They created a file folder benignly labeled "Miscellaneous notes made by J. T., 1954.") Virtually all of the $63 million went to
covert action, although the CIA secured approval of Appropriations chairs
and the Budget Bureau to use $300,000 from the fund to support purchase
of air conditioning in some agency buildings, claiming that the temperatures
during summer months were so high as to affect staff performance. The CIA's
total budget for Fiscal Year 1952 remains unknown, but Taber's notes show
$78.9 million was spent for "intelligence" purposes and $206 million on "Cold
War" (i.e., covert action) efforts. His notes imply some other spending and
do not include administrative costs, so the agency had been granted at least
$435 million for Fiscal Year 1952, and probably much more, by President Tru-
man and a Democratic Congress.

During Fiscal Year 1953, with the agency budget still crafted by Democrats but carried out mostly under Republican guidance from Congress and
the White House, none of the $183.5 million contingency fund was used,
according to CIA documents in Styles Bridges's files. However, Taber's notes
(and a document in Mahon's papers), while indicating that the CIA left
unspent much of the money it had been budgeted for the year, also suggest
that some reserve moneys may have been used. Also, they indicate that $103.4
million was budgeted for "intelligence" and $164 million for "Cold War"
efforts. An additional $136 million for administration and other purposes
had been granted to the agency by Congress and the president for Fiscal Year
1953, totaling over half a billion dollars.

For Fiscal Year 1954, crafted in 1953 by the Republican administration and Congress, Taber's notes list $110 million in the reserve fund, $166.7 million budgeted for planned "Cold War" activities (of that, $57 million toward "paramil" activities and $109.6 million toward "pol & psych" warfare), and $114.3 million for "intelligence." They also list $25 million for "administration," suggesting that the agency budget for Fiscal Year 1954 was approximately $416 million. None of the Fiscal Year 1954 reserve fund was used in the first half of that year, though. Looking ahead, Bridges and Taber, who monitored the fund, permitted Dulles in summer 1954 to plan on transferring $4.1 million from the 1955 account to the FBI for counterintelligence purposes.[9]

Taber and his subcommittee members' knowledge of critical intelligence matters is further suggested by his notes about subjects covered in the February 1954 subcommittee hearing with a large but indeterminate number of Appropriations Committee members and staffers present. (Taber raised the number of attendees in February over what it had been in 1953 for reasons unknown, despite the leak to Gannet newspapers. The issue of large attendance would soon come up again.) Taber's notes suggest detailed discussion of the types of intelligence functions to be funded: "para mil[itary]" activities, "pol. + pscy." warfare; "covert" and "overt col[lection]" of intelligence; the numbers and purposes of CIA field offices in the United States (which interviewed returning international travelers); the numbers of U.S. intelligence personnel — civilian and military — in the "field" overseas, the numbers of persons (not including "employees" of the CIA) in some way on the agency "payroll"; Soviet and Chinese military aircraft capabilities; and discussion of "new sta[tions]" in Africa, Australia, India, and Europe. On these and related subjects, plenty of budgetary figures are listed. A separate handwritten sheet in the same file from 1954 indicates discussion of Soviet nuclear war–fighting capabilities. The most intriguing portion reads, "Soviet threat 3 yrs., by 1957 can launch all of fissionable material in stock pile," a prediction not far off, in light of the Soviets' first intercontinental ballistic missile launch three years later, on top of its substantial bomber aircraft holdings.[10]

Bridges's files have the most detailed documents on crafting the Fiscal Year 1955 CIA budget in the spring of 1954. They show that, of the $335 million eventually appropriated by the House and Senate subcommittees in late May, $225 million for the agency's "normal operations" was to be hidden in the budgets of the army ($25 million in the "Project 2712 Classified Project"), the navy ($30 million in "Activity 10 Contingencies of the Navy"), and the air force ($110 million in the "Project 120 Aircraft Component Spares and

Spare Parts," $20 million in "Project 891 Contingencies of the Air Force," plus $40 million from "Prior year funds available from Aircraft and Related Procurement"). One hundred and ten million dollars that had been unused in the CIA's previous contingency reserve account (and hidden in the air force's "Project 120, Aircraft and Related Procurement" account) was carried over to the Fiscal Year 1955 budget. Therefore, out of the $335 million total, $150 million was unspent from previous years' budgets, so (as the CIA's comptroller noted in summarizing Taber's thinking), "this, in effect, allowed the Committee to show a cut in appropriations of $150 million."[11]

Since Taber and company were moving toward granting the agency $335 million for Fiscal Year 1955, far less than the $500 million-plus budget of two years earlier, the DCI presumably would face an obvious question: how would the quality of American intelligence fare? Before he could do so, though, Dulles's and Taber's staffs clashed as they had in 1953 on how many should attend the next hearings scheduled for March 24 and 25, 1954. Ken Sprankle called Pforzheimer on March 22 to indicate that Dulles and associates would appear not before the CIA subcommittee, but before Appropriations' full eleven-member subcommittee on Armed Services, plus three staffers. Sprankle "requested that 15 copies of the 'black book' containing our budget information be delivered to him that afternoon."

Pforzheimer seems not to have argued at length but passed on the problem to Red White, who telephoned Sprankle with the counteroffer that the books be delivered the next day and that the CIA take custody of them overnight. "Mr. Sprankle said that this arrangement would not be satisfactory, inasmuch as the staff had to work on the books probably well into the night," White wrote.

By late afternoon, Dulles was on the phone to Taber, expressing "concern." Come to my office tomorrow morning, said Taber. At 9:00 a.m. on Tuesday, March 23, White joined Dulles in greeting the chairman. (The CIA leaders' visit to Capitol Hill would not, of course, make the newspapers. Instead, readers of the *Washington Post* on the morning of the 23rd encountered an alarming page-one story: "The FBI has alerted police officers throughout the country against enemy agents trying to smuggle midget atomic weapons into this country for sabotage.") In the comfort of his office, Taber explained his thinking: "information had reached members of the Armed Services subcommittee involved with the budget for the National Security Agency (which had requested $ [amount censored] for Fiscal Year 1955) that CIA was also involved" in signals intelligence. They "therefore had the impression that there was duplication of effort in this field between NSA and CIA."

The DCI explained that it was "through our relations with foreign intelligence services" that the CIA "did obtain NSA-type information of great value . . . which we turned over to them, and that NSA had advised us that it would cost approximately $30 million, if they had to obtain the same information by actual monitoring." There is no duplication of effort, he insisted.

On a related subject, Taber told Dulles that another agency was "planning to spend money duplicating facilities which the American Telephone and Telegraph Company already had." He trusted that he would not discover "such duplication in CIA's budget, whereupon he was assured that (a) whenever possible, we used Department of Defense trans-ocean facilities, and (b) our money went primarily into maintaining base stations communicating with a large net of agents, and (c) that we felt sure we were perfectly clean on this score."

Dulles and Taber compromised on the most contentious issues: the DCI and aides would testify before the large subcommittee and staff, as planned, but would say less than originally planned about details of "operations," about specifics of the Plans Directorate's budget, and about personnel figures for all directorates. Overall figures would do, said Taber, who accepted Dulles's suggestion that the CIA leadership testify again a couple weeks later before the smaller CIA subcommittee (whose members were also on Appropriations' subcommittee on Armed Services) and give all such details. In the meantime, "we also agreed to furnish Mr. Sprankle any additional information which either he or the Chairman felt he should have." The CIA could keep the "black books" each evening.[12]

Some of Dulles's testimony before the sizeable subcommittee (and five staffers) on March 24 and 25, 1954, is unusually well documented. Dulles had over a year's experience of Chairman Taber's aggressive and suspicious nature under his belt, plus the subcommittee staff's off-and-on studies of the CIA. He brought to the hearings what he described to agency subordinates as a "high level" document that described successes but also failures of the CIA in the sensitive areas of espionage, counterintelligence, and covert operations. After giving his standard brief history of U.S. intelligence, including the explosion of intelligence activities and expenditures during the Korean War, Dulles explained to the subcommittee that all the major types of clandestine activities previously described to them in 1953, "FI — the classical spy business," "PP — covert political and psychological activities," and "PM — covert paramilitary activities," continued to be carried out by the CIA. Then he ventured into a discussion of recent failures:

> Our experience in 1951 and 1952 demonstrated that a rapid expansion and intensification of operations . . . was not profitably possible, and might be risky or even unwise for the long pull of the Cold War. This applied equally to PP, FI, and PM activities. We found that additional money and personnel were not the sole factors involved; that the severity of Soviet bloc security controls, the dearth of capable agents to work behind the Curtain, the requirements of proper cover and documentation, and the thoroughness of our planning and preparation were in reality the limiting factors. We were reminded that prerequisites to successful PP and PM operations included counter-espionage activities against hostile security and intelligence services, the careful collection of operational or tactical intelligence on opportunities or suitable objectives, and the development of sound doctrine and techniques that will afford a reasonable chance of success.

Dulles was admitting that all had not gone well in recent years: "Although we can report successes during the period of intensification, we learned many lessons from a pitched battle with an adversary having ample funds and 35 years of experience, as against our less than five years." After detailing the strengths of Soviet intelligence agencies, the DCI moved to the topic of "reappraisal, for the long pull of the Cold War": "As a result of these lessons, the Agency reappraised its capacity for rapid expansion. The result was a self-imposed policy of retrenchment and cut-back in those areas where we considered that we were over-expanded. Thus, the total funds expended for Clandestine Services in FY 1953 dropped about 30% from the high of FY 1952, and were still further reduced for FY 1954."

Next, Dulles directed subcommittee attention to "charts of successes and failures of FI, PP, and PM operations," and continued: "Analysis of our operations shows that those carefully planned and supported over a period of time were usually successful, while the unplanned, urgent, one-shot operations not only usually failed, but also disrupted and even blew our careful preparations for longer range activities." Since the "threat of early general war has receded somewhat," it was clear "that we must prepare now for the Cold War over a long period of time, with special attention to the preparation of plans and development of assets to enable the government to take quick and decisive action at some later time to accomplish its long-range objectives." The CIA would continue "efforts to place undercover agents in strategic positions who may be activated at some later time when their services are most needed."

In effect, Dulles seemed to be admitting that "rollback," much talked about by Republicans in 1952, was on hold. In the meantime, the agency would "still give emphasis to elimination of the causes of our failures; this requires improvement of cover, documentation, and authentication facilities. The field of covert training, where we are woefully behind the Soviets, will be strengthened." Perhaps in a year or so, he suggested, the CIA would be better at clandestine activities and might "propose a modest increase in some of our most profitable type of activities." Perhaps in conjunction with the Defense Department, the CIA would consider "certain countries in the Near East, South Asia, Africa, and Latin America which might require expansion of activities to meet the developing situation. In any event, the committee is assured that whatever we ask for in the way of funds will be within our capacity to absorb and use efficiently in the Cold War."[13]

Taber (and Bridges, who received a private DCI presentation, as did his Appropriations subcommittee subsequently that year) probably accepted what Dulles said. The DCI's subsequent encounter with Taber's smaller CIA subcommittee (eight members, plus Cannon and Taber) remains undocumented, except for Dulles's suggestion (according to White) that "the Agency had reached its peak strength and, in fact, could get along with a considerable reduction in its personnel strength" — this would have been music to Taber's ears — and Taber's complaint to the DCI that "he had reports from two sources that some of CIA's personnel overseas were extremely heavy drinkers and were, in other ways, not a credit to the United States."

Though the DCI spoke of a "self-imposed" retrenchment at the hearing, the two chairs (Taber especially) and Eisenhower (assisted by his Budget Office) had contributed to the tightening of CIA spending in 1953 and 1954. Dulles, following Eisenhower's guidance, had long ago warned Wisner, "The approval of myself of projects . . . does not in any way relieve any official of this Agency from his obligation to insure that all expenditures are appropriate and authorized and all actions taken under any project are perfectly correct." Still, CIA files from 1954 show that fiscal progress was imperfect, at best. Senator McCarran received an anonymous letter from someone at the CIA detailing wasteful spending of millions of dollars on three agency projects. An assistant to the Deputy Director for Administration (DD/A) wrote in his diary, "Will have to discuss this with the Director. . . . anyone having this much accurate information must be a fairly knowledgeable CIA employee." Another apparent misuse of agency funds that year by covert operators, uncovered by an executive branch study, led one CIA administrator to say he "shuddered to think" what might have happened had a congressional committee learned of it — Allen Dulles might have been "crucified." Instead, the DD/A called a number of meetings to deal with "inept administration" of the project. It was known as PBSUCCESS.[14]

Guatemala: Sterilizing a "Red Infection"

One of the paradoxes of legislative oversight of intelligence in the early Cold War period was that the U.S. Congress could give strong support of aggressive covert action while, with the exception of a few leaders, not really knowing which such policies were being carried out. Guatemala was a perfect example. Following its 1944 revolution, which brought democratically elected leftist governments to power, the country faced an increasingly hostile neighbor to the north, the United States. Guatemala's treatment of U.S.-based corporations, especially the United Fruit Company, in expropriating land and other assets, did nothing to improve relations. Elites in Guatemala helped persuade U.S. journalists, members of Congress, and executive branch leaders that the Central American government was veering further and further leftward toward communism in the early 1950s.

Late in the Truman presidency, the U.S. government aborted an attempt to support Guatemalans who aimed to overthrow President Jacobo Arbenz. Those at CIA headquarters who were involved in the effort felt "grimly" about that "horrifying" turn of events, one agency leader noted in his diary. But new administration leaders — President Eisenhower and the Dulles brothers among them — also believed that the Guatemalan government was Red. The CIA leader had help from the Board of National Estimates, which informed him on April 22, 1954, "The Communists now effectively control the political life of Guatemala."[1] A deal made by Arbenz's government to purchase Soviet-made armaments from Czechoslovakia that spring only sealed the matter in the American leaders' minds.

In May and June 1954, Washington used CIA officers and Ambassador John Peurifoy to support and direct Guatemalan military leaders in overthrowing Arbenz's government. They employed psychological warfare — cleverly deceptive efforts to persuade Guatemalan citizens and political/military leaders that a major invasion force was steadily moving toward the nation's capital. This so unnerved Arbenz and others that the government fell without much of a battle.[2]

While the overthrow of Arbenz was unfolding, the U.S. government pretended to have nothing to do with it. In the year or so after President Castillo Armas's anticommunist government was brought into power with agency assistance, the CIA quietly judged that his government was "inept," despite his "virtually dictatorial powers," and that there were growing "public demands for a return to constitutional democracy." Still, while American news reports and congressional debates began to acknowledge that the United States had been involved, the overthrow became one of the CIA's "successes." *U.S. News and World Report* reported on July 16, 1954, "CIA's one big success, according to prevailing opinion in Washington, is its role in the recent revolution in Guatemala." By early 1956, a *Washington Evening Star* article also labeled Guatemala a triumph for the CIA and was more forthcoming with details. Even critics of the CIA in the 1950s and 1960s declined to challenge that interpretation of events.

In the late Cold War period and since, however, the American overthrow of the Arbenz government has come to be widely seen as shameful. This is mostly because the governments that followed the 1954 coup in the subsequent five decades were far more repressive than Arbenz's elected government. Even intelligence scholar Christopher Andrew, an Eisenhower admirer, describes the Guatemala affair as a "disreputable moment" — Eisenhower was "directly responsible" for "death and destruction" yet showed no signs then or later of embarrassment over his "bullying of a banana republic." In 1999, President Bill Clinton would visit the Central American country and say, "Support for military forces and intelligence units which engaged in violence and widespread repression was wrong."[3]

There were other unfortunate legacies of the Guatemala "success": Allen Dulles would use it as a model in advising President Kennedy seven years later to pursue the Bay of Pigs invasion of Cuba, which failed miserably. Also, the event would vastly exaggerate the CIA's reputation worldwide for causing all sorts of havoc.

A Congressional Role?

It is accurate to view CIA involvement in overthrowing the Guatemalan government as mandated by higher political authorities in the U.S. government, but it is a mistake to assign responsibility and blame for the covert operation solely on the Eisenhower White House. While direct evidence of what congressional leaders knew of the operation before, during, and immediately after its occurrence is fragmentary, a suggestion that they did not know something of what was happening is thoroughly implausible. Congressional intent — judged by speeches, votes, and interactions among the administration and key legislators — was clearly that the U.S. government should do whatever it might take, short of outright war, to stop ongoing "Soviet aggression" in Central America.

In the winter and spring of 1954, a number of congressional leaders had frequent private contacts with the Dulles brothers and the White House about Guatemala. Among these was Senator Alexander Wiley, chair of the Foreign Relations Committee, who believed that a "communist octopus" had for years used its tentacles to control events in Guatemala. "Home grown communism" was a myth, according to Wiley: "There is no communism but the communism which takes orders from the despots of the Kremlin in Moscow." The Wisconsin senior senator was far less known than the *other* senator from his home state, but he garnered somewhat more respect within the Senate itself. In his two years (1953–1954) as chair of Foreign Relations, Wiley persistently urged the Eisenhower administration to go beyond limp diplomatic means to get rid of Arbenz's government. A few years before things came to a head, Wiley had explained the urgency behind his unchanging and unambiguous views to colleague Theodore Green (D-RI): "It seems to me that Guatemala is going to be a source of Red infection throughout Central America and the sooner we help sterilize that source, the better."[4]

Wiley readily agreed to the DCI's request to go public in describing the shipment of Soviet-made armaments from Czechoslovakia to Guatemala in May as "part of the master plan of world communism." On his own initiative, Representative Patrick Hillings (R-CA) claimed on May 21 that other arms-laden ships from behind the Iron Curtain were on their way to Central America. "It is obvious from recent developments," he said, "that the Kremlin is stepping up its drive to establish a beachhead on this continent." A member of Charles Kersten's Communist Aggression Committee, Hillings soon hit the road. "Despite assurances to the contrary, Congressman Hillings has visited Guatemala," wrote Pforzheimer on June 5. Agency heads feared such publicized travel would inspire "hearings on Guatemala." Hillings knew nothing, apparently, about CIA operations there, but favored some type of U.S. intervention: "There is no question that the leaders of Guatemala are taking orders from Soviet Russia." The Dulles brothers and Vice President Nixon successfully persuaded him that issuing a report that month would be "detrimental to U.S. interests." Senator George Smathers (D-FL) spoke up, too, relying on "information gathered by me and my staff." The senator did not mention one of his sources, the CIA. But he did warn that "the Politburo of Guatemala" was "taking orders from Moscow." The cargo ship that left Stettin,

Poland, on April 17—laden with armaments—and arrived at Puerto Bar-
rios, Guatemala, on May 15 was concrete evidence of Soviet intervention. "Are
we not solemnly pledged to prevent and to frustrate such intervention?"
he asked.

Various senators' urgency and frustration with what seemed like a slow-
moving Eisenhower administration was shared across parties and by many on
the other side of the Capitol. Covert action's leading public proponent, Representative Kersten, had been meeting with Dulles across the past few years.
In his opening weeks as DCI, Dulles had told staffers that Kersten would be
"inquiring into this field." Predictably, the legislator was among those pushing the administration in the spring of 1954 to act decisively. As historian
Richard Immerman explained, Kersten reasoned that "the Guatemalans had
a right to revolt against the Communists, [so] . . . the United States had a right
to assist the revolt."[5]

The Johnson Resolution

A long-forgotten debate in June 1954 over a sense-of-Congress resolution
displayed this unambiguous intent. The resolution's author was a man who
would become famous ten years later for fathering another overwhelmingly
supported, hastily passed resolution to enactment—Lyndon Johnson. The
Senate minority leader was reacting to the published reports of Guatemala's
arms purchase from Czechoslovakia. In consultation with the State Department, Johnson offered his colleagues and those in the House an opportunity to give unstinting support to Eisenhower with "an unmistakable
warning that we are determined to keep communism out of the Western
Hemisphere."

Johnson's and other senators' language was immoderate, to say the least;
the challenge facing the United States in Guatemala was "a new type of
imperialism," "an open declaration of the aggressive designs of international
communism." Therefore, the United States had to "support" the Organization of American States (the OAS, much influenced by the United States),
which fought against the "upsetting of sovereign governments by the international Communist movement or conspiracy."[6]

The rhetoric was no less fervent in the House. Senator Johnson took
"firm and constructive action," showing "leadership and statesmanship on
a high level," said Minority Leader John McCormack. Support for the reso-

lution was urgent, said Jack Brooks (D-TX), since "a communist-dominated government in Guatemala is only 700 miles" from his home state. Fellow Texan Martin Dies agreed: "The Soviet government . . . has challenged the Monroe Doctrine. To that challenge there can be but one response."[7]

When the House voted on June 29, the result was a unanimous "yes." No one referred to the CIA or the possibility that the United States was interfering in the internal affairs of Guatemala. Only slightly less gratifying to the Eisenhower White House was the Senate vote, where only one member voted "no." It was William Langer, who was widely dismissed as an old-fashioned isolationist. Langer's explanation of his vote — at a time when Joseph McCarthy's anticommunist crusade was in full flower — is, in retrospect, not easily dismissed:

> I do not think the United States should jump into the Guatemala situation, a sensitive and very grave threat to world peace, with such elephantine delicacy. I do not believe that the members of the Senate have been adequately informed as yet as to what is going on. . . . Is there a foreign invasion of Guatemala, or is there a civil war? If it is a foreign invasion, exactly who are the invading forces, and who are behind them? I ask any Senator if he can answer those questions, and answer them intelligently? . . . There has been much talk about the malevolent influence of the $548 million United Fruit Company in Guatemala, which some have charged is bigger than the government itself. . . . We ought to be committed to the principle that every sovereign nation has a right to determine for itself its own form of government.

Langer's statement and his vote were the talk of Capitol Hill, but no senator replied to him on the floor, a sign of how at odds he was with the political times. After all, as Smathers had said a few days earlier, proposals for a "hands-off" approach were "unrealistic and naïve."[8]

Press and Congressional Knowledge

While congressional intent — that Arbenz should be removed from power — was clear, congressional *knowledge* of specific, unfolding events remains obscure. It would be a mistake to think that Congress at large was simply ignorant, however. Since the time the Eisenhower administration issued innumerable claims that a conflict wholly involving Guatemalans was unfolding, U.S. newspapers had tended to accept that view in their editorial pages and in many news stories. However, they also reported claims from the Guatemalan and Soviet governments and from many newspapers in Latin America and others that the United States was behind the conflict. Even the British government expressed reservations about the U.S. account of the Guatemalan crisis. Any interested member of Congress at least knew that the U.S. government was being charged with a hidden-hand role in the affair.

But the words "Central Intelligence Agency" hardly ever showed up in newspapers. During the entire month of June 1954, the *Washington Post* never suggested — in news stories, editorials, opinion columns, or letters to the editor — that the agency played a role in the Guatemalan crisis. The *New York Times* was a much better newspaper than the *Post* in the 1950s, with reasonably comprehensive treatment of events in Washington and internationally. One early Cold War analyst of the press found the *New York Times* being "described on Capitol Hill as 'everyone's Bible of information' and 'every man's CIA.' "[9] Still, both papers' editorials stridently argued that the United States had to stop the Soviet Union from solidifying its Guatemalan "beachhead" in Central America. Neither newspaper explained specifically how this was to be done. The writing in both papers resembled editorials in other major newspapers; the *Philadelphia Inquirer* wrote that Guatemalan exiles were "streaming back into their own country with the avowed purpose of smashing the Russian plot and liberating Guatemala from the most dangerous threat the Western Hemisphere has had to face."

The *Times'* news pages, more than most American newspapers, prominently featured accusations from around the world that the U.S. government was behind the little war in Guatemala. On June 20— when Allen Dulles let Eisenhower know that events were coming to a head in Central America but that the outcome was "very much in doubt" — front-page stories read that (1) the State Department "said that it had no evidence indicating that the violent developments of the last twenty-four hours were anything but a 'revolt of Guatemalans against the government' "; (2) the Foreign Minister of Guatemala said that "the aggression" had the "firm support" of the United States Department of State; and (3) the Soviet Union charged that "the United States had 'prepared and inspired' the attack on the Guatemala government."

Furthermore, the newspaper did actually mention Allen Dulles and the CIA in connection with the crisis, though just twice, and only on its op-ed page. The first reference to Dulles came from James Reston, also on June 20, in his regular Washington column. Titled "With the Dulles Brothers in Darkest Guatemala," it began, "John Foster Dulles, the Secretary of State, seldom intervenes in the internal affairs of other countries, but his brother Allen is more enterprising. If somebody wants to start a revolution in, say, Guatemala, it is no good talking to Foster Dulles. But Allen Dulles, head of the Central Intelligence Agency, is a more active man." Though he underestimated Foster Dulles's role, Reston's column was a rare case of realism in the U.S. press about the parties behind the conflict in Guatemala. While he recognized that a coup would not solve Guatemala's problems, the *Times* columnist was no critic of Allen Dulles or the CIA:

> Moscow is now definitely fishing in these long-troubled waters. It sees the possibility of Latin America's disillusion. It resents the strong Latin American support for the United States at the United Nations. It fears United States bases of operation near its own frontiers and is now obviously trying to establish Communist governments near ours.
>
> Mr. Dulles (Allen, that is) can no doubt help block this objective in Guatemala, but it will take Foster Dulles and the Congress to bring about a policy change that will deal with the central economic problems of the hemisphere.

The *Times* ignored the CIA's role in the Guatemalan crisis in a June 21 editorial and instead gave credence to U.S. claims that the crisis was purely a matter of freedom-loving Guatemalans versus Communists. (The *Times* also kept reporter Sydney Gruson, based in Mexico City and learning about U.S. activities to the south, out of Guatemala during the coup, at the request of Allen Dulles.)

The second prominent *New York Times'* mention of the CIA in relation to Guatemala came in response to that editorial. With prime placement on the June 24 op-ed page, a reader castigated the newspaper for its inconsistencies: "We will not escape the consequences of this aggression by proxy by taking a 'who, me?' attitude. In your issue of June 20, James Reston frankly admitted Allen Dulles's role in the invasion of Guatemala. Ambassador Peurifoy's cynical answer to the Guatemalans' complaint about American planes bombing and strafing Guatemalan towns that 'there are American planes everywhere in the world' will be thrown into our teeth wherever and whenever we try to persuade people that our presence serves exclusively peaceful ends."

Given the *Times'* near-universal readership on Capitol Hill, the CIA's involvement in the Guatemala affair was a widely suspected "secret," even among legislators with little seniority and power. Still, none talked publicly about the agency's suspected activities.[10]

The Barons

Among leaders in Congress, what more specific knowledge was there of the CIA's covert action against Guatemala? Walter Pforzheimer said years later, "I'm sure the committees were informed." Without claiming a specific memory, Pforzheimer says Taber's House Appropriations subcommittee on the CIA would have been mostly closely consulted, and there would have been "no holding back of details."[11]

About Guatemala, two documents in declassified CIA files show some interactions between agency personnel and unspecified congressional committee staff members in February and April 1954. The staffers were passing on information from individuals who themselves had information on persons inside the Guatemalan government. The staffers provided the names "as possible assistance [to] KUBARK [i.e., CIA] activities." Agency leaders passed on the information to PBSUCCESS leaders in Guatemala. Regarding those sources revealed to the agency by the congressional figures, the CIA wished in April to "obtain names of most likely defection possibilities in WSBURNT [Guatemalan government] hierarchy plus information on their personalities, weaknesses, plus channels and methods of approach." Congressional staffers exchanging information with CIA leaders about Guatemala did so, presumably, with the knowledge of their superiors.

Richard Immerman writes that a few powerful legislators — especially Senate majority leader Knowland and Appropriations Chair Bridges, Senators Wiley, Johnson, and others — interacted with Eisenhower or State-CIA leaders, pressing them to do "more" about the Guatemalan government, and were given at least oblique assurances that such was being done. Anticommunist crusader Charles Kersten, not a baron in Congress, but chairman of the House Select Committee on Communist Aggression, was similarly advised by Eisenhower's national security adviser, Robert Cutler, in late May. Cutler then informed Allen Dulles and others that Kersten had pledged that his committee "will not raise any question again about Guatemala" for at least a while.[12]

What these legislators and CIA subcommittee chairs and ranking minority members Taber, Russell, and Saltonstall knew of specifics is unclear. Saltonstall's son and legislative aide, William, *assumed* in a memo to his father some years later that the senator had had prior knowledge of the CIA's role in overthrowing Arbenz. His assumption was credible, for rumors of past CIA involvement in Guatemala were among topics scheduled to be discussed in an apparently unrecorded meeting of the subcommittee with Allen Dulles on March 22, 1954.[13]

In sum, available evidence suggests that Congress — counting both leaders (who knew far more of events unfolding between the CIA and Guatemala's government) and followers — had not just a permissive, but an enthusiastic attitude toward getting rid of the Arbenz government.

The CIA's View of Congressional Intent

Dulles, Pforzheimer, and others could easily judge legislative preferences in the *Congressional Record* and in conversations with leaders. They never doubted, later on, that the CIA's 1954 operation had reflected those preferences. But what documentary record is there of CIA views of congressional sentiment at the time? The best evidence comes from notes of one of the weekly PBSUCCESS meetings in March, with attendees (their names were "sanitized" from the document at twentieth century's end) from the CIA, the State Department, and possibly other organizations. This, of course, was a time when more and more members of Congress, Senator Margaret Chase Smith, for example, vocalized on Guatemala: "We might as well do away with the diplomatic niceties right away." And Eisenhower had already assured Knowland that he anticipated dealing soon with a new government in Guatemala. In this political atmosphere, the March 9 meeting's participants connected congressional opinion to the coming months' imperatives in Guatemala:

> Mr. [name deleted] then stated that he and Mr. [name deleted] were there to take stock of the present situation, to determine where we stand now and what are the future prospects. Are things going downhill so fast in Guatemala that PBSUCCESS, as it now stands, may not be enough? Consideration must be given to the much greater pressure which may come from Congress and public opinion on the present Administration if the situation in Guatemala does deteriorate. It may be necessary to take more calculated risks than before. . . . Mr. [name deleted] then asked Mr. [name deleted] exactly what was meant by possible additional calculated risks. Messrs [name deleted] and [name deleted] replied: (a) We might reconsider exploiting the conclusion arrived at by [Dominican Republic leader Rafael] Trujillo last year and transmitted to [Venezuelan leader Marcos] Perez Jiminez that the best way to bring about the fall of the Arbenz

government would be to eliminate 15–20 of its leaders with Trujillo's trained pistoleros. . . . [Name deleted] then expressed himself as opposed to the elimination of 15–20 Guatemalan leaders as a possible solution to the problem, although stating that such elimination was part of the plan and could be done.[14]

CIA leaders in Washington and Central America, along with members of the State Department continued to discuss the assassination option off and on in the three months leading up to the overthrow of the Arbenz government. It appears that no assassinations occurred, however.

The notable feature of the March discussion is that participants linked the necessity of "more calculated risks" such as assassination to "pressure which may come from Congress." Five weeks later, as the possibility still loomed that the operation might be cancelled, Frank Wisner presented the same view at a State Department meeting:

> Both State and this Agency would be immediately faced with the $64 question: "What are we going to do about Guatemala, and what can we do that would be effective?" We are on notice of the fact that in the upper echelons of the Administration it is expected that something will be done — of a drastic nature — to remove the menace of communist-controlled Guatemala. Moreover, there seems to exist a considerable degree of expectation in certain quarters of the Congress that something is brewing, and in any case, that something must be done.

While the extent of discussions about Guatemala between the CIA and congressional leaders may never be known, there was little doubt at the agency or the White House as to overarching congressional intent before or after the overthrow. Senator Smathers reflected legislative sentiment when word emerged on June 30 of the Guatemalan government's fall: "In all candor, we must admit that the democratic nations of the Western Hemisphere could not permit the continued existence of a Communist base in Latin America, so close to home." Lingering views that U.S. policy toward Guatemala in 1954 was simply the product of a hawkish executive branch, with Congress having little complicity in that policy, can safely be put to rest.[15]

Mr. Mansfield Goes to the Senate

Early on as DCI, Allen Dulles predicted to a group of air force officers that Congress would soon "want more and more to look at this intelligence picture as a whole. . . . We've got to get our ducks in a row as we come up before future Congresses." Speaking those words, he may have had in mind not just the elites of Capitol Hill, but young reformers like Mike Mansfield. The freshman senator had a mild-mannered exterior atypical of Congress but cared passionately about democratic governance. A veteran of service — beginning at age fourteen — in the army, navy, and marines, Mansfield went on to be a history professor in his home state before winning election to the House of Representatives. He moved to the Senate after election in 1952 and ignored the tradition of new members keeping silent on the floor. This was partly because he was appalled that any government agency — whether doing crucial work in foreign affairs, or handling domestic matters — might escape genuine oversight by the nation's legislature.

Specifically, in just a few years since he had told Deputy DCI Dulles at a House Foreign Affairs Committee hearing that the CIA should proceed aggressively and secretly in covert operations, Mansfield had become skeptical of the agency's competence and adherence to the law. The reasons for this shift remain unclear. Though the senator was more idealistic than most of his peers, he had a deep pragmatic streak. To fellow senators, he defined recent history this way: "By 1947, most Americans realized that the United States was confronted with a foe which would use any means to attain its aim — the conquest of the world. Information on the capabilities and intentions of aggressive nations became imperative, especially in view of the developments in atomic energy. The need for the Central Intelligence Agency is seldom questioned any longer, and I certainly am not challenging it now."[1]

Mansfield was prepared, though, to challenge the idea that the agency was properly monitored. Congress was unable to judge whether or not the CIA functioned legitimately, he claimed, and should create a ten-member joint committee on intelligence, similar to the Joint Committee on Atomic Energy, and supported by a proper staff. (Probably more than Mansfield understood, his citation of the JCAE as a model rubbed Eisenhower the wrong way. Among the topics the Joint Committee pushed hard on in 1953 were specific results of two recent Soviet nuclear tests and the undesirability, in the JCAE's

view, of continued sharing of nuclear secrets with Britain. A reporter summarized Joint Committee thinking: "Any facts given to London would soon
find their way to Moscow." The president tried to limit what Allen Dulles told
the Joint Committee. Dulles's solution, usually, was to give the most sensitive
information to the JCAE chair, and hope that he would not tell all to Joint
Committee members. Following CIA testimony at a hearing about the USSR's
first hydrogen bomb test explosion in August — which seemingly upset the
American public less than the first Soviet atomic bomb test in 1949— a JCAE
member assured the press that the United States was well ahead of the Soviet
Union in atomic and hydrogen bomb development and "will continue to be.")[2]

DCI Dulles had predicted to his audience of air force officers that Leverett Saltonstall's Armed Services Committee would not even vote on Mansfield's resolution because "the Committee is naturally and properly jealous
of its prerogatives in this field." He justified this, saying what Saltonstall and
his partner, Richard Russell, believed: "Anything that's known to 15 or 20
people is certainly going to be known to the Alsop brothers." Indeed, Saltonstall soon told Mansfield it would be "impossible" for the busy committee
to consider the resolution. But Dulles knew, too, that Mansfield would not
give up. In late July, Inspector General Lyman Kirkpatrick prepared a "suggested list" of potential members for such a committee, if it were to be created in the coming year. Among the names on it were Mansfield, Richard
Russell, John McCormack, and the young Michigan Republican representative, Gerald Ford. Later in 1953, Pforzheimer and an ally from the White
House Budget Office discussed "several of the CIA's legislative problems,"
including Mansfield's "known tenacity." L. K. White warned others in September, "It seems reasonably clear that Congress is going to insist upon
knowing more and more about our business," then wrote in his diary in
November, "Mr. Dulles requested that personnel not comment on Senator
Mansfield's proposal. . . . He said that we did not like this proposal in its present form, but that we did not want to appear to fight it."[3]

Mansfield again brought a resolution to the floor the following March.
By 1954, he and his cause had gained some admirers, although Pforzheimer
thought him a "dreary punk. I wouldn't call him an idealist." Mansfield again
faced a tough battle in gaining attention for his cause — Joseph McCarthy
was engaging in his one-man version of aggressive legislative "oversight" of
the CIA. The agency, meanwhile, was deeply involved that spring in
Guatemala and tracking events in Indochina. But Mansfield had done home-

work and politicking in his first year in the Senate, so the national news media and colleagues paid some attention this time. (In the House, similar ferment emerged, with some legislators asserting that the CIA and other intelligence agencies were "entitled" to a "continuous, constant, and stable relationship with the Congress."[4])

Newspapers were full of stories about McCarthy's worsening relations with fellow Republicans on March 11, but an impassioned Mansfield managed to gain the attention of a "hushed and attentive" Senate (as described by reporters), charging that the agency was "freed from practically every ordinary form of congressional check. . . . secrecy now beclouds everything about CIA — its cost, its efficiency, it successes, and its failures." This had led to extreme arrogance; the agency seemed "to have marked out for itself a setting above other government agencies, the Congress, and the public." "Neither do we know," he added, "if CIA is staying within the limits established by law." The agency appeared to have become more than a provider of information; it was "an instrument of policy," engaging in mysterious "activities" around the globe.

The Montanan's speech and campaign for oversight reform exemplified an emerging pattern in the CIA's early years: news reports shaping the variations in intelligence oversight, month to month, and year to year. Mansfield's lengthy March 1954 critique was shaped by and explicitly drew on news reports, opinion columns, and editorials published over the preceding two years. These included one columnist's claim in late 1952 that "legislators who have been in close contact with the CIA believe that there is much deadwood in the organization" and that the CIA had become "so topheavy and unwieldy that it should be scrapped altogether." During Mansfield's 1953 attempt to reform intelligence oversight, the *New York Times* reported that two CIA agents had given incorrect information to the FBI a year earlier that Owen Lattimore (an influential academic suspected by McCarthyites of betraying the United States) was soon to flee the country. Later, Beetle Smith directed CIA officials to refuse to testify in court about the matter; although the judge held them in contempt of court and sentenced them to jail, President Truman pardoned them. This was troublesome on three counts, Mansfield said: the CIA report was incorrect; it showed the CIA illegally getting into domestic matters; and CIA leaders would feel they could defy courts of law.

Mansfield also cited with satisfaction a series of *Richmond News-Leader* editorials that castigated the CIA and Congress for perpetuating a dangerously inept system of oversight. (Although Mansfield did not know it, Dulles had telephoned Virginia's Senator Harry Byrd, read him one of the editorials, and said its description of the CIA as a "free-wheeling outfit" was unjustified. Byrd replied, "If you're not a free-wheeling outfit, why aren't you?")

Assuming that such charges were reasonably accurate, Mansfield said, "until we create some sort of 'watchdog committee' . . . we will have nothing but continued anxiety about the Central Intelligence Agency and its widespread activities."[5] Careful as he was to avoid attacks on Allen Dulles or those in Congress then mandated to do oversight, and for all the characteristic dryness of his delivery, Mansfield nonetheless had given one of the most withering critiques ever voiced against the agency-Congress relationship.

Some thought Mansfield's 1954 campaign was having little effect, but colleagues kept signing his resolution. On March 18, Pforzheimer informed Dulles that liberal Democrats Warren Magnuson and Henry Jackson, both of Washington state, and conservative Republicans William Langer and Charles Potter (MI) had become cosponsors. A worried Leverett Saltonstall soon decided to have Dulles appear before his CIA subcommittee. Committee staffer William Darden sent word to the CIA that Dulles's presentation "should look toward answering various problems raised by that speech. He felt that Mr. Dulles' statement should be a lengthy one, up to one hour if necessary, prior to questioning." The CIA accepted the suggestion.[6]

DCI appearances before the subcommittee were not unusual, of course, occurring one to three times annually, although the main theme of the hearing would be. Saltonstall relied on Darden, a Georgian initially hired by Russell, to arrange the hearing. He and Pforzheimer quickly clashed over the staffer's suggestion that a written transcript of the hearing be made. Saltonstall learned, if he did not already know, that Darden could be a skeptic about the agency. Some of this may have been personal. Pforzheimer recalls, "We just didn't get on." But Darden put the case in nonpersonal terms to Saltonstall: "In the absence of some record of the hearing, my impression is that Senator Mansfield's expressed concern over undue secrecy and lack of adequate congressional supervision is supported. This is especially true since the Committee receives highly classified material and the reporters [i.e., stenographers] have all undergone a full field investigation by the FBI."

Except for the JCAE, the practice of transcribing hearings with CIA testimony was irregular. If a transcript of the March 22, 1954, hearing was made, it has never been declassified. The only part of the hearing that survives is a copy of Saltonstall's opening remarks, which read as if they were prepared by Darden: "I think it is safe to state that our legislative oversight of CIA has extended almost altogether to consideration of bills affecting the CIA and has not resulted in our receiving very complete information relative to CIA operations."[7]

Despite it having twenty-seven cosponsors, the Armed Services Committee shelved the Mansfield resolution in late May. The *Times'* Hanson Baldwin cited the opposition of Saltonstall as a primary reason and guessed that Russell, Styles Bridges, and Allen Dulles had something to do with it. Eisenhower said nothing publicly on the issue, but his views on congressional "meddling" were well known by Washington insiders. Baldwin, meanwhile, was becoming a regular critic of the agency and its oversight by Congress: "It is curious that Mr. Mansfield's measure, introduced for the second year, received short shrift at the very time when the activities of the Central Intelligence Agency have been emphasized by the crisis in Indochina and the Army-McCarthy hearings. . . . Such a committee is particularly needed at this time, not only to assist in improvement of the agency but also to safeguard it against irresponsible attack."

Weeks after the resolution was shelved, and as McCarthy waged ferocious attacks against the CIA, the *Times* reported, "Mr. Dulles . . . was not nearly so adamant as formerly against the idea of a joint congressional committee to look after his agency." The *Times* published other lengthy articles that month, assessing relations among the agency, President Eisenhower, and the Congress, in light of challenges from Mansfield and McCarthy. (Buried in one article, without elaboration, was a journalistic landmark — a mention of "assassination" as one of the "hostile activities" carried out by the agency's "secret intelligence operation.")[8] In another article, Baldwin judged the agency (whose annual budget he overestimated at $1 billion) not yet "adequate" in its performance. The CIA had erred badly in its analyses of Indochina, including the Battle of Dien Bien Phu, he claimed. Labeling McCarthy a "bull" in a CIA "china shop," Baldwin noted the essence of the problem at hand: "Intelligence services cannot work, except in secrecy. Yet this very secrecy, unless somehow scrutinized, can breed inefficiency or danger to a democracy."

Gently, Dulles tried to correct and persuade Baldwin. In a "purely personal" letter on June 7, 1954, he said that the budget estimate printed in the *Times* was "so many times out of line as to be thoroughly damaging," that CIA estimates on Indochina had been "reasonably accurate," and that he harbored no ill will toward Mansfield: "I am convinced that Senator Mansfield, whom I know well and respect, has at heart the desire to improve our intelligence and to protect it from destructive attack."[9]

Mansfield would be back with a similar resolution two years later. Eisenhower and Russell would remain firm opponents, but Saltonstall and Dulles would begin to wonder if the history professor from Montana was right.

Joseph McCarthy: The CIA's Other Would-Be Senate Overseer

Even as Allen Dulles dealt with Mansfield's advocacy, he suffered through the far more aggressive campaign of Joseph R. McCarthy to clean up a CIA supposedly beset by "dishonesty, subversion, treason, etc." While the agency was not usually the main target of McCarthy's anticommunism crusade during its prime years of 1950–1954, it never left his short list, either. Dulles would respond with careful skill.

Citizens could observe just the proverbial tip of the iceberg of the interactions between one side — McCarthy, his aides, and his extensive underground in Washington — and the other — Dulles, his assistants, his allies in Congress, and the White House. Surprisingly, the struggles have never been systematically explored. (Many relevant records were destroyed or remain classified.) It was not unusual, though, for the DCI to complain to his similarly besieged brother, the secretary of state, about CIA assistants having to be "on the phone constantly with McCarthy's cohorts" and under pressure to give documents to the Permanent Subcommittee on Investigations, part of the Government Operations Committee.[1]

In hindsight, seeing *any* legitimacy in McCarthy's various investigations can be hard. Nonetheless, his subcommittee had a substantial mandate to investigate irregularities in the executive branch. Its parent committee, successor to the old Committee on Expenditures in the Executive Branch, had, like its House counterpart, received authority from the Legislative Reorganization Act of 1946 to conduct such investigations. Two prime goals set out by the new chairman and his chief counsel, Roy Cohn, in 1953 were to look into "instances of waste and inefficiency" and "evidence of subversion."[2]

In the early months of the new Eisenhower administration, many in Washington foresaw an inevitable break between the Republican McCarthy and his president and party leader over the communists-in-the-executive-branch issue and, more pointedly, over who had the responsibility to address the issue. It was widely suspected that Eisenhower loathed the senator for his "coarse familiarity" (as Richard Nixon later wrote) and because of the "gutter" techniques of his crusade. Nothing had so pained and aggravated Eisenhower in the 1952 presidential contest as campaigning in Wisconsin with McCarthy, who earlier had attacked Eisenhower's former mentor, General George C. Marshall, as a traitor.

In seeking the presidency, Eisenhower had acknowledged that communist infiltration *was* a problem; an enthusiastic and shrewd consumer of intelligence during World War II, he understood the importance of countering enemy countries' intelligence efforts. In McCarthy's presence before a Wisconsin audience, candidate Eisenhower probably exaggerated his own fears of communist subversion, though, suggesting that a tolerance for communism in the United States had led to "contamination in some degree of virtually every department, every agency, every bureau, every section of government." Still, Eisenhower said that the executive branch had prime responsibility for rooting out communist sympathizers and agents within its ranks.

In January 1953, as the Eisenhower-McCarthy struggle began, the senator increasingly worked and drank too hard. Biographer Thomas Reeves wrote, "Armed with a zealous subcommittee staff, a large budget, and the power to subpoena, Joe was sometimes entangled in several probes and skirmishes at once. . . . The increasingly frantic pace of his daily life, fed by an ever-growing sense of mission and self-importance, did not permit even brief pauses for the most elementary reflection."[3]

McCarthy became convinced early in the year that a comprehensive congressional investigation of the CIA was warranted. Such decisions were not merely cynical calculations, according to Reeves — after McCarthy thrust himself into national prominence in 1950, he really believed that communist agents and sympathizers threatened U.S. security. (Indeed, most American political leaders so believed at the time, and some historians of a half-century later judge these concerns to have been warranted.)

One of his top subcommittee aides, Don Surine, collected documents and gathered information in winter-spring 1953 from various sources in and out of government. With others, Pforzheimer speculated that McCarthy had "a small underground in CIA, like he had everywhere else." DCI Dulles worked on that unpalatable assumption. Former CIA personnel were also among McCarthy's sources. As Inspector General Lyman Kirkpatrick later wrote of the period leading up to the Eisenhower-Dulles era,

> General Smith had established what was known by the rather unsavory title of "The Murder Board." He had charged this organization with completely reviewing a major segment of the Agency's work and with making recommendations as to what should be continued and what should be stopped because it was either

marginal or unproductive. This board had lived up to its name and, as a result of its work, many activities were canceled. Naturally, some of those involved in these activities felt an injustice had been done and, with their jobs no longer in existence, went to Senator McCarthy to attack the Agency.

Based on allegations made to him by these and other people, the senator and his associates became convinced that an infiltration problem plagued the agency, carried out by agents of the Soviet Union's KGB. "Our files contained allegations gathered from various sources," Cohn later wrote, "indicating that the CIA had unwittingly hired a large number of double agents — individuals who, although working for the CIA, were actually Communist agents whose mission was to plant inaccurate data." Similarly, Representative Timothy Sheehan (R-IL) spoke on April 1 of strong evidence that "Russian sympathizers entered the employ of the Central Intelligence Agency when that Agency was created in 1947." He asked, Are they still there? But Sheehan lacked McCarthy's flair for the dramatic and the prominence of a Senate seat, so his charges and questions gained little notice.[4]

All the more busily, though, Surine lined up potential witnesses for hearings that, he and McCarthy hoped, would be held jointly with Styles Bridges. For the powerful Appropriations chair, with its secretive little subcommittee on the CIA, to agree to conduct hearings jointly with McCarthy would have been bad news for the agency and the president. Bridges had helped make McCarthy more or less respectable within the Senate. One of the very few who had known early on about the Manhattan Project, Bridges thought McCarthy was absolutely right in charging that communists had successfully injected themselves into leading agencies, the CIA included.

The Appropriations chair agreed, too, with McCarthy's professed standard in judging whether a person ought to hold a top government position: "The test is not whether a man or woman is guilty, beyond a reasonable doubt, of espionage or Communist party membership, but whether the circumstances are such that we cannot take a chance when we are dealing with a sensitive post in a sensitive area." Pforzheimer warned Allen Dulles on April 6 that nothing would preclude Bridges from "telling Senator McCarthy anything which the latter desired to know about CIA." Still, Bridges apparently failed to persuade Carl Hayden (D-AZ) and other pillars of his CIA subcommittee to endorse joint hearings with McCarthy, so the idea died.[5]

This, of course, did not stop the Wisconsin senator, who planned investigations and hearings by his own subcommittee and told Cohn that no topic interested him more than the CIA's problems. On March 17, at McCarthy's request, Dulles appeared before an Investigations subcommittee hearing that was closed to the press. Perhaps in anticipation of that hearing, Dulles had (on March 3) asked an attorney friend, Peyton Ford, to research the "right of a congressional committee to demand papers and information from the Executive Branch." Upon receipt days later of an analysis that noted the ambiguities of the Constitution and history of such legislative-executive struggles, Dulles replied, "I hope I shall not have occasion to use it frequently." He presumably did use it, but those attending the March 17 hearing kept its interactions secret, except for McCarthy's comment to reporters that "this does not mean we are investigating CIA."

Dulles surely encountered lively interest on McCarthy's part; Kirkpatrick, who typically accompanied the DCI to such meetings, later wrote of McCarthy, "Whenever he met with Mr. Dulles, it almost always consisted of a monologue on McCarthy's part, with allegations and denunciations, but not facts." The *New York Times* speculated on March 18 that the subcommittee, already investigating the State Department, might start probing the CIA. This seems to have been the occasion recalled by Kirkpatrick of McCarthy, "at the height of his demagoguery," summoning Dulles "one day to hand him a list of twelve names of people whom he said were working for the CIA and whom he claimed were security risks. Mr. Dulles brought the piece of paper back to the office and handed it to me, and told me to follow through on it."[6]

At this time, Pforzheimer warned Dulles that it would be a mistake to "seem to ignore" McCarthy's request, since the senator might pursue "more drastic action." Kirkpatrick investigated and learned that only two of the persons worked for the agency. The "list of twelve" was revealed, after a time-consuming internal inquiry, to be a worthless rehash of an older list of "subversives." Dulles was enraged at having to follow through on McCarthy's "request." The DCI's friend, columnist Joseph Alsop, claimed that there was more to the "list" incident: the CIA head had gone to the president and told him "that no intelligence agency could possibly continue to operate effectively if its employees were subject to congressional inquisition. He pointed out the impossibility of maintaining secrecy, of keeping 'cover,' of doing the intelligence job. He said that he would have to resign if the President could not protect the CIA from such investigators as McCarthy. Eisenhower then promised to support Dulles to the limit."

The DCI was almost certainly the source for the story, which Alsop would not publish until Dulles faced a more trying dispute with McCarthy in the summer. In the meantime, the DCI often projected nonchalance about the McCarthy threat; at an off-the-record luncheon, he told Overseas Writers Club members that his agency "may have a little trouble with McCarthy, but not as much as my eminent brother is having."

What seemed to McCarthy and his allies like gross negligence on security matters looked radically different to those working on such cases at the agency. The CIA conducted "careful, painstaking" investigations, Kirkpatrick later claimed: "I sat on many, and chaired several, loyalty and security boards for the CIA and it is to the credit of that organization that it went about the business of 'purifying' itself in a calm, careful manner." But early-1950s Washington, DC, evoked (Kirkpatrick wrote) "something of the atmosphere that must have been present during the French Revolution."

McCarthy's staff faced an increasingly emboldened CIA across the spring, perhaps because of Eisenhower's quiet support. Pforzheimer told Dulles on May 5: "I informed Mr. Flanagan, General Counsel of the . . . McCarthy subcommittee that CIA would not be able to furnish any information to the committee in reply to its request for information as to the newspapers and periodicals to which CIA subscribes." Pforzheimer also turned down an older, pending request from McCarthy's subcommittee to question a CIA officer serving on a governmental committee examining shipping issues.[7]

When McCarthy revealed his investigation plans at an executive session of the subcommittee, Stuart Symington urged him to clear such a move with the White House. It is doubtful that a warning from Symington, a friend of the CIA and Dulles and one of McCarthy's enemies, had much impact. Meanwhile, Eisenhower wrote a friend that spring that McCarthy wanted "above all else, publicity. Nothing would probably please him more than to get the publicity that would be generated by public repudiation by the President."

Eisenhower moved more toward a public reproach of McCarthy in early July 1953 when a leading staffer of the senator's subcommittee published an article claiming that Protestant clergymen were "the largest single group supporting the Communist apparatus in the United States today." When McCarthy hesitated to remove the aide, Eisenhower issued a statement that, without mentioning the senator, condemned "generalized and irresponsible attacks that sweepingly condemn the whole of any group of citizens."[8]

The senator's growing tensions with agency leaders became public on July 9, when a dispute erupted over the CIA's youngish, brainy William Bundy. He had done impressive signals intelligence work during World War II and later set aside thoughts of becoming a historian by joining the CIA in 1951. By 1953, he was a top assistant to Dulles, attached to the Board of National Estimates and serving as liaison to the National Security Council. In anticipation of also taking on liaison duties with the Atomic Energy Commission, Bundy was under review by a board (that included an FBI officer) for the highest level of clearance. Not insignificantly, he was also the son of a former State Department official and son-in-law of former Secretary of State Dean Acheson.

A moderately liberal Democrat, Bundy was a friend and former law partner of Alger Hiss's brother, Donald. Like many other Democrats, Bundy had harbored doubts that, as a State Department official, Alger Hiss had worked on behalf of the Soviet Union. Bundy had contributed to the Hiss defense fund, prior to the latter's eventual conviction for perjury. Bundy had admitted this when joining the CIA, along with the fact that, in 1940 — while working for the Library of Congress — he had briefly been a member of the United Public Workers Association, which McCarthy later listed as a communist-front organization.

On the morning of July 9, having learned from the FBI of Bundy's history and the proposed enhancement of his security clearance, McCarthy had Roy Cohn telephone Walter Pforzheimer. The aide demanded, "Get him up here!" To McCarthy and Cohn, it seemed obvious that a friend of the Hiss family should not have access to critical military and intelligence secrets. Bundy should come before the Investigations subcommittee that morning, Cohn demanded of Pforzheimer. Subsequently, the main protagonists had somewhat different versions of the course of events during the rest of the day. An angry McCarthy provided his account that afternoon on the floor of the Senate: "We called Mr. Pforzheimer, the liaison between CIA and Congress, and told him we wanted Mr. Bundy to appear at the meeting; and Mr. Pforzheimer indicated Mr. Bundy would appear. Later, Mr. Pforzheimer called back. . . . we were notified that Mr. Bundy had suddenly gone on vacation. Mr. Pforzheimer said he did not know where Mr. Bundy went. . . . We wish to subpoena Mr. Pforzheimer."

McCarthy did not detail his (accurate) suspicion that the DCI had sent Bundy on an unanticipated vacation as a way of stalling on McCarthy's requests and subpoenas. But he announced a plan to subpoena Dulles also, because "I cannot believe that the head of one of our most important executive agencies would take it upon himself to say, 'None of our employees can be subpoenaed by a congressional committee.' "[9] "This I never said," Dulles told his friend, journalist Walter Lippmann. The DCI's account was that "I was notified of this request just as I was leaving for a meeting of the

National Security Council. I sent back word through a member of our legal staff that I did not wish Bundy to appear until I had an opportunity to consider the matter."

Things happened less sedately than Dulles admitted. In the midst of the DCI's meetings that July 9 with Bundy, Pforzheimer, and others at CIA to discuss McCarthy's request, Pforzheimer told his boss that he would not commit perjury about Bundy's whereabouts that day, if called before McCarthy's subcommittee. The legislative liaison had plenty of experience in dealing with McCarthy and Cohn, though it took awhile for him to discover that Dulles had informally appointed Lyman Kirkpatrick to deal with McCarthy also. Neither Pforzheimer nor Kirkpatrick relished dealing with the senator. Years later, however, Pforzheimer claimed, "I had no trouble with Joe. I remember the first time I ever saw him was at a baseball game out at old Griffith Stadium. He was so drunk he could hardly stand up." Pforzheimer had a blunt, affable, but not always fully forthcoming manner with McCarthy and his aides, which usually worked well. Still, it was one thing to lie over the phone, another to do so under oath. As Deputy Director of Intelligence Robert Amory (on whom Dulles also relied during the crisis) said to Cohn, when the latter accused him of perjury regarding Bundy, "It wasn't perjury because I wasn't under oath. I just lied." When someone at the CIA would ask Pforzheimer during the height of the affair, "How are you and Joe doing today?," he would respond, "Well, I'm not in jail."[10]

Dulles quickly told Bundy to leave the agency building immediately, speak to no one, and go on vacation out of town at once. "Be out of touch" were Dulles's parting words for his young assistant. He then had Pforzheimer place a call to McCarthy, coolly confirming that Bundy was on vacation and unavailable. By that afternoon, Bundy was back in his hometown, north of Boston, playing golf with his father and worrying that his career might be in ruins.

That afternoon, Pforzheimer received a subpoena. The DCI could not order all of his assistants to leave town, nor would Dulles have Pforzheimer testify that he had lied about Bundy, so the decision to fight McCarthy became concrete. President Eisenhower said nothing publicly about the Bundy affair, and any conversations he had on the subject with Allen Dulles remain undocumented. The DCI did speak with Ike's national security adviser, Robert Cutler, with whom Bundy had interacted on NSC matters and who had been an admiring friend and coworker of Bundy's father during World War II. Through such intermediaries, Eisenhower backed up the

DCI. Incongruously, Eisenhower also saw the senator the next day, July 10, when he attended a White House bill-signing ceremony. Spotting McCarthy in the back row of a group of legislators, Ike waved and called out, "Hello, there." McCarthy waved back.

That same Friday, Dulles took CIA legal counsel Lawrence Houston along to Capitol Hill to see McCarthy and Republican members of his subcommittee. Dulles told the chairman, "Joe, you're not going to have Bundy as a witness." Later in the day, Foster Dulles called his brother, asking how he "came out with McCarthy." The senator was in "an ugly mood," said the DCI. "The general tenor of McCarthy's statement was that CIA was neither sacrosanct, nor immune from investigation." McCarthy told reporters later that day that he had assured the DCI that if he or other CIA leaders were called before the subcommittee, "we will not expose their secret, classified operations." Allen Dulles judged the meeting "something of a draw," and noted that Karl Mundt (R-SD) was "helpful," Charles Potter (R-MI) "mum," and Everett Dirksen (R-IL) "absent." In other words, none of the subcommittee's Republicans aided their chairman that day. Potter was unlikely to help McCarthy either — he met off-the-record with Eisenhower a couple of days later.[11]

Dulles and McCarthy would meet again the following Tuesday, July 14. The DCI also contacted Vice President Nixon, whose anticommunist credentials rivaled those of McCarthy. Nixon had a good relationship with McCarthy and knew that Eisenhower "was reluctant to plunge into a bitter personal and partisan wrangle, aware that if he repudiated McCarthy or tried to discipline him, the Republican Party would split right down the middle." The DCI called and (Nixon later wrote) "asked me if I could do anything to help prevent a confrontation. He said that he had complete confidence in Bundy and that his main interest was to keep the CIA out of the newspapers." Nixon agreed, but he, too, had a condition that boxed Dulles in — Bundy should undergo investigation by a new Civil Service security board. Dulles and Bundy had little choice but to accept the condition. Nixon then approached the Wisconsin senator:

> I told McCarthy that I had seen Bundy's performance in several National Security Council meetings and he seemed to me a loyal American who was rendering vital service to the country.
>
> "But what about his contribution to Hiss?", McCarthy persisted.
>
> "Joe," I said, "you have to understand how those people up in Cambridge think. Bundy graduated from the Harvard Law School, and Hiss was one of its

most famous graduates. I think he probably just got on the bandwagon without giving any thought to where the bandwagon was heading."

The next day, I had lunch with McCarthy and the other Republicans on his subcommittee.

There, Nixon twisted arms. The vice president assured the four Republican legislators that Eisenhower firmly backed the DCI.

Leaks to the press made Ike's views public, too. Joseph Alsop reported on July 13, "The real Eisenhower, the man of courage and high principle, who does not appease and will not yield to blackmail, at last seems to be taking charge." With such presidential backing, Nixon insisted to McCarthy and his colleagues that a publicized congressional investigation would "damage national security, harm our relations with our allies, and seriously affect CIA operations." As Nixon later wrote, McCarthy reluctantly "agreed to drop his investigation of Bundy and the CIA."[12]

McCarthy had *his* conditions for resolution of the crisis, however, in talks with Dulles on July 13 and 14. The two men agreed that the subcommittee would relay all information it had on Bundy to the agency, which would then make that a part of the CIA's (and the loyalty board's) effort to "re-evaluate Mr. Bundy's status." Dulles also agreed, according to a public McCarthy statement cleared with the DCI, that there was a "right of Congress to subpoena witnesses and uncover graft, corruption or subversion in any branch of the government." But the Investigations subcommittee "postponed" any attempt to subpoena Bundy.

Asked by reporters if he felt he had won a victory or suffered a defeat, McCarthy replied, "It is neither." But, as the *Times* noted, "The agreement reached today between Messrs. McCarthy and Dulles was necessarily very general and posed questions that might result in controversy between the CIA and the subcommittee." This judgment was more astute than most others that showed up in the press over the following weeks. The common view was that Dulles and the CIA had "won." In a sense this was true, since so many people thought so. And, in fact, the DCI had more or less stood up to McCarthy. Alsop wrote that the senator had "suffered his first total, unmitigated, unqualified defeat." Without describing any sources or evidence, Alsop reported, "President Eisenhower flatly refused to permit McCarthy to subpoena Bundy." The event was "so politically meaningful" in light of the administration's past deference to McCarthy that the "incident may well be remembered as the turning of the tide" against the Wisconsin senator. There was an element of wishful thinking in Alsop's analysis — one top Eisenhower aide would worry in his diary about the president's "disastrous appeasement" of McCarthy the following November — but the column was widely noted.[13]

Among those probably happy to read Alsop's analysis just eight days after the Bundy crisis erupted was Allen Dulles, who — on the very day of the column's publication — worriedly reminded Foster Dulles that "McCarthy hadn't actually abandoned his right" to subpoena CIA leaders. The DCI may well have been a source for the latest Alsop column. (Dulles kept a copy of it in his personal files for the rest of his life.) He was no amateur in the game of shaping perceptions in Washington. The director asked an aide to "communicate to all that the DCI stands behind all CIA employees," but cautioned "that there is to be no gloating about the recent McCarthy business." Another satisfied observer was Saltonstall, who was appalled at McCarthy's attacks on the CIA and Dulles. The Massachusetts senator was characteristically polite, though faintly snobbish: the loud, crude McCarthy — with rural, midwestern, and Irish Catholic roots — was not his type. Saltonstall and the DCI played golf, kidded each other about their mutual Ivy League backgrounds, and had drinks ("a little hospitality") at each other's homes to do business. Saltonstall had enjoyed dinner with Dulles and his wife just two weeks before McCarthy went on the attack.

Even as the nation read of McCarthy's "complete cave-in," he and the DCI almost immediately discovered their different understandings of their agreement. Especially, the senator was angry to learn that Bundy, though about to undergo the new investigation, was not suspended from his job, pending the outcome of that probe. That, McCarthy thought, would have been standard procedure.[14]

For the remaining weeks of the congressional session that summer, McCarthy bombarded Dulles with demands for information on, and harsh treatment of, Bundy. Their correspondence was not immediately publicized, but constituted an outright rupture, with the senator making the most serious possible charges against the CIA head. It began calmly on July 16, when McCarthy submitted the "information" he had on Bundy. But McCarthy did not want to wait for a drawn-out investigation by the CIA to learn why Bundy had made contributions to the Hiss defense fund. Was he, in fact, a member of a communist-front organization? If so, why had he joined, and why did he leave? If the alleged facts are untrue, McCarthy wrote, "then I feel it is very important for your organization and for Mr. Bundy that the matter be cleared up immediately. If those facts are true, then I am sure you will agree that he should not be holding a top job in the Central Intelligence Agency."

While confirming on July 22 what was already known — that Bundy had contributed to the defense fund and briefly joined the United Public Workers — Dulles otherwise gave McCarthy a polite brush-off. "Further comment," he wrote, should await the "re-evaluation of Mr. Bundy's case . . . the outcome of which will be communicated to your Subcommittee."

But "the fact you have now confirmed to me . . . that Mr. Bundy did contribute $400 to the defense of Alger Hiss . . . raises the gravest question," responded McCarthy on July 27. Should Bundy be "holding a sensitive post in an intelligence agency, a good part of the work of which must involve the detection of activities of people such as Alger Hiss?" McCarthy added, "I would appreciate knowing what reasons he now gives" for having contributed to the Hiss defense fund.

Dulles resisted again in an August 1 letter. "I note your refusal," a furious McCarthy responded on August 3, "to give up any information in regard to the connection between Hiss and Bundy." Reminding Dulles of their July 14 agreement that "information should be available to the Committee if such information in no way endangered the security of your agency or impeded its work," McCarthy accused the DCI of gross impropriety:

> I understand that Mr. Bundy now holds a top position in your organization and has access to all secret information coming . . . from various parts of the world. I further understand that he did not come with your organization until after Alger Hiss was in jail. For that reason, his contacts and association with and his contributions to Alger Hiss were of necessity prior to his employment by you, unless, of course, he has had contact with Hiss since he has been in jail. . . . Unfortunately, the Congress is going out of session tonight, so that no action can be taken in the case of your protection and cover-up of Bundy. However, the full matter will be submitted to my Committee and undoubtedly to the Senate upon its return.
>
> I might add that it would seem that the last man in the world who would try to protect and hide the facts about one of his top officer's associations with and contributions to a convicted traitor would be the head of the CIA.[15]

McCarthy publicized his ominous threats on August 4 but could do little for the time being about CIA handling of the matter. He was livid to learn, just days after his scorching correspondence with Dulles, that Bundy was to vacation in Europe. This, of course, required a passport; for weeks McCarthy had thought Bundy should be denied one. In fact, he thought the CIA officer should be arrested at dockside.

Allen Dulles took it in stride when John Foster Dulles, who was much more cautious in dealing with the Wisconsin senator, telephoned from his State Department office during the height of the Bundy crisis, with the intense McCarthyite director of security, Scott McLeod, hovering a few feet away. Unusually, McLeod also served as personnel director at the State Department, leading the well-connected diplomat Adolf Berle to observe in his diary that, with "one of McCarthy's stooges" holding both positions, "in practice this meant that McCarthy and not Dulles was directing Foreign Service and the careers of the men in it." As McLeod listened, Foster Dulles told his brother (according to State Department records) that "a letter had been prepared to McCarthy saying that if the subpoena were served [on] Bundy, we would be glad to be notified, because we did not normally issue passports in such instances." This, of course, was precisely the sort of response to McCarthy that Allen Dulles did *not* want. Calmly, the DCI persuaded his brother and other State Department officials to let Bundy take the European vacation. Asked by a reporter where Bundy and family were planning to travel, the defeated McCarthy replied only, "I know where I'd like to have them go."[16]

Many at the CIA had similar thoughts about McCarthy, and one made the mistake in September 1953 of thinking out loud about how much simpler life would be for the agency and the nation if there were no Joseph McCarthy. Well past 5:30 on Friday afternoon, September 20, when many at the CIA had gone home for the day, Horace "Pete" Craig invited his subordinate, psychologist Dr. William J. Morgan, to stick around for some conversation. Little is known about Craig, except that his CIA duties involved Eisenhower's Operations Coordination Board. Morgan had been with the OSS during World War II, then with the CIA (doing psychological assessment of job applicants). He was on the army payroll as of 1953 but detailed to work under Craig at the agency.

With McCarthy making life unpleasant for many at the CIA, Craig paced the floor in Morgan's presence and asked his thoughts about the problem. This surprised Morgan, who claimed to know little about McCarthy, but voiced the impression that "what we are trying to do and what the Senator is trying to do is the same." Craig, however, thought the CIA should "penetrate" McCarthy's subcommittee staff. In fact, Craig said, he had decided on just the right person and would probably explore getting that unnamed young man placed with the subcommittee. Morgan suggested this was a bad idea and said the CIA should instead try to befriend McCarthy, perhaps "indoctrinate him."

The suggestion of penetrating McCarthy's staff had shocked Morgan, but not nearly so much as the still-pacing Craig's next words. The senator had done great harm to America's reputation abroad. "It may be necessary to liquidate Senator McCarthy, as was Huey Long," he said. Reflectively, he added, "There are madmen who would be willing to do it for a price." The psychologist was used to hearing strange statements but was at a loss for words, as he thought: "*Is Pete serious about this thing, or is he sounding off? He must be losing his mind.*" The two men soon parted, with Morgan the more disturbed of the two. After apologizing to his wife for being late for dinner, he told her of Craig's remarks. "He is out of his mind!" she responded.

Upon thought, Morgan wondered if Craig had been trying to determine, in a bizarre fashion, whether or not the psychologist was part of the much-talked-about McCarthy Underground. Morgan had claimed not to have any connections with the senator, but he did something that was consistent with Craig's suspicions — he told no one at the CIA about Craig's mention of "liquidation" but went to a member of McCarthy's staff a month later. The psychologist was called before the Investigations subcommittee the following March. Senator Potter chaired in McCarthy's absence. Among the staffers present were Roy Cohn and Robert Kennedy. Morgan recounted the story, due to his desire to serve the "national interest," but claimed to have "had a debate with my conscience." Knowing that Dulles had warned CIA employees about going to McCarthy, Morgan told the subcommittee, "The fact that I am here jeopardizes my own stay in government. If I am a government employee a year from now, I will really be amazed."

Senators and staff took the psychologist in other directions during his private testimony. Potter raised a question about Matt Baird, director of training for agency officers: "Did he have any personal traits that would be objectionable in normal society?" While admitting that he had no "facts that he is a homosexual," Morgan spoke of Baird as having been "looked upon as a queer" and said Baird had been discharged from prior employment at a boys' school for "teaching the boys how to masturbate properly." (Baird's reputation at the CIA was decidedly heterosexual, according to Pforzheimer's later recollections.)

Don Surine, who had been investigating the CIA for the past year, moved the hearing closer to its central topic: "Do you know of any projects of liquidation that CIA has engaged in abroad, in a general way?" Initially, Morgan was responsive ("yes sir, I do") but within a moment contradicted himself, and then hinted why he did so: "When men are liquidated in intelligence, you must not refer to it. . . . The question of liquidation of enemy agents is never referred for official discussion."

Ultimately, Senator McClellan pressed the central question that had led to the hearing: Had Craig's mention of liquidating McCarthy been something of "substance" or was it something that had "no significance and should not be pursued further?" Morgan claimed that no purpose would be served in making the story public yet ventured that Craig's remarks had been serious: "He didn't say it in jest. He said it in a reflective sort of way."

Whether Allen Dulles ever heard of Morgan's approach to McCarthy's subcommittee is unknown. Anyone who leaked damaging information to the senator would be fired, the DCI had promised six hundred top employees at a mid-July 1953 agency convocation. Pass the word on, he told them. Except for the few McCarthy devotees among CIA officers, the response of most who heard the speech was exultant. "It was a brave act," Kirkpatrick recalled, as "Dulles' remarks were almost sure to get back to McCarthy." Sherman Kent, who headed the Board of National Estimates on which Bundy worked, expressed gratitude in a note to his boss for the "stirring . . . magnificent" speech.

The Investigations subcommittee seems not to have pursued the "liquidation" matter much further. The senators held no public hearings, and no one leaked the sensational subject matter to the press. William Morgan would continue to create tests for CIA use with potential officers until 1957, and Horace Craig would stay with the agency until 1958, as would Matt Baird until 1965.[17]

McCarthy faced the raw political fact by August 1953 that Eisenhower, with Nixon and Allen Dulles among his chief agents, had damaged his subcommittee power base — Republican members would not support their chair's attempt to subpoena CIA officials or to investigate the agency. Nor would Democratic members; they had walked out of a subcommittee hearing days before the Bundy affair broke.

A lull in the battle with McCarthy permitted some fruitful reflection on the part of Dulles, journalists, and, uniquely, William Bundy. With the help of staffers, the director of central intelligence monitored commentary in Congress and the press. Senator Mike Monroney (D-OK) attacked the notion that the Wisconsinite had "a monopoly within this Government of despising, exposing, and prosecuting Communists and their fellow travelers." But one citizen admonished Monroney, "Drop dead, you lousy S.O.B. You have the blood of 300,000 American boys dripping from your stinking hands." Other outspoken anti-McCarthy legislators were a lonely few and rarely coordinated their attacks.[18]

In the press, Dulles was not surprised to find himself portrayed as a near-traitor in outlets like the conservative *Chicago Tribune*, which charged that he and the agency had "an appalling record of bringing Communists into . . . public service and protecting them there." But he was a hero to many liberal and moderate newspaper columnists, editorialists, and broadcast commentators. The DCI took time to thank some, including Elmer Davis, who had remarked on ABC Radio, "It looks as if this vital government agency will not be kicked to pieces, as McCarthy has kicked the State Department." Dulles no doubt pondered at greater length critiques by Hanson Baldwin in the *New York Times* and Walter Lippmann in his syndicated column. Baldwin would continue through the 1950s to be the *Times'* most regular correspondent to cover the CIA; by 1955, a Dulles aide would be preparing lengthy summaries and caustic analyses of Baldwin's work. But on July 30, 1953, he was hardly anti-CIA. "We must know our enemy, or die," he wrote. "Whether we like it or not, the Central Intelligence Agency is necessary." It would be "unthinkable" to have McCarthy "let loose" among agency files. On the other hand, the Bundy "incident confirms the need for the establishment of a Joint House-Senate Committee, akin to the Joint Committee on Atomic Energy."

Lippmann rejected "the argument that the CIA is something apart, that it is so secret that it differs in kind from the State Department or, for that matter, from the Treasury Department." This was absurd, Dulles thought. "The mere disclosure that a particular person is working for us may destroy an entire operation. This has already happened to us in connection with other congressional investigations," he wrote his friend, promising details when their summer vacations ended.[19]

In the meantime, Bundy went about his daily duties at the CIA as if all were well. Still not granted the "Q" clearance for atomic intelligence, he remained under investigation for the rest of 1953 and into the next year by a "loyalty board" composed of civil servants. A face-to-face encounter between

Bundy and the board was many months off. As that probe moved methodically along, Bundy made a personally and politically significant choice — remaining a friend of Donald Hiss.

Awkwardly, Dulles was among nine hundred guests at Senator McCarthy's September wedding in St. Matthew's Cathedral. The weather was perfect that day in Washington, and thousands gathered outside the church to observe the famous and infamous arrive and depart. Dulles's thoughts during the long nuptial mass about the groom, who had charged him with near-criminal negligence, can be imagined.[20]

Through that fall and into the winter, McCarthy's aides regularly contacted the CIA. As Dulles had agreed in his July meetings with McCarthy, and as had always been the case with authorized committees, Congress had a right to secure information from the agency. And so staffers of the Investigations subcommittee marched on, telephoning and otherwise making requests for information and written analyses from CIA officials. Oftentimes, they obtained the information they wanted.

One topic intriguing them was the agency's information on shipping and other trade-related interactions between "Red China," as the People's Republic of China was almost universally known in the United States, and allies of the United States. The British were suspected to be among the top shippers and trade partners, which infuriated McCarthy and others, since the United States had been in combat against Chinese forces for the preceding three years in the just-concluded Korean War. CIA estimates of such trade activities came under sharp scrutiny by McCarthy's subcommittee, especially differences between the agency and naval intelligence. Fretting over potential damage to relations with allies, Foster Dulles called his brother one afternoon in December 1953, asking if he might not stop his underlings at the CIA from providing requested information to McCarthy's subcommittee. Allen Dulles had been dealing with the McCarthy shipping problem since February. While the DCI said he could, of course, control what "official announcements" his people made, it would be a mistake to forbid them from "talking" with McCarthy's staff on the issue. It would surely lead the subcommittee to "ask" CIA personnel for formal testimony, a forbidding road. By the way, the DCI added, "British trade is the largest single item."

According to Cohn, McCarthy understood "the importance of maintaining close relations with our allies. But some action had to be taken." The subcommittee staffer handling the China trade issue for McCarthy was young Robert F. Kennedy, who drafted a strongly worded letter urging Eisenhower to speak out on U.S. allies' trade with China. McCarthy told an aide that, on this issue, he would "not take 'no' for an answer." Richard Nixon again intervened, though, persuading McCarthy to "withdraw" the letter — already at the White House — so that Eisenhower could avoid having to answer it and thereby escape giving offense either to the British or to anti-communists at home.[21]

McCarthy also created a brief stir in the fall of 1953 when he publicized rumors that the United States might soon have Lavrenti Beria — the infamous former security chief of the Soviet Union under Joseph Stalin — in its custody. Beria had been arrested early in the summer, the loser in a power struggle after Stalin's death in March. An informant in Spain, supposedly in touch with Beria, had used an American reporter to contact McCarthy. The plan was for McCarthy to "guarantee" Beria's "conditions of surrender to the United States" and for the senator to accompany him and two companions to the United States. Supposedly, Beria insisted that his presence in Spain and his wish to defect to the United States were "under no circumstances" to be made known to the CIA or the State Department. McCarthy agreed, sending signed guarantees through intermediaries, but the scheme leaked to the press on September 19. Foster Dulles, annoyed by reporters' questions about it, called the DCI. The CIA had followed the post-Stalin turmoil as closely as it could, with little success. Allen Dulles assured the secretary, though, that "the whole thing is a fake. . . . the informant is second-rate." The DCI was right. Soon, the senator put as much distance as he could between himself and the hoax. Far from defecting to the United States, Beria was executed in a Soviet prison in December.[22]

As 1954 began, McCarthy renewed his interest in the CIA. Had he known of the latest events regarding Bundy, the senator would have salivated over the prospects ahead. Bundy endured questioning while being wired to a "lie-detector" and spent a full day before the loyalty board in February. Weeks later, it judged that no evidence suggested treason by Bundy but recommended nonetheless that he be fired, lacking the character suitable for intelligence work. Bundy's loyalty to Alger Hiss's brother had apparently been too much for the board members. In return, Bundy thought his judges were "a bunch of second-rate hacks." He and Dulles surely feared that the board's finding would leak. But Dulles eased the pain of the news by informing Bundy that he would put the board's recommendation before another panel to judge the appropriateness of his "character."[23]

McCarthy had other agency topics to examine, meanwhile. As chair of the Investigations subcommittee, he could not unilaterally authorize formal investigations. Still, one of his discretionary powers was to direct staff members to initiate "preliminary" inquiries, of which there had been over four hundred during his leadership of the subcommittee. McCarthy authorized another one in late spring 1954, with staff member Surine in charge. By this time, the famous, televised Army-McCarthy hearings were well under way, exploring McCarthy's charges of communist infiltration in the U.S. Army. The very sensational nature of such charges inevitably led the hearings to focus, as well, on the questionable legitimacy of McCarthy's anticommunist crusade.

On June 2, during the twenty-fifth day of the army hearings, McCarthy renewed grave charges of subversion against the Central Intelligence Agency. There was new evidence, he said, of Communists having served in the old OSS and then being "blanketed" into the agency. "The worst situation we have now," he added subsequently, "is not in the military. It is in the CIA." His words still had the power to electrify the national press. The June 3 lead story in the *Times* said, "Implicit in Senator McCarthy's assertion that communist infiltration was 'much more serious' than in the Army was an indication he soon might ask his investigating subcommittee to look into the ultra-secret agency devoted to counter-espionage." Thus, there emerged a new "conflict of secrecy versus public accountability."

The DCI wasted no time in responding, consulting closely at this point with Senator Saltonstall. Within an hour of seeing the Associated Press account of McCarthy's charge, the DCI edited a response. After trying out different wording, he scrawled "O.K. AWD" on a statement for the press whose first sentence was simple and blunt: "McCarthy's charge that CIA is penetrated by communists is false." The prediction from "highly placed Republicans," said the *Times*, was that "a final, decisive showdown between Senator McCarthy and President Eisenhower" was on the way.[24]

At the White House, it was not at all clear where events were leading. The angry national security adviser, Robert Cutler, met on Saturday morning, June 5, with White House chief of staff Sherman Adams and perhaps others to try to grab control of the situation. Adams later wrote that Cutler was "one of the strong enemies of McCarthy on our team," while the chief of staff tended to agree with Eisenhower that McCarthy was best treated with public indifference. Details of the Saturday meeting seem lost to history, except for Cutler's impassioned follow-up letter to Adams. There he spoke of "arrangements . . . for obviating public investigation of CIA by the McC Committee. If worked out as feasible, [they] would satisfactorily dispose of that issue." Cutler clearly left the meeting in frustration, though, convinced that "insulation of CIA by the proposed arrangements will not deter McC from continuing his past practices at will in other fields." The larger question and problem, Cutler thought, was, "How long is the legislative function to continue to be abused and perverted to serve the ends of one senator, determined to gain personal publicity at *any* cost?" Cutler soon thrilled to Eisenhower's response (recorded in press secretary James Hagerty's diary) a few days later: "My boys, I am convinced of one thing. The more we can get McCarthy threatening to investigate our Intelligence, the more public support we are going to get. If there is any way I could trick him into renewing his threat, I would be very happy to do so and then let him have it." Ike summoned Allen Dulles and Senator Knowland to the White House on June 8 to hear that the CIA could not be "constantly subjected" to congressional investigations. The senator predicted overwhelming support on Capitol Hill for the president against McCarthy.[25]

The president and advisers devised two arrangements to substitute for McCarthy's threatened investigation: one, a secretive committee headed by General Jimmy Doolittle, the famed World War II air commander, to examine CIA competence in clandestine work; the other, by retired General Mark Clark's subcommittee of Herbert Hoover's Commission on the Organization of the Executive Branch, would look at the agency's performance in other areas. As Eisenhower reported to Adams later in June, Hoover told the president that "he would probably try in advance to contact Senator McCarthy to secure" his permission that no further effort would be made to investigate the CIA, on the assurance by Hoover "that he and his Commission would do a good job." Such assurance would not have satisfied McCarthy, who hoped that the evidence gathered by Surine would persuade a majority of the Investigations subcommittee's members to approve a full-scale investigation. He soon encountered severe Republican pressure. Alert listeners heard a death knell for McCarthy's proposed inquiry when his subcommittee colleague, Karl Mundt, told reporters on June 26, "I predict our committee will not vote to investigate the CIA." Senator Alex Smith — a Dulles friend who knew something of the CIA's ongoing covert action projects — told the DCI a few weeks later, "I have a definite assurance from Senator McCarthy that ... they have turned over to the Hoover Task Force the problems of the CIA."

Later in the summer, Dulles called Bundy into his office and reported that the second review panel had rejected the loyalty board's findings. Bundy retained his job and reputation and finally gained the "Q" clearance, the pursuit of which had led to the controversy.[26]

A deflated McCarthy turned over "evidence" on the CIA to the Hoover subcommittee later in 1954. By then, McCarthy's days as a national leader were over. When the Senate censured his conduct in September, its two key overseers of the CIA split. Armed Services chair Saltonstall voted "yes." Appropriations chair Bridges remained convinced that McCarthy had been right on the big issue of communist infiltration and voted "no."

After the censure, McCarthy spiraled downward in alcoholism, dying three years later at age forty-eight. In retirement, Eisenhower would write, "Measured against all the mental anguish unfairly inflicted upon people . . . the benefits flowing from the McCarthy 'investigations' do not loom large." Of course, a very few of those accused *had* been communists or sympathizers of the Soviet Union, though McCarthy never uncovered any spies. When William Bundy later looked back on the period, he said of Dulles, "I did not thank him at the time, but made my gratitude and respect amply clear over the years." Brooding in his own post-agency years over growing questions about CIA efficacy during his directorship, Dulles began writing a memoir. Before dropping the project, he would create notes titled "Sketches of My Life and Its Points of Decision," including a list of thirteen events in which he took great pride. Number six on the list read simply, "McCarthy and Bill Bundy."[27]

"You, Who Championed Our Cause"

A bizarre story from early CIA history, still cloaked in secrecy, concerns an outside intelligence-gathering agency that the CIA subsidized and employed in the early 1950s — to the tune of over half a million dollars one year — only to be forced by congressional leaders to continue the subsidy after agency heads judged the group's intelligence reports inadequate. The group — one of a number of organizations that the CIA paid for information in the early Cold War years — never had a formal name, but supporters and critics sometimes referred to it in writing as the Organization. While a few other legislators had close relations with the group, the best-documented ties are those of Styles Bridges, whose McCarthyite conservatism made the president view him as a second-rate leader (as he did many other congressional Republicans). Nonetheless, Bridges's chairmanship of Appropriations and its informal CIA subcommittee and his influence over other Senate conservatives meant that deference had to be paid.[1]

The Organization has rarely been described in print. However, Lyman Kirkpatrick wrote in his memoirs:

> One of my most onerous duties as utility case officer for Mr. Dulles was that of dealing with an organization which had been established in World War II as a competitor to the OSS. General George V. Strong, the G-2 of the United States Army in 1942, hated the OSS (and later the CIA) and vowed that he would not rely upon its intelligence collection system, but established his own in 1942. This resulted in one of the most unusual organizations in the history of the federal government. It was developed completely outside of the normal governmental structure, used all of the normal cover and communications facilities normally operated by intelligence organizations, and yet never was under any control from Washington.

The Organization had a fairly extensive network of intelligence operatives in Europe, Asia, and elsewhere. Many were businesspeople, some fanatically anticommunist. Like many persons used by the CIA around the globe, some were opportunists. Still, the group compiled an intelligence-gathering record that satisfied the army during the war and thereafter through 1947 and then the State Department, which began subsidizing the Organization in early 1948. Along the way, one of the group's leaders, Colonel John D.

"Frenchie" Grombach, testified against the creation of a *Central* Intelligence Agency in 1947. He told congressional leaders, "If we had a thin cord here, would you, any of you gentlemen, like to be thrown out of the window with one string of cord, or prefer to be thrown out of the window with three or four thicknesses of cord?"

Grombach mostly lost the argument, though the CIA was less central in American intelligence affairs than it might have been. Kirkpatrick writes that, during Beetle Smith's tenure, Organization leaders sought to "work with and for CIA." Memoranda by Organization leaders claim that the CIA forced the State Department to hand over its sponsorship of the group. In either event, as of April 1951 the Organization worked for the CIA but was nearly free of its control. As Kirkpatrick writes (and Organization papers confirm in less critical language), "They insisted on giving up their reports with no indication of the place of origin and flatly refused to reveal the sources on the grounds that the CIA was insecure." In 1951/1952, when Kirkpatrick acted as case officer, he changed the method of handling the Organization twice and "found myself constantly attacked by the outsiders for what they thought were CIA errors, and by the insiders for tolerating what they thought was a nonprofessional intelligence organization."[2]

Smith had approved CIA sponsorship of the Organization after an extensive study and recommendation by Allen Dulles and Kirkpatrick, "to see what they could produce of value." This reasoning, voiced by Kirkpatrick, was defensible. Certain army and State Department leaders had been convinced that the Organization's intelligence had merit. Beetle Smith agreed, though the Organization's account (passed on to Bridges) of Smith's enthusiasm for some of its achievements may have been exaggerated: "This Organization obtained the top secret cipher systems of an important [Soviet] satellite for the ridiculously low sum of $30,000 at considerable risks. General Walter Bedell Smith, as Director of CIA at the time, commended the co-director of this Organization and stated that this was one of the two most outstanding secret intelligence accomplishments since World War II."

It was another signals intelligence matter that may have caused the final rupture between CIA and the Organization. The latter group went to Bridges and his Appropriations CIA subcommittee in summer 1953, claiming that "had CIA lived up to its prior agreements and arrangements calling for an initial payment of $50,000 . . . this Organization would have obtained the top secret Soviet diplomatic ciphers which CIA, with over 60 times more money and personnel has never been able to obtain." As one Organization leader wrote separately to Bridges, the CIA's "refusal to speculate $50,000" for the ciphers was "almost unbelievable." The trickiest part of the Organization's argument to Bridges was that they sought the forcible subsidy from an agency that they viewed as having a dangerous monopoly: "Since CIA not only evaluates and disseminates but also collects intelligence, with a monopoly on covert collection, it is vitally important that there be at least one separate, positively insulated, covert collection organization, which in addition to collecting intelligence will provide a safety check on CIA." Kirkpatrick claims that by this time the CIA had decided that, while a few of the Organization's sources occasionally produced useful information, many were "paper mills," i.e, "organizations of refugees or émigrés producing alleged intelligence reports from interrogating other refugees and émigrés or from the 'cocktail circuit.' They were worthless and unreliable and most frequently dedicated to selling a point of view."

The Organization told Bridges, though, that CIA actions during Dulles's first year as DCI led to an inevitable question: "Are there interests still in the Government who do not desire the mistakes of the past to be known, or the infiltrations in this country to be uncovered?" Organization leaders posed this question when Joe McCarthy was riding high, though they denied "trying to hold a pistol" to the CIA's head "in the form of a threat to go to Senator McCarthy." And they claimed to have had other intelligence successes that surpassed those of the CIA, including a penetration into the Presidium of the Soviet government. "Does CIA claim to be able to continue this source or reproduce it," they asked Bridges.

It is tempting to dismiss the Organization's account, given its McCarthyite leanings, and believe Kirkpatrick's memoirs, given his enduring, solid reputation. Still, Organization leaders offered Bridges some critiques of the CIA that hold up well. Among them was the claim that British intelligence had engaged in "activities" that were sufficiently "detrimental to United States interests" as to be considered a "penetration" of the agency. Whether they knew of the Kim Philby case is unclear, although the Organization's closeness to J. Edgar Hoover may have led to such knowledge.

Allen Dulles would not have cared much in 1953 and 1954 that the group thought he had been "taken in . . . by Communists or pro-Communists" if it were not clear that Bridges and a few other powerful legislators might intervene on the Organization's behalf. What if the legislators not only insisted on continued money for the group, but also followed its suggestion of creating a "Joint Senior Committee of Congress"?

The group was willing to accept far less subsidy than it had received at its peak in 1951 or 1952— $650,000— but its leaders continued to refuse to identify its sources and told Bridges that the agency had conducted reckless, illegal investigations of Organization leaders. Such sticking points had led to a previous rupture late in Smith's time as DCI. This, of course, was a time when CIA leaders were becoming aware that their fast-paced expansion of clandestine activities was wasteful and inefficient; a retrenchment was already under way. The Organization had sought and received the intervention of JCAE chair Sterling Cole, who held a hearing. Cole may have been persuaded by Smith and Dulles that the Organization was flawed, but other friends of the group — including former Undersecretary of State Norman Arthur and Ambassador David Bruce — subsequently pressured the new DCI Dulles to restore the Organization's contract. But by the spring of 1953, relations were frayed yet again.

After interactions, including with Bridges's CIA subcommittee hearing, with Organization leaders in late May or early June, the Organization was able to approach the CIA with renewed confidence. One of their leaders told a CIA liaison of a subcommittee meeting with Bridges, Karl Mundt, and Pat McCarran present, "The chairman . . . urgently requested me to advise him promptly if it appeared that termination was to be definite or if it appeared that negotiations for continuance were being unduly deferred." In mid-June, Dulles privately discussed Grombach's complaints with Bridges. The agency and its supposed subsidiary agreed on a new contract on August 16, 1953. The Organization's annual budget would be only 46 percent of the previous year's. As Grombach later wrote, Senator Bridges had "played such an important part in preventing our termination by CIA."[3]

By 1954, though, the senator told the *Washington Daily News* that he was considering a "full-scale inquiry into the secret operations" of the CIA. Some Appropriations colleagues had urged this, based on "complaints" they had heard, including one that the agency did poorly in "cloak and dagger" work. This threat emerged as Dulles again decided not to renew the Organization's contract beyond that year. Perhaps, in part, this was because the Organization's McCarthyite leanings had become more obvious, even as McCarthy's fortunes had peaked. Or maybe it was the details of a dispute over the Chateau Project, another (still obscure) signals intelligence effort carried out by the Organization. The Chateau offerings, whatever their nature, were evaluated by the CIA and British intelligence. At some point in 1954, Dulles told an unidentified member of Congress that the Chateau material was of no value. Organization heads hotly disputed this. Whether the dispute was ever examined by the Appropriations CIA subcommittee remains unknown.

The last letters between Organization leaders and Bridges to be found in the late senator's files are from summer 1954. Grombach and a colleague claimed in June not to want further intervention by the senator but asked that Bridges let them know if there "should be an effort to discredit this organization or its principals . . . so that we may go out assured that you who championed our cause know that our record is clean and clear." But, pathetically, they sought his intervention yet again in early September, asserting "the potential value of this organization, never fully availed of, as a continuing and running check on, and test of, the intelligence produced and disseminated by the CIA monopoly."

Bridges met in his home state of New Hampshire with another of the group's leaders, John Clements, on Sunday, October 9. Whether he planned to resume advocacy on behalf of the group soon would not matter as much. A few weeks later, the Democratic Party would win a majority of seats in the Senate. Come the following January, Bridges would no longer chair Appropriations or its CIA subcommittee. The new chair, Carl Hayden (who "does not talk very much" but "wields a great deal of influence behind the scenes," noted Pforzheimer), would lean toward more senior, less ideological members of Appropriations to fill the CIA subcommittee. Also, the specter of McCarthy had faded. For these and other reasons, undoubtedly including Dulles's determination to rid himself once and for all of what seemed a chronically troublesome group, the Organization died.[4]

By the end of Eisenhower's first two years as president, the CIA had garnered widespread support in Congress and the press. The *Saturday Evening Post* said the CIA's covert operatives were "hitting the Russians where it hurts." Reporters Richard and Gladys Harkness judged that "a helping hand in the rescue of one country such as Guatemala or Iran from communism is worth CIA's annual budget many times over." The Soviet government, they wrote, gave top billing as "villain" to Allen Dulles and his "dirty tricks" department but continued to "single out for attack" the U.S. Congress for passing the Kersten Amendment a few years earlier.

Similarly, the clerk of the Senate Appropriations Committee told Pforzheimer in 1954 that he "had heard no rumblings or criticism of CIA." Though it sometimes bored him, congressional relations were a challenge for Dulles, who made it a high priority. After becoming director, he had agency subordinates provide him with lists of their friends and acquaintances in Congress, so that the CIA could better use its assets there. He also reinstituted Beetle Smith's practice of hosting groups of legislators for breakfast or lunch. Only rarely did he stumble. The *New York Mirror* relished reporting an embarrassing moment the DCI had toward the end of summer 1953 upon encountering a senator who served on McCarthy's subcommittee: "While lunching at a D.C. bistro, he spotted a law-maker and his wife at another table, so he ambled over and after passing a few complimentary remarks, said, 'Well, so long Senator, and it was nice to see you again, Mrs. Moody.' The Senator replied, "Mr. Dulles, I am NOT Senator Moody. I am Senator Potter, and I defeated Senator Moody in the last election." More substantively, Allen Drury of the *Washington Star* described Dulles in a 1954 column for out-of-town newspapers as "a man of notoriously thin skin who is not above trying to get the jobs of newspapermen who criticize his agency."

Dulles ended the year knowing also that there were congressional critics besides Mansfield, McCarthy, and Bridges. One was Representative Fred Busbey (R-IL), who had helped shape the CIA on the Expenditures Committee in 1947 but told an Internal Security subcommittee of the Senate Judiciary Committee in autumn 1954,

> I believe it is time that somebody looks into CIA and cleans up the mess down there. . . . I do not believe the intelligence that we are getting from our so-called listening posts all over the world through CIA will amount to a tinker's damn. The proof of that is this: Show me one instance where the information secured by the CIA has been of assistance, or has done one thing to contain or stop this march of the Marxist communists in their program for world revolution.[5]

Barons Restored

Dwight Eisenhower professed not to be terribly upset when the Democrats regained comfortable control of the House and a narrow hold over the Senate in the November 1954 elections. Of course, neither he nor anyone else could foresee that many of the new committee chairs would hold those jobs through and well beyond the 1950s. Sam Rayburn, taking the House Speakership again, told the once-again minority leader, Joe Martin, "I'm tired of all this shifting around," so the surprised Republican leader happily kept his more-spacious suite of offices.

Of the specific committee changes, it is not hard to see why the president lost little sleep. At Senate Foreign Relations, having the bipartisan Walter George (D-GA) in charge, rather than little respected Alexander Wiley (R-WI) was no great loss. Richard Russell again took control of Armed Services in the Senate, trading places with Leverett Saltonstall. While Russell disliked foreign aid programs, his renewed accession to power was otherwise no great reversal for the White House. By this point in his twenty-three-year-long career in Washington, Russell was, wrote the *New York Times'* William S. White, "incomparably the most influential man on the inner life of the Senate." White thought that Russell, unlike most other leaders, "could actually command the votes of others upon many matters." In 1957, Lyndon Johnson would coach Eisenhower (whom he had urged to invite Russell for a private White House session) on the senator's personality — "He is shy, reticent, sensitive personally."[1]

On the Appropriations Committee of the Senate, Carl Hayden of Arizona replaced the prickly Styles Bridges as chair. At age seventy-seven, Hayden was still crafty, yet beloved among most senators. Politically moderate, he valued the give-and-take of senatorial politics and lacked Bridges's habit of leaking to columnists. "It was part of Hayden's nature to shun publicity" and "work quietly in his office," according to a former Senate staffer. "He shied away from photographers with the truthful comment, 'I look just like Mahatma Gandhi.'"

Administration leaders, including those at the CIA, would soon come to discover that they liked and trusted Hayden. Because of his age, Hayden's energy and effectiveness would begin declining by the late 1950s, but he worked hard, taking care of his wife, who could not walk, in a home near the Capitol and handling Senate business in his office six or seven days a week. Despite his work ethic, Hayden would pay less attention to CIA oversight than any other subcommittee chair of the 1950s.[2]

In the House, a vigorous seventy-one-year-old Carl Vinson of Georgia again took the chair of Armed Services from Dewey Short. Respected and feared, Vinson loved heading the committee. "No twist or turn in the chaotic tale of American military preparation through three wars . . . escaped his monumentally faithful and incredibly perceptive eye," wrote one Washington reporter. White House legislative liaison Bryce Harlow had once worked for Vinson and occasionally heard from him. At one apparently dull White House meeting, Harlow and two other aides communicated messages on the same piece of paper. The liaison wrote, "Vinson called — insists that DDE be told his *and* Russell's viewpoint that Army *not* go below 900,000 — that ships be decommissioned, etc. instead of further Army reductions. I have to be in his office at 11 a.m." One of his associates wrote, "You will undoubtedly have a very interesting meeting," and then drew a picture of an atomic bomb explosion.

The *Times* noted of the "Swamp Fox" — one of Vinson's many nicknames — that he was "a tall, affable man of much force and personality. For Sunday afternoon relaxation, he likes to sit on the front porch of his frame bungalow." Vinson had cooked for his physically handicapped wife, read to her, and attended to her many other needs until her death in 1950. Now he lived, uniquely, with a young aide and his family in suburban Chevy Chase, Maryland. For the childless Vinson, they became his family. When he went back to Georgia, he stayed in a home without a telephone.[3]

At Appropriations, the seventy-five-year-old Clarence Cannon of Missouri regained the chairmanship from John Taber. Cannon was less systematic and more secretive than Taber in dealing with the CIA, whose heads would rarely encounter more than five Appropriations members and would deal with fewer staffers in 1955. Nonetheless, the committee would continue its long tradition of trying to guard the government's treasury against big spenders and retain (in the words of one scholar) its reputation as "hardworking, even by the most craftsmanlike House standards."

Also on the House side, "rollback" enthusiast Charles Kersten, chairman of the Select Committee on Communist Aggression, was defeated for reelection from his Milwaukee district. Dulles had met occasionally with the legislator and his aides (one of whom once explained to the bored DCI that communism really was an "international criminal conspiracy"). A few days after the election, Pforzheimer advised Kirkpatrick, "You may wish to mention to the DCI that Congressman K may wish to see him shortly and may be looking for a job." Kersten ended up working as a "consultant" to the White House on psychological warfare.

The four new Democratic Appropriations and Armed Services chairs would work hard but, like others in Congress's long history, would not easily find enough time to monitor executive branch bureaucracies. Neither Cannon, Vinson, Hayden, nor Russell spoke frequently before the House or Senate, and all eschewed fashionable Washington social circles. They would be targets of careful attention by Allen Dulles for the remainder of the Eisenhower presidency, though, as would their ranking minority colleagues.

So would Democrats George Mahon and Paul Kilday (both Texans), soon to be designated by their House Appropriations and Armed Services chairs, respectively, to monitor many CIA matters. Mahon, especially, became influential in relation to the CIA by mid-decade, heading Appropriation's Subcommittee on Defense, whose most senior leaders (plus Cannon) constituted the subcommittee on the CIA. William S. White judged Mahon "a truly submerged great national figure" in the 1950s and early 1960s, no less significant than a succession of secretaries of defense. His Defense subcommittee dealt with a far bigger slice of the national government's budget than the twelve other Appropriations subcommittees. Mahon drove a decade-old Chevrolet and often took his own lunch to Burning Tree Club on Saturdays for golf with partners that sometimes included Richard Nixon and Dwight Eisenhower. Within the House, Mahon generated esteem and affection. Outside of Washington and his congressional district, he was unknown.[4]

By mid-decade, Dulles increasingly had private encounters with legislators who had traveled abroad. On rare occasions, agency staffers even accompanied the travelers. Legislators who visited the Soviet Union would be briefed and debriefed most carefully by the CIA before and after their travel. Unsurprisingly, in light of how highly his colleagues viewed Richard Russell's intellectual capacities, the CIA showed more than the usual interest in his observations from an eighteen-day-long trip to the Soviet Union in 1955. Upon Russell's return in late October, Dulles asked him to allow the heads of Army and Air Force Intelligence to join in the scheduled debriefing.

The most unusual observation made by Russell and the two aides traveling by train was of a Soviet aircraft's seemingly near-vertical ascent. This was at a time when world public opinion was much impressed by sightings of "flying saucers." The senator had no fear of little green men, but he knew the United States was working with Britain and France on inventing "flying saucer"–type aircraft and that U.S. intelligence had heard stories of such Soviet efforts. This was on top of deep concern among many in the United States over Soviet progress in developing "normal" military aircraft.

Within days of Russell's return, Assistant Director of the Office of Scientific Intelligence Herbert Scoville and an aide interviewed the senator and his assistants about the odd sighting. Russell had been resting in his train compartment, Scoville later reported to Dulles, when "he suddenly noticed a greenish-yellow ball rising rapidly. He rushed into the next compartment stating that he had seen what he thought was a flying saucer. . . . The rest of the party was initially skeptical. However, suddenly a second ball was noticed rising rapidly and then the other members of the party were convinced." Prior to meeting with Russell, Dulles sent word: "After an analysis of all of the reports on the particular incident you described, we are not disposed to conclude that there is evidence that anything radically new in this field has been developed, although we are following up all clues with care." Scoville and aides judged that Russell had probably seen nothing more than "the exhausts of normal jet aircraft in a steep climb."[5]

Enough members of Congress journeyed to the Soviet Union in 1955 that Dulles had subordinates debrief them in their hometowns late that year rather than wait until most returned to Washington. Some legislators served as virtual spies for the agency. Around the time of Russell's meeting with the DCI and other intelligence heads, Deputy Director for Intelligence (DD/I) Robert Amory wrote an analysis for Dulles of reports submitted by "Senator [name deleted]" from his visit to the Soviet Union. "You can compliment him enthusiastically on the material he has gathered and the precision with which he has reported it." Amory singled out the senator's reports of meetings, including "that with [name deleted] as adding materially to our understanding of this very important but barely known member of the Presidium . . . and that with [name deleted] of *Pravda* (this talk adds much to our knowledge as to how the party line is set)."[6]

Leverett Saltonstall also interacted with the CIA about his fall 1955 travels. Before he left, Charles Cabell — acting in Dulles's absence — coordinated Saltonstall's briefing by the agency. A follow-up note from Cabell to Saltonstall said, "We have cabled your date of arrival and have asked our station chief to contact you in each of the following places: Paris, Berlin, London,

Rome, Istanbul, Beirut, Cairo, Madrid and Bonn. In each instance, the station chief has been asked to tell you about our organization and operations and to plan the briefing in accordance with the demands on your time." With George Mahon, who went to Europe later in the 1950s and met assorted CIA officers there, Dulles claimed to be "sure you have some ideas which will be helpful to us all" and arranged to call at the congressman's office for a private talk.

Most legislators' thoughts from traveling abroad were of less interest to the CIA than those of Russell, Saltonstall, or Mahon, but Dulles took care during his long tenure as DCI to meet personally with many of them. Late in 1955, he directed all station chiefs abroad to be systematic about reporting on all briefings of Congress members, including their "reactions . . . and, most particularly, the atmosphere which prevailed and the general attitude" of the legislators. In 1957, apparently the first year when the CIA kept thorough records, the agency debriefed fifty-three just-returned lawmakers, with Dulles handling five of them. John Warner, the new legislative counsel, wrote the next year that few such interviews produced "positive" intelligence — meaning information on other nations' capabilities and intentions — except in those cases where the members of Congress had "traveled to Soviet Russia and Iron Curtain countries." One representative even provided the name of a person (in a country not specified by Warner) to assist the CIA with covert action.[7]

Senator Allen Ellender (D-LA) made himself valuable to the CIA by touring the USSR in 1955 and 1956, even spending a couple of hours with Nikita Khrushchev in the latter visit. Dulles joined fourteen others from the CIA, the State Department, and the armed services in January 1957 to debrief the senator for three hours. "The youth of Russia, particularly as a result of education, are beginning to question the policies and actions of the leadership," a CIA note-taker reported Ellender saying. A few days later, Dulles, Robert Amory, and six agency analysts spent two memorable hours with Representative Jamie Whitten (D-MS), a future Appropriations chair. He had spent thirty-eight days in Eastern Europe and the USSR, just before the 1956 Hungarian uprising. Whitten was struck more by the "very real and significant Russian weaknesses" and castigated the CIA for "the lack of a balanced intelligence picture" of the USSR in most congressional testimony. "This fear of the Russians reflected itself so effectively in the preceding Congress that the last budget resulted in the unique spectacle of granting the Secretary of Defense considerably more money than he even asked for," Whitten said.

It was more than just politic for Dulles to pay attention to returning members of Congress: American intelligence knew far too little about the Soviet public, government, and military, especially. Dulles admitted this periodically at the White House, in congressional testimony, and even in public speeches. Therefore, the CIA debriefed innumerable other world travelers, too — business persons, tourists, academics, etc. Among those in 1955 was Supreme Court Justice William O. Douglas, whose Soviet trip roughly overlapped with that of Russell's. He, too, was all eyes during a layover at Semipalatinsk airbase. A CIA summary of Douglas's report to them, later passed on by Dulles at a NSC meeting, noted, "Numerous jet medium bombers seen at airfield." Also, "Train loads of Chinese going west seen at Petropavlovsk." The point emphasized most strongly by Douglas was that visits by "Asian and Near East peoples" were having a "great effect on these visitors." The justice predicted, "Given ten years of peace, Asia will be lost to the USSR." Told of this prophecy decades later, a former member of the clandestine services laughed and recalled that, upon hearing of such warnings, "you were ready to mount up the horses and charge."[8]

"Dodging Dead Cats"

In the mid-1950s, Eisenhower preferred the CIA subcommittees and even that occasional thorn in his side, the Joint Committee on Atomic Energy, over having a large, generously staffed joint intelligence committee oversee the agency. Allen Dulles usually agreed. The director already spent plenty of time dealing with Capitol Hill, most of it on individual contacts — in person, by telephone, or in crafting just the right language for a letter. The subject matter varied, from the crucial to the picayune. Of the latter, inquiries from legislators about disgruntled former CIA employees were a chronic irritant for Dulles. They were also, a CIA officer told others, inevitable: "An employee leaves; he retains legal residence in the state; he has a congressional representative; the congressional representative has to depend on his constituents to return to Congress. The ex-employee gets in touch with his congressman, and — zowie! — the letter comes. 'John Jones is unhappy, and claims A, B, C, D, and E; and I would appreciate your advice, Mr. Dulles, as to what brought this situation about.' "[1]

One of a multitude of cases that took Dulles's time arose when CIA regulations endangered true love. Agency employee Juan J. Ryan, originally from New Jersey, married an Irish immigrant, not waiting for the CIA to investigate her background, and was fired for it. Representative Hugh Addonizio (D-NJ) promptly and loudly called for a congressional investigation. Speculation arose in the press that the agency was somehow anti-Irish. Soon, Carl Vinson summoned CIA officials for an explanation, at which point Ryan regained his job.

Though there might not have been more than ten to fifteen hearings in a comparatively quiet year like 1955, they took more of Dulles's time than most understood. A Dulles aide told fellow officers that such appearances were "like an iceberg. The DCI might appear before a Senate Appropriations Committee for two hours, and you would think that was a long session in itself, but the major portion of the iceberg is below the surface; the man may have to take six, eight, or ten hours to be properly briefed in order to give a two hour presentation and answer questions from the committee table."[2]

Though licking his wounds after almost two years of threats from Joe McCarthy, Dulles had briefly developed some appreciation in late 1954 for

Mike Mansfield's joint intelligence concept. With Dulles's knowledge, Inspector General Lyman Kirkpatrick and George Carey, the assistant director for operations, consulted around the agency about how to "best phrase a recommendation . . . which would provide us with a congressional committee." When Walter Pforzheimer challenged Carey on such thinking, the assistant director predicted that, while existing arrangements had worked well enough in the past (a "Saltonstall, if properly briefed, could intercede for us"), the agency "could not always count on having a friend at court" in the future.

Within months, though, Dulles turned away from the joint committee idea. The president would tell Nelson Rockefeller in May 1955 that "one of the leaders of Congress came to him with some scheme whereby Congress could be assured of what CIA was doing." Ike said he "would have no part of it." The DCI, in moving toward advocacy of such a committee earlier in 1954, would have informed the president at some point. Such a conversation would have halted Dulles's support.

For this and possibly other reasons, Dulles soon pronounced himself fully satisfied with existing oversight. In notes prepared for an off-the-record speech in late January 1955 to American Legion leaders, Dulles wrote, "Our relations with Congress are constantly misunderstood. . . . Our budget is carefully scrutinized by Appropriations. . . . As far as 'watchdog' is concerned, we prefer subcommittees of Armed Services. A permanent committee has two major disadvantages: it would be overlooking the policymaking of the Executive; a permanent staff would present security problems."[3]

The latter two points were often voiced by Eisenhower and Richard Russell, to Mansfield's skepticism. The Montanan, something of a Senate insider by his third year in office, offered a new resolution in mid-January 1955. He had thirty-two cosponsors. At first, the White House seemed to take little notice. On January 19, Dulles wrote Sherman Adams, "Mike Mansfield has stirred up considerable impetus back of his resolution, and it seems important that I should know the President's attitude — at least for my confidential guidance." Bryce Harlow, who handled legislative liaison for Eisenhower, noted to a colleague, "In the past, this type of effort has been vigorously opposed by the Administration; I don't know whether or not it is still an issue." But after Mansfield announced new cosponsors for the resolution on February 5, Harlow warned his coworker that the senator's effort was "a powerful move."

To Russell, the joint committee idea seemed absurd and dangerous. To counter it, the Armed Services chair moved toward slightly more openness on February 3. The *New York Times* reported:

Senator Richard B. Russell said today that a Senate group had been keeping a close check for years upon operations and activities of the supersecret Central Intelligence Agency. The Georgia Democrat . . . named a three-man subcommittee to, as he phrased it, "continue the work." The members are Mr. Russell, himself, and Senators Leverett Saltonstall, Republican of Massachusetts, and Harry F. Byrd, Democrat of Virginia.

Mr. Russell's statement that there had been a continuing check on the CIA came as a surprise. Numerous members of Congress had complained they were kept completely in the dark about CIA activities.

One committee staffer, Bill Darden, would assist the subcommittee, as in previous years. On March 4, some members of the group — expanded to include Styles Bridges and Lyndon Johnson — met at CIA headquarters with Dulles and others. There they discussed the CIA's "organizational structure" and "security, personnel, and fiscal practices." Another meeting was planned some weeks later to "go into greater detail [over] . . . intelligence production, and to discuss some operational problems in various parts of the world."[4]

Roughly overlapping the shift of power to Democrats in Congress in late 1954 to early 1955 was the issuance of reports on the CIA by the previously noted Doolittle Committee and the Clark Task Force of the Hoover Commission. For Jimmy Doolittle, the president had delineated his responsibilities and those of Clark's group: "You will deal with the covert activities of the CIA . . . and your report will be submitted to me. General Clark's Task Force will deal largely with the organization and methods of operation of CIA and other related agencies. . . . Reports of the Hoover Commission are made to the Congress." They would go to Eisenhower as well, with a censored version to be publicly released. The group headed by Mark Clark would examine topics that impinged on covert action, including the entire CIA budget and the Plans Directorate's activities other than the specifics of its covert operations.

Eisenhower directed Dulles to make "facilities" and "access to any and all information relating to covert activities" available to Doolittle's group. The White House did not even disclose the existence of the committee, which was first reported by the *Times* in October 1954. Doolittle was famous for his exploits as a World War II general. He and three colleagues did their work, which involved extensive international travel, in the summer and fall. Having been outed by the *Times*, the group created — under White House supervision — a statement of its findings about the CIA for the public in late

October: "In spite of the limitations imposed by its relatively short life and rapid expansion, it is doing a creditable job." Unspecified "areas" and "operations" could be improved, though.[5]

To Eisenhower, the committee unabashedly advocated that the United States surpass Soviet covert action capabilities but warned that his Operations Coordinating Board (OCB) was not "giving the Agency adequate guidance and advice on the more important covert projects." Allen Dulles, they said, had "unique knowledge" and "his whole heart" in the CIA's work. But (according to notes of a White House meeting) Dulles's "weakness, or the weakness of the CIA is in the organization — it grew like topsy, sloppy organization. Mr. Dulles surrounds himself with people in whom he has loyalty but not competence. There is a lack of security consciousness throughout organization. Too much information is leaked at cocktail parties." The DCI was too emotional, Doolittle and his colleagues added, especially in defending his staff from the committee's criticisms.

Neither Frank Wisner, Charles Cabell, nor Richard Bissell came off well in the report, which bothered the president. Certainly, Eisenhower was not an uncritical consumer of intelligence during tense Cold War events. On March 11, 1955, for example, as the president wrestled with the perennial problem of how to protect Taiwan, he would complain bitterly to the Dulles brothers and Goodpaster about "conflicting intelligence information coming to him." Still, to the Doolittle group, he defended Dulles: "The President said he had never seen him show the slightest disturbance. . . . We must remember that here is one of the most peculiar types of operation any government can have, and that it probably takes a strange kind of genius to run it." The committee also met the DCI himself, who was required by Eisenhower to report on reforms made at the agency in relation to the Doolittle Report (and, subsequently, the Clark Report).[6]

Some histories have unfairly treated the congressionally mandated Clark Task Force investigation as a sham. Actually, the investigation was unpleasant for many at CIA. Two full-time Clark assistants spent days aggressively roaming around agency buildings. One of them brusquely informed CIA leaders that the investigation began with a working assumption that their agency was "not performing the functions for which it was created, but it is actually devoting most of its efforts to the performance of covert functions" for the State Department. It seemed to one CIA leader that the investigator "wanted to put everyone on the defensive, and his manner was so critical that some embarrassment could not be avoided." The Geographic Area, one of many agency bureaucracies that geared up to deal with the Clark Task Force, spent over sixteen hundred man-hours doing so.

In spring 1955, the Clark group gave the agency and its director a modestly favorable review. Dulles was "industrious, objective, and selfless," but, "in his enthusiasm, he has taken upon himself too many burdensome duties and responsibilities on the operational side of CIA's activities." The Clark Task Force recommended creation of a small, permanent bipartisan committee composed of respected lawmakers and "public-spirited citizens" to oversee the CIA. The group found no illegalities committed by the agency but thought the suggested committee would limit the "possibility of the growth of license and abuses of power." The larger Hoover Commission agreed on the need for more intelligence oversight, but with Styles Bridges as a member, instead endorsed Mansfield's concept of a congressional committee.

Also, the Clark Task Force was "greatly concerned over lack of adequate intelligence data from behind the Iron Curtain," something all three DCIs in the agency's history had admitted on Capitol Hill. General Clark and his colleagues rejected Joseph McCarthy's allegations, so prominent in 1953 and 1954 but old news by 1955, that CIA and other intelligence agencies were seriously infiltrated by communists. McCarthy, himself, had turned such "evidence" over to Clark in January, much to the concern of agency leaders who thought the retired general treated McCarthy too credibly. In June, Eisenhower told legislators and subordinates, "It's no longer McCarthyism, it's McCarthywasm." (Over a year later, though, Dulles worried to Senator Russell that McCarthy had turned over more documents to the Internal Security Committee headed by Senator James Eastland [D-MS]. Russell told the DCI to forget about it.)[7]

When the time came for its report to go to Congress, the Government Operations Committee wanted to receive it on behalf of the Senate. Richard Russell told a concerned Armed Services aide, "Let it go."

The most revealing, unpublicized reaction at the CIA to the Doolittle and Clark investigations, following McCarthy's commotions and amid Mansfield's efforts, came from Wisner, who had handled covert operations since the Truman presidency. Wisner had held Hillenkoetter in contempt and then suffered under Beetle Smith's severity. Though Allen Dulles shared his enthusiasm for covert action, Wisner had an uneasy relationship as well with this DCI, who seemed too much of a publicity hound.

For Wisner, fighting the secret battles of the early Cold War era was a distinctly moral enterprise, despite the tactics employed. Addressing his fellow assistant directors and Dulles on July 18, 1955, he pugnaciously summarized an assessment he had given senior staffers in the Plans Directorate. Notes of the talk provide a unique inside-the-agency view of the national press and Washington's political arena:

> The Clark Committee findings . . . are by no means as adverse and derogatory as some newspaper reporters and columnists would lead one to believe. . . . Some writers who are apparently unfriendly to the Agency have seized upon portions of the published material and have enlarged upon it, quoted passages out of context, and otherwise managed to create the impression that the Agency was found egregiously wanting. . . . Twice within a very short space of time the Clandestine Services have been thoroughly investigated and in each case — although the approach and motivation were different — we have come off clean and whole. . . . All enemies of the Agency and people with special axes to grind were given full opportunity by the Clark Committee to be heard, with the result that just about every "dead cat" that could be thrown was, in fact, cut loose at us — but without appreciable adverse effect. . . . Under the circumstances, the personnel of this Agency are entitled to feel very reassured and, in fact, proud to belong to an organization which has so successfully withstood the acid test of these unprecedented investigations. . . . The time has now arrived when this Agency can and should go over onto the attack against its irresponsible critics. This is, of course, a matter which must be handled with the greatest of care. . . . We should let it be understood that the "open season" on CIA is closed, and that it is no longer a fashionable or profitable pursuit to sling mud at our people.

Not everyone at the CIA shared Wisner's siege mentality in 1955, but his memo contradicts later published descriptions of a supposed Golden Era when CIA heads were not bothered by outsiders asking questions. Wisner's prescription for attacking the agency's "enemies" and "critics" seems not to have troubled Dulles or Richard Helms, who had the analysis widely distributed at the CIA.[8]

"They Have to Have a Building"

In Fiscal Year 1955, the Central Intelligence Agency functioned with a $335 million budget, the same as in 1954, when substantial moneys went unspent for the second year in a row. The agency had far less money than suspected by some observers, who spoke or wrote of half-billion-dollar budgets. The number of agency personnel had also shrunk, at least somewhat, since the Korean War. At the beginning of Fiscal Year 1955, according to the Doolittle Report, "approximately 20,000" individuals were engaged in agency activities. In addition to American CIA officers and other personnel, this included foreigners who worked full- or part-time in espionage or other roles. Full-time staff members numbered 13,306, as of June 30 of that year.[1]

In May 1955, investigators for the Clark Task Force judged that the agency was "able to obtain from Congress the approximate funds" needed. This was true, usually. At an otherwise unrecorded March House Appropriations hearing, for example, members "were very critical of the publicity in connection with our proposed headquarters building," noted a Dulles aide, but he predicted "that we would have no trouble getting approval" of the CIA's proposed Fiscal Year 1956 budget. Nor did the CIA have a difficult time on the Senate side that year. Many of Carl Hayden's CIA subcommittee members had interacted with Dulles at two or more hearings held in the spring by Armed Services subcommittees (one handling the CIA's request for a new headquarters building), so they approved the CIA budget in June without summoning Dulles to a hearing. Leverett Saltonstall telephoned Dulles, though, to suggest that he call Senator Henry Dworshak (R-ID), an Appropriations member who "might cause us some trouble." (Dulles would soon appear before a Senate Appropriations subcommittee.)[2]

Still, agency leaders felt somewhat encumbered on personnel matters. A recurring theme in surviving 1955 agency records, and in years just before and after, is their struggles to hire as many persons as they wished — this, at a time when the agency's business hummed along. One agency bureaucrat wrote late that year about the Cable Secretariat, "During FY 1955, 13% more cables were processed than during FY 1954. Each month, January through August 1955, has seen a new high established in the number of cables processed."

The phrase "Taber limitation," referring to the former House Appropriations chair, was rarely spoken in 1955, but the problem remained. It could not be solved by using the substantial funds in the DCI's unvouchered account; CIA still lived under the ruling from the Comptroller General that unvouchered funds had to be used only for unforeseen intelligence emergencies or projects. Such realities do not support the belief that later arose, that — to quote an unnamed source in the Final Report of the Church Committee — the CIA's budget "got a free ride" in the 1950s from a Congress that "rarely" required DCIs even to testify.[3]

The periodic tendency of legislators to question the agency's personnel levels affected its efforts to obtain funding for a new headquarters building in Langley, Virginia. Obtaining a new headquarters had been on the minds of DCIs since the days of Roscoe Hillenkoetter. As noted earlier, Beetle Smith secured authorizing legislation but failed to shepherd appropriations legislation through Congress in 1951. He failed in another attempt in 1952. In 1953, House Appropriation's chief clerk, Kenneth Sprankle, rejected agency leaders' quiet request for an endorsement by Chairman Taber or the full committee of the headquarters concept.

Allen Dulles got serious about trying again in 1955, appearing in June and July before subcommittees of the Senate's Armed Services and Appropriations Committees and the House Appropriations Committee to argue his request. His and others' testimony fills hundreds of still partly classified transcript pages. Dulles faced pointed questioning from Senator John Stennis (D-MS) and Representative Errett Scrivner (R-KS), according to CIA notes, about "the need for the present strength levels, and Mr. Scrivner expressed the hope that a cut of between 25% and 40% might be possible when CIA's headquarters personnel are efficiently brought together in a single building." Scrivner told Dulles he hoped the building would "enable you to do much more work so much better, with so many fewer people that the sheer savings of people alone . . . would pay for itself — [in] just a matter of years." This fanciful idea, which Dulles had promoted in prior years, would dog him for the rest of Eisenhower's presidency.[4] Former Deputy Director for Support (DD/S) Lawrence K. "Red" White recalls that Chairman Vinson of the House Armed Services Committee almost unquestionably supported a new building. In a hearing, "he said to Allen Dulles — he called him 'Doctor' — 'Doctor, you are here to ask us for a new building, and I think you ought to have a new building. . . . You probably are going to ask us for about $25 million.' Allen said, 'Mr. Chairman, we're going to ask you for $50 million.' Vinson replied, 'My, my, that is going to be a nice building.' "

Despite such memories, Congress did not resolve the issue in 1955. Indeed, at a June 17 hearing of the full Senate Armed Services Committee, the hearing transcript shows, those members who were not on the CIA subcommittee were shocked to learn of the nearly 14,000 employees who worked in agency offices in Washington. "The number is fantastic," said Margaret Chase Smith. "I believe those fellows are getting in each other's way," Ralph Flanders (R-VT) mused. Flanders's homely advice was to "follow the policy which Mrs. Flanders follows in buying my clothes. She does not buy them. She goes with me. She always insists that the waist measure be tight. That controls my diet. Perhaps we can make the waist measure tight for this CIA building."

Russell and Saltonstall disliked discussing CIA matters in so large a setting. Saltonstall stumbled through an explanation that the CIA "coordinates and draws up and works out all the information coming from all the departments every day and that requires a great number of people." Russell observed, "They have to have a building. The number of employees and the size of the building is unrelated to that." Even Smith agreed that it was "disgraceful that they should be in 34 locations." Chairman Russell won unanimous agreement that there should be one building, but John Stennis, who chaired Armed Services' Real Estate and Military Construction subcommittee, was otherwise stubborn: while Dulles had been "impressive" in making the case for a new building, whether CIA needed one so expensive was questionable.[5]

Ultimately, the agency received authorization to proceed with construction, but legislators appropriated only $5.5 million in 1955 for planning purposes. (As executive branch leaders know from painful experience, congressional *authorization* is generally a prerequisite to, but does not guarantee, that *Appropriations* committees and the Congress, itself, will actually grant the money.) The CIA would have to return to Capitol Hill the following year. Meanwhile, construction costs were rising. Meeting in September 1955, Pforzheimer and Red White hoped to obtain the funding from legislators early in 1956. Otherwise, "the boys will really have their knives out."

As late as mid-January, though, Dulles hesitated to initiate the legislative attempt, possibly because of a little sideshow in the Senate — someone on the Foreign Relations Committee spread the rumor that the Dulles family would profit from the sale of land for the new headquarters. To squelch the rumored "family CIA matter," Alex Smith volunteered to pose questions privately to Secretary of State Dulles. On January 26, 1956, he received a long-winded "no" as a response to the rumor. Smith conveyed the answer to Walter George, chair of Foreign Relations (and no doubt to others), disposing of "the strange tale one of our colleagues told us."[6]

Meanwhile, Dulles talked quietly to reporters about his agency's inadequate offices. The *Washington Star* reported in February 1956, "Headquarters of the Agency is a group of aged brick buildings at 2430 E Street, N.W. Its location is no secret. Any cab driver can take you there." After the CIA approached Congress, it suffered the embarrassment of John Stennis going to the Senate floor to publicize and oppose the latest request of money. The previous year's figure of $46 million had "seemed a little high," he said, and the number of agency employees was "shocking," but he had gone along with it. "I am further shocked and somewhat chagrined to learn that the CIA is asking for an additional $10 million. . . . The only justification given for this item is that building costs have gone up 5.72 percent within the past 12 months. However, the increase in the request for appropriations is 21.7 percent."

The House remained mostly on Dulles's side in his long struggle for the appropriation. Clarence Cannon wrote the DCI, "I have not always been impressed by the efficiency of the Central Intelligence Agency," but allowed that "if you have to have the new building, the sooner it is available, the better." George Mahon had told Dulles in 1955 he hoped the building would be a "down-to-earth, minimum-type building, and not a show place" but was otherwise supportive.[7]

The Senate's inclination toward a "tight waist" provoked some turmoil at the CIA over congressional relations. Martin Claussen, an assistant to Dulles, warned a colleague in the spring that the agency had done poor planning for congressional presentations on the issue. The latest set of briefing materials was "far from adequate, if it is intended for the critical (and sympathetic) eyes of Congressmen and congressional committee staffs."

This must have been the reaction of Stennis and Senate colleagues, including Richard Russell, for they approved only $46 million ($4 million less than the House had recently appropriated), with language requiring, as CIA leaders had feared, "that the Agency shall plan to house all headquarters personnel" in the new building. That was "a practical impossibility," Dulles warned Carl Hayden. "According to present cost estimates prepared by the Public Buildings Service, we cannot accommodate all of our personnel in a modern $46,000,000 building, no matter how austere," he wrote. He could live with a $46 million headquarters (though he again suggested more), but the stipulation about all personnel "would force me either to abandon the building or to reduce our personnel strength to a point where we could no longer carry out essential functions."

Ultimately, Dulles received somewhat less money than he wished, but a conference committee agreed to live with the CIA's vague pledge to make "every effort" to accommodate its personnel in the new building. Construction began and would take up the remainder of Dulles's service in the Eisenhower presidency and beyond. (Early in 1957, Dulles would actually approach Russell, Vinson, and others about possibly obtaining $10 million more for the project. Vinson would support the idea; Russell and others, including Senator Harry Byrd, would openly doubt in the DCI's presence that the CIA needed so many personnel and would refuse to support the proposal. The DCI would also become enthusiastic in 1959 about constructing a director's home on the Langley property but would find little support from his own subordinates or among leaders in Congress.)

In terms of drama, CIA-congressional interactions from 1951 to 1956 over a new headquarters hardly rival many other better-known intelligence stories. Nonetheless, in contrast to published accounts implying that Dulles easily worked his magic "over highballs with the men who mattered" in Congress, his headquarters victory was incomplete and had come only after difficult planning, lobbying, and testifying.[8]

As to broader budgetary questions dealt with by Congress, the 1955 to 1957 period was an expansive one for the CIA, with considerable covert operations and technical innovations, including the U-2 spy aircraft. CIA budgets for Fiscal Year 1956 and 1957 have neither been declassified nor discovered in archives, but some facts can be constructed. By 1955, with the CIA budget at $335 million, it had devoted 67 percent of its dollars since 1947 to the Plans Directorate and its covert action predecessors; 12.1 percent had gone to the Intelligence Directorate, and 20.9 percent had gone to the Science Directorate.

Remarkably, documents mentioning preparations for the Fiscal Year 1956 agency budget refer not only to continuing personnel "ceiling problems," but also planned *reductions* from the CIA's 1955 budget. Through a subordinate, Dulles informed agency leaders, "The amount of new obligational authority as proposed in the 1955 budget or as enacted by the Congress will be reduced in 1956, so that the levels of Government employment and operations will be lower in 1956 than 1955."

Minutes of the Geographic Area staff meeting of August 8, 1955, refer to a CIA leader informing "the group that there will be a budget cut in the 1956 operating budget, which affects the Geographic Area, as well as the rest of the Agency." There followed discussion of various possible cuts, limits on overtime, etc. Responding that week to the same news and noting that cuts would apply to "the 1956 Operating Budget and the 1957 Estimates," Intelligence

Directorate head Robert Amory informed Allen Dulles, "I am resubmitting a revised request representing a total reduction [words censored] positions. I believe the new figure represents the minimum that we should plan on for the DD/I area, considering the many new and expanded requirements which have been placed upon the offices."

Amory clearly hated the budget cut news. In November, a new indignity arose, which he promptly shared with his assistants: "As a result of inquiries from the Congress, the DCI has directed that a survey of manpower utilization be made with the Agency. The Inspector General has been appointed Chairman of a Special Committee to conduct the survey and submit recommendations to the DCI by December 10." The survey was important to higher-ups, Amory told his subordinates. He did not tell them that more than an "inquiry" was at hand; a congressional committee had already suggested the 10 percent personnel reduction.

Inspector General Kirkpatrick's committee soon required Amory to describe how DD/I would function following such a reduction. It would require a reorganization, he replied, one that would cause "disruption of efforts, the loss of key personnel . . . and other confusions." Indeed, "for the DD/I area as a whole to perform at maximum efficiency, a total *increase* in manpower [words censored] is required," for example, "to improve coverage of foreign guided missiles, nuclear energy, and basic science programs." The missiles topic would inflame CIA-congressional relations within two years. Similarly, Amory told Dulles that the proposal "would leave the Agency open to the charge of having been very short-sighted if, following Russian incursions into Eastern Europe, we were suddenly called upon to provide information on the industrial plants which had fallen into Russian hands."

Conceivably, such resistance provided Dulles with the necessary support to avoid significant reductions. A declassified in-house history says, "The funds requested were the same as those appropriated for the two preceding fiscal years, except for a [number censored] reduction in the contingency fund. CIA's budget was now on a plateau of Cold War operations." Specifically, funds available for covert action remained "the same as for the two preceding years, but with the reduction of the reserve fund."[9]

Such budgetary limitations were rooted in larger trends in national government — the president viewed a balanced budget as a matter of national security. Legislators who dealt with appropriations were similarly minded. "The United States Treasury is as important a part of national defense as the armed services," said Clarence Cannon. Yet, they — like Eisenhower — wanted the CIA to learn the capabilities and plans of the Soviet Union, China, and other worrisome countries, carry out appropriate covert actions, and counter other nations' intelligence efforts aimed at the United States.

Predictably, in such an era, tensions arose between the legislative and executive branches over how to do all of the above while also supporting a strong military. In early 1957, for example, Cannon's Appropriations Committee voted out a defense appropriations bill that was $300 million less than that requested by Eisenhower. If Cannon had had his way, the cuts would have been greater. Citing "a recent United States intelligence estimate," Cannon said that, in the unlikely event of a United States–Soviet war, it would be a large nuclear one, initiated by Soviet bombers based above the Arctic Circle. "When they come over that Pole, what can the Army do? What can the Navy do?" America's fate in such a war would be determined by the performance of the air force. The House and Senate eventually gave the Pentagon more than the Cannon committee wished, though.[10]

Fiscal Year 1957's budget, crafted in 1956, continued one trend: the proportion of CIA employees involved in "Cold War activities" had dropped from one-third to one-fourth across three years, while the proportion doing "intelligence activities" grew from two-thirds to three-fourths. Similarly, from Fiscal Year 1953 to Fiscal Year 1957, "the principal increase in intelligence activities was for covert intelligence collection, and the principal decrease in Cold War activities was paramilitary activities." In another respect, Fiscal Year 1957 was different — the agency won a significantly increased budget, despite Dulles's worry (professed at the White House in April) that Congress would "cut the CIA budget to bits and that this would have a serious effect on our anti-subversion programs in weak nations." Other U.S. intelligence agencies increased their spending, too — Robert Macy of the Bureau of the Budget reported to a colleague that "costs of foreign intelligence activities, excluding most communications support, are estimated . . . about 20% higher than Fiscal Year 1956." The increased spending benefited "the military departments, the National Security Agency, the Central Intelligence Agency, the Department of State," and others. It resulted "in large part from a growing investment in the technical means of intelligence collection, with no comparable reduction in the more traditional methods of collection. . . . Foreign intelligence costs may be expected to increase another 15 to 20% in FY 1958 over 1957."

At about the same time, an NSC staffer summarized the costs of "foreign, positive, strategic intelligence activities," which were poorly defined and left out much of what the CIA did. Nonetheless, they show enlightening trends, especially for the National Security Agency, whose budget rose from $370 million in Fiscal Year 1956 to $450 million in Fiscal Year 1957. The cost of the CIA's "positive, strategic" activities (i.e., examining the plans and capabilities of other countries) went from $150 million to $157 million.

As President Eisenhower and top intelligence advisers agreed in an early 1957 Oval Office meeting, there were "large budgetary problems involved" in running an extensive intelligence establishment. Secretary of Defense Charles Wilson expressed bafflement about how "to get better information without spending more money." Secretary of the Treasury Humphrey "said that he was numb at the rate at which expenditures were increasing in the field" and warned Dulles that progress in making intelligence agencies' efforts better coordinated and more efficient "had better be quick, or Congress would take over with a committee similar to the Joint Atomic Energy Committee."

The discussion was revealing, as well, about Eisenhower's preference not to know too much about covert operations. While some advisers thought such operations needed better management from the top, Eisenhower questioned any change that would result in "adding more people who would know about such programs." The president also said that "there were some things which came up in the . . . field which it was better that the President and the Secretaries should not know about, so that they could be in a position to disavow them, if necessary." Eisenhower allowed that "he or some other responsible official should know about the idea, but nothing else concerning the details of the program."[11]

As for Congress, the obvious fact is that leaders of subcommittees on the CIA — Cannon, Mahon, Russell, and others — knew and approved the details of the higher CIA budget for 1957, with only some complaints. In the Congress at large, though, some suspected or knew something of the trend and protested. Representative Robert Sikes (D-FL), a fairly senior member of Mahon's subcommittee on Defense, complained publicly that the CIA spent "hundreds of millions of dollars a year. . . . I question seriously that it is earning its keep." His colleague Eugene McCarthy (D-MN) agreed: "The average member of Congress knows no more about the CIA than what he reads in the papers. We don't know how much the group spends or what it produces, and that disturbs many of us."[12]

The New Mansfield Resolution:
Two Surprises

Senator Mansfield's campaign to create a joint committee on intelligence took two unexpected turns by early 1956. The first was its sheer momentum. In January, referring to sentiment on Armed Services toward Mansfield's resolution, Richard Russell informed Carl Hayden, "Nearly all of our Committee are co-authors of the bill." Even Allen Dulles's Senate friend, Alex Smith, had at one point in 1955 sponsored a bill to create an oversight committee (though he would later scrawl on a memo about that bill, "Why did I introduce this?"). More significantly, Styles Bridges, the top Republican on Appropriations, continued to support the concept. News reporters predicted in December 1955 and beyond that not only the Rules Committee, then considering the resolution, but the full Senate would vote "yes." Nonetheless, the White House was late and disorganized in mobilizing to defeat the resolution. The second surprise would not emerge until senators debated the resolution in April.

Mike Mansfield was no back-slapper, but he was smart and trusted by most senators. The roguish George Smathers later described him as "the most saintly guy I know." Mansfield had "little vanity and great stoicism," observed a longtime Senate staffer. As the Montanan's stature grew in the Senate, so the prospects for his resolution improved. Throughout 1955, in writing and in person, the junior member of the Rules Committee had urged colleagues to consider if existing oversight practices might be a "hodgepodge system." Mansfield shared Richard Russell's fundamental belief, though, in the Senate's norms of courtesy and shrewdly kept him informed of his plans for the resolution.[1]

The CIA had been alert to Mansfield's lobbying in 1955 and to reports that he had over a third of the Senate as cosponsors. Dulles wrote Eisenhower in November, "I have had many discussions on this subject with Senator Russell and Senator Saltonstall." Like them, "I would prefer the status quo." Instead of a joint committee, Dulles had "gathered that you favor the designation of a high-level committee of civilians — a kind of Board of Visitors — to meet with the CIA at intervals of their choosing."

For public consumption, the DCI only mildly questioned the wisdom of Mansfield's proposal, but he was — according to *New York Times* reporters — already preparing that year for a "vigorous behind-the-scenes fight" in 1956. But he would fail, the *Times* predicted. The newspaper's editorials favored the resolution, as did the *Washington Post* and the *Wall Street Journal.* So did many less prominent newspapers, from the *Washington Daily News* to the *Milwaukee Journal,* the *San Francisco Examiner,* and the *Butte* (Montana) *Standard.* News articles in the *Times* were hardly objective on the subject — Hanson Baldwin and Allen Drury openly sided with Mansfield.

Late in 1955, Drury dismissed the work of the Senate and House Armed Services subcommittees on the CIA, claiming that they were "always driven off with the cry of 'secret work' when they attempt to delve too deeply into CIA activities." Former reporter Stanley Grogan, who had served high-ranking army officials as a press liaison in World War II, now worked as Dulles's aide. Occasionally setting up off-the-record encounters between his boss and leading journalists, Grogan collected the Drury article as part of his role of monitoring articles published nationwide about the CIA. Dulles had complained previously to Drury about an earlier story; the reporter half apologized but added that his information "came from sources on the Hill and from within your organization." As the time drew near for Senate action, Grogan prepared a lengthy, critical study of Drury's and Hanson Baldwin's writings on the CIA since 1947. Baldwin, he wrote, had "seriously breached the security of the Agency"; Drury had become "biased" after joining the *Times.*[2]

On January 11, 1956, Theodore Francis Green (D-RI), chair of the Rules Committee, sought Hayden's and Russell's comments on the resolution, prior to a hearing scheduled for two weeks later. Since Appropriations chair Hayden was also a Rules member, the Committee published his views. Sometimes, though, the defenders of existing arrangements were their worst enemies. Hayden admitted that his Appropriations subcommittee was not especially assertive, because of the "active interest" of the Armed Services subcommittee, which had "continuously" maintained "supervision over the operations of that Agency to an entirely adequate degree." (Inaccurately, he claimed that House Appropriations had been as inactive as his own.) It hardly mattered that Hayden wrote, "No information has been denied, and all desired information has been candidly supplied," when he added, "Committee members have, from time to time, refused proffered information because such information has no relation to the normal legislative procedures of Congress."

Russell wrote to Green, knowing that seven members of his own Armed Services Committee cosponsored the Mansfield Resolution. They were "colleagues whose opinions I hold in high regard." However, the CIA had demonstrated a willingness to keep the four relevant congressional subcommittees "fully informed" on agency activities. Russell noted correctly that the proposed joint committee would be composed of those who previously had sat on the four CIA subcommittees. "It appears," he noted, "that the only new persons to be immediately responsible for the activities of the CIA would be staff of the proposed Joint Committee. . . . It is difficult for me to foresee that increased staff scrutiny of CIA operations would result in either substantial savings or a significant increase in available intelligence information." Russell expressed a belief that conflicted fundamentally with Mansfield's: "If there is one agency of the government in which we must take some matters on faith, without a constant examination of its methods and sources, I believe this agency is the CIA." Nonetheless, Russell claimed that his subcommittee had required agency leaders to respond candidly to "the specific complaints and criticisms that have been voiced in Congress and the press."

Mansfield told the Rules Committee on January 25, "I realize full well, because of the very nature of the duties of the CIA, that there has been no public scrutiny of its activities. This may be necessary in this day and age, but I believe that a Joint Congressional Committee should be created for the purpose of seeing that good management is maintained in the CIA and also to keep a constant check on its intelligence policies." Saltonstall also testified but reported to Dulles that he "had not been able to accomplish much." The Rules Committee, which had hardly noted Mansfield's previous version of the resolution in 1954 before rejecting it, now supported it, 7 to 2. Hayden and Thomas Hennings (D-MO) dissented. All four Republicans, including Joe McCarthy and William Jenner — who told Saltonstall that the CIA worked "against the interests" of the United States — voted "yes."[3]

It was "an unexpected turn of events," national security adviser Dillon Anderson wrote to Vice President Nixon, and the National Security Council (which he called "the statutory 'Board of Directors' for the CIA") had been slow to act. "Allen Dulles felt reluctant to take a position until he had received NSC guidance; the legislative people on the White House staff needed NSC guidance before making their contacts on the subject." Given Eisenhower's animosity toward the Mansfield resolution, the "necessity" of a formal NSC vote before launching a counterattack suggests uncharacteristic incompetence at the White House. Finally receiving a mandate, legislative liaison Bryce Harlow went into action.

News accounts of the emerging struggle were hardly the stuff of newspapers' front pages — when the Rules Committee approved the resolution, newspapers were reporting prominently on the bus boycott by blacks in Montgomery, Alabama. Reports inside some newspapers, though, suggested that the director of central intelligence was already working against the resolution before the NSC and Rules Committee votes. In February, he wrote a friend, "There is no letting up in the work, and I now have to battle for my appropriations, a congressional proposal for a 'watchdog' committee, etc." (Dulles or his deputies — not including the CIA legislative liaison, who visited Capitol Hill regularly — testified before, or met with, legislators on at least twenty-five days in 1956.)

Because Mansfield had thirty-four announced cosponsors, and given the overwhelming vote in the Rules Committee, the resolution's success had come to seem assured in the Senate. Pforzheimer advised the DCI, "There is only one way to beat the Mansfield Resolution — that is to peel away its co-sponsors, one by one." Dulles allies like Richard Russell and majority leader Lyndon Johnson might have the requisite influence to do the peeling. Pforzheimer was then leaving the legislative liaison's position but advised Dulles to contact Alben Barkley (D-KY) and Stuart Symington, both having served on Truman's NSC and digested many CIA reports. Pforzheimer did not trust Symington, and "you had to pray" that former Vice President Barkley "wasn't tanked up that day." Still, they could be useful.[4]

Right in the middle of the January events, President Eisenhower announced the creation of the President's Board of Consultants on Foreign Intelligence Activities (PBCFIA). In his diary, Eisenhower recorded an intent that the board would "be able to satisfy the President, the Congress, and, if necessary, the public, on the value and suitability of our intelligence efforts." The previous November, Allen Dulles had told Eisenhower that appointment of the board prior to Senate handling of the resolution might deflate Mansfield's momentum.

Exactly the opposite happened. The *Times* reported in February that Senate Republicans indicated

> that they would give active, and possibly unanimous, support to the basic principle of a bill by Senator Mike Mansfield. . . . The Republican senators obviously

were miffed by what they regarded as the President's implied lack of trust in Congress' discretion in handling super-secret intelligence matters. . . . Styles Bridges of New Hampshire, chairman of the Senate Republican Policy Committee, told reporters after the regular weekly luncheon of all Republican members that the group had been advised the President was "very much opposed" to the Mansfield bill. "He said it was too sensitive for Congress to take it up," Senator Bridges declared.

William F. Knowland of California, the Senate Republican leader, told the policy group of the President's views. Senator Bridges said that the news did not impress him.

To Eisenhower, Knowland and Bridges personified the weaknesses of Capitol Hill Republicans, but it had not been his plan to alienate them.[5]

Weeks earlier, Saltonstall had gently outlined for the president a dilemma resulting from the creation of the Doolittle Committee and the subsequent board — the very fact that Eisenhower had appointed them "seemed to show the need . . . to supervise" the CIA. As the president knew, Saltonstall was no great legislative strategist. This would have crossed Eisenhower's mind in recalling a January 31 legislative conference at the White House, at which Saltonstall had implied that the president would have Bridges's support. Saltonstall also admitted that, in Senate maneuverings over the issue, "I may have hurt more than helped." It might be better to let the resolution pass in the Senate and go on to the House, where it would face likely defeat.

Eisenhower avoided giving the legislators advice on tactics and strategy that day. He fumed, though, over the "constant furor" to create a joint committee. Allen Dulles reported, "as he should," to what the president called the "military committees. I think that's as far as we should go." Of Mansfield and his allies, Eisenhower asked, "Why can't they trust their military affairs committee?"

In the president's presence, House leaders took the lead on January 31 in fashioning the administration's legislative strategy. Democrat Paul Kilday rebuffed Saltonstall: "We should try to stop it in the Senate." Kilday and the White House would urge Speaker Rayburn, House minority leader Martin, and Carl Vinson to make their antagonistic views of the resolution known in the Senate. Vinson soon assured Senator Hayden that, if the resolution made it to the House, he would "oppose the matter in every possible way." (He did not disclose what he had told Dulles in a recent subcommittee hearing that

had covered the CIA budget, ongoing covert action, and Soviet missiles —
namely, that "the House always came out second best in any joint committee
arrangement.")[6]

Press critics were no more impressed by Eisenhower's announcement of
the President's Board than were most Republican senators. Hanson Baldwin
responded, "There have been so many intelligence failures, so much friction,
and such sharp criticism, particularly of the CIA, that the appointment of
the citizens' board should not preclude the establishment of a continuing
and permanent congressional watchdog committee."

For over two months after the Rules Committee vote, the White House,
the CIA, and Senate leaders worked to slow down Mansfield's seeming
momentum. Dulles's lobbying was considerable but discreet. In March, he
invited all of the members of the four CIA subcommittees (plus staffers
authorized "to have full access to information on our activities") on a two-
day inspection trip to a CIA center in Virginia where training "is given to
Agency personnel prior to their assignment in sensitive posts abroad." The
trip was to take place in late April, after the forthcoming Senate vote, but the
CIA hoped that hostile members of the subcommittees like that of Bridges
could be mollified by such plans. Few of the busy legislators or their staffs
would take part in the outing.

In early April, the *Times'* William S. White — an intimately connected
chronicler of Congress — wrote that "formidable bipartisan Senate forces"
were readying for the showdown with the administration. "The most
informed estimates today were that Mr. Mansfield's project would prevail in
the Senate, notwithstanding the objections of President Eisenhower. The
consensus thus was that what happened later in the House of Representatives would determine whether a 'watchdog' committee would in fact be
thrust upon the Administration." As Eisenhower understood, a president has
no formal say on how Congress organizes itself.[7]

Senate debate started on Monday, April 9, the day after Washington had
completed its annual Cherry Blossom Festival, which was marred by icy rain
and winds. The dozen or so senators who spoke that day and the following
Wednesday disagreed on key questions, among them, Was the CIA doing a
good job? Was there "secrecy for secrecy's sake" at the agency? Did Congress
monitor the CIA appropriately? If not, was the oversight system or its leaders to blame? How well would a joint committee work? How widely would
knowledge of CIA activities disperse under the new system?

Mansfield and Saltonstall dominated the first debate. Mansfield had the "highest regard for Mr. Allen Dulles" but said that he could not determine whether or not the CIA "has any part in making policy." He suspected it did. Nor could he, as a senator serving on the Foreign Relations and Rules committees, find out "how large CIA is." Everything about the agency was "clothed in secrecy," which "invites abuse." It seemed likely, though, that "all is not well with the CIA," given the recent report by the Hoover Commission, which emphasized "a woeful shortage of information about the Soviet Union."

Saltonstall countered that the CIA most certainly was not a "policymaking body," since its work was done "under the orders of the President and the National Security Council." Saltonstall's remarks implied that the CIA performed competently, though he never quite said so. As to the prevailing oversight system, the Massachusetts Republican said its goals in relation to the CIA were clear — "seeing that its funds are properly spent and that its activities are properly carried out in the way intended by Congress." A member of both Senate subcommittees on the CIA, Saltonstall said that they had "gone into the subject to the degree we believe necessary to determine that CIA is functioning properly. If we do not do our work, we should be the ones to be criticized."

Mansfield recognized the political minefield of attacking his elders, though, and pronounced the membership of the subcommittees first-rate. He noted that the proposed committee of twelve overseers would be made up entirely of senior members of the existing subcommittees on the CIA. A key addition, though, would be "a small, selective staff of persons having the highest possible clearance," who would "assist the committee members in making checks and appraisals on CIA and its operation."

Mansfield provoked what became the historic moment of the first day's debate. Addressing Saltonstall, he said, "I wonder whether the question I shall ask now should be asked in public; if not, let the Senator from Massachusetts please refrain from answering it: How many times does the CIA request a meeting with the particular subcommittees of the Appropriations Committee and the Armed Services Committee, and how many times does the Senator from Massachusetts request the CIA to brief him in regard to existing affairs?" Richard Russell was not there to hear Saltonstall's response, but he probably cringed when he read it in the *Congressional Record* the next day: "I believe the correct answer is that at least twice a year that happens in the Armed Services Committee, and at least once a year it happens in the Appropriations Committee. I speak from my knowledge of the situation of the last year or so; I do not attempt to refer to previous periods."

Allen Dulles had indicated readiness at all times to answer any questions that senators might wish to ask, said Saltonstall. However:

> The difficulty in connection with asking questions and obtaining information is that we might obtain information which I personally would rather not have, unless it was essential for me as a Member of Congress to have it.
>
> Mr. Mansfield: Mr. President, I think the Senator's answer tells the whole story.

Saltonstall went on to repeat that, when necessary, he had chosen to "have" high-level intelligence, but the mention of personal reluctance to ask certain questions — when "the lives of American citizens" might be at stake — gained the attention of Mansfield and other critics of the CIA and its legislative overseers for years to come.

For all the interest of the CIA, the administration, and Senate leaders in how the eventual vote would go, the news media gave the Mansfield Resolution scant attention. Front pages featured coverage of the race between Estes Kefauver and Adlai Stevenson for the Democratic presidential nomination, a forthcoming vote in Congress on a farm subsidies bill, and an assault on Nat King Cole as he sang before an all-white audience in Birmingham, Alabama.

When debate resumed two days after Saltonstall's speech, Richard Russell took center stage. After opening with predictable courtesy, emphasizing "such high regard" for Mansfield, the Armed Services chair went on the offensive in a way that Saltonstall had not. "I have read in the *Record* all that occurred" in the previous debate, he said, "and I do not find that there was advanced one substantial argument, predicated on established facts, which would justify the Senate in adopting the concurrent resolution." Was the CIA too powerful? Russell was "dumbfounded" to read of such a charge. "By no stretch of the imagination can the CIA be considered a policymaking agency," he said; it answered appropriately to the National Security Council. Of course, CIA personnel "undoubtedly waste some money. They make mistakes. They have not been able to penetrate behind the Iron Curtain and gather to the last detail as to the strength of the Russian forces." But the CIA was bringing in information of "vital value." One "bit of information" — which Russell would not describe — "has been used on two or three occasions" by the government and was "well worth the total cost of the administration of all our security agencies."

How well did Russell's own Armed Services subcommittee on the CIA perform its job? "I hope I have not been derelict in my duty," Russell said, but he made a case that Saltonstall had not:

> We have had before us the head of the Central Intelligence Agency and his staff. We have never had them fail to respond to a single question we have asked them. . . . *We have asked him very searching questions about some activities which it almost chills the marrow of a man to hear about. . . .* I doubt very much whether the heads of many of the independent agencies have spent more time with the committees to which they are supposed to report, over the course of the average year, than Mr. Dulles, as Director, has spent before my committee.

And Russell suggested — so briefly that few noticed — that Saltonstall might not have been at every meeting of the subcommittee with the CIA. Russell also offered an olive branch of sorts, if Mansfield's resolution should lose:

> I shall endeavor, to the best of my ability, to keep in touch with what the CIA is doing. I do not mean to say by that that I intend to undertake to find out whether or not we have an agent in some foreign country — perhaps a satellite — who is tapping the telephone of some foreign embassy, or anything of that nature. However, I shall undertake to exercise as close supervision over this Agency as is ordinarily exercised by the parent committees of the Congress in dealing with agencies which are responsible to them.

Given Russell's view that Congress was not systematic in monitoring most agencies, this was less than the promise that it might have seemed.

What about the right of the entire Congress and the general public to know of CIA activities? This question was raised by one of Mansfield's most eager allies in the first day's debate. Wayne Morse (D-OR) argued that all senators, even all citizens, ought to know of CIA activities. In making that case, Morse charged Saltonstall with supporting an "American police state system. Never will my voice be raised in defense of it!" Russell responded, two days later: "We have not told the country, and I do not propose to tell the country in the future, because if there is anything in the United States which should be held sacred behind the curtain of classified matter, it is information regarding the activities of this Agency. . . . It would be better to abolish it out of hand than it would be to adopt a theory that such information should be available to every member of Congress and to the members of the staff of any committee."

Carl Hayden agreed: "How it would be possible to keep the American people fully informed and at the same time keep our Communist enemies in Moscow in the dark, it is difficult to imagine."

What about the proposed staff, costing $250,000 per year? Mansfield had assured the Senate that it would be small, highly competent, and trustworthy. But Russell countered, "It is next to impossible, when a committee is created, to keep the staff down to the size intended originally. . . . Most of us are, instinctively, empire builders." When Mansfield wondered aloud if Russell even had any staffers present when the DCI testified before his subcommittee, Russell referred to Bill Darden, though not by name: "I have had one staff member present, and only one, who has been with the committee since I have been a member of the committee."

It was during the second day's debate that many journalists and others who considered themselves Washington insiders had a surprising realization — votes were shifting. Conceivably, the certitude of Russell's allies, Stuart Symington and Alben Barkley, that a joint intelligence committee would harm national security, affected some senators' thinking. But Mansfield's cause suffered not just from their opposition and Morse's extreme language, but from having another "ally," Joseph McCarthy. The alcoholic senator was chronically ill by 1956 and mostly ignored by fellow legislators. He often sat at his desk, observed veteran Senate staffer Richard Riedel, "a piteous specter with a bloated face." But, when Republican minority leader Knowland awkwardly announced a change of mind about the Mansfield resolution, repeatedly citing Russell's speech — McCarthy had a burst of his old energy: "I have roughly 100 pages of documentation covering incompetence, inefficiency, waste, and Communist infiltration in the CIA, which I am holding in the hope that a committee will be established so that I can turn the information over to it. . . . I think the able Senator from Montana has arrived at the proper answer to this problem."

One of the debate's observers was a remarkably mature sixteen-year-old Senate page, Frank Madison, who kept a diary. Of McCarthy's pile of evidence against CIA, "No one seemed dreadfully impressed." Other Republican leaders joined Knowland in abandoning it. Styles Bridges spoke with deceptive mildness in saying, "I do not agree particularly with the way the President has proceeded" but claimed that he could not agree with Mansfield either.

Other senators clumsily defended their abandonment of Mansfield, some quoting Russell: "If we . . . establish a new joint committee, we are going to dry up sources of information." Mansfield, while gracious about his suddenly impending loss, was outraged at the logic behind his opponents' arguments: "Do Senators think the executive branch trusts Congress? I think that is immaterial. The question I want to ask is, 'Does Congress trust itself?'"

Fifty-nine senators, including pillars like Lyndon Johnson, most members of the CIA subcommittees, and ten of the resolution's cosponsors, voted "no." Twenty-seven senators, including future national leaders Hubert Humphrey (D-MN), John F. Kennedy, Henry Jackson, J. William Fulbright, and Sam Ervin (D-NC), voted "yes."[8]

Who engineered the huge change of sentiment leading to Mansfield's defeat? No doubt lobbying by Russell, Johnson, Dulles, and others had a far greater effect on the vote than did the debate. Mansfield had complained angrily (and reporters agreed), "We have the CIA doing everything it possibly can to defeat this resolution." But the *Times'* William S. White later explained it by distinguishing between the Senate's ruling "Inner Club," whose most prominent member was Russell, and other senators. The Club members "decided, for no very perceptible reason except that they felt they had been inadequately consulted, that a joint committee would not do at all. Under their bleak and languid frowns, the whole project simply died." Mansfield gave a similar explanation: "What you had was a brash freshman going up against the high brass."[9]

"We Have a History of Underestimation"

When a reporter asked Dwight Eisenhower in February 1957 if the Soviet Union might launch a surprise attack against the United States, the president showed exasperation: "Oh, for goodness sake! Of course, anything is possible in this world in which we live." Moving past his irritation (which would only increase in coming months at such questions), he assured journalists that such an attack was unlikely: "Any such operation today is just another way of committing suicide."

Long before the Soviet Union surprised much of the world by launching its Sputnik satellite in October 1957, animosity between the two superpowers had become chronic. Although Presidents Truman and Eisenhower exercised some rhetorical restraint toward the Soviet Union in the early Cold War years, many other U.S. leaders did not. Styles Bridges had begun the 1950s worrying that the United States would soon "become a satellite slave state, operated by the criminal conspiracy in the Kremlin." Clarence Cannon claimed in 1956 to fear "that the President elected this year may be the last President in the history of the United States. . . . The sinister shadow of communism is engulfing the world and the United States." That same year, Stuart Symington asked, "Would we like our children to be in the sealed boxcars now moving across Russia to Siberia, loaded with young men and women from Hungary?" The communists, he said, have a clear objective — "world domination."

Carl Vinson also observed world politics somberly: "The sinister forces at loose in the world today are far more dangerous to the very existence of our country than were the forces of Nazi Germany." Richard Russell concurred: "Stalin merely took up where Hitler left off." Such views, all spoken publicly, were thoroughly common in Congress during the late 1940s and 1950s. Legislators who oversaw the CIA always did so in light of such fears. The agency would, they hoped, uncover and help to counter such dangers facing the United States.[1]

One danger that American political leaders occasionally addressed in the mid-1950s was Soviet development of nuclear-armed missiles. Those concerns were initially overshadowed by a related fear — that the USSR had surpassed the United States in building bombers that could reach the United States or its bases in Europe or elsewhere. The connection between the two concerns was commonsensical, rooted in fears of a surprise nuclear attack. Since bomber aircraft were a well-established military technology, it is not surprising that intelligence, political, and bureaucratic struggles over a possible "bomber gap" would emerge earlier than such fights over missile technologies. On this, the CIA would find itself in a complex set of disputes, risking the displeasure of key legislative overseers and Eisenhower.

The issue crystallized in early 1956. The House, following Clarence Cannon's and George Mahon's Appropriations Committee in February, set the Fiscal Year 1957 budget for the air force at slightly under the administration's request of $15.7 billion. This was close to half of the entire defense appropriation coming from the House, $33.6 billion, and vivid evidence of U.S. reliance, under Eisenhower's (and Congress's) "New Look," on air power for national defense.

Usually, reporters' eyes glazed over in boredom during budget debates. But Cannon — who heard Allen Dulles's views on the Soviet threat a few times per year — livened up a House debate with lurid commentary on the nature of war, if it came, between the United States and the Soviet Union. To the Appropriations chair, a political moderate, this was not some distant danger. He told a story already circulating publicly and persistently on the U.S. side of the Cold War: "Twenty-five years ago in Moscow, the secretary of the executive committee of the Comintern declared: 'War to the hilt between communism and capitalism is inevitable. Today, of course, we are not strong enough to attack. Our time shall come in 20 or 30 years. To win, we shall need the element of surprise.'" To Cannon, it seemed entirely possible that the time had nearly arrived for war. Both superpowers were "arming desperately for the last and final conflict." Historically, the United States had "accepted war only when it was forced upon us," but a surprise attack by the Soviets could be imminent. Uniquely, he claimed that "Russia is drilling troops to operate on paved highways. There are no paved highways in Russia — only dirt roads. So, it is possible that Russia is preparing to follow up such a colossal simultaneous attack by bombers with paratroopers." "The battle," he estimated, "will be won or lost in the air. And it will be largely over in one afternoon."[2]

Despite those views, Cannon's committee and the larger House essentially agreed with Eisenhower that, with a near-$16 billion budget, the air force would have all the money it could handle in Fiscal Year 1957 to build more long-range bombers. This, despite the air force's damning the appropriation with faint public praise as "austere" but "adequate." Privately, its allies in the Senate geared up to persuade the nation that planned levels of aerial warfare spending reflected complacency about the Soviets' capacity and possible intentions. Many newspaper columnists raised the same alarm, prominently among them the brothers Stewart and Joseph Alsop. Throughout the 1950s, a recurrent theme in their columns was steady Soviet progress and lesser U.S. strides under Eisenhower. A typical column, on January 13, 1956, said: "Very few Americans realize that the great SAC [Strategic Air Command] force, which is the mainspring of American and free world strategy, is not really a long-range air force. . . . about 80 % of SAC's fighting aircraft are medium range B-47s." The Alsops' thinking carried weight in the Congress, though not with Eisenhower, who assured a friend, "I have no time to read them." The president was confident that he would never "have to defend myself against the charge that I am indifferent to the fate of my countrymen."[3]

Just days after the House vote, Richard Russell charged the administration with taking "very long chances with security" and appointed a special subcommittee "to investigate the adequacy of United States air power." He did so at the request of Symington, onetime secretary of the air force under Truman, who became the subcommittee's chair. Among those joining him on the new body were Saltonstall, who could be counted on to protect White House interests, and Symington's ally, Henry Jackson. The new chair had warned the previous year that it was "clear that the United States . . . may have lost control of the air." This had happened, he claimed, because the Eisenhower administration made fiscal restraint a higher priority than national security. "It was," he said on February 25, 1956, "a secret policy, never explained and never justified." All the while, Symington claimed, the USSR was reaching a point where it could simply destroy the United States.

At the White House, Eisenhower listened to Secretary of Defense Wilson predict on March 29 that the months-long hearings would be "difficult." "Agonizing," the president predicted. Yet Eisenhower's sympathy for Wilson was limited; he had severely pressured the secretary to force the military services to cut spending and had criticized him before the entire National Security Council on March 22 for his poor performance. Wilson had a dilemma: he agreed with intelligence estimates showing dramatic Soviet aerial progress. Tactfully, at the NSC meeting, he offered to show Eisenhower what he had learned from "a complete review of all our existing intelligence material." No response from the president was recorded.[4]

In 1955, Allen Dulles told a senator that it was not the CIA's job to judge "the relative position" of the U.S. and Soviet programs. Still, one of the agency's central duties was to rate the abilities of other nations. Among the over one hundred witnesses to be called by the Symington subcommittee in 1956, therefore, were past and present intelligence leaders. Former DCI Smith would testify that the Soviets had "closed the gap" in training technical personnel and in doing weapons-related science. But it was the current DCI whose views would most interest the subcommittee. Not surprisingly, Dulles resisted Symington's request for testimony.[5]

The DCI had been in a bind over the matter of congressional relations since January, when he told the president that the Military Applications subcommittee of JCAE was also seeking a classified briefing on Soviet capabilities at two hearings scheduled for that month. Eisenhower advised him to tell legislators that "such a briefing would be contrary to the interests of national security" by "inevitably" revealing intelligence sources. Further, Ike suggested, "it might be well for one man to be designated to do all the testifying by Defense on the missile question."

That argument did not impress legislators. At the first JCAE subcommittee hearing, Chairman Henry Jackson took the lead in insisting that Dulles could not avoid speaking about Soviet bomber and missile strength at the next week's session since, after all, "we have a history of under-estimation." While willing to share atomic weapons intelligence, Dulles suggested that "it may be more useful from your angle" if someone from Defense did the bombers-missiles briefing. When two subcommittee members began to accept that Eisenhower-style logic, Jackson would have none of it: "Let's get the record straight on this — CIA obviously has its source of information on this." It would be "archaic and stupid" to separate consideration of warheads from their delivery systems. The DCI also implied that perhaps only the Armed Services committees had jurisdiction to hear about "instruments of delivery." This further angered Jackson: "We have gone over this thing. We have appropriate jurisdiction because we have to know." Moreover, questions about committees' jurisdiction could be posed only by legislators: "The Executive Branch can't raise it." By January 18, 1956, Eisenhower had partially given in: he and six other administration leaders met to prepare Dulles for the second JCAE subcommittee hearing. Records of it were destroyed or remain classified.[6]

Meanwhile, Dulles had met with Carl Vinson and other House Armed Services members on January 16 and would soon be back before their CIA subcommittee. Notes from the first session show little except the chairman's intention to have hearings with agency heads once a month (a plan that almost surely was not followed). In the subcommittee meeting, Dulles told Vinson, five associates, and committee counsel Robert Smart "that there were no secrets between himself and the members of this subcommittee, and that he would brief the members on all aspects of CIA activities in which they had any interest." In giving a "detailed explanation of the organization of CIA," he provided "frequent examples of covert operations."

The DCI, "at the request of the committee . . . gave a detailed report of the Soviet guided missile program" and so violated Eisenhower's proscriptions. One member asked about "the potency of the atomic warhead in various missiles to which the Director referred." Dulles probably hoped that Vinson and subcommittee member Sterling Cole, the ranking House Republican on JCAE, would excuse him from giving an answer. After "consultation" with them, however, "the Director gave this information, which he read from a . . . briefing of the Military Applications Subcommittee of the Joint Committee on Atomic Energy."[7]

Eisenhower hated the law that required the executive branch to share atomic intelligence with the JCAE; even more did he hate such intelligence being given, as in the Armed Services hearing, to seven others on Capitol Hill. At a February 9 session of the National Security Council, a disgruntled president forced the DCI to justify the openness of his testimony. A White House note-taker recorded the scene as Dulles

> reminded the President that he had discussed this briefing with him before he had made it, and also stated that the contents of the briefing had been coordinated by the responsible intelligence authorities. Moreover, said Mr. Dulles, he had done his utmost to protect the sensitive sources. . . . He then proceeded to describe the main points which he had made in this briefing
>
> . . . . [Deputy Defense] Secretary [Reuben] Robertson commented at the conclusion of Mr. Dulles' remarks that certain members of these committees had been told about the sources of U.S. intelligence about Soviet missile developments. The President said, with a sigh, that he did not know what more we could do to protect ourselves against skunks. If anyone was caught revealing the slightest shred of information about our sources of intelligence . . . we ought to get him "on the trigger."[8]

The president did not often view his DCI as a skunk, but then he was unaware that Dulles had also committed to a four-hour dinner with two dozen journalists at Washington's Carlton Hotel on March 2. Two invitees were from the *Times*, Baldwin and Drury not among them. At such events, he discussed sensitive intelligence estimates, counterintelligence problems, and sometimes even covert action. Stanley Grogan summarized the "firm background" arrangements he had made for Dulles: nothing reported "will be attributed to you or any government official; there will be no mention of any meeting or dinner; and nothing will be published until at least 48 hours after the conclusion of the dinner." Grogan suggested he discuss the Mansfield Resolution (which Congress addressed simultaneously with the supposed bomber gap), Soviet attempts at "subversion in Italy and France," and whether "recent speeches" (presumably the anti-Stalin ones by Nikita Khrushchev) signified a "new" Russia. He could also "do some counter-propaganda."[9]

Around the same time, Dulles attended two days of House Appropriations CIA subcommittee hearings. The first one, on February 27, 1956, went on for over three hours and was attended by five Appropriations members and one staffer, with Dulles flanked by seven CIA aides. Many such meetings went unrecorded, but a budget officer made note of most questions posed that day. After Cannon complained, not for the first time, about the publicity surrounding the CIA headquarters building proposal, he gave his annual warning against future Korean-War–style surprises. As increasingly happened at Appropriations hearings, legislators wanted to talk most about intelligence matters and let budgetary questions slide. What were the chances of mainland China attacking Formosa, asked John Taber, who also inquired about the CIA's recent "Cold War" activities, meaning covert action. Furthermore, "Why does the government always under-estimate Soviet abilities?" How much effective information has been obtained from double-agents, wondered Harry Sheppard (D-CA). Is the Soviet bomber, the Bison, as good and effective as the B-52, asked Cannon, and, How close have your agents been to the Bison? The chairman ruminated on the growing difficulties of obtaining "information" about Soviet missiles and atomic capabilities. Was it CIA or another agency that determined that the USSR had 400 submarines, asked George Mahon, and, What is the quality of Soviet machine tools? When 5 p.m. neared, Cannon announced that another hearing would soon address the CIA's budget "in somewhat greater detail."[10]

"Gentlemen, the doors are now shut," said Chairman Symington at 10:05 a.m. on Wednesday, April 18, 1956. The setting was the Senate Office Building's huge, ornate Caucus Room, with marble walls and a thirty-five-foot high ceiling. Almost three months had passed since the White House had acknowledged it could not prevent Dulles from testifying before the air power hearings. With the Senate about to consider increasing the air force budget beyond that approved by Eisenhower and the House, Dulles's remarks, to be drawn from the latest National Intelligence Estimate (NIE 11-56), could have a potent effect. Uncharacteristically, he agreed to give testimony without securing advance agreement that it would remain secret.

Five others senators and six staffers joined Symington in facing Dulles and three others from the CIA, plus seven Defense Department leaders. (The DCI would also go before the senators on April 23 and 24 and apparently once more the following month.) His thirty-one-page statement in hand, marked up to coincide with slides showing major figures on Soviet bombers, the DCI began by promising "as graphic a presentation as possible." Unusually, Dulles's hand-edited, prepared remarks survive in archives, as do substantial hearing transcripts. He offered an analysis of Soviet ability to (1) "undertake penetration of Western defended air space," (2) "resist penetration of Bloc-defended air space," and (3) "engage in fighter-versus-fighter contests for control of air space." The first topic most concerned legislators.

Drawing on NIE 11-56 (approved by the Board of National Estimates, representing the intelligence establishment), Dulles tried not to be alarmist. The Soviets faced considerable obstacles, he stressed:

> Present Soviet capabilities for an air attack on continental U.S. are restricted by the small numbers of operational heavy bombers, the limited capacity of forward bases, the limited availability of megaton-yield weapons, and the probable lack of an operational in-flight refueling capability. By mid-1959, however, the USSR could have made considerable strides to overcome each of these limitations.

But to the legislators, even the current status of Soviet air power was worrisome, for Dulles told them that there were presently forty-five or more operational Bisons, heavy bombers "roughly comparable to the B-52. With inflight refueling, the Bison would range over the U.S. as far as Los Angeles and Detroit on two-way missions from forward bases." Additionally, up to 45 Soviet Bears, "inferior to the Bison in speed and altitude capabilities" but with superior range, "could reach virtually any target in the United States on two-way missions from forward bases without refueling."

The news about the sophisticated Bisons was shocking: U.S. intelligence had only first sighted "a Bison fuselage on the ground" in mid-1953. On May Day 1954, one Bison had flown over the annual parade in Moscow. Only in early 1955 had intelligence identified the plant near Moscow that produced them. On May Day that year, the Soviets flew thirteen Bisons over their parade, or so it seemed. A Defense Department press release announced that the Soviets had "elected to expose some new aircraft developments in air parade formation over Moscow. These observations establish a new basis for our estimate of Soviet production of the heavy jet bomber." Soon, the Defense Department would step up production of B-52s. Only later would the United States realize that the Soviets had flown a few Bisons in a large circle.

The testimony of Air Force Intelligence at the subcommittee hearings, interspersed with Dulles's, raised a more alarming estimate, that at least one hundred Bisons had already been produced, though many were not yet operational. After legislators' questioning, Dulles checked with CIA analysts and reported back to the subcommittee that he concurred with the air force estimate. He added a proviso, though, later summarized in a CIA memorandum: "Accuracy of data not as precise as specific numbers quoted would indicate." In other words, U.S. intelligence did not know how many Bisons existed.

Such awkward moments hinted at the struggles of previous weeks and months in the intelligence establishment. At one point, late in the process of creating NIE 11-56, the CIA found itself in the middle of a dispute involving Air Force Intelligence on one side and the State Department (assisted by navy and army intelligence representatives) on the other. To the nearly completed NIE, the State Department wished to add a footnote that, as a CIA analyst noted, "asserts that a radically different estimate would be equally probable." As the analyst told Dulles, this would be an absurd response from an intelligence group to "the mission assigned to it by the President," which was to estimate "the most likely size and composition of the Soviet Long-Range Air Force as of mid-1959." Such differences were papered over, for the time being, with the creation of NIE 11-56.

What were U.S. intelligence projections of Soviet heavy bombers by 1959? Dulles told the legislators that the Soviets would likely have four hundred operational Bisons by the middle of that year, almost nine times the estimated number for 1956. About the other heavy bomber, the Bear: he predicted three hundred operational aircraft, almost seven times as large as the current fleet. Hundreds more of both bombers would be in production by 1959, also.

There were other ominous warnings from Dulles. The CIA believed, for example, that "the Soviets are psychologically capable of undertaking one-way missions, if required." This meant that over a thousand other Soviet bombers were a threat as well. Their crews "enjoy many special privileges, and morale is believed to be high," he said. Most could probably navigate "to reach major cities and industrial centers in the U.S." What sort of warheads could the aircraft deliver? "We estimate that all the estimated 700 heavy bombers could be equipped with large-yield nuclear weapons," Dulles said. The DCI's bombing scenario was not unlike the one laid out more vividly by Clarence Cannon two months earlier.

Ballistic missiles were not the focus of the hearings, but Dulles touched on them briefly. The Soviets had had short-range missiles with a 350-nautical-mile range since approximately 1954; a medium-range missile "capable of reaching targets 850–900 miles distant, could now be available in limited quantities"; and "by 1958–1959, the Soviet Union could have ready for series production an intermediate-range ballistic missile [IRBM] with a range of 1,600 nautical miles. Large-yield nuclear warheads for ballistic missiles will probably be available in limited quantities in 1959–1960."

Dulles's prepared testimony made no mention of long-range missiles. But, in response to a senator's question on April 18, he offered a prediction with significant hedges: "An intercontinental ballistic missile [ICBM], with a range of 5,500 nautical miles, could be ready for series production in 1960–1961. That is our best estimate, and that would be subject to check as we get further intelligence, and that date may be altered one way or the other as we get firmer intelligence." Under further questioning, Dulles admitted that he did not know whether the Soviets placed a higher priority on IRBMs, which could reach U.S. bases in allied nations, or ICBMs, which could hit the United States.

Even before the first day's testimony ended, Symington told testifiers, "There seems to be a discrepancy between the figures that have been presented [in February] by the Secretary of the Air Force to the committee, and the figures which are being presented today by the Director." The figures concerned the Soviets' MIG-17 and the range of Russian intermediate missiles. With Senator Herman Welker (R-ID) in vigorous agreement, Symington observed, "We seem to be pretty well mixed up." Dulles knew that senators suspected that the CIA downplayed Soviet capabilities and that the air force was being more truthful, so he said it would be a "pleasure" to resolve the discrepancies with the air force secretary.[11]

Overall, Dulles's analysis struck the legislators as ominous, though they said little, publicly, about his remarks. At his next appearance, on April 23, Dulles entertained senators with personal memories relative to Nazi Germany's development of missiles: "On the eighth of September 1944, the first operational firing of a V-2 against London — I remember that quite well. It just happened I was there on that day and having lunch with Bill Donovan at Claridge's Hotel, and that V-2 hit London. It was the first one that came down." This led Saltonstall to reminisce about visiting the "V-2 underground pits" after the war: "I saw the number of people that had been killed in making those things . . . and it ran up into the thousands of people, mostly prisoners of war and forced labor."

Dulles also clarified for the senators the apparent discrepancies between his numbers and those of the secretary of the air force. His explanations were regarded as so sensitive, though, that they were not transcribed. Inevitably, a senator pushed Dulles to say whether the United States or the Soviet Union had "done less or more work in the field of ballistic missiles," but the DCI responded, "I keep out of comparisons." Senators tried on three subsequent occasions that day and the next to get Dulles to relent, but he would not. "I am no war-gamer," he told Symington, but the senator complained about being "mystified" by differences between public statements from the Eisenhower administration and "classified information we get, both from you and Department of Defense." It looks to me, he said "as if they are way ahead of us in the missile field." About the only admission of error that senators could extract from Dulles was when Senator Jackson observed that the United States had "never over-estimated" Soviet capabilities. The DCI judged that the "tendency was to underestimate the Soviets up to, say, around two years ago."

As the DCI went back and forth with various senators, Symington interrupted him at one point to announce, "It has just been coming over the wire, and was handed to me, that Khrushchev announced in Birmingham, England — boasted — that the Soviet Union is now building a guided missile with a nuclear warhead." It was a surreal moment, as everyone quickly turned back to the ongoing testimony, but Symington took a moment to write a note to reporters outside the caucus room: "If true, it is a significant and terrible warning." Dulles later told the senators that Khrushchev "bursts out and says things which I believe they all regret that he has said."

When Dulles concluded his April testimony, Symington declared, "I bow to no one in my respect for the Central Intelligence Agency." Still, he had never forgotten how "terribly shocked" Americans were when the USSR first exploded an atomic bomb. He criticized "what has been done with the intelligence" by the Eisenhower administration, but did not claim that the CIA's "intelligence was wrong." Dulles insisted, "There has been no tendency to discount the Soviet power and potential." It was "a pleasure to be before the committee," though.[12]

Obviously senators would be influenced by the DCI's testimony, but whether they could refer to it in coming debates to explain their views had not been settled during his appearances. Dulles acted on May 8 to close off any such public airing of high-level intelligence, writing Symington a letter which was, itself, classified as "Secret": "The intelligence which we collect here in the Central Intelligence Agency . . . comes not only from other intelligence operating units of this government, but also from many friendly foreign sources. If those foreign sources are put on notice that intelligence which they may share with us is subject to public release through congressional hearings or otherwise, it would, in my opinion, tend to dry up these invaluable sources."

Symington quickly telephoned Dulles to concur. Dulles told Goodpaster at the White House who, in turn, informed Eisenhower a few days later.[13] That small victory for the CIA and the White House did not deter Symington, Jackson, Russell, and other senators campaigning to enlarge the air force budget. The opponents of the increase, Saltonstall and Bridges among them, would be on the defensive; among their problems, they told the White House, was being "treated like poor relations" by the air force. Indeed, not everyone with the air force wanted to hew too closely to White House statements. On May 26, General Curtis LeMay, head of the Strategic Air Command (SAC), faced Symington's question of when the Soviets could, "if the present programs go along," be in a position to destroy the United States. His estimate was "definite — 1960 — he can do it with a complete surprise attack."

Chairman of the Joint Chiefs of Staff, Admiral Arthur Radford — whose navy was less involved in missile/bomber matters — offered an opposite view: "Our intelligence is actually very poor. . . . there is good reason to believe that we normally overestimate the Communist capabilities, and in almost every respect." Defense Secretary Wilson, who had warned Congress in a Chicago speech "not to go off the deep end in our national security programs," met the subcommittee in June, saying that U.S. military strength "in general" and its long-range bombing capacity were "superior to that of Russia." The lack of consensus within the Pentagon on U.S. and Soviet air strength was obvious.[14]

Toward the close of hearings, Symington looked Wilson in the eye and announced "inescapable" conclusions, one of which was that "either you . . . or responsible military officials of the Defense Department are misleading the American people as to the relative strength of the U.S. vis-a-vis the Communists." Symington did not quite shield his suspicion that Wilson was the guilty party.

Symington and allies brought their budget cause to the floor in June 1956, as the air force subcommittee continued to take testimony. Its members had had almost two months to pass on, discreetly, what they had learned from Dulles and others to interested fellow senators. In debate, legislators never explicitly cited the DCI's analysis. Indirectly, they did, though, in unexplained references to "estimates," while openly debating the merits of LeMay's and Wilson's differing views. One flustered member of Symington's subcommittee referred on the Senate floor to "the latest intelligence estimate of the Russians' force," then quickly added that he had "heard so much testimony, classified and unclassified," that he was "afraid to say anything more."

Though the press did not note it, this was a debate in which key senatorial overseers of the CIA figured prominently, with a rare split along partisan lines. Parallel debate occurred in open sessions of the full Armed Services Committee, which were reported by Senator Dennis Chavez (D-NM) to the rest of the Senate: "It was the opinion of the majority of the committee, at least, that General LeMay, because he is in command of the Strategic Air Force is in a better position to tell the Congress and the country what is actually needed in order adequately to protect . . . the United States than is anyone else of whom we know." Knowland soon responded to the implied insult against the nation's commander-in-chief: President Eisenhower "would not knowingly recommend to Congress anything which would adversely affect the security of the American people." The "great General LeMay," by contrast, "may give undue emphasis" to air force concerns.

Richard Russell, normally reticent in debates, figured centrally in this one. "I do not think I have earned a reputation as a spendthrift," he said, with understatement. But, "I am not satisfied with the small number of planes we are getting. . . . I would be much better satisfied if I thought we were getting as many as it has been estimated the Russians are producing." Russell's soaring opinion of General LeMay's SAC starkly contrasted with his assessment of Secretary of Defense Wilson. "The greatest single factor in maintaining the peace and preserving this nation — and I challenge anyone to deny it successfully — has been the Strategic Air Command," he claimed. But "my patience has been sorely tried by the attitude of the present Secretary of Defense . . . a man so completely inept and unequipped for this responsible position."[15]

The CIA and Dulles were hardly mentioned in the June 25–26 debates. Dulles's name had come up on June 18 on the Senate floor, because he had done an interview, conducted by Representative Harold Ostertag (R-NY). In a television studio in the Old House Office Building, Dulles blundered by pronouncing his usual "I'm not really in the job of making comparisons" stance, then saying he would "depart" from that "philosophy" in the interview. "Overall, in the atomic field, I feel quite sure they aren't ahead of us." When Ostertag specifically pressed the ICBM topic, Dulles said, "I have no evidence that they're ahead of us."

The interview aired on June 17 on just three upstate New York television stations. Later in the evening they would have more entertaining programs, including "What's My Line?" and "The Bob Hope Show," but Ostertag's office sent transcripts to news organizations. An outraged Symington sought and received a transcript of the interview from CIA officers who so informed Dulles (out of the country for a few days). Henry Jackson went to the Senate floor, describing Dulles as "partisan" to offer the analysis, in so public a fashion, to a Republican legislator, when the DCI had "always declined to discuss such matters publicly before congressional committees." The JCAE, on which Jackson served, immediately issued an "invitation" — accepted by CIA staff on the director's behalf — to appear a few days later. Meanwhile, Charles Cabell cabled Dulles, "No word from Symington yet," but a committee staffer warned the assistant DCI that some of the DCI's recent testimony in the air power hearings might have to be made public after all.

By chance, covert action head Frank Wisner and his wife threw a birthday dinner party on June 21 in honor of the senator, who had kept a public silence about Dulles's television appearance. A "troubled" Wisner (who had known nothing of the telecast) recounted Symington's fury for the DCI:

> He was extremely annoyed with your having made certain statements on this television program which you had either refused to make to his committee or declined to allow him to quote you for (it was not too clear which was the case). He said that his own irritation was considerably surpassed by that of Senator Jackson and Senator Anderson, and that a lot of other senators were irritated. . . . Stuart seemed to take special exception to some statement of yours to the effect that you did not believe that the Russians were ahead of us in the field of intercontinental ballistic missile development. . . . Stuart then launched into a considerable review of the numerous times and occasions on which he has come to the defense of the Central Intelligence Agency. He reminded me of how he had

stood up against Senator McCarthy in our defense during and before the McCarthy-Army hearings. He said that he had prejudiced his close personal friendship with Senator Mansfield in siding against him on the issue of the Mansfield Resolution, and he recited other incidents, all of which are, of course, accurate. He said that he had done these things not merely because of his admiration and friendship for you and certain others in the Agency, but because of his belief that the Central Intelligence Agency was entitled to be treated in a special and separate category. However, if it is the policy of this Agency to engage itself on one side or the other of highly controversial political issues, he would have to revise his views.

It would be worth the DCI's time, Wisner said, to reassure "Stuart and perhaps certain of his Democratic colleagues."[16]

Naturally, the White House would have been pleased with Dulles's televised remarks, but by June 26, William S. White reported of the ongoing bomber debate that "Democrats, for the first time, were successfully challenging the President on a matter involving military judgment." Even many Republicans were deserting Eisenhower by proposing a compromise increase in the air force budget, one smaller than the Democrats'. After that attempt — led by Bridges and supported by Saltonstall — failed, the Senate voted, 48–40, for the extra $800 million appropriation favored by Russell and Symington. The House followed suit on June 29. The increased funding would, Congress intended, "expedite production of heavy bombers, tankers, and other essential Air Force weapons to the optimum limit of existing facilities." Sherman Kent, director of the Office of National Estimates (ONE), suggested to Dulles that NIE 11-56, on which the DCI based his secret testimony, and from which LeMay publicly and privately drew, had helped produce the congressional vote. Eisenhower signed the $34.6 billion Fiscal Year 1957 federal budget bill, saying not a word about the air force appropriation, but was furious over it.[17]

Except for Eisenhower's anger, the vote's connection to the NIE might not have been too problematic for Dulles. Unfortunately, the estimate had been wrong. On July 2, only three days after the vote and two weeks after Symington fumed over the DCI's television appearance, Kent summarized for Dulles "the latest developments in a problem which relates to your April testimony before the Symington Committee, and to your possible obligation to bring that testimony up to date. The significant point is that intelligence received since you testified has not only caused CIA to lower its former estimates of heavy bomber production, but is now also causing AFOIN [Air

Force Intelligence] to re-examine its former estimates." The evidence was coming that summer from varied sources — the National Security Agency, from "occasional" but sometimes "intensive attaché observations" of a production plant, from one of the first flights by the new U-2 spy aircraft, from "intelligence acquired during the rehearsals for the abortive May Day fly-bys," and even from Air Force Chief of Staff Nathan Twining, who visited the USSR in July.[18]

After Dulles had testified, but before Congress's vote on the air force budget, views of intelligence leaders were shifting. For most of June, Air Force Intelligence downplayed the need for a revised NIE but by the end of the month — just as Congress voted — informally admitted to the CIA the necessity of a "sharp downward revision" of the number of likely Soviet heavy bombers. Nonetheless, when Twinings appeared before Symington's subcommittee on July 19— its last hearing on the bomber topic — the air force chief correctly, but misleadingly, referred to the "latest agreed national estimate on Soviet bomber strength" as that from the preceding April. He was not eager to disclose the embarrassing and difficult ongoing process of revising NIE 11-56.

Symington was well-connected to air force leaders, though, and clearly had heard something about a possible revision of the national estimate. He suspected that the national intelligence process was being politicized by the White House. A member of ONE captured the Twining-Symington encounter at the hearing:

> Gen. Twining was asked to re-state his numerical estimates of Soviet heavy bomber production and strength in operational units for the present and mid-1959. He repeated the figures used in the DCI's previous testimony, and made no mention of the likelihood of any change in those estimates. Senator Symington then asked him for a complete listing of the latest agreed numerical estimates on each type of Soviet aircraft, which Gen. Twining evidently did not have available. Symington then said . . . "If there is any change in national intelligence as a result of recent pressures, we would like to know when the changes were. . . . So, let's put it this way: Let us have the figures of national intelligence as of March 1, and then the changed figures on national intelligence subsequent to that, with the justification . . . as to why that was done." Twining agreed to supply this for the Record.[19]

Dulles would have eventually informed Symington's subcommittee about the changes, but the senator had been so specific and assertive about any such possible revision that the DCI — even more than Twinings — had been put on notice that he would need a detailed set of records to explain the necessity of a new estimate. Therefore, when members of the Board of National Estimates approved the secret NIE 11-4-56 on August 13, 1956, the CIA faced the task of justifying the new analysis.

Congress had adjourned two weeks earlier and Dulles was off on an eight-week trip as of August 19. Before he left, the DCI ordered the preparation of a "complete review of accuracy of previous estimates on Soviet weapons development." One of the categories in the review would be "overestimates" — the "previous Bison estimate" was to be an example. Two weeks after the DCI's return, the CIA's legislative counsel hand-carried a memo to the Symington subcommittee's counsel informing him about NIE 11-4-56. Probably Dulles also informed Goodpaster at the White House, although the DCI did not do a briefing there on the new estimate until the following month. The NIE said that U.S. intelligence no longer believed that there were at least forty-five Bisons in operational units; a likelier number was thirty-five. There had not been a "cumulative production" of one hundred Bisons, after all; probably there were forty. However, it still predicted that the Soviets would have four hundred Bisons and three hundred Bears, all operational, by mid-1959.[20]

"The complexities of estimating on the wide scope of Soviet programs and strengths are," Dulles later wrote Symington, "such that, from time to time, predictions regarding specific Soviet programs must be modified in the light of new evidence." In conveying word that "Bison and Bear production in 1955 and 1956 was at a considerably lower rate than we had previously believed it to be," Dulles also warned Symington that the new estimate "was based on new evidence and not on any extraneous considerations." What seemed incredible or implausible to Symington and the few other legislators in the know seemed to Dulles more a case of how "responsible opinion differs as to whether intelligence has overestimated or underestimated Soviet strength." He warned Symington and colleagues, further, that "there is no way of predicting the direction or degree of change which this new information will dictate" in future estimates.

The revised estimate was hard for the Air Force subcommittee chair to swallow. Maybe Air Force Intelligence had come around to the CIA's new views, but he and his sometime patron, Senator Russell, remained skeptical. The president was not surprised, though. He had never been reluctant to criticize intelligence analyses. One time, he verbally demolished an agency estimate as something that might have been written by high school students. His aide, Andrew Goodpaster, later recalled that Eisenhower "made his own determinations in this regard. Very quickly we found that the Bomber Gap had a tendency to recede. It was something that each year was going to occur next year."

Symington had succeeded in getting more money to the air force, but he had lost politically, as the administration let word filter out in early 1957 that the USSR's current bomber strength was not so menacing after all. By the time his subcommittee issued its formal report, which said that the "defenses of the United States have been weakened . . . because of a tendency to either ignore or underestimate Soviet military progress," Symington became the target of editorialists. One newspaper described the Missourian and his allies as having shown "shocking gullibility" in relying on "inexcusably mistaken" information. Without a hint of irony, a "surprised" Symington complained to the DCI about "publicity in the press" on an intelligence issue.

To Symington's frustration, the "bomber gap" issue, which had never really concerned most ordinary Americans, faded. Dulles may have been satisfied with the outcome, but he would soon face an even more aggressive Symington. The president would remain convinced that Dulles had erred in permitting early national estimates to exaggerate Soviet bomber strength, thereby wasting taxpayers' money. "As it turned out," a CIA historian later wrote, "The Soviets never demonstrated the level of interest in heavy bombers that the West assumed, and by at least the late 1950s had decided to concentrate on ICBMs."[21]

Hungary and the Suez: "We Had a Very Good Idea, Senator"

On July 21, 1956, Allen Dulles had a long, late-afternoon conversation in his office with an academic friend who served as a part-time adviser to the CIA. A month earlier, police in Poznan, Poland, quashed a massive workers' demonstration, killing scores of demonstrators and sparking the world's attention. Whether citizens in Soviet-dominated European nations would ever revolt successfully against their oppressive governments had long been debated in CIA offices. The agency, of course, had tried but failed at "roll-back" efforts years before. By 1956, the CIA had "some papers we've been getting out" on tensions in the Soviet Bloc, Dulles told his friend, but "we never get anywhere." There were "a lot of people I disagree with here in my own shop" who thought the peoples of Eastern Europe had "lost hope and courage." The latest Polish events showed "that the younger generation and the working people were quite willing to take risks to improve their lot."

Of course, people "were killed in that Poznan affair. You've got to take some risks, you can't make an omelet without breaking eggs." Dozens had died in demonstrations demanding free elections in East Germany in June 1953, for example, but (the DCI claimed), "I got very angry with some of my people for not sending others" there after the event. "I sometimes think people are too frightened." In contrast, in an apparent reference to 1953 protests in Soviet-dominated Czechoslovakia, Dulles coolly observed, "The horrible thing in that Czechoslovakian thing was that nobody got killed. I'd have felt much better about that, and the Czechoslovakian people would have stood much higher in the world's estimation, if there had been a thousand or ten thousand people killed in that. We kill more people on the roads every day for no purpose."

There was hope, though, on both sides of the Atlantic. At the CIA, "we're building up in psychological warfare. . . . it's really going along very well," though he claimed not to be "much in touch with that now." And despite the crackdown in Poland, others living in the Eastern Bloc seemed inspired by the Poles. Citing unnamed Hungarians that recently "took over this granary," Dulles explained, "They're young people. That brings new light. That took planning, thought, and courage."[1]

Ten days later, Dulles's yacht-owning friend Charles Wrightsman wrote from France, "With Congress out of the way, when may we expect you to visit us at Antibes?" Mansfield Resolution and bomber gap concerns were more or less out of the way, and Dulles needed a rest. Offering to "send the Learstar to Paris to pick you and Clover up," Wrightsman joshed, "You had better join us and then we can outline the future of the Suez Canal."

The DCI could not anticipate that the American presidential election campaign would be nearly overshadowed in its final days by two overlapping Cold War crises. One was Soviet military intervention in Hungary to stop the government and populace from moving more and more in anti-Soviet directions. In response to massive demonstrations and other unrest, the USSR initially agreed in October to Hungarian demands that Soviet troops already in the country be removed; the Soviets even suggested a new policy of noninterference in the affairs of other nations. This was one of the most significant and promising statements to come out of the USSR since the end of World War II, the DCI told Eisenhower. However, the Suez Crisis then flared up, with Britain and France working secretly with Israel to coordinate attacks on Egypt, which had nationalized the Suez Canal, a crucial passageway for oil to Europe. The Soviet Union rhetorically supported Egypt's leader, Gamal Abdul Nasser, and completely reversed itself regarding Hungary, with massive movement of tanks and troops into the country. The bloody outcome there left the separatist movement and thousands of citizens dead.[2]

For U.S. officials, the events in Hungary were painful, yet they held some promise. The worst aspect of the utter defeat dealt Hungarian freedom fighters had been the fact that U.S.-supported radio stations, especially the CIA-funded Radio Free Europe (RFE), had occasionally given encouragement to the rebellion by hinting at U.S. intervention. As the uprising failed, many Hungarians bitterly blamed the United States for not moving in. Still, Eisenhower and others thought the sheer ugliness of the incursion demonstrated the emptiness of Soviet anticolonial rhetoric and might ruin its standing in Third World and neutralist nations. In Allen Dulles's words to Eisenhower, other administration leaders, and the congressional leadership, Russia "had lost a satellite and gained a conquered province. . . . in the outside world, the myth of sweet reasonableness of communism has been destroyed."

When the United States' allies then colluded to attack Egypt, shielding many of their maneuvers from the United States, Eisenhower was bitterly disappointed. What a tragedy it was, John Foster Dulles mused to the president, that "just when the whole Soviet fabric is collapsing, now the British and French are going to be doing the same thing." He and Eisenhower knew that those two countries and Israel were betting that the United States would not dare to oppose them. But the United States would be a "nation without honor," the president told his advisers, if it did not vigorously oppose the action. Despite initial military successes, the Suez affair was a disaster for the British and French, who were eventually compelled to withdraw their forces.[3]

To what extent did the CIA alert top policymakers that the Hungarians would revolt, that the Soviets would intervene, and that U.S. allies would attack Egypt? After both crises eased somewhat, Dulles faced these questions from some in the press and Congress. With most legislators at home for the campaign season, the initial congressional reaction was muted. Only Mike Mansfield prominently questioned CIA performance, while the Senate Foreign Relations Committee summoned the DCI.

The CIA had appeared before the committee infrequently in the past. During especially big crises, though, Dulles thought he could not profitably refuse such "invitations." Grudgingly, Eisenhower agreed. He had Goodpaster give the DCI permission to convey "a general picture of what has happened to date in the Middle East, but nothing on our estimate of future developments or on what we as a government plan to do." Dulles could also "indicate in general terms whether we knew about the events before they happened, but nothing at all should be said on how we knew or the exact extent of what we knew." Dulles met with the committee, chaired by Democrat Walter George (GA), on Monday, November 12. Among the other members who returned to Washington for the session were Mansfield, two future chairs — Theodore Green and J. William Fulbright — plus Wayne Morse, William Langer, Bourke Hickenlooper, and John Sparkman. By the time of the hearing, the Soviet military had squashed the remaining Hungarian resistance.[4]

Mansfield, skipping niceties, quickly asked Dulles: "Is it true that we were caught by surprise by events in Poland?" The DCI barely answered — offering unpersuasive words on a "spontaneous combustion" that was "extremely difficult to predict" — when Mansfield interjected, "Well, were we caught by more surprise in Hungary by events than we were in Poland?" Dulles offered no coherent answer, at one point saying, "We were not caught by surprise as to the general condition or the general reactions, except in

Hungary [where] it went beyond what we expected. As to the exact time, I cannot say that we predicted it was going to happen on a certain day." Moments later, he contended, "I rather predicted that Hungary would move first."

The DCI was putting the best possible face on an embarrassing situation. Few if anyone in the executive branch thought the agency had predicted a major anti-Soviet turn by the populace and government of Hungary in late 1956. A 1955 NIE, for example, described Hungary as showing signs of "popular unrest" but found that "active and organized resistance is virtually impossible, because of elaborate and effective police controls." Early in 1956, another estimate noted continued tensions in Hungary and other satellites of the USSR but said "none of these difficulties will jeopardize either the control by Moscow-oriented communists or the implementation of Soviet policy."[5]

As Allen Dulles told Foreign Relations, much of the intelligence out of Eastern European satellites came from U.S. embassy personnel. The judgment of one diplomat — Edward T. Wailes, minister to Hungary — was that "our isolation from so many of the Hungarian people naturally contributed heavily toward the failure of our intelligence to gauge the temper of the Hungarians." Even as the European and Middle Eastern crises were unfolding, that was the view at the State Department. Notes from a November 2 staff meeting read: "*Intelligence Failure* — Mr. [Robert] Murphy [deputy undersecretary for political affairs] said that it should not go unremarked that in the three separate crises of Poland, Hungary, and the Middle East, there had been no notice whatsoever from intelligence sources and that there seemed to be a complete lack of any intelligence which could have permitted an anticipation of events." But Murphy and Undersecretary of State Herbert Hoover Jr. avoided any such mention of intelligence lapses when they joined Dulles in the Foreign Relations hearing.

The DCI, in fact, had taken a somewhat different tack regarding Hungary as an intelligence failure when he told the NSC a few days earlier (according to a White House note-taker): "In a sense, what had occurred there was a miracle. Events had belied all our past views that a popular revolt in the face of modern weapons was an utter impossibility. Nevertheless, the impossible had happened, and because of the power of public opinion, armed force could not effectively be used." After the USSR's military intervention a couple of days later — "ruthless and brutal to the last degree" — he predicted correctly to the NSC that the rebellion would be "extinguished in a matter of days." And with the Foreign Relations Committee, he frankly admitted that, on the topic of what changed Soviet policy toward Hungary, "We have nothing definite on that."[6]

Regarding the Suez, Mansfield was similarly direct: "Mr. Dulles, were we caught by surprise by events in the Middle East?" Dulles's one-word evaluation of "the performance of the intelligence community" was "satisfactory." Specifically, he claimed, "We were quite well informed with regard to . . . the events leading up to the Israeli attack [words censored]; and we were not caught by surprise, from the intelligence angle, when the British and French forces moved in." Here again, the director of central intelligence was not straightforward with the committee. It was true that the CIA had a good sense of what Israel, which initiated its attack before the British and French, might do. As Eisenhower recorded in his diary, "Our high-flying reconnaissance planes have shown that Israel has obtained some 60 of the French Mystere pursuit planes, when there had been reported [to the United States] the transfer of only 24." The president wrote one friend, "Our intelligence showed that Israel was completing a very extensive mobilization," but told another, "We had no idea what France and Britain were doing." If anything, just before the joint attack, "we did think that, so far as Britain and France were concerned, there was some easing of the situation."[7]

Even the DCI's brother thought the Suez was a partial, though perhaps excusable, intelligence failure. Upon the initiation of British-French attacks on Egypt, Foster Dulles told Senator Knowland that he had had "no intimation of it." Allen Dulles claimed, then and later, that while the English and French closed off their interactions with the U.S. government before the attacks, U.S. intelligence had nonetheless uncovered and predicted their likely plans. Many writers have accepted the DCI's claim — one Dulles biographer even writes that Eisenhower's indignation over the British-French attack was "pure hypocrisy" — but the substantial declassified records of the Suez crisis do not especially vindicate the CIA head. In fact, on the night of October 29, when the Israelis were well into their invasion of the Sinai Peninsula, the DCI was less proficient than his brother at forecasting at the White House what would come the next day. Foster Dulles said (according to Goodpaster's notes), "The Canal is likely to be disrupted, and pipe lines are likely to be broken. In those circumstances, British and French intervention must be foreseen." The DCI instead repeatedly suggested that "the Israelis might still be planning to withdraw — that the operations thus far have been in the nature of probing action." No doubt Allen Dulles accepted that the Europeans' intervention was probable, but he and his agency displayed no special predictive powers before the event, except for the monitoring of heavy French assistance to the Israeli mobilization. His claim to Mansfield — who repeatedly tried to pin him down on what the CIA knew in advance of the British-French action — that "we had a very good idea, Senator" was evasive, at best.

In facing the committee, Dulles knew he had an audience that was mostly sympathetic to Israel while hostile to Nasser and, as always, the Soviet Union. So, his opening remarks emphasized the extent to which the Egyptian leader had become beholden to the USSR: "The origin of the present crisis is the Soviet effort to move into the Near East." Nasser, he said, had succumbed to the "Soviet temptation of big armaments" and "seriously miscalculated the British and French positions, as well as that of the Israel." Soviet adventurism, plus "the military alliance of Egypt, Jordan, and Syria . . . all tended to make Israel feel it was only a question of time before Israel's existence would be seriously threatened." Dulles's seeming defense of Israel was so strong that Russell Long, with the support of a couple of colleagues, reminded the DCI that "Egypt was not the aggressor." Without kind words for the performance by the administration, the CIA, or Dulles, Senator George ended the hearing after three and a half hours.[8]

In the weeks following the Hungarian and Suez crises, Mike Mansfield and scattered news periodicals highlighted the CIA's apparent failures. On an ABC News program, the senator showed his complete disbelief in Dulles's words: "We were caught by surprise in Poland, caught by surprise in Hungary, caught by surprise in the Middle East." It was tempting, he said, to renew his crusade for a joint committee to monitor "delinquent" intelligence agencies.

More distressing to Allen Dulles were comments from the White House suggesting that British and French actions in the Suez had been a surprise. Administration leaders were really commenting on the deviousness of U.S. allies, not on the CIA, but agency leaders took offense at the remarks. They engaged in massive counter-leaking, with Dulles leading the charge. Stanley Grogan arranged another private dinner for the DCI and journalists on November 19. Soon, *U.S. News* reported: "Twenty-four hours before Israel invaded Egypt and 48 hours before Britain and France intervened, a 'top secret' report from the Central Intelligence Agency was delivered in writing to the White House. It said that: Israel would not attack Jordan, Israel would attack Egypt, [and] Britain and France would attack in the Suez Canal area. This document climaxed a whole series of warnings from Central Intelligence, all pointing in the same direction."[9]

Other news outlets agreed, but some dissented. The *Indianapolis Times* editorialized, "They didn't know what was brewing in the satellites — bad enough. But they were completely in the dark about what our friends Britain, France, and Israel were up to. [Senators] who voted last spring against setting up a joint congressional watchdog committee . . . should be feeling a twinge of conscience." The *New Republic* said, "A housecleaning is in order. Congress must take a hand in the matter." Dulles limply defended CIA performance at Yale Law School a few weeks after his Foreign Relations testimony. "Such criticisms have to be left unanswered, not because they are justified, but because the information available to us cannot be advertised before the event."

He would have to be more forthcoming with details at further congressional inquiries early the following year. One is well-shielded from history. After Richard Russell privately asked Dulles in February 1957 "whether CIA was on top of the Middle East situation when it erupted last October," they quickly agreed that a hearing should occur soon. The only evidence of the event, though, is a long analysis by Grogan, predicting questions his boss would face. Among them, assuming the CIA warned the White House twenty-four hours in advance of the Suez attacks, "Why could not an equally positive warning have been furnished by CIA much earlier than this, in view of (a) extensive newspaper discussion of the evident British-French preparations and intentions all through August, September, and October; and (b) rumors appearing in newspapers as early as September 30 that British and French leaders had ceased to furnish information to U.S. authorities regarding their Middle East activities?"[10]

House Appropriations apparently held hearings in January, May, and June 1957. Notes by legislative liaison Normal Paul (who briefly succeeded Pforzheimer) show Chairman Cannon in January pursuing "areas in which we were most deficient." Except for needing to "know a lot more about what is going on within the Kremlin" and to "focus more" on Africa and Latin America, Dulles did not admit "deficiencies." Cannon then tweaked the DCI with the claim that subcommittee member Jamie Whitten had taken photographs "without any limitations whatsoever" while visiting the USSR, and "asked the Director why CIA was unable to get any of this type of information." The agency had "stacks of photographs," probably of the same things that Whitten had seen, Dulles claimed, while adding that he hoped to debrief Whitten soon.

Hungary and Suez were on Cannon's mind, too, and Dulles's defense of

CIA performance in the first hearing did not satisfy those doubts. John Taber warned Dulles on May 1 to expect a call from the chairman "any minute" to arrange hearings. Also (a CIA note-taker wrote), Taber "advised him that Mr. Cannon would, without a doubt, accuse the Agency of falling down in its prediction and reporting on the Hungarian and Polish riots and also 'our failure' in the [words censored]." At a June hearing, CIA subcommittee member Harry Sheppard handed Dulles a list titled "46 Questions" about agency functioning. Dulles told associates that the Appropriations staff had given CIA "about 10 days" to prepare replies. "The Director commented that a number of the questions deal with some of our most sensitive activities. . . . he first wished to see full answers to all of the questions, after which he would decide what questions should be answered in writing and those for security reasons replied to orally." Dulles also approved Robert Amory's suggestion of informing the White House "that we had been asked a number of questions by the House Committee on Appropriations regarding CIA activities which we intended to answer." Nothing more survives about the hearings and "Questions," except an August diary entry by L. K. White that he had been informed that Cannon told a friend of plans "to undertake a complete review of the Central Intelligence Agency."[11]

About Eastern Europe, as elsewhere, Dulles gathered intelligence wherever he could, including from legislators. After Representative John Blatnik (D-MN), a former OSS member, returned from Yugoslavia in 1957, he visited the DCI and tattled on the State Department, to the effect that when President Josef Tito went into seclusion, then had a long visit from the USSR's Defense Minister, and soon announced Yugoslavia's diplomatic recognition of East Germany, the U.S. embassy in Belgrade had had no idea what was unfolding. Dulles kept a poker face during Blatnik's indictment of State but was surely amused when the legislator conveyed — based on "off the record, informal talks" — what the Soviets had told Tito: "Now, look, we're having trouble in Poland, and we're not going to have no goddammed more Hungarys around here, if we can help it!"

Stanley Grogan tried to convince the DCI that, on the journalistic front, Hungary and the Suez had not been disastrous for the CIA. Summarizing three volumes of attached clippings from "350 newspaper, magazine, and broadcast comments" on the Hungarian issue, he admitted that many "American press reports consistently suggested that the U.S. government and the State Department, in particular, were surprised at the revolt." While twenty-one mentioned the agency, "only four comments assert or imply that

CIA was surprised." On the "broader question, whether the United States had . . . contributed to the outbreak of the revolt . . . CIA has evidently not been mentioned a single time [by U.S. news media] as an alleged factor behind the revolt, while in the communist radio and press media . . . CIA has been repeatedly attacked as a prime mover." Overall, Grogan judged, "CIA has had a relatively 'good press,' domestically, on Hungary" and a "somewhat better press than it had on the concurrently developing situation in the Middle East."[12]

Regarding the threat of more attacks from Mansfield, Lyndon Johnson and fellow Democrats intervened, selecting him as the Senate's new assistant majority leader in 1957, after their party retained control of the House and the Senate in the same 1956 election. At the same time, Eisenhower became the first reelected president in the twentieth century to face an opposition-controlled Congress. Perhaps because of his leadership duties under Johnson, Mansfield's activism in relation to the CIA would never again be the same. Even when he would learn from his staff in 1958 that the CIA was engaged in an activity that raised "grave questions of legality" — subsidizing a domestic group, the American Friends of the Middle East — Mansfield would not make the joint committee idea a top priority.[13]

Still, leaders at the agency could not anticipate this. Coming off Foreign Relations' Suez-Hungary hearing and facing the one coming in the spring, agency heads began the year 1957 spooked by the initially widespread support a year earlier for Mansfield's joint committee proposal and congressional assertiveness regarding the "bomber gap" issue. Carl Vinson privately told Dulles and his top aides that the new Congress would be "bad" but pledged to have his CIA subcommittee meet frequently with agency heads in order to ward off further joint committee resolutions. Vinson's analysis of the new Congress was inconvenient for agency leaders who desired congressional approval of an early retirement and other benefits bill. Dulles and his deputies knew personnel who had suffered physically and mentally from their demanding work abroad.

A rare, surviving transcript of a February 7 conversation among CIA leaders about the encounter with Vinson shows Inspector General Lyman Kirkpatrick, Legal Counsel Lawrence Houston, Legislative Counsel Norman Paul, Deputy Director for Intelligence Robert Amory, and others vividly evaluating the young 85th Congress:

Mr. Paul: Mr. Vinson . . . seemed to feel that bringing up a large package of legislation for CIA would simply bring us out onto the floor once more and open it up to all kinds of debate, which might bring in the joint committee [issue] and a lot of other things. The idea is to keep us off the floor, if at all possible. The Director said he agreed with Mr. Vinson. Mr. Vinson also made a very significant statement that we should try to stretch our [existing] legislation to the very limit —

Mr. Houston: — of existing authorities.

Mr. Paul: Yes. And the Director noted that, and said he would do what he could. Now, we haven't seen Senator Russell and discussed this specifically with him, but I think the Director feels, and I certainly feel, that he would probably go along with that one hundred percent.

Houston wondered if they should follow Vinson's suggestion to "find" the maximum possible authority in existing law to alter employee benefits. Kirkpatrick responded: "Yes, sir! . . . If it was last year, I would say push it, but this year I would say if our friends up there, Vinson and Russell, want us to stay off that subject, that we will pull out immediately, because there are a couple of laddies up there waiting for a good peg to hang us on." Another CIA leader (his name deleted) agreed: putting legislation before Congress would give "our enemies up there, or those who want closer supervision of the Agency — whether they're enemies or not — a real hook to hang their arguments on, and a pretty good one."

Exploiting the National Security Act of 1947 and Central Intelligence Agency Act of 1949 to the hilt in legally justifying the CIA's financial practices made some agency leaders uncomfortable. Houston told his colleagues, "There are certain things we are doing now that are certainly technically improper." Seemingly to persuade himself as much as the others, Houston repeatedly said, "It doesn't bother me too much."[14]

Even as Dulles would deal fairly successfully with others problems coming along in 1957 and 1958, he would display lingering insecurities about the Hungarian and Suez incidents. To George Mahon, he wrote, "The references by the President and other high officials, to the general effect that they were not informed beforehand regarding the Suez development, was intended to apply to the fact that they had not been informed by the British and the French. . . . This fact has not effectively gotten over to the press or the public." And during a private chat in his office with actor and sometime-diplo-mat Douglas Fairbanks Jr. — with whom Dulles had experienced "great fun" in autumn 1957 on a yacht owned by Greek shipping tycoon, Stavros Niar-chos — an expansive DCI would talk shop so confidentially that whole pages of his remarks would remain censored in the conversation's transcript half a century later. Still, Dulles had lost his cavalier interventionist views of East-ern Europe. When Fairbanks reported a backhanded compliment from the Polish ambassador to the United Nations that U.S. radio broadcasting to Poland had been "potent," the director recoiled, then said, "Yes, I think it has been, but I think it's been quite careful. I mean, there has been no incitement to revolt. . . . We're not anxious to incite the satellites to revolt."[15]

Sputnik

"As Sputnik whirled serenely overhead, a startled world looked at Russia with new respect." So said *Time* magazine on October 21, 1957, in response to the USSR's launch of a rocket putting a 184-pound sphere into orbit around the earth. The new Soviet leader, Nikita Khrushchev, loved it: "People of the whole world are pointing to the satellite; they are saying that the U.S. has been beaten." As perceptions of the Soviet Union seemingly improved in many nations, numerous U.S. citizens and legislators cast unusually critical eyes on the president. Some on Capitol Hill wondered yet again how well the CIA had been doing its job of forecasting significant events. For, even without the Russian rhetoric, Sputnik was all too suggestive to ordinary Americans that the ability to launch a metallic object into orbit signified another likely capability — to destroy — quickly, massively, and from far away.

Such judgments may now seem exaggerated or even hysterical, but it would be hard to overestimate the concern provoked in the United States by launch of the earth's first man-made satellite. *Time* wrote, "As the slowly shifting orbit carried Sputnik over the east coast of the U.S., hundreds of early risers in New England saw the sunlit speck sweep across the pre-dawn sky." The sight produced awe and fear. Newspapers and other media engaged in innumerable fearful analyses of the launch's implications. *Newsweek* put Sputnik on three consecutive covers. For the United States, the event was a "defeat in three fields: in pure science, in practical know-how, and in psychological cold war," its editors wrote. It was obvious that "a couple of dozen such rockets, equipped with dirty H-bombs instead of radio transmitters and batteries, could with very few technical changes be made to spew their lethal fallout over most of the U.S. or Europe."[1]

The pessimism was even greater on the two leading television networks' news programs. NBC and CBS traditionally gathered their most prominent journalists at year's end for an hour-long, prime-time review of major news stories. Though 1957 had seen important events, including the use of federal troops to enforce integration of Little Rock's public schools, both broadcasts focused almost exclusively on the Sputnik launch seven weeks earlier. For Edward R. Murrow, summarizing his CBS colleagues' reports, the nation's "lack of leadership was showing," given the Soviets' lead in long- and intermediate-range missile capabilities. Sputnik had occurred, said Eric Sevareid, "in the teeth of . . . very apparent intelligence information available to them as to every-body else. I have a feeling there has been a response here not to objective facts enough, but too much to subjective illusions." At NBC, too, Chet Huntley turned viewers' and colleagues' "attention to the major event of 1957, the first launching of a satellite into space by the Russians, which permeates every aspect of our national and international existence." The "laughter in Russia was raucous and triumphant," said reporter Joseph Harsch. Psychologically, Sputnik was "another Pearl Harbor." Irving R. Levine, though, reminded Huntley that "Russia has as many headaches as we do."[2]

Congress was out of session when Sputnik went up, but many members reacted loudly. On October 10, Henry Jackson said, "This is a week of shame and danger for America. . . . We are behind [in missile capabilities] and we are falling further and further behind. We are now voluntarily abdicating world leadership to the Soviet Union." For Stuart Symington, the USSR's achievement was "another case in which the truth of the greater progress cannot be officially concealed by an atmosphere of disbelief." He suggested that Eisenhower "be more frank" about "the present situation" and call a spe-cial session of Congress to address it. Symington and Republican Styles Bridges asked Richard Russell to authorize an investigation by the Senate Armed Services Committee. But Russell and House Armed Services chair Carl Vinson were less unnerved by Sputnik. Initially, Russell resisted calls for an inquiry. Vinson was unmoved after two months of building pressure to "do something" about Sputnik. "It now appears," he said as 1958 began, "that the word 'Sputnik' has an English synonym known as 'hysteria.' "[3]

Eisenhower tried at a press conference to reassure the nation: Sputnik "does not raise my apprehensions, not one iota." But the president had health problems. He was recovering from a heart attack two years earlier, and he was to suffer a mild stroke just weeks after Sputnik. These lessened his energy and effectiveness and took away his ability to speak quickly. Far less usefully, out-going Defense Secretary Wilson labeled Sputnik a "nice technical trick," while White House Chief of Staff Sherman Adams said that the United States had no intention of playing "an outer space basketball game" with the Soviets. At a dinner a couple of weeks after the satellite launch, Budget Bureau Director Percival Brundage predicted to Allen Dulles that Sputnik would be forgotten in six months, but their dinner companion, former minister to Luxembourg Perle Mesta, responded, "In six months we may all be dead."

Eisenhower doubted the much-alleged military superiority of the Soviet Union, for plausible reasons. The United States had its own substantial missile development programs, spending three billion dollars in 1957, with more planned for the future. Still, some press reports about what Eisenhower knew and when he knew it were troublesome: on October 16, a Dulles aide noted a "Friday night radio broadcast and subsequent article in Saturday's Washington *Post*, reporting on the fact that CIA had advised the President and the National Security Council several months in advance of the Soviet launching of the earth satellite."[4]

The president's confidence regarding U.S. security was in spite of a post-Sputnik warning that Dulles passed on from his panel of scientific consultants. Having studied the CIA's best intelligence on missile programs of the USSR and examined such U.S. capabilities, the four scientists warned Dulles that "the country is in a period of grave national emergency" that would last for years. The Soviet missile program "has been thoroughly thought out and followed for years." There would probably be a dozen operational ICBMs in the USSR by the end of 1958; the United States was "lagging by *two to three years*." The government needed to become better at making missiles, they said, and added: "We cannot emphasize too much that increased efforts by the intelligence community, both overt and covert, are mandatory to counter this threat."

It could not have been easy for Dulles to forward the letter to the White House. Eisenhower soon appointed a special assistant to head a new presidential science advisory committee. Announcing the appointments in a televised speech, Eisenhower again tried to soothe fears: "We are well ahead of the Soviets in the nuclear field, both in quantity and in quality. We intend to stay ahead." Just hours before the speech, Eisenhower even considered publicly disclosing how the U-2 aircraft gave him confidence in estimates of Soviet military strength but decided against it.[5]

Although Sputnik's launch brought the words "missile gap" into common usage, certain members of Congress, the executive branch, and the CIA had long worried about Soviet missiles. In 1955 Senator Clinton Anderson, who chaired the Joint Committee on Atomic Energy, and Senator Henry Jackson, who chaired its subcommittee on Military Applications, raised the matter with Eisenhower. Their letter, shared with the CIA, was immediately classified as "Top Secret," but an agency summary of it survives: "We fear that the USSR may achieve the first ICBM before the US does. Consider their long experience with ballistic missiles, possibility that they began top priority work to develop an ICBM in 1946, while we didn't until 1954." It is "entirely possible, and even probable, that they will achieve the ICBM well ahead of us." Make such long-range missile development a top priority, they urged the president. In 1956, Jackson told the Senate, "We do not know exactly when the Russians will get the ballistic missile, but there is grave danger that they will get it before we do. We have consistently underestimated the Soviets."[6]

Anderson's and Jackson's concerns clearly reflected their interactions with air force leaders; John Prados writes of a clandestine 1955 meeting in which two air force officers "armed with a briefcase of documents, described to Jackson the relative missile progress of the U.S. and Russia." Jackson and Anderson had access to CIA estimates, also. How often agency leaders testified before the JCAE or its Military Applications subcommittee in 1955 is unknown, but in 1956 and 1957, according to its own incomplete records, the CIA testified about "Soviet guided missiles" on five occasions. Agency heads also addressed the topic in three 1956–1957 hearings held by the Senate Armed Services Committee or its subcommittees. The House Armed Services subcommittee on the CIA also heard testimony on missiles in January 1956. Most records of these remain classified or are nonexistent.

Satellites seem not to have been the focus of much discussion in such testimony, although estimates prepared by the CIA in conjunction with other intelligence agencies — and which provided much raw material for such presentations — briefly noted in the 1955–1957 period that a satellite launch was possible. A March 12, 1957, estimate said that the USSR had the "capability" of doing so that year.

The one certain case of a congressional body interacting with the CIA in advance of Sputnik on the satellite topic was that of George Mahon's House Appropriations subcommittee on the CIA. Following its relatively new practice of giving long lists of questions to be answered by CIA leaders following subcommittee appearances, Mahon's group referred in summer 1957 to the "meagerness" of information on Soviet aircraft, ship, and guided missile production and asked whether the United States actually had any "good" operations within the USSR. In a reply — still mostly censored at twentieth century's end — the CIA referred to "Soviet earth satellite programs."[7]

Clearly, in describing Soviet missile programs to certain legislators and the White House, the agency's focus had been the danger of nuclear strikes against the United States or allies. Few had pondered the "threat" of a Soviet satellite. As Carl Vinson said after the USSR's success, "None of us fully realized the psychological effect of being first in orbit." Actually, a 1955 NIE had acknowledged that such an event would have "psychological . . . significance," but the point had not loomed large with intelligence leaders.

Nonetheless, after Sputnik went up, the CIA knew that members of Congress would hear from the public — Saltonstall received a "tremendous number of inquiries" from fearful constituents — and that the agency would hear from Congress. At a November 1957 meeting of deputy directors with the DCI, a Dulles aide noted, "Mr. Bissell stated he was strongly of the opinion that there should be a comparative estimate of U.S.-Soviet guided missile capabilities, since to his knowledge there is no one place where all this information is drawn together. Mr. Kirkpatrick pointed out that, with the convening Congress, it was certain that its members will be constantly seeking such information." "I'll talk to the President about it," Dulles told them. Within days, meanwhile, agency leaders leaked information demonstrating, as *Newsweek* reported, that "government officials right up to the top were tipped on Soviet satellite plans and progress."

Knowing that public opinion, not to mention legislative and journalistic pressure, seemed to demand congressional investigation, Richard Russell authorized a semi-public investigation by Lyndon Johnson's Preparedness subcommittee. In doing so, Russell protected his CIA subcommittee from what would have been extensive publicity, had it been the sole Armed Services body to examine Sputnik. Russell may well have wished to increase Johnson's national stature, in anticipation of a 1960 presidential campaign, but he also had more faith in Johnson than in most others on his committee, especially Symington. The Missourian would have raised "a lot of hell, but it would not be in the national interest," Russell said privately.[8]

After Russell's decision, Dulles approached Goodpaster at the White House with news that the Preparedness subcommittee had requested the CIA's presence. Dulles would be asked to give "an intelligence evaluation as to Soviet missile capabilities, and what this evaluation has been in the past." The hearing would seek to elicit "presentation by CIA of the historical record" and "recognition of consistent underestimation" of "Russian scientific and military progress." In effect, Preparedness would inquire as to what the White House had known from the CIA and when it had known it.

Following his discussion with Dulles, Goodpaster consulted two other White House aides and possibly the president. They agreed that "although it would be preferable to avoid having CIA give substantive intelligence in this way, there is no practical alternative but to do so." Dates were set for testimony by Dulles and others from the CIA on November 26 and 27. Dozens from other agencies would also testify eventually. Twelve Armed Services members, many not on the Preparedness subcommittee, would attend all or part of the hearing, as did eleven legislative staff members (all having or soon to receive Top Secret security clearance) and two committee consultants.[9]

Dulles testified for two hours on the evening of November 26 and for four hours the next morning, calmly puffing on his pipe through it all. As he and his associates spoke, two CIA security officers guarded the doors. Only one day had passed since the nation had learned of Eisenhower's stroke and three weeks since the USSR had launched yet another Sputnik weighing 1,121 pounds and carrying a dog named Laika. Herbert Scoville (by then head of the Office of Scientific Intelligence) shared the duty of delivering the opening statement, outlining Soviet missile capabilities in detail. Most of his and Dulles's time was spent responding to questions from Johnson and others. While only fragments of the latter portion of the hearing have made their way to archives, the entire opening statement has. Dulles began with an estimate that the Soviet economy — despite its inefficiencies and smaller size, when compared to that of the United States — would continue to grow faster than the American economy. The Soviet economy would continue to permit "production of military goods and services . . . roughly equal to that of the U.S."

The DCI and Scoville offered three key explanations of how the USSR, which "had no known guided missile program at the close of World War II," could have advanced so quickly. First, the Soviet government "exploited the German guided missile program," relying heavily on "400 German missile specialists." By 1948, the USSR had a missile program that equaled "that which existed in Germany at the close of World War II." (In fact, although the DCI did not say so, Russian interest and research into rocketry stretched back to the beginning of the century.) Second, "the Soviet science program continues to be fed by the Soviet educational system, which is now out-stripping that of the U.S. in developing a scientific-technical manpower pool." He explained:

Every Soviet student, by the time he finishes high school, has had to take five years of physics, five years of biology, four years of chemistry, and ten years of mathematics. . . . In the year 1957, the Soviet Union added 140,000 [college] graduates in science and engineering, compared to only 100,000 in the U.S. Our rate of growth is thus appreciably lower and unless this trend can be reversed, which would be very difficult, if not impossible, within the next five years, the U.S. will be placed in an increasingly unfavorable technological position vis-a-vis the Soviets.

Dulles's brief history lesson suggested that the United States had been in a position of "scientific inferiority" in the 1930s, but "in the space of 10 to 15 years" had achieved "overwhelming dominance in relation to Western Europe. The Soviets will endeavor to duplicate this feat vis-a-vis the U.S." This latter factor served as Dulles's third underlying explanation of the USSR's ability to launch Sputnik.

Scoville calmly detailed the fragmentary raw intelligence on which the CIA and others in the intelligence establishment based their estimates. He noted, too, the intelligence agencies' contrasting answers to certain questions about the Soviet program. Still, he repeatedly used the word "vigorous" to describe missile launches at the Kapustin Yar test range. There had been "at least 300 ballistic missiles . . . flight tested" since mid-1955, and "as many as 22 separate missile firings have been conducted in one month . . . four in one day, five in a 24-hour period. Very few flight test delays or failures have been detected, indicating an extremely high overall flight test reliability. . . . This we believe a very important factor in assessing Soviet capabilities."

While the CIA's evidence "that could be specifically related to Soviet development of an ICBM has been quite sketchy," analysts' "current belief" was that the Soviets placed "top priority on achieving an operational ICBM." Khrushchev had announced, and U.S. intelligence believed, that "two ICBM vehicles have been flight tested" successfully. There was no doubt at all, Scoville said, that the Soviets had a new long-range missile test range facility.

What did this mean for the future? Here Scoville admitted that member agencies of the "intelligence community," as policymakers optimistically call it, had "not yet completed the resolution of differences of interpretation of . . . data" relevant to the future. So, he told the legislators, the Soviets would likely have an operational, nuclear warhead–equipped ICBM by 1958, 1959, or 1960. And when might the USSR have significant numbers of such ICBMs? "The Intelligence Community is not as yet in agreement as to the probable dates," but Scoville was prepared to offer a "belief" that "100 ICBMs could be available for operational use between the middle of 1959 and 1960, and 500 ICBMs could be available for operational use between the middle of 1960 and 1962. CIA, at the present time, believes that the earlier dates are the more likely, but the whole problem is under urgent review at this moment."[10]

Scoville and Dulles did not mention the U-2 aircraft, which made CIA tracking of Soviet military capabilities somewhat easier. Russell and Saltonstall, but possibly no one else on the parent Armed Services Committee, already knew of them. Probably, though, Dulles and Scoville discussed American radar facilities near Samsun, Turkey. Their existence had been prominently publicized shortly after the Sputnik launch by *Aviation Week* magazine: "The General Electric–operated radar near Samsun has provided data on the type of Russian missiles being launched . . . their speed, altitude, track and approximate range." An accompanying editorial said that the existence of the radar facilities in Turkey proved "conclusively that the officials of the executive branch of the government knew positively of the basic facts in the onrush of Soviet science in developing ballistic missiles and the hardware associated with the Sputnik satellite. They not only failed to warn the American people . . . but, at the same time, they deliberatively and unmistakably took action that is seriously weakening both our airpower in being and the quantity and quality of our future aerial weapons."[11]

Scoville had one other piece of bad news for the senators — while the CIA had "little direct evidence" of Soviet submarines with "supersonic cruise-type missiles," it seemed likely that they already existed or soon would, posing "a very serious threat to the U.S. and our overseas bases."

Dulles said that the intelligence establishment continued to judge "that the Soviet Union does not now intend to initiate general war deliberately and is not now preparing for general war as of a particular date." However, after the DCI's Preparedness subcommittee appearances, Styles Bridges said publicly that he had heard "very unpleasant information." He predicted that the subcommittee report following its weeks-long hearings would "shock any complacency out of various officials."

CIA leaders viewed Dulles's prepared testimony as so secret that they destroyed twenty-three of their twenty-five copies of it. The DCI edited a heavily sanitized written summary of the hearings that Johnson could release publicly. It stressed Soviet scientific and military progress, excellent science-related education in its schools, healthy economic growth, and obvious missile advances. What Dulles's pen deleted from the testimony summary was more politically sensitive: CIA said the intelligence establishment "*had* estimated the Soviets would have the capability of orbiting earth satellites during the year 1957, employing for that purpose the same propulsion developed in their missile program."[12]

If released, the statement would have further embarrassed and angered the president and probably led to additional public and private debates over the clarity of such prior CIA warnings to the White House. The statement was accurate, though. On March 12, 1957, Dulles had issued NIE 11-5-57 on Soviet guided missile programs: "The USSR will probably make a major effort to be the first country to orbit an earth satellite. We believe that the USSR has the capability of orbiting, in 1957, a satellite vehicle which could acquire scientific information and data of limited military value." When Dulles had casually mentioned this to the NSC at the White House two months later, Eisenhower leaned forward and carefully discussed the implications for U.S. national security of a missile that could put a satellite into orbit.[13]

Dulles also deleted mentions of the Soviets' "steady progress" in building nuclear warheads for its diverse missiles and references to Soviet submarines. So heavily censored a release of the DCI's testimony angered Symington, whom Eisenhower by now regarded as a demagogue and chronic irritant. On many a day, Johnson viewed Symington in much the same light, but the former air force secretary was a national figure with a good chance for the Democratic presidential nomination in 1960. In fact, House Appropriations chairman Cannon said that Sputnik and other Soviet missile advances had "automatically nominated" his fellow Missourian for president. Symington insisted to the press in late November that Dulles's testimony constituted a "sad and shocking story" and "the sooner the American people know about it, the better." On nationwide radio, though, commentator Fulton Lewis said that Johnson thought Dulles's testimony was so disturbing that it "can never be released to the public." (Lewis also painted the CIA as "one of the great weak spots of the government," since its "force inside Russia is known to be very sketchy, probably non-existent.")

Unlike the majority leader, Symington was not on Russell's CIA subcommittee, which had an impeccable record of bipartisanship and confidentiality. Johnson knew that Russell wanted the Preparedness subcommittee to emulate that record, despite the troubled political environment. Informed by reporters of Symington's outburst, Johnson calmly said it had been healthy "to take a good look at certain procedures of coordination between CIA and the services and Congress." Of course, he admitted, Dulles's account had been worrisome: "I shall do all that I can to see that the American people receive all the information on the record, consistent with the national interest."[14]

Very quickly, the public did know: on December 1, Rowland Evans reported in the *New York Herald-Tribune* that Dulles's testimony had persuaded some subcommittee members that crucial "intelligence reports had never had the proper attention of high administration officials until after the Russians proved their rocket capability with Sputnik I." Senator Joseph O'Mahoney responded to the report: "Either this information supplied by Mr. Dulles . . . has been suppressed before it got to the President or, having reached the President, because of his illness, he was unable to handle it." Eisenhower's stroke had occurred after Sputnik, so O'Mahoney's grasp of events was hardly perfect either, but he advised the president to hand over his duties to an acting president Nixon, at least temporarily. Wayne Morse, meanwhile, said that Ike should simply resign. Grogan warned Dulles, "The Democrats have obviously taken your testimony before the Johnson committee to embarrass the President."

Newsweek, too, detailed the DCI's testimony:

> Soviet Russia today has enough land-based intermediate-range missiles — on hand and ready to fire — to damage or destroy almost all overseas bases of the U.S. Strategic Air Command. . . .
>
> Russia could, if it chose to push the button for World War III, launch missiles with atomic or hydrogen warheads from submarines 500 miles at sea that would all but wipe out New York City (or, for that matter, any other city on the Eastern Seaboard).
>
> The Central Intelligence Agency has reported these and other facts of Soviet missiles development to the National Security Council since mid-1953 — but with no apparent result.
>
> These were the most significant highlights of the secret testimony Allen Dulles gave Lyndon Johnson's subcommittee . . . during the open phases of its inquiry into the U.S. missiles lag. Seldom had a congressional committee been handed such a large dose of unvarnished fact. . . .
>
> What bothered the senators as much as anything was Dulles' statement that the "hard" information gathered by the CIA had, seemingly, evoked no response from the National Security Council. The intelligence agency, he said, couldn't get the significance of its data across; no one would listen.
>
> They began to listen, Dulles added, when Sputnik I went up.[15]

The story angered the White House and its defenders on the subcommittee, who did not deny the report's accuracy. Still, there is something highly improbable about a depiction of Dulles criticizing Dwight Eisenhower's NSC to a group of senators. Nonetheless, the DCI contacted Democratic and Republican leaders of the subcommittee to express exasperation over the *Newsweek* article. In a Preparedness subcommittee hearing, Prescott Bush (R-CT) blasted the "failure of this subcommittee to safeguard secrets entrusted to it in executive session." In view of the leak, he asked, "What government official can be sure that classified information he provides us will not be turned over to Russia via the press?" Dulles had privately guessed to Bush that a certain Democrat had been the leaker. This provoked a "little bit of an argument" (as Bush referred to it) in the subcommittee between him and Johnson. LBJ ventured that the leaker was probably a Republican but that when he and Bush could "learn to control senators, why, you will have a formula that I have not been able to obtain." In any case, Congress never "provides as many leaks as the Executive Department does." (Johnson had no idea how correct he was. Years later it would be revealed that an army colonel passed on National Intelligence Estimates to the Soviet Union in the late 1950s and early 1960s. The *Newsweek* story would have provided scant illumination to Russian leaders.)[16]

The tempest passed quickly that December day. Possibly with White House encouragement, Dulles prepared a cold letter to Johnson, criticizing the leaks' endangerment of "the security of the intelligence we . . . obtain and our means of obtaining it." But the agency had no interest in alienating the majority leader and would-be next president. Dulles scrawled on the typewritten letter, "Not Sent, AWD."

Overall, the hearings had gone well for the CIA but painted a picture of Eisenhower and other administration leaders as complacent and stingy. Specifically, the Defense Department appeared plagued with interservice rivalry. Dulles probably hoped that the limited spotlight placed on the CIA would now fade. But, as Eisenhower later wrote in his memoirs, 1957 ended unhappily for the United States, with the two Sputniks in orbit not "matched by successful United States launchings. Instead, a month earlier, in a glare of publicity, a Vanguard had failed a scheduled test two seconds after takeoff. It had caught fire, fallen back to earth, and was totally lost."[17]

Of equal disappointment to Eisenhower was a classified report he received one month after Sputnik from a commission headed by H. Rowen Gaither, head of the Ford Foundation. When it had been appointed by Eisenhower in early 1957, the group's mandate was to focus on civil defense in the event of a surprise nuclear attack. However, the commission drew on CIA and other intelligence reports to say, "By 1959, the USSR may be able to launch an attack with ICBMs carrying megaton warheads, against which SAC will be almost completely vulnerable under present programs." The

Gaither report recommended sharp increases in military spending on missiles and the SAC. By December, its pessimistic essentials leaked to the press, creating additional pressure on Eisenhower and Congress to spend more.

Robert Sprague (who succeeded Gaither as the panel's director) personified the report's dire contents. Meeting with John Foster Dulles early in 1958, he said the United States had to choose between two options: "preventive war" or conducting a "hot" negotiation — "threaten the Soviet Union that if it did not settle on US disarmament terms, we would change our present policy against preventive war." Dulles could scarcely conceal his impression that Sprague, a longtime consultant to the government on defense policy, had lost his mind.

Eisenhower told his NSC that "before we get done with this Gaither thing, we could find ourselves obliged to do things we normally would never think of doing." He did not worry about being pushed into a preventive war but was annoyed that Lyndon Johnson wanted access to the Report, which, he said, was "a classified report to the President, prepared confidentially by a board of consultants appointed by the President." National Security Adviser Cutler warned Eisenhower that Johnson and other leaders in Congress would especially want to see "timetables" of future U.S. and Soviet nuclear war–fighting capabilities. "The President replied in exasperation," according to a note-taker, "that he was sick to death of timetables. . . . they never proved anything useful." Despite Vice President Nixon's judgment that what newspapers had already published about the report was "fantastically worse than what the Gaither Report actually said," Eisenhower refused Johnson's request.

At the end of Eisenhower's presidency, a CIA officer familiar with Congress would note a "marked increase over the years in the number of appearances . . . before congressional committees." Sputnik had been the "significant turning point." Similarly, Eisenhower told an associate at year's end that "crisis" had become "normalcy." And in the privacy of his office, Dulles confided to a friend that the United States should spend "billions" more to deal with the Soviet threat: "They're getting ahead of us in the guided missile field, apparently." Unbeknownst to him, the Senate Foreign Relations Committee was set on exploring just such implications of Sputnik in January, when the Preparedness hearings would close.[18]

An Early "Year of Intelligence"?

The phrase "Year of Intelligence" would not gain currency until 1975, when the press and Congress would discover, investigate, and publicize the CIA's past questionable handling of covert action, counterintelligence, and analyses. In many respects, though, 1958 was an earlier such year for those in the agency and at the White House, due to perceived intelligence failures and resulting widespread dissatisfaction in Congress and the press. Late in the year, a CIA leader would write that he and colleagues "appeared more frequently before congressional committees, provided more information, and made more official contacts with the Congress" than ever before. It was a hectic and often unpleasant year for agency leaders who knew something that historians have not understood — that even in the long "Era of Trust" between the CIA and Congress that stretched from 1947 through the 1950s and well beyond, legislative oversight of the agency varied from one year to the next. "Alarms" set off by publicized incidents led to more energetic monitoring of the CIA than that occurring in quieter times. Allen Dulles and Dwight Eisenhower would be fatigued and frustrated by Capitol Hill's responses to unexpected events in the Soviet Union, the Middle East, and South America in 1958. The DCI, especially, would gain a foretaste of congressional relations to come in the next few years.[1]

His biographer Peter Grose writes that the DCI's "grip over the intelligence service he had built was faltering" by 1958. Dulles "could no longer sustain his chosen part of the spymaster; he had become a bureaucrat, a role for which he was ill-suited, enmeshed with competing bureaucracies across the government." Similarly, the sixty-eight-year-old Eisenhower, while not the amiable incompetent suggested by some journalists and Democrats, was no longer at the peak of his capabilities nor a master of details.

Styles Bridges allowed himself to be drawn into a discussion of this on a Sunday morning talk show in March when a reporter spoke of the president perhaps not being well-informed. There was "a White House Palace Guard," Bridges responded, and it had not kept Eisenhower sufficiently briefed on some issues. "*I* have not withheld information from him," wrote National Security Adviser Robert Cutler, who blasted Bridges for his "slanderous indictment" of the White House staff. "I have long had a feeling of deep respect and friendship for President Eisenhower," Bridges responded. "Nevertheless, there have been various occasions where not only I, but others of the President's friends, have felt that he was not well enough informed on matters of importance."

Gordon Gray (who soon succeeded Cutler as special assistant for national security affairs and worked with Staff Secretary Andrew Goodpaster in helping Eisenhower manage national security matters) thoroughly admired his boss. In private memos, though, he periodically described an out-of-touch president. In June 1959, he would write of a covert operation that "disturbed" the president, who "assumed that it had been approved by the 5412 Group. I reported that it had not been approved by the Group within the last 11 months." As Gray informed Ike, the Group included "the Under Secretary of State, Deputy Secretary of Defense," and Gray, "all in an advisory capacity to the Director of Central Intelligence."

Gray and the President's Board of Consultants on Foreign Intelligence Activities, headed by retired General John Hull, occasionally suggested to Eisenhower that the Group, which decided on proposed covert operations, functioned unevenly, despite Dulles's claims to the contrary. When Gray told the president that he endorsed the board's offer in late 1958 to examine those review processes, Eisenhower became confused. "The President expressed doubt about this and said he thought that he had a group which reported to him annually on such matters who might be more appropriate. I sought to convince the President that what he had in mind was the Hull Board, but without success." Weeks later, on Christmas Eve, when Gray wondered if any CIA "programs" had been approved regarding turmoil-ridden Cuba, Eisenhower (due to an eventual meeting with the Hull Board and a December 23 National Security Council session) admitted to Gray that "he had not known until the NSC meeting that the view of the U.S. government was that of wishing to oppose Fidel Castro." Gray may not have told others that Eisenhower sometimes failed to grasp important intelligence-related details, but he decided (with the president's blessing) to monitor those particulars more closely. Gray would tell Dulles and others in January 1959 of his conviction that "the President would expect some initiative in the 5412 Group. As long as I have been a member, there has been practically none of this."[2]

During the first two months of the new session of the 86th Congress, Dulles and CIA compatriots testified at a flurry of hearings. January and February were always relatively busy for the agency on Capitol Hill, but in

1958 there was even more to talk about in the first private hearings of the subcommittees on the CIA since Sputnik. Still, unlike the Preparedness subcommittee's recently ended hearings, most of these occurred with very little publicity. Few records of them exist or are declassified, but a CIA document prepared at the White House's request shows their dates: on January 6, CIA leaders appeared before Vinson's House Armed Services CIA subcommittee; on January 15 and 17, CIA leaders testified before the JCAE; on January 28 and 29, Dulles and others appeared before George Mahon's Defense subcommittee of the House Appropriations Committee, probably with committee chair Cannon in attendance (senior members of the group constituted Appropriations' CIA subcommittee); on February 5, the CIA was back before the JCAE. On February 7, the Senate Foreign Relations Committee questioned agency leaders, as did the Senate Appropriations Committ ee or its CIA subcommittee on February 26. All were closed to the public and press by a Congress that had kept over a third of *all* its hearings private since Eisenhower's presidency began.[3]

Prior to the two days of his subcommittee hearings, Mahon revealed his thinking about the CIA in two letters to a New York resident. She apparently had written to criticize CIA handling of intelligence on Soviet missiles and urged him to read *U.S. News'* coverage of the USSR's burgeoning nuclear war fighting ability. On January 13 Mahon promised to do so, but added, "I think the Central Intelligence Agency is doing a good job. . . . the NSC has tended to discount the seriousness of the intelligence reports." However, after reading the magazine, which concluded that the "U.S., today, is far behind Soviet Russia in the big race for superrockets," Mahon wrote again the next day about the CIA: "I have faith in the integrity of the people who operate it; but I don't think there is any doubt but that many mistakes are made and that there is much room for improvement."

Customarily accommodating to fellow House members, the Texan had also promised Edna F. Kelly (D-NY) that he would soon discuss her firm belief — of "laxity existing in United States intelligence services today, when a rigid, cohesive intelligence organization could be the means to our very survival" — with the DCI. Kelly had been dismayed to discover, after the Sputnik launch, that various journalists had suggested in early 1957 that the USSR would soon launch an earth satellite. Especially, she noted (and sent to Mahon and Paul Kilday of House Armed Services' CIA subcommittee) an article in *America* magazine, in which a Fordham University professor had written in May 1957 that Soviet scientists "openly admitted that they will launch several artificial satellites" in the near future. (Dulles responded to Kelly and her colleagues that the article's information had been "carefully considered" in creating intelligence estimates in 1957.)

Mahon or one of his trusted assistants would have had private talks with agency leaders before the two days of hearings. Walter Pforzheimer had always regarded Mahon as "so secure" in keeping secrets that he was "tremendous." The two men interacted on a first-name basis. Still, Pforzheimer remembers that "there were things that George took up with us that he didn't like, that were wrong." By 1958, the new legislative liaison, John Warner, found Mahon "a good politician, but very conscientious." Warner recalls, "Many times, Mahon would say, 'Find out about this. I don't want to hold a hearing on it, but find out about it.' A lot of things I would handle that way." Before responding, "I was always sure I had the facts, and knew what the Agency had done or not done." Mahon's assistant, Bob Michaels, also had trustful relations with Warner.[4]

On January 29, Theodore F. Green, chair of the Senate Foreign Relations Committee, invited Dulles to brief his committee on February 7 of the "relative military, political, and economic strength of the United States and the Soviet Union." Dulles was sick at home the day after receiving the invitation but sent word to Goodpaster, "This will require some thought." Goodpaster consulted with Bryce Harlow, who managed the White House's congressional relations. Days earlier, Harlow had warned CIA General Counsel Lawrence Houston of his "concern over the number and type of briefings which were being given to various committees of the Congress in recent weeks." Houston later told Dulles that, when he asked if Harlow was requesting the CIA to *do* something, the presidential aide said it was "a White House problem" but observed that Dulles's "directness and honesty before the committees were commendable, but created certain problems."[5]

Nonetheless, administration officials and Dulles decided that the agency could not decline the request, in light of the Sputnik hysteria. The director, accompanied by two associates, sat before the committee of ten senators and five staff members a week later at ten in the morning and pronounced himself "glad" to answer any questions (at a rare hearing whose records would survive).

Filling in for the elderly Green that day, J. William Fulbright pledged that nothing the DCI said would be made public without his permission. Early in his testimony, Dulles described Sputnik as "a spectacular demonstration of the great technical competence of the USSR." He claimed that the satellite launch "did not come as a great surprise to us in the intelligence business, and it has not caused us to make any basic changes in our estimates of Soviet capabilities." Dulles surely knew that his understated comment would not be enough.

As he had just over a year earlier regarding the Suez and Hungary, Mike Mansfield bluntly asked for specifics: "How long ahead of time did the CIA know about the Soviet ICBM and the Soviet Sputnik?"

> Mr. Dulles: With regard to the Soviet ICBM, it . . . was a question of taking known capabilities and predicting . . . in the light of our own best scientific judgment, not only from the CIA, but of our scientific advisers as to what they could probably do in a particular length of time, based on the fact that they had proved up missiles in the range up first to 700, and then to about 1,000 miles. And estimates were made and given to the Congress, certain committees of the Congress . . . about when the ICBM might be available. . . . On the earth satellite, we had many statements of the Soviets and we had a good deal of knowledge with regard to their propulsion engines and the power of them, and what we thought they could do.
>
> Senator Mansfield: Is it safe to say that before the . . . first Sputnik that the CIA and its coordinating agencies had brought to the attention of the proper officials in this Government . . . that there was a strong possibility that these events might occur?

Robert Amory assured Mansfield that the CIA had shared that prospect. Relevant congressional committees had been alerted, too, Dulles said. Foreign Relations members learned from Dulles that, except for the more hysterical analyses, much of what they read in reputable newspapers and magazines about Soviet missile capabilities was accurate: "This extensive ballistic missile flight testing . . . has aided them tremendously and will continue to be vital to the success of their earth satellite and ICBM programs and, of course, to their military deployment of missile systems." But he assured them that "the intelligence community is in agreement that the Soviet leaders would not deliberately initiate a war against the United States, at least during the next five years, unless they should make some unforeseen technological breakthrough." Soviet leaders, the "dominant" one being Khrushchev, "almost certainly still believe that we have a greater capacity than they for waging nuclear war." In deference to CIA and White House concerns, the senators did not ask Dulles to evaluate U.S. capabilities, which JCS chair General Nathan Twining covered in a separate hearing.

Committee members freely raised other questions with Dulles. If they concerned what he called "very delicate" topics, such as actions the United States might take to increase tensions between the USSR and China or the "tracking system in Turkey which for the past several years has been able to take note of these missile developments" (raised by Mansfield, due to his reading of *Aviation Week*), Dulles's answers were censored from the transcript. He claimed, though, that such articles "affected our ability to gather intelligence." He later warned the committee that Soviet espionage "persists" in the United States, noting the recently completed trial and conviction in U.S. federal court of Colonel Rudolf Abel of the USSR for spying against the United States since 1948. Notably, Dulles described "significant modifications in Soviet society," with forces being released that Soviet "leaders have found it difficult to control." In the long run, it was doubtful "that the Soviet citizen who has been educated to a higher level and encouraged to exercise initiative will continue to submit without question to the decisions of his leaders."

After discussion of other USSR-related topics ("over a period of time, eventually, conflicts are going to arise between Communist China and Russia," said the DCI), the legislators took Dulles to matters including South Vietnam ("doing extremely well"), Africa, and Indian neutrality. As the near-three-hour-long hearing moved toward its conclusion, senators pronounced themselves delighted with Dulles's testimony. It had been "excellent" (Fulbright), "a wonderful seminar" (Morse), and "one of the most heartening experiences" (Humphrey); Mansfield was "very impressed." The DCI probably had mixed feelings about the praise, for Fulbright asked if it would be agreeable to appear before the committee again within weeks. "Entirely so," said the DCI, who said nothing of predictable White House opposition and worriedly reminded the senators, "The briefing I gave was a top-secret briefing."

The fears provoked by the late-1957 Sputnik launch, so evident in the Foreign Relations hearing, would endure through and past 1958. In a repeat of recent years, the Senate overwhelmingly passed a Fiscal Year 1959 defense appropriations bill of over $40 billion in spring 1958, authorizing more missiles, submarines, and aircraft than the White House wanted. Simultaneously, senators and representatives resisted a White House plan for reorganizing the Defense Department. Eisenhower was incensed at senators who thought their knowledge of national security surpassed his.

The House eventually reduced the Defense appropriation somewhat, but Eisenhower hated signing legislation that, as he publicly admitted, spent a billion dollars more than was militarily necessary. He did so at a time when a Gallup Poll showed a plurality of citizens supporting Congress over the president on defense issues, "if it comes to a showdown." Ike's job approval rating had fallen to an unusually low 54 percent, and "missile gap" had entered the American lexicon.[6]

"I Cannot Always Predict When There Is Going to Be a Riot"

From late May through June 1958, the CIA was back in the headlines, due to its performance prior to Vice President Richard Nixon's nearly fatal "good-will" trip to South America. The tour had been scheduled largely at the insistence of Secretary of State Dulles, who consulted frequently with the vice president about politics and foreign policy. But the trip, which would include all but two South American nations, was purely symbolic. Of all the foreign journeys that Nixon was called on to make, it was "the one I least wanted to take . . . because I thought it would be relatively unimportant and uninteresting." The CIA gave "no intimations of any possible violence," he later wrote.

The tour's early days went well. The vice president did encounter hostility and some violence in Peru, and he managed to get in one solid kick into the shins of a demonstrator who spat point-blank into his face. The CIA sent a warning to Nixon's party that Venezuela, where an American-backed dictator had been overthrown by the military a few months earlier, would be rough: "Information has been received relating to rumors of a plot to assassinate the VP in Venezuela." The vice president brushed aside the information; more specific CIA warnings seem not to have reached him, by choice of the U.S. ambassador in Venezuela who believed the police there "had everything under control." But, on arrival in Caracas on May 13, the Nixon party—which included Mrs. Nixon and eight government officials and assistants plus about twenty-five reporters—found it difficult to move past angry demonstrators at the airport. The Americans had attempted to stand at attention for the playing of the Venezuelan national anthem. "As we stood," Nixon recalled, "I had the sensation that rain was falling—but it was an absolutely clear day." The "rain" was human spittle—"dirty brown, coming from a tobacco-chewing crowd" on an observation deck above. Pushing their way through crowds with the assistance of the Secret Service but with no help from the disappearing Venezuelan police, Nixon and the others were taken on a route that was supposed to lead to a wreath-laying ceremony at the tomb of Simon Bolivar.

The progress of the motorcade was soon halted by mobs, though, which "seemed to materialize out of nowhere. The Venezuelan and U.S. flags were ripped from the front of our car." After Secret Service agents hauled demonstrators off Nixon's car at two different blockades, the motorcade continued its "wild and weird ride," running into the third and worst roadblock, less than a mile from the Bolivar memorial. A mob, which grew to about 4,000 participants, pelted the cars with rocks and larger objects. The side windows of Nixon's limousine began to crack and break under the assault. Spittle on windshields was so thick that chauffeurs used their windshield wipers. As Nixon sat in his car with a panicking Venezuelan foreign minister (whose eyes were injured by flying glass) and others, including interpreter Vernon Walters and Secret Service agent Jack Sherwood, the crowd grew louder and more aggressive, egged on by leaders riding the shoulders of others.

The vice president and Mrs. Nixon remained calm during the twelve-minute, but seemingly endless, attack: "Pat appeared to be talking to the Foreign Minister's wife as calmly as though the trouble was no worse than an afternoon traffic jam on the Hollywood freeway," Nixon noted. The worst moment occurred when "one of the ringleaders — a typical tough thug — started to bash in the window next to me with a big iron pipe. The shatterproof glass did not break, but it splattered into the car. Walters got a mouthful and I thought for an instant, 'There goes my interpreter.' Sherwood was hit. Some of it nicked me in the face. Then we heard the attacker shout a command and our car began to rock." For an instant, the realization crossed Nixon's mind — "We might be killed."

Miraculously, it seemed, the motorcade began inching ahead. This was due to the driver of the vehicle ahead, who cleared a path for the vice president's car. Nixon quickly directed his driver, a Venezuelan who "had done a superb job," to leave the planned route, on the logical assumption that things would only get worse if they proceeded according to plan. He was right. "Since a mob is not intelligent, but stupid," Nixon later explained, "it is important whenever possible to confront it with an unexpected maneuver." The American party was soon safely away from demonstrators.[1]

The tour had not exactly improved U.S. relations with Venezuela or Peru, but the vice president was greeted by over fifteen thousand people, including Eisenhower and half of the Congress, upon his May 15 return to the Washington airport. Meanwhile, sustained attacks against the agency had erupted on Capitol Hill. The House was debating part of the 1959 appropriations bill when what began as an attack on the State Department for not anticipating the violence in Caracas turned against the CIA. On the widespread assumption that the largely youthful, violent mob in Caracas was organized by Venezuelan communist "cells" that were beholden to the Soviet Union, a predictable question arose: "Why have we not penetrated these organizations? Failure to do so indicates incompetence, in my opinion." So said Representative Price Preston (D-GA), who was on the Appropriations Committee but not its CIA subcommittee.

A rhetorical shellacking of the CIA by six House members followed, while three others defended the agency. Preston illuminated for the House the difference between membership on Appropriations and membership on its CIA subcommittee, saying that he knew virtually nothing about the agency except what he gathered from an unnamed source (probably Mahon or Cannon):

> Although we are appropriating unbelievably large sums for the Central Intelligence Agency, we are not getting from this agency the kind of information we are entitled to have for the money we spend. I want to inquire of the gentleman from New York [John Taber] . . . how many members of the House of Representatives know the total amount we appropriate for the CIA?
>
> Mr. Taber: I think five.
>
> Mr. Preston: Five members. I thank the Gentleman. If we were getting real results from this agency we might put up with the luxury of the hoodwinking and the blindfolding of Members of the House as to this Agency, but we are not getting it, so I think it is time we turned the light on them and found out how many employees they have, where they are operating, how many in Peru, how many in Venezuela, what they are doing, how much money they have.

Both Preston and Taber had already interacted with the CIA since the attack on Nixon — Taber to clarify what the agency had said to administration leaders about conditions in Venezuela prior to the riots and Preston regarding an invitation to visit the CIA for a briefing on the crisis. Taber continued,

> There never has been a single instance where they failed to produce information and lay it before the proper officers of the Government as to the facts on any of these things that have come on. I have checked that very carefully.
>
> Mr. Preston: Before whom did they lay the information about the insults that were going to be hurled at Vice President Nixon?
>
> Mr. Taber: They laid the whole information with reference to the people down in South America before the State Department before he left.

Before the debate ended, other House members indicted the CIA: "None of the major upheavals of recent years have been known to the American government and the American people until we read it in the papers, despite the fact that we are spending several million dollars a years on this Agency," said Robert Sikes (D-FL). "It is for that reason that I have today introduced a bill (H.R. 12534) to establish a Joint Congressional Committee on Foreign Intelligence," Peter Frelinghuysen (R-NJ) said. He also put a lengthy *Harper's* magazine article by Warren Unna into the *Congressional Record*. The article typified a new willingness in the press to critically analyze the history of the CIA, "the only major United States government agency entirely free of congressional scrutiny." This was unlikely to change soon, Unna wrote: "One of the Senate's leading liberals, speaking off the record, explained his own opposition by stating bluntly that he didn't think his colleagues could be trusted with such secrets."[2]

On the Senate side, reaction began the very afternoon of the mob attack against the Nixon party. Oregon's Wayne Morse ("a Nixon-hating Democrat," said *Time* magazine), who often spoke on a nearly deserted Senate floor late in the afternoon because news organizations in his home state were still at work in a time zone three hours earlier — assessed the attack: "I make this statement as the chairman of the Subcommittee on Latin American Affairs of the Committee on Foreign Relations. . . . While not a political supporter of the Vice President of the United States in American politics, I am a supporter of the Vice President whenever he appears on behalf of our country anywhere in the world. . . . I think we need to learn from the State Department why, apparently, our intelligence was not better." Worse still, he said, the United States had perhaps attracted such violent reaction because of "the support we have given to dictators in Cuba, the Dominican Republic, and elsewhere in Latin America." Mike Mansfield believed "that there is communist inspiration behind this well-developed pattern" of unrest in South America but added that U.S. foreign policy needed reexamination.

The next day, Lyndon Johnson paid tribute to Richard and Pat Nixon, then pronounced it "incredible" that "there was so little advance warning of the dangers into which our Vice President was walking." A few days later, Styles Bridges said that "now is a good time for a review" of the agency and its "advance preparations" for the Nixon trip. Stuart Symington asked for a "full investigation" of "intelligence agencies" that "failed to the point they apparently did."[3]

Notably silent in the few days of what the *New York Times* called the "CIA fight" were Chairmen Cannon, Vinson, Hayden, and Russell. The agency, though, mounted a public relations offensive with legislators and journalists in late May, and Stanley Grogan monitored the results. Some in the Congress rallied around the CIA within days, as Taber had. Representative Charles Porter (D-OR), without specifying his source, said that the agency "specifically cautioned" Nixon against motorcades and informal appearances. Senator Hubert Humphrey predicted, "You'll probably find the CIA had forewarned everyone." Others, like Representative Charles Chamberlain (R-MI) remained silent but informed Dulles of "correspondence from constituents" about failed "intelligence operations preceding the South American tour."

While the evidence is reasonably clear that the CIA did issue proper warnings about the explosive environment in Venezuela, this was not obvious to informed citizens at the time. Nixon declined to criticize the agency publicly; privately, he believed that CIA and State Department personnel were unable to "discover" that the "Communist high command in South America had made a high-level decision" to mount a "massive pay-off demonstration in Caracas" in reaction to the relative success of Nixon's Lima visit. Journalists were split over the judgment shown by the CIA, the State Department, and even Nixon, himself, over allowing the tour to occur. To the influential columnist Walter Lippmann, it was "manifest that the whole South American tour was misconceived, that it was planned by men who did not know what was the state of mind in the cities the Vice President was to visit." The Senate Foreign Relations Committee should investigate this "diplomatic Pearl Harbor," he said. *U.S. News* claimed that the agency "missed completely the Communist plans for attacking Nixon in South America," while *Newsweek* seemed to accept the claim made to them by CIA officials that "they warned the Administration of Latin American unrest."[4]

President Eisenhower increasingly feared throughout his presidency that, as the CIA testified before legislative bodies other than the regular Appropriations/Armed Services bodies, those "irregulars" would request agency testimony more and more. His fear was on-target in May 1958— Senate Foreign Relations insisted that Allen Dulles testify about the Nixon trip. Dulles also agreed to testify soon thereafter before Morse's subcommittee. The DCI went before the full committee just four days after Nixon's return to the United States. Assisted by covert action chief Frank Wisner and others in preparing for his testimony, Dulles began by quoting from Venezuelan Communist Party documents and putting them into context: "The pattern of international communism since the days of Lenin has been to destroy the free governments of the world." He described a recent meeting in Moscow of

> Latin American Communist Party leaders under the supervision of a Soviet Communist Party official who stressed the need for an action program and for stimulation of anti-American sentiment. . . . Implementation of this action program became quickly evident in the calling of a clandestine regional meeting of Communist Party leaders of Latin America in Cuernavaca, Mexico. . . . We have found since that time that the step-up of Communist activity in Latin America has been very marked.

The CIA "had warnings that the Communists in South America would endeavor to create incidents in connection with the Vice President's visit. We were in very close touch with the State Department and with the Secret Service before and daily during the trip," he said. In those countries where "reasonable police protection was afforded, no serious incident occurred." Venezuela's new government, "established under a junta, well intentioned, but weak . . . made beautiful promises to us. On paper, the security forces seemed to be adequate. In practice, they fell down."

Perhaps to deflect an attack on his and the agency's performance, Dulles admitted, "Maybe we should have known that. It is very hard to predict. How can you tell that a policeman is going to stand his ground or whether he is going to run in case of a mob? . . . I admit in the Central Intelligence Agency I cannot always predict when there is going to be a riot or what a riot is going to do." Dulles alluded specifically to Venezuelan students' animosity toward the United States for reasons including "our support of dictators in Cuba, the Dominican Republic, and Paraguay" and "the support of United Fruit and intervention in Guatemala."

During two hours of questions after his statement, Dulles educated senators about Venezuela:

> There is a hard core of the Communist Party that went underground and went abroad during the days of the Perez Jimenez regime. Then it flocked back after that regime fell [in January 1958]. That apparatus in Venezuela is in turn, through couriers and in other ways, radio, directly in touch with Moscow, and to a large extent takes its orders from Moscow in matters of this nature.

The Chairman [Senator Green]: It is supposed to be secret?

Mr. Dulles: Oh, yes.

The Chairman: But is it kept secret?

Mr. Dulles: Not entirely. We have penetrated Communist Parties in various parts of the world.

Apparently committee members accepted Dulles's view that Moscow was largely to blame for the riots. About the only unhappiness expressed in the hearing was that of Morse, who complained about it being "very cursory." But, referring to forthcoming hearings before his subcommittee, he expressed an intention to be "fully briefed as to the Nixon trip" and said a "thorough study" would be necessary. For Dulles, though, senators voiced only praise for his "frankness." Even Morse told Dulles and the State Department's Robert Murphy (who also testified), "You are two great professors." After the hearing, Morse told reporters that the Nixon trip had been "unwise," in light of intelligence reports that "there would be trouble." (While the press and senators hailed his forthcoming "investigation," records of agency testimony before Morse's subcommittee have not been found.)[5]

A few days after Dulles's May 19 Foreign Relations appearance, he went before the combined CIA subcommittees of the Senate Armed Services and Appropriations Committees, which Richard Russell chaired. (The Georgian had recently celebrated his twenty-fifth anniversary as a senator, feted by dozens of colleagues on the Senate floor. "He is the epitome of what many of us in this body would like to be," said Mansfield. Karl Mundt liked "the idea of eulogizing a colleague in the Senate while he is still with us.") Dulles and five aides faced Russell, Saltonstall, Hayden, Bridges, and staffer Bill Darden. Lawrence Houston's memo of the meeting was heavily censored by the CIA, which released it in 2003. In response to a question from Saltonstall, the only "failure" Dulles admitted to was neglecting to "appraise properly" the security precautions taken by the Venezuelan government. Notes of a discussion following a Hayden question on "repercussions" in Latin America were almost entirely censored, except for Houston's observation, "Senator Russell remarked that this was one which they, the senators, should stay out of." At a hearing four weeks later of the Inter-American Affairs subcommittee of the House Foreign Affairs Committee, Dulles repeated his main theme: "The promised police protection was not furnished."

After all that testimony, some grumbling continued on Capitol Hill; the *Washington Star* reported on May 23, "Senator Kefauver . . . said last night that if Allen Dulles, head of the Central Intelligence Agency, didn't have the correct information in advance on the kind of reception Vice President Nixon would receive in South America, 'then he ought to be fired.'" But Kefauver, for all his fame as a would-be president, had little influence in the Senate. And newspaper columnists soon gave up on the Nixon trip intelligence failure topic. Grogan reported happily to his boss that some influential columnists, including Joe Alsop, never "mentioned CIA in connection with the Vice President's trip."

By admitting some fallibility in response to the outcry in Congress, Dulles had pretty well dodged a bullet. Many legislators accepted his view that the Nixon incident had alerted the U.S. and Latin American governments to new threats. Senator Alexander Wiley summarized: "This has probably brought home to us and also to the South American countries the insidious penetration of the Communists."[6]

Four weeks later, on June 18, 1958, the DCI met with an unhappy President Eisenhower, whose chief of staff, Sherman Adams, was under fire in the press and would eventually resign for improperly using his influence with government agencies on behalf of a gift-wielding friend. Joining Dulles and Ike in the session were national security assistant Goodpaster and White House legislative liaison Harlow. Besides Dulles informing the president about impending testimony before the JCAE that the CIA was revising downward its previous estimates of Soviet missile and bomber aircraft capabilities, the meeting was the latest in a series called to warn the DCI against too frequent Capitol Hill appearances. About the revised estimates, Eisenhower groused at Dulles that "the Soviets have done much better than have we in this matter. They stopped their Bison and Bear production, but we have kept on going, on the basis of incorrect estimates and at tremendous expense in a mistaken effort to be 100% secure." Dulles seems not to have argued the point, remarking that the Soviets appeared "to be looking to the guided missile rather than to the heavy bomber as their major weapon for the future."

After that opening, Goodpaster suggested consideration of "what committees Mr. Dulles should appear before, what their security record is, and how the problem of conflict in testimony" between the CIA and the State and Defense departments could be avoided. The topic was timely, as the DCI or his representatives were to appear that very day before a House subcommittee. While Dulles emphasized the "very good" security of the CIA subcommittees, someone (not named in Goodpaster's notes) reminded him of "security violations" after his appearance before Lyndon Johnson's Preparedness subcommittee seven months before.

Goodpaster then raised Dulles's testimony before the Foreign Affairs/ Relations committees, which had troubled Eisenhower by publicizing the CIA's and Defense Department's seemingly different estimates of Soviet military strength. While the DCI claimed that coordination between the two agencies had been "very successful," no one else in the meeting supported this view. Eisenhower eventually gave "general assent" to Dulles giving such testimony, so long as it was "thus coordinated." But on all "political matters," he said that the State Department should do all such briefings. When Dulles defended his and Murphy's recent appearance before Senate Foreign Relations, "The President, while recognizing that such testimony might be necessary on occasion, reiterated his view that it would be better for the State Department to testify." Eisenhower again warned the DCI against testifying "too frequently," as Congress would "tend to inject itself into matters of operating detail and executive decision." He urged Dulles, "Keep as aloof as possible."

After that chastisement, Dulles had Herbert Scoville review for Eisenhower what the CIA would say to the JCAE about recent Soviet tests. The next day, CIA heads appeared before a Senate Foreign Relations subcommittee.[7]

Iraq: "Our Intelligence Was Just Plain Lousy"

Throughout the following June and early July, the U.S. government faced new problems in the Middle East. The pro-Western government of Lebanon had been struggling to put down an uprising that received at least strong rhetorical support from President Nasser of Egypt — a figure viewed with extreme anxiety by the Eisenhower administration and many in Congress. "If he was not a Communist," Eisenhower later wrote, "he certainly succeeded in making us very suspicious of him." Earlier in the year, Egypt and Syria had announced plans to form a new United Arab Republic (UAR). Soon thereafter, the pro-Western monarchy of King Faisal in Iraq announced its plans to form the new Arab Union (AU) with Jordan, headed by Faisal's second cousin, King Hussein. Eisenhower thought both kings were "courageous"; he judged Iraq as "the more powerful" of the two nations: "This was the country that we were counting on heavily as a bulwark of stability and progress in the region."

The president and Secretary Dulles made policy toward the Middle East, knowing that they had Congress behind them. A year earlier, members had overwhelmingly endorsed the Eisenhower Doctrine, which (in Eisenhower's later words) resolved "to block the Soviet Union's march to the Mediterranean, to the Suez Canal and the pipelines, and to the underground lakes of oil which fuel the homes and factories of Western Europe."

On Monday morning, July 14, Eisenhower was "shocked to receive the news of a coup in Baghdad" against King Faisal's government: "The army, apparently with mob participation, had moved upon the royal palace and had murdered Crown Prince Emir Abdul Illah." Soon Eisenhower learned that the king and his premier, Nuri al-Said, had also been killed. Ironically, the crown prince had recently suggested a partnership of the United States, Iraq, and Syrian dissidents in covert action to take Egyptian "pressure off . . . Lebanon." "This somber turn of events," Eisenhower later wrote, "could, without vigorous response on our part, result in a complete elimination of Western influence in the Middle East."[1]

Much as Eisenhower feared, Iraq would move into a distinctly new political era, eliminating decades-old (and U.S.-supported) British influence. The coup, in fact, fomented what one scholar later described as "a social, political, and cultural revolution" in Iraq. The looting and burning of the British embassy was appropriately symbolic. More shocking was the treatment of Nuri's body after his execution in the streets of Baghdad — a British diplomat observed as "a car was driven backwards and forwards over it, until it was flattened into the ground."

Eisenhower had been hesitant about intervening in Lebanon during weeks of political turmoil and intrigue, although he had already virtually promised the Lebanese government of President Camille Chamoun that he would do so if conditions warranted. Terrified by the latest news from Iraq, the Lebanese leader quickly vented fury on the American ambassador for the hesitancy of the United States. Robert McClintock cryptically described the encounter in a cable to the State Department: "Chamoun said he did not wish any more inquiries or specifications or conditions re our intervention. . . . He wanted the 6th Fleet here within 48 hours or else he would know where he stood re assurances of support from West." While Eisenhower asked the British government to refrain from intervening, the United States quickly prepared to send troops into Lebanon.[2]

The same day that the president learned of the Iraqi coup, he invited congressional leaders to briefings by the Dulles brothers on Iraq and to discuss the likely U.S. intervention in Lebanon. Some of the legislators — Senators Fulbright, Green, and Wiley of the Foreign Relations Committee — had mulled over the decline in Lebanon's stability with Secretary Dulles three weeks earlier. Dulles had expressed hope that intervention could be avoided, as it might endanger "the position of our friends in other countries in the Middle East." He had warned administration colleagues, including his brother, that "what was at stake here was the whole periphery of the Soviet Union."

No senator seems to have disagreed with Secretary Dulles on any point on June 23. Rather, once-classified meeting notes show:

> The Secretary was asked whether we had any ability through CIA to organize our indigenous forces which could be used to combat the insurrectionists. It was suggested that many Turks and others from the area looked like Lebanese and could perhaps be infiltrated as counter forces. The Secretary did not give a direct answer to this question, although he did mention that consideration had been given sometime ago to the formation of a 'freedom corps' made up of nationalities which could be used for occasions such as this. He also made

reference to the difficulties of this kind of covert activity, citing humiliating experience which [Saudi Arabian] King Saud had recently undergone when an operation of his backfired.

Eisenhower and the Dulles brothers addressed familiar faces at the White House on July 14, among them the most prominent and would-be overseers of the CIA, including Russell, Bridges, Saltonstall, Mansfield, Cannon, Taber, and Vinson. The DCI's detailed report — duplicating his remarks to Eisenhower earlier in the day — cited one report that the Iraqi crown prince had been "torn limb from limb." The coup was carried out by "pro-Nasser elements," including junior army officers and "leftist" civilian members of the Baath Party. While the "hand of Nasser" was evident, there was "some question" as to whether the coup had been "dictated by Egypt." This was an understatement, as Nasser was actually completing a visit to Yugoslavia.

Dulles concluded, according to notes that he closely followed: "If the Iraq coup succeeds, it seems almost inevitable that it will set up a chain reaction which will doom the pro-West governments of Lebanon and Jordan and Saudi Arabia, and raise grave problems for Turkey and Iran. . . . The Soviet Union will undoubtedly welcome these developments and do what it feels it safely can without direct involvement in overt hostilities to support this chain reaction."

While most of the subsequent discussion focused on the risks and merits of intervening in Lebanon, something the legislators knew had already been requested by Chamoun, Fulbright raised the question of "whether CIA had notice of the coup in Iraq." Even after decades, the CIA has prevented release of Dulles's answer to this question. However, Sherman Adams's memoirs make it obvious that Dulles's answer to Fulbright's question was some version of "no": "The Central Intelligence Agency and the military intelligence sources had given the President no forewarning of the sudden revolt in Iraq, and the Congressmen did not hesitate to point this out at the meeting."[3]

The weather was stormy the night after the briefing, and Senator Alex Smith slept poorly. A devout, lifelong Episcopalian, perhaps he was bothered by a headline in the previous day's *Post*: "[Archbishop of] Canterbury Says God May End Human Race in an H-Bomb War." For thirty-one years, Smith had awakened early each morning to pray and write in his diary. At 3:00 a.m., he wrote, "The Iraq situation is terrible. Allen Dulles, CIA do not seem to know anything about it." A good friend of the DCI, Smith added, "I am seeking God and his guidance in a terrible crisis. The 'coup' in Iraq has caused a threat to us all and world peace."

Adams and Smith were accurate regarding the CIA and the rest of the intelligence establishment — they *had* failed to predict the coup. Just days earlier, the CIA's clandestine services chief, Frank Wisner, had told the State Department's director of intelligence that while "articulate public opinion" in Iraq was preponderantly hostile to the government there, activists were small in number and badly organized or easily controllable by "firm government action." Happily, he thought, Iraqi internal security forces and leaders had improved distinctly over the past year. No wonder that Secretary Dulles told Eisenhower just after the coup happened that he had "no ideas, because it happened so fast." The secretary was unhappy with "reluctant" U.S. generals and admirals who planned a move into Lebanon. He told Vice President Nixon: "All they think about is dropping nuclear bombs and they don't like it when we get off that. They say Lebanon exhausts their possibilities." Nixon said, "We are prepared for the war we probably will never fight and not for the one which will be lost."

At the White House session, congressional leaders mostly supported intervention. Carl Vinson told Eisenhower, "We must make up our minds to go the distance. . . . free government is on trial." Fulbright questioned whether the Iraqi coup had been "Soviet or Communist-inspired." The president admitted that "there is not enough hard intelligence to be sure." Bridges thought "control of the Middle Eastern oil is of determining effect on the free world's future." But the group left the intervention decision up to Eisenhower. The president said that neither intervention nor a hands-off approach was "attractive," but the latter policy would be a "Munich approach. I am sure that if we do not move, this continuing crumbling will go on. If Iraq goes, all the pipelines go." When the legislators returned to Capitol Hill from the two-and-a-half-hour session, the *Washington Post* described them as "tight-lipped, but visibly shaken." The director of central intelligence seemed unfazed by events, though. Coming out of the White House later in the day, reporters asked if he could describe the meetings that had occurred. Dulles responded laughingly, "I never tell anything."

None of the "shaken" legislators had countered Speaker Rayburn's comment that "only one person should make a statement" about the meeting "and that one should be the President." However, within hours, as Eisenhower joined key advisers to work out details of the intervention in Lebanon, press secretary James Hagerty informed him that "congressmen who were in attendance this afternoon have already been leaking to the press." Thus it was no surprise to the American public when Hagerty announced the next day that marines had landed in Beirut to "protect American lives" and "assist the government of Lebanon to preserve its territorial integrity and political independence."[4]

Over the next few weeks, as ordinary Americans debated the merits of the Lebanese incursion, administration leaders wrestled with its propriety too. Privately, it pained Eisenhower that "the people" in Arab countries were "on Nasser's side," but General Nathan Twining assured him that sometimes intervention was the "right thing to do." Ike agreed, "so long as the action rests on moral ground."

An angry debate gained momentum on the floors of the House and Senate over the following three weeks: Had CIA incompetence deprived Eisenhower and others of critical advance warning of the Iraqi coup that inflamed the Lebanese crisis? Was the United States facing the "greatest challenge since Pearl Harbor," as one senator phrased it, due to flawed agency performance? The seriousness of this debate is reflected in CIA papers from July–August 1958. Never had the agency made such thorough records of legislative and press responses to an alleged intelligence failure. Grogan listed for the DCI every member of Congress and every newspaper editorial or column in the nation known to have addressed the "Iraqi 'surprise' issue." Grogan's records tracked "the general coverage and climate of congressional opinion in which the CIA has once more been publicly involved" from the day of the July 14 Iraqi coup through the following August 14.

Among the critical comments Grogan noted: "Rep. Charles B. Brownson . . . introduces House resolution somewhat similar to Mansfield's, July 16." "*Philadelphia Inquirer,* July 17: reports that Congressmen are 'deeply disturbed' about 'a serious failure of intelligence.'" "New York *World Telegram and Sun,* Roger Stuart, July 16: reports . . . CIA is 'a sore point with a rather large number of Senators and House members.'" A minority of nationally prominent columnists were sympathetic to the CIA: "New York *Mirror,* Walter Winchell, July 18: praises DCI, says that CIA is being made 'scapegoat.'"

It was not just influential newspapers that Grogan reported on to Dulles. If the DCI wanted to know how the *Greensburg* (Pennsylvania) *Tribune-Review*'s editorial page assessed the agency performance in the Iraqi crisis, Grogan's reports had it: the wave of criticism "appears to be justified. . . .

we — and especially the CIA people — cannot afford to be politically naive." Or if Dulles was curious about the *Saratoga Springs* (New York) *Saratogan*, Grogan had its analysis supporting congressional scrutiny of the CIA: "Something seems terribly wrong."

Grogan similarly followed newspaper columnists and broadcast commentators — famous ones like Winchell and Howard K. Smith of CBS Radio ("the state of our continuing intelligence shocked the world") and less influential figures like Douglas Smith of the *Pittsburg Press* and Aaron Benesch of the *St. Louis Globe-Democrat*. In fact, Grogan noted and attached photocopies of hundreds of press responses, favorable or not, to the government's and especially the CIA's handling of the Iraqi crisis. His reports, occasionally getting handwritten amendments from Dulles, were so thorough as to list even newspapers and columns that had *not* commented on the issue.

Of those in the press and the Congress that had analyzed the issue, the DCI's aide said, many had been restrained and temperate. But this was a positive spin on his own numbers. On July 18, Grogan had reported to Dulles, "In all, 73 press and congressional comments have appeared since last Monday on the 'surprise' issue. Of them, seven have been friendly to CIA and 30, unfavorable." Others were "neutral." As of July 28, by Grogan's count, sixty-seven legislators had spoken publicly about some aspect of the Middle East crisis. Of those, "16 senators and 12 representatives have publicly commented on CIA or U.S. intelligence. . . . Most of these comments have been unfavorable." By August 15, with Grogan compiling 466 cases of journalistic and legislative comments on the Iraqi "surprise," unfavorable comments on Capitol Hill and in the news media continued to be more than double the favorable ones.

Grogan's quantitative analysis was suggestive of the prevailing congressional anger. In the Senate, Mike Mansfield said, "The events in Iraq of yesterday have burst upon us like a bombshell." The majority whip reintroduced his old resolution calling for a joint congressional committee on intelligence, something he had viewed as impolitic since the resolution's defeat two years earlier. Hubert Humphrey warned on July 17, "We must take into consideration that there could be a terrible war, even the beginnings of World War III." And while speaking well of Dulles and suggesting that the CIA had probably improved its intelligence performance over the years, he endorsed Mansfield's idea. Wayne Morse said, "Our intelligence was just plain lousy." In the House, Representative Armistead Selden (D-AL) recited a litany of CIA failures:

Only a few weeks ago, the life of our Vice President was endangered in Latin America. The CIA apparently did not supply him with a very definite warning as to what to expect. Back in 1950, the Committee on Foreign Affairs was told by the head of the CIA only a few days before the outbreak of fighting in Korea that there was no immediate threat in that area. There is doubt in my mind and in the minds of many others that the CIA was aware of the situation in Hungary before the tragic revolt in that country or that the President and the Secretary of State were adequately informed of events before the invasion of Suez by Israel, the United Kingdom, and France. . . . The people of the United States would have more confidence in the CIA if they knew that there was close congressional supervision of CIA operations.

Representative Charles Brownson (R-IN) called Iraq the "final straw" in a series of intelligence failures. Then, referring to members of the Armed Services/Appropriations subcommittees on the CIA, Brownson said intelligence oversight ought not to be "delegated to a few men, a very few men. These men are terribly busy because they are on two of the most overworked committees in Congress."[5]

After two weeks of legislative assaults on the agency, George Mahon sent Dulles the critical views of a fellow legislator and made a request: "I would like to know whether or not our government failed to know about probable developments in Iraq; and, if so, was the CIA responsible for this failure." Dulles appeared secretly before Mahon's subcommittee a few days later, with Clarence Cannon attending. There, according to Red White's diary, "Most of the session was taken up on . . . our alleged failure in Iraq." Also, "there was some discussion as to how the Committee could be kept briefed on a permanent basis, whether they should put a man down with us full time or whether we could distribute to them our weekly and daily reports." But, he added, "no agreement was reached." Toward the meeting's end, Cannon suggested that the agency's personnel and — by implication, its budget — should be cut. Dulles took offense at this, saying he was trying to cut personnel but could not guarantee success. Furthermore, "he expected to come back in January asking for $40 or $50 million more than we had asked for in Fiscal Year 1959." Later in the year, Mahon warned Deputy Director Cabell and John Warner that (as the legislative counsel noted)

he heard considerable criticism of the Agency from his colleagues, some of whom wondered if the Agency had too many people and whether or not it was incompetent. Therefore, he felt he would like to talk with some of our field representatives to learn more of our activities abroad. Mr. Mahon made a particular point that while he knew Mr. Dulles and General Cabell discussed matters frankly with him, he would like to be assured that our representatives abroad would talk with him in the same frank manner. General Cabell assured him they would receive word on this.

The DCI also went before Vinson's Armed Services subcommittee on the CIA on July 30, a subcommittee of the House Foreign Affairs Committee on August 5, and Senator Russell's CIA subcommittee on August 8. Records of all those encounters are still classified, if they exist at all, but Dulles must have been in top form at the Foreign Affairs hearing — CIA critic Wayne Hays (D-OH) said afterward that Dulles's testimony left him "far more satisfied" with the CIA's performance than before.[6]

Predictably, the one written record of Dulles testimony over the Iraq issue comes from the Foreign Relations Committee. Of course, if Allen Dulles and the White House had had their way, there would have been no such testimony. Presumably, the DCI read Drew Pearson's July 22 column (passed on by Grogan) predicting that Dulles would "definitely" have to go before the Senate committee soon. Judged retrospectively, the accuracy of Pearson's columns in the two weeks after the coup is impressive. He claimed, correctly, that rather than anticipating the Iraqi event, the United States had such high regard for Iraq's army that it had devised plans to use it in Lebanon. For "failing to learn of the revolt in Iraq until 2:00 a.m. of the day it happened," Dulles would have to explain himself. (The columnist also claimed, mysteriously, that Dulles would "fire his intelligence chief in Iraq — if he can ever find him." The mystery was apparently solved some years later, when a Dulles biographer reported that those who murdered the Iraqi leaders "also killed the local CIA station chief.")

When Foreign Relations did invite him, Dulles complained to his brother on the morning of July 25 that he was being "pressured hard" to comply. He noted that Armed Services Chairman Russell typically tried to limit such appearances, sometimes telephoning colleagues and asking them not to examine the CIA. Dulles hoped the senator might save him from Foreign Relations testimony this time, too. According to State Department notes of his morning conversation with Secretary Dulles, the DCI telephoned Russell, but the senator "would not give him support not to go." On the contrary: "He thought AWD should go. AWD does not like to go, but does not know what to do about it." Nor did the Secretary like it, but in light of Russell's distressing conclusion, there was, by Dulles's own account, no other choice. Three days later, the DCI notified the Committee; it would be his third Foreign Relations appearance in 1958.[7]

On the afternoon of July 29, in the chandeliered room normally used by Foreign Relations for executive sessions, the DCI sat before the soon-to-retire Chairman Green, Senator Fulbright, who would succeed him, ten other committee members, and three staffers. Always capable of uttering polite untruths, Dulles expressed his "appreciation" for the "opportunity to appear before your committee" and pledged "as full a fill-in as you may wish." He admitted with some frankness that the agency had not been especially successful. The CIA had alerted "the highest levels of the Government" on March 6 that "existing trends" in Jordan, Iraq, and Saudi Arabia suggested grave danger to those governments. But "rumors of plots and assassinations" were common in the Middle East, he said, so it was "very hard to separate the wheat from the chaff." "At that time, we considered the situation in Jordan to be the most shaky . . . in Saudi Arabia to be the second most shaky, and the situation in Iraq to be shaky but probably less shaky than in the other two countries."

At least in the uncensored portions of the hearing, Dulles did not blame other agencies for the CIA's failure of prediction — asked if the Agency's reporting had been based on State Department or other reports, Dulles said that the CIA had relied primarily on its own "secret channels." It was obvious in his testimony that the CIA had relied too much on the Iraqi government's analyses and supposed military strength: "We appraised the Iraq situation as somewhat stronger than the others because it had a strong leader, because it had a better Army . . . and because that leadership in Iraq had extreme, and as it turned out, exaggerated confidence in its own ability." As to the timing of the coup, Dulles claimed that it "could probably not have been predicted." Conceding that it was not an "alibi," he noted that the Iraqi "government itself, which was one of the few governments in the Middle East that had a reasonably good security service, was caught entirely napping." Even Nasser had been surprised by its timing, the CIA believed.

Most members were fairly deferential to Dulles, but not William Langer, who took exception to Dulles's terminology and its political implications:

> Senator Langer: Mr. Chairman, the witness several times has used the expression "mob." Do you mean by that the patriotic people of Iraq who are

sick and tired of having those in control of Iraq bribed by the United States government?

Mr. Dulles: I am not sure I caught the question, Senator.

Senator Langer: The question is, you several times have used the expression here about the mob —

Mr. Dulles: The mob, yes.

Senator Langer: Yes. Do you mean the patriotic people of Iraq who were sick and tired of having 2 percent who were in control there, who were being bribed by the United States government to run the country?

Mr. Dulles: I do not think that those who took part in the pretty brutal murders on the day of the coup were necessarily the patriotic citizens of Iraq to which you refer.

Senator Langer: The Secretary of State several times has told this committee that the one solid Arab country we could bank on was Iraq. What have you to say about that now?

Mr. Dulles: Well, I do my own testifying, Senator. . . . All I can say is that among the Arab countries, Iraq did appear to be, until recently, the most solid, among a group of countries, none of which has been or is too solid or has been for many years.

Much of the remaining discussion was of Nasser. Reacting to one senator's statement that the Egyptian leader was "a complete tool of the Kremlin," Dulles replied that, while Nasser "has come under a good deal of the influence . . . he is not yet the tool of Moscow." The DCI told senators something they seemed not to already know, that the U.S. ambassador to Egypt talked frequently to Nasser. Dulles also spoke of a "friend" who was then serving as his go-between with Nasser. "If nothing was done" (i.e., if the United States had not intervened in Lebanon), Dulles added, he had advised the president "that Lebanon and Jordan would shortly follow the fate of Iraq, and that Saudi Arabia would also fall . . . very shortly thereafter." Additionally, Dulles told Fulbright about countries of the Middle East in which the CIA and the Soviet Union did or did not have agents. Mansfield pressed the DCI on the problem of CIA figures working at "cross purposes" with State Department personnel abroad. Dulles replied to Mansfield's satisfaction (though not entirely honestly): "If they do, I get them out. . . . I rap them over the knuckles and I do that quite often."

Perhaps because the Iraqi event really was a failure for the CIA, senators did not praise Dulles's testimony effusively, as they had in the year's two previous hearings. The *New York Times* indicated that Dulles and the senators mostly kept quiet after the meeting, though Fulbright did say that the CIA had " 'considerably more information' about the new leaders in Iraq than it did at the time of the revolt," and Langer complained about the secrecy surrounding the hearing.[8]

Within another week or so, the furor of the latest "surprise" issue began to die down, as members of Congress started heading home. Still, the sheer volume of legislative criticism in late summer 1958 suggests that the agency's reputation had suffered. This provoked some anger at the CIA. A Plans Directorate leader warned Dulles that "the extensive press and congressional criticism" created a danger that "some stations may react to the clamor by habitually predicting disaster, in the manner of Joe Alsop, to cover their number." At year's end, another Dulles aide would face a nearly impossible request: could not the CIA start giving "an occasional intelligence briefing where the Agency foresaw the possibility of some event," asked House Armed Services staffer Robert Smart. As for the press, Grogan indicated to his boss, "CIA has been caught, once again (as in the Hungarian and Suez situations in 1956) in a rash of press accusations, innuendos, skepticism, and doubt-raising comments about intelligence performance."

The CIA's (and Eisenhower's) reputation might have suffered more if the Lebanese intervention had gone very badly. The worst of it had been the embarrassment of U.S. troops storming a Lebanese beach full of unconcerned sunbathers. The country saw an eventual transition to another elected leader, and the United States withdrew its troops, in line with a United Nations resolution. Iraq's new government, under General Abdul Qassim, who had led the coup in July, would turn eventually on both Nasserites and the Communist Party there in an effort to stay in power. The Foreign Relations Committee would question Allen Dulles about this later in the year.

Eventually, many analysts thought Eisenhower had overreacted by intervening in Lebanon. This crossed his mind, too, after the man who had helped lead the Lebanese rebellion in 1958, Rashid Karami, showed up as a likeable and not-so-radical Lebanese premier visiting the White House in 1959. There, he told Eisenhower that the landing of 15,000 U.S. troops had been unnecessary, that the skillful U.S. diplomat Robert Murphy could have done equally successful work without the American military there. Afterward, Eisenhower wrote, "I could not completely smother the thought that, if one visitor's statement had been true, every one in my administration could have been saved a lot of anxious hours."[9]

Return to Missile Gap

No member of Congress put President Eisenhower in a worse mood during the last couple of years of his administration than W. Stuart Symington III. The two men had once been friendly, toiling in the fields of national security during the Truman era, but that time had passed. The Missouri senator — tall, elegantly dressed, articulate, and ambitious — lived with his wife in a Georgetown home decorated with Renaissance art. It was no small trick for Symington to have won the confidence of political bosses, wealthy elites, and ordinary voters in Missouri in 1952, mastering the concerns of constituents such as farmers by learning the intricacies of agricultural policy. However, from his days as secretary of the air force, then head of the National Security Resources Board under Truman, and ever since, his passion had been national defense.

Yale-educated, the son-in-law of a former senator, and hardworking, Symington impressed many as a substantial legislator. When he walked onto the Senate floor in 1953, Joseph McCarthy was in his heyday. Symington quickly took on the Wisconsin senator, though to no great effect, and soon feared the impact on his own career. By the late 1950s, Symington longed for the presidency. Some thought he would get it, but others saw little depth and a lack of consistency to the senator, despite his focus on defense. Joseph Alsop was a Symington ally on defense issues but told friends that the senator was "really too shallow a puddle to jump into." Drew Pearson, once friendly with Symington, came to regard him as lacking courage, someone who "just won't stand up."

Edward P. Morgan, an observer of 1950s Washington, wrote that Symington had initially been "at the threshold of the Inner Club . . . that elite, invisible group with a somewhat southern accent, which, under the aegis of Lyndon Johnson, seems to influence to such an extent the destinies of the Senate." All through the years of Bomber Gap and now Missile Gap, Symington seemed sure of his righteousness. After winning reelection in 1958, he told a friend in Washington, "At times, I seem to be about the only man in this town fighting for an adequate defense." This conviction helps explain Morgan's assessment of Symington in the Senate, that he "never quite passed through the door" into the "Sanctum" of its most powerful leaders. His preoccupation with military matters would "bore one colleague" and "make another jealous of his expertise." George Reedy, who worked for Richard Russell and Lyndon Johnson, later wrote that the Missourian, for all his intelligence and competence, had little impact within the Senate. "Nobody had any anecdotes about Symington."[1]

No one was more prominently associated in the press with the missile gap issue than Symington, though. While Russell shared some of Symington's fears about weaknesses in American defenses, he harbored a quiet opinion that Symington indulged in too many leaks and dabbled in demagoguery. John Kennedy and Lyndon Johnson also made much of supposed U.S. vulnerability and frequently complimented Symington's leadership on the issue. But they tried to elbow him (and each other) out of the way toward the Democratic presidential nomination in 1960.

Symington and Allen Dulles had found it surprisingly easy to talk during their periodic conflicts in the mid-1950s. By 1958, as the DCI knew, the senator was increasingly worried about missiles. On what Symington would later describe as "one pleasant summer night" that year, the director invited the senator to the CIA to hear the latest on Soviet missiles. So, as the senator later said of the invitation, "I took it."

On July 21, Dulles gave Symington a briefing based (the DCI would tell Eisenhower) "upon coordinated estimates of the Intelligence Community and not solely estimates of the Central Intelligence Agency." Working from a document written for the occasion, Dulles told Symington what U.S. intelligence knew, what it believed, and what it predicted. Among the few things known with certainty was "the existence of a new 3,500 nautical mile ballistic missile test range" in the USSR. Dulles did not tell Symington how that knowledge was acquired, though.

With only a little less certainty, the DCI reported to Symington, "We believe that six ICBM vehicles have been successfully flight-tested on this range and that all three Soviet earth satellites were launched from there. We have good evidence that at least the last four ICBM firings reached the general impact area." Analysts also believed that the USSR was developing an ICBM which, when operational, could carry a nuclear warhead 5,500 nautical miles.

Dulles predicted, "Some time during the year 1959, the USSR will probably have a first operational capability with up to 10 prototype ICBMs.... We cannot, however, disregard the possibility that the Soviets may establish in the latter part of 1958 a limited ICBM capability with missiles of unproven accuracy and reliability." He added that what the CIA and other agencies did *not* know was critical. It was also remarkable, in light of all the publicity on a supposed gap: "We have no firm evidence of the construction of bases for launching ICBMs or of their deployment." Nonetheless, the intelligence establishment believed that ICBMs could "probably be produced, launching facilities completed, and operational units trained at a rate sufficient to give the USSR an operational capability with 100 ICBMs about one year — 1960 — after its first operational capability date, and with 500 ICBMs about two or three years — 1961–62 — after first operational capability date."

Bureaucracies commonly treat grave matters with unemotional language, but Symington would not have missed Dulles's meaning — the Soviet Union probably would have the ability to launch a highly destructive nuclear attack against the United States in 1959, if not in the very year in which they were speaking. By 1960, the USSR "probably" could rain utter destruction across most of the United States. Also, it would "likely" have "nuclear weapons delivery systems capable of reaching the majority of our overseas bases" with nuclear warheads on shorter-range missiles sometime in 1958.[2]

Symington was an audience of one that day in Dulles's CIA office, an unusual setting with multiple exits, entrances, and nearby waiting rooms to accommodate the occasional need for confidentiality about who was visiting. The senator was no such mysterious guest, but he was a strong-willed one, seeing the DCI's report as confirming a missile gap. After all, the United States would not be able to launch a nearly instantaneous nuclear attack against the Soviet Union for a few years. The early 1960s looked to be especially dangerous — while the United States might well match the Soviets' ten ICBMs in 1959, projections (from the Defense Department) for 1960 showed the United States with thirty such missiles, seventy fewer than those the USSR would likely have. The gap was projected to be far larger, in the hundreds, in 1961 and 1962. The awkward truth for Allen Dulles, the man whose name was on National Intelligence Estimates, was that U.S. intelligence leaders *did* imply a missile gap. President Eisenhower's instincts, though, told him that any gap would be small and insignificant, in light of both countries' overall military capabilities.[3]

Even assuming that intelligence estimates (for both countries) were accurate, the interpretation of them depended very much on how one viewed the Soviet and U.S. governments and their respective military forces. Historian Edgar Bottome suggested that "three schools of thought originated in 1957–1958, in response to the possibility of a shift in the strategic balance of power" between the two superpowers. Those in the first group said the USSR "was planning a surprise attack on the United States as soon as they felt they had gained a definite superiority in nuclear striking power." The air force's Thomas S. Power, one of Eisenhower's least favorite generals, typified the group, saying of the Soviets, "They will use it against us when they think they are stronger than us." Many academics made up a second school of thought, which held that, since "no nation could be certain of destroying its enemy's nuclear striking force, no nation would attempt a surprise attack." A third group, including many analysts of Soviet military doctrine, thought that the USSR's leaders had repudiated surprise attack strategy as "likely to endanger the survival of the Soviet Union, itself." The Soviet leadership "had assigned its long-range ballistic missile to the defensive mission of deterring a United States attack on the Soviet Union."[4]

Symington feared that the first group of analysts was right. So too did his ally, Harvard professor Henry Kissinger, then publishing alarming missile gap articles. Eisenhower never denied that long-range missiles equipped with nuclear warheads constituted the "ultimate weapon" but told two of his scientific advisers in early 1959 that it "would be at least a few years before the Soviets could conceivably have enough missiles so as not to have grounds to fear retaliation." Moreover, Eisenhower and the Dulles brothers strongly believed that the USSR would not launch a nuclear war. "No matter what differences in culture and tradition, values or language, the Russian leaders were human beings, and they wanted to remain alive," Eisenhower later wrote.

While the president accepted the need for a substantial American deterrent, he did not believe that the United States required the same numbers and types of weaponry held by the Soviets. With persistence and occasional anger, he often reminded Defense Department officials of this. Late in 1958, he responded to Chief of Naval Operations Admiral Arleigh Burke's argument at an NSC session for pushing ahead with the Polaris submarine missile program: "The President said that if what he [Burke] had stated was correct, then it was toward the Polaris program objectives that we should be building hard, but at the same time we are also trying to buy time with our Atlas missile, the Titan missile, and practically everything else. How many times do we have to calculate what we need to destroy the Soviet Union?" Ike often wondered aloud how many times he had to say that balancing the budget was a matter of national security, for unbalanced ones would weaken the national economy. "The U.S. defense system has got to be one that this country can carry for forty years," he told his NSC. He also worried that creating too huge a military would fundamentally alter American culture, society, and politics. Some in the administration privately differed with Eisenhower on these points, but he did not agonize over this. He knew who was president, and who was not.[5]

Symington's fears turned to alarm on August 5, when he met with Thomas Lanphier, an old friend who had served as his assistant secretary of air force and was now vice president of the Convair Corporation, which worked on the Atlas missile program. Lanphier remained well-connected to the air force, serving as a colonel in the reserve. Symington obviously shared a good deal of his recently acquired, highly classified intelligence on Soviet capabilities with Lanphier, who claimed to be aghast — *his* information, picked up from persons within the military services, the Atomic Energy Commission, and the CIA, indicated far more extensive missile testing and more sizable Soviet nuclear war fighting arsenals than suggested by Dulles.

Symington urgently telephoned Richard Russell, receiving clearance to pursue the matter with the DCI, whom he then called. The next day, Symington and Lanphier met Dulles at the CIA. Howard Stoertz, of the Office of National Estimates staff, took notes (still heavily censored by the CIA):

> The Senator expressed his great confidence in Lanphier, based on long personal association. Lanphier had come to him only the day before with information on Soviet IRBM and ICBM progress which did not agree with what the DCI had told him a short time before. . . . The Senator felt the only thing to do was to lay the problem on the table with the DCI. . . . Lanphier added that Senator Symington and the DCI were the first people to whom he had voiced his concern. The Senator indicated that they both planned to talk with Henry Kissinger that night. . . . Lanphier several times made it clear that his information was hearsay from people in the intelligence business, although he said not all of it was from any one source. He believed it was sufficiently different from the DCI's official position, and apparently so much more alarming, that he and his informants were concerned. The DCI, on the other hand, stated that he did not feel that he was minimizing the danger, and that he could not go along with Lanphier's figures on test firings.

When the DCI asked the two men where they obtained their "intelligence," Symington responded, "From your own and other elements of the national intelligence system." Two unnamed sources, in particular, claimed that the Soviets had engaged in far more test firings of ICBMs than the DCI believed. Dulles "doubted that Lanphier's figures could be backed up in any intelligence component in the government." Annoyed at Lanphier's access to highly classified figures and emphasis on worst-case possibilities, Dulles refused to debate U.S. intelligence estimates with a defense industry leader and eventually required Lanphier to leave his office, so that he could try to persuade Symington of the more balanced conclusions that might be derived from current estimates. This failed. Following a determined point raised by the senator, the DCI acknowledged that "if the Soviets achieved a first operational capability in the latter part of 1958, they might have 500 at the end of 1960."[6]

Two days later, Dulles also evaluated Soviet capabilities before Richard Russell's CIA subcommittee — with Symington attending at Russell's invitation. Afterward, Symington remained steadfast in his belief that trends would "leave ourselves and our allies subject to overt political, if not actual military aggression from the Sino-Soviet alliance, with a relatively slight chance of effective retaliation against such aggression between 1960 and 1962."

Fearing an intelligence failure at best, and intelligence politicization at worst, the senator asked to see Eisenhower. This request, too, was soon granted. With a long letter to the president in hand, Symington greeted him in the Oval Office on the morning of August 29. As any visitor to the president knew that day, Ike had a variety of troubles on his mind — Governor Orval Faubus of Arkansas was defying a federal court order to integrate public schools in Little Rock, and the Peoples' Republic of China was threatening to invade the islands of Quemoy and Matsu, held by the noncommunist Republic of China. The senator and president were joined only by the trusted Goodpaster, who took notes. Symington repeated what he had told Dulles and reported that, despite frank discussions, he "had not resolved with Mr. Dulles the disagreement over the estimates."

After listening patiently, a skeptical Eisenhower told Symington of his own "knowledge of this matter." Indeed, he had read some of Symington's writings on the missile topic. Without bragging, the president spoke further of himself, saying "it would be out of character for him to be indifferent to valid assessments of Soviet strength," no matter the source. As for Lanphier, the colonel "cannot possibly get information that reflects the full process of the evaluation system."

Eisenhower also needled Symington about his past performance on defense issues. "Of course," he noted, "differing interpretations can be reached" when looking to the future. "He cited the great error," Goodpaster recorded, "that had been made two years ago in estimating Soviet Bear and Bison programs, which resulted in mistakes being made in our own programs, inasmuch as the Soviets actually carried out only a small fraction of what *certain people* estimated at that time." Furthermore, while the Soviets had started their missiles program "as early as 1945," the United States had only gotten serious during his administration. The implication that Symington and his Truman administration associates might have worked harder to create long-range missiles was hard to miss.

Symington was hardly passive in meeting with a war-hero-turned-president. He expressed astonishment "at the things Allen Dulles did not seem to know." This charge left Eisenhower unimpressed, provoking a presidential lecture on intelligence bureaucracies, which must function "very much on a line, rather than a staff basis. As a result, individuals at lower levels in the structure do not have an evaluated assessment of bits and pieces of reports, many of dubious reliability, of which they have heard."

Only once did the senator impress the president, when he mentioned that an American Atlas missile "had been fired the previous night with very successful results." Ike knew nothing of it, but blandly observed that he understood the Atlas program was "making good progress." American ICBMs would be available "a year or two later" than might be preferable, he added, but "this is the cost of having delayed until 1954 or 1955 in doing what the Soviets started in 1945."

Perhaps to signal their meeting's close, Eisenhower suggested that Symington see Secretary of Defense Neil McElroy about his concerns. But before leaving, Symington reminded Eisenhower of his singular worry that McElroy could not solve — "the intelligence estimate of Soviet test firings is much lower than it should be, to be consistent with the estimated growth of their ICBM operational capability." He would be happy, the senator said, to "come in again if he could be of further help in this matter." Ever the skeptic of legislators wanting to "help" on intelligence matters, Eisenhower merely repeated that "this, too, is a matter that could well be discussed with Mr. McElroy."

After Symington's departure, Eisenhower picked up the telephone and asked the operator to find either McElroy or his deputy, Donald Quarles. Eisenhower's diary records, "Quarles took call. The President said one thing that disturbed him in his discussion with Senator Symington this morning was that Symington had mentioned a completely successful firing of the Atlas. This occurred last night, and at eight this morning, Symington knew it; the President knew nothing about it. Quarles said the report was true; that Defense had failed in its communications to the President. . . . Missile was made by Convair (Tom Lanphier organization). Whatever information Symington had was accurate."⁷ Eisenhower also examined the detailed, six-page, single-spaced letter Symington had handed him. It specified the two unnamed intelligence sources' claims that the Soviets had conducted scores of ICBM test firings in 1957 and 1958. Its summary read:

> The United States plans to have 24 operational ICBMs by 1960, and 120–130 by 1962. In the same time period, the CIA estimates the Soviets will have 500 ICBMs by 1960 or 1961. Based on these accepted figures alone, we believe our currently planned defense programs are insufficient to meet the threat which the CIA estimates the Soviets will pose by 1961.
>
> But if we are correct in our belief that the Soviet ballistic missile testing program has been much greater than as estimated by the CIA, and if construction of Russian ICBM launching sites is as advanced and as wide-spread as we understand to be the case, it is clear that our planned defense programs are even more insufficient.

Eisenhower wrote on the letter, "To CIA. Return Please. DE." Bryce Harlow informed Symington that the president was having the letter "taken under analysis and evaluation, the results of which will be made known to you as promptly as possible."

On October 10, 1958, Dulles evaluated Symington's letter for Eisenhower. This followed a whole new round of discussions he had not only with senior CIA associates, but with "intelligence officers of the Army, Navy, Air Force, and JCS, and the State Department, and the Atomic Energy Commission." Unanimously, they agreed (he told Eisenhower) that Symington's "presentation, together with Mr. Lanphier on August 6, leads me to believe that they provide no basis for changing our estimate on Soviet guided missiles." Symington assumed that "a long time lag" was inevitable in assessing Soviet test firings of ICBMs, but Dulles reminded Eisenhower that "information as to the actual occurrence of an ICBM firing involves no time lag." This was due to American spy technologies in Turkey and in the air, about which Symington knew little to nothing. "Reasonable men could differ" about estimates of future missile arsenals in the USSR, Dulles said, but — confident that Symington was wrong about the numbers of tests — the DCI smelled blood: "The Intelligence Community would, of course, welcome the opportunity to receive directly from the sources to which Senator Symington and Mr. Lanphier refer, any information they may have on this vitally important subject." This invitation Dulles would press on Symington, to his discomfiture, in coming months. Meanwhile, Dulles assured Eisenhower, yet another "re-examination of evidence on the Soviet ICBM program is under way at the present time to determine the possible impact on our estimates of the apparent recent lag in test firings."[8]

That reexamination was to be by the Guided Missile Intelligence Committee (GMIC). With congressional support, Dulles had created the interagency committee in 1956, in response to severe wrangling between Air Force Intelligence and the CIA over the missile threat. Thereafter, as John Prados wrote, the GMIC "produced analyses of technical characteristics of Soviet missile systems that contributed to NIEs." Dulles directed the committee to answer twelve questions, thereby assessing Symington's charges and concerns. One question was, "What is the degree of likelihood that through deception or concealment, the Soviets have prevented us from discovering the true magnitude of their ICBM test-firing program?"

Though U.S. intelligence could only wonder about this at the time, the Soviet government seems intentionally to have engaged in exaggerations of their missile capabilities. Khrushchev was one of many prominent Russians claiming in 1959 that, for example, a single Soviet factory could produce two hundred and fifty missiles in one year. Some Americans, including journalist Lloyd Mallan, having traveled and interviewed widely in the USSR, suspected bold Soviet deception. Mallan published a series of three articles in *True* magazine, detailing the various exaggerations and distortions. Despite the Sputnik launches, Soviet bomber and missile capabilities were generally unimpressive, he claimed. It would be years before the Soviets would have the ability to destroy the United States with a missile attack. Many Soviet "achievements" were skillfully exaggerated by the government of the USSR and widely believed by the U.S. press and public. Sometimes, Mallan wrote, the Soviets simply lied: On January 2, 1959, the USSR claimed that it "had successfully launched a rocket toward the moon. The Russians also claimed that this rocket, which they dubbed 'Lunik,' subsequently went into orbit around the sun." But it was not true: "The Russians did not fire a rocket past the moon on January, 1959." Whether or not he had any doubts about the Lunik achievement, President Eisenhower publicly congratulated the Soviets.

In reaction to the Mallan articles, Clarence Cannon sent Dulles some questions: "Did this man actually visit with Russian scientists as freely as he claims, and if so, why wasn't he an agent of our intelligence? Do we send such people, either reporters, scientists, or educators, on fact-finding missions into Russia? If not, why not?" When Symington read the articles, he asked Russell to request a CIA analysis and response. The agency, which might have wanted to ally itself with a published report that essentially endorsed Eisenhower's skepticism about Soviet aerial progress, did not. An aide reported to Symington, "The CIA asserts that in no items of importance does Mallan's evaluation coincide with theirs." Perhaps the aide was skewing the report to suit Symington's preference: Early in 1959, the CIA's Herbert Scoville and colleagues would testify before the JCAE on supposed Soviet nuclear-powered aircraft, which Mallan labeled another "Big Red Lie." Later, they would testify about a CIA document labeled the "Lunik hoax" before another congressional subcommittee.[9]

The GMIC met an October 31 deadline for reporting to Dulles and the Board of National Estimates. By the second week of December, Harlow informed Symington that the detailed analysis "of the information presented in your August 29 letter" had been completed. "Recently, the President asked me to let you know that the conclusions reached as a result of this analysis are substantially at variance with the information you were furnished." Eisenhower would have Dulles call Symington to arrange another meeting. Symington "read with regret" Harlow's letter but thanked him and Eisenhower on December 15, 1958, and sent Christmas greetings.

Even before the senator learned of Eisenhower's and Dulles's conclusion, aides to the DCI had prepared a ten-page presentation for Dulles to use in briefing Symington. In his office on December 16, Dulles was flanked by the board's Howard Stoertz, the heads of Air Force Intelligence and the GMIC, and Scoville. Symington had company, too — as Stoertz noted in a memorandum, "Senator Symington brought Mr. Lanphier to the DCI's office, clearly expecting that he would be included in the briefing." Dulles did not brief "representatives of industry," he said coolly. Symington defended Lanphier's importance, grumbled that he might appoint him as a staff member just to get him security clearance, but submitted to Dulles's stance. Symington was further annoyed to learn from Dulles that he was expected at the Defense Department just after his visit to the CIA to hear the latest on American arsenals. With Lanphier still in the room, Symington expressed "complete ignorance of such an arrangement." Anyway, he said, there ought to be "one official who would give the Congress a comparative briefing on what we were doing and what the Russians were doing in weapons systems." Dulles suggested that there were people at the NSC and Defense Department who could do such comparative analyses, but "the Senator continued to press for the identity of some single person, saying he wished the DCI would do it, himself." Again, Dulles claimed to be "not competent on U.S. weapons programs."

After Lanphier stepped out, the DCI turned to the business at hand, assuring Symington "that everyone in the intelligence community takes with the greatest seriousness the Soviet capability in ballistic missiles." And, just so Symington would know that intelligence leaders did not dismiss concerns about a missile gap, he said, "Our estimate warns that the U.S. now faces the possibility, soon to be a probability, that the Soviets have operational ICBMs, and we have stated our belief that, upon achieving an initial ICBM capability, the Soviets would build toward a substantial force of ICBMs as rapidly as practicable." But, "I have no evidence that there has been any effort within this intelligence community to suppress evidence or to prevent the fullest analysis of the views of any competent person with information to contribute." On the contrary, "subsequent to your report to the President, we have conducted a thorough re-analysis of all evidence on the Soviet ICBM program, to determine the possible impact on our estimates of an apparent recent lag in test firings." Only six had been detected so far.

The United States had a "highly sophisticated, integrated intelligence collecting system, combining scientific and conventional methods. Because of its nature, certain details of this system [are] known to only a limited number of persons in the intelligence community." Based on that system, he and intelligence colleagues stood by the earlier conclusion that "no significant number of test firings to 3,500 nautical miles has passed unnoticed." There was simply no evidence available to "responsible analysts at any level with competence in this field" to support Symington's claims of fifty-five to eighty test firings in that range by the Soviets. Dulles was "at a loss" to understand how figures suggested by Symington could come "from our own intelligence sources."

Despite the lag in Soviet testing, the "United States Intelligence Board continues to estimate, without dissent, that the USSR will probably achieve a first operational capability with 10 prototype ICBMs at some time during 1959." With 1958 coming to an end in two weeks, Dulles noted that prior intelligence concerns that the Soviets might have operational ICBMs that year appeared to have been unwarranted. Especially in the area of production and deployment of missiles, U.S. intelligence was "unsatisfactory," but a "highest priority" attempt "to acquire the information we must have" was under way. Still, intelligence leaders had no evidence to support Symington's claim that the Soviets' construction of fixed and mobile ICBM launching sites was "advanced" and "widespread."

As to future projections, Dulles reminded Symington how tenuous they were: "Since there is no direct evidence on Soviet plans for quantity production of ICBMs, we have selected the figures of 100 and 500 operational missiles [in 1960–1961 and then in 1961–1962] as yardsticks to provide a basis for measuring capacity to produce and deploy those weapons. These figures do not represent an estimate of Soviet requirements or intentions; in fact, it is possible that the Soviets themselves do not as yet have fixed plans in this regard." Still, Dulles used the word "estimate" in relation to those numbers, and concluded, "It is . . . the opinion of the qualified consultants with whom we have conferred that, in light of such data as we have on the Soviet program, our estimates of the pertinent Soviet capabilities are reasonable."

Dulles's presentation included other intelligence morsels, including the belief that the Soviets had experienced four unsuccessful space launch attempts in addition to its three successful Sputnik launches. Symington, though, was interested in the ICBM topic. Based on what he had heard from Dulles on tests, it looked "as if the Soviets were slackening up in their ICBM development," something the senator refused to believe. Though Dulles assured Symington that "there was no delay in receiving information on a firing," Symington was not mollified. As Stoertz noted, "Senator Symington's view was that the intelligence picture was incredible. . . . the Soviets couldn't be making ICBMs if they weren't firing them. Considering the estimated cutback in bomber production in conjunction with our figures on ICBM firings, it sounded as if Khrushchev was violating Teddy Roosevelt's principle of speaking softly but carrying a big stick." This Symington did not believe. "The slackening of ICBM testing and cutback in bomber production was a wonderful thing to believe," he sarcastically noted, "if it was more important for the U.S. to balance the budget than to have national defense." Symington then asked how his letter of August 29 to the president had been wrong. The DCI was too clever to wander in that direction, noting that "he wasn't saying who was right or wrong, but was giving the Senator the intelligence we had."

The briefing over, Lanphier was readmitted to Dulles's office to face questions from Scoville about his "sources." Nobody at CIA Intelligence Directorate thought the Soviets had fired fifty-five ICBM tests, said Scoville, who shared Dulles's thinly veiled contempt for Lanphier's unnamed suppliers of information. The Convair official admitted that "his original report had been based on information floating around in the intelligence hierarchy. . . . he assumed the number of firings he had reported were extreme, and that he had quoted them to get the DCI to take a look at the intelligence system." He clung to the belief, though, that the United States had "fallen a generation behind in the ballistic missile field." No doubt to Dulles's annoyance, Lanphier and Symington then repeated all of their concerns to the group — the "U.S. was deluding itself," "the lack of a clear picture would be the death of the country," "the Soviets were not going to give up their missile lead, but the intelligence story on testing made it look as if they were." He would have to make a speech about the problem, Symington said. The DCI and the senator both indicated that they would tell Eisenhower about their conversation.

With White House permission, Dulles would also soon report to two Armed Services barons about what he called "the history of the controversy with Senator Symington." With Leverett Saltonstall, Dulles pondered Symington's probable speechmaking in coming weeks, and to Richard Russell, the DCI suggested an early January meeting of the CIA subcommittee.[10]

From the Pforzheimer Era to the Warner Era

By the end of 1958, Eisenhower had plenty of reasons to ponder the management and oversight of intelligence. His two-year-old Board of Consultants on Foreign Intelligence endorsed the ongoing U-2 flights over the Soviet Union, for example, but criticized Dulles's management of the CIA and the larger intelligence establishment. Especially, board chairman John Hull reminded Eisenhower of the "serious gaps in our knowledge of the capabilities and intentions of the Soviet Bloc" and questioned the management of covert action. The Plans Directorate "may be incapable of making objective appraisals of its own intelligence information, as well as of its own operations when it is involved in Cold War activities which are the subjects of its own reports."[1]

This critique would gain particular resonance three years later, after the agency attempted to overthrow the government of Cuba. But even in 1958, it had acute relevance — the CIA had tried unsuccessfully that year to overturn the neutralist government of President Sukarno in Indonesia. Many in the executive branch (and those few who spoke up in Congress) saw that country heading toward communism. HUAC chair Francis Walter observed in February, "The majority of the people in Indonesia are desperately trying to forestall eventual subjugation by Communist China and the Soviet Union." Representative Harold Collier (R-IL) urged aid to "the gallant rebels" opposing Sukarno. As John Foster Dulles admitted in the White House, though, the "directing forces" behind Sukarno were not communist but simply "favorable personally" toward him. The operation was larger than, and as politically ambitious as, the 1954 coup overturning Arbenz in Guatemala. The State Department and Secretary Dulles were involved, as was the U.S. military. Allen Dulles lacked the enthusiasm he had shown in the Guatemalan case.[2]

Things went badly for months, hitting rock bottom when Sukarno loyalists shot down an American pilot and found papers linking him to the CIA. Agency operatives soon abandoned the Indonesian dissidents they had been encouraging and supporting. The President's Intelligence Board, more than the toothless dog that Mike Mansfield had anticipated in 1956, was not much

impressed, telling Eisenhower in mid-December: "There was no proper estimate of the situation, nor proper prior planning on the part of anyone, and
in its active phases the operation was directed, not by the Director of Central Intelligence, but personally by the Secretary of State, who, ten thousand
miles away from the scene of operation, undertook to make practically all
decisions down to and including even the tactical military decisions."

By this point in his presidency, Eisenhower had come to view outside
consultants as frequently unrealistic, but he did not ignore this group.
Assisted by Goodpaster, Gray, and the board itself, he kept pressure on Allen
Dulles either to reorganize the agency in certain respects or to explain why
the board's suggestions were not appropriate. Gray, in particular, would push
the 5412 Group to manage covert action more systematically. As for Congress, Allen Dulles almost certainly had conversations about Indonesia with
the CIA subcommittee heads, but the surviving record on this is blank. His
brother, though, simply lied to the Congress and the nation — March 1958
was just one of the times he assured legislators that "we are not intervening
in the internal affairs of this country." In April, President Eisenhower told a
press conference that American policy was one of "careful neutrality."[3]

In November, in response to CIA judgment that Congress might revive and
pass the joint intelligence committee idea, Bryce Harlow warned Dulles that
Eisenhower was "utterly appalled" at the thought. The DCI went to the White
House again to discuss the covert action and Congress topics on December 26,
1958, seven weeks after Democrats had scored a huge victory in congressional
elections. (The new 86th Congress would have 64 Democrats in the Senate and
only 34 Republicans; the House would have 283 Democrats and 153 Republicans.) Goodpaster and Gray joined Eisenhower, who directed Dulles to cooperate in the 5412 Group's more active process. "One reason for the foregoing,"
Goodpaster reported the president as saying, "is to obviate any tendency for
congressional groups and their staffs to get into these activities."

Eisenhower thought some in Congress were too aggressive, not just about
the CIA's "intelligence," but also its "substantive operations." Indeed, a few
months later, the House Appropriations' CIA subcommittee would submit
written questions as a follow-up to one of its hearings. Among the questions
for the agency: "Why is there a reduction in [words censored] operations in
the Near East?" and "Go into the [words censored] a little more thoroughly,
and give us a rundown on the specific activities as to where, by whom, and
how much." The president spoke with envy and admiration at the December

meeting of how the British government kept "knowledge of specific activities confined to a small handful of people." The "tendency toward 'supervisory' activity on the part of the Congress over the substantive operations and intelligence of CIA would be most harmful" to him.[4]

Dulles had suggested to Goodpaster days earlier that the White House start keeping records he forwarded to them relating to Stuart Symington and the agency, implying that there would be more to come. He had earlier sent a list of dates when the CIA had testified so far in 1958 before legislative bodies. It showed over two dozen days with such hearings, virtually all of them secret, but many with committees that were not regular overseers of the CIA.

Coincidentally, Eisenhower had recently heard from J. William Fulbright, new chair of Senate Foreign Relations, seeking testimony from the DCI in the new year on the Soviet Union's capabilities and intentions, plus political unrest in Asia and Africa. The President seemed in no mood at the December gathering to accommodate *more* congressional assertiveness. He had confidence in Democrats Russell, Hayden, Cannon, and Vinson, plus most senior Republicans on the CIA subcommittees, but not many others.

Dulles would continue to contact Russell and Vinson, especially, to discuss keeping the oversight process limited. He knew this would have limited effect, though — as he occasionally pointed out to the White House, each of the 1958 hearings had occurred with the permission of the subcommittee barons. Briefly, as 1959 began, the DCI would inform the White House in advance of his congressional contacts, but he quickly dropped the habit. He had "plunged into the problems incident to the new session of Congress," he wrote a friend. The DCI would testify before six different congressional committees in January, one of them Fulbright's and only two of them CIA subcommittees.[5]

Such expansion of oversight did not necessarily signify congressional unhappiness with the agency so much as it did unhappiness of subcommittee members with their own oversight. Mahon and some colleagues on the House Appropriations subcommittee were unhappy, sometimes aghast, with Cannon's informality in questioning Dulles at annual budget hearings. "I could see the pain on Mahon's face and Jerry Ford's face," former legislative liaison John Warner recalled of one meeting. He arranged for Mahon and two others to have follow-up meetings with agency leaders. Afterward, no doubt choosing their words carefully, the legislators sought and obtained Cannon's agreement that the CIA, in addition to the budget hearings — typically taking two days — should brief the subcommittee on international conditions each year.

Dulles reported to Goodpaster in the fall of 1958 that the subcommittee (along with unnamed other legislative bodies) wished to learn more "concerning our estimate of critical world situations and, in varying degrees, to disclose the role played by this Agency in those situations." Chairman Cannon had "specifically requested that I provide him with a plan as to how this objective can be accomplished," he noted. Dulles seems to have delayed responding to the request, but Red White noted in his diary that Mahon warned the DCI in January 1959 that he was "opposed" to members of the subcommittee "standing up and defending CIA, inasmuch as this caused him trouble with other members of the Appropriations Committee who were not privy to CIA information."

Nonetheless, at a White House meeting in June 1959, Dulles was virtually instructed to continue ignoring requests for more hearings, unless (as he wrote) "there was further pressure from Congress." Such pressures did continue, at least from Mahon and Cannon. Apparently without telling the White House, Dulles attended an Appropriations' "intelligence meeting" in which "no financial matters are to be discussed" later that summer. By December, Dulles would further accede to the pressures from Appropriations, at a meeting in Cannon's office. Two days of "intelligence" hearings were scheduled for January 1960 before an expanded subcommittee membership.[6]

Cannon has been treated unfairly in histories as utterly irresponsible in failing to monitor the CIA. His oversight was uneven and informal, but the Appropriations chair was not normally a pushover — Allen Dulles learned this when he asked yet again for money to build a home for the Director of Central Intelligence along the banks of the Potomac. Cannon and his CIA subcommittee gave "quite a negative reaction," according to a Dulles aide. More importantly, in May 1958, Cannon had asked Dulles in a hearing to provide "an overall estimate of the expenditures of the U.S. intelligence community." It was not a new topic in Agency-congressional relations — back in 1953, Robert Macy of the Bureau of the Budget warned intelligence agency heads that unnamed Congress leaders had asked that the Bureau screen "government-wide intelligence activities" to eliminate "gross duplications." Only a modest increase in Bureau monitoring of the intelligence establishment seems to have come of the request then, and to Cannon's seemingly reasonable 1958 request, the DCI had to admit that he "did not have jurisdiction over the expenditures of any of the intelligence components of the government other than CIA." He knew of "certain computations" made by the BOB about community-wide spending but was otherwise not fully knowledgeable.[7]

Dulles's attempted brush-off failed: Cannon "practically demanded a copy" of the Bureau report. As the DCI told heads of the other intelligence agencies a few days later, "in view of Mr. Cannon's insistence," he would have to respond more fully. Apparently coincidentally, President Eisenhower (and his Intelligence Board) had also periodically asked Dulles and the Bureau of the Budget to provide a detailed accounting of overall U.S. intelligence spending. Later in 1958, Dulles provided the Appropriations subcommittee with an initial report indicating spending by each agency of the intelligence establishment, which had expended "65,027 man-years and funds in the amount of $431,130,000" in Fiscal Year 1958. Dulles and other agency heads seem not to have been dishonest in addressing the costs issue — constructing a single accounting system for the far-flung intelligence establishment's procedures was hard. One leader noted that the word intelligence "means different things to different people." Still, it "would have embarrassed everyone" if Congress had "gone behind the figures."

Cannon would not give up while waiting for a fuller report. In a 1959 hearing, he would insist on treating the director of central intelligence as the true head of all U.S. intelligence agencies: Drawing from the report he had received, he asked, "What do these 20 people do in the Office of the Secretary of Defense?" "What do these 39,000 employed by the Army do?" "National Security Agency, 8,586?" Dulles's answers are unrecorded. After a series of other interim responses, Deputy Director Cabell would provide Cannon with a reasonably comprehensive "Estimated Foreign Intelligence Costs" memo in spring 1960 and virtually whine to the chairman that it had "been very difficult to compile." CIA comptroller E. R. Saunders, who headed the committee created to fashion the cost estimates, told colleagues that Cannon's subcommittee had "put great pressure on CIA."[8]

Before joining the CIA, John Warner had worked at the OSS late in World War II, then at CIG, and had helped draft the National Security Act. In 1957, he took on the direction of the agency's legislative relations. While changes in legislative oversight had occurred incrementally across the CIA's first decade, the differences between Pforzheimer's early work in the late 1940s and that of Warner a decade later seemed substantial to the latter liaison: "Walter had one person helping him — a secretary or administrative assistant. I had three people working the Hill with me, plus backup in the office, and we were busy as hell."

The growth in the legislative liaison staff at the CIA was an inevitable outcome of Congress's increased monitoring of the agency. Similarly, more congressional staffers interacted with the CIA than a decade before. One agency leader wrote in March 1959 of "a large number of staff people on various committees who have a fairly intimate knowledge of the workings and activities of the Agency." At House Appropriations, the three most important staffers were Kenneth Sprankle, Samuel Crosby, and Robert Michaels. When Mahon heard about one of Khrushchev's periodic boasts about reading American intelligence reports, it was Crosby who looked into this. On one occasion in 1960 (and perhaps others), Clarence Cannon sent Crosby to spend some weeks in Asia to investigate CIA stations. Informed of this plan by the chairman, Dulles persuaded him that the CIA's comptroller should go along. John Warner and Sprankle slipped away from Capitol Hill occasionally for a few drinks at lunchtime, but the liaison especially admired Michaels, who also visited one or more CIA stations abroad. At Senate Appropriations, Frances Hewitt and Michael Rexroad handled CIA relations for Chairman Hayden. When the CIA wished to clear a "proposed transmitter sale" to a foreign nation in 1958 (its identity still classified over four decades later), Warner briefed the two aides and then Hewitt discussed it with Hayden.[9]

Though he was aware that other CIA subcommittee heads used more than one staffer to handle agency relations, Richard Russell insisted that chief clerk William Darden would be his only staffer to do so. However, other leading Armed Services members, such as Lyndon Johnson and Stuart Symington, had their own security-cleared staffers handling CIA matters. Most importantly, Kenneth BeLieu was the Preparedness subcommittee's go-between with the agency. Able, energetic, and likeable, BeLieu had been badly wounded in the Korean War and walked with a limp. Warner recalls that Johnson, the Preparedness chair, was "not one to pay much attention to detail. At times, details became important, and Ken would help." In November 1959, when Houston conveyed "information pertaining to events south of the border," he wrote BeLieu, "We trust that this information can be restricted to Senator Johnson and yourself. . . . we can make available some of our people to discuss all aspects of it with you personally."[10]

Warner also had a close and admiring relationship with House Armed Services' chief counsel Robert Smart, "a very senior kind of guy." Having served with distinction in the Army Air Forces during World War II, Smart had impressed Dewey Short (a fellow Missourian) as "the best Missouri has to offer" and joined the committee staff in January 1947. Soon, he won the trust of Democrat Carl Vinson, who regained the chairmanship from Short in 1955. Dulles was mortified to learn in October 1958 that an agency station chief in Europe had somehow neglected Smart, who (as Red White reported in his diary) "sat in his hotel for two days, waiting for someone to contact him." Dulles complained about the foul-up for weeks, saying "someone should be disciplined about this," before directing a subordinate "to prepare a sanitized memorandum which could be shown to Bob, explaining what had happened." Smart would direct a significant investigation of the CIA in 1959. Warner wrote in March, when estimates on Soviet missile capabilities had drawn significant dissents from some members of the U.S. Intelligence Board, that "Mr. Smart requested that he be provided with a tabulation for 1958 of the total number of NIEs with the number of dissents or footnotes and who dissented." Yet, for all the time that Smart and other congressional staffers spent dealing with CIA, they had other duties as well.[11]

Although congressional staffers have usually been unpopular with those working in the executive branch, Warner claims that relations between the CIA and congressional staffs were generally good. William Darden agrees. Occasional friction was unavoidable. Walter Pforzheimer, who relished the informality of those relations through 1956, scarcely concealed his dislike of Darden, who sometimes urged his bosses, Russell and Saltonstall, toward more systematic oversight of the agency. Warner later thought Darden was almost impossible to dislike but had been "too sensible" for the opinionated Pforzheimer's taste. (Decades later, in separate interviews, Darden graciously asked about Pforzheimer's well-being, while the latter said, "I never liked Darden.") Another case of animosity flared up in August 1959, when an agency budget official and two House Appropriations staffers traded angry charges. The staffers worked "in an insecure manner," said the CIA man. Kenneth Sprankle and another Appropriations staffer denied it all, "resented the implication," and derided the CIA as "too sensitive."[12]

Much of the increased workload for the liaison's office in the late 1950s was as mundane as that handled in Pforzheimer's day. Warner and assistants sifted through thousands of proposed laws each year to find those few "of direct interest to the Agency." Since 1947, legislators had also requested hundreds of times that the agency consider hiring their constituents. Whether they came from influential or obscure members of Congress, the CIA treated the requests carefully and kept legislators informed of eventual personnel decisions. Most of the constituents were not hired, and some complained to their senators or representatives, but the CIA quickly developed procedures for dealing with that. In 1958, the Office of Legislative Counsel received 208 telephone inquiries about personnel cases and responded in writing on 168 of them.

One involved Francis Walter, "the most powerful member of the House on all immigration matters" (an aide told Dulles), who inquired about a young constituent. Warner reported to Dulles, "He has known this boy and his family for many years." But the agency had not hired him — "he is 50 pounds overweight, has albumin in his urine, and has hypertension." Since Walter had clout, Warner let Dulles decide who should respond to the chairman. In this instance, as in most, the DCI let the liaison handle it, which may have been a mistake. Dulles had previously been warned by an aide, "Agency relationships with Mr. Walter are not good. He has taken a position that he will not sponsor any private bills in which we are interested." Walter would remain angry and have a showdown with Dulles two years later.[13]

Another common duty of the Office of Legislative Counsel was handling requests for information. Legal counsel Houston summarized for Dulles such activities in the first ten months of 1958: "There were 96 telephone requests from the Congress for information. On 88 occasions, documents on these subjects were personally delivered to the requester. There were 24 personal visits with members of Congress and 64 meetings with staff members."

For discussion of sensitive issues, Dulles or top associates usually met with powerful legislators in their offices. Warner's summary covering most of 1958 indicates that "senior Agency officials personally met with 36 members of Congress . . . on 30 different occasions." Some such meetings were to "debrief congressmen traveling abroad." Such travel was limited in election year 1958, but in fall–winter 1957, thirteen senators and forty just-returned representatives gave their observations to the agency, which informed the President's Intelligence Board that "considerable useful information was obtained by the Agency, and several specific items may develop into operational assets."

In formal hearings from autumn 1957 through autumn 1958, Warner's memo notes, agency heads testified on approximately twenty-seven days. "It has been determined that CIA made appearances before 16 *different* congressional committees or subcommittees whose membership totals 168. . . . 109 *different* members of Congress actually attended: 41 senators and 68 representatives." Dulles testified at the vast majority of those hearings.

Warner evaluated congressional oversight in autumn 1958 for Dulles. Given the "stepped-up interchange between the Agency and the Congress in the past year," Mike Mansfield's joint intelligence committee idea would surely come up again. In part, this was because many legislators "have been unaware that any hearings on CIA are ever held." (Warner was right — by mid-February 1959, legislators would introduce fifteen different joint committee proposals.) He added that most members of the CIA subcommittees knew too little about "the full nature of the intelligence structure, the method in which it operates, and the problems it faces." Warner blamed the "extremely busy" CIA subcommittee chairs for such problems. It was time, he suggested, to inform most or all CIA subcommittee members about the U-2 program. Dulles tentatively agreed and said that Warner's staff should prepare a "dry run of the overall presentation" but reserved to himself and the president the right to decide whether all subcommittee members would be told.

Warner also recommended that, after each future hearing, Dulles "request the chairman of the subcommittee to report the fact of the briefing and review of agency activities by the subcommittee" to the committee and to the full Senate or House. The CIA, meanwhile, should start giving regular "briefings from our Station Chiefs abroad" to the subcommittees. Usually, subcommittee members only met station chiefs during foreign travel. A few months after digesting the liaison's memo and talking to Cannon and others, Dulles told subordinates (according to White) that the agency should provide "one or more places on Capitol Hill where our 'Weekly Bulletin' would be available to selective key members, as well as a knowledgeable CIA individual who could answer further questions, etc." But such innovations would require White House approval. Goodpaster would kill the idea in June 1959, almost certainly at Ike's direction.[14]

Earlier that year, the president told future DCI John McCone — who headed the Atomic Energy Commission and interacted frequently with the JCAE — that he wondered if "the executive branch" was becoming "too subservient to that committee." The CIA had just testified before the JCAE and would appear before Fulbright's committee days later. Red White wrote in his diary on February 4 of "a ground swell developing for more frequent briefings of these committees on some systematic basis." Ike would continue to complain.[15]

Subordinating Intelligence?

At the Pentagon, they shudder when they speak of the "gap," which means the
years 1960, 1961, 1962, and 1963 . . . because in these years, the American
government will flaccidly permit the Kremlin to gain an almost unchallenged
superiority in the nuclear striking power that was once our specialty.

— Stewart and Joseph Alsop

On the cold morning of Friday, January 23, 1959, Stuart Symington moved closer to open confrontation with the Eisenhower White House and Allen Dulles, after Secretary of Defense Neil McElroy accurately reminded an open hearing of George Mahon's Defense Appropriations subcommittee that there was still "no positive evidence" that the USSR had an operational, nuclear-armed, long-range missile. Symington responded at the Senate within hours, landing himself and McElroy in the *New York Times'* lead story the next day, with photographs. He implied that McElroy based his claim on "a recent down-ward revision in intelligence estimates of Soviet ICBM capability" for the next few years. Nothing "could be more certain to lessen our chances of survival than to subordinate our intelligence evaluation to our budget policies."[1]

Eisenhower and Dulles steamed for weeks at Symington's suggestion. Ike grumbled in the White House on February 9 about "self-appointed military experts" who were "either honest or dishonest neurotics." The next day, he lashed out to science advisers, including James Killian (plus a note-taking Goodpaster), "on the way irresponsible officials and demagogues are leak-ing security information and presenting a misleading picture of our secu-rity situation to our people. Some of our senators seem to be doing this. In turn, the munitions makers are making tremendous efforts toward getting more contracts and, in fact, seem to be exerting undue influence over the senators." Though he could not remember Thomas Lanphier's name, Eisen-hower thought that Symington — "being accompanied in various official conversations by a man who is a Vice President of Convair" — was a prime example. The activities of the two men, and the readiness of Congress to spend more than Eisenhower wanted on the military, led Eisenhower to ponder the influence of what he would later call the Military-Industrial Complex.[2]

One concrete way that Symington and Lanphier were having "undue influence," the president thought, related to a program they may have known nothing about—the U-2 missions. After two and a half years of periodic reconnaissance over the USSR, Eisenhower began to doubt their further utility. In December 1958, the president had reminded his Intelligence Board that he had been "highly enthusiastic" about the program. U-2s had revealed much about Soviet military installations, prime targets for the United States in a nuclear war. But (recorded Goodpaster), "he expressed a concern that the U-2 has been tracked." The question "which he is facing is whether the intelligence which we receive from this source is worth the exacerbation of international tension which results." There should be "a complete reevaluation" of the program. But he heard little support for this from his Board that day. Furthermore, the U-2 and Turkish radars had not yet answered the "most important" question, posed weeks later by McElroy to Eisenhower, Dulles, and others: when would the Soviets attain "an initial operating capability of 500 ICBMs." This was the glaring weakness of national intelligence estimates, McElroy thought. "Congress was continually concerned over the basic premises employed by the Defense Department, that is, our intelligence estimates. . . . he therefore requested the President to consider the matter of additional overflights of the USSR."[3]

Eisenhower wavered in his approach to such U-2 missions in the early months of 1959, owing to tensions over Berlin, China, and elsewhere. Always in the forefront of his thinking was the desire to leave the presidency two years later having transformed superpower relations. In the first week of April, Eisenhower approved two U-2 flights one day, then reversed himself the next, calling in CIA's Richard Bissell (who managed the program) and McElroy to the White House to explain himself. Both men routinely had urged more U-2 flights over the Soviet Union. With Goodpaster present, Eisenhower explicitly connected U-2 usage to the pressure created by legislators: "He agreed on the need for information. This need is highlighted by the distortion several senators are making of our military position relative to that of the Soviets, and they are helped in their 'demagoguery' by our uncertainties as to the Soviet programs."[4]

Almost no one in the Senate—aside from Russell and Saltonstall, probably Bridges, Hayden, and Johnson, and possibly a few others on CIA subcommittees—knew of the U-2s, but congressional questions about U.S. intelligence on Soviet war-making capabilities pressured Ike to use them more systematically. On many a day in 1959 and 1960, he worried over "the terrible propaganda impact that would be occasioned if a reconnaissance plane were to fail."

Allen Dulles understood the competing pressures on Eisenhower and his response to them. The DCI was galled for weeks over Symington's implication that NIEs had somehow been "subordinated" to budget concerns. The charges affected public and congressional opinion, he thought — Grogan kept feeding him memos summarizing the outbursts of concern about the "predicted 'gap' between U.S. and USSR programs in ballistic missiles." When Dulles testified before his subcommittee on February 2 and 3, 1959, even the good-natured George Mahon noted the obvious uncertainty of Dulles's prediction, specifically that the DCI kept saying, "We believe, we believe." Too, Mahon remarked about Soviet missile tests, it "seems strange — none since May 1958." Really, he wondered, "have you recorded all the tests?" Further, Mahon — among the House elect who knew of U-2 — believed that there were "a number of military targets within Russia that are not precisely identified as to location, and that these would require aerial reconnaissance prior to bombardment." This he had been told by unspecified CIA sources and had raised with the air force chief of staff, General Thomas White.

Mahon was no demagogue. On the same day that Symington predicted the United States might soon be in a "hopeless" position vis-à-vis the USSR, Mahon spoke less apocalyptically — Eisenhower's missile program was "not adequate." Congress ought to add one or two billion dollars to the proposed $41 billion defense budget for Fiscal Year 1960, though it would probably only obtain a half billion increase, he said.[5]

The DCI decided to confront Symington in two ways: first, expressing his resentment over Symington's "intelligence subordination" remark; second, by questioning Symington again about *his* sources of information. The first opportunity came on February 4, 1959. That morning legislators woke to a front-page *New York Times* story from Moscow that began, "Marshal Rodion L. Malinovsky, Minister of Defense, told the Communist Party congress today that Soviet missiles armed with hydrogen warheads could strike 'precisely any point.' " It was also the day after Dulles had completed his testimony before Mahon's subcommittee, barely a week after he had addressed missile concerns, the rise of Cuba's Fidel Castro, and Chinese tensions with the USSR before Fulbright's Foreign Relations Committee, and nineteen days after admitting to Russell's CIA subcommittee that "our" intelligence on Soviet production and deployment of ICBMs was "unsatisfactory."[6]

Having addressed those and other committees in recent weeks, Dulles may have thought himself so well-versed as not to need the extensive briefing notes that staffers had prepared for his meeting with the Preparedness subcommittee. The DCI, though, walked into one of the most hostile congressional hearings of his professional life. Well before he had covered the main points of his planned presentation, Dulles was peppered with questions about revised national intelligence estimates. Clinton Anderson interrupted Dulles's early reference to previous and new numbers predicted for the USSR by 1960, asking, "Now, where do you cut back down to these other figures [in the new NIE] and who cuts you down?" Dulles bristled, "Nobody 'cuts me down.'" Anderson persisted: "Now, who put you to the later figure? Who gets you to take the later figures?"

Anderson would not be brushed off, so Dulles tried to explain: "In agreeing to the estimates which I will now give you, I have changed, we have changed our position in the CIA somewhat because of the fact that from May of 1958 until the present time, to the best of my belief — and I feel confident about it — they haven't successfully tested any missiles, and I changed my views when I believed the basic evidence changed. I do not stick to a thing because I have said it once." Here Symington joined the discussion. He was in a feisty mood, because Defense Secretary McElroy had just told the subcommittee days earlier that the United States had no intention to match the USSR "missile for missile." As a Dulles associate later recalled, the exchange between Symington and Dulles "became lively":

> Symington: When I saw you with other people who know their subject, in July and August and again in December [1958], we offered you what we thought were evidences of more testing.
> Dulles: But gave me no evidence.
> Symington: Well, we thought it was evidence. Let's not get into that.
> Dulles: You gave me assertions. I want to make that point perfectly clear.

After disagreeing on what had been said and not said at their previous meetings, Dulles moved to put Symington on the spot:

> I want to comment very directly on the statement that you made [on January 23] . . . that you were making an investigation to see whether the Estimate had been changed for budgetary considerations.
> Symington: I did not say that. I said that I asked if it had been. I asked the Secretary of Defense if there had been any change in the Estimate because of budgetary considerations. That is a proper question to ask.

Dulles: Do you want to ask me too?

Symington: I did and you said "no," so I wasn't going to bring it up, but I will be damned glad to ask it if you want to hear it.

Dulles: I do want to hear it.

Symington: Then I will ask it.

Dulles: I say the implication that there has been any change, even the question that an estimate has been changed, out of budgetary or out of other considerations, I consider an insult to the Agency. . . .

Symington: Well, I was told —

Dulles: —and I would not stay a minute on this job —

Symington: I see now why you wanted me to ask the question —

Dulles: Mr. Chairman, can I finish?

Senator Stennis [presiding in Lyndon Johnson's absence]: Finish your statement.

Dulles: The integrity of the Central Intelligence Agency has to be preserved, and if there is any senator who feels that I am changing estimates, or any of [us] are changing estimates for budgetary, political, or any other considerations, that would be ruinous to the Agency, and I consider a mere question as to whether that has been done a very, very serious matter and I hope that the Senator would be willing to withdraw even the question. . . .

Symington: Now just let me say this to you, that if I have any question about your integrity, I won't ask it, I will say it. I just want you to understand that, you see.

Dulles: Good.

But Symington, while acknowledging the CIA's unusual, crucial status, was unwilling to concede Dulles's claim that certain "mere questions" should never be asked:

I will say to you that if I hadn't felt that somebody had overruled your intelligence, your estimates, that I probably wouldn't have asked the question, although I think the question was entirely proper, and I did not put the deductions on it that some of the newspapers stories did.

Dulles: You realize that the maintenance of the integrity of our organization, its freedom from political, budgetary, and other considerations, is absolutely vital to its existence?

Symington: I certainly do.[7]

By swearing and interrupting each other, Symington and Dulles had violated the courteous norms valued by the likes of Russell and Mahon. It was the most hostile exchange between an agency leader and a legislator since Joseph McCarthy charged Dulles with dereliction of duty five years earlier.

In retrospect, there seems to have been no distortion of intelligence to which Dulles and the CIA were a party. Still, the DCI's exchanges with Symington (and others) highlighted the fact that U.S. intelligence agencies *had* gathered new information and revised their analytical methodologies somewhat regarding operational ICBMs, and so produced estimates that were modestly revised. As a result of legislators' questions about the revisions, CIA staff produced a primer a few days later for Dulles, Scoville, Warner, and others to use to better explain this to congressional groups and members. It noted the complexities involved in reaching "first operational capability" [FOC] with ICBMs. In December 1957, a "special estimate devoted solely to the Soviet ICBM program" had estimated (the primer explained) an FOC of ICBMs would occur in the "mid-1958 to mid-1959" period; a "500 operational capability" would probably occur in "mid-1960 to mid-1961, or at the latest, mid-1962." In late May 1958, a revision to that estimate suggested that the FOC would "probably" occur in 1959; the 500 operational capability would be in "1961 or, at the latest, 1962." It moved back the FOC by six months because test firings by the Soviets "had not been as high as expected." In November 1958, a revised estimate — the "intensive re-examination" provoked by Symington's questions — said that the FOC was still likely in 1959; the 500 operational ICBM capability would probably be in "1962, possibly as early as 1961." Largely because of the complexities involved in creating operational missiles and launching facilities, the U.S. intelligence establishment had shifted "from two years to three the probable time period required by the USSR to build from a first operational capability to an operational capability with 500 ICBMs."[8]

Dulles tried to explain this to legislators at the next Preparedness hearing on March 18, 1959, called specifically to "clarify" answers given at the February hearing and before other committees. He noted correctly that there had not been "any drastic or radical recent change in our estimates" on the FOC. The shifting back to 1962 as the likeliest year for the Soviets having five hundred fully operational ICBMs was not insignificant, he explained, but had been done for substantive, not political/budgetary reasons. He reminded them, too, that the unending handicap facing U.S. intelligence was that it had "insufficient evidence to judge the magnitude and pace of a Soviet ICBM production and deployment program." If Dulles found it tricky doing these explanations of a complex and politicized topic, he was at least being prepared for a more difficult round of explanations that would be required following the next year's more radical changes in methodologies and estimates.

Regarding Symington, badly advised (the DCI thought) in airing agitated claims about subordinated intelligence, Dulles would not mind seeing him eat crow. But the DCI avoided any hint of such a motive when he pursued Symington further at the March meeting. When, he inquired of the senator, could he talk to the sources that had told Symington of scores of ICBM tests carried out by the Soviets, or at least see their evidence? If the Soviets were carrying out such extensive tests, there was a "very vital" national security problem at hand — "the intelligence community has no information at all to bear out that." The CIA had detected one new successful ICBM test, plus a failed one by the Soviets, since Dulles appeared before Preparedness six weeks earlier. This he reported to them, but if the overwhelming amount of testing claimed by Symington "could be demonstrated or were demonstrable," it would serve the national interest. Extending an olive branch, Dulles was even willing to ask the CIA's own outside consultants to have their names revealed to the senator. Symington, though, was reluctant to make a trade of source names.

Lyndon Johnson watched both men spar, then asked, "Why don't you all work that out, talk to each other about it, talk to your sources, and see if both sources are willing to have their names used? And on this other information you are talking about, if that has not been obtained in confidence, if it can be used, I am sure Senator Symington will be glad to do it."

Symington, though, claimed to be offended by "Mr. Dulles' recent comments about me personally and what I have done," and asserted that all his efforts had been proper. "Now," he asked, "what you would like to have me do is to disclose to you information which I presented to you in July and to the President in August, is that correct?"

> Mr. Dulles: No, no, it is not information.
>
> Senator Symington: The sources?
>
> Mr. Dulles: I want some of the background on which this information was adduced. I mean, the raw information cannot be estimated by the intelligence community — if someone says there are 55 firings, there must be some evidence of those firings. What is the evidence?
>
> Senator Symington: And you would like for me to disclose, in effect, therefore, my sources?
>
> Mr. Dulles: No. If you will bring the evidence that your source has on what he bases the 55 and 80 firings, that would be very helpful.

Senator Symington: You would like me to tell you where I got my information?
Mr. Dulles: If that information is true, all this [the latest NIE] is wrong.

Senator Symington: That is right; that is exactly right. . . . Let me assure you
that I don't say that my information is right, but I have no intention of disclosing people who felt it was their obligation to come and tell me things that had
to do with what we are discussing. I will make one final statement, and that is,
since I have last talked you, additional people have given me information which
I believe justifies the basis of the letter that I presented to the President after talking with you.

Johnson's persuasive powers had limited effect — after Symington's further complaints, he gave Dulles (in a "Dear Allen" note) just one source's
name. The DCI quickly learned that that production "expert" had no information at variance with that held by the intelligence establishment. He
reported to Goodpaster, "The Senator has never given me any information
as to the basis of his 'intelligence' regarding ICBM testing, etc." He also let
Symington know (in a "Dear Stuart" letter) that his "revelation" of one
source had been of no value.

In July, Symington inquired of Richard Russell if he had heard new "findings" from the CIA and was told "yes." "Could I ask Dulles to give me the latest news on Soviet missile progress," Symington asked. Russell agreed. So
Symington telephoned the DCI, called him his "dear friend," and (as Dulles
noted) "said he would like to drop by and find out what the information is
and 'would like to lick his wounds.'" Symington heard the latest intelligence
from Dulles that same day — it was apparently not earth-shaking — and
their relationship was quiet for the remainder of the year.[9]

In and Out of Hearing Rooms

But relations were not exactly calm between the agency and Congress in the months following Dulles's explosive encounter with Symington in March 1959. There were at least twelve or thirteen more committee or subcommittee hearings with CIA participation that year, plus at least two other occasions when Allen Dulles joined groups of legislators for informational sessions. That made for an annual total of at least thirty or thirty-one agency appearances before formal legislative bodies (plus two informal groups sessions), apparently the highest number in the CIA's thirteen years. Records of such meetings are imperfect, so there were probably more. Also, the legislative liaison's office was unable to keep track of CIA-congressional exchanges occurring outside of hearings — in person, in writing, or by telephone. John Warner recalls being aware that Dulles would often stop by Saltonstall's home for drinks and a talk after work. Warner adds, with a laugh, though, "He never told us."[1]

Similarly, much of Clarence Cannon's oversight occurred not in hearings but in his office, alone with Dulles. How often these occurred is unknown, but two Dulles memos about 1958 sessions survive. In January, Cannon summoned Dulles not to discuss "our budget problems, but . . . in particular, Soviet advances in the armament field." Cannon's questions "covered the field of missiles, submarines, aircraft, etc." When the chairman "asked about my views as to our general situation vis-à-vis the Soviet Union . . . I said that I saw no reason to get panicky, but that a special effort would be required to close the gap with the Soviets in the field of ballistic missiles." The United States was "probably stronger than the Soviet Union in the overall military field," though. Otherwise, Cannon was "interested in the Soviets' submarine development" and "the question of foreign aid." Dulles "stressed the extent and nature of the Soviet drive to take over uncommitted and undeveloped areas of the world." Cannon barely asked about forthcoming Fiscal Year 1959 CIA budget requests, wondering (Dulles wrote) "whether I had enough money," to which he replied that "we were asking for a slightly smaller appropriation in FY '59 since our reserve had been built up to the safety point."

In a December 1958 session, Cannon wanted to talk about "signals sent by the satellite, Sputnik," Dulles noted, and "we had a long talk about France." Otherwise, it was "danger spots around the world — Cuba, Venezuela . . . the

Berlin situation, Indonesia," then India. The meeting closed with a discussion of Missouri-made corncob pipes that the two men owned. In both meetings, Dulles indicated readiness to meet with the Appropriations subcommittee as often as Cannon might wish, but the chairman showed no particular response to the offers. He did summon Dulles to his office a few weeks later, in January 1959, for a missile gap talk.

By then, Dulles had "plunged into the problems incident to the new session of Congress," he wrote a friend, "getting to know some of the many new faces there." But old faces mattered more. *Time* magazine reported that Cannon had "presided over the spending of more than a trillion dollars — exactly $1,040,597,183,594.75 — in his 18 years as chairman of the House Appropriations Committee." *Time* added that Cannon, while "perhaps" the most unpopular member of the House, was also its "hardest working member (roughly, from 10 a.m. to midnight, seven days a week) and one of its ablest." Appropriations would have fifty members in 1959, the largest congressional committee in U.S. history. Its fourteen subcommittees conducted virtually all of their business in secret. Despite Cannon's power and his recurrent hostility toward many military leaders ("they always want to fight the next war with old weapons," he said), the Senate Appropriations Committee frequently restored cuts made in the foreign/defense policy budgets by Cannon's committee.

The DCI predictably declared to the chairman at the January session "that I did not feel competent to make comparative appraisals" but quickly did just that: "I told Mr. Cannon that, in my opinion, the Russians were probably technically somewhat ahead of us, as they had devoted more time and energy to the guided missile program and all its components, since they had taken over a large share of the German assets at the end of the war." However, within a few years, "we should be able to narrow the gap with them in the guided missiles field." This and other accounts of the 1958–1959 Cannon sessions belie published claims that the missile gap was purely an invention of Symington and other ambitious legislators.[2]

Transcripts from early 1959 hearings dealing with the agency's Fiscal Year 1960 budget have never been declassified or do not exist, but some records of informal budget interactions have survived. They suggest that, initially, the CIA faced pressure in 1958–1959 — from Eisenhower aides and members of CIA subcommittees — to reduce its spending in 1960. Red White of the CIA recorded in November 1958 that "Mr. Stans and Mr. Dulles had agreed that our budget figure for Fiscal Year 1960 should be revised downward very substantially. . . . General Cabell buzzed me to say that he had decided that we should cut our [word censored] Program in half . . . and that our personnel strength in Europe would be cut by about 50%."

Dulles soon turned against such plans and engaged Maurice Stans in a showdown two weeks later, at which the director of the Bureau of the Budget opined that the CIA had "exaggerated the costs of our regular operations" for years, wrote White, who attended and was all ears. Dulles "emphasized the necessity for good intelligence inasmuch as if, according to present estimates, we did not get at least 15 minutes early warning in the event of a hostile attack on the United States, the result would be catastrophic." Neither director budged. At the meeting's end, "Mr. Dulles stated that when he went before the Appropriations Committees in the Congress, he was always asked whether he thought he had enough money to carry on his work and that, in prior years, he had always been able to give an affirmative answer. He explained to Mr. Stans that, if he were required to adjust his budget request along these lines, it would be impossible for him to give an affirmative answer if that question were asked of him again this year." Stans said he would be taking this issue, among others, to the president in a few days. But the pressure on the CIA seemed to have eased somewhat. A week later, Eisenhower approved a Fiscal Year 1960 CIA budget based on the assumption of "personnel reductions of at least one percent in 1959 and 1960, respectively," but Dulles wrote six weeks later that he had told Cannon — the man who regularly posed the "enough money" question — that the budget "would be up a bit from last year, largely in part because of the pay raise which would be reflected in our ordinary budget for the first time in FY 1960. I told him that we were making a very real effort to . . . see whether we could effect any personnel cuts. I stated I wanted him to know this because, as he well knew, any people whom we dismissed ran first of all to their congressman and I would need some support from the Congress, if I were going to be able to carry through any personnel reductions. He laughed at this and said he fully realized the problem."[3]

Many informal CIA-congressional interactions in 1958, like other years, involved presentation of information requested by legislators or reaction to *their* "intelligence." Dulles himself spent time getting an appropriate CIA analysis prepared and delivered for the White House to provide to Senator Homer Capehart (R-IN) on "Communist political and economic penetration in Latin America" and faced a request from Eisenhower to analyze Representative Frank Becker's (R-NY) report that Spain's Francisco Franco indicated to him that he had "a large supply of Russian guns and ammunition that could and should be fed to Russia's satellite countries through the underground." Meanwhile, Dulles's associates in the Office of Research and Reports (ORR) spent considerable effort preparing a report on tire production in the USSR ("antiquated by U.S. standards") for Representative Glenard Lipscomb.[4]

A sample of informal interactions in 1959, besides Cannon's and Symington's private meetings with Dulles, might begin with Paul Kilday, who chaired the House Armed Services subcommittee on the CIA (at the request of Carl Vinson, who usually attended) beginning in January 1959, after twenty years' service in Congress. Kilday had earned Vinson's respect so thoroughly by the time of the Korean War outbreak, nine years earlier, that the chairman openly admitted his reliance on the junior member when others were leaving Washington for their home districts: "The crisis in the world is so acute that I must ask that you remain in Washington during the recess period in order to assist me personally," he pleaded. Well before 1959, Kilday had been one of those trusted by Vinson to be part of the informal and thoroughly secretive subcommittee on the CIA. The tall Texan, who rarely spoke on the floor of the House, was (wrote columnist Arthur Krock) "rated by his colleagues as one of the ablest and most sincere members of Congress."

Eisenhower, too, respected Kilday, though in early 1958 the promilitary congressman had opposed portions of the president's Defense Department reorganization plan, which, he said, contained "too many dead cats." With uncharacteristic sensationalism, he claimed to fear the proposed strengthening of powers held by the Secretary of Defense and Joint Chiefs of Staff — it could create a military leadership like the one that "took Germany into two world wars and lost them both." But Kilday helped craft a compromise bill that Eisenhower signed.[5]

The seven others who joined Vinson and Kilday on the CIA subcommittee were not newcomers to Congress, but they were not chosen simply on the basis of seniority. It was primarily Vinson's estimation of members — in consultation with ranking Republican Les Arends (IL) regarding GOP members — that led to their selection. Kilday saw Dulles and others from the CIA early in 1959 in preparation for planned subcommittee hearings. Warner recorded Kilday saying that Sam Rayburn "had received considerable pressure for action" on eleven resolutions introduced in the new Congress for a joint intelligence committee, and therefore the "reconstituted" CIA subcommittee "would function on an active basis." Kilday also renewed a naive suggestion that his staff had asked of the CIA: "It might be extremely useful if it could be stated that the subcommittee had in its files a report on a certain situation prior to its occurrence so that the subcommittee could so state. In this connection, he specifically mentioned the Iraq situation."

Later in the year, Kilday saw and kept an October report by newspaper columnists Robert Allen and Paul Scott:

> That unpublicized House investigation of the super-secret Central Intelligence Agency has uncovered some jolting disclosures. One of the most astonishing is an almost incredible story of the CIA forking over more than $1 million for hidden ore in Japan, in exchange for super-duper Communist information, only to find that both it and the ore were virtually worthless. . . . Another startling discovery is that CIA is now one of the biggest contractors in the government. In 1958, on the basis of one study in the probers' hands, the Intelligence Agency was the third largest federal purchaser, being exceeded only by the Defense Department and the Atomic Energy Commission. Practically all of the CIA's buying is in foreign countries. . . . The probe is being made by a special seven-member Armed Services Subcommittee, headed by Rep. Paul Kilday. . . . An expert staff has been compiling data about CIA for months in preparations for hearings at a still-undetermined date.[6]

Indeed, Kilday and his subcommittee staffers had plenty of interactions with the CIA in 1959. Dulles met with the subcommittee on four or five days in February, joined on different days by colleagues including DDI Amory, Inspector General Kirkpatrick, covert action leaders Richard Bissell and Richard Helms, and others. While one day's hearing focused on "world affairs," according to a CIA document, three other days' meetings concerned "Agency activities." In March, Kilday wrote that his subcommittee had held "quite a number of meetings, and has additional meetings planned for the immediate future." One agency leader worried (excessively) on February 20, "It is beginning to appear that there may be a briefing such as this every month or every two weeks." Another Kilday subcommittee hearing with CIA leaders present occurred the following June 30. Most specifics on 1959 hearings seem lost to history, though records suggest that Senator Alex Smith played some role (that remains obscure) in the mysterious payments for "worthless" ore.[7]

Kilday was almost certainly not the person who leaked to reporters Allen and Scott; Warner recalls him as "acutely conscious of the need to protect legitimate secrets of CIA." So, Kilday was probably unhappy to receive mail from members of the public congratulating him on that year's investigation. One letter said of the CIA, "It is essential that their activities be scrutinized and I commend you for your efforts." Kilday fended off such correspondents with word that his subcommittee's activities were secret.

Despite the secrecy, evidence exists on some of the topics that were on Kilday's mind and how he dealt with them mostly outside of committee hearing rooms. "The Kilday subcommittee has raised the question of an improved audit by the General Accounting Office (GAO)," noted Lawrence Houston in October 1959. The Comptroller General (CG) headed GAO, an arm of Congress, and had (as noted earlier) grudgingly accepted during DCI Smith's tenure that the GAO would stay out of many or most covert action projects, especially those funded by the DCI's unvouchered account. On the other hand, the GAO had prohibited Smith from using his unvouchered fund to support "normal" CIA projects.

With the passage of nearly a decade, the CIA-GAO relationship had frayed, largely because of changes at the GAO. CG Joseph Campbell, though a Republican, won the respect of Democratic-led Congresses after taking the helm at GAO in 1954, for the Office was an outstanding source of information on the executive branch. While previous CGs had been attorneys, Campbell had an accomplished accountancy background. Across the mid- to late-1950s, he expanded so-called comprehensive audits that improved on a previous approach, which merely examined agencies' vouchers for expenditures. Fred Mosher writes that Campbell had "an almost passionate concern to find, to disclose, and to force the correction of inefficiency and waste of public funds." He was not "enthusiastic about working cooperatively with the executive agencies and officials."

The comptroller general decided in 1959 that the CIA, too, should undergo the comprehensive audits. Campbell advised Kilday in May 1959, "The expanded work would include an examination of vouchered expenditures, and, at the outset, the controls and procedures used in processing unvouchered expenditures. Also, we would propose to make a limited examination of the support for unvouchered expenditures. . . . We have heretofore carried out only limited audit work at CIA, and we do not believe such limited work should be continued." Kilday's subcommittee could be helpful, the CG said, by "advising the Agency of your interest in broadening the audit performed by the General Accounting Office."

This major challenge to the CIA's budgetary autonomy could succeed only if Campbell persuaded Kilday and Vinson, plus barons of the other legislative subcommittees on the CIA, to support the new comprehensive role for the GAO. Those other leaders would have been a tough audience for the Office in an outright conflict with the CIA, for Richard Russell and Carl Vinson remained determinedly deferential to Eisenhower on big national security questions. In a spring 1959 White House meeting, during one of the periodic Berlin crises of the era, the two Armed Services chairs could hardly contain themselves in deferring to the president, with Russell assuring Eisenhower that any decisions about war were wholly the president's — "consultation with Congress would not be necessary." In turn, Eisenhower singled out the "two committee chairmen" — among other legislative leaders present, with Allen Dulles watching — for an invitation to "call him directly" if they ever felt the administration had been "remiss in informing them."

Campbell did gain support from the new chair of the House Armed Services CIA subcommittee, for Kilday informed Dulles on June 18 that, after a series of subcommittee meetings, its members had "informally concluded that (1) the degree of audit of vouchered funds performed by GAO representatives in the Central Intelligence Agency was considerably less than had been thought; (2) for the protection of the Agency and the assurance of the Congress, the audit function should continue; (3) that more senior representatives of the General Accounting Office should be assigned to this function." Kilday directed Dulles to negotiate the issue with Campbell.

During the course of many meetings and exchanges of letters between the CIA, the GAO, and Kilday and Vinson on Capitol Hill, Dulles initially agreed that the GAO could expand its audit "in a considerable portion of the Agency," and suggested that he and Campbell "reach agreement on certain fundamental aspects." But later in the year, having informed Eisenhower of the "problems" created by Kilday and Campbell, Dulles rebuffed the comptroller general's proposed comprehensive audits of even vouchered CIA accounts, saying they would "necessarily reach into the confidential operations."

Only if Vinson and Russell had solidly backed the GAO would Dulles have been forced to relent. But Vinson had not given full CIA-related authority to Kilday; the hard-working seventy-six-year-old chairman viewed *all* Armed Services matters as his business. Mosher writes that no requests the GAO received were considered a higher priority than those coming from committee chairs, but an unambiguous "request" from Vinson or Russell that the CIA fully accede to Campbell seems not to have materialized. The General Accounting Office (and Kilday) failed at their reform effort.

Handling of the GAO issue is suggestive of the extent to which congressional-CIA relations were often carried out informally. Of the many CIA-GAO-Congress interactions of 1959, only one of them, in June, is known to have been in an actual subcommittee hearing, presided over by Kilday and featuring Dulles, Bissell, and others. All other treatment of the issue by Kilday and subcommittee colleagues and staff occurred in meetings between subcommittee staff and GAO staff, in subcommittee meetings without CIA testimony, and in correspondence. (Committee staff head Robert Smart summoned a CIA accountant to his office in March for questioning about CIA accounting practices at home and abroad and its relations with the GAO. The accountant was warned by his boss, Comptroller Edward Saunders, "not to withhold any information," and Smart seemed satisfied with the responses.) Kilday and Vinson talked among themselves and with Dulles about the GAO question. These were surely the most crucial exchanges on the topic.[8]

Without any known hearings, Kilday also discreetly addressed two other topics in 1959— a contract for Air America and a disturbing boast by Nikita Khrushchev. On the first issue, Kilday monitored an awkward situation in which a member of Congress represented the interests of a commercial air transport company, Arctic Pacific, Inc., which claimed to have lost under "suspicious circumstances" to Air America in a supposedly open bidding process for an airlift contract with the U.S. Air Force. Parts of the CIA's budget were, of course, hidden in the air force budget and those of other military branches. Air America and its corporate parent, the Pacific Corporation, were secretly owned by the CIA. Representative Steven Carter (D-IA), who had served in the Pacific during World War II, seems to have known this. He challenged the air force for contracting out to Air America for certain "airlift services to be performed . . . generally in the Far East and Western Pacific." Air America was born in 1959, when the CIA's also-secret Civil Air Transport (CAT) was divided into smaller airlines. Air America worked mostly in Southeast Asia. After the 1950s ended, Brigadier General Edward Lansdale would write in a classified memo of CAT: "It has had some notable achievements, including support of the Chinese Nationalist withdrawal from the mainland, air drop support to the French at Dien Bien Phu, complete logistical and tactical support for the Indonesian operation, air lifts of refugees of Mainland China and Tibet, and extensive air support in Laos."[9]

One of Dulles's deputies noted on June 24, 1959, that he had met with air force and agency leaders "about Congressman Carter, who has caused a lot of trouble." Dulles instructed the deputy that Carter "could not be briefed as to CIA's interest in CAT and that the Air Force should go ahead and award the contract. . . . It is possible that Congressman Carter may cause further trouble, and if he has gained a knowledge of our interest in CAT in some unauthorized manner, he may drag us into it." Carter apparently had some inkling of Air America's unique ownership and role, and (according to an agency memo) "threatened" to discuss it on the floor of the House. "Mr. Kilday immediately took action to protect our interests, including standing by on the floor to cope with the congressman." Carter never did speak of the CIA before the House.

It was left to chairman Chet Holifield (D-CA) of the Military Operations subcommittee of the Committee on Government Operations to deal with the conflict in a low-key fashion, with Kilday watching. On June 19, Holifield found that "the award to Air America does not appear to be improper." Kilday had something to do with the quiet resolution of the issue, as his surviving files have Air America correspondence and documents. None of them mentions the Agency, but Kilday scrawled "CIA" on them for proper filing.

There are two footnotes to the little episode involving Congress, the CIA, and Air America in 1959 that could stir the hearts of conspiracy theorists. The first is that Colonel Fletcher Prouty of the air force's Office of the Director of Plans was a player in the outcome of Carter's challenge. Prouty, who later became an extravagant conspiracy theorist of the Kennedy assassination, served in the late 1950s as a liaison to the CIA and Congress on matters relating to air force support of covert action. In addition to whatever else he did on the Air America–Congress issue, Prouty kept CIA's Lawrence Houston informed as to the specifics of the air force's response to Carter's challenge. Houston's office, in turn, kept Kilday abreast of matters. The second footnote: Carter died the same year that he challenged the Air America contract at the age of forty-four, having served less than a year in the House. His death in a Washington area hospital was attributed to cancer.[10]

The other incident demanding Kilday's discreet attention in 1959 occurred in September. "There on American soil was Nikita Khrushchev," wrote *Time* magazine, "short, bald, and portly, wearing a black suit, Homburg, and three small medals, accepting a 21-gun salute, parading past a guard of honor." Khrushchev showed "the politician's adeptness at choosing which questions to answer, dodge, or bull through," said *Time*. In the nation's capital, he was honored with the largest white-tie dinner ever hosted during the Eisenhower administration, though the premier dressed down for the event.

Among Khrushchev's other scheduled events in Washington was a late afternoon tea on September 16 with members of the Senate Foreign Relations Committee and selected guests, including Richard Russell. (Committee chair Fulbright would send a "practically verbatim" transcript of the session to DCI Dulles.) By the time Khrushchev arrived, the Capitol was mostly deserted, but not the ceremonial Capital room, which was filled with twenty-five alert congressional leaders. The Soviet leader began by saying, "I feel that I have known practically all of you a long time but, until now, you have been sort of ethereal beings to me. Now you appear in the flesh." Moments later, after extolling Abraham Lincoln as one of humanity's most progressive leaders, he said that the progress of communism against capitalism had surely "disappointed" the senators ("who of us has not been disappointed sometimes in life as when a daughter was born instead of a son?"). When Khrushchev complained about "appropriations by the Congress of funds for subversive activities" against the USSR, Fulbright said, "I'm afraid I don't understand you." Russell responded with a straight face, "I know of no appropriations anywhere for any subversive work in Russia."

Russell raised his own topic of interest. Was it true, as Vice President Nixon had recently claimed, that the Soviets had experienced failures prior to getting a rocket launched past the moon? The question put Khrushchev into a sarcastic mood: "Since the Vice President seems to know more about it than I do, you had better ask him." Though he wagged his fingers at the legislators now and then, the session was mostly good-humored.[11]

In Los Angeles, Frank Sinatra sang "Live and Let Live" for the premier, and then said, "It's a marvelous idea!" While in California, Khrushchev needled Henry Cabot Lodge, ambassador to the United Nations, with claims that the Central Intelligence Agency had been compromised. "The Soviet Union has even got money from the United States for its intelligence work," he said during a city tour in which one of the other passengers was a local official. While Lodge disregarded Khrushchev's remarks, the Los Angeles official — Victor Carter, a member of the Board of Fire Commissioners, who also happened to head a film studio and was a native-born speaker of the Russian language — was alarmed. He told a fellow L.A. political figure — Kenneth Hahn, a member of the Los Angeles Board of Supervisors — who, in turn, spread Carter's account far and wide. To various legislators, Hahn wrote,

> During this trip, Mr. Khrushchev boasted to Mr. Lodge that the United States Central Intelligence Agency is a complete farce. He claimed that important

diplomatic and military communications to and from the United States have been intercepted by Soviet agents. Mr. Khrushchev told Mr. Lodge that recently, when a secret message was sent by President Eisenhower to Prime Minister Nehru of India, the Soviet government knew the contents of this message. He also stated that the Soviet government also intercepted a secret message from President Eisenhower to the Shah of Iran.

When Mr. Lodge diplomatically doubted Mr. Khrushchev's statements, the Soviet Premier offered to send copies of the documents to Mr. Lodge to prove his point. Mr. Carter also said to me that Mr. Khrushchev stated the American intelligence agents of the Central Intelligence Agency, working in Europe and the Middle East, are working for the Russian government also, and that much of the money that is being sent to these agents is handed over directly by them to the Soviets. After this statement, Mr. Khrushchev humorously inquired why does not the American government send the money directly to Russia, or save it and reduce American taxes?[12]

Those receiving the story included Allen Dulles, George Mahon, and Paul Kilday. If Khrushchev's boast was authentic, there would be repercussions for other agencies, in addition to the CIA, including the National Security Agency and the State Department. But, receiving "several inquiries concerning the letter circulated by Mr. Kenneth Hahn," Dulles initiated contact with congressional leaders. The DCI had relished meeting Khrushchev at a White House reception prior to the Los Angeles visit but now felt some embarrassment. As *Time* reported, upon shaking hands with Khrushchev, Dulles said, "Mr. Chairman, you may have seen some of my intelligence reports from time to time." Khrushchev responded in kind: "I believe we get the same reports, and probably from the same people." "Maybe," Dulles retorted, "we should pool our efforts!"

Before Dulles reached Mahon, concerned enough in Texas to write a brief memo after reading that "the Russians had broken a top secret code of the U.S.," the House Appropriations CIA subcommittee chair directed a staffer in Washington to contact the agency. The CIA's response to Mahon, probably handled personally by Dulles, is undocumented. Meanwhile, in Washington, Armed Services colleagues urged Paul Kilday to determine (as CIA subcommittee member Charles Bennett [D-FL] wrote) "just what the facts are and what corrections may be instituted as needed." Bennett was impressed by Hahn's judgment that Khrushchev's "offer to present documentary proof of his statements to Mr. Lodge" gave his claims ominous credibility. Since

Congress budgeted millions for intelligence, Hahn wrote, "I believe it is absolutely imperative that the proper congressional committees thoroughly investigate this situation."[13]

Just as Kilday prepared to contact Dulles, he heard from him. The Soviet premier's claims were "part of a deliberate campaign to discredit U.S. intelligence and thus leave a clearer field for communist subversion." Khrushchev probably hoped to "draw out any information that any official reply or action might supply." The DCI wrote of Kilday's understanding of intelligence:

> You recognize, of course, that from time to time, agents are exposed and apprehended. This often happens to Soviet agents. These agents sometimes carry both money and ciphers known as one-time pads. These pads are useful solely for communications between that agent and his home base, and do not affect any other communication system. As far as we are concerned, Khrushchev has not got much comfort out of us in this respect; in fact, nothing comparable to what we have gained from Soviet defectors and agents. As far as the general communications systems of the U.S. government are concerned, they are protected between sender and recipient by a variety of means, none of which were made suspect by Khrushchev's remarks. We are constantly calculating the protection given to such communications by the inherent security of the devices used and are constantly alert to interpret and exploit any information which would alter our calculations.

Although Kilday scribbled the words "CIA Sub-comm." on his Khrushchev-related correspondence with Dulles, there is no record of a hearing on the topic. More likely, the "investigation by the appropriate committees of the Congress" suggested by Hahn was conducted instead by discreet conversations and correspondence between the DCI and the likes of Kilday, Mahon, Russell, and possibly a few others. Probably, Kilday and the rest felt reassured by Dulles's evaluation of Khrushchev's CIA claims. Even decades later, the truth of those claims is impossible to evaluate authoritatively. Kilday was possibly unaware of security problems in 1959 at NSA, although it was answerable to the House and Senate Armed Services committees. In fact, that agency, created in 1952 by Truman, was (as James Bamford writes) "infested by moles and potential defectors" during most of its early years. Kilday would begin to learn this soon, and his usual informal modes of communication with intelligence agencies would not suffice.[14]

Other heads of CIA subcommittees resembled Kilday in conducting much of their agency business outside of hearings in 1959. When Senators

Russell, Hayden, and Saltonstall observed Henry Dworshak erupt in a July Appropriations Committee meeting that it was "outrageous" that he knew nothing about the CIA's budget, Chairman Hayden moved to squelch the discussion and assured Dworshak that he "certainly would know about it." Hayden had Saltonstall telephone Dulles, who recorded in a memo that "Saltonstall suggested that the Director might want to consider calling up Senator Hayden or Senator Russell and asking them if they didn't think it would be a good thing for him to go around and see Dworshak and tell him the story; it might calm him down." Since Dworshak was not on Appropriations' CIA subcommittee but wanted to know "the total number of employees and the total amount of money included in the CIA budget," Dulles demurred. It "would be setting a precedent and would be opening the floodgates to numerous other requests," he told Saltonstall. House leaders Cannon and Taber had "stood firm against requests such as this," he said, and "quieted all questioners, many of whom were as tough as Dworshak." Dulles advised Saltonstall "that the Senate adopt this same position."

Saltonstall waffled in response to the DCI's suggestion, but following further talks with Russell, Hayden, and Styles Bridges, he persuaded Dulles to write Hayden a "memorandum in general terms." As the senator told the DCI of Hayden, "If he wants to show it to Dworshak, that's his business and not yours." Dulles disliked the solution, though, so he appealed the next day to Chairman Hayden, "If Senator Dworshak has the information, the other members of the Appropriations Committee would have an equal right to know." The conversation evolved into a rare, private deadlock between Dulles and Hayden, until the exasperated chairman said, "I am a very busy man." Knowing that Hayden almost never showed anger, Dulles later acceded to his desire to pacify Dworshak.[15]

Former agency personnel recall that only up to a point did George Mahon view hearings of his House Appropriations subcommittee as appropriate for review of sensitive topics. A sample of this comes from a rare document found years later in his papers — a partial transcript of an Appropriations subcommittee hearing. Whether it was Mahon's Defense subcommittee or the smaller CIA subcommittee is unclear. The hearing occurred on an unspecified date in 1959 and featured an interaction between a CIA figure, perhaps pseudonymously named Dr. Heathcotte, and "the Chairman," presumably Mahon but possibly Cannon. (Like Vinson, who kept Kilday on a leash in heading the Armed Services' CIA subcommittee, Cannon often attended Appropriations' subcommittee meetings chaired by Mahon. Thus, for a period of time, there were two "Mr. Chairmans" for each subcommittee.) The initial topic in the transcribed hearing was an apparatus that, as part of a "Project Cannon Ball," was being tested in relation to different conditions in the atmosphere, the earth's surface, and underground. A second project, "Operation Walnut Tree," also came up. One or both of the projects apparently had some major counterintelligence purpose.

The transcript begins with the chairman wishing to "digress for a moment" to question "Dr. Heathcotte, who I see is in the room":

> The Chairman: We all know, Doctor, that the "Cannon Ball" project is highly classified, but I don't believe we would violate the security involved if you could tell us briefly how that undertaking is progressing.
>
> Dr. Heathcotte: I hesitate to make any response, Mr. Chairman, in view of the tight restrictions that have been placed around the matter you mention. The fact that a "Cannon Ball" project has been well under way for some time is widely known, but the highly sensitive matters involved are known to but a few people outside of those actively participating in it and the members of this Subcommittee.

With the chair seeming to favor some discussion of the project and Heathcotte resisting, the ensuing discussion was kept off the record. When the stenographer resumed work, the chairman tried again:

> In the limited manner we have just discussed, I believe security restrictions would be observed if you were just to touch on the scientific aspects that are not directly connected with the real and ultimate purpose of the work that is now being done.
>
> Dr. Heathcotte: I will try, Mr. Chairman, but it is going to be rather difficult for me to do so. As you gentlemen know, and as we in this particular specialized field are aware, no other country in the world has given attention to the possibilities involved in this project. We have reached the point now where the realm of possibility has been hurdled; we have established the fact that our goal is a proven reality. We have been highly successful in our sub-surface studies, both underground and under the rivers and oceans, and the results achieved regarding atmospheric phenomena stagger us a bit.
>
> The Chairman: Has your area of probing been wide enough to include both fertile and frozen waste of land and both cold and hot water so that the necessary comparisons are available for required adjustments?
>
> Dr. Heathcotte: Certainly, Mr. Chairman, we have enough information now

to conform the apparatus for any given condition. We are very much encouraged. It was discouraging for the first eighteen months, but then suddenly, like hitting an oil well, things began to unfold in our direction.

At this point, when Project Cannon Ball's supposed success was apparently described and discussed, the discussion again moved off the record. When the stenographer resumed transcribing, Heathcotte was describing future plans:

> We will need more money for the Bolivar Heights installation because of our ability to create conditions there that you might find in any given place in the world. We can do it whether land, water, or atmosphere is involved. It is our plan to bring into the Bolivar Heights center within the next six or eight months, all of the teams we have had operating on the scene where the land and water is the coldest. We have the problem of duplication licked now. Of course, the lunar expedition and its logistics support must remain intact for at least another year.

Though CIA veterans could not, years later, explain the reference to a "lunar expedition" or other topics in the testimony, Mahon and company seemingly understood the subjects discussed. But when the chairman asked if the CIA representative could tell about another project, "Operation Walnut Tree," he ran into a stone wall. Dr. Heathcotte responded, "That I cannot, Mr. Chairman, under any circumstances. Just be assured we are happy with the money you have allowed for 'Walnut Tree' and have faith in us. We are moving forward." Perhaps sensing less than complete "faith" on the chairman's part, Heathcotte added, "I think it would be very healthy for the members of the Subcommittee to be in attendance at the bi-weekly meetings we have been holding with the President and the Security Council ever since these projects came into being more than three years ago. That is the only forum where we are permitted to go into these matters without restraint." The chairman showed scant enthusiasm for that suggestion and then asked more questions about the functioning of the mysterious Bolivar Heights facility — whose nature remains obscure. Expansion of Bolivar Heights, which was apparently an hour's plane ride from Washington, was inevitable, Heathcotte indicated. The payoff would be a better "reservoir of information and experience."

Dulles was apparently not at the hearing, which is not shocking, as there were at least eight hearings with CIA testimony in 1959 without him present. Perhaps the cryptic Dr. Heathcotte and his CIA colleagues thought that

Mahon, who thanked them for "preserving the security of our country in the face of physical hazards and risks," was satisfied with their explanations, but he was not. In addition to making a notation to raise the subject again at a hearing early in 1960, he called Dulles about the "Cannon Ball" and "Walnut Tree" projects. What the legislator and DCI said to each other remains undocumented, but afterward a Mahon staffer wrote, "James Angleton of CIA came up to Committee to discuss it" with Mahon.

Angleton headed counterintelligence for the agency from the 1950s through the mid-1970s. Given exceptional autonomy by Dulles and later DCIs in hunting for traitors and foreign agents within the CIA, he was an agency legend in his own time but not a frequent testifier on Capitol Hill. Indeed, the document from Mahon's files is virtually the only instance of Angleton's name showing up in any CIA-related papers found in files of 1940s-to-1960s agency overseers. Of the former high-ranking CIA officials who have looked at the surviving transcript from Mahon's papers, none has been able to explain the nature of the two projects or why James Angleton was chosen by Dulles to discuss them with George Mahon.

The congressman's documents are suggestive, as the 1959 files of Kilday, Russell, and others are, that the most sensitive topics were often handled outside of hearings by CIA subcommittee leaders. Whatever transpired in Mahon's telephone call to Dulles and in his meeting with Angleton would have been more detailed than that which occurred in the hearing. Unfortunately, for the purposes of history, such conversations were even less well documented.[16]

"Who Are Our Liquidators?"

The Senate Foreign Relations Committee summoned the CIA to three closed sessions in 1959, almost matching the previous year's four or five such occasions, despite Eisenhower's continuing hostility. The briefest hearing was the most interesting. The new chair, J. William Fulbright, invited Allen Dulles to educate committee members in late April 1959 about Tibet, from which the Dalai Lama had escaped just weeks earlier. Also, the committee wished to ask about Adbul Qassim's year-old, unstable government of Iraq.

About Tibet, Dulles assured senators that the CIA had been following the "situation very closely since 1956, when we began to receive reports indicating the spread of the Tibetan revolt against the Chinese Communists." In fact, since 1957, the CIA had been training Tibetans in guerrilla warfare, a topic about which Dulles did not usually speak before Foreign Relations. After initially training six Tibetans on the northern Pacific island of Saipan that year, the agency recruited and brought many more Tibetans to an old World War II army base in Colorado in the United States. When the Chinese government cracked down on the brewing rebellion in Tibet — which had been occupied by Chinese troops since 1951 but had suffered China troubles for centuries — the Dalai Lama fled his palace near the capital city of Lhasa in the spring of 1959. As Dulles explained to the committee in April, "As late as March 17, the Dalai Lama still hoped for a peaceful solution. But when shells fell near the summer palace, he decided the time had come to leave. The Dalai Lama, his mother and younger brother and two sisters slipped out of the palace on March 17 and joined the escape party. . . . Serious fighting began on March 19 in Lhasa and continued for several days. On March 22, the rebels were driven from Lhasa."

CIA leaders believed that some of its Tibetan trainees aiding the escaping group were partly responsible for the success of the Dalai Lama's long passage through high mountain passes to India. Dulles briefly related the escape story, "a rather dramatic one," he said. His ensuing account was almost completely censored from the surviving transcript, presumably because of the DCI's inclusion of the CIA's role in the event. The only reason Dulles's account can be judged to have been brief is that when he offered to elaborate with a "somewhat detailed account of just what took place in

Lhasa and how the Dalai Lama got out," Chairman Fulbright brushed off the topic: "This is interesting, but I don't believe we can do a thing about it."

Before giving up on the subject, Dulles politely countered that there *were* things the United States could do. This subject again was mostly censored in the transcript, except for Dulles's explanation that the CIA was functioning as an intelligence conduit: "For example, we have played back information that we received to the Dalai Lama and then from the Dalai Lama to Nehru and to the Indians." Dulles also apparently stressed the "propaganda value" of the Tibet tragedy in educating Southeast Asian leaders about China, as it was those two words that Fulbright used in response to the DCI's prescription regarding the Tibet problem. When Fulbright again sounded skeptical about doing anything more for the Tibetans "like direct physical assistance," Dulles did not argue the point further. He would not give up on Fulbright, though.

Responding to Mike Mansfield, Dulles revealed that the CIA was "in close touch" with two brothers of the Dalai Lama who lived in the United States. When Mansfield asked off-handedly if they were at Johns Hopkins University, Dulles's initial response was guarded: "I don't think they are in educational institutions. They have been pretty busy recently on other matters." When Mansfield pursued the subject, Dulles apparently leveled with him, as his next response was censored. If he was truthful, Dulles would have revealed that all three of the Dalai Lama's older brothers were activists in the Tibetan resistance and had interacted with the CIA; the eldest, Takster Rinpoche, had been meeting with CIA and State Department officials since 1952. He and another brother, Gyalo Thondup, had agreed with the agency in 1956 on the pilot program to train and support a half-dozen Tibetan resistance fighters. This evolved by late 1958 into far more extensive CIA support, including American-piloted air drops of thousands of pounds of materiel and training of resistance fighters. The Dalai Lama knew of such things but resisted learning details.

Dulles had often declined to make unambiguous predictions at congressional hearings, but on two points raised at the 1959 Foreign Relations gathering he was blunt. Pressed by Fulbright to say if there was any chance that the resistance could succeed against a "determined" Chinese offensive, Dulles said, "No." (Two months later, Dulles would deliver a message the CIA had obtained from the Dalai Lama, addressed to Eisenhower and Herter, along with the gift of a white silk scarf. "Please confer and plan whatever strategy is necessary in regard to giving Tibetans independence," he wrote.) About the possibility that the Dalai Lama might respond to the Chinese government's entreaties to return to Tibet, the DCI told senators, "I don't think there is the slightest likelihood that he will go back."

Perhaps Dulles felt free to be forthcoming because there was widespread support in Washington for supporting the Tibetans against "Red China." Many U.S. supporters were idealists, while others had power politics on their minds. When the Tibetan resistance, made up of twenty-eight different groups, gained steam, Eisenhower's Operations Coordinating Board (OCB) labeled the revolt "a windfall for the U.S." At the beginning of 1959, Tibetan fighters controlled large portions of central Tibet, with the Chinese on the defensive. Partly due to Chinese airpower, though, this changed within months. On this development, too, the DCI was frank with the committee: "The Chinese are now engaged in mopping up the rebels outside the key strong points. I regret to say they are having a great deal of success in doing that."

In describing the desperate straits of the resistance's "tribesmen" from the vicinity of the city of Chamdo, Dulles raised the far more sensitive fact that the CIA was not merely analyzing the Tibetan situation but was a party to the struggle. Normally, he would have been stingy about describing difficult covert action to Fulbright's committee, given Eisenhower's views about Congress. Normally, too, his remarks would have been censored from the transcript (made by committee staff) at the CIA's request. But, just as part of the Dalai Lama escape story survived censors' attention, so did the DCI's explanation of how he knew about conditions on the ground with the Tibetan fighters: "We have had messages from our people who are with the Chamdo tribesmen." This mention of "our people" — CIA-trained and -equipped foreign nationals, in this case Tibetans, fighting a guerrilla war — was precisely the sort of topic that Dulles would discuss, if asked, with the four subcommittees on the CIA but rarely with other legislators. An uncensored transcript of the hearing would presumably reflect Dulles giving some elaboration of what "our people" were up to. As a former CIA officer later wrote of the Tibetans, "In addition to their instruction in guerrilla warfare and tactics and the use of small arms, they had learned how to operate the RS-1 hand-generated crystal radio transmitter and receiver, and to use radio signal plans, telecodes, and one-time encoding and decoding pads that each team carried to convey intelligence from the rebel areas, transmit requests for specific assistance, and guide the planes to their airdrop delivery sites."

The DCI spoke emotionally some moments later about the Tibetans' plight: "We have pathetic reports about the condition of the people on the frontier. It is comparable, in a sense, to the Hungarian operation. . . . they haven't the ammunition, they haven't the organization. They may be able to reassemble in certain mountain areas there and hold out for some time. But it is terribly difficult country. I mean, there is no cover." These were not easy words to voice, as many at the CIA felt a continuing sense of failure and guilt over not having done more for the Hungarian resistance. While the CIA had done and would do much more for the Tibetan resistance — airdrops of supplies would continue for four years — the DCI was effectively admitting that CIA support of the Tibetans was failing to make a crucial difference.

That legislators showed no surprise about the DCI's reference to "our people who are with the Chamdo tribesmen" in Tibet suggests that Dulles had earlier described, in a censored part of the hearing, the CIA's ongoing role in Tibet. In the approximately forty minutes of discussion of Tibet that morning, no senator seems to have criticized CIA involvement there. Even before the hearing occurred, Hubert Humphrey had inquired of the State Department about "supporting guerilla military action against the Peiping regime." This, of course, was already being done by the CIA, though the State Department did not say so. Also prior to the CIA hearing, Mansfield urged U.S. recognition of any government created by the Dalai Lama. Some weeks later, the State Department assured another congressional supporter of the Tibetans, Representative Stuyvesant Wainwright (R-NY), that it "received with an open mind any CIA proposals designed to exploit the situation in our national interest" and that it did not impose "any policy restrictions which would inhibit CIA from support of the Tibetan resistance movement."

What of Fulbright's skepticism and his comment that nothing could be done? The senator prided himself on knowing world politics and was no stranger to questions about irregular warfare. In 1952, well before winning the chair of Foreign Relations, the Arkansas senator had requested and received CIA analysis of "the amount of propaganda, bribery, etc., that the [Soviet] bloc is engaged in, country by country." Some months after the April hearing, Dulles asked the Tibetan Task Force's political officer, John K. Knaus, to go to Fulbright's home to show him film taken by a CIA-trained Tibetan during the Dalai Lama's escape journey. The film had been conveyed to the agency by summer 1959. So one evening, Knaus met Fulbright for a businesslike encounter in his living room. Among other things, the film showed a ceremony inside Tibet but close to India, presided over by the Dalai Lama, with a thousand people in attendance, consecrating a newly announced government of Tibet.

Knaus later wrote that, after showing the film to "the usually reserved" Fulbright, "he asked, 'What do you expect me to do about this?' When I replied that the CIA sought support for its program to aid the remnants of the resistance in Tibet, the laconic senator said, 'All right.' In those days, this was sufficient to constitute endorsement by the Senate Foreign Relations Committee, which he chaired." Fulbright's support was not nearly as essential as that of Appropriations and Armed Services leaders, but it helped.

The passage of time and, especially, the tumult of the 1970s over U.S. intelligence has obscured the extent to which times were not so great for Allen Dulles and the CIA in the late 1950s, when its handling of Suez, Sputnik, Indonesia, Iraq, and other matters had harmed the agency's reputation. Even more would the CIA face criticism in 1960 and 1961, but in 1959, Tibet was an almost politically perfect issue for the agency. Knaus writes of a "certain sense of romance attached to the Dalai Lama and his cause, a 'Shangri-la factor' that permitted free range in sustaining operations, as long as they harassed the Chinese Communists and, by extension, the Soviet Union, the monolithic nature of the communist empire then being an article of faith in Washington."

The resistance would be virtually destroyed by the Chinese in the coming few years, as Dulles predicted to the senators. The Dalai Lama later observed that the Americans' "assistance had been a reflection of their anti-Communist policies, rather than genuine support for the restoration of Tibetan independence." He was also grudging in his later published accounts of CIA assistance to Tibet, which his brothers had largely arranged, calling the air-dropped materiel "almost useless." Even of his escape from Tibet, which the CIA had aided and regarded with pride, the Dalai Lama wrote,

> Almost everyone but myself was heavily armed, including even the man appointed as my personal cook, who carried an enormous bazooka and wore a belt hung with its deadly shells. He was one of the young men trained by the CIA. So eager was he to use his magnificent and terrible-looking weapon that, at one point, he lay down and fired off several shots at what he claimed looked like an enemy position. But it took such a long time to reload that I felt sure he would have been made short work of by a real enemy. Altogether, it was not an impressive performance.[1]

On Iraq, Dulles was again more forthcoming at the April 28 hearing than Eisenhower would have wished. The news from that country had not gotten better for the United States since the 1958 coup that replaced a pro-Western government. Americans, not just at the CIA, had initially tended to view the government headed by Abdul Qassim as both pro-Nasser and pro-Soviet but came to learn that the truth was more complex. While in the long run Qassim would repress local communists, in the shorter run his and Nasser's governments became openly hostile. Qassim turned to the USSR for military and other aid and removed many Nasserites from the Iraqi government, replacing them with figures thought by the United States to be communist and/or pro-Soviet.

The tenor of Dulles's analysis and senators' remarks in the Foreign Relations session was that events had gone from bad to worse. Iraq's "general atmosphere," the DCI said, was a "terror typical of a descending Iron Curtain." The Russians were "trying to drive down into the Middle East into the heart of the oil-rich lands through Kurdistan, Iraq, down to Kuwait, Saudi Arabia and that whole area. I think it is a very dangerous move, and that it is probably the most dangerous area facing us today." Dulles, who had long claimed to abstain from "policy making," suggested to senators that the United States had no choice but to try to "save" Qassim from communist influence and to pursue rapprochement with Nasser. "If you must choose," he asked, "isn't it much safer to try to play with Nasser, even endanger the oil, than it is to let Communist Russia come in?"

Only Russell Long objected: "Nasser does about the same type of thing Khrushchev does. He says one thing and really has something else in mind. It appears to me that to play that kind of game with Nasser is just the kind of thing that Nasser would like." But Dulles responded, "One has to choose somewhere along the line," and Fulbright heartily agreed, reminding Long, "It isn't a matter of whether either one of them are nice friendly fellows. You have to make a choice. It's much safer for us to have a weaker country like Egypt in control of Iraq and the oil than it is to have Russia in control."

The ebullient Hubert Humphrey had by far the most provocative contribution to the discussion. Reminding Dulles of the long-established "Russian oppression of the . . . Moslem population in the southern part of the Soviet Union," he asked the DCI, "Are we able to find any refugees from these Moslem minorities who are of any help to us?" Dulles's answer was censored in the transcript published years later, but — whether the director was forthcoming or not — the senator was only starting to think out loud. Stating bluntly that Iraq faced communist control, Humphrey, too, wanted to "save" Qassim from the supposedly more violent, ruthless, and increasingly successful Iraqi Marxists. He then moved the discussion in a direction that Dulles possibly found entertaining:

> You said a while ago that we are 'builder-uppers,' that it is more difficult for us. We try to build up a country, the communists try to destroy it. Well, if Iraq is being taken over by the communists, then we are not building it up. We ought to be trying to destroy what they have there.
>
> In other words, who are our liquidators? This is what it gets right down to. You know, this is like running a police department against the hoodlums. I mean, whom do you have? Do we have people that shake them up, or are we just going to talk economic and political doctrine? Because, in answer to Senator Fulbright's question, if the Prime Minister of Iraq is afraid of assassination, or if we have some reason to believe that this conditions his thinking, then there is only one way that you handle that, and that is for some other people to be a little afraid of it, just like when those Norwegians announced that every Communist Party member in Norway had two people assigned to kill him; on the day the Russians struck, two Norwegians were to kill one communist, so if the first one missed, the second one would get him. That had a tendency to deplete the ranks of the Communist Party.

Probably surprised by Humphrey's discussion of assassination, no other senator endorsed his point. Dulles remained silent, except to inform Humphrey that Qassim had "not said to us that he is afraid of assassination." On the other hand, said the DCI, "I have the hypothesis that if he tried to break with the communists, he would be in danger of assassination." Qassim's future was very much in doubt, one way or another, according to Dulles. When Humphrey asked if Qassim was already "gone," the DCI said, "I don't see how he is going to assert himself in an anti-Communist way without 'going.'"

In fact, Qassim would soon turn against communist "supporters." The Soviet Union accepted this, having no enthusiasm for the Iraqi communists either. Relations between the USSR and Iraq were sufficiently cooperative over the following few years so that CIA leaders arranged for Qassim to be "incapacitated" by a poisoned handkerchief. Whether or not it ever reached him, the plan failed. One assassination attempt, also believed to be supported by the United States, included Saddam Hussein, Iraq's future dictator, among its plotters. It, too, failed. Qassim would not "go" until 1963, executed by Iraq's army.

To demonstrate that the Soviet Union was reaching out to repair relations with Nasser, the DCI read a lengthy, detailed summary of a letter Nikita Khrushchev had sent the Egyptian leader just eight days earlier. Dulles explained that the letter "was obtained through secret channels . . . from the man who read the letter and then gave us an account of it." He then read portions, including Khrushchev's claim to Nasser that "what the USSR is doing in Iraq today is no more than the UAR asked it to do for Iraq when Abdul Nasser was in Moscow in July 1958." This, of course, was the time when the Iraqi coup bringing Qassim to power had occurred. But Khrushchev recognized Nasser "as the only leader in the Arab world and is willing to help him become strong." "A clever letter," said Humphrey. "It is a rather clever letter," agreed Dulles.[2]

Dulles's most publicized congressional testimony of 1959 was before a subcommittee of the Joint Economic Committee, which invited him to describe the strengths and weaknesses of the Soviet Union's economy. The subcommittee was engaged in a comparative study of the American and USSR economies, a topic that (Dulles told them) aroused "heated controversy." The DCI and his aides were determined that the presentation, to be delivered by Dulles himself in a rare open session, would not be jargon-laden, dull, or inaccurate. In its final form, the analysis provided warnings and reassurances and revealed differences of emphasis between Dulles and President Eisenhower on the matter of large military spending.

Dulles faced subcommittee chair Representative Richard Bolling (D-MO) and others from the House and Senate on Friday afternoon, November 13, in the old Supreme Court chamber in the Capitol building. A capacity audience heard the CIA testimony, which indicated that the USSR would not approach American standards of living for decades. To Khrushchev's boast a month earlier that the Soviet Union would surpass U.S. living standards by 1970, the DCI said, "This is a gross exaggeration. It is as though the shrimp had learned to whistle, to use one of his colorful comments."

On the military ramifications of future Soviet economic growth, Dulles projected, "If the Soviet industrial growth rate persists at eight or nine percent per annum over the next decade, as is forecast, the gap between our two economies by 1970 will be dangerously narrowed, unless our own industrial growth rate is substantially increased from the present pace." The U.S. rate had been less than 3 percent for six of the seven preceding years. The DCI added that if, by 1970, the USSR's industrial production were 80 percent of the United States', the Soviets would have so strong a military production capacity as to require a drastic increase in U.S. military effort. Therefore, he said, "we must increase our recent rate of growth." This from a director of central intelligence who normally abstained in secret congressional testimony from speaking to domestic issues.

There was an almost admiring quality to Dulles's reference to Soviet "concentration on those aspects of production and of economic development which . . . leaders feel will enhance their power position in the world." Once Khrushchev and company "determined upon a high priority project — and they have fewer echelons of decisions to surmount than we before the final go-ahead is given — they are able to divert to this project the needed complement of the ablest technicians in the USSR which the particular task demands." While the American public enjoyed far greater material comforts, Dulles judged that U.S. "production of the consumer-type goods and services . . . add little to the sinews of our national strength." An early draft of Dulles's statement had him making an Eisenhower-style observation that "the vast resources being devoted to military expenditures throughout the world, if diverted, would form a pool of development capital that would promise the end of poverty within a generation." One of the DCI's underlings ridiculed the latter statement as "quite a promise!" and the prediction was dropped.

Newspapers around the country reported Dulles's testimony on their front pages. A *New York Times* photograph showed a smiling Dulles before the subcommittee, but its headline read, "Soviets Closing Output Gap, Allen Dulles Warns U.S." On that same day, in a less prominently placed story, the newspaper reported that in Wisconsin unannounced presidential candidate John F. Kennedy had accused the Eisenhower administration of encouraging the American people to become "complacent, self-contented, easy going" over the preceding "seven gray years."[3]

"I'd Like to Tell Him to His Face What I Think about Him"

If not the CIA's most tumultuous year during Eisenhower's presidency, 1960 was certainly a contender. Far more than any other year since creating the agency, Congress subjected it to publicized debates, hearings, and investigations. CIA leaders would spend parts of at least twenty days testifying there. While there had been twenty-eight or more days with testimony in 1959, there would be enormously more discussion of the CIA on House and Senate floors in 1960, due to the missile gap, the U-2, and Cuban controversies. Eisenhower continued to hate this trend. "The longer he stays in this city, the more he finds the most disappointing thing to be the lack of respect one feels for the Congress as a whole," Goodpaster wrote.[1]

The year began with a resurgence of missile gap charges when Joseph Alsop wrote of the "very fishy . . . downgrading of intelligence estimates" of Soviet missile strength. The "sponsors of our business-as-usual defense budgets, headed by the President, are playing a vast game of Russian roulette with the national future." Alsop's attack in late January was anticipated by administration leaders, Allen Dulles especially. On January 7, the DCI presented summaries at the White House of two new National Intelligence Estimates of Soviet capabilities and policies. One, titled "Soviet Capabilities for Strategic Attack through Mid-1964" troubled Dulles, not because of its methodologies and conclusions, which he defended, but because it was politically explosive. He told Eisenhower and other NSC members that the NIE "raised many questions which will be raised in this session of Congress, particularly as concerns the missile issue." But Dulles, himself, caused trouble by giving Eisenhower and associates a positive spin on the significance of the Estimate's numbers. While saying that mid-1961 would be "the point of maximum threat," he added, "The missile gap doesn't look to be very serious." This suited Eisenhower, who thought the "gap" was illusory.[2]

Actually, the Alsops and Symingtons of the political world would agree with the written Estimate that "in another year or two, the Soviet leaders may feel that their long-range missiles give them a political advantage which they may wish to test by attempting to win concessions from the West." Still, this prediction did not erase the new Estimate's dynamite — testimony in

1959 had relied on an NIE that assumed a possible "crash" Soviet missile program and predicted the USSR might have 500 intercontinental ballistic missiles by the middle of 1961. The new NIE predicted that the USSR would only have 140 to 200 operational ICBMs by then. There were honest but complicated reasons for the changes, including better evidence, more nuanced assumptions, and refined methodologies. Also, an agency historian wrote, "as more evidence came in, it was necessary to address the question of what the Soviet program probably was, rather than what it could be."[3]

A note-taker at the January 7 NSC meeting recorded the secretary of defense designate, Thomas Gates, worrying that "last year Secretary McElroy had admitted to a missile gap on the basis of an intelligence estimate of Soviet capabilities. It now appeared that the intelligence estimate had undergone a considerable change and that it now virtually says there is no missile gap." Congress would be "very much interested."

This would become more apparent a few days later when Senator Thruston Morton (R-KY) would tell the president that ordinary Kentuckians feared that the United States was becoming militarily weak. An amazed Eisenhower would agree to urge Gates and the Joint Chiefs chair, General Nathan Twining, to address such fears in their coming congressional appearances. In the meantime, Ike gave Dulles testimony guidance — don't emphasize the higher numbers of Soviet ICBMs that Air Force Intelligence would have preferred to see in the NIE. Following an NSC member's suggestion, the DCI said he did not plan to mention misfires of Soviet missiles, which might lead to congressional questions about failed American launches. But Dulles would find it necessary to go against such guidance in the days to come.[4]

The DCI could easily guess that his most difficult testimony that January would be before the Preparedness subcommittee, where no one was so determined as Stuart Symington to promote the missile gap idea, or so blunt in questioning Eisenhower's handling of intelligence on the USSR. By this time, too, the CIA had put into writing its "Procedures for Briefing Appropriate Members of Congress on Soviet ICBM Firings." Each month, the Office of Scientific Intelligence briefed legislative counsel John Warner about recent missile/satellite launches. In turn, Warner briefed staff heads for the Senate and House Armed Services Committees, plus the Preparedness subcommittee at the Senate. The staffers were then charged with keeping chairs and other "appropriate members" like Symington informed.[5]

Prior to going before Preparedness late in January, Dulles testified before four other congressional bodies. There are no records about his encounters with the Joint Committee on Atomic Energy or the House Astronautics and Sciences Committee, but George Mahon's notes of the first day of his Appropriations subcommittee's hearings on January 11 and 12 survive, and the Senate Foreign Relations Committee created a transcript — less censored than usual — of Dulles's testimony there on January 18.

Before Mahon's group Dulles seems to have chosen his words carefully, but he described the new numbers and revised methods used by the CIA and its fellow intelligence agencies. As Mahon summarized the DCI's remarks on the new "Soviet Capabilities" NIE, "Last yr's basis dealt with capability. This year it is estimate of what [the USSR] would have." Then Mahon scrawled the NIE's numbers that had just been presented at Eisenhower's White House four days earlier. And Dulles summarized the intelligence establishment's view that in "1961— USSR has most favorable chance to build up vis-a-vis U.S.," but "they would not have a decisive superiority. They would consider U.S. strong enough to counter attack in adequate way." Still, "pressure and threats . . . may become pronounced. Danger of miscalculation might increase." Regarding the years after 1961, Dulles took Eisenhower's advice and stressed uncertainty. Mahon recorded from the DCI's presentation, "After 1961— speculation — estimates differ." But, not following Eisenhower, Dulles added specifics: "Majority think mid-1962— 2 5 0 to 350 ICBMs, 450 in 1963" and made clear that those numbers meant operational missiles on launchers.

Mahon's eight pages of detailed notes show a primary focus on the Soviet missile threat in Dulles's testimony but also a world tour touching on Iraq ("Qassim seems not to be able to govern successfully"), Chinese-Soviet relations ("quarreling, but still a meaningful alliance"), China's influence over neighboring countries ("has gone down in Asia — Japan, Ceylon, India, etc."), and other places.[6]

Dulles reminded Fulbright's Foreign Relations Committee that the estimates he would draw on were produced by the U.S. Intelligence Board, reflecting "consensus views of the entire community." But, he said, "I assume full responsibility for what I say." As well, he reminded the senators that predictions regarding the Soviet Union's missile program continued to draw on "inadequate" evidence. "We know little about the deployment of ICBMs," he said, then added:

> We have that as the highest priority, but we have not picked up any evidence on fixed ICBM bases, or for that matter movable bases, because there would have to be

some sort of pad or fueling station even if they were on railcars, except of course for the two testing sites, about which we know a good deal — the Tyura Tam missile range, from which they have shot these long-range missiles, and the Kapustin Yar range, on which they have tested some 500 of the shorter-range missiles over the years, and on which we have had pretty complete evidence since 1953.

Description of four long-range missile tests was based on "absolutely accurate" information, he said. He then violated his recent White House pledge: "There have been, of course some failures. I have on this chart only the successful tests. There have been about 15 to 20 percent failures, and maybe more because failures are hard to pick up. And may I say in this room that the monitoring of failures is much more unsuccessful than the monitoring of successes. They pretty well know we pick up their successes, but they don't know what we get on their failures." Dulles elaborated the CIA belief that the Soviet Union had two or three nuclear-powered submarines. "We estimate," he added, "that in the 1961 to 1963 period, the USSR will achieve a weapons system combining a nuclear-powered submarine with a 500- to 1000-nautical mile ballistic missile, capable of launching from submerged positions." Since the United States had six such subs at the time, however, U.S. intelligence judged that the Soviets "have not been at all anxious to say, 'We have one submarine.' "

During Dulles's almost three hours before Foreign Relations, one question went unasked — had the administration manipulated intelligence in deference to budgetary priorities? Perhaps because the DCI sounded fairly alarmed — indicating that, in 1961, the USSR would "probably have its most favorable opportunity, through the rapid buildup of ICBMs, to gain certain military, political, and psychological advantages over the United States" and that "the present Soviet ICBM program would provide some 140 to 200 ICBMs on launcher in mid-1961" — the senators did not view him as a party to intelligence distortion. The DCI also had a humbling admission: "We in the CIA are inclined to accept Khrushchev's statements both as to his present manpower strength in the Army, which is about 600,000 lower than we had been estimating, and as to his program for his military forces." Khrushchev had spoken just four days earlier to the Supreme Soviet, also indicating a greater reliance on missiles and a virtual end to strategic bomber production.

In his spoken tour of the world, Dulles claimed that a big problem for Soviet citizens was boredom. "I wish I could tell you that I thought there was general unrest there," he added, but "I don't think there is." About Iraq's leader, the DCI indicated, "Anything might happen to Qassim . . . which might not be an unmitigated evil." There was no suggestion of apparently ongoing CIA actions against Qassim. On Cuba, Dulles said, "We have a grave crisis at our door," in light of Fidel Castro's "continually increasing anti-American policy." Elsewhere in Latin America, there had been "meetings of communists at which Soviet agents have been present. We are pretty well informed on those meetings, and there is no doubt that the Soviet Union and Communist China are being quite active in this hemisphere." From China, he reported, there had been very few defectors in recent years, which surprised him. By contrast, he said, the United States had obtained "extremely valuable inside information" from a few recent defectors from the USSR. (Uniquely in this hearing's transcript, this topic was heavily censored, at CIA request, by the committee before its eventual declassification.) He explained:

> We have received more defectors in 1959, that is, those who leave for ideological motives, most of them, or for other motives, but who have certain intelligence potential. We had 47 of them during 1959, 11 of them from the Soviet Union [sentences censored].
>
> This was shortly after the military attaché of the Soviet Union in Rangoon tried to defect, but was captured by the Soviets and returned for punishment to Moscow. [Words or sentences censored.] . . . Possibly the prize catch of the year from the point of view of defectors was a [words or sentences censored] authorities and later asked for asylum in the United States, which was granted to him. He has given us more and better information in [words censored] fields with regard to the Soviet Union than any other man that has come over to us.

When Senator Frank Lausche (D-OH) asked Dulles to elaborate, Dulles hesitated and then responded. Censors' deletions are again heavy, leaving intact just the report that a particular defector "came over to us with a vast amount of files, and most of the information we got from him, and a good deal we got from [words censored] is of quite a highly technical nature with regard to the building up to their [words censored], who they use and how they operate, and it has been invaluable to us in that way." One of the defectors presumably described by Dulles was Aleksandr Kaznacheev, a Soviet diplomat granted asylum in 1959 by the United States. Kaznacheev gave the CIA an unusual look at intelligence operations in Soviet embassies, as well as the USSR's disinformation and covert psychological warfare campaigns.

Mike Mansfield, beginning his third year as majority whip of the Senate, raised one of the most obscure questions ever posed by any legislator in the Truman-Eisenhower era to a director of central intelligence: "Could you tell the Committee, based on the Nerchinsk Treaty of 1689 and other treaties entered into between the Manchus and the Czars, how much Chinese territory in those years was taken by Czarist Russia from the Manchu empire?" Dulles was momentarily at a loss: "I can't answer that. Maybe Mr. Amory can." Indeed, the deputy director of intelligence could, at length. After the hearing, Fulbright told reporters that Dulles was not one to "gloss over the hard facts of life."[7]

The senators' willingness to raise varied questions and their lack of interest in the intelligence distortion issue demonstrate that not everyone in Washington shared Symington's and Alsop's deepest suspicions. This did not deter them or their allies, though. The senator, considering a candidacy for the Democratic presidential nomination, did not wait for the Preparedness subcommittee hearing on January 29 to lower the boom. On January 27, he held an unusually well-attended press conference, then took to the Senate floor to repeat "a serious accusation, which I make with all gravity." The intelligence books, he said, "have been juggled so the budget books may be balanced." Unlike his "intelligence subordination" speech a year earlier, there was no ambiguity:

> I realize fully that my statements on this vital matter may be labeled as politically motivated by those who prefer to conceal the facts, and by others who do not know the facts. I choose to face that risk. It is an insignificant risk, indeed, compared with the unwarranted risk which this policy of misinformation has brought down upon our country.
>
> Occasionally, after the administration's inaccuracies have been clearly and publicly labeled as such, top officials have modified their previous statements, such as occurred in the case of Secretary McElroy's admission last year about the three-to-one missile gap. Mostly, however, the administration has served up reassurances and complacency; and most recently, when the existence of a serious missile gap was being generally accepted, the administration proceeded to change the ground rules for evaluating the facts.

Symington was referring to quickly declassified testimony by Defense Secretary Gates days earlier before three committees. Following Eisenhower's suggestion that he allay public fears, Gates claimed that McElroy's 1959 statement about a three-to-one ICBM gap favoring the USSR had been based "on estimates of what the USSR could produce and was not an affirmative statement of fact. . . . we do not now believe that the Soviet superiority in ICBMs will be as great as that previously estimated."

Hearing of Gates's words in contrast to some of Dulles's private remarks in the same period, Symington had become darkly suspicious. He continued, "The new policy is to compare Soviet intent in the ICBM field as against our ICBM schedules. Prior to this, the comparison had been based upon Soviet capability in the ICBM field, as against our ICBM schedules. This amazing change to intent from capability in the method of using intelligence data enabled the administration further to cut down substantially the estimate of Soviet ICBM production." On page one, the *Washington Post* agreed: "Newsmen and many military officers expressed some incredulity at the announcement of this new basis of estimating intelligence data. They thought it had been abandoned after Pearl Harbor." A *Post* editorial suggested that Gates's analysis had "overtones of a political gimmick." The unfortunate defense secretary could not describe some of the most credible evidence that analysts relied on to assert that the Soviet Union was not engaged in a "crash" missile production program — ongoing U-2 flights showed no such drastic effort — so the NIE assumed that an "orderly" production effort was under way.[8]

Reasonable persons could disagree about the best way to estimate future missile strength of another nation, but Symington was correct, at least, that there was a decidedly new estimate of Soviet strength, relying on somewhat different methodologies. Dulles, himself, had publicly explained and defended it just a day earlier. His starting premise was, "Facts have no politics." In seeming contrast to Gates's words, he claimed, "We have not downgraded this [Soviet missile production] system this year as contrasted with last year's." He explained,

> The analysis of any given Soviet weapons system involves a number of judgments. These include Soviet capability to produce the system; probable Soviet inventories of the weapons system as of today; the role assigned to this system in Soviet military planning; the requirements the Soviet high command may lay down for the weapon over the future. All these judgments are to some degree interdependent. . . . Consequently, in our estimates, we generally stress capabilities in the early stages of Soviet weapons development and then, as more hard facts are available, we estimate their probable programming, sometimes referred to as intentions.[9]

It was not obvious to all that the new approach made sense. Lyndon Johnson complained, "The missile gap cannot be eliminated by the mere stroke of a pen." But Symington's January 27 speech was more aggressive and accusatory: "Through this process, the administration has given the people the impression that the missile deterrent gap has been sharply reduced and possibly eliminated. In fact, able and responsible reporters have been given such impressions." Secretary of the Air Force Dudley Sharp, for example, told CBS News it was "doubtful" that the Soviets would have more operational missiles than the United States at any time from 1960 to 1963. This, Symington said, typified the administration's "manipulation of data," which was less expensive than a "decision to accelerate our own ICBM program."

If Symington had proof of such budgetary calculations by Eisenhower, Dulles, or others, he did not divulge them. Certainly, the president had achieved only modest success in restraining defense spending. It had been 62.9 percent of the entire federal government budget in 1955; by 1959, it was down to 57.5 percent, but rose to 59.1 percent in 1960. Still, Eisenhower was wrong to claim later that the missile gap controversy had been nothing more than "a useful piece of demagoguery." After all, Symington drew accurately from the NIE and Defense Department testimony when he said, "If we compare the ready-to-launch missiles attributed to the Soviets on the new intelligence basis with the official readiness program for U.S. ICBMs, the ratio for a considerable length of time will be more than three-to-one."[10]

If intermediate-range ballistic missiles were included, "the Soviet advantage would be even greater." Symington concluded, "I charge this administration with using intelligence information in such a manner that the American people have been given an inaccurate picture of what is necessary for our national defense. I regret that it is necessary for me to make this serious charge." The Democratic senator never named his presumed targets — Allen Dulles, the Central Intelligence Agency, Gates, and (especially) Eisenhower. Despite claiming to understand the gravity of his charges, Symington apparently did not. He showed surprise when a reporter logically asked if the president should be impeached for such manipulations. "Unthinkable," he responded. Hours later, Eisenhower labeled promoters of the missile gap thesis "political morticians."[11]

Thinking that Symington had slandered the president and associates, Leverett Saltonstall emerged in fighting form the next afternoon:

> There are, in my opinion, no more trustworthy citizens and public officials than Mr. Allen W. Dulles, Director of CIA, Thomas B. Gates, Jr., Secretary of the Defense, Maurice Stans, Director of the Budget, and, finally, the President of the

United States, Dwight Eisenhower. It is inconceivable, in my opinion, that any of these dedicated men would "juggle" intelligence so that budget books may be balanced. . . . Implicit in the Senator from Missouri's speech of the other day is the idea that capability is no longer being taken into consideration by our defense officials. It is important to point out that this is not at all true.

Symington took sharp exception to Saltonstall's implication that he had spoken untruthfully: "I do not wish to invoke any Senate rules unnecessarily, but I wish to know . . . is the Senator saying that the statement in my talk was not true?" Saltonstall was not intimidated. Passing up the opportunity to note the irony of the situation, he brushed off the suggestion that he had questioned Symington's integrity.

"I have never attacked anyone's character," Symington claimed, but Saltonstall highlighted "the short sentence the Senator put in his speech . . . that the intelligence books have been juggled so the budget books may be balanced. That statement, in my opinion, is not an accurate statement." Symington tried again: "I have not questioned anything that Mr. Dulles has done." The Missourian was not going to win a character argument in which the reputations of Dulles and Eisenhower, especially, were in contention, but he stood by his charges: "Based upon the testimony which was given by Secretary Gates as to what the Soviet intentions are, and comparing those intentions with our own production scheduled, I do not believe our deterrent capacity in 1961, for example, will be adequate to maintain the security of the United States." And he would not relent from the claim that "the American people are being given a false impression in public, contrary to what we are told in classified meetings."

"That is an opinion —" Saltonstall started to say, but Symington interrupted, "It is not an opinion; it is the product of clear mathematical analysis." Among those doing the best analyses as "a service to the people of the United States," he said, was Alsop. By contrast, he said, "The administration is playing 'ducks and drakes' with our national security. I may say to the Senator from Massachusetts that I do not believe in attempts to meet facts with assertions about character. With all due respect to the character of the persons to whom he referred, I have sometimes found people without high character entirely right on certain subjects, and also people of the highest character who were not entirely correct on certain subjects." Maybe, said Saltonstall, but "I think it *is* a question of character." Those who questioned the judgment of Eisenhower and his colleagues "must bear the burden of proof to show that they are wrong."

Saltonstall had always wanted to be of help to the president and the CIA in the Senate. In 1956, he had mostly bungled his defense of prevailing oversight practices. Now, he successfully drew a line that others, if they wished to make the missile gap into a character issue, would cross only with trepidation. Soon, the *Washington Post* parted company with Symington's "juggling" charge in an editorial.[12]

Nonetheless, the president would seethe for weeks over the senator's remarks, and the DCI was hardly off the hook, as substantive questions remained. Congressional hearings had produced "as sharp a conflict as ever raged around the greatest single issue of these times," said *Newsweek*. A day after Symington's attack, General Thomas Power, head of the Strategic Air Command, claimed publicly that there could be little doubt that the Soviets were producing missiles at the "high rate" they claimed. Within two years, they conceivably could deliver a "massive" attack on the United States. When reporters asked Eisenhower about this, he said, "Too many generals have all sorts of ideas."[13]

Even before the supposed disparities between public and private administration announcements were subjects of newspaper headlines and newscasts, the DCI had agreed to testify before a joint session of the Preparedness subcommittee and the Aeronautical and Space Sciences Committee. Then Richard Russell decided that his CIA subcommittee should also join the January 29 hearing. Predictably, Dulles's appearance was one of the least secret of his many visits to Capitol Hill. "No record of Dulles' testimony will be kept," reported the *Post* (inaccurately), "and nothing of what he says is expected to be made public."

It was just a year earlier that the DCI and Symington had come to verbal blows in a Preparedness hearing over the senator's milder suggestion of intelligence "subordination," but the intervening, shocking events had made it a long year for Dulles and fellow intelligence professionals. Chalmers Roberts of the *Post* could not get the DCI or colleagues to go on the record about Gates's infamous testimony and related public remarks, for example, but he reported their private reactions: "What Gates had to say about the new method of evaluating intelligence raised a furor among the men who produce intelligence from the flow of bits and pieces which reach Washington." The unnamed officials took special offense at Gates also discussing the controversy at Republican "Dinner With Ike" events — "they felt he had cast aspersions on their efforts to be factual and non-political."[14]

Dulles would later deny that such animosity guided his testimony, but he would present a detailed chart of numbers from the NIE that Gates not only did not present but had never seen. Still, the director and Symington struggled somewhat less colorfully in the 1960 hearing than a year before. The senator reminded Dulles that the new "Soviet Capabilities" NIE projected thirty-five Soviet ICBMs by the middle of the current year, while the Strategic Air Command hoped to have a dozen such operational missiles by that time. The DCI again refused to engage in comparative analyses. Not to be put off, Symington asked Dulles a simple mathematical question — what happens when you divide 36 by 12? The DCI answered. Symington thought this a victory of sorts. It was only a start, though, for Dulles's figures could be read alongside Defense Department projections to suggest an even larger missile gap. Symington addressed the DCI:

> What worries me is — and again let me emphasize I am in no way criticizing the Central Intelligence Agency — that as a result of many articles in the papers, the people have the impression that we have eliminated the missile gap. . . . Now, based on the figures that you give us and that we get from the Pentagon building, the missile gap [as of] the middle of July is 12-to-1 this year and 9½-to-1 a year from next July. Don't you think it is unfortunate, therefore, that this type and character of information has been handled in this way?
>
> Dulles: Senator, I think that is for others to judge.
>
> Symington: Now, Mr. Director, I have been very frank in assuring you that I had no criticism of information you have given. . . . Isn't it disturbing to find out, based on your figures and the Pentagon figures, that there is a gap many, many months from now of 9½ -to-1, instead of 3-to-1?
>
> Dulles: I stick to my job of trying to report on what we can find out about the Soviet Union, and I don't deal with gaps.
>
> Symington: I think you are a little hard-hearted this afternoon . . . but my point is that General Power, if he is correct . . . to destroy all our deterrents, they could do that this summer, late this summer, with the number of ICBMs they have, if their accuracy was as much as ours, could they not?
>
> Dulles: That gets into war-gaming, and that is out of my field.

Senator Clair Engle (D-CA) told Dulles, "the thing that troubles me is that I have been unable to discern anything in the things that you have said that discourage the validity of the statement made by General Power. . . . Now, if that is true, we are in very sad shape, indeed."[15]

Symington emerged from the closed hearing later in the day and, not bothering to find a hideaway for carefully directed leaks, told reporters gathered that Dulles's testimony "completely confirms my position." Henry Jackson agreed: The DCI testified that the Soviets had and would continue to have "a quantitative and qualitative lead in intercontinental ballistics missiles. . . . some of the rosy color that Mr. Gates had in his presentation has been taken out."

Richard Russell did not forbid Symington and others from commenting publicly on the day's testimony, but it probably crossed his mind that no senator had ever emerged from *his* CIA hearings and sought out reporters. On balance, though, the Armed Services chairman had a finely tuned sense of when intelligence matters should be dealt with absolutely confidentially, which was almost always, and when public controversy required that they become semipublic. This was one of those latter occasions.

The DCI's testimony was secret, but leaks from the day-long hearing were so authoritative that Dulles would privately describe them as of "real value to the Soviets." Press reports tended to emphasize that, as Drew Pearson wrote, "He gave bleak intelligence figures which not only completely refuted Secretary Gates, but also the rosy assurances which Ike, himself, has been giving the public." Pearson also claimed that when Eisenhower read a transcript of the director's testimony, "The blood rose on the back of his neck. Intimates described his reaction as the biggest explosion since nuclear tests were suspended."[16]

Gates, just weeks into his job, felt beat up. *Time* magazine described a recent, lame attempt by Gates to explain "the new cheerfulness about the missile gap" to journalists as "one of the roughest press-conference pummelings that veteran Washington newsmen could recall." It seemed that Dulles, with his exclusive chart, had betrayed him. Following his own testimony before other committees but before going in front of the Preparedness subcommittee, Gates asked to see Eisenhower. Goodpaster took notes, as usual. His upcoming testimony before Johnson and Symington would be "the roughest of all," Gates worried. The secretary said top Pentagon witnesses "were being subjected to severe attack, and were receiving little support or defense. They are being charged with complacency, introduction of politics into defense affairs, and with having downgraded our intelligence." Perhaps worst of all, "Mr. Dulles last Friday had given figures to the Congress that Defense had never seen prior to that time, and that had not previously been disclosed to the Congress." Eisenhower had been calm until this point but "stated with vehemence that he has been opposed to giving such detailed figures to congressional groups — particularly those whose only interest seems to be to misuse them and misrepresent their meaning." The flash of anger passed, though. An amiable Ike said, "I know you're having a tough time. . . . I'm trying to help you in my press conferences." And he reminded Gates "not to forget his sense of humor in this situation." Inevitably, Gates will sometimes find his "foot in the fly paper" because "some other people are talking too much."

The secretary needed that encouragement but "came back to the point that he and other top Defense officials are embarrassed because of the new figures given by Mr. Dulles to the Congress. The President said he is very troubled about this, and about the indication that Mr. Dulles may be giving too many figures to the Congress." Preparing to leave, the dejected Gates added, "With all the activity going on, it was hard to avoid a few mistakes." The president assured him that he was doing just fine.[17]

Whether the president subsequently reproached Dulles for frankness at the hearing is unclear. He pressured the DCI to do something about leaks, though, especially those going to Joseph Alsop. Days after Dulles appeared before the Preparedness subcommittee, Alsop published a column in the *Post* and newspapers around the country titled, "The Dulles Testimony." The "hard, disturbing facts and figures . . . can now be revealed on undoubted authority," he wrote. Alsop proceeded to review figures from the "Soviet Capabilities" NIE and accurately quoted and summarized Dulles's thinking, which, careful readers might have noticed, was far less "disturbing" than Alsop's. For example, Dulles said that if the NIE's projections and assumptions were correct, "there will be no moment when the Kremlin can risk a nuclear strike at the United States." But, Alsop wrote, Dulles was not sure that those projections and assumptions were accurate. What if one or two Soviet plants producing ICBMs had workers going twenty-four hours a day, rather than proceeding on the "orderly" basis assumed by Dulles? The "whole outlook would be hideously transformed" by such a "trifling error in the American intelligence estimates," he claimed.

Eisenhower resented Alsop's influence. He criticized the columnist so vehemently while talking with John McCone early in 1960 that Goodpaster's notation of one Eisenhower remark (on his "extremely low opinion . . . of Alsop's integrity and moral character") was censored for decades. Presidential press secretary James Hagerty matched Eisenhower's animosity toward Alsop, a homosexual who — very much in accord with his times — was closeted. "He's a fag," Hagerty once blurted out to another journalist during the missile gap controversy, and threatened, "I'm going to lift his White House pass." When Goodpaster discussed the Alsop column with the president,

Eisenhower directed him to have Dulles tell Lyndon Johnson, "Until this is cleared up, I cannot again appear before your committee." But the Eisenhower anger blew over yet again and he changed his mind. Dulles sent Johnson a more temperate protest of the leaks: "This publicity is definitely detrimental to our intelligence work." Let's talk, he suggested, "in order to see whether together we can find any leads as to how the information disclosed could have been obtained."[18]

Dulles (and Eisenhower, in his calmer moments) knew that little or nothing would come of such a chat, though. Ike groused a few weeks later to his friend, Prime Minister Harold Macmillan of Britain, that "despite repeated efforts, it had proved to be almost impossible to track down responsibility for such leaks." Predictably, the DCI derived no use from an investigation by the CIA's Office of Security, which reported that Alsop had inquired of committee staffers about getting a hearing transcript and almost certainly had seen one, courtesy of someone on Capitol Hill. Shortly thereafter, Alsop approached Dulles "on a business matter which may give you the creeps," as the columnist wanted to discuss the "estimate-producing machinery." Such an invitation always carried a thinly veiled threat from Alsop, who had once written to a Dulles associate at the CIA that it was "the duty of men in your position to see that vital facts become known as rapidly as possible" and who now stressed that he was "anxious to avoid being unfair" in what he wrote. Probably without telling Eisenhower, Dulles soon had "a general talk on the subject" with the columnist.[19]

As weeks passed in February, Eisenhower brooded over Symington's intelligence distortion charge. In interactions with the press that month, the president did not conceal his mood. "His blunt replies seemed at times to border on the splenetic," wrote one journalist. On February 11, Eisenhower told reporters raising missile gap questions, "I have been in the military service a long time. I am obviously running for nothing." Most citizens agreed with Eisenhower's implication — his personal history was relevant in any such defense/intelligence debate. Even though a plurality of Americans surveyed for a poll that month thought the USSR was "farther ahead in the field of long range missiles," 71 percent of the public thought Eisenhower was handling his job effectively.

While reporters raised missile gap questions with the president many times in January and early February, they failed to ask specifically about Symington's "juggling" charge until a journalist did so toward the end of a February 17 press conference. In response, Eisenhower (in the words of a

Times reporter) "appeared to control himself with effort." "Despicable," the president said. "If anybody — anybody! — believes that I have deliberately misled the American people, I'd like to tell him to his face what I think about him." The headline for the *Times*' leading front-page story the next day read, "Angry President Denies He Misled U.S. on Defenses." A small article inside that same edition quoted Symington claiming, "I don't know anybody who said the President misled the nation." Also receiving less attention was Eisenhower's assurance to the nation, "Our defense is not only strong, it is awesome, and it is respected elsewhere."[20]

Dulles, meanwhile, thought he was through with the Preparedness subcommittee for awhile, but the Defense Department testimony in open and closed hearings in the weeks after his testimony so confused senators as to make them wonder if they had misunderstood the DCI. One reason for the confusion was that various civilian and military leaders within the Defense Department, plus certain senators, were more interested in defending their allies' and their own reputations than in clarifying matters. But Senator Alexander Wiley, ranking Republican on Foreign Relations, defended his president and admonished Symington, who had just been citing NIE figures at one closed hearing: "I trust when the facts are given, they are not given with such an emotion as we have had it given." The Missourian was undeterred: "The administration does not have the right to imply or to state that there has been a major change downward in the Russian missile readiness potential when actually the change has been upward."

Later, after audaciously claiming that there had never been a leak out of Preparedness, Symington publicly warned colleagues, "If that assertion is disputed, I am going to release the percentage of increase for this year's Estimate over last year's Estimate as given to us by Mr. Dulles." The threatened leak of CIA information was something that no chair of a CIA subcommittee would ever do: Around the same time, Mahon fretted over classified "nuclear aircraft" information in his office, telling an aide, "I do not want secret stuff left with me unless proper steps are taken." Have someone "come over and look at this stuff and take necessary steps."

Richard Russell kept his silence about Symington's menacing remark, but the Republican National Committee tried to bring just such eminent Democrats more squarely into the fray: if Symington was about to perpetrate "an act of total, reckless irresponsibility" by publicizing secret intelligence, it was "the responsibility of the Democratic leadership to see that no such information reaches his hands." Similarly, Republican senators were aghast at Symington's threat.[21]

Often, questions and answers intended to clarify matters at the Preparedness subcommittee hearings and thus reassure those who did not have set views about missile gaps and juggled books were anything but reassuring. At one session in February, Senator Thomas Martin (R-IA) asked the head of Air Force Intelligence, General James Walsh (who dissented from portions of the NIE), "Do you have access to any intelligence information that is not available to Mr. Dulles' organization?" "I have not," Walsh responded. "Do you have access to all intelligence information to which they have access?" Martin continued. "I like to think so" was Walsh's limp response. Similarly, when committee counsel Edwin Weisl asked air force chief of staff General Thomas White to describe the views of his superior, Joint Chiefs chairman General Nathan Twining, on a particular point, White politely and respectfully declined: "After all, I have to live with these people." To this, Symington responded, "The Congress might as well fold up and go home, then."

Perhaps the most glaring surprise of the hearings was the failure of coordination between the Defense Department and the CIA. Once, when Symington questioned Admiral Arleigh Burke about the "Soviet Capabilities" NIE, a point arrived at which Burke said, "We must have different figures." On a number of occasions, those testifying *did* have different numbers from those offered days or weeks earlier by Dulles. Knowing this and wanting to demonstrate in public sessions that the missile gap was genuine, Symington became more relentless and theatrical. On February 9, without disclosing figures on a "Top Secret" sheet in his hand, he eyed Twining and said, "Now I have here the official figures that were given us. . . . Show me any evidence, if you will, in opposition to what was given us by the Director of Central Intelligence Agency." Speaking then to Captain L. P. Gray, an assistant to the general, Symington said, "Will you take this piece of paper, please?" Not sure what was unfolding, Gray asked, "Do you want me to show it to the General, Senator?" "Yes," Symington answered, "I would like to see if there is anything there that justifies the American people believing that any missile gap is being closed." Looking again at Twining, Symington said, "You have a representative of the Joint Chiefs on the National Intelligence Board. There are the figures." Then he waited for a response. But Twining would not take the bait: "There is no way to answer this in open session, Senator."

Hours later, in an executive session, senators showed Twining the chart of figures shown to the committee by Dulles nine days earlier. The embarrassed general said of the chart's numbers of "on-launcher missiles" that they had "never been shown before, to my knowledge." "Then you have been misinformed," said Weisl. While some Republicans tried to save Twining, suggesting a postponement in testimony, Weisl — answerable to Lyndon Johnson — would not give up. Examining figures on the chart seemingly derived from the "Soviet Capabilities" NIE, the counsel asked what their origins might be. Twining responded, "We don't know why the CIA did it." Saltonstall appealed to Stennis, who chaired temporarily in Johnson's absence: "I don't think it is proper to ask him questions and make assumptions when he has already stated to this committee that he didn't know where those figures came from." Stennis admitted that the "cross-examination" was a bit "severe," but said "the General is capable of taking care of himself." Stennis, himself, had to leave soon thereafter, so the onslaught continued with Symington chairing. Eventually, Weisl said, "It is apparent, isn't it, Captain Gray and General Twining, that you don't understand the Dulles figure?" Twining threw in the towel: "That is right. It is confusing." After a full day of testimony by Twining on February 9, Symington warned that "we are getting our country in exactly the same kind of a position the British got their country into in the late 1930s."[22]

When Gates's turn came to appear before the committee, Symington and Weisl insisted on talking exact numbers and ratios. The secretary tried to beg off: "I do not really believe it is possible, I certainly do not want to add to the confusion, I don't believe it's possible to talk about ratios. I don't believe it is possible. I think the difference [between projected U.S. and Soviet missile strength] has narrowed."

Symington dealt more quickly with Gates than he had Twining:

It is my understanding, based on what I have heard this morning, and before, that you have said that the new intelligence analysis had narrowed the gap. It is also my impression, in listening to Director Dulles, that the reverse was true. The testimony of Secretary Sharp on a national telecast implied that the gap had either been narrowed or eliminated. It is my impression from the testimony of Director Dulles that the reverse is true. . . . Is there any reason why this year, in order to clarify this matter, you don't announce publicly the ratios based on our best estimates of the number of ready-to-launch ICBMs the Soviets have, as compared with the number we plan to have?

Secretary Gates: I think that the ratios are misleading, Senator, and I don't know how to announce them in a way that wouldn't cause more confusion.

In contrast, a major theme underlying Symington's questions of Dulles, Twining, and Gates was that, as he told Prescott Bush, "In a democracy, the people have a right to know."[23]

All parties to the missiles hearings agreed that confusion had been rampant for days. The DCI would later take some responsibility for the hearings' mess: "I made a mistake. I took an estimate prepared for 1959 and one in the process of preparation and tried to put them on the same basis to simplify them. I extrapolated. The old estimate had little information on ICBMs but lots of IRBMs. In the old estimate, we said we thought they would have a certain capability within a certain period of time. It was a reasonable extrapolation, but one that had not been given to the Department of Defense before." Coming after the testimony by Pentagon heads, though, Dulles's acceptance of responsibility did not resolve their Preparedness torture.

Fortunately for Dulles, he had not been forced by Eisenhower in early February to swear off future testimony before the subcommittee, for Lyndon Johnson agreed to a request by Saltonstall to summon the director again to remedy the senators' discombobulation. In the overheated political atmosphere that month, such an invitation could not be declined, even though it would be Dulles's ninth day in a congressional hearing that year. The DCI, accompanied by a half-dozen assistants, appeared on February 24, announcing a mission of clearing up "any questions in your mind." His written presentation, marked up and apparently used, stressed that "improved intelligence" permitted him and the United States Intelligence Board to decide to "deal not primarily with capabilities, but with probable Soviet programming." As always, despite the considerable details Dulles provided the dozen or so senators, he could not tell them about the U-2. A CIA historian later wrote of this very time frame: "The estimates had agreed on January 1960 as the date for initial operational capability, and NIE 11-8-59 had estimated that by mid-1960 there would be some 35 missiles on launchers. With this deployment, it should be possible to find some confirming evidence. Nevertheless, a U-2 mission on February 5, 1960, which covered some 4,500 miles of Soviet railroads in the Volga River valley, had revealed no identifiable deployment."

Dulles told senators what he could. It was true, as Congress, the press, and the nation by then knew, that "the old Estimate concluded that the Soviets could have in inventory a larger number of missiles than our new estimates indicate they probably will have." But he defended such conclusions in detail. Overall, the CIA historian with access to a hearing transcript found the February 24 event unremarkable: "Much of the same ground was covered again, with Senator Symington trying to get Dulles to support his missile gap theory and Dulles refusing to get into net estimates."[24]

Symington continued his public attacks on the Eisenhower administration, as well, especially in a late February Senate speech. As the *New York Times* reported, he "repeated earlier charges against the administration defense policy and deliberately used the word 'misled' " in relation to the American public, which he said was being given "false statements." The senator also slipped in a remark that was hardly noted in the press but would have further raised Eisenhower's blood pressure if he read it: "To the best of my knowledge, there are no persons who served with President Eisenhower in responsible positions in World War II who agree with the present defense policy of this country."

Two senators compared Symington to Winston Churchill that day. Many news commentators, Democrats, and some Republicans treated the missile gap as a fact. Walter Lippmann portrayed Eisenhower as "talking like a tired old man who has lost touch with the springs of our national vitality." Still, Symington could not fail to notice that virtually no one in Washington had endorsed his specific claim of "juggled" intelligence books. Even John Kennedy, running for the Democratic presidential nomination and a missile gap believer, said in late February that he did "not charge anyone with having intentionally misled the public for purposes of deception." And *Newsweek* reported earlier that month its survey of hundreds of "the most influential individuals" in all fifty states showing "a continuing confidence in the U.S. and its leaders, a firm feeling that the nation could still take care of itself on the economic front, and — if need be — in a cataclysmic nuclear war." Symington would soon assure Dulles in a telephone call that he did not believe that there was any "monkey business" going on at the CIA.

Nonetheless, the hearings and controversies on missile gaps and intelligence juggling put considerable pressure on Eisenhower to authorize more U-2 flights. Little had changed since a White House meeting a year earlier when Defense Secretary McElroy "requested the President to consider the matter of additional overflights of the USSR" because "Congress was continually concerned over . . . intelligence estimates."[25]

U-2: "We Have Felt These Operations Were Appropriate"

Typical of agency-Congress relations in the early Cold War years, the first notification of a legislator about the U-2 program occurred informally in the mid-1950s, over drinks, followed some time later by a more formal but equally secret affair on Capitol Hill. That member of Congress was Leverett Saltonstall, who later wrote,

> Dick Russell trusted me, as we had worked together for years on problems of defense. When a new CIA project was in the air about which we wanted precise information, he would sometimes say, "Lev, you do it." I would call up Allen, and he and his security man would stop at my house at the day's end or I would go to his home in Georgetown. We would have a little hospitality; I would ask him questions, and he would tell me what the CIA was up to, and the next morning, I would pass on the information to Dick Russell in his office. In this way, he and I learned about the U-2 planes.[1]

On Friday, February 24, 1956, some time after Dulles's chat with Saltonstall, the DCI traveled to Capitol Hill to meet with Russell's Armed Services CIA subcommittee. On the *New York Times'* front page that cold morning, one headline read, "Democrats Want Dulles to Inform Congress Better," referring not to the CIA chief but to the secretary of state. Another lead story that day described Eisenhower's first major foray onto a golf course since his 1955 heart attack.

Either before or after the February 24 session, Dulles met with just Russell and Saltonstall and, according to a CIA in-house history, "shared with them the details of Project Aquatone," then the U-2 program code name. No one at the CIA seems to have written an account of the meeting until almost two years later. But the agency history reports that Dulles asked Russell's and Saltonstall's opinion on who else in Congress should be informed about the U-2. They are said to have recommended that House Appropriations leaders Cannon and Taber — but no one else — be so informed.

This occurred three days later on a cloudy Monday afternoon, following a three-hour House Appropriations CIA subcommittee hearing. Five Appropriations members and one staffer had attended, with Dulles flanked by seven

CIA aides. Cannon had posed his usual warning of "No more Koreas!," and others questioned the effectiveness of U.S. intelligence and covert action. Before taking his leave as 5 p.m. neared, Dulles approached the chairman and asked to speak alone with him and Taber. The latter had inquired minutes earlier, "Why does the government always under-estimate Soviet abilities?" Cannon and Taber were gratified to learn of the U-2 program, certain "ELINT operations," and another operation whose identity was still censored by agency officials half a century later. Before departing, Dulles told the chairman and ranking Republican that they could decide whether or not to inform other subcommittee members.[2]

While the agency history claims that only those four legislators knew of U-2 between 1956 and 1960, substantial evidence suggests otherwise. Dulles insisted in retirement that others on the CIA subcommittees knew. He told one interviewer, "People said Congress can't keep a secret; I don't believe it. I told Congress about the U-2 five years before it came down. So I know they can keep a secret." To another reporter, Eric Sevareid, who asked about Clarence Cannon's subcommittee, Dulles said, "We told the House committee about the U-2, which was the most secret thing we had, and the best kept secret for five years of any operation that I've ever known." William Darden, chief clerk of the Senate Armed Services Committee for much of the 1950s and 1960s and completely trusted by Russell and Saltonstall, sat in on agency subcommittee meetings. Darden was careful years later, in retirement, not to overstate his memory of, or role in, events. But of U-2 and the subcommittee, he says, "They knew about that." So did Darden, who felt "an admiration for the technology involved and sort of a reassurance that we knew something about the Soviet capability."

The CIA's legislative liaison, John Warner, also later claimed, "They were aware of the program." Asked if "they" included not just Russell and Saltonstall but "others like Vinson, Cannon, Mahon, too," he responded, "Oh, yeah, because that was an expensive program for us in those days, and it had the potential, as it eventually did, for being explosive — the amounts of money, and working with the Air Force. They probably weren't briefed in detail, but I'm sure that they were briefed." While the briefings initially included only "the chairman and the ranking minority member" of each subcommittee, this extended to include, "eventually, others." Apparently, each CIA subcommittee's chair decided which of its members would be brought into such knowledge.[3]

In one respect, U-2s were widely known — NASA used them for publicized and (as the Senate Foreign Relations Committee would later note) "extremely valuable . . . upper altitude weather research." But most legislators knew nothing of U-2's critically important espionage flights over the USSR, although a few stumbled into information on the program or had a close call. Once, in the late 1950s, Senator Estes Kefauver, a former presidential and vice-presidential candidate, traveled to West Germany. Despite his prominence, Kefauver displayed such pronounced, combined traits of sanctimonious religiosity and sexual promiscuity as to offend colleagues. One Senate heavyweight privately spoke of Kefauver "out running for president with his cock in one hand and the Bible in the other." In Germany, though, Chancellor Konrad Adenauer invited the well-known senator for a chat.

Little did Kefauver know, as he waited outside Adenauer's office for the meeting, what was occurring inside: Arthur Lundahl and John Bross of the CIA were explaining the U-2 program and showing the chancellor photos of Soviet military sites. "Fabulous, fabulous!" said Adenauer. When his secretary came in to announce that Senator Kefauver was waiting outside, Adenauer asked if the senator might join their meeting. No, Bross said, the senator was not "cleared" for information. An agency historian writes, "The Chancellor's stoic face broke into a smile."[4]

Stuart Symington, too, heard rumors about the U-2 in 1959, but could not get Dulles to talk about it in a private meeting. When the senator visited Germany just before Christmas, he tried to wring information about the program out of an air force colonel at Adana Air Force base, from which U-2s flew. The colonel refused to tell Symington anything, then heard the senator recite his credentials as former secretary of the air force and a current member of the Armed Services Committee. The colonel still would not budge. Symington was impressed.[5]

As Warner suggested, the U-2 program was too expensive to hide for very long from top legislators. At a crucial White House meeting in November 1954, Eisenhower had formally approved the production of thirty U-2s at an estimated cost of $35 million. According to Goodpaster's notes, "Dulles indicated that his organization could not finance this whole sum without drawing attention to it, and it was agreed that Defense would seek to carry a substantial part of the financing." That late in the year, except for the Senate's consideration of the McCarthy censure, Congress was essentially finished for 1954. Perhaps the DCI wished not to discuss U-2 at all with congressional leaders in 1955, although his conversation with Saltonstall occurred that year or very early in 1956. (Over four and a half decades later, the agency still censored records of its U-2 funding. Clearly, though, much or all of the CIA's portion of the U-2 budget came from the DCI's special unvouchered account; the air force covered the rest.)

The program, headed by Richard Bissell, was so secret that, even within the CIA and in Eisenhower's NSC and White House, only those who had to know of the project were so informed. (Among those aware of U-2 were presidential aides Goodpaster and his own assistant, John Eisenhower, who joined the staff in 1958.) The president had warned the DCI that he was quite willing to kill the program if it did not remain secret. Even those in the know often had gaps, Bissell later recalled, "It was completely compartmentalized in the interest of security and walled off. Allen Dulles knew less of what went on in that component of the Agency than he did about any of them." Vice President Nixon only learned specifics of the program after Eisenhower's heart attack in fall 1955. In August 1956, Goodpaster conveyed Eisenhower's renewed and strongly worded directive to Dulles: "There is to be no mention of the existence of this project or operations incident to it, outside the Executive Branch." Whether the DCI told Eisenhower that he had already described the U-2 program to Appropriations subcommittee leaders and possibly a few others is unclear, but the president's hostility helps explain why, after the Sputnik event a year later, Dulles decided not to go through with a "special briefing" on U-2 that aides had prepared for delivery to twenty-five congressional leaders, including Symington and Mike Mansfield.[6]

Within a few years beyond the initial U-2 flight over the USSR, the program established itself as a prime U.S. intelligence asset. Bissell would summarize the U-2's contributions:

> The intelligence collected allowed Eisenhower to remain calm during a period of great international tension. He was able to avoid bellicose rhetoric or acts of aggressiveness, secure in his knowledge that the Soviet bomber and missile threat was significantly less than the public sometimes feared. . . . Militarily, the U-2 provided invaluable information on the Soviets' capabilities and the deployment of their forces. In the event of war, we would be equipped to strike at the heart of their military-industrial complex far better than they at ours. The U-2's contributions to our economic security are also important. . . . Eisenhower repeatedly frustrated the attempts of America's military-industrial complex to gain financing for larger and more expensive weapon systems.[7]

Still, from 1956 through spring 1960, a conflicted president often suspended flights over the USSR for months at a time. In turn, his advisers at the CIA, the State and Defense Departments, and on the NSC staff tended to favor more frequent use of the U-2. In February 1959, when Neil McElroy cited "continual" congressional concerns over the legitimacy of "our intelligence estimates" in lobbying for more U-2 flights, the president responded (according to his son's notes) that "to continue reconnaissance flights . . . is undue provocation. Nothing, he says, would make him request authority to declare war more quickly than violation of our air space by Soviet aircraft." In an April meeting with McElroy and Bissell, Eisenhower acknowledged the great "need for information . . . highlighted by the distortions several senators are making of our military position, relative to that of the Soviets, and they are being helped in their 'demagoguery' by our uncertainties as to Soviet programs." Nonetheless, he rejected "certain reconnaissance flights" that had been proposed. An October 26, 1959, Eisenhower-Dulles encounter revealed another presidential concern (recorded by Goodpaster):

> Dulles came in to propose the conduct of a U-2 reconnaissance flight over a key area of northern European Russia. The President said that, recognizing that there may be substantial intelligence values involved, there is a basic and broader question — either the Soviets in the present circumstances would contemplate general warfare or they would not. If they would not, it does not seem necessary to him to conduct these searches for any missile sites they may have. In fact, it is in the nature of provocative pin-pricking, and it may give them the idea that we are seriously preparing plans to knock out their installations.

A few days later, Goodpaster notified Bissell that Eisenhower had vetoed the proposed flight.[8]

By early 1960, Eisenhower increasingly wished to transform Soviet-American relations before leaving office, although members of his administration battled bitterly over the wisdom of, and means to, such a goal. The president took note, more than they, that when Khrushchev had completed his 1959 trip to America, he had told 17,000 cheering party members (plus millions of Soviet citizens by way of radio and television): "President Eisenhower has displayed wise statesmanship in assessing the present international situation. He has shown courage and valor. . . . I got the impression that the President sincerely wanted to liquidate the Cold War."

Just months later, though, Khrushchev had reason to doubt Eisenhower's intentions and his control of the U.S. government. In March 1960, SAC chief General Thomas Power told Mahon's subcommittee that Air Force Intelligence was "reasonably sure" that it had identified at least twenty-six operational Soviet ICBM sites. In other settings, air force leaders suggested that the USSR had as many as one hundred long-range missiles deployed. While Dulles told Mahon's subcommittee that the CIA had identified only two Soviet missile launching sites, one legislator (who seemed to speak for others) complained that his testimony was "fuzzy." Pressure grew on Eisenhower to approve more U-2 missions to settle the dispute. He had already permitted one in February, despite believing that his "one tremendous asset in a summit meeting" would be his "reputation for honesty." That U-2 flight had not revealed new missile sites but did not settle the controversy. In response to a request for four more overflights, Eisenhower allowed one on April 9. There was, one intelligence leader claimed at the time, "a reasonable chance of completing this operation without detection."[9]

The flight photographed new Soviet radars and a new missile launching area, but it did not go undetected. One official soon warned Bissell that future penetration of Soviet airspace "without detection . . . may not be as easy in the future." Khrushchev, meanwhile, was appalled and embarrassed by the flight. His government had quietly protested earlier overflights, to no avail, but the latest ones seemed a slap in the face. After his return from the United States, he had publicly asked the United States and its allies to take no action before the summit that would "worsen the atmosphere" and "sow seeds of suspicion." Khrushchev later wrote that the Americans "were making these flights to show up our impotence. Well, we weren't impotent any longer." Khrushchev upbraided Soviet air defense officials for failing to knock down the April 9 flight but expected other chances.

Indeed, even before that flight, one last pre-summit U-2 flight had already been approved by Eisenhower for later in the month. When bad weather loomed, the president was sympathetic but directed (in Goodpaster's words) that "no operation is to be carried out after May 1." Such specific directions from the president were common; he had often pored over maps and proposed schedules with Dulles, Bissell, and others. In this instance, he balanced intelligence requirements against diplomatic ones — the Paris summit was to begin on May 16. The president could only hope that the Soviet leaders would tolerate one more U-2 flight.

After weather delays, the approved flight was to begin on Sunday, May 1, in Pakistan, following a route with the "best chance of photographing suspected locations of Soviet ICBM sites" at Tyuratam and elsewhere, plus other sites, including Stalingrad, a nuclear plant in the Urals, and a submarine shipyard, and then land in Norway. It "would be the most adventuresome overflight to date because it proposed covering so much of the Soviet Union," a CIA historian added. "The pilot selected . . . was Francis Gary Powers, the most experienced U-2 pilot in the program," who had "flown 27 operational missions in the U-2, including one each over the Soviet Union and China, as well as six along the Soviet border."

Since May Day was a major holiday in the USSR, there was relatively little Soviet air traffic. Powers's flight was detected and tracked, as the Soviet Air Defense Command was finally well prepared to respond. An SA-2 rocket exploded behind the U-2, damaging but not destroying it. Soon Powers, who had barely escaped from the aircraft, was on the ground, as was the U-2. Both were in surprisingly good shape. Even as Khrushchev reviewed the May Day parade in Moscow, a military commander whispered that a U-2 had been shot down.

Dulles, in New York that Sunday morning to receive the Golden Rule Award "for distinguished government service and dedication to Christian ideals" from the St. George Society of the New York Police Department, missed hearing the news until he returned home that afternoon. By then, Eisenhower had heard from Goodpaster that the flight was "probably lost." The president and others hoped that the Soviets might keep the U-2 story secret, to avoid the embarrassment of acknowledging that American spy flights had traveled across the USSR.

In an appropriately strange setting, Eisenhower would learn much more a few days later, courtesy of Khrushchev. Eisenhower, his NSC members, and other high-ranking officials did a drill evacuation from Washington early on Thursday morning, May 5, to an elaborate underground command post in Virginia's Blue Ridge Mountains for use in the event of nuclear war. There, an eerily calm and routine NSC meeting proceeded, without addressing the unfolding story. At the same time, press secretary Hagerty phoned Goodpaster from the White House with breaking news that Khrushchev had announced the shoot down. Quickly, the administration was in disarray— reporters tried furiously to get a statement out of Hagerty, but Goodpaster told him to say nothing for the moment. It was a prudent choice, since Goodpaster knew that Hagerty was uninformed about the spy aircraft. After an hour passed with Hagerty still on a leash, the hard-drinking, chain-smoking press secretary exploded with anger, mistakenly convinced that Goodpaster had not yet even informed the president of the latest news. When Eisenhower returned to the White House late that morning, Hagerty told him and Goodpaster that the president should immediately go before the press to deny Khrushchev's charges. Soon, Hagerty would learn how uninformed he had been, and why his suggestion went nowhere.

Khrushchev's announcement was before a long-planned gathering of the 1,300-member Supreme Soviet in Moscow's Great Kremlin Palace. Among the prominently seated guests was U.S. Ambassador Llewellyn Thompson. For over two hours, Khrushchev addressed domestic issues, then reminded delegates that he and Eisenhower were soon to meet, along with the heads of France and Britain. Success at the May 16 summit was crucial "if a solid basis is to be laid for peaceful co-existence between states with different social systems." Then he sprang the news:

> Lately, influential forces — imperialist and militarist circles, whose strong-hold is the Pentagon — have become noticeably more active in the United States ... Comrade Deputies! On the instruction of the Soviet government, I must report to you on aggressive actions against the Soviet Union in the past few weeks. . . . The United States has been sending aircraft that have been crossing our state frontiers and intruding upon the airspace of the Soviet Union. We protested to the United States against several previous aggressive acts of this kind.

Of the most recent flight's scheduling, Khrushchev said, "The day they chose for this was the most festive day for the working peoples of all countries — May Day! . . . The government said, 'The aggressor knows what he is in for when he intrudes upon foreign territory. . . . shoot the plane down!' This assignment was fulfilled." Looking at his American guest in the audience, Khrushchev said, "Just imagine what would have happened had a Soviet aircraft appeared over New York City, Chicago, or Detroit. . . . How would the United States have reacted?" Then the premier raised another crucial question: "Who sent this aircraft across the Soviet frontier?" He was prepared to believe that Eisenhower had not ordered the flight, for "I do not doubt President Eisenhower's sincere desire for peace." After the four-hour talk, Khrushchev departed the hall to ecstatic applause, never having revealed the equally significant news of Powers's survival and capture.[10]

Pouring Oil on Fire

In the following hours and days, the Kremlin, the White House, and Congress all staggered their reactions to U-2 events, producing a fine mess. In Washington, the apparent loss of the aircraft had already been misleadingly announced before Khrushchev spoke. Under guidance from the White House, the State Department, and the CIA, NASA claimed on Tuesday, May 3, that a U-2 flight originating in Turkey and studying "clear air turbulence" was missing. American newspapers barely noticed. On May 5, in quick response to Khrushchev's much-publicized speech, the State Department issued a brief statement (crafted by Dulles and a State Department leader) indicating that a U-2 aircraft doing meteorological research and "having a failure in the oxygen equipment which could result in the pilot losing consciousness" might have "accidentally violated Soviet airspace."

Then NASA issued yet another statement explaining how the U-2 studying "gust-meteorological conditions found at high altitude has been missing" since May 1. In a follow-up press conference, a NASA spokesman said the mission was "wholly peaceful, scientific weather research." Minutes later, the State Department received a "Most Urgent" cable from Ambassador Thompson in Moscow. He had assumed that Powers and his U-2 had been incinerated in the sky but overheard Soviet Deputy Foreign Minister Jacob Malik tell a Swedish diplomat that the pilot was being questioned![1]

That same day, Lyndon Johnson became the first legislator to speak on the floor of either house of Congress about the U-2. He did so late in the morning, with Mike Mansfield presiding over the Senate. Johnson had to choose his words carefully. The majority leader and chairman of the famed Preparedness subcommittee was Russell's protégé and served on his secretive CIA subcommittee. Johnson knew something of the U-2 program and could guess that NASA's announcement was intended to camouflage the actual purpose of the May 1 flight. He knew nothing of the pilot's survival but was ready to stick with the administration's cover story, hoping it would suffice. Somberly, Johnson announced: "I have asked the Administration to give us full particulars. . . . I note that Mr. Khrushchev's statement says that the plane which was shot down was unmarked. If I am correctly informed, all National Aeronautical and Space Administration planes are clearly marked, and are on strictly peaceful missions. It may be that Khrushchev is simply using this incident in an attempt to apply leverage for the coming summit meetings." Mansfield, knowing less than Johnson that May 5, spoke more bluntly: "Did it occur to Mr. Khrushchev that the plane might have been engaged in perfectly legitimate pursuits, and might inadvertently have gone off course and over the border?" Then, Mansfield turned his ire on the United States government: "First reports indicate that the President had no knowledge of the plane incident. If that is the case, we have got to ask whether or not this administration has any real control over the federal bureaucracy."[2]

Only Mansfield and Johnson spoke of the downed U-2 on the floors of Congress that day. But others were angry about Khrushchev's speech, as the *Washington Post* reported. Styles Bridges, the most senior Republican on the Appropriations subcommittee on the CIA knew something of U-2 flights but feigned ignorance and anger — telling reporters that Eisenhower should not attend the Paris summit unless the Soviets provided "an immediate explanation and response" — while privately hoping that the White House would admit nothing about the aerial espionage program. Senator E. L. Bartlett (D-AL) took offense at the "rude, crude, provocative remarks of Khrushchev." Leverett Saltonstall stayed quiet on the Senate floor but sought out Dulles on the evening of May 5 and again by telephone the next morning for cryptic, inconclusive conversations about "that subject." He had never forgotten the DCI's briefing of him and Russell some years before on U-2, he said. Now, he was being asked what Khrushchev's speech could really mean, and he "assumed that other members of the Senate had also." The DCI promised to brief Saltonstall privately, and soon.

On Friday, May 6, Johnson advised all American and Soviet leaders to avoid angry public accusations. The Soviet government, after all, was "a sovereign government, and it must be respected as such." Khrushchev "may well have thought the flight of the plane was a deliberate intrusion on our part. If that were even a remote possibility, we, too, should be taken to task for allowing it just before the summit meeting, or at any other time." His remarks made obvious, in retrospect, the administration's difficulty in coordinating not only its own response to the incident but those of legislative supporters.

More than others on Capitol Hill, though, Mansfield had outlined the dilemma that Eisenhower now probably knew would not go away — he could admit knowledge and take responsibility for the U-2 flight, thus probably ruining his relationship with Khrushchev and the chances for detente, or deny any knowledge of the flight and imply that he did not control his own administration. If the U-2 would have been thoroughly demolished in its shooting and had fallen to the earth, and if Powers had died, perhaps the story and dilemma might have faded. Dulles and Bissell had, after all, previously assured Eisenhower that no U-2 or its pilot could survive if shot down.[3]

Some in the administration foresaw the dangers of the rising, ill-informed rhetoric in Congress. National security adviser Gordon Gray was aghast at ongoing relations with Capitol Hill. Richard Bissell, especially, wondered how long Eisenhower could accept a situation in which the Senate majority leader was speaking of taking the United States to task if it ever deliberately sent aircraft over the USSR. Bissell reached out to George Kistiakowsky, the president's science adviser, who had learned of the U-2 loss on May 3, but refrained from penning his usual diary writings until May 6, because "the matter was so hush-hush." He then wrote:

> Short visit from Dick Bissell to exchange commiserations on the U-2 plane mishap. Both Dick and I, and according to him, Allen, feel that the President should take congressional leaders at least partly into his confidence to prevent the building up of indignation in Congress, which would only pour more oil on the fire. I called Andy [Goodpaster] about it afterwards, and he said that this has been considered and flatly rejected because the Boss thinks that these congressional fellows will inevitably spill the beans.[4]

Even before news emerged that Powers was alive — made public by Khrushchev in another speech on Saturday, May 7— Dulles probably knew that the secrecy surrounding U-2 was gone. For one thing, some reporters had learned of the program in the preceding two years. Hanson Baldwin, the longtime military intelligence reporter for the *Times*, discovered the U-2 flights and their purpose during a 1958 visit to Germany. Back home, Baldwin virtually summoned the CIA's Robert Amory to lunch and informed him that a U-2 story was soon to appear in the *Times*. "Jesus, Hanson, no!" begged Amory. It had been one thing for *Model Airplane News* to publish an accurate speculation two years earlier about U-2s "flying across the 'Iron Curtain' taking aerial photographs" but would be quite another for the *Times* to do so.

Eventually Baldwin and his editors agreed to remain mum, but warned the CIA that the story was "ready to go, if we hear that a Drew Pearson or anybody is about to publish it." By May 6, Baldwin lessened his frustration by writing a story on the missile gap. Without naming the U-2 aircraft, it described U.S. knowledge of Soviet long-range missiles and implied how that knowledge emerged: "no operational sites are known to exist, despite intensive and at least partly successful efforts to penetrate the Iron Curtain." Dulles was sophisticated enough to know that the rest of the story would emerge soon from the *Times*—where columnists James Reston and Arthur Krock also knew of U-2—and elsewhere.

Once Khrushchev spoke on May 7, this was even clearer. On that Saturday, he told the Supreme Soviet, "The pilot of the American plane is alive and well." Anyone wishing to understand the U-2's mission, he advised, should "seek a reply from Allen Dulles, at whose instructions the American aircraft flew over the Soviet Union." He claimed to be relieved, though, at Hagerty's May 5 statement that Eisenhower "knew nothing about the incident." The door to the Paris summit was still open, Khrushchev implied.[5]

News about a surviving pilot and substantially intact spy aircraft was "unbelievable," Eisenhower later wrote. Some legislators initially refused to believe it. Of Khrushchev's claim that Powers was on a spy mission authorized by Dulles, Representative Craig Hosmer (R-CA) snorted the words "fairy tale." His colleague J. Carlton Loser (D-TN) endorsed the sentiments of the *Nashville Banner*, which demanded the release of Powers and a "full apology" from the Kremlin. Now it was all the likelier that Eisenhower would have to decide whether it was less damaging to admit or deny his knowledge and authority over U-2. Resisting a clear choice between those two options, Herter had another cover-story statement that the president grudgingly authorized for release on May 7:

> As a result of the inquiry ordered by the President, it has been established that, insofar as the authorities in Washington are concerned, there was no authorization for such flight as described by Mr. Khrushchev.
>
> Nevertheless, it appears that in endeavoring to obtain information now concealed behind the Iron Curtain, a flight over Soviet territory was probably undertaken by an unarmed civilian U-2 plane. It is certainly no secret that, given the state of the world today, intelligence collection activities are practiced by all countries, and postwar history certainly reveals that the Soviet Union has not been lagging behind in this field. . . . It is in relation to the danger of surprise attack that planes of the type of unarmed U-2 aircraft have made flights along the frontiers of the free world for the past four years.[6]

The cover story was shocking, not so much for its seeming dishonesty, but for its clumsiness and the implication that U-2s could go over the Soviet Union without the permission or knowledge of "Washington authorities." The statement led the *Post* to wonder if Powers could have engaged in the mission "on his own" or on orders of "local American intelligence or military authorities" in Turkey. In the aftermath of Khrushchev's and the State Department's words, Washington was a "sad and perplexed capital," said the *Times*. Eisenhower, himself, would regret the May 7 State Department statement for years to come. "I didn't realize how high a price we were going to have to pay for that lie," he said with great feeling to a reporter years later.[7]

Congress probably would have exploded with questions about such an intelligence-political mess, if the statements had not emerged on a Saturday. Some members spoke to the press that night or soon thereafter, though. Without knowing who had authorized the flight, Representative Chester Bowles (D-CT), a foreign policy adviser to presidential candidate John Kennedy, called the supposed rogue flight "dangerous and hurtful. . . . The role of clandestine operations is inherently difficult for a democracy . . . but that is an argument for greater presidential control, not less." Senator Alexander Wiley observed, "The President, the Secretary of State, and the nation deserve an answer not only for scheduling of such a flight, not only for such deep penetration into Soviet territory, but also for reaching such a decision at this critical time in international affairs." Such emotion and confusion displayed in the Sunday and Monday *Times* overshadowed Baldwin's latest analysis that the U-2 "probably has been one of the most successful reconnaissance planes ever built."[8]

Khrushchev also still wondered who authorized the U-2 flight. While it was still morning in Washington on Monday, May 9, the Soviet premier sought out Ambassador Thompson at a Moscow diplomatic reception, greeted him warmly, and took him aside. Khrushchev said he "could not help but suspect that someone had launched this operation with deliberate intent of spoiling summit meeting," Thompson cabled Washington. The premier expressed dark suspicions of Dulles and said he had taken note of Senator Mansfield's remarks. Khrushchev also confirmed that his government had known of previous U.S. spy flights and explained (accurately) that when the USSR had complained to the State Department, it "had blandly denied any knowledge of them."

Like many presidents, Eisenhower frequently cursed up a storm in the White House, but he was uncharacteristically quiet and depressed that Monday morning. The only words he spoke to his secretary were, "I would like to resign." An hour or so later, after meeting with a group of Republican legislators, Eisenhower heard an intriguing story from one of them, Senator Francis Case (SD), during a nine-minute Oval Office talk. Case thought he should inform the president that while the senator had traveled with other legislators in an air force plane from Moscow to Warsaw in 1959, some crew members had distracted accompanying Soviet officials with cockpit conversations, while other air force personnel used "high powered camera equipment" to photograph Soviet territory. The episode occurred "only a few days prior to Mr. Khrushchev's visit here." Eisenhower agreed with the senator that it had been improper to "take advantage of guest status while traveling through Russia."[9]

The president seems not to have known that his own brand-new presidential aircraft, built by Boeing in time for his planned trip to the Soviet Union, was equipped with sophisticated concealed cameras to take photographs that would match or surpass those from U-2s. Project Lida Rose, costing $1 million, seems to have been an initiative of Allen Dulles and Defense Secretary Gates. Historians of the project write that "Dulles had not necessarily set out to deceive the President. But sometimes, as he knew, it was a boon to political superiors if they were kept in the dark."[10]

The president made up his mind on one thing later on May 9: while insisting that it be done "without apology," Eisenhower accepted Dulles's view that congressional leaders must be brought into some confidence on the U-2. No wonder — news services quoted the usually circumspect Richard Russell, at home in Georgia, as describing an overflight of the USSR just before the planned summit as "almost incredibly stupid." Also, if the president looked at the day's *Times* he would have seen Styles Bridges heading a front-page story titled, "Angry Congressmen Urge Inquiry on Spying Activity." Bridges was about as unpopular as ever at the White House and with many at the CIA. DD/I Robert Amory, who favored U.S. recognition of Communist China, was overheard at an embassy party earlier in the year referring to "that goddamned old do-do up there, Bridges, who is the fellow that pulls the strings every time to keep us from any progressive move." Respected or resented, an assertive Russell or Bridges could not easily be put off.[11]

Anticipating approval of some sort of legislative encounter, the director of central intelligence had virtually insisted to a reluctant Eisenhower that he be permitted to show photographs taken by U2s to Congress leaders. The president initially balked, until Dulles said, "If I can't show the photos, I would rather not do it at all."

On short notice that same day, eighteen Capitol Hill barons and one ill-informed backbencher headed to Senate Appropriations Committee hearing room F-82, knocking on a locked door as they arrived. Their names were checked against a list of invitees before admission for a briefing to feature Herter and Dulles. Senator Frank Lausche (D-OH) showed up, thinking that all members of Foreign Relations were invited: "To my embarrassment, I had to leave. A newspaperman asked me why I was leaving and, facetiously, I said, 'I was thrown out.'" The briefing was, in fact, intended for the formal leaders of the House and Senate, the chairs and minority leaders of the House and Senate Appropriations and Armed Services Committees, and the heads of the congressional committees on foreign affairs.

Carl Hayden allowed a gray navy blanket to be hung over the room's doorway to muffle any escaping sounds of voices. When the DCI approached, a reporter spotted him and asked, "Any statement?" "About the usual," chuckled Dulles, as he moved on. He and Herter entered the room full of what seemed to the accompanying photographic interpretation specialist, Art Lundahl, to be "angry or combative" legislative barons. Dulles and the secretary told the assembled legislators that the United States had been engaged in aerial espionage with U-2 aircraft for some time. As Herter would also tell the nation just after the briefing, this had been done pursuant to "presidential directives to gather by every possible means the information required to protect the United States and the free world against surprise attack." Under those directives, "programs have been developed and put into operation which have included extensive aerial surveillance by unarmed civilian aircraft, normally of a peripheral character but, on occasion, by penetration. Specific missions of these unarmed civilian aircraft have not been subject to presidential authorization." Although Eisenhower later wrote that Herter's presidentially approved statement to the legislators and the country had been "meticulously accurate," it was dishonest — U-2s had flown along the periphery of the USSR, but "penetration" had been more than occasional. Also, Herter and Dulles underplayed the involvement of a president who had studied maps of proposed flights and ruminated over proposed flight dates: the DCI said that the "details and timing" of U-2 flights were "left to technicians."

Some legislators wanted to know how many U-2s had flown over the USSR. When Dulles declined for reasons of "high security" to be more specific than "a considerable number," the leaders pressed him, and he relented by giving an approximate number (which remained censored by CIA decades later). No member of Congress in the hearing room questioned the necessity of reconnaissance, though the meeting's atmosphere was "disturbed" and "troubled," according to two congressmen there. Among the most unhappy was Speaker of the House Sam Rayburn, who asserted twice that May 1 was a "doubtful time to release such a flight, with the summit conference coming on." Unsatisfied with Herter's and Dulles's defenses, Mr. Sam (as he was widely known) returned to an earlier question: who gave the order for this flight? Dulles evaded the question again, saying such decisions were sometimes made "in the field" and "sometimes by Washington." The DCI also apologized to the Speaker for never having briefed him about U-2.

When some legislators suggested that the United States should not have publicly acknowledged its U-2 program, Herter responded, "It was one of the most difficult decisions I ever made in my life." That statement, too, was dishonest — Eisenhower made the decision that Herter would speak on Capitol Hill and publicly about U-2. As to the future, Herter disturbed some members of Congress by implying that the aircraft would continue going over the USSR. (Walter Lippmann would soon write that such a policy "makes it impossible for the Soviet government to play down this particular incident because now it is challenged openly in the face of the whole world.") Dulles and Herter listened with poker faces as the legislators urged them to center "responsibility" in someone before such future activities occurred. With greater emphasis, some members questioned how anyone could have timed the flight so badly and speculated that Washington-based intelligence officials must have made that decision purely on the basis of "good weather conditions — without any thought of the impending summit meeting," as the *Post* reported. It must have pained Dulles to be a party to such speculation. Nor could he mention that Eisenhower had refused his offer to take the blame for the U-2 mess and resign.

About Powers's competence and loyalty, legislators aggressively asked: Had he brought the plane down from the normal 70,000 feet altitude before the shooting, and if so, why? Why had Powers not killed himself, in accordance with what they believed to be "intelligence tradition"? Why did he not at least use the "destruct" button (which Dulles had described) to destroy the aircraft? Although Dulles seemed to believe, mistakenly, that if Powers had pushed the button, all of the plane and its contents would have been destroyed, he strongly defended the pilot. However, the legislators' repeated, skeptical questions virtually forced Dulles to pledge that he would not be "ruling anything out" in future investigations of Powers.

The DCI was all the more glad that, after the not entirely satisfactory opening testimony and exchange with the Congress leaders, he could say, "Mr. Lundahl will now give you a briefing on what we've accomplished." He then whispered to his chief photographic interpretation assistant, "You've got to be good!" Former CIA photo interpreter Dino Brugioni wrote that Lundahl ("the most respected and honored intelligence officer in the intelligence community") had typically done rounds of briefings following earlier major U-2 missions. His first "audience" was always the president, followed by the secretaries of state and defense, the Joint Chiefs of Staff, heads of other intelligence agencies, and unnamed "congressional leaders."

Showing large photographs of the earth's surface inside the Soviet border to the legislators on May 9 and explaining detailed views of missile sites and other facilities, Lundahl aimed to be as "good" as Dulles hoped. Early on, though, angry legislators interrupted him. Mike Mansfield wanted to know if "any Cabinet members knew of this flight?" Dulles said he believed not. Well, then, was Powers "under the command of some colonel in Turkey?" Getting no straight answer from the DCI, Mansfield rephrased the question: "Who was Powers' boss?" This, too, failed to get a clear answer from Dulles, although Herter more explicitly misled the congressional leaders by asserting that Eisenhower was "not involved" in the May 1 flight. Others, including Senate minority leader Dirksen, seemed untroubled by Dulles's and Herter's apparent obfuscation and were intrigued to learn of the U-2's less-publicized mission of gathering "Russian electronic emissions" and "missile telemetry."

Eventually, the leaders permitted Lundahl to continue his presentation, which *was* good. When it ended, the small audience gave Dulles and associates a standing ovation, so surprising the DCI that he dropped a pipe onto his lap. He, Lundahl, and Herter smiled and accepted the applause while Dulles simultaneously batted out smoldering ashes. Gratified, the DCI asked that the CIA's section of the briefing be considered off-the-record. Rayburn announced firmly that he would give news reporters waiting outside "no comment whatever." Though the session had ended well, the DCI exited the Appropriations room alongside Herter, murmuring, "That was a rough one."[12]

After the session and upon the public release of Herter's statement, many legislators readily reacted to the latest version of an explanation. Those doing CIA oversight were split in their public reactions; supporters of the CIA and the Eisenhower administration included Saltonstall ("international communism's traditional aggressiveness make overseas intelligence operations necessary") and Cannon ("why shouldn't we try to find out what they are up to, in an effort to prevent a sneak attack which would kill hundreds of thousands?"). Paul Kilday, by contrast, thought the government erred seriously in authorizing Powers's flight just before the planned summit and in having "admitted the purpose of the flight." Still, "getting that information is not a very pretty business, but it is an essential business." The next day, he told Dulles that when the United States was caught doing "dirty business," then "we should look dumb, and blink our eyes, and not admit anything."

Richard Russell, George Mahon, and Carl Vinson said nothing about the administration's latest explanation, but Lyndon Johnson pointed out the next morning that there were "many unanswered questions." Johnson had been unable to attend the legislators' group briefing on May 9, but Dulles, Bissell, Lundahl, and others would go to Capitol Hill the next day to brief him. Hours before that session, Johnson told the Senate, "If blunders have been made, the American people can be certain that Congress will go into them thoroughly." But there would be no partisanship and no rush to judgment, he emphasized. A gratified Richard Nixon — aware that he and Johnson might be opponents for the presidency later in the year — stepped down from his Senate president's rostrum and shook the Texan's hand.[13]

Faithfully, Speaker Rayburn voiced not a word of criticism after the May 9 briefing. Later that afternoon, though, he visited the White House at Eisenhower's invitation, where the president implored him to save an endangered foreign aid bill. As he had to Dulles, Rayburn expressed anger over never having been told about the U-2. No one in the House or Senate, not even Cannon, Taber, or Mahon, had known of World War II's Manhattan Project before Rayburn. Though Eisenhower would not have known this history, in June 1943, President Roosevelt had stressed to General Leslie Groves that the Manhattan Project "be even more drastically guarded than other highly secret war developments." But, within six months it became obvious that the hugely expensive atomic bomb program could not continue to be funded without explaining it to *someone* in Congress. At Roosevelt's specific direction, Secretary of War Henry Stimson and General George Marshall went to Rayburn's office in February 1944 and detailed the A-bomb program. The Speaker then summoned the House majority and minority leaders to that same meeting to hear the news. They, in turn, soon passed on the sensitive information to Cannon and Taber and urged their support for "an inscrutable appropriation." (Stimson and colleagues would also shortly approach a handful of Senate leaders.)

Such appropriators would be filled in on more details the following year and even visit the Project's headquarters in Tennessee. Rayburn had no interest in the inspection ("I would see a lot of buildings and pots and pans and jars that nobody could explain to me," he later said), but he was proud to have been the first legislator in the know and that he and other House-Senate leaders had secretly funded the atomic project. Cannon, Taber, and others felt the same way. Days after Leslie Groves picked up George Mahon at his house on May 23, 1945, for a trip with a few other members of Congress to Oak Ridge, Tennessee, the Texan wrote a memo of the event, titling it "A Fantastic Interlude." It noted, "The first bomb will be dropped on the Japanese from an airplane." Rayburn's ignorance of the U-2 was partly his own fault: unlike House majority leader McCormack, who had always liked having private lunches with DCIs every year or so, the Speaker had not seemed "desirous" of briefings, in the words of a CIA official. Nonetheless, Rayburn told Eisenhower he would be a good soldier, help with the foreign aid bill, and back him through the developing Soviet-American crisis.[14]

Others bitterly criticized the administration or the CIA in the day or so after word spread of the legislators' briefing. "Why have we had so much misinformation in connection with this matter?" asked Homer Capehart, a loud, hawkish senator from Indiana. His Democratic colleague, Eugene McCarthy, said that "the decision to fly a plane across the heartland of Russia is one which should have been made at the highest levels of government." The youthful Senator Frank Church (D-ID), a future investigator of the CIA, mocked Eisenhower for the administration's "penchant for not letting its right hand know what the left hand is doing." Mike Mansfield, though, thought himself enlightened by the Dulles-Herter presentation, commending Eisenhower, Herter, and Khrushchev, too — the latter for "his perspicacity in recognizing that the President had no advance knowledge of this action."[15]

"Their Answer to That Demand": Congressional Paternity?

No reaction from Congress to the U-2 affair received the press attention that Clarence Cannon's would, and for good reason. The House Appropriations chair had briefly and bluntly endorsed the administration's aerial espionage policies to reporters (bumping into each other and barking out questions) immediately after the Dulles-Herter presentation. Cannon had been surrounded by other congressional barons, though, and the experience had not stilled his anger at Khrushchev or American critics of the U-2 program, nor lessened a new sense of mission.

Shrewd, scrappy, and eighty-one-years old, the chairman was not a frequent orator in the House and remained infamous for his occasional fistfights and verbal sparring. Once, during the Republican 80th Congress, Frank Keefe (R-WI) had called Cannon a liar during an exchange on the House floor. When Cannon moved to have the remark stricken from the *Record*, members voted along strict party lines, rejecting his motion, 171 to 120. Keefe maintained for years afterward that this was the only time that the House had ever "voted one of its members a liar."

By 1960, after thirty-one years on Appropriations and fifteen years heading it, Cannon was one of the two or three most powerful House members. He continued to keep agency leaders on edge by summoning them on short notice for hearings or private briefings. In March, he had thrown Dulles a curve by asking the DCI to testify *alone* at a budget hearing. Dulles called Mahon and admitted that he did not know "everything" going on at the CIA. The Texan's advice, which Dulles followed, was to bring his top associates to the Capitol and have them "stand by, in case they were needed to help on some details." With Cannon's permission, Dulles would summon comptroller E. R. Saunders and covert action chief Richard Bissell to answer certain questions. Another time that year, when the CIA tried to get a compensation plan through a late session of Congress, only Cannon could have enabled this by skipping Appropriations' CIA subcommittee consideration of the legislation and summarily granting his committee's endorsement. But when an aide explained the CIA's plan to the chairman, he cut him off: "I am against it."[1]

Some CIA leaders thought Cannon's considerable intellectual ability had lessened by 1960, but the chairman had observed the obvious on May 10: nine days had passed since Powers's capture, and not once had anyone in the administration stated publicly how long U-2 flights had been occurring. Nor had they confirmed that the U-2 flights were a CIA program, though Herter had implied as much when he told reporters that Dulles would join him for the May 9 congressional leaders' briefing. Worst of all, administration defenses of the U-2 flights had been halting, unclear, and defensive. Without consulting agency heads, Cannon decided to publicize basic information on the U-2 and speak more frankly than any fellow legislator ever had about Capitol Hill elites' support and knowledge of covert CIA matters.

When Cannon stood to address the House on May 10, other leaders and members, including Taber, his longtime Appropriations partner and rival, gathered round. Reporters did the same in the gallery. Cannon began without fanfare:

> Mr. Chairman, on May 1 the Soviet government captured, 1300 miles inside the boundaries of the Russian empire, an American plane, operated by an American pilot, under the direction and control of the U.S. Central Intelligence Agency, and is now holding both the plane and the pilot.
>
> The plane was on an espionage mission authorized and supported by money provided under an appropriation recommended by the House Committee on Appropriations and passed by the Congress. Although the members of the House have not generally been informed on the subject, the mission was one of a series and part of an established program with which the subcommittee in charge of the appropriation was familiar, and of which it had been fully apprised during this and previous sessions. The appropriation and the activity ... [were] under the aegis of the Commander in Chief of the Armed Forces of the United States, for whom all members of the subcommittee have the highest regard and in whose military capacity they have the utmost confidence.
>
> The question immediately arises as to the authority of the subcommittee to recommend an appropriation for such purposes, and especially the failure of the subcommittee to divulge to the House and the country the justifications warranting the expenditure and all details connected with the item at the time it was under consideration on the floor.
>
> The answer of the subcommittee is: absolute and unavoidable military necessity, fundamental national defense.

Cannon followed with a somewhat mangled account of how a member of Congress and a newspaper had revealed U.S. capability to decipher Japanese cables during World War II. Cannon misstated the harm done, since the Japanese government apparently never learned of the leak, but he credibly argued the continuing dangers of such revelations. Then he gave a more accurate history of his subcommittee's handling of critical secrets, rooting it in the context of World War II and the early Cold War, when the United States enabled itself to destroy whole cities in an instant: "This subcommittee, including the same personnel with the exception of two members who have since died, was the same committee which — for something like three years — provided in the annual appropriation bills a sum which finally totaled more than $2 billion for the original atomic bomb."

The surprise beginning of the Korean War, Cannon claimed, was the other formative experience shaping congressional treatment of U-2:

> There was no shadow of war; not the slightest cloud appeared on the horizon. The sudden rush of a vast army of well-armed, well-trained, and well-munitioned communists across the border made it necessary for us to throw precipitately into battle raw and untrained troops who were wholly unable to protect themselves or hold their positions. And there followed one of the most disastrous periods in the history of American arms.

Cannon then staked a claim that historians have since ignored — that the U-2 program was created in response to congressional demands following that Korean debacle:

> Each year, we have admonished the authority, the CIA, that it must meet future situations of this character with effective measures. We told them, "This must not happen again, and it is up to you to see that it does not happen again," that the American forces must be apprised of any future preparation for attack in time to meet it. And the plan they were following when this plane was taken is their answer to that demand.

Khrushchev came in for particular disdain from Cannon:

> He yesterday characterized the policy of the United States as stupid and blundering. His fury is incited by the fact that it is neither stupid nor blundering. On the contrary, it has been infinitely successful and effective. . . . His discovery that since 1956, for four years, CIA has been sending planes across his border — and as

far as 1,300 miles into his interior without his knowing it — is the occasion of this outburst. It completely disproves his vaunted ability to stop SAC at the border.

The Appropriations chair closed his twenty-five minutes of remarks by designating "the most gratifying feature of the entire incident":

> The world has always recognized the remarkable success of our form of government. It has been the wonder and admiration of mankind. But always they have said that it was at a great disadvantage in a war with an authoritarian dictatorship. We have here demonstrated conclusively that free men, confronted by the most ruthless and criminal despotism, can — under the Constitution of the United States — protect this nation and preserve world civilization.

Hearing these words, Democrats and Republicans uncharacteristically rose to applaud Cannon. When the ovation subsided, Taber called Cannon's remarks "the most magnificent and courageous speech I have heard on this floor in many a day." The United States and the USSR had a right, he added, to "inspect and examine what the situation might be on the other side. When the leader of Russia refused us that right, the only method we had and the only chance we had was to get out and do just what was being done by this pilot. It was nothing, compared to the spy work that was carried on by the Russians — nothing at all." Such speeches and that of Lyndon Johnson that same day signified "a closing of congressional ranks in support of the administration's basic position on the U-2 incident," said the *New York Times.*[2]

Joseph Alsop equaled Cannon in his unabashed pleasure over U.S. capability to photograph the Soviet Union's military bases. Alsop titled his May 11 column, "The Wonderful News." He seemed unembarrassed by a revelation that signified to many that there was little or no missile gap: "The American government's national intelligence estimates of the Soviet military posture now have an entirely new look. For many years after the war, the estimates consistently erred on the optimistic side. . . . Those who remembered the past errors, like this reporter, were bound to suspect present errors. But the fate of the U-2 that fell near Sverdlovsk has broken a great, corrective secret." Eisenhower would have all the "power cards" at the Paris summit. Still, Alsop admired Dulles, the CIA, and "all the brave men" who flew before Powers, not the president. The "balance of terror," recently tilting toward the USSR, had been "shockingly neglected by the present administration."[3]

Almost half of the twenty-six citizens writing Chairman Cannon in the days following his speech criticized his U-2 cheerleading, though. A few treated him as a warmonger. One thought that the U-2 espionage was "the most provocative imaginable," adding, "I consider your speech neither magnificent, nor courageous. It strikes me as the same old unimaginative display of jingoism that has blighted so many statements from both sides during recent years." Other legislative defenders of the flights heard from the public; most were laudatory, but the critics were fierce. One acquaintance of Leverett Saltonstall wrote with such strong language that the Massachusetts senator rebuked him for becoming "emotionally aroused."

Some in the Congress, though, agreed with those angry citizens. On May 12, Representative Paul Jones (D-MO) sent Cannon and Dulles a copy of a speech he had prepared but did not deliver. In it, Jones argued that "many are ashamed that this administration, or at least someone in a very high position, felt compelled to resort to a lie in attempting to justify the presence of an American plane over the Soviet Union." Columnist Drew Pearson, admitting not to have known of the U-2, similarly wrote on May 11 that the CIA had once again "severely disrupted U.S. foreign relations. . . . We have two secretaries of state. One is the official Secretary of State, Christian Herter. The other is Allen Dulles, head of the Central Intelligence Agency." Unfortunately, he added, legislators treated the CIA as "sacrosanct." Eisenhower, if he had read Pearson's article, would have regarded it as predictably replete with errors and half-truths. Probably, the president had not seen it; he told reporters on the very day that Pearson's weekday column was published in the *Post* (in its usual place by the comics) that he only read Sunday papers and carefully studied their news analyses.[4]

Nonetheless, the column typified a growing belief that the president did not rule his own administration. That notion had to be squelched, Eisenhower thought. Also, Ike feared that critiques of the sort voiced by Congressman Jones to Cannon and Dulles had merit. Long before most legislators had heard of the U-2, the president had frequently worried aloud over the consequences for his and the nation's reputation for honesty and fair play if an aircraft were to be shot down over Soviet airspace. Early on in the U-2's existence, when it became clear that the Soviets could detect the flights, Eisenhower warned Dulles that he had "lost enthusiasm" for the program. Despite its great value in illuminating Soviet capabilities, the U-2 went against his desire to have the United States follow a "correct and moral" position. What if the American people learned of what was going on? "Soviet protests were one thing," Goodpaster recorded the president saying, but "any loss of confidence by our own people would be quite another."

After extended, gloomy reflection, Eisenhower decided that he must go public, ignore his own doubts about the four-year-old aerial espionage program, and defend it. This would be unprecedented: members of Congress had occasionally spoken in the House and Senate about American espionage — and Cannon had just celebrated it, gaining Eisenhower's admiration for "straight talk" and Dulles's pledge to circulate the speech text to "my people" — but no president had done so. Still, it was long-ingrained in Eisenhower to take responsibility for any important failure occurring on his watch.[5]

Eisenhower stepped before reporters in an Old Executive Office Building auditorium on Wednesday, May 11, one day after Cannon's speech. A *Post* reporter, one of 275 present, wrote that the president — "attired in a lightweight blue suit" — seemed "not greatly excited over the uproar in Moscow." With prepared notes in his hand and eyeglasses on, Eisenhower began his 185th presidential news conference by complimenting leaders of both parties for "statesmanlike remarks" and then giving "four main points" intended to "supplement" Herter's prior statements:

> The first point is this: the need for intelligence-gathering activities. No one wants another Pearl Harbor. This means that we must have knowledge of military forces and preparations around the world, especially those capable of massive surprise attacks. Secrecy in the Soviet Union makes this essential. . . . ever since the beginning of my administration, I have issued directives to gather, in every feasible way, the information required to protect the United States and the free world against surprise attack and to enable them to make effective preparations for defense.
>
> My second point: the nature of intelligence-gathering activities. These have a special and secret character. They are, so to speak, "below the surface" activities. They are secret because they must circumvent measures designed by other countries to protect secrecy of military preparations. These elements operate under broad directives to seek and gather intelligence, short of the use of force — with operations supervised by responsible officials within this area of secret activities. . . . Third point: how should we view all of this activity? It is a distasteful but vital necessity. We prefer and work for a different kind of world — and a different way of obtaining the information essential to confidence and effective deterrents. Open societies, in the day of present weapons, are the only answer. . . . My final point is that we must not be distracted from the real issues of the day by what is an incident or a symptom of the world situation today. This incident has been

given great propaganda exploitation. The emphasis given to a flight of an unarmed nonmilitary plane can only reflect a fetish of secrecy.

Eisenhower spoke truthfully in his first three points. As his many private comments indicated, though, he knew that the Soviet response to U-2 reflected more than just a "fetish for secrecy."

Though he insisted he would say nothing else in relation to U-2 that morning, Eisenhower's voice quickly rose, reacting to the Soviets' claim that the United States had acted provocatively: "They had better look at their own record. And I'll tell you this: the United States — and none of its allies that I know of — has engaged in nothing that would be considered honestly as provocative" as the spying on the United States by Rudolf Abel. America, by contrast, was using the U-2 merely in relation "to our own security and our defense." Despite his anger, Eisenhower told reporters that he still planned to travel to Paris for the summit meeting with Khrushchev and the heads of Britain and France.

Most citizens, editorialists, and members of Congress seemed satisfied with the president's analysis. He had been "valiant," thought editorialists at the *Times*. "Lucid," said the *Post*. True, the NASA cover story had made "a liar of the government. It does not follow, however, that all covers are inept or that the Central Intelligence Agency on this account needs overhauling. Indeed, we think that the restraint shown by congressional leaders in the face of cries for 'investigation' is altogether wise." Stuart Symington, Eisenhower's bane, wished out loud for "a president eager to shoulder the full responsibilities of the office," even as he pledged to stand behind Eisenhower. "It is very important to try to find out everything we can about what's going on behind the Iron Curtain," he added, as he also praised Dulles to the hilt. Still, one lonely House member suggested that the "topmost leadership" of the United States should "thank God that the world is not in ashes today."[6]

What of Cannon's claim that a handful of legislators on the Appropriations' CIA subcommittee held some responsibility for the creation and usage of U-2s — that the program was the agency's "answer to that demand" by Cannon and colleagues that the United States be protected from future surprise wars? Did Cannon's repeated warnings following the Korean surprise of 1950— "this must not happen again, and it is up to you to see that it does not happen again" — play a role in the American government's dramatic, innovative, and risky aerial espionage policy of that era? No doubt, some historians and partisans of the CIA or Eisenhower would ridicule such a claim. Even many respected analysts have written about U.S. foreign policy — in intelligence and in other areas — as simply a product of the executive. Michael Beschloss's admirable U-2 history only mentions Cannon once, in the often-repeated story of the chairman asking Dulles, "Are you sure you have enough money?" The neglect of Congress occurs, in part, because the executive branch is far more conveniently researched and chronicled, given the ease of keeping track of a president and advisers versus researching scores of relevant legislators.

Cannon, like other overseers of the CIA in that era, is often remembered fondly but patronizingly by CIA counterparts decades later. The agency's first legislative liaison, Walter Pforzheimer, recalled in the 1990s, "I used to laugh, because it was like a ritual every year when Cannon's first question always was, 'How did you people miss out on the Korean War?' " Some writers treat Cannon as essentially an old fool who was (in the words of authors David Wise and Thomas Ross) "such a good friend and great admirer of Allen Dulles that much of the secret CIA hearings during Dulles' tenure were taken up with mutual congratulations." Since members of Congress sometimes gave speeches more-or-less authored by agency personnel, some even wondered if the CIA did so for the octogenarian chairman.[7]

Others, including Dulles and former inspector general Lyman Kirkpatrick, would later describe Cannon as supportive but formidable, and not to be crossed under any circumstances. Cannon "seemed to feel a proprietary interest in the organization throughout his life," wrote Kirkpatrick. "A more careful watchdog of the public treasury can hardly be found," Dulles claimed. Deference went both ways between CIA and congressional barons, he suggested. About Cannon's U-2 speech, itself, Deputy Director Charles P. Cabell was later adamant: "This came as a surprise to us, as it did to his staff, for he had done his own research and prepared his own speech." Cabell added that the Appropriations chair was "most knowledgeable" on intelligence and "would grill us unmercifully over items which he did not completely understand or accept."

Nor can it be doubted that Cannon meant what he said in his landmark U-2 speech. The following day, just to reinforce his points, Cannon went to the humble Washington work space of Hearst newspapers' reporter Ed Edstrom. The journalist was startled as the "venerated Appropriations chairman pounded the desk of this reporter with an angry vigor that belied his

81 years." To demonstrate his subcommittee's knowledge of state secrets, Cannon "said the last report on the flights of U-2 planes was made six weeks ago." (About this, Cannon was apparently truthful — Dulles and Bissell had gone before an Appropriations CIA subcommittee hearing on March 28.) American "espionage holds surprises that would amaze Premier Khrushchev, if he knew about them," Cannon added.[8] Dulles noted of a May 16 private session, in which a "keen" Appropriations leader further questioned the DCI about aspects of Powers's flight, "He did rather wistfully indicate that he felt a little let down at the President's statement that these flights would be discontinued." The chairman added that "it was necessary to continue to gather intelligence by available means, with which I thoroughly agreed."

This takes us back to the question of why the CIA developed and flew U-2s over the USSR for four years. Early in his tenure, DCI Dulles was unenthusiastic about his agency taking on the U-2 project. When Edwin Land, head of an intelligence study group, went to Dulles in late October 1954 with a proposal for what later became the U-2 aircraft and program, he ran into resistance. In-house CIA historians wrote: "The DCI strongly believed that the Agency's mission lay in the use of human operatives and secret communications, the classic forms of intelligence gathering. Land came away from this meeting with the impression that Dulles somehow thought overflights were not fair play."

Dulles's standoffishness was striking, considering that Land's group was specifically confident that the proposed project could "find and photograph the Soviet Union's Bison bomber fleet and, thus, resolve the growing 'bomber gap' controversy" brewing on Capitol Hill. Land and colleagues took the U-2 idea to the president, who doubted that the military should run such an operation, so gave an initial go-ahead, directing that it be run "in an unconventional way." Land then wrote Dulles, "This activity is appropriate for CIA, always with Air Force assistance. . . . You must always assert your first right to pioneer in scientific techniques for collecting intelligence — and choosing such partners to assist you as may be needed."

Historians have not closely examined the early-to-mid-1950s domestic political environment — Congress especially — that would have further enthused the president about U-2 and brought Dulles around. There on Capitol Hill, Cannon was hardly alone in admonishing the CIA and others in the administration to prevent surprise attacks. One of many was Californian William Knowland, the Senate Republican leader through 1958 and an outspoken, conservative anticommunist thorn in the president's side.

Knowland has had the misfortune to be remembered in history as the man about whom Eisenhower said there was no final answer to the question, "How stupid can you get?" At the very same time that U-2 was emerging as an option, Knowland had criticized the administration for being ready to do "nothing more than merely send notes to Moscow" after the USSR shot down a U.S. B-29 aircraft that had crossed its border. The flight's path had been intentional, to examine Soviet war fighting abilities, but Eisenhower was unwilling to reveal that to Knowland or the public. "You apparently think we are just sitting supinely," Eisenhower admonished the senator in a White House meeting. "There is a very great aggressiveness on our side that you have not known about," Eisenhower explained, "and I guess this is on the theory of 'Why put burdens on people that they don't need to worry about and therefore make them fearful that they might give away something?'" It enraged the president in 1954 and later that Knowland and some other legislators lacked most citizens' confidence that Eisenhower would always put national security ahead of every other concern.

Cannon's critiques, more than Knowland's, were usually offered in discreet settings. While records that might support or demolish the Appropriations chair's claim that some in Congress helped father U-2 are insufficient or not yet declassified, it should not be dismissed out of hand.[9]

"My Opinion of the CIA Went Skyrocketing"

A day after Cannon's speech, Paul Kilday — who had attended the senior legislators' briefing and was telephoned by Dulles — chaired a secret House Armed Services subcommittee hearing featuring the DCI, Lundahl, and others. No record of the event has surfaced, but it appears that this was the first time the full subcommittee had been told about U-2. (Carl Vinson and his senior Republican colleague on Armed Services, Les Arends, may well have been told of the U-2 by Dulles in a December 1957 meeting. It is entirely likely that Kilday learned of U-2 well before May 1960, though documentary evidence is lacking.) Months later, Kilday wrote Lyndon Johnson: "The subcommittee, in closed session, examined all phases of the incident. It would hardly be possible to overemphasize the value to the United States of the U-2 flights over Russia. . . . The difficulty lies in the fact that President Eisenhower, Secretary Herter, and others participating 'panicked.' . . . Thereafter, the President admitted fully the responsibility of our government for the entire program. This was a colossal blunder." In his long indictment of the administration's "stumbling, blundering, and hesitant conduct of foreign affairs," Kilday never criticized the CIA or Dulles.[1]

Less than a week after the Kilday hearing, Senator Thomas Kuchel (R-CA) would pronounce May 16 "a sad day in this melancholy world." On that day, Eisenhower met his British, French, and Soviet peers in Paris, and Khrushchev's speeches made it obvious that he would want an apology from Eisenhower. The Soviet leader was angry, too, that Vice President Nixon had said that "such activities" as U-2 flights "may have to continue in the future."

Interacting with U.S. leaders in Paris, British prime minister Harold Macmillan thought they "were in considerable disarray." In advance of the four leaders' meeting, he worked to persuade Eisenhower to state that U-2 flights would not resume. Though open to this, the president also warned French president Charles de Gaulle that he would not "crawl on my knees to Khrushchev." When de Gaulle told Eisenhower of Khrushchev's threat "to deal shattering blows" against nations that might permit basing of U-2s in the future, Eisenhower responded, "Bombs can travel in two directions." The American president's anger about "this goddamned plane" was directed not only at

Khrushchev. He confidentially told Herter and a few others in Paris that intelligence leaders in his administration "had failed to recognize the emotional, even pathological, reaction of the Russians regarding their frontier."[2]

The summit opened disastrously: Khrushchev castigated the U-2 program as the product of "a small, frantic group in the Pentagon and militarist circles" and told Eisenhower that the Soviet people would not be able to receive him with "proper cordiality," thus effectively disinviting him for a scheduled visit. Further, the premier insisted that Eisenhower explain the policy "that such acts" as U-2 flights would continue. The president — livid but displaying a calm exterior — then read a prepared statement precluding future flights over the USSR during his presidency. Still, Eisenhower followed through on his determination not to apologize. Khrushchev — as unrestrained in volume and language as Eisenhower was the opposite — finally said to the president, "We don't understand what devil pushed you into doing this provocative act to us just before the conference."

Without an agreement on the apology issue, the conference was doomed. Eisenhower was so livid for the rest of the day that his son John and members of his administration would remember for years his tirades against the "son of a bitch" Khrushchev. After Eisenhower invited the State Department's Livingston Merchant for a stroll outside his temporary residence in Paris that evening, the diplomat was shaken by Eisenhower's mood. Merchant's account, given to Dulles, was that Eisenhower said "something like . . . if it were not for my responsibility to posterity, I would be ready to have the showdown right now — i.e., launch the nuclear attack."

Eisenhower might have felt better had he known how overwhelmingly complimentary most members of Congress were over the past few days, both of his efforts toward resolving the crisis and his refusal to apologize for the U-2 flights. In the Senate, where news arrived quickly on May 16 of the disintegrating summit conference, Democrat Albert Gore said, "The American people can trust President Eisenhower to react as the gentleman that he is." Kenneth Keating mocked the Soviet leader: "I suppose Khrushchev expects Congress to impeach the President of the United States and sentence Allen Dulles to 20 years at hard labor." Less loftily, Pennsylvania Republican senator Hugh Scott, observed, "This is not a time in our country for sissies or pantywaists or timid apologists." Most of the press agreed. A *New York Times* editorial said, "Let us have done with the whimpering about espionage being a departure 'from the code of responsible international behavior.'"[3]

The next day, though, Senate majority whip Mansfield made it clear that once the Paris conference was history and Eisenhower was respectfully and warmly welcomed back to the United States, hard questions would be asked. "The blunders" of the U-2 incident and its handling "are for this nation to face. Responsibility for dealing with them rests, not with Mr. Khrushchev, but with the politically responsible President, with the politically responsible Congress, and with the American people who hold both accountable." Senator George Aiken spoke for many Republicans, though: "Leave it to history and future revelation to fix the responsibility for this failure."

A huge crowd greeted Eisenhower when he arrived at Andrews Air Force Base on the afternoon of May 20. Tens of thousands more cheered him during the ride to the White House. It crossed the mind of Senator Stephen Young (D-OH) that administration leaders with U-2 responsibilities "should have been seated in automobile directly following that of the President. . . . it would have been appropriate to have draped that automobile in mourning."[4]

Hours later, comfortably ensconced in his living quarters, Eisenhower received Henry Cabot Lodge, the ambassador to the United Nations, for a long talk. The president said nothing to indicate that he had come to believe that his son, John, was correct in placing the blame for the U-2 fiasco on Dulles, and that the DCI should be fired. But Eisenhower did remark "that the administration and training of some of our intelligence units were weak." By the way, the president added, Lodge might want to "hint" to the U.N. that the United States now had better "methods" than the U-2.[5]

On the evening of Wednesday, May 25, Eisenhower spoke by television to the nation. Taking "full responsibility for approving all the various programs undertaken by our government to secure and evaluate military intelligence," he also raised a question for Khrushchev: "Why all the furor concerning one particular flight?" The president even showed a U-2 photograph, impressive in its detail, of a California naval station, and assured viewers that, although he had stopped aircraft flights over the USSR, "new techniques, other than aircraft, are constantly being developed."

That theme had parallels in congressional speeches that week. Congressman Paul Dague (R-PA) had already announced "that, in a few short months, we will have in orbit observer satellites that can collect all the information to be gleaned by a U-2 plane." Any complaints would be "academic, in light of the Russian space vehicle presently passing over most of the countries of the world every 90 minutes."

The U-2 crisis also spilled over into the ongoing presidential campaign, far enough along that John F. Kennedy and Richard Nixon were clear frontrunners for the Democratic and Republican nominations. On the Democratic side, Senators Johnson and Symington, along with former presidential candidate Adlai Stevenson, hoped that the controversy would demonstrate the need for maturity in a possible Democratic presidency. As Theodore White wrote, "From his offices of Majority Leader of the United States Senate, Lyndon B. Johnson watched the unfolding events of May and June like a man trapped. He, like Stevenson, enjoyed an instant appreciation in political weight as the world events, beginning with the collapse of the summit, made the youthful Kennedy seem ever more like a boy." But on the night of May 10, hours before Eisenhower's press conference on the U-2, the Catholic Kennedy was the surprise winner in heavily Protestant West Virginia's primary over Hubert Humphrey, and all seemed well for his campaign. Just hitting his stride, and soon to celebrate his forty-third birthday, Kennedy then created his own U-2 crisis.

He campaigned on May 18 in Oregon, where Symington and Johnson were on the ballot but not campaigning and native-son Wayne Morse was determinedly fighting Kennedy, as he had (unsuccessfully) in the Maryland primary days before. At a high school in the town of St. Helens, Kennedy arrived too late for a breakfast event but spoke to a gathering of excited students and others. Some students wanted to talk about U-2 and the disintegrating Paris summit. Kennedy told them that the timing of Powers's flight was not "defensible" and suggested that Khrushchev would not have broken off the summit if there had not been a U-2 crisis. A young woman then asked the senator what he would have done in Paris as president. Kennedy noted that Khrushchev "said there were two conditions for continuing." One of them Kennedy rejected: putting those responsible for the flight on trial. Of the other condition, "that we apologize," Kennedy said, "I think that that might have been possible to do." He quickly substituted other wording, though: If Khrushchev "had merely asked that the United States should express regret then that would have been a reasonable term. . . . I would express regret that the flight did take place."

A news story in the next day's *Portland Oregonian* began, "If Senator John F. Kennedy of Massachusetts were President, he might apologize to Soviet Premier Khrushchev for the U-2 spy incident." Coming at a time when newspaper, radio, and television reports around the nation were full of the rupturing summit in Paris, however, Kennedy's remarks gained little notice initially. But by the following Monday morning, news of Kennedy's words reached Republicans in the Senate. Their leader, Illinois' Everett Dirksen, in a deeply resonant voice, slowly repeated Kennedy's statement, then — to "let this amazing statement speak for itself" — placed the *Oregonian* article in the *Congressional Record*. Dirksen's greatest ire, though, was for Stevenson, whom he thought had suggested a dangerously "soft" approach for the United States at the Paris summit in a recent interview.

Minority whip Hugh Scott, former chairman of the Republican Party, took to the floor that morning without alerting Kennedy's office — the candidate was to return later in the day — and attacked both Democrats: "It is my hope that neither the distinguished Senator from Massachusetts nor that other candidate . . . will, either one of them, brand himself as a 'turnquote.' It is my hope that they will relieve themselves of the curse of suspicion of appeasement." Just fifteen years after World War II and not even a decade after McCarthyism had peaked, "suspicion of appeasement" and any variation on "turncoat" were fighting words. Supporters of Kennedy were furious. Many mistakenly believed that the candidate had not even uttered the word, "apology." The normally mild-mannered Mike Mansfield actually began shouting on the Senate floor: "The idea of calling these men appeasers!" Both men had records of wartime military service, Mansfield reminded Scott, who was "doing a disservice to the country when he puts words in the mouths of Stevenson and Kennedy which were never uttered." Scott was unyielding: "If they are appeasers, let the record speak for itself."

A *Times* reporter described "angry Republicans and Democrats popping up on both sides of the aisle in an effort to get into the fight." The administration's handling of U-2 had been "muddleheaded, mentally inert, and inept," said Stephen Young, adding that Eisenhower operated "the presidency on a part-time basis." Republican John Butler (MD) seemed never to have heard of the oversight concept: "Does the legislative branch have the authority to investigate the executive? I think not." Morse, having survived Kennedy's Oregon primary triumph in feisty spirits, said Congress should recognize that the U-2 flight was "aggression," rather than "wave the American flag into tatters over it." Senator John Carroll (D-CO) voiced a suspicion that would remain alive for decades in some quarters, despite a dearth of evidence: "Was there someone in the Central Intelligence Agency who wished to torpedo the conference?"

Lyndon Johnson, increasingly pursuing the Democratic presidential nomination, was absent early that day, and Mansfield had already lost his temper, so other elders tried to calm the storm. Republican George Aiken said, "We have gone too far not to have a discreet, judicious, and careful inquiry," but "if we shoot off any more fireworks around here, we will not have any left for the Fourth of July." J. William Fulbright, planning to propose just such a U-2 "inquiry" to his Foreign Relations Committee the next day, came onto the floor after the raucous dispute erupted: "I think we ought to be careful in what we say, and ought not to inflame anyone's thoughts."

Reporters asked Scott later in the day if he was calling Kennedy and Stevenson appeasers. He insisted that he had not. But the Associated Press reported that Scott thought both Democrats should be called before some "investigating committee to testify on their views." Speechmaking took on its normal, dull routine on the floor for some hours. Kennedy returned by midafternoon, as did Johnson. He and Richard Russell talked agriculture, ignoring the bloodletting that preceded their public dialogue. Off the floor, Kennedy and Scott spoke, the details seemingly undocumented, but the Pennsylvanian provided his own notes of his earlier remarks to Kennedy. Eventually, well after four o'clock, Kennedy addressed the Senate. "I note that the Senator from Pennsylvania and the Senator from Illinois are in the chamber." Eyeing Scott, Kennedy continued, "I will ask the Senator if he believes that I am under suspicion of appeasement?" "On the contrary," said Scott, "I suggested that the Senator from Massachusetts may relieve himself—and I made the suggestion in good will—of the suspicion of appeasement. . . . In my opinion, it would be appeasement to have the President apologize."

Someone at St. Helens High School had recorded the candidate's speech, so Kennedy did not deny using the word "apologize." He claimed, though, "No one deduced from my answer that I wanted the President to apologize to Khrushchev." Obviously, the reporter for the *Oregonian* did make that deduction, so Scott would not absolve Kennedy. However, "if the Senator from Massachusetts feels that he had no intention to appease by making the statement, I will accept the Senator's version as my own." Kennedy responded, "I accept the Senator's somewhat grudging response." It was "not grudging at all," said Scott, who would soon be portrayed by the *Post* cartoonist Herblock as receiving guidance from the ghost of Joe McCarthy. Everett Dirksen also castigated Kennedy's Oregon remarks, but when a Democrat tried to associate him with that day's "chicanery," Dirksen replied, "I love the Senator from Massachusetts too much to do that under any circumstances." The Illinois senator smiled at Kennedy and pledged, "If I say anything about him, it will be only to toss him a dainty bouquet."[6]

The exchange left some people unsatisfied in and out of the Senate. "Let us not fall under the spell of our American Hamlets," said Barry Goldwater

(R-AZ). The campaigning Kennedy soon encountered "a teen-aged girl with a Kennedy-for-President placard and a perplexed expression on her face. 'Why,' she asked, 'did you say that President Eisenhower should apologize to Khrushchev?'" Eisenhower never commented publicly on Kennedy's statement. Privately, he thought the senator had "some intelligence" but lacked the "judgment" required for the presidency.

Lyndon Johnson tried to take advantage of such critical sentiment. By now seeking delegates for the presidential nomination, though still an unannounced candidate, Johnson asked audiences in a number of western states, "Would you apologize to Khrushchev?" Predictably, the loud response was, "No!" But Johnson's campaign against a clear front-runner did not excite many reporters or citizens. Because Kennedy, widely popular with reporters, had stepped back from his apology idea, coverage concerning his Oregon remarks quickly diminished.[7]

Another event that moved the Kennedy story out of the news was publicity about a possible hearing by the Senate Foreign Relations Committee. Eisenhower was dubious about the prospect. Only by the morning of May 24, when the Kennedy-Scott debate and other congressional speeches were in the newspapers, had Eisenhower accepted that hearings and some level of White House cooperation were inevitable. Shortly before an NSC meeting, Gordon Gray recorded Eisenhower as saying that "he felt he would have to amend his earlier directive about no conversations about the U-2." Gray agreed: "I said it appeared to me that there was no longer any hope that congressional committees could be restrained from conducting investigations of the U-2/summit matter."[8]

Given that an "investigation could not be stopped," Eisenhower told the NSC, testimony about U-2 before Fulbright's or anyone else's committee should "include information which the USSR is presumed to know," "should not jeopardize any other intelligence sources or methods," and should "not be expansive as to details or other intelligence activities." There should be "no apologies" and no implication that "any other nations were involved in this U-2 activity." Finally, "while making clear that the basic decision regarding the U-2 program was made by the President, the impression should not be given that the President approved specific flights, their precise missions, or their timing." With this guideline, Eisenhower required his people to understate, to the point of dishonesty, his knowledge of U-2 missions. The president also showed some pique toward Dulles at the NSC meeting because Powers "had a flight plan with him when he landed" and "started talking as soon as he touched the ground." But the director told the president and NSC that "a flight plan was, of course, necessary to the operation" and that each U-2 pilot had been instructed, in the event of capture, to "reveal whatever he himself knew, including the fact that he worked for CIA."

Once Eisenhower agreed to the hearing, it was all the easier for Republicans on the committee to assent, agreeing unanimously with Democrats at "a very peaceful meeting" to seek administration testimony. Not all thought that the director of central intelligence should be among those invited, but Fulbright insisted and noted that such testimony had become routine for the committee following significant international events in recent years. At the CIA, Dulles's assistants prepared him as never before for a Foreign Relations' appearance, profiling the committee's members (Lausche was "miffed," Morse "extremely critical," Gore "hangs on like a rat terrier").[9]

On May 25, the House Foreign Affairs Committee also requested Dulles's presence for a hearing on June 1, the day after Fulbright's hearing. This, too, was accepted, and agency personnel prepared profiles for Dulles of that committee's members, including William Meyer (D-VT), who had asserted "a constitutional right to know details" about CIA and U-2.

Eisenhower invited congressional leaders to breakfast prior to the closed but much-publicized hearings. On May 26, they joined him and Secretaries Herter and Gates (but not Dulles) in the State Dining Room of the White House. Despite much talk in the nation's capital and the press that Eisenhower was a part-time president, he was very much at the center of the dialogue that morning. While he had already warned Dulles, Herter, and others not to mention any allied nation's involvement in U-2 at the pending hearings, the president led a discussion about the longtime willingness of leaders in Pakistan, Norway, and other nations to allow basing of U-2s. Styles Bridges was annoyed that such leaders had publicly disavowed and denied knowledge of the spy flights, but Eisenhower assured him that they were "fine" allies and Herter added that their governments were merely going through the motions of disavowal.

Eisenhower claimed to "heartily approve" of the Senate hearings opening the next day with Herter's appearance but insisted to the legislators that the decision to use U-2s, going back almost four years, had been his alone. He worried (James Hagerty noted) "that the members of Congress, in conducting the inquiry, would try to dig into the interior of the CIA and its covert operations." Eisenhower repeatedly used the word "investigation," leading Mansfield to assure the president that "an investigation in the ugly sense of the word" would not occur. Fulbright agreed, but both senators made use of this rare chance for dialogue with the president about intelligence.

Mansfield "wanted to ask one question: what would the President think if there were to be established in the Congress a joint congressional committee which would oversee activities of the CIA." Politely, but firmly, Eisenhower noted the "delicate and so secret" duties of the CIA that required it to be "kept under cover." Less tactful in addressing Mansfield was Richard Russell, who reminded those present that he had known of the U-2s for a long time and warned that (as Hagerty recorded) "any leaks of this nature from the staff would endanger the lives of men going into Russia and that he did not want it on his conscience." Carl Vinson also expressed "complete disagreement with Senator Mansfield," as did Hayden.

Then Fulbright spoke up. According to a pair of knowledgeable journalists, the Foreign Relations chair was, at the time, "distant, at times moody, pessimistic, and frustrated by his lack of influence." The senator had occasionally been at the White House for consultations, though, and had even been invited by Herter to join the Paris summit before it broke up. Now Fulbright asked "whether it was wise for the President to take responsibility for the U-2 flights. He said that he, himself, thought that disavowal would probably have been better."

> The President [Hagerty wrote] said that when the plane was first missing, no one knew what had happened. It had been thought that if the plane got into trouble it would be destroyed, all material on board would be destroyed, and that the pilot would be free of any such material. On this assumption, the story of a weather plane would have been able to stick. But, he added, the assumptions were incorrect. Within a few days, the balloon was up.
>
> Senator Fulbright said that he still didn't think it was wise to take full responsibility.

Somewhere during this exchange, Eisenhower lost his famous geniality and matched Fulbright's sour directness: "Look, Senator, this is modern-day espionage. In the old days, I could send you out or send a spy out and if he was caught, disavow him. But what do you do when you strap an American-made plane to his back?" Hagerty's notes had the president asserting a bottom line: "If he didn't take responsibility, someone else would have had to. He said he agreed that Khrushchev had tried to give him an out on this, but that he looked upon it as his responsibility. . . . Anyone sitting in his chair wouldn't want to put the CIA on the spot, and would not want to disown the CIA."

Just as Hagerty finished making notes of the president's response to Fulbright, Vinson leaned over to him and whispered that Eisenhower was "dead right," that Fulbright was "all wrong." You could count on Ike to take responsibility, Vinson added, "that's the kind of man he is, anyway."

None of the Hill leaders present took Fulbright's side or disagreed so sharply with the president that morning. Lyndon Johnson, though, posed a question that millions wondered about — why weren't U-2 flights stopped well before the summit? The previous flights had been successful, Ike responded. Powers's flight had to "take advantage of the weather to get the needed information that would not be available later on, and the decision was to go ahead. It was just bad luck that the flight had failed."

Toward the end, Eisenhower showed more of his sunny side, joking that the only way he could be punished for the U-2 failure was by way of impeachment. "You haven't got long enough to go for that," Sam Rayburn responded, also in good humor. Besides, the Speaker added seriously, "We are all in this together." Later in the day, the president couldn't help but gloat to his cabinet about "Mr. Fulbright's unsupported position in the morning discussion."[10]

On the same day that Ike reached an understanding with legislators about the upcoming Foreign Relations hearing, Dulles and five other agency leaders went before Cannon and Mahon's House Appropriations CIA subcommittee to discuss U-2 and a project code-named "Isolation." Details about the hearing have never surfaced, but the Powers incident seems to have put Mahon in a reflective state of mind. "The cat is fairly well out of the bag," he wrote a friend back in Texas. He and a "few" others had "known for years a great deal about this operation. . . . Those of us in Congress who work with the CIA and with the military have never discouraged the overflight programs. We have felt that these operations were appropriate, under the circumstances. I do think the overflights should have been suspended for quite some time prior to the . . . summit conference."

Mahon's Republican colleague on the CIA subcommittee, Gerald Ford, had already told his constituents in a newsletter, "Because this business inevitably involves deceit, misrepresentation, falsehood, intrigue, and every devious avenue of approach, public officials may not jeopardize the national security by publicizing the true facts . . . but when a given situation (no matter how embarrassing) becomes public knowledge, we commend a frank and honest disclosure."[11]

Also prior to Dulles's May 31 appearance before Fulbright's committee, State Department leaders testified there for a few days. During a public portion of one early session, the chairman illuminated his position on covert action and espionage, telling Herter that all nations in history had engaged in the "black arts of intelligence operations . . . lying, cheating, murder, stealing, seduction, and suicide . . . not because they want to, not because they believe these acts are moral, but because they believe such activities are essential to their own self-preservation." No one from State matched Fulbright's frankness about such moral horrors.

CIA's Richard Helms observed it all. The deputy director for plans thought Herter had been ineffectual and ill-informed in his testimony and suggested to Dulles, "You should go over to the attack and answer in your initial statement as many of the outstanding questions as you possibly can." Senator Gore "was a bloodhound" with Herter on the question, "Who had the final say?" The secretary of state "stuck to the point that his role was advisory, and told the senators that they would have to ask you about the point of final authority." Contrary to Eisenhower's guidance, Helms suggested, "The less you have to take cover on grounds of security, the better."

Before the DCI showed up at the New Senate Office Building (costing the fantastic sum of $27 million), its fourth floor hearing room had been "swept" for listening devices, blankets were again hung over its doors to lessen the chance of sound escaping, and (as *Time* reported) "an electric Shredmaster waited to chew secret papers into meaningless pablum," as necessary.[12]

Reporters crowded the corridor outside the room prior to Dulles's arrival. The DCI — accompanied by Deputy Director Cabell, Helms, and others — hoped that what he and others said might be kept secret, for the committee promised to release nothing from the planned all-day hearing without his permission. Dulles's long opening statement had been carefully reviewed and edited by Goodpaster at the White House to enhance its ambiguity as to Eisenhower's knowledge of individual U-2 flights. The presentation covered what was, to anyone reading substantive newspapers, detailed but familiar material on the history and purposes of U-2, Powers's background, and what was known of the shoot down. He closed by anticipating Fulbright's line of questioning: Eisenhower's "decision taken to assume responsibility in this particular case was the correct one," Dulles claimed, although he admitted that he had been ready "to assume the full measure of responsibility."

The chairman would use his prerogative to engage the DCI in far more dialogue than other senators. (Not all members were present: Kennedy attended to his campaign that day, and Morse was absent, simplifying Dulles's life.) Fulbright prefaced his questions with compliments: "I have heard nothing but praise with regard to your part in this whole matter, and particularly the effectiveness of the U-2 program. . . . What I regret more than anything else is that we seem to have finally gotten ourselves into a position where we are committed as a country not to do it any more."

The chairman also reminded Dulles, "I don't know how much money you get. I don't know how many employees you have. I know very little, except what you have told us in the briefings, and I have taken the position it wasn't my responsibility to do it, and it was perfectly proper." Of Fulbright's one big objection — against Eisenhower's taking responsibility for U-2 flights over the USSR — Dulles could not persuade him that the president had acted appropriately, but he reassured the committee that U-2 would probably not "be a precedent. . . . I would not expect that the high authority would assume responsibility in the ordinary type of clandestine operations."

More effectively than Fulbright, Frank Lausche explored with the DCI how many other current "operations in which you are indulging" had the same level of hazard "as the one we are discussing." There were "some" that were "equally hazardous," Dulles revealed, but only "one or two" had the sort of "broad political implications that I think questions would be raised, if it were done without the President's knowledge." Most covert operations were "readily deniable. You lose an agent, this or that, you deny it." To Russell Long, who asked if "some of our agents have been caught before," Dulles said, "Oh, yes." "Did we uniformly deny all those instances?" Long wondered. "Always, certainly," the DCI assured him. This seemingly eased senators' concerns over presidents potentially being "required to lie" very often about clandestine work.

Few legislators in this or other sessions had the illusion that they learned comprehensively about the CIA. As an aide to Lyndon Johnson noted months later, "Now, as in the past, the briefers have been frank enough, if proper questions have been asked, but have seldom volunteered information." In many respects, though, Dulles leveled with senators, not pushing the White House/State Department line that there had been "occasional" penetrations of the USSR by U-2s. On the contrary, there had been "a very considerable number" over the years, he told Homer Capehart, who did not insist on knowing the exact number. With Lausche, Dulles had a blunt, if perhaps confused, exchange about the law:

Senator Lausche: Has it ever been suggested to you that, in acquiring intelligence, you must comply with international law?

Mr. Dulles: No, sir. Or domestic law, for that matter.

Senator Lausche: What if I were to introduce a bill saying that you were not to operate except in conformity with Federal law and international law in the acquisition of knowledge? That is a rhetorical and an oratorical question.

Mr. Dulles: Do I have to answer that, sir?

Senator Lausche: No, I think it answers itself.

Dulles presumably had in mind domestic laws of other countries, but he did not say so.

And he essentially refused, with elaborate politeness, to answer a central question from Capehart and Gore: what was Powers's flight, scheduled so close to the Paris summit, trying to detect? The DCI had already described the mission as related to "capability for surprise attack." Trying to be obvious that missile sites were the objects of concern, without violating Eisenhower's testimony guidelines, he said, "I think I can go this far. . . . it is very much easier to get definite information on certain things during the period of construction, rather than after they have been constructed and camouflaged and protected." Gore thought U-2 had been a "marvelously successful" program but took Dulles's remark as a rebuff. It was the first question "I have ever asked you, to which you did not supply a satisfactory answer. . . . It seems to me that either the members of this committee or the chairman are entitled to this information."

Dulles also would not answer Fulbright's question, "Have you made similar overflights of China?" Fulbright did not insist on an answer, which would have been "yes," since the question violated the hearing's ground rules by getting away from the Powers incident and the summit. Nor did Fulbright criticize Dulles for asking that another question — about Pakistan's knowledge of the intelligence nature of U-2 flights originating in that country — "not be pressed." But it was the refusal to explain fully the purpose of Powers's mission that would grate on some committee members for years to come. Still, the May 31 hearing ended at 5:10 p.m. without any real criticism of the CIA voiced. "You have carried out your responsibility in the U-2 incident very effectively," Fulbright said.[13]

The senator seemed to accept fully a familiar Dulles claim, telling reporters afterward that the CIA should not be held responsible for U-2 flight decisions because Dulles "does not pass on the wisdom of policy but confines himself to the furnishing of information." To a reporter inquiring about the special treatment accorded the CIA by Congress, Fulbright said, "It's very wise." Dulles could not have hoped for more from Fulbright, or for a better lead headline in the next day's *Times*: "Fulbright Holds CIA Blameless for U-2 Incident." This led Eisenhower's national security adviser, Gordon Gray, to tell a colleague that the committee was "after the President."

On June 1, Dulles went before the House Foreign Affairs Committee, chaired by Thomas Morgan (D-PA), which had rarely heard from the DCI during the Eisenhower presidency. "What you hear today is for your ears and your ears alone," Morgan told committee members. Dulles then repeated the briefing he had given Foreign Relations, with accompanying testimony and photographs analyzed by Lundahl. Some members known for skepticism toward the agency were supportive that day — Edna Kelly told Dulles, "No matter what happens, I am in complete accord on spying on the enemy under all conditions, and I hope we continue it to whatever degree is necessary." Representative Marguerite Church (R-IL) said, "I am getting in my mail the most tremendous expression of almost national pride that we were able to do it, aside from any ethical questions involved." They did not know, of course, that Dulles more-or-less lied (as other administration figures had) about the president's role in authorizing the May 1 flight. "The final decision was left to us in CIA," Dulles told Church.

Lundahl's late-morning photographic presentation was "extraordinary," said one member. It gave another member "a great, heartening sense of security." Of Eisenhower's decision to cancel further U-2 flights over the USSR, Representative Stuyvesant Wainwright (R-NY) told the DCI during afternoon testimony, "I am surprised that we cancelled them after the wonderful information we had this morning."

Few Foreign Affairs members criticized Dulles that morning, but he faced heavy skepticism in the afternoon. Representative Leonard Farbstein (D-NY) pressed the DCI repeatedly on the political folly of sending a spy flight across the USSR shortly before the planned summit. Since Dulles inaccurately claimed responsibility for authorizing the Powers's flight, he manufactured an explanation: "It wasn't considered from the political angle." Farbstein was amazed: "Don't you think it is a bit of a weakness to allow a flight to be made without a political evaluation being made at such a critical period in political history of the world?" Dulles's testimony would fuel speculation in some quarters, said Representative William Meyer, that "this may have been used as a device to break up the summit." Dulles recoiled at the thought, insisted that no one "could have gotten into my organization and fouled that thing up in that way." Meyer was unsatisfied: if the U-2 incident had not occurred, Eisenhower's trip to Paris to meet Khrushchev might have been "*the* trip" to revolutionize U.S.-Soviet relations. Dulles doubted it: even without the U-2 affair, "the prospects of achieving results over Berlin were very slim."

About the president's eventual admission that he authorized the U-2 program, Dulles said that the publicity surrounding Powers's shoot down had made it appropriate. Still, "I don't think the President should be drawn into the ordinary espionage situation. In fact, I would not think of going to consult the President as to whether I could send an agent to either X, Y, or Z." Most operations are "disavowable. You send in an agent. You have an operation of this or that kind. Disavow it, forget it. The President doesn't have to know anything about it."[14]

Senator Fulbright, unlike the House's Morgan, planned to issue a public committee report on U-2 and the failed summit. He tried to craft one that all Foreign Relations members could endorse. The job took three weeks, with highly publicized results that were, as the chairman noted, "probably not wholly satisfactory to any member of the committee." The title of Senate Report No. 1761, *Events Relating to the Summit Conference, Together With Individual Views,* gave away the fact that Fulbright failed to achieve a consensus. In the report, issued on June 25, twelve of the committee's fifteen members said of Powers's mission that there was "good reason to conclude that the flight should not have gone." Probably, they believed, the summit would have occurred had there been no U-2 incident, though Khrushchev might well have found other reasons to avoid constructive talks at Paris. Without quite saying that Eisenhower was wrong to have taken responsibility for the U-2 flight, the committee found his action "unprecedented" and approvingly noted Dulles's offer to take responsibility. Otherwise, the report hardly mentioned the Central Intelligence Agency.

The committee found that coordination of the cover stories issued after the shoot down clearly "broke down" and expressed "disappointment" that the administration would not disclose the "very special" goal of Powers's flight that justified its hazardous timing just before the summit. "A government based on a separation of powers cannot exist on faith alone," the committee said, before turning around and recognizing "that the administration has the legal right to refuse the information under the doctrine of executive privilege." Furthermore, the committee said the overall U-2 program was "one of history's most dramatic and successful intelligence operations." White House partisans could not have been happy with the report, since (as the *Times'* Russell Baker wrote in the lead page-one story) it charged "the administration with having mis-handled the U-2 espionage plane incident at almost every important point."

Three Republicans dissented in some fashion. With customarily forceful but awkward language, Homer Capehart said the report harmed "the best interests of the United States and international relations" and so voted against it entirely. Ranking Republican Alexander Wiley, whose intellectual capabilities inspired Fulbright's contempt, had his "additional views" stated toward the end of the 19,000-word report. The Wisconsin senator had developed something of a mantra in the weeks after the U-2 incident. It was the first of the dissenting section's eight points: "The members of Congress who have been responsible for reviewing the details of our intelligence-gathering activities knew of these flights and approved of them." Wiley continued, "Bad luck, not bad judgment, was the true cause of the May 1 incident. . . . every past experience justified the conclusion that it would not fail." Furthermore, if the president "had to make a statement, *he had to state the truth*" (emphasis in the original). Democrat Frank Lausche joined in making those points.[15]

It was a few days before Fulbright or Wiley went to the floor of the Senate to tussle over the report. Fulbright — freed from the constraints of crafting sentences that would satisfy over a dozen other senators — was first, on June 28. He charged Eisenhower with a "grave" mistake in assuming responsibility for the flight. After all, "one reason intelligence agencies exist is to serve as a whipping boy in cases of this kind." As a result of the U-2 "bumbling and fumbling," the prestige of the United States "among nations has reached a new low." Most originally for a legislator in the early Cold War era, Fulbright viewed the incident from the vantage point of a Soviet leader:

> Suppose a Russian counterpart of the U-2 had come down over Kansas City on May 1. This event in itself, I daresay, would have brought speeches in the Senate powerful enough to rock the Capitol dome with denunciations of the perfidy of the Soviets on the eve of the summit conference and with demands that the President not go to Paris. But then, Mr. President, reflect how much more violent the reaction here would have been if Mr. Khrushchev had said he was personally responsible for the flight, and at the same time left the impression that he had every intention of trying again.

The "smug self-righteousness" of the United States "must have been unbearably provocative to the Soviet government and contributed substantially to the violence and intemperate bad manners of their representative, Mr. Khrushchev, at Paris." "Strangely," observed Wiley three days later, Fulbright was "second only to Moscow" in making "the biggest noise and greatest effort to pin blame on the U.S." Wiley then expressed intelligence-related views that at least equaled those of Fulbright for their originality: "This is a new day in a changing world that calls for honesty and integrity in world diplomacy. Thank God, the President of the United States demonstrated it."[16]

Russell Baker predicted in the June 26 *Times* that the committee's U-2 report would "become one of the basic documents in the coming campaign debate over foreign policy." It did not. Nor did the larger set of U-2 events loom large in the fall presidential oratory. Kennedy had established himself since the mid-1950s as a critic of Eisenhower's defense policies, a "bomber gap" and "missile gap" believer who wanted to build up the military. But having used hawkish language and then — however briefly — the word "apology" in the spring, he would gain no advantage from harping on U-2 in the fall. Citizens polled a month after Powers's flight was shot down thought, by a two-to-one margin, that the administration "handled it well." Eisenhower's approval rating was still high, at 68 percent. Richard Nixon would occasionally refer in the fall to Kennedy's onetime use of the A-word, but since most press commentators and government officials thought the administration's initial handling of the U-2 incident had been inept, the vice president, too, saw little political profit there.

At the CIA, Dulles proudly told associates in late May that he had received 110 letters about U-2 from citizens, almost two-thirds of them favorable, and job applications were up. The CIA's personnel director, however, told Red White that the influx had been "odd ball" letters. Most legislators also found that citizens generally supported the administration, including the CIA, and despised Khrushchev. Many wondered, according to Wiley, "How are we going to know what is going on inside Russia?" He answered that satellites would soon outperform the U-2. A few legislators claimed that most of their mail criticized the administration. Senator Edmund Muskie (D-ME) read portions of six angry antiadministration letters into the record, including one saying, "We had better start electing presidents who are young enough to keep their wits until they finish their terms."[17]

Dulles would apparently not meet with some members of Richard Russell's Senate Armed Services subcommittee until late in the summer. The

Georgian had written Clair Engle early in the crisis that "the timing of the ill-fated flight of the U-2 is incomprehensible." His CIA subcommittee would "meet with Mr. Dulles in the near future," he promised Engle (and later the press), but "I did not want to complicate the already delicate summit situation by having a meeting with him before the President left for Paris." Despite the "stupid" timing of Powers's flight, he hoped that the incident would "not become a club which will impair the effectiveness" of the CIA. He wrote to Fulbright, "The CIA has failed in many instances," though not in all cases that critics charged. Russell would not announce the date or other details about his forthcoming hearing, and records of it seem lost to history. However, Deputy Director C. P. Cabell would later write, "We were in the closed Committee room for a long time and gave them complete information."

The attitude of Russell's leading colleagues on Armed Services and Appropriations had not changed, either. Saltonstall never criticized the CIA publicly during the U-2 affair and barely said a word about the performance of Eisenhower's White House. He and the DCI talked privately about U-2, and late in the summer, "supper with Allen Dulles @ 7:30 p.m." was on his calendar. Hayden told one constituent who criticized Eisenhower that the Constitution gave the president "sole direction over our relations with other nations."[18]

As the U-2 crisis faded across the summer, Dulles found time for other business. Among his routine contacts were telephoning young Senator Frank Church (D-ID) to inquire about his secret three-hour meeting with a Soviet diplomat. The DCI also helpfully offered to inform J. Edgar Hoover's FBI about "this contact," since the Bureau was known to "maintain a certain amount of watch." Church accepted the offer.

Dulles mostly avoided involvement in a much-publicized affair involving the National Security Agency. Two of NSA's cryptologists defected to the USSR in July, and that agency was tardy both in discovering this and in informing congressional leaders. When Francis Walter of HUAC publicly implied that the CIA had played a role in the hiring of the two men, the DCI telephoned to complain. It resulted in a rare outright argument between Dulles and a congressional leader, with Walter actually hanging up on the DCI. But Dulles successfully persuaded more important legislators like Richard Russell that it had been the Pentagon's "primary responsibility" to run NSA.[19]

Still, Dulles surely heard stories of executive branch figures criticizing the agency for the remainder of the summer and into the fall. The Washington grapevine carried word that General Twining confidentially called CIA handling of U-2 "disgraceful," and an FBI subordinate told J. Edgar Hoover of supposedly widespread opinion that CIA "stupidity" caused the incident. But, after reviewing transcripts of "various hearings before congressional committees . . . at the time Powers went down in May 1960," CIA general counsel Lawrence Houston wrote that "no congressmen expressed either moral or policy objection to the principle of overflights by the U-2." The DCI could take some credit for this.

Though painful, Eisenhower's plan to demonstrate his control of the administration and to protect the CIA — by taking responsibility for the May 1 flight yet leaving legislators and the public unclear about his level of involvement — succeeded. Prior to his remarkable press conference, one occasionally heard legislative grumbling to match that of the *Chicago American*'s complaint about CIA "stupidity" or *Newsweek*'s claim that "CIA never has been popular with Congress." But most such judgments vanished after the May 11 Eisenhower press conference. Stuart Symington so flattered Dulles in mid-May that the DCI sent a "deeply appreciative" note for going "out of your way to express confidence in our organization" and himself. But, days later, the senator said, "By a series of blunders, each surpassing its predecessor, the President of the United States became a bound and living sacrifice for such public denigration and humiliation as no occupant of that high office had ever before experienced." Still, it suited Eisenhower that few in Congress or the press resurrected the joint intelligence committee idea; Mansfield in the Senate and Clement Zablocki in the House tried, and *Aviation Week* editorialized that "the need for a congressional or some other 'watchdog' operation over CIA was never more apparent," but the would-be reformers garnered little attention or new support.

For Congress, the U-2 incident became by far the most discussed issue of its thirteen-year shared history with the CIA. Legislators filled over two hundred pages of 1960's *Congressional Record* with remarks, debates, and news articles on the topic, over four times the verbiage resulting from the 1958 Iraqi "intelligence surprise." Shocking as the affair had been, especially in demonstrating that Eisenhower could be dishonest with the American people, most congressional resentment against the CIA went unspoken in public. What *was* spoken and written about the U-2 usually had a different tone. As Barry Goldwater said, "My opinion of the CIA went skyrocketing when I heard about it."[20]

Part Three

Cuba, the CIA, and Congress:
1960–1961

Castro: "This Fellow Is Bad and Ought to Go"

The news of April 15, 1959, was replete with Cold War imagery. Dwight Eisenhower, on a golfing vacation in Georgia, had learned in a morning telephone call from John Foster Dulles that doctors had found that the secretary's abdominal cancer — diagnosed a couple of years earlier — was metastasizing. The implications were obvious to Dulles and the president, who immediately decided to hold an unusual out-of-town press conference. An hour later, reporters expecting to see press secretary Hagerty at a hotel press headquarters encountered a moist-eyed Eisenhower. Dulles had "definitely made up his mind to submit his resignation," he said. A reporter wrote, "Mr. Eisenhower, tears brimming, spoke in a voice choked with sorrow: 'I can't tell you how much regret I feel about this.'" It was a seven-minute press conference.

That evening, pictures of Ike's tears and the declining Dulles dominated the television network newscasts, by then reaching millions of American households. Later that evening, cameras recorded Fidel Castro raucously arriving at Washington's National Airport, wearing his trademark green fatigues and sporting ten-inch cigars in his breast pocket. Brushing past policemen and Assistant Secretary of State Roy Rubottom Jr. there to officially welcome him, the Cuban leader shook hands with hundreds of admirers waiting behind a fence. The "roar of welcome carried clear across the Potomac," said *Newsweek*.[1]

The thirty-two-year-old revolutionary was already a legend. On New Year's Day of that year, his guerrilla forces had ousted the corrupt government of Fulgencia Batista, who had long been friendly toward the government and big business interests of the United States. In return for Batista's alliance and concerned for his government's stability, the CIA and the State Department had pushed the dictator toward political reforms in the mid-to-late-1950s and aided his attempt to crush Castro's rebellion. That movement had fragile beginnings in the early 1950s but took on an air of inevitability by 1958, as not only poor but also middle class and some elite Cubans joined the cause. The State Department ended arms sales to Batista that year. Privately, a senior member of the administration spoke of substantial "opposition within Cuba to Batista" and of "considerable congressional and public sentiment in the U.S.

opposed to shipment of arms to Batista." Senators Morse, Mansfield, and Fulbright "were particularly outspoken in their criticism of U.S. aid to Latin American dictators. In view of all these considerations . . . the State Department had decided to apply rigidly a policy of non-intervention in Cuba."[2]

Not all in Congress were pleased by this. Senator Allen Ellender visited Cuba in December 1958 and seemed to believe those Cubans who told him (according to his own notes) "that Castro has been riding high because of the favorable publicity he received from the American press" and that few Cubans "would trust him to be President and successor of Batista." Ellender was not the only one out of touch with the momentum of events in Cuba. Later that month, Gordon Gray recorded that Eisenhower "expressed a feeling" to Dulles and Goodpaster that, "for one reason or another, the main elements of the Cuban situation had not been presented to him." Within weeks, Batista was out.[3]

In late January 1959, DCI Dulles spoke of the Cuban events before the Senate Foreign Relations Committee: "I do not think Intelligence did badly in that situation. We felt that Batista was on the losing end of the stick weeks before it came to an end." Now, he said, "they are going through a little French Revolution." Robert Amory offered the senators a memorable explanation of Castro's triumph: "The army of Batista was a mercenary army drawn from the lowest dregs of Cuban society, mostly Negroes, and when they got into combat in the jungles, they would not go anywhere." When Homer Capehart pushed Dulles on "the reason for Castro's executing so many people," the DCI responded, "When you have a revolution, you kill your enemies." Castro had "shown great courage" and showed no "communist leanings," although the CIA was suspicious about "this fellow, Che Guevara, the Argentinian who has been fighting with him."

No one in the hearing told Dulles that the United States ought to intervene in Cuba, though a few days earlier the irrepressible Representative Wayne Hays had suggested consideration of imposing an economic embargo and sending U.S. troops to the island nation. Apparently, though (said Dulles), Castro "has very wide popular backing throughout the island, and this situation may work out, but we may have more trouble." American intervention in the revolution "would have had disastrous effects throughout the whole hemisphere."[4]

Dulles's hopes that the U.S. government and Castro might coexist evaporated in Washington throughout 1959 as the Cuban government continued its widespread executions of political prisoners and included communists

in its ranks. Still, with Castro touring the United States in April, signing auto-
graphs for admirers, and talking to reporters and editors, optimism for an
accommodation arose. "We aren't communists," he told a group of editors,
adding that those executed in Cuba had been guilty of war crimes, that there
would be no confiscation of foreign-owned private industries, and that Cuba
would have a free press. "The first thing dictators do is to finish the free press
and establish censorship," he said. However, Cuba would provide "hospitality" to exiles from other Latin American countries who sought to overthrow
dictators in their homelands. During a Sunday afternoon meeting at the vice
president's ceremonial Capitol Hill office, Richard Nixon urged the Cuban
to hold free elections. Castro knew that the American-supported Batista had
staged a coup to take power in 1952, when it became clear that he could not
win power through elections. He told Nixon, "The people of Cuba don't
want free elections; they produce bad governments." By the time Castro
exited his office, the vice president was already an enthusiast for overturning the Cuban government.[5]

Most U.S. government officials were not so quickly dismissive. When
chairman Fulbright of the Foreign Relations Committee learned from intermediaries that Castro wanted to meet top legislators, he immediately invited
the Cuban to a hearing that would also include House Foreign Affairs Committee members. Within hours, on April 17 (a *Post* reporter wrote), "there
were cheers from a crowd of tourists, as Castro made his way to a Senate
committee room. Uniformed police and security officers lined the Capitol
entrance wing and the crowded Senate corridor." Inside the book-lined committee room, the atmosphere was less warm. Of the eighteen legislators present, ranking Republican Alexander Wiley peppered Castro with the bluntest
questions: "What is your connection with communism, if any?" "None," said
Castro. Then, two other questions came. Did Castro intend to confiscate
American property? Would he attempt to take over Guantanamo, the Amer-
ican-held naval base in Cuba? Castro gave unqualified answers of "no." But
was Castro planning to take over other Caribbean countries, Wiley asked.
The sole "trouble" in the Caribbean was dictators, Castro responded, and
Cuba's only role in its home region would be one of "example."

Throughout the hour-and-a-half session, Castro remained relaxed,
warm, and confident. Representative James Fulton told Castro that he had
entered the meeting feeling "neutral and suspicious," but now regarded him
as his "amigo nuevo." Fulton told reporters afterward, "I think we should
help him all we can." Castro "made a very good impression," Senator John

Sparkman remarked. All in all, a journalist wrote, Castro's visit had been "one of the most remarkable sessions with the head of another country anyone could recall at the Capitol."[6]

Not everyone was charmed, least of all George Smathers. Tall and suave, the moderately conservative Smathers's interest in Cuba had obvious geographic roots, since no state was closer to the island nation than Florida. Also, Smathers's law firm had long represented corporations with interests in Latin America. More than any other senator in the Eisenhower and Kennedy eras, Smathers would publicly and privately lay out the grounds for American intervention against Castro. Given his big business connections, this earned Smathers a sinister reputation in some quarters, although a recent biography suggests that the "most noble aspect of his career" was the "pursuit of democracy in Latin America." Many of Smathers's colleagues at least regarded him as an authority on the region.

A Democrat, Smathers had been one of a handful of senators invited to Castro's trials of "war criminals" in Cuba earlier in the year, an invitation he declined with a warning: "Your name will be judged in history, not so much on how many demonstrations are held, but rather upon how well you lead the people of Cuba down the road to a better economic position, a greater democracy, and a recognition of personal rights." Smathers later recalled of the Foreign Relations encounter with Castro:

> I wasn't on the committee at that time; I got permission from Fulbright to do it, because I wanted to ask Castro these questions. After Frank Lausche got through — Lausche took forever, Wayne Morse took forever, talking to him. But Fulbright cut me off. Castro said he had to go, he was speaking to the National Press Club at twelve o'clock, and it got to be about five minutes of twelve and I said, "Well, Mr. Chairman, let me just ask two or three questions — Fidel Castro, when are you going to have an election? When are the people of Cuba going to have an opportunity to vote for who should be their leader rather than have somebody like you take over?" And he said, "They would re-elect me, overwhelmingly." I said: "Well, in that case, why are you afraid to set a date?" He said, "I'm not going to answer that question."

Afterward, Smathers allowed to reporters that Castro might be a "good man," but he proceeded to the Senate floor to observe that the Cuban had communists "peppered throughout his government." Smathers's reaction was no great shock to observers — days earlier, he had charged that Cuban leaders were planning to invade other Latin American countries. Even before Castro was out of the United States, his brother Raul publicly labeled the senator one of the "enemies of the revolution."[7]

Increasing numbers of Americans, on and off of Capitol Hill, thought the United States should intervene in Cuba, especially after Castro did nationalize U.S.-owned properties later in 1959. But Fulbright wrote one such constituent, "Any kind of intervention in the manner of Teddy Roosevelt would only be self-defeating, not only in Cuba, but elsewhere in the hemisphere." Still, as Castro developed relations with the Soviet Union later in the year, no members of Congress spoke further of him as an "amigo." In October, President Eisenhower approved a program urged on him by the State Department and the CIA to support Cuban exiles and dissidents who wished to topple Castro's government. Soon there would be scattered raids by sea, launched from the United States, against Cuban coastal facilities. It was just a beginning.[8]

If the Central Intelligence Agency's involvement in the overthrow of Guatemala's government in 1954 ranks as perhaps its most notorious covert action "success" from the early Cold War period, the Bay of Pigs intervention of early 1961 is surely that era's most infamous agency failure. As many analysts have shown, two presidents and their aides crucially shaped that policy. What has never been adequately explored, though, is the remarkably hostile congressional sentiment toward Castro's government, much less CIA leaders' interaction with legislators on the topic. In the later, unpublished words of Allen Dulles, "Congress was restive, and the demand for some sort of action was mounting. Here was a reservoir of anti-Castro strength."[9]

Growing congressional hunger for Castro's removal, some legislators' anger at presidents Eisenhower and Kennedy for "softness" toward Cuba, and Allen Dulles's alert to a subcommittee that a covert intervention was in the offing constitute part of a lost history. Numerous legislators' habits in the late 1940s and early 1950s of urging more aggressive covert action did not change as the latter decade approached its end. In 1958, Styles Bridges told Dulles in a CIA subcommittee meeting that "we should do more of the Cold War activities," although Leverett Saltonstall worried that this might "impair" the agency's intelligence-gathering. In 1959, a House member having lunch with Dulles and six others at the CIA "wondered why the West had never 'pinched off' Albania." After explaining that this might harm relations with

Yugoslavia, the DCI assured the legislator (as Lawrence Houston noted) that "nevertheless plans had been made against the event that national policies might desire operations in Albania." By the time the United States would attempt to remove Castro from power, Congress would — with one prominent exception — signal in a multitude of ways its support for such a move.[10]

As 1960 began, Allen Dulles was no longer blasé about Castro. "We have a grave crisis right at our door," he told Fulbright's committee on January 18, adding that Castro was trying to organize "a congress of the under-developed states which would be directed against the United States." The CIA was "pretty well-informed" on meetings between Cuban and other Latin American communists and Soviet officials. Days later, Eisenhower told reporters that the United States followed a "policy of non-intervention in the domestic affairs of other countries, including Cuba." Even as the CIA secretly wrestled with new ideas about how to push Castro out of power, the State Department continued to pursue and publicly emphasize traditional diplomatic options. This angered Smathers. The senator probably knew little of CIA covert activities but, having just traveled in Latin America for three and a half weeks, was thoroughly dissatisfied with publicized administration policies.[11]

On February 18, he said so to Eisenhower, who was just about to visit South America and the Caribbean. As he was aware, Cuba had been on Smathers's lengthy itinerary, but the senator had been clearly if unofficially disinvited by its government. This, at about the same time that Soviet deputy premier Anastas Mikoyan had a successful, much-publicized visit to Cuba. Bryce Harlow's notes show Smathers indicating in the Oval Office that he

> wanted mainly to discuss with the President our policy, or lack of policy, in respect to Cuba. He said he had just left the Senate Committee on Foreign Relations, where Mr. Rubottom and others from the State Department had been discussing this very problem. He stated that he asked the President in every South American country he visited what he thought ought to be done in respect to Cuba and Castro, and that without exception each president had stated that it is important now for the United States to develop a firmer policy toward Castro. He mentioned a wide-spread belief that Castro represents a growing effort to overthrow existing governments in South America.

Smathers complimented "the President's action in the Middle East" — the 1958 intervention in Lebanon — "describing it as tough and decisive."

Eisenhower claimed to agree with the senator but said there was a "serious missing link," namely the lack of a request from the OAS to "do something about Castro." Displaying a talent for evasion that would have shocked most citizens at the time, Eisenhower complained that "although everybody says something should be done, they seem to want it done clandestinely — a policy, the president explained, approximating gangsterism." (In giving Smathers the impression of rejecting clandestine American action against Cuba, Eisenhower followed the sort of advice he would give Dulles and others four weeks later. Of "preparations of a para-military force" to deal with Cuba, Goodpaster's March 17 notes indicate, "The President said that he knows of no better plan for dealing with this situation. The great problem is leakage and breach of security. Everyone must be prepared to swear that he has not heard of it.")

Whether Smathers discounted the president's February 18 "gangsterism" comment is unknown. He responded that surely the State Department could share intelligence with OAS member countries so that the Organization would soon be "calling upon America to intervene in Cuba." Eisenhower endorsed this hope and voiced the thought that, by visiting privately with the president of each country on his itinerary to push an OAS initiative, "almost anything would become feasible."

Eisenhower urged Smathers, in the meantime, to demonstrate in a planned Senate speech that "the situation in respect to Cuba is intolerable. The President pointed out that a senator can talk more freely on such matters than people in the executive branch." Yes, said Smathers, his good friend Dick Nixon had "explained to him how embarrassing it is for people in the executive branch to deal effectively with situations of this kind." But Eisenhower assured the aggressive-minded Smathers that the new secretary of state, Christian Herter, "isn't lacking in guts." Not wanting to end the private conversation on an unpleasant topic, "The President and Senator Smathers then talked enthusiastically about new golf clubs designed by Spalding, the first set of which had been given to the President."[12]

At Eisenhower's direction, Herter soon saw Smathers, which may account for one part of the senator's lengthy February 25, 1960, speech indicating that the United States had "begun to take a firmer position" toward Castro. It had been "wise" not to intervene in Cuba at the time of the revolution, but now Castro had "identified himself as being pro-communist." With other senators, including Barry Goldwater, Spessard Holland (D-FL), and Richard Russell urging him on, Smathers had another label for the Cuban leader — "Fuehrer

Fidel." "Are we going to continue taking abuse, grinning all the while like a sick ape?" he asked. Still, Smathers expressed caution about "acting unilaterally against Cuba" and pinned his hopes, for the time being at least, on the OAS.

To some, though, the president (and, by implication, even Smathers) was too soft on Cuba. Responding to news of what seemed a bland Eisenhower speech to Brazil's Congress, Representative Daniel Flood (D-PA) said the president did "not go far enough." Congress should interpret existing treaties among western hemispheric nations as allowing "any one or more" of them to take whatever action they thought necessary against "the subversive forces known as international communism and its agencies in the Western Hemisphere."[13]

Upon his return, Eisenhower again urged the State Department to win OAS authorization of collective action against Castro. Smathers, meanwhile, was disturbed in March to learn that, after bringing the U.S. ambassador home for a few months in protest of Castro's actions, the State Department was sending him back to Cuba. Just fifteen years after World War II's end, Smathers described the latest decision as "Chamberlain-umbrella appeasement." Of the Cuban leader, he told the Senate, "Apparently, most of us agree that this fellow is bad and that he 'ought to go,' " so why offer "the intangible support of sending an ambassador to Cuba, so that Castro can prate and brag to the world, 'I brought the United States to its knees by abusing it.' " The United States should turn over to the OAS "all the information available to us from the CIA and military intelligence agencies," because "if we were to work through that Organization, we could probably get rid of this fellow, and we would not be working unilaterally."[14]

No less fervent than Smathers was his colleague Olin Johnston (D-SC) who, on June 18, called the Cuban situation "the most bitter pill that we have to swallow." The senator was not subtle in assigning blame within the U.S. government: "The very success of the communists in Cuba represents a downright failure of our Central Intelligence Agency to have adequate knowledge of what was going on under the covers." Castro needed to know that if his government engaged in "infiltration" of other nations, the United States would "move in with force to stop him." Administration planning for this should "not wait until after the election."

New York Republican Kenneth Keating, who would gain national fame in 1962 for correctly asserting that the USSR was placing offensive missiles in Cuba, earned uncharacteristic applause on the Senate floor two years earlier by raising such alarms about Castro. On June 24, Keating warned, "Communist operations in Cuba represent the boldest challenge to freedom in the Western Hemisphere that we have known in 60 years." Specifically, there was

> a steady movement of Soviet engineers and technicians bound for the Caribbean through East Berlin, their main project to be the construction of an airstrip on the southern coast of Cuba. Russia's helping hand to Cuba in this respect began eight weeks ago. My information is that about 250 Soviet technicians have been cleared through East Berlin, en route to Cuba since then. . . . The airstrip being built by the Soviets is designed to handle the largest types of aircraft. It is located near Matanzas, and my information is that it has a 12,500-foot runway, with an unusually heavy concrete base.
>
> I simply do not see how we can close our eyes and pretend that all this just is not happening.

Among those applauding Keating was Smathers, whose self-described "weak little voice" for a hard line against the "Soviet satellite" to the south had gained no attention from the State Department, he claimed. By now, the Florida senator had given up on State, sending a message through an aide to Nixon that he "hated to use the hackneyed phrase that they are 'soft on communism,' but this appeared to be the only way to say it." Smathers added a dire, unexplained reference to "the exchange of atomic information with Cuba"; the senator was "correctly diagnosing it as a direct pipeline to Russia," said a Nixon aide, who passed on Smathers's final warning: "Something should be done, and done soon, because this is something that will blow up in our face." But Keating gained no particular respect from the Republican administration, either, it seemed — the Defense Department said it had no knowledge of "any airstrip being built in southern Cuba," although it admitted that a base for ships or submarines might be under construction.[15]

The most explicit congressional endorsement in 1960 of U.S. action against Castro's Cuba came the next day when L. Mendel Rivers of South Carolina took the floor of the House of Representatives. While a few in Congress may have known something of CIA's covert plans against Cuba by the summer of 1960, Rivers almost certainly did not. With almost twenty years' seniority, he was a leading member of the Armed Services Committee and would become its chair in five years. Still, Carl Vinson had not yet appointed him to the secretive subcommittee on the CIA, perhaps because the colorful, alcoholic representative could not always keep a secret and sometimes went missing for days on end. Drew Pearson once reported that Rivers "had run around the corridor of the Savoy in London in his underpants, chasing girls." Though a Democrat, the conservative Rivers had endorsed Eisenhower for reelection in 1956, without apology and suffering no political harm in his home district. (About the only record of Rivers's having interacted with the CIA is Pforzheimer's account of talking to a friend of the congressman interested in distributing foreign-made beers in the United States. "The two beers were creditable products," Pforzheimer recorded, but the CIA steered clear.)

Rivers had lost patience with the Eisenhower administration, though, and reserved an hour's time on the House floor to say so. On June 25, he began by drawing on poet James Lowell: "Once to every man and nation comes the moment to decide, in the strife of truth with falsehood, for the good or evil side."

> Ninety miles from the United States, the most deadly form of government is daily, methodically, and successfully being set up. Its principal aim is the infiltration and takeover of all the countries of Latin America. Mr. Speaker, this must not come to pass. Time is running against us — tomorrow is too late for this country to act affirmatively, forthrightly, and positively. . . . America's survival must not be determined by what the United Nations thinks, or what Russia thinks, or what the world thinks. We should deliver an ultimatum to Communist Castro that we expect an immediate guarantee that the property and lives of Americans must be protected and guaranteed. Failing in this, we should, under international law, be prepared to occupy this island to protect these vital rights.

Rivers was just warming up. Castro was a "bearded pipsqueak," his regime suppressing "those who voice any criticism." The United States "would be committing suicide in allowing any unfriendly regime in Cuba," which would establish "military bases of the Soviet universal empire 90 miles away from our shoreline." This would constitute "not only a threat to the Cape Canaveral missile center," but could subject American cities to the danger of bombing. "Send a company of Marines down there and take over," Rivers advised. Predicting that future generations of Americans would read his speech, if only "this country lasts that long," Rivers ended, "Let us give our leaders whatever spinal injections they need. Let us back them up. Let us make them lead."

The tragicomic Rivers was not ignored by colleagues that day. Eight members congratulated him on the floor and similarly advocated ridding Cuba of Castro. One was Frank Bow (R-OH) of the House Appropriations CIA subcommittee, which earlier in the year had an unrecorded, apparently brief dialogue with Allen Dulles about Cuba. Responding to Rivers, Bow noted the impending change in trade relations between the United States and Cuba. For years, Cuba had exported huge amounts of sugar to the United States at a price well above that prevailing in international markets. American law mandated this to ensure steady access to sugar and provide price supports to U.S. sugar producers. Congress was soon to permit Eisenhower to change those trading terms, to Cuba's great economic detriment. Castro, not surprisingly, had complained at the prospect of this. Bow noted, "We read daily in the paper that Fidel Castro has said that, unless we subsidize his sugar and pay great sums to Cuba, that he will take over American plants." This was blackmail, Bow thought, and "when somebody tries to blackmail you, you go down and face them." The U.S. government ought to say, "Mr. Castro, you are not going to take our property, and if you attempt to do it, we will come over and take it away from you." The other legislators used words that day like "mollycoddling of the communists," "Khrushchev is laughing," and "Oh, how I pray for a Teddy Roosevelt" when referring to administration policy, and phrases like "this bearded wonder," "this Red military base 90 miles from the great city of Miami," and "this danger to the Free World" when discussing Castro and Cuba.[16]

Perhaps because Rivers spoke on a Saturday afternoon, as Congress rushed to pass bills and adjourn before the Republican and Democratic nominating conventions, the *Washington Post* and the *New York Times* ignored the rhetorical assault on Castro. Rivers's prediction that future generations would note his speech has proven utterly mistaken, although this says as much about flaws of the historical record as those of the South Carolinian. Still, many newspapers around the country published wire-service reports of it. Within days, hundreds of citizens sent Rivers letters that he hauled onto the House floor the following Friday. Overwhelmingly, he claimed, the letter writers wanted the United States to get tough on Castro. There seemed to be no other course but to "occupy Cuba." Immediately, House members joined in on another verbal attack on Castro. Few used language so blatant as Rivers in supporting American intervention, but only Barratt O'Hara (D-IL), who fought in Cuba in the Spanish-American War, dissented: "It is not for us to intervene in the internal affairs of another nation."[17]

Rivers cared little about diplomatic organizations like the Organization of American States. But Senator Keating, despite the similarity of his anti-Cuba rhetoric to that of his House counterpart, joined George Smathers and others in hoping for most of summer 1960 that the United States would be able to act with OAS support or participation against Castro. Like Eisenhower, they and others in Congress were soon disappointed. The Organization addressed "threats of extra-continental intervention" late in August, at the request of the United States and against Cuba's lone opposition, but it also took up the matter of the Dominican Republic's long-standing but failing dictator, Rafael Trujillo. The result was an OAS condemnation and diplomatic isolation of Trujillo's regime, a rejection of communism in Latin America, but no mention of Cuba or Castro.

Eisenhower lamented that there was "no alliance in which indecisiveness is so great, or in which it seems so hard to generate an initiative." Despite his repeated badgering of Herter, the president's two-track policy of planning a Cuban intervention and seeking an endorsement by the hemisphere's key alliance had half failed. For the rest of his presidency, State Department leaders would tell Eisenhower that the OAS might come around, but he probably knew better. In any case, Ike endorsed further U.S. planning of Castro's overthrow. As he told Dulles, Bissell, and a few others who had outlined the projected costs of the covert plans on August 18, "If we could be sure of freeing the Cubans from this incubus, $25 million might be a small price to pay." The president thought "we should be prepared to take more chances and be more aggressive," wrote Gordon Gray. But how sad, Eisenhower reflected the following autumn, that Latin American public opinion would be against any such American intervention, and that governments there had not been "more active in teaching their people about the problem."[18]

Smathers disliked the OAS results, too, but he had American culprits in mind. "The State Department and — I do not like to say this — the administration" had "miserably failed." He even blamed the administration for Castro's rise: "Having failed to encourage a peaceful transition from the dictatorship of Fulgencio Batista to a genuine democracy, our State Department precipitated Batista's overthrow and the installation of Fidel Castro." Then he placed a journalist's analysis of the OAS outcome in the *Congressional Record*, a significant portion of which he read aloud for his Senate audience, including the final sentence: "The end result has been to leave the United States to seek alone a solution that will insure peace."[19]

Administration loyalists would occasionally remind overheated colleagues that the Cuba topic was, in Senator Prescott Bush's words, "very sensitive." But, across 1960, although no legislators were as persistent as Smathers or as colorful as Rivers, most members' speeches were sweeping indictments. Congressman Armistead Selden (D-AL) said Cuba was furthering "the international communist conspiracy" that had as its goal the "complete control and domination of the individual countries of the western hemisphere." Representative James Oliver (D-ME) told colleagues and constituents back home that Cuba was soon "to be a Russian naval and missile base poised at the very heart of our country." How, Senator Holland asked, could Castro be so hostile toward the United States when "we have been their best friends." Representative Richard Poff (R-VA) said, "We can no longer compromise with this evil. Appeasement is folly." Why, Senator James Eastland (D-MS) asked, had the United States taken "only half-hearted measures against the communist dictatorship which has been established in Cuba under Castro?" Senator Ellender uttered the word "Munich." Senator Gordon Allot (R-CO) agreed with Richard Russell: "We cannot stand idly by." The nearest thing to a favorable remark that year was Representative Charles Porter's judgment that Castro's government was "still honest," in contrast to Batista's corruption. But his otherwise deeply critical speech, and a "Dear Fidel" telegram he had recently sent the Cuban, wondered when Castro would hold elections.

Of course, the Eisenhower administration had not been particularly passive toward Cuba, but few on Capitol Hill knew that. Nominated to head the Democratic Party's ticket in the forthcoming election, Senators Kennedy and Johnson probably learned something of agency planning that summer. George Smathers had recently been brought into some level of knowledge by the Eisenhower administration, but it did not satisfy him. Those heading CIA subcommittees may also have known of Cuba preparations in 1960, but the evidence is lacking. Certainly those powerful legislators remained publicly circumspect. When a constituent inquired about Carl Hayden's views early in the summer, the Senate Appropriations head first wrote, "I am not yet in favor of sending the Marines to Cuba, because I hope that with rope enough, Castro will hang himself." It was best "to join with the anti-communist governments of Latin America in sending armed forces to Cuba of ample strength to accomplish that result." On reflection, though, Hayden edited his response to read simply, "I have not had the opportunity to keep in close touch with what is going on in Cuba." Later in the summer, although George Mahon remained silent about Cuba, he forwarded Eisenhower a petition from scores of constituents asking the president to "give financial and armed assistance to all honest Cubans who wish to return the island of Cuba back to the Cuban people." If necessary, "occupy the entire island of Cuba with military forces."[20]

"What Is the Rationale behind That?"

It increasingly seemed to Eisenhower in late 1960 that the United States was not yet sufficiently organized to intervene in Cuba before his presidency's end. Whether to force the CIA to act while he was still president or perhaps to influence his successor's hand, Eisenhower told Dulles in November that the plans should be "expedited." Soon, Dulles informed president-elect Kennedy of the expanding CIA plans (though he knew of them from other sources by then). By December and January, Eisenhower knew perfectly well that Castro and the growing U.S. covert action force of Cuban exiles were more JFK's problems than his own.[1]

Kennedy quickly settled one question — whom to appoint as CIA head. Right after the election, Dulles acceded to his telephoned request to stay on as DCI. Eisenhower was unenthusiastic about this, but Dulles's choices were increasingly beyond his control. Eisenhower broke diplomatic relations with Cuba on January 3, 1961, his last important act in relation to Castro. Something made the president even more hawkish toward the very end of his presidency. Perhaps it was his own impending liberation, but another factor was his meetings with William Pawley, a wealthy international businessman, former U.S. ambassador, and confidante of presidents for decades. Pawley, who had spent part of his childhood in Cuba, played an important, unofficial role in support of U.S. covert action against Guatemala in 1954. Moreover, as one historian has noted, "Eisenhower turned repeatedly to Pawley when Communism threatened to spread to the Western hemisphere — America's backyard and Pawley's."

By 1960, the energetic Pawley had long since allied himself with Smathers, egging the administration toward firmer action against Castro; on May 13, they had done so together at the White House. As the year drew to a close, Pawley, acknowledged as a "zealot" by the president to advisers, had nonetheless persuaded Eisenhower to inform his Cuba planners that he did "not share the State Department's concern about 'shooting from the hip.'" Are we being "sufficiently imaginative and bold," the president asked Dulles and others. The United States "should be prepared to take more chances and be more aggressive." And Ike directed Dulles to be "in constant touch with Mr. Pawley." Weeks later, on January 19, 1961, with little elaboration of the difficulties inherent in overthrowing Castro's government, Eisenhower told

Kennedy that the United States had helped the assembled anti-Castro forces "to the utmost." Plans for the operation should be (a Kennedy note-taker recorded) "continued and accelerated."[2]

On January 20, Kennedy took the oath of office. Two weeks earlier, Smathers had urged him and secretary of state–designate Dean Rusk to "prevent the importation of all dutiable Cuban exports in order to deprive the Castro regime of as many United States dollars as possible." The initiative would win approval, but was small potatoes compared to the covert action brewing against Cuba. The Florida senator — who knew from another friend, Dick Nixon, of Eisenhower's more aggressive Cuba plans — already had a history of urging Kennedy to think hawkishly about Castro. On a golf outing immediately after the election, Smathers had tried to "get something moving" regarding Cuba and Latin America. During the fall campaign, he had written Kennedy that "another Guatemala" might be required. "Anything less circumspect" would be problematic.[3]

Kennedy and Smathers had been close since entering the House of Representatives in January 1947. When JFK, suffering from World War II back injuries, struggled to walk on crutches from his House office to the floor for votes, Smathers often assisted him. More than Kennedy, who was frequently sick and had seen much tragedy in his short life, Smathers exuded a devil-may-care attitude. "I love Smathers! He doesn't give a damn," Kennedy would tell friends. Both men soon won seats in the Senate. In that "club," some had not a single close friend. Smathers was no such loner. His charms were at least as considerable as Kennedy's — the Floridian had, after all, managed to become and remain close friends with three men who were not, themselves, intimates: Kennedy, Johnson, and Nixon. Still, he never aspired to lead the Senate, firmly refusing LBJ's offer of the majority whip position in the mid-1950s.

Smathers later described the beginnings of his friendship with Kennedy as "a natural chemical reaction. . . . We had a lot in common. We'd walk to the floor together to vote, talking about legislation, events of the day, girls, and so on." "Girls," especially, interested the two young men. In 1953, Smathers had been the only senator in Kennedy's wedding party. He would nominate Kennedy for the vice presidency at the 1956 Democratic convention and work hard for his election in 1960, after an awkward preconvention period in which Johnson, Kennedy, and *another* close friend, Stuart Symington, competed for the presidential nomination.[4]

Meanwhile, shortly before Kennedy's inauguration, Leverett Saltonstall wrote in his pocket calendar, "Dulles @ 8." The DCI would also be at the senator's home for drinks and dinner in February. Saltonstall could therefore knowledgeably write a constituent that, while the United States faced "the problem of expanded Soviet activities" in Cuba, "intelligence reports described ever increasing opposition to the Castro regime."

Not coincidentally, Dulles conveyed the same two points six days later to Kennedy and advisers — "Cuba is now for all practical purposes a communist-controlled state," but there was "a great increase also in popular opposition" to Castro's regime. A "rapid and continuing build-up of Castro's military power" was under way, and (as Eisenhower had also been told) "the present estimate of the Department of Defense is that no course of action currently authorized by the United States government will be effective in reaching the agreed national goal of overthrowing the Castro regime." At that meeting, Kennedy directed the Joint Chiefs of Staff to "review" with the CIA "proposals for the active deployment of anti-Castro Cuban forces on Cuban territory." Meanwhile, his national security adviser noted, "the President particularly desires that no hint of these discussions reach any personnel beyond those most immediately concerned within the executive branch." Kennedy's standard for secrecy, like Eisenhower's, would not be met by Dulles.[5]

In all the available documentation of CIA-Congress interactions from 1947 through the Bay of Pigs period, some fragments, occasional indirect written evidence, and a few recorded memories survive of discussions about covert action. Only one verbatim record of a DCI telling a legislative group of a forthcoming covert action exists: a partial transcript of an early 1961 hearing of the House Armed Services subcommittee on the CIA, which continued its relatively assertive ways under Paul Kilday. There, Dulles alerted members to a likely intervention in Cuba.

At 10:00 a.m., Friday, March 10, in Room 314 of the Old House Office Building, chief counsel Robert Smart joined Kilday, ranking Republican Les Arends, Charles Bennett (D-FL), George Huddleston (D-AL), Melvin Price (R-IL), James VanZandt (R-PA), Bob Wilson (R-CA), and Frank Osmers (R-NJ). Most would have seen front-page reports that the USSR (in the *Post*'s words) "took another step today toward putting a man in orbit. A five-ton space ship carrying a female dog circled the earth and landed safely." None of that day's published news was as momentous, though, as that learned by the members when they faced Dulles, Deputy Director Cabell, Intelligence Directorate head Amory, the Operations Directorate's number two man, Richard Helms, legislative liaison Warner, and a CIA stenographer. Such meetings were not usually transcribed, Warner later recalled, evidence that Chairman Kilday and Dulles understood this session's special nature.[6]

It was common for Dulles to divide his opening presentations to congressional groups into different subject matters, including "intelligence" (a tour of world hot spots) and "operations" (a review of covert action and significant spying in various countries). Less lurid topics, such as the almost-completed CIA building and desired changes in agency personnel policies fell into the "administration" category. The DCI would have started on March 10 by addressing intelligence findings, assisted by Amory. Then the surviving record starts with Dulles saying:

> On operations — Cuba, first of all. This is also very classified, although obviously a certain amount of it has gotten to the press, but not its attribution. Beginning just about a year ago now, the decision was made in the high political level that Cuba had passed the point of no return, that it was a communist-dominated society, that there was no reason to believe that they were going to change, that their stock in trade was hatred of and attempt to degrade the United States in every possible way, and that the objectives of Cuba were far beyond the confines of Cuba itself, that they were trying to extend their communist revolution to neighboring countries, particularly in the Caribbean area, and therefore we were asked to start to develop, working covertly, a force-in-being of Cubans and a political organization of Cubans and a propaganda attack on communism in Cuba — really a three-pronged attack: one was military, one was the political, and the third was the propaganda.
>
> To start with the last first, we developed the radio equipment on Swan Island, which you have heard a great deal about. That has been going on now for about six months and is, we think, very effective.

Of the "political" task of uniting Cuban exiles, Dulles said:

> We have been working very hard to try to bring the Cuban leaders together in some sort of organization. We have organized what we call The Frente under [Manuel] Verona. During the last few weeks we have been enlarging the base of that and we hope to have together — hopefully, this week — have together a stronger group, more representative of all the Cuban resistance parties. It's terribly difficult to get these people together. There are over 100 separate, different

Cuban groups, all of which aspire to leadership; there are at least 100 people that think they ought to be the next president of Cuba. We have been expending a certain amount of funds in this operation, and we really feel now there is some ground for hope.

But "the third facet, and probably the most important of all, is the preparation of a Cuban force," which Dulles had Cabell explain:

> That involves all three elements — ground, naval, and air, because we have to have those capabilities. Essentially, the size of our ground force is roughly in the neighborhood of a thousand Cubans, already recruited, organized and in training in Guatemala in a base there. And they have, by this time, attained a very high degree of proficiency, under Latin standards, and our judgment is that it's probably the best force to ever develop in Latin America, as far as its firepower and its maneuverability and all is concerned.
>
> In connection with that, we have developed an Air Force. It, too, is based in Guatemala and under training — recruited from Cuban pilots, both commercial and military crews. As far as flying aircraft is concerned, they are at a fairly high degree of training, but we run into, particularly there, the normal Latin characteristics of lack of precision and determination and all, and their ability to get through on a given mission and to do the things that they are supposed to do leaves much to be desired.

Much of Cabell's testimony remains censored by the CIA. Looked at in context, it seemingly was an elaboration of preparation for air support of the planned invasion and an admission of the risks of hostile political reactions in Latin America. (Four decades later, Warner examined the censored transcript and also surmised that Cabell may have indicated the importance of naval and air cover for the invaders. This would remain a fierce area of disagreement between defenders of the CIA and those defending the reputation of John F. Kennedy, who ultimately authorized far less aerial and naval support than most CIA leaders preferred.)[7]

In response to questions from Osmers, Dulles took over from Cabell and indicated that Castro had "developed a very large militia — about 200,000 in Cuba," of whom "thirty to forty-thousand" had "pretty good fighting qualities." More ominously, the "great rank-and-file of the people" seemed pro-Castro, despite criticisms by Cuba's Catholic hierarchy. "We are very disturbed at the general trends," he said. Of the potentially negative side effects of intervention in Cuba, Dulles added, "That is purely a political question, and beyond us. We have tried to carry out our particular side of the man-date we were given, but recognize the extreme difficulty in effect on Latin America, etc." The remaining anti-Castro "resistance inside Cuba," the DCI said, was "not strong enough, of itself, to rise up against this militia force that they have created. . . . If there is any hope of having it rise, it will have to be sparked. In some way or other, you have to light the fuse, and do it fairly dramatically — then that involves the possible use of these forces."

Kilday established through repeated questions to Dulles that the Cuban militia had "a tremendous amount of arms" from the Soviet Union. Kilday had a drinking problem but was smart and performed sufficiently to earn respect in the House. His sharp questions on the morning of March 10 came just days after another attempt to create a joint congressional committee on intelligence had arisen in the House. Its sponsor, Foreign Affairs Commit-tee member Edna Kelly, told the House Rules Committee, "CIA makes its own policies and procedures, spends as much money as it may require, reviews its own errors as its conscience so dictates, and selects such reme-dies as it deems proper to correct its errors and to improve its operations." Kilday denied it all: his subcommittee, he told Rules members, met regularly with Dulles to receive "full and current reports" and operated in nearly as much secrecy as the agency. Kelly's resolution did not make it out of Rules, but the debate there reminded Kilday, other barons, and Dulles that the CIA had a mixed reputation on Capitol Hill.[8]

After Kilday questioned Dulles at his subcommittee's March hearing, Robert Smart's turn came. Outgoing and intelligent, the heavyset chief coun-sel often represented Vinson and Kilday in meetings with agency leaders. Though favorably disposed toward the CIA, he was no pushover. Facing Dulles and the other agency heads at the 1961 hearing, Smart asked, "What is the rationale about the size of the force in Guatemala under training? A thousand troops against the size of the Cuban army, plus the militia — is it to be considered adequate? Or is that all we can get?" Cabell's first defense of the CIA-trained force's size was the need to "retain any semblance of non-attributability." This was of no small concern to President Kennedy. All those present knew that the *New York Times* had published a story that did not mention the Central Intelligence Agency but described U.S. planning for a covert intervention in Cuba. Additionally, Cabell suggested, recruiting more men would have required lowering "the standards as to what we consider to be the individual reliability of those men, and motivation." The thousand or so trained Cubans were "not just street bums."

When Smart inquired as to what so small a force could achieve, Cabell spoke of it as the "nucleus . . . of an amphibious operation in seizing a portion of Cuban real estate, and that enclave then would be used — the existence of it, the knowledge of it, and the presence of it — would be a rallying point, both visible to Cubans to spark resistance in other parts of the island, because they would have this example in front of them, and an actual, physical enclave people could join." Frank Osmers was not satisfied. The New Jersey representative usually kept a low profile at subcommittee hearings, but this morning Osmers questioned whether "a force of 1000, however well-trained, would be able to hold . . . a sizeable enough piece of Cuban real estate to permit that." He added, "I admit a thousand is a thousand times better than none," before Cabell interjected, "Our judgment is affirmative on that." Representative Bob Wilson observed that, after all, Castro had begun with only thirty-two fighters years before. But Dulles could see that Osmers, Kilday, Smart, and probably others on the subcommittee had their doubts about what a ground force of a thousand Cuban exiles could achieve, even with air support, so he revealed that the U.S. military had given its evaluative "help, because we don't consider ourselves competent military authority in the United States." The CIA had sought and received "the very highest and effective support of that kind." Maybe in Dulles's mind the CIA really had "sought" the military's evaluation of its plans; most everyone else in the administration thought the initiative came from President Kennedy.

A few years later, brooding over the blame he and the CIA faced for over-optimistically pushing Kennedy toward what became the spectacularly failed Bay of Pigs operation, a retired Dulles would write, "I know of no estimate that a spontaneous uprising of the unarmed population of Cuba would be touched off by the landing." Without quibbling over the meaning of words, this was misleading, at best. It was the director of central intelligence who told the Kilday subcommittee on March 10 that the remaining anti-Castro "resistance inside Cuba" was "not strong enough, of itself, to rise up against this militia force that they have created. . . . If there is any hope of having it rise, it will have to be sparked." And Dulles had watched Cabell tell Smart that the "nucleus . . . of an amphibious operation in seizing a portion of Cuban real estate" would be "a rallying point" to "spark resistance."[9]

The partial transcript does not show Amory or Helms saying anything about the Cuba plans. Dulles had denied Amory's Intelligence Directorate a significant analytical role in the lead-up to Bay of Pigs; it must have been interesting, and was certainly rare, for Amory to hear Dulles and Cabell explain the plans. Though second only to Richard Bissell in the Operations Directorate, Helms had barely concealed his doubts in conversations at the agency about the brewing plans. He, too, was kept at a distance from them.

Whatever else the agency leaders told Kilday's subcommittee that day, presumably including more on "operations" worldwide, and whatever other questions arose, they remain classified "Top Secret" early in the twenty-first century. Nor is there any surviving written record of agency interactions with other CIA subcommittee leaders, such as Mahon and Russell, about Bay of Pigs preparations. Dulles sent Clarence Cannon a thank-you note about "discussions" they had during the last week of Eisenhower's presidency, but the topics remain unknown. John Warner guesses that the CIA probably briefed the Cannon/Mahon subcommittee (or its most senior members) as it had Kilday's group about the Cuba project. Similarly, of the Senate Appropriations and Armed Services subcommittees, which functioned jointly, Warner believes that "we would have held a meeting with Russell, Saltonstall, and maybe a few others" about it. (Russell had continued to voice hostility toward Castro publicly and privately. In a closed session of Armed Services on April 5, with General Lemnitzer testifying, but CIA's Warner observing, Russell "stated that he believed that, as soon as it became apparent that Cuba was communist-dominated, we should have invoked the Monroe Doctrine," which meant intervene. "He was very strong in his views on this," wrote Warner the next day, "and was joined by senators Case, Symington, Thurmond, and Bush.")

Warner's estimate about advance word to the Georgia senator is consistent with what Russell would say after Bay of Pigs, when anyone would have had reason to deny advance knowledge of what proved to be a disastrous affair; Russell would say only that he had not had prior knowledge of its "timing." This is what Dulles told the Kilday subcommittee on March 10— the timing of such an order could only be determined at a "high political level." All knew this to be Kennedy.[10]

A president could also decide which confidantes to tell about plans for Cuba. A ready audience for Kennedy, when he wished to think out loud, was Smathers. With the presidential election over, the long, joyous Kennedy-Smathers congressional association — when they played practical jokes on each other, traveled the world, and engaged in sexual escapades — came to a close. "Jack" was now "Mr. President" and relaxed in Florida with Smathers less often. Still, the friendship endured.

Smathers let DCI Dulles know a few days after the Kennedy inauguration that he was as convinced as ever that Castro's government had to go. The words in that conversation were warm but amounted to a set of warnings for the DCI. A CIA note-taker wrote that Smathers "indicated that he is 'crowded' when he returns to Miami by those who are not entirely pleased with the way things are going," meaning Cuban exiles groups who worked (often contentiously) with the CIA toward an overthrow. Manuel Antonio de Verona, leader of the group that Dulles was to describe to Kilday's subcommittee, "had been out to the Senator's house the other day. . . . He was critical of certain things. The Director indicated that we were trying to do a lot of things for him." Smathers "stressed that he did not think at this time there should be any appeasement shown to Castro; no softness of any kind." He had just offered the same opinion to the president, he said, with the Reverend Billy Graham as his "witness." Dulles pledged to get Smathers's "wisdom" on the situation soon, adding that he was "working closely" with William Pawley. Hearing those reassurances, Smathers claimed to be "satisfied."[11]

Records of Kennedy's White House visitors are imperfect but indicate that Smathers saw the president there twice in March 1961. It was on those occasions, apparently, that Smathers, who admittedly "talked too much" about Cuba with Kennedy and sent him "memorandums at the rate of about two or three a week about something," had two unforgettable conversations with him. The senator would later recount them in interviews, including one in 1964 for the John F. Kennedy Presidential Library and another in 1975 for the Senate's Church Committee, which investigated alleged intelligence abuses in prior decades. He recalled that in March 1961 (the same month that Kilday's group heard about CIA plans), the president twice raised the taboo topic of assassination. The first conversation occurred inside the White House, but as Smathers recalls, Kennedy was "essentially an outdoor man," and so it was on the lawn of the presidential residence that the second and, for Smathers, more memorable discussion occurred: "The question came up about Cuba — what are we going to do about Cuba? I don't know whether he brought it up or I brought it up. We had further conversation of assassination of Fidel Castro, what would be the reaction, how would the people react, would the people be gratified. I'm sure he had his own ideas about it, but he was picking my brain on this particular question. . . . As I recollect, he was just throwing out a great barrage of questions. He was certain it could be accomplished — I remember that — it would be no problem." Indeed, Kennedy said he had been "given to believe" by CIA leaders that Castro would be dead by the time Cuban exiles landed on the shores of their native country.

Did Kennedy actually want Castro assassinated? Given Smathers's love for the dead Jack Kennedy, his awkward description of this part of the walking conversation can be taken with a grain of salt: "I talked with him about it and, frankly, at this particular time I felt, and I later on learned that he did, that I wasn't so much for the idea of assassination, particularly where it could be pinned on the United States." Whether or not Smathers later downplayed his and Kennedy's enthusiasm for killing Castro, he never denied his eagerness for intervention in 1960–1961. Seemingly unimpressed by the CIA's small-scale intervention plans, in that same walking conversation on the White House lawn, the senator pushed an alternate "plan of having a false attack made on Guantanamo Bay, which would give us the excuse of actually fomenting a fight, which would then give us the excuse to go in there and do the job."

While documentary evidence has never surfaced to substantiate Smathers's memories of the assassination conversations, there is little reason to doubt them: the CIA's Bissell authorized at least two attempts to assassinate Castro prior to Bay of Pigs. Nor can there be any doubt that Smathers knew in spring 1961 that some kind of Cuban intervention was forthcoming. Days before the event, he would try to provide a further justification for it, openly talking of "irrefutable evidence that missile bases are being built in Cuba."[12]

The only other legislator not on an Armed Services or Appropriations CIA subcommittee known to have heard authoritative advance word of the covert action was J. William Fulbright. The Foreign Relations chair probably heard no such thing from Dulles, under strict confidentiality orders from Eisenhower and Kennedy. Indeed, when the director readied himself for a January 11, 1961, appearance before Foreign Relations, Eisenhower complained at length and for the umpteenth time (a State Department notetaker recorded) that "we allowed ourselves to be pushed around to an unwarranted extent by congressional committees." The president "ruled that Mr. Dulles should testify, but that he should insist on no record being kept and no one else being present other than members of the committee and the Chief Clerk."[13]

Fulbright had read news accounts predicting a covert invasion of Cuba and may have checked their accuracy with Richard Russell, who would have known something of CIA preparations, but — as with Smathers — it was the new president himself who told Fulbright that the stories were essentially accurate. It happened by coincidence, when the president and Fulbright had plans to travel to Florida on March 30 for their respective Easter vacations. Kennedy offered the senator a ride on Air Force One. Fulbright accepted the invitation and then prepared for it by authoring a lengthy memo. It said that the much-rumored intervention would violate international law, be impossible to keep secret, undo "the work of 30 years in trying to live down earlier interventions," open "an endless can of worms," and fail to dislodge Castro.

After he read the memo, Kennedy said little about it to Fulbright on the plane ride. A junior member of Fulbright's committee just months before, Kennedy knew that it was no minor problem to have the chairman oppose a major covert action. When they flew back to Washington a few days later, Kennedy invited Fulbright to join him for a State Department meeting that afternoon. It turned out to be a large gathering — second-level foreign policy bureaucrats (including the CIA's Richard Bissell), White House staffers, and now Fulbright were there, along with Secretary of State Rusk, other members of the National Security Council, and the president. Though some of them later claimed to have had severe doubts about the operation's prospects, only Fulbright clearly opposed it, repeating to the group what he had said to the president in writing. No decision emerged from the meeting, although Kennedy urged the CIA to scale down the size of the operation so that it would more plausibly "appear as an internal uprising."

Without explicitly urging the president to abandon the Cuba plans, his speechwriter and all-purpose adviser Arthur Schlesinger wrote Kennedy a few days later, "The people who fail to understand the pressing necessity for this action include the Chairman of the Senate Foreign Relations Committee (and that he has said that the only members of his Committee whom he thinks would support the action are Senators [Thomas] Dodd and Lausche — which perhaps suggests the kind of people to whom the idea will automatically appeal.)"

Even if the U.S.-backed rebels should experience initial success, Schlesinger added, administration officials would "presumably be obliged, in the traditional, pre-U-2 manner, to deny any such CIA activity." But to avoid repetition of the Eisenhower administration's post–U-2 disarray, Kennedy should see to it that officers of his government fully grasped "the line we are prepared to take and stick to." That raised questions, including, "What about the Senate Foreign Relations Committee? What about the House Foreign Affairs

Committee? What about senators and congressmen in general? Someone should begin to think what they should be told."

Also, Schlesinger and Kennedy knew that some in the executive and legislative branches and among Cuban exile groups persistently assumed that, if early setbacks in a covert invasion of Cuba arose, JFK surely would authorize overt military intervention. Schlesinger reminded Kennedy on April 10 that "if the rebellion appears to be failing, the rebels will call for U.S. armed help." Then, "members of Congress will take up the cry." When that happens, "our people must be primed to oppose this demand." Two days later, the president told reporters, "There will not be, under any conditions, an intervention in Cuba by the United States armed forces."[14]

"I Agree That You Had to Replace Dulles"

Within hours of the intervention's beginning, it looked like a disaster for the United States and its Cuban associates. Given press reports, especially in Latin America, that some type of invasion loomed, Castro had ordered the arrests of thousands of political dissidents who might have sparked "resistance in other parts of the island" (in Cabell's words to Kilday). The fourteen hundred Cuban exiles who walked ashore or parachuted into their native homeland met strong resistance from Castro's military and were permitted little air support by Kennedy.

UN ambassador Adlai Stevenson initially denied Cuban and Soviet charges of U.S. intervention, as administration leaders struggled over what further actions Kennedy should take in support of the would-be liberators of Cuba. At a late-night White House reception for members of Congress on Tuesday, April 18, with the invasion still largely unknown to most legislators and the public, Robert Kennedy pulled Smathers aside from his dance partner, Jacqueline Kennedy. "The shit has hit the fan," the attorney general told him. At one Oval Office session, Smathers joined Mike Mansfield, Robert Kennedy, and the president in a desperate struggle to find a solution. When Smathers advocated massive aerial bombing to support the invasion, the attorney general profanely questioned his sanity. Smathers's advocacy and Fulbright's earlier cautions quickly leaked to the press.[1]

Over a hundred members of the brigade died in the fighting, with the rest captured and imprisoned. Even as a nearly simultaneous crisis in Laos developed, with Soviet-backed forces on the offensive, President Kennedy publicly assumed responsibility for the Bay of Pigs. Only eleven months had passed since Eisenhower's U-2 admission.

A few days after the failed intervention, at the Kennedy administration's request, the House expedited consideration of $600 million in foreign aid to Latin America. But members talked more of Castro and Cuba than they did the planned recipient nations. Otto Passman (D-LA) said of Castro's name, "It is a profanity." The bill passed 329 to 83, after scant discussion of the money's purposes. It was an "unheard of performance," said the *Washington Post*, "the administration's one tangible dividend so far from the Cuban crisis." Another result of Bay of Pigs astonished many, Kennedy included: his approval rating in the Gallup Poll jumped to 83 percent.[2]

The response to the failed invasion on the floor of the Senate and House was that of skepticism over its feasibility, mixed with a good deal of sympathy toward Kennedy and/or the CIA. An exception was Wayne Morse, who chaired the Latin America subcommittee of the Senate Foreign Relations Committee. When Bay of Pigs first unfolded, Morse had appeared on NBC's "Today Show" and faithfully drew on the president's and secretary of state's public statements to insist that the United States was not intervening in Cuba. Sadder and more knowledgeable on April 24, he told the Senate, "I hope we have not come to a pass when we have to keep a dictionary at hand and refer to it for an analysis of possible semantics or concealed meanings in statements issued by the White House and by the Department of State." It was not enough that the president had conferred "with one or two individual senators" before authorizing the invasion.

Perhaps the most unusual response came from Allen Ellender. In a Senate hearing, the Louisianan told air force secretary Eugene Zuckert and chief of staff General Thomas White that communist infiltration in Cuba was Soviet "retaliation" for being surrounded by American air bases: "We are reaping a lot of trouble for things we did in the past. People are squealing like pigs because of what happened in Cuba. We've been doing that to Russia for seven or eight years, haven't we?" Zuckert and White were too stunned by Ellender's remarks to respond. But few in the Congress agreed with Morse or Ellender. More common sentiment came from Senator Dodd: "The first attempt to liberate Cuba from the Castro tyranny failed for the simple reason that we had yet to make the stern resolve that this fight must not be permitted to fail."[3]

Decades later, few differ from the analysis of Aleksandr Fursenko and Timothy Naftali that the most tragic consequence of Bay of Pigs was the

> ascendancy of a Cuban security service dominated by the Soviet Union. For over a year, Fidel Castro had backed away from initiatives that could have transformed Cuba into a police state. Confronted with an increase in counterrevolutionary activity in the fall of 1960, however, Castro had taken the first important steps. The Bay of Pigs operation accelerated these changes, creating a momentum toward the building of a surveillance state that Fidel Castro had once considered avoidable.[4]

For the rest of 1961, CIA faced the inevitable investigations. The president appointed one group, headed by General Maxwell Taylor and including Robert Kennedy, Arleigh Burke, and Dulles. With the latter two men dissenting, the Taylor Report concluded that "under the conditions which developed, we are inclined to believe that the beachhead could not have survived long without substantial help from the Cuban population or without overt U.S. assistance." More secretly and bluntly, CIA inspector general Lyman Kirkpatrick concluded in an in-house review that agency leaders had failed the new president by not telling him that the operation's "success had become dubious" by spring 1961 and not recommending the operation's cancellation.[5]

At Fulbright's closed Foreign Relations hearings on May 1 and 2, just as former President Eisenhower publicly counseled against a "full-scale investigation" of Bay of Pigs, Dulles and Bissell essentially blamed President Kennedy and the Joint Chiefs of Staff for the debacle. Of the Cuban exiles, Dulles told a senator: "They had been trained together as a force. They knew their fire power, which was very high and, as I say, the general military estimate of the situation was that if they got ashore with the equipment, they could hold this beachhead for a considerable time, until they could have been substantially reinforced. That seemed to be the military judgment at the time, and people who have come back from the beaches have said . . . [t]hey could have handled the situation, if they could have had the ammunition and the air cover." Homer Capehart was incredulous that "our high military people" would have approved "what would appear to me to be a Boy Scout operation." Dulles claimed, "I do not want to put responsibility or blame on anyone else, but I can say we took the highest, the best military advice that we could get." When Capehart tried to clarify the respective roles of the CIA and the Joint Chiefs ("CIA did not particularly direct this invasion, did they, or train those people?"), Dulles left the senator mired in ignorance and ire toward the JCS by replying that the CIA had played "a part" in directing and training the invaders. "The plans were considered, as has been already indicated, at a very high level, and that consideration included high military men."

This bewildered Morse: "What I do not understand is why it was thought that twelve to sixteen hundred people, backed with three supply ships, plus these other three ships . . . could possibly establish a beachhead in this area of Cuba or two beachheads in this area of Cuba, when we knew, and we knew this from past briefings, that Castro had built up a considerable amount of artillery and tanks and defensive emplacements?" Dulles continued to shift blame to others: "The judgment as to its feasibility was concurred in, sir, by the various Americans who were familiar with these plans, and this included, of course, the military officers who helped formulate the plans, and also the Joint Chiefs of Staff."

Stuart Symington endorsed Dulles's and Bissell's defense of the agency against newspaper columnists who "have had a field day in socking the CIA" but wondered if "based on history, didn't we know that if they did have any fighter defense, that our position would be difficult, if not hopeless?" Bissell used this as an occasion to criticize the president (although never mentioning his name): "We did, indeed know that, sir, and we counted on knocking out their air strength on the ground before this operation started."[6]

The CIA leaders testified for almost four hours. Afterwards, Russell Long said that JCS chairman Lyman Lemnitzer should be fired, but Fulbright judged that there had been a "collective responsibility" for Bay of Pigs. Like other Foreign Relations members, he seemed satisfied by Dulles's and Bissell's words, telling the reporters, "I know all I want to know." Pressed by reporters whether Dulles conceded that the CIA had made a mistake, Fulbright paused, then provoked laughter by saying, "He conceded that the operation was not successful." Fulbright soon enjoyed many newspaper columnists' accolades for having opposed the invasion. He was "the only wise man" among Kennedy's advisers, wrote Walter Lippmann.[7]

Some of the subcommittees on the CIA in Congress looked more quietly into the matter. Kilday summoned Dulles and other CIA heads for a private and presumably unrecorded briefing. A week later, he told the Texas Chamber of Commerce that, after other bodies were finished, his subcommittee would seriously examine "a number of questions posed by the Agency's operations during the last 14 years." Ending CIA responsibility for carrying out secret operations against other nations "might be one area Congress should explore." A constituent warned Kilday that a whitewash would be "tragic in the extreme." Another wrote, "Since the horrible Cuban invasion fiasco, it seems unbelievable that the sleuths of the CIA should be allowed to continue to operate." Wherever Kilday's own eventual investigation led, his subcommittee published no reports and left behind very little paper trail.[8]

The House Appropriations CIA subcommittee called in Dulles and associates twice in May, the first time (May 12) to talk about Bay of Pigs and the second time for a budget hearing. (Another budget hearing would follow on a Sunday afternoon in June.) The first meeting left subcommittee members "still very well-disposed toward the Agency," Red White wrote in his diary. George Mahon — also briefed individually by Dulles and telephoned by President Kennedy following the invasion — had received scores of letters critical of the U.S. government. He wrote one corresponding friend that

America's "Cuban policy for the past several years has been characterized by a series of blunders. I am making known to appropriate officials the content of the messages which I am receiving, and expressing my own views." At the president's request, Mahon also authored an analysis of U.S. capabilities to fight limited wars. In sending it along, the subcommittee chair told JFK, "Command me, if I can be helpful."[9]

Agency overseers on Capitol Hill remained unanimously hostile toward Castro after Bay of Pigs. Styles Bridges wrote a friend and publicly stated, "We must act soon to rid this hemisphere of the threat which Castro represents." Uncharacteristically, for someone who had accused JFK of "appeasement with Communist Russia" eight days after his inauguration, Bridges abstained from denigrating the president after the Cuba disaster.

The subcommittee leaders were split in their privately expressed views about who should be blamed for the invasion's failure. Carl Hayden concurred with the "general agreement that what happened can be principally attributed to the Central Intelligence Agency, which failed to perform the function for which it was created and for which it should be held accountable." When Senator Albert Gore wrote President Kennedy that it would be wise "to abolish the name and the Agency (CIA) and to disperse its functions for a period of time," Richard Russell told Gore that he "generally" agreed, especially regarding the name change. (Whether due to the senators or not, Dulles discussed the name change idea in May with the President. Kennedy left the decision up to the DCI, who let the suggestion die.)[10]

Apparently without insisting on Dulles's removal immediately after Bay of Pigs, Russell told Kennedy in person, "The position of Director of Central Intelligence in these troublous days is second in importance only to the presidency." Responding by telephone from his home in Georgia later in 1961 to JFK's request for an evaluation of John McCone, his nominee to replace Dulles, Russell wondered if McCone "has the imagination it takes — that job requires a peculiar type of operator." But, when the president began to defend his removal of Dulles, Russell cut him off: "Oh, I agree that you had to replace Dulles." Clarence Cannon, by contrast, wrote the outgoing DCI that the CIA "was made the scapegoat of the Cuban fiasco to save those in policy making activities who really sponsored the project." To no avail, he, Mahon, and other members of the House Appropriations CIA subcommittee had written Kennedy after Bay of Pigs, endorsing Dulles's "exceptionally reliable, efficient, and competent" performance. After it became clear that Dulles would go, Mahon wrote him, "In my judgment, you did a wonderful job as Director of the Central Intelligence Agency. . . . you will continue to have a top place on my list of friends."[11]

The *New York Times'* editorial page blamed Bay of Pigs on executive branch agency leaders and unnamed "senators who should have used their influence" to stop the intervention. Although not saying so publicly, some legislators knew that, by fiercely urging presidents Eisenhower and Kennedy to do "something" about Castro while downplaying the complexities involved, they had been complicit in the policy. Some had the *Congressional Record* and their own past correspondence and press releases checked to see if they had or had not suggested an intervention. An aide to Mahon reported, "Nothing in our files shows anything to indicate that Mr. M favors invading or staying out of Cuba."[12]

With the encouragement of others, Senator Eugene McCarthy introduced a joint intelligence committee resolution on April 27. A *Times* reporter asserted on May 2 that "the attempt to overthrow Premier Fidel Castro's regime in Cuba revived increased congressional uneasiness over the Agency's activities" and that support was increasing for a joint intelligence committee. Some of the resolution's supporters thought that since Kennedy had supported the similar Mansfield resolution in 1956, he would back McCarthy. But now, the new majority leader (and Kennedy loyalist) Mansfield said, "This is no time for a congressional investigation," and the president reactivated Eisenhower's old Foreign Intelligence Advisory Board. This was part of an attempt "to dampen demands for closer congressional supervision and investigation," said the *Times*. Naively, the newspaper's editorial page wrote that Mansfield was "unaccountably failing to press this idea, just when it may have a chance of adoption." By the summer, a Kennedy administration figure privately wrote, "There is no real strong move in Congress to do anything about CIA." As the year moved toward a close, Clark Clifford, an important part-time adviser to the president, listed five top priorities for the next DCI — one was to "stoutly and intelligently" resist efforts to "establish a joint congressional committee on foreign intelligence" as it "could seriously hamper the efficient and effective operation of our intelligence activities." Not until five more years' worth of intelligence controversies unfolded would the resolution go before the full Senate.[13]

By year's end, the *Times* had published a record amount about the CIA — fifty-seven articles, columns, editorials, and letters. There was little mention in the press, though, of the topic that had arisen quietly at the CIA and the White House when Kennedy talked to Smathers — an assassination attempt against Castro. Exceptions were Drew Pearson and Stewart Alsop in the *Post* (and, through syndication, scores of newspapers around the country). As the Bay of Pigs invasion crumbled, Pearson wrote, "Fidel Castro now sleeps in his office, his bodyguard doubled. He is deathly afraid of assassination. His fears may not be unfounded." A few days later, filling in for his brother, Stewart Alsop wrote a column titled "If You Strike at a King." It said, "The prestige and even the honor of the United States are now obviously and wholly committed to Castro's ultimate downfall. There is hardly anybody in the higher reaches of the Kennedy administration who does not agree that this commitment to Castro's destruction now in fact exists."

Days later in the same newspaper, though, Chalmers Roberts predicted that the president would not "get his fingers burned again" in Cuba but worried that Congress evidenced a "new chauvinism ... born of frustration" that could be "troublesome to the President and dangerous to the nation's future." Roberts probably did not know it, but Kennedy was specifically troubled by Smathers's "pushing, pushing, pushing." This continued until one night early in 1962, when the Florida senator joined Kennedy for a private meal: "The President was actually fixing our own dinner, and I raised the question about Cuba, and what could be done and so on. And I remember that he took his fork and just hit his plate, and it cracked, and he said, 'Now, damn it, I wish you wouldn't do that! Let's quit talking about this subject.'" The senator who had most aggressively pushed two presidents to rid Cuba of Castro promised never to broach the topic again with Kennedy. He apparently never did.[14]

The former president that had approved the program that came to be known as Bay of Pigs warmly received a briefing on the Taylor Committee Report at his Gettysburg home from Taylor and Dulles in June 1961. Dwight Eisenhower had not changed his views toward Congress and covert action. Taylor noted after the visit, "I received the impression that General Eisenhower perceives the need of suppressing further public debate of the Cuban operation." Ike "expressed disapproval of the recent TV appearance" by Senator Joseph Clark "in which the Cuban operation was argued."

The idea of Cuba as a threat to the United States would not vanish. In July, Styles Bridges warned the Senate, "Soviet MIGs have begun arriving in Cuba." That same month, according to Red White's diary, "Ed Saunders received a telephone call from Sam Crosby, staff member of the House Committee on Appropriations, who said the Committee had received reports that 'the U-2 flights over Cuba last week revealed missile bases under construction.' Mr. Crosby requested that he be briefed on this subject." The CIA briefed him two days later, apparently, and then briefed Bob Smart of Kilday's staff. What they were told remains unknown, but Eisenhower's old "missile gap" nemesis, Stuart Symington, saw an *Army Times* story later in 1961 claiming that the Soviet Union had constructed four launching pads for intermediate missiles that "could hit as far north as Washington and inland from 1000 to 1200 miles." After Symington or a staffer contacted the agency about the report, the senator scrawled a note: "CIA does not believe so."[15]

Afterword: Alarms

It may be routine someday for histories of U.S. foreign policy (and the narrower realm of intelligence) during the early Cold War era to show how Congress mattered, occasionally, as much as the occupant of the Oval Office. I hope that this book contributes to that goal. No doubt, future analysts will reach some conclusions that I will not share, which is fair enough. Having rummaged for the better part of a decade through the "attic" of Congress and the CIA for documents, though, I offer a few thoughts.

Much of the Conventional Wisdom about Congress and the CIA Is Accurate

Legislative oversight of the CIA was not comprehensive. Particularly on the Senate side, Carl Hayden's agreement to "combine" his Appropriations subcommittee with that of Richard Russell's Armed Services subcommittee meant, in effect, that the CIA would escape close scrutiny of its budget and activities by Senate Appropriations from the mid-1950s onward. Senator Russell's reluctance to employ more than one staffer in keeping up with the CIA necessarily limited the monitoring performed by the Armed Services subcommittee as well.

There is virtually no evidence to suggest that legislators knew of CIA involvement in domestic affairs, including the subsidy of American think tanks and other intellectual enterprises, the opening of mail of U.S. citizens, and certain drug tests on human subjects. (Possibly, someday, researchers will find documentation suggesting that members of Congress did know of such activities.)

Most of the time, Congress deferred to presidents and leaders of the CIA on crucial intelligence issues. As virtually all scholars agree, legislators of that era shared a belief common among the general public and in the press that presidents and their top assistants should lead in foreign affairs. Furthermore, as John Warner stressed to me in an interview (as he had to Allen Dulles decades earlier), senior members of the Armed Services and Appropriations committees were busy — and often overworked. Even the elderly Carl Hayden was a hardworking and extremely busy legislator. Had Hayden headed a formal committee on intelligence, he might have been effective as an overseer of the CIA. But, as Mike Mansfield understood all too well, Hayden chaired an Appropriations Committee charged with setting the budgets of all executive branch agencies.

Congress rarely fought along party lines about the CIA. Democratic and Republican CIA subcommittee leaders' cooperation was especially strong.

Much of the Conventional Wisdom Is Wrong or Incomplete

Congressional oversight was not simply passive or static across the CIA's first fifteen years. Citizens and the press barely knew of variations in oversight practices at the time, and they have never been explored in published histories. Still, the preceding pages make it obvious that monitoring of the agency had become decidedly more extensive in the late 1950s, for example, than it was a decade earlier. The reasons for this are not hard to fathom: much-publicized intelligence "failures" had occurred every year or so, setting off discontent in the public and press and leading to congressional complaints or questions about the agency's performance. After a string of such events — Bogota, the Soviet A-bomb, Korea, Hungary, Suez, Sputnik — Mike Mansfield's joint intelligence committee idea had robust appeal (even after its 1956 defeat), leading the CIA subcommittee chairs to promise more in the way of oversight.

In other words, the American political environment had thus become increasingly conducive to the development of improved intelligence oversight. If and how that might occur remained highly contingent, though, on Congress and the powerful chairs of the House and Senate Appropriations and Armed Services committees. Russell and Hayden seem to have barely altered their procedures, while House chairs Cannon and Vinson appointed trusted junior colleagues to head their CIA subcommittees. Those bodies made considerable use of staffers in subsequent monitoring of the agency. This fits with what scholars of the era knew, and as one wrote, "The House has developed over the years a corps of members who are devoted subject-matter experts to a degree quite unusual in the Senate." Overall, in my judgment, the House carried out more effective oversight of the CIA than the Senate did in the early Cold War era.[1]

Still, congressional assertiveness/passivity toward the CIA varied across those years in both branches. Matthew McCubbins and Thomas Schwartz would later capture the essence of legislative oversight of the executive branch, characterizing it as historically having been limited and best compared to the alarm systems used long ago in cities to permit those who discovered fires to report them. In essence, when the public or the news media or interest groups are energized to complain about problems badly handled by government bureaucracies, they pressure Congress to investigate. Oversight activities are thus a function of the "alarms" being set off in a given time frame. The notion that the post–World War II Congress has been or is continuously and vigilantly on "patrol" for agencies' poor performance is naive.[2]

McCubbins and Schwartz never mention the CIA, but the events described herein mostly fit the pattern they describe. Congress was more assertive toward the CIA following apparent failures to estimate events and conditions properly. No matter how informal, the recurrent congressional inquiries into those lapses prodded DCIs all the more toward the goal of competence in doing estimates, or (in the words of many a legislator) avoiding "another Pearl Harbor." In quieter times, of course, Congress was comparatively passive and deferential.

Congress was hawkish about covert action. This was true not only of almost all leaders with knowledge of the CIA, but also of others who knew little. In all of my explorations of published and unpublished materials, I very rarely encountered a legislator privately telling a DCI or president that the agency should avoid covert action. But I discovered a couple of dozen cases where members of Congress advocated the "quiet" option.

The significance of Congress formally endorsing covert action, by way of the Kersten Amendment, has been neglected in the history books.[3] So has the prevalent opinion of powerful legislators, in the aftermath of that amendment's passage, that Congress should avoid "going public" again about covert action.

Overall, I believe that, in addition to presidential directives, congressional attitudes helped move the CIA toward assertive covert action.

Congressional oversight looked far different to Allen Dulles and most other CIA leaders than it did to later critics. If DCIs rarely had to worry about Hayden or even Leverett Saltonstall, they gave substantial time and energy to keeping Richard Russell, Clarence Cannon, John Taber, Paul Kilday, George Mahon, Styles Bridges, Mike Mansfield, and quite a few others satisfied. Those that could not be accommodated, like Joseph McCarthy, nonetheless demanded and received attention.

Also, while Dulles understood that nothing mattered more on the Senate side than being responsive to Richard Russell, he knew that the Armed Services chairman might farm out oversight duties during times of public controversy, anointing Stuart Symington's subcommittee to explore bomber gap concerns and Lyndon Johnson's subcommittee to explore the implications of Sputnik.

Whether it was Cannon, Vinson, Russell, Taber, or almost anyone else, early DCIs understood their intent regarding a few overarching priorities: the CIA should detect plans by enemy nations to attack or otherwise harm the United States or its allies. A DCI presiding over a failure to do so risked being forced out, not just by the president but by leaders in Congress, as happened to Roscoe Hillenkoetter. Too, the directors understood that the agency should carry out effective covert action in support of American foreign policy.

Was Congress Irresponsible in Its Oversight of the Early Cold War CIA?

A simple answer is not obvious, in my view. In the mid-1970s, the Senate's Church Committee and the House's Pike Committee found that Congress had been grossly negligent, both in the quantity and quality of its monitoring of the agency. Most histories of the CIA, although barely touching on legislative oversight, have accepted the committees' analyses. Such critiques have honorable roots: Congress pronounced in the Legislative Reorganization Act of 1946 that its oversight of executive branch agencies should be "continuous," "vigilant," and "thorough."

If the events described in this book suggest anything, though, it is that Congress was more assertive in relation to the CIA than has been understood. Its oversight of the agency in the early Cold War era was limited and informal, hardly matching the standards that Congress set for itself in 1946 or in the 1970s, but far from nonexistent.

Quantity does not equal quality, of course. Joseph McCarthy aggressively monitored CIA activities, but few think that he did so responsibly. The legitimacy of Stuart Symington's assertiveness on the missile gap issue is also widely questioned by historians.

Furthermore, legislators did not prevent the agency from engaging in certain abuses of its charter. Nor did presidents. Indeed, historians have made clear in recent decades that many of the CIA's legally questionable domestic activities and morally questionable foreign activities were carried out in response to presidential directives. Evidence may even show someday that the Richard Russells and Clarence Cannons of the era joined with presidents in

suggesting that the CIA involve itself in domestic affairs as a matter of supposed national security. Of course, they may have warned agency leaders
against such activities.

Whether or not sufficient documentation ever emerges to settle the question, it seems fair to suggest that if the Congress of 1947–1961 should be held
accountable for CIA failures and misdeeds, then it should be credited for
CIA successes. These were not negligible. Perhaps most important are the
agency's many estimates that the Soviet Union, for all its military might and
expansionist tendencies, was not planning to launch offensive war against
the United States. In an era when many feared surprise nuclear attack by the
USSR, the CIA consistently (and we may now say "correctly") estimated that
such an attack was highly unlikely for as far ahead as its analysts could predict. On innumerable occasions, DCIs shared this judgment with legislators,
thus lowering the fear on Capitol Hill and around the nation.

Finally, despite my best efforts over the past decade to unearth documentation about the CIA and Congress, evidence is still extremely scarce about
crucial interactions. Actual notes, much less transcripts, of agency heads' testimony before the Armed Services and Appropriations subcommittees have
rarely been declassified. Whether they even exist in CIA files is unclear. (With
one notable exception, my attempt to obtain such papers under the Freedom of Information Act failed.) While a few memoranda of discussions
between DCIs and congressional leaders have surfaced, they are just that —
few. No one doubts that Senator Russell was a noteworthy figure in relation
to the agency, but did he ever (responsibly) provoke reforms at the CIA? We
do not know.

Perhaps the best frame of reference for answering the responsibility/irre-
sponsibility question is provided by Senator Mansfield's joint intelligence
committee proposals of the 1950s. Possibly, a reasonably staffed single committee would have performed more effectively than the variety of CIA subcommittees. Arguably, that committee might have approved and supported
the agency's notable production of estimates on conditions and threats in
world politics. Perhaps such a committee would have discovered and forced
the discontinuation of agency involvement in domestic affairs. The committee might have urged a distinctly different approach to covert action, though
this seems unlikely.

On the whole, although Senator Russell's fear of a leak-prone staff was
warranted, I think congressional oversight in the early Cold War era would
have been somewhat more responsible if Mansfield had prevailed. Still, if

the system of oversight in place since the mid-1970s, which features House and Senate intelligence committees, shows anything, it is that effective congressional monitoring of intelligence does not easily occur under any imaginable set-up. Long before the events of September 11, 2001, there was a well-established history of complaints about ineffective oversight by those two large, well-staffed committees that had extensive interactions with the CIA and other intelligence agencies.[4] After that massive terrorist attack, widespread calls to reform the system would emerge yet again. Among the ideas: a joint congressional committee on intelligence.

Notes

FIRST HIDDEN, THEN LOST

1. Frank Smist's *Congress Oversees the United States Intelligence Community, 1947–1994*, 2nd ed. (Knoxville: University of Tennessee Press, 1994), touches only briefly on the early days of the CIA and Congress.

2. George Galloway and Sidney Wise, *History of the House of Representatives*, 2nd ed. (New York: Crowell, 1976), p. 216. Roger Davidson and Colton Campbell, "The Senate and the Executive," in *Esteemed Colleagues: Civility and Deliberation in the U.S. Senate*, ed. Burdett Loomis (Washington, DC: Brookings, 2000), p. 213.

3. Citations for all quotes can be found in the chapters that follow.

4. Doolittle Report excerpts, in William Leary, ed., *The Central Intelligence Agency: History and Documents* (Tuscaloosa: University of Alabama Press, 1984), pp. 143–45.

NO "AMERICAN GESTAPO," BUT "NO MORE PEARL HARBORS"

1. *Congressional Record* (hereafter *CR*), 7-7-47, pp. 8295, 8299, 8320, 9421, 7-19-47, p. 9419. Members of Congress surely had the Soviet Union on their minds but did not say so in the floor debates.

2. *CR*, 7-24-47, p. 9913.

3. DCI Vandenberg's January–May 1947 diary, CIA Records, National Archives (hereafter NA).

4. J. Adams to Leverett Saltonstall, 9-5-47, Box 162, Leverett Saltonstall Papers. Pforzheimer to Hillenkoetter, 5-29-47, and memo for record, 6-19-47, U.S. Department of State, *Foreign Relations of the United States* (hereafter *FRUS*), *Emergence of the Intelligence Establishment, 1945–1950* (hereafter *Emergence*), (Washington, DC: GPO, 1996), p. 573. David F. Rudgers, *Creating the Secret State: The Origins of the Central Intelligence Agency, 1943–1947* (Lawrence: University Press of Kansas, 2000), p. 144. Pforzheimer, work diary, 3-26-47, CIA Records Search Tool (hereafter CREST), NA.

5. Walter Pforzheimer, author interview. Pforzheimer to Busbey, 4-29-47, CIA Records, Historical Source Collection (hereafter CIA/HSC), Box 1, NA.

6. Pforzheimer, memo for record, 6-19-47, and memo to Hillenkoetter, 5-29-47, *FRUS: Emergence*, pp. 573–74, 576. Donovan to Gurney, 5-7-47, Box 5, CIA/HSC. *Current Biography, 1950* (Gurney) (New York: H. W. Wilson Co., 1950), pp. 207–9.

7. Vandenberg statement, 4-29-47 (Expenditures), and 5-1-47 (Armed Services), Box 5, CIA/HSC.

8. Executive hearing, 6-27-47, Box 399, House Committee on Expenditures Papers, NA. *Current Biography, 1947* (Brown), pp. 66–68.

9. Deputy Director Edwin Wright's diary (JFK), 7-21-47 and 7-29-47, Pforzheimer,

diary, 5-9-47 and 7-18-47 (JFK), 1-10-49 (Gurney), and 2-23-49 (Sasscer), 2-17-50 (Pepper), Assistant Deputy Director for Administration (hereafter ADD/A) diary (Taber), 5-16-52, all in CREST. Pforzheimer, author interview.

10. Edson testimony, partial transcript by Pforzheimer, 6-17-47, Box 5, CIA/HSC. Pforzheimer's memory of the "borrowed" transcript is backed up by Wright's diary, 7-8-47, CREST. Rudgers, *Creating*, p. 145.

11. Pforzheimer, author interview; memo for record, 4-29-47, Box 13, and "Excerpts . . . Hearings of the House Committee on Expenditures," 5-8-47 and 6-24-47, Box 5, CIA/HSC. Hillenkoetter to Gurney, 6-3-47, *FRUS: Emergence*, pp. 574–75.

12. Thomas Troy, *Donovan and the CIA: A History of the Establishment of the Central Intelligence Agency* (Frederick, MD: University Publications of America, 1981), p. 385. Pforzheimer, memo for record, 4-29-47, Box 13, CIA/HSC.

13. Houston to Hillenkoetter, 9-25-47, and notes by Arthur Darling on conversations with Houston, 1952 and 1953, Boxes 12 and 13, "Excerpts from Hearings," 4-1-47, Box 5, all in CIA/HSC. Expenditures agreed that the Armed Services Committee should handle future legislation detailing CIA powers (*CR*, 7-19-47, p. 9445).

14. *New York Times* (hereafter, *Times*), 11-22-47, p. 7. Fredric H. Cowart, "Mahon and Manhattan: Sharing the Secret" (unpublished paper), 5-6-92, Reference File, George Mahon Papers.

15. E. K. Wright, diary, 6-6-47, CREST. NIA minutes, 2-12-47 and 6-26-47, W. Eddy to Marshall, 2-15-47, and M. Leva to Marshall, 4-15-47, all in *FRUS: Emergence*, pp. 492–93, 494–95, 775–76, and Supplementary Documents microfiche.

16. NIA leaders to Hoffman, 6-26-47, Hillenkoetter to Gurney, 6-3-47, Minutes of NIA meeting, 6-26-47, all in *FRUS: Emergence*, pp. 311–12, 575, 775–76.

17. Dulles statement, 4-25-47, Box 398, House Expenditures Committee, NA.

18. *Times*, 7-7-47 and 7-8-47, p. 1. *CR*, 7-7-47, pp. 8295, 8320.

19. *CR*, 7-19-47, pp. 9430, 9444–45, 9448.

20. *CR*, 7-19-47, p. 9444.

21. *FRUS: Emergence*, pp. 576–78, 775–77. *CR*, 7-19-47, p. 9412. Rudgers, *Creating*, pp. 143–48.

22. George Gallup, *The Gallup Poll: Public Opinion, 1935–1971*, vol. 1 (New York: Random House, 1972), pp. 665–66.

INITIAL OVERSIGHT: BUDGETS AND COVERT ACTION

1. Lovett, summary notes of NSC meeting, 6-3-48, *FRUS: Emergence*, p. 695.

2. *U.S. News and World Report* (Hillenkoetter), 7-21-50, p. 26. Pforzheimer, diary, 12-11-47, CREST.

3. Nelson Polsby, *How Congress Evolves: Social Bases of Institutional Change* (New York: Oxford University Press, 2004), p. 149. Stephen Horn's *Unused Power: The Work of the Senate Committee on Appropriations* (Washington, DC: Brookings, 1970), pp. 38–40, 76, 97–100, 127, 135, 178, 186, notes that legislators "often acquire vested interests" in the agencies they oversee.

4. Richard Fenno, *The Power of the Purse: Appropriations Politics in Congress* (Boston: Little, Brown, 1966), pp. 137–38.

5. Pforzheimer, memo for record, 10-25-51, Michael Warner, ed., *The CIA under Harry Truman* (Washington, DC: Center for Study of Intelligence, 1994), pp. 441–43. William Darden, author interview.

6. The Joint Committee on Atomic Energy received estimates regarding Soviet nuclear progress two or three times a year in the late 1940s. Hillenkoetter provided Senator Ralph O. Brewster with a "secret" CIA analysis of civil aviation capabilities of a group of foreign nations. See Hillenkoetter to Brewster, 12-10-47, Box 4, CIA/HSC.

7. Darling, notes on interview with Sidney Souers, 12-9-52, Box 13, CIA/HSC. See also NSC meeting notes, 6-3-48, showing Secretary of the Army Royall's distaste for covert action in peacetime, in *FRUS: Emergence*, pp. 696–97.

8. Gallup, *Gallup Poll*, vol. 1, pp. 721, 726. Kennan to Lovett and Marshall, 5-19-48, and to Lovett, 5-25-47, *FRUS: Emergence*, pp. 684–85, 690.

9. Hillenkoetter to NSC, 5-24-48, *FRUS: Emergence*, pp. 688–89.

10. Houston to Hillenkoetter, 9-25-47. On February 13, 1953, Houston interpreted his 1947 memo to mean that Congress might have wanted legislation or "or least to have its committees on expenditures informed in general terms regarding the operation." See Darling's summary of Houston's remarks, Box 13, CIA/HSC.

11. "Memorandum for the President," reporting discussion in NSC meeting, 5-20-48, and another NSC meeting, 6-3-48, *FRUS: Emergence*, pp. 686–87, 694–98.

12. Quotations are from "Early Mention of CIA Covert Action Activities to the Congress," Pforzheimer (then CIA consultant) to DCI William Colby, 5-16-75, CIA Records, Troy Papers, Box 12, NA. Hillenkoetter's subcommittee testimony was on 4-8-48.

13. *CR*, 3-25-48, pp. 3525–26. Bridges, cited in "Memorandum for the President of Discussion . . . National Security Council," 5-20-48, in *FRUS: Emergence*, pp. 686–87; and in *Current Biography, 1948* (Operation X), p. 65. James Richards (D-SC), subsequent House Foreign Affairs Committee chair, met with Acheson in the latter's office on January 9, 1950, to urge vigorous covert operations. See *FRUS: Memoranda of Conversations of the Secretary of State, 1947–1952*, Microfiche Supplement (Washington, DC: GPO, 1988).

14. Executive session of Foreign Relations Committee, 11-17-47, in U.S. Senate, Committee on Foreign Relations, *Foreign Relief Act: 1947* (Washington, DC: GPO, 1973), pp. 152–54. Thomas Powers, *The Man Who Kept the Secrets: Richard Helms and the CIA* (New York: Knopf, 1979), p. 326.

15. Kennan to Lovell and Marshall, 6-16-48, *FRUS: Emergence*, p. 709. NSC 10/2, *FRUS: Emergence*, pp. 713–15.

"A SOUTH AMERICAN PEARL HARBOR"

1. Beaulac to Marshall, 3-22-48, and to Lovett, 4-9-48, *FRUS, The Western Hemisphere, 1948* (Washington, DC: GPO, 1972), pp. 22–23, 39. *CR*, 4-15-48, pp. 4559–61. *Newsweek*, 4-26-48, pp. 22–23. *Times*, 4-13-48, pp. 3, 24, 4-14-48, p. 11.

468 Notes to Pages 34–42

2. *Times,* 4-13-48 (editorial), p. 26, 4-17-48 (Mansfield), p. 7. Brown, statement to press, Box 14, CIA/HSC. *CR,* 4-15-48 (Jackson), p. 4560.

3. E. K. Wright, diary (Taft), 4-12-48, CREST. *Public Papers of the Presidents: Harry S. Truman, 1948* (Washington, DC: GPO, 1966), p. 216. *Times,* 4-13-48 (Dewey), p. 24, 4-15-48 (Lovett), p. 15.

4. "Statement of . . . Hillenkoetter," 4-15-48, Records of NSC, Harry S. Truman (hereafter HST) Library. *Times,* 4-16-48, p. 1. Grogan to A. Dulles (apology), 5-16-58, Box 3, CIA/HSC.

5. *Times,* 4-16-48, pp. 1, 6. CIA, "Bogota Riots" history, Box 14, CIA/HSC.

6. DCI-State memo of conversation, 4-16-48, *FRUS: Emergence,* pp. 312–15. *Times,* 4-18-48, p. 25. Souers to President ("Protection"), 5-20-48, NSC Records, HST Library.

7. NSC reports to Truman, 5-20-48, Kennan to Lovett, 5-25-48, *FRUS: Emergence,* pp. 686–87, 690. *Times,* 4-16-48, p. 19. K. McDuff to S. Spingarn, 4-13-48, Box 1, Spingarn Papers, R. Blum to Hillenkoetter, 4-14-48, Souers to NSC members, 4-23-48, Records of NSC, HST Library. *CR,* 4-15-48, p. 4550 (Italy), 4-21-48, p. 4721. Pforzheimer to A. Schwartz, 5-6-48, in Warner, *CIA under Harry Truman,* pp. 197–98. On management of covert action: memos to Truman, 6-3-48 and 7-7-49, *FRUS: Emergence,* pp. 696, 985. William S. White, *Home Place: The Story of the U.S. House of Representatives* (Boston: Houghton Mifflin, 1965) (Marcantonio), p. 14. Christopher M. Andrew, *For the President's Eyes Only: Secret Intelligence and the American Presidency from Washington to Bush* (New York: Harper Collins, 1995), pp. 154–64.

8. J. R. Steelman to President, 4-24-48, B File, CIA, HST Library. Ironically, Forrestal had argued to Hillenkoetter that "criticisms in Congress and elsewhere" spurred the need for new management of covert action, resulting in OPC's creation. In turn, Hillenkoetter would assert in 1949 that "the Bureau of the Budget and the Congress last year had questioned duplication in the administration of the Central Intelligence Agency." Hillenkoetter added, "Consequently . . . CIA had changed to a single administration for secret operations and administrative affairs." J. Lay to M. Leva, 9-21-48, Records of NSC, HST Papers, Box 9, H. Hurley to J. Steelman, 2-7-49, HST Papers, Official File, Box 1259, all in HST Library.

"THIS IS AN ESPIONAGE BILL"

1. R. Lee to Taber, February 1949, John Taber Papers. *CR,* 6-19-48, pp. 9107–8. Nelson Polsby, *Congress and the Presidency* (Englewood Cliffs, NJ: Prentice-Hall, 1964), p. 39. Richard Helms, "Present at the Creation," in *In the Name of Intelligence: Essays in Honor of Walter Pforzheimer,* ed. Hayden Peake and Samuel Halpern (Washington, DC: NIBC Press, 1994), p. 288.

2. Pforzheimer, memo for record (LBJ), 4-8-48, *FRUS: Emergence,* p. 600. *Times,* 7-20-48 through 7-25-48, analyzed by S. Grogan for Hillenkoetter, undated, Box 15, CIA/HSC. Pforzheimer, "Early Mention," CIA Records, Troy Papers, Box 12, NA; and Church Committee, *Final Report,* Book One, pp. 493–94.

3. Arthur Darling, *The Central Intelligence Agency: An Instrument of Government, to 1950* (University Park: Pennsylvania State University Press, 1990), p. 285. Pforzheimer, "Early Mention," 5-16-75, CIA Records, Troy Papers, Box 12, NA; and Church Committee, *Final Report,* Book One, pp. 493–94. Pforzheimer to CIA Executive Director, 3-30-48, and F. Howe to P. Armstrong, 12-29-48, *FRUS: Emergence,* Microfiche Supplement. *CR,* 3-7-49, pp. 1944–46, 5-27-49, pp. 6949–51.

4. *CR,* 3-7-49, pp. 1942–49. *Times,* 3-7-49, p. 2, 3-8-49, p. 3. Pforzheimer, memo (McCarran's Judiciary subcommittee request), 3-24-49, CREST.

5. *CR,* 5-27-49, pp. 6950, 6952, 6955, 3-7-49, pp. 1945–47. Church Committee, *Final Report,* Book One, p. 495.

6. *CR,* 3-7-49, p. 1949.

7. *CR,* 5-27-49, pp. 6949–56. On Langer, see Pforzheimer diary, 3-21-49, CREST; Drew Pearson, *Diaries: 1949–1959,* ed. Tyler Abell (New York: Holt, Rinehart, and Winston, 1974), pp. 132–33; and *American National Biography,* vol. 13 (New York: Oxford University Press, 1999), pp. 151–52.

8. *CR,* 3-7-49, p. A1289, 5-27-49, pp. 6947–56, 6-7-49, pp. 7368–70. On March 23, 1949, Representative Arthur Miller (R-NE) offered a negative critique of the CIA, drawing from the "Eberstadt Report" of the Hoover Commission, and suggested creation of a joint intelligence committee (*CR,* pp. A1663–64). Office of General Counsel, "Historical Study of the Use of Confidential Funds," undated (from 1952–1954), p. 8, Box 7, CIA/HSC. *Times,* 3-8-49, p. 3, 5-28-49, p. 5, 6-8-49, p. 15. On Dickstein, see Allen Weinstein, *The Haunted Wood: Soviet Espionage in America* (New York: Random House, 1999), pp. 140–50, 228, 341. CIA to NSC, 2-28-49, *FRUS: Emergence,* p. 940. DCI-Alsop correspondence, 1948–1949, CREST.

9. Houston to Hillenkoetter, 5-7-48, *FRUS: Emergence,* pp. 602–3. Houston and Pforzheimer to Hillenkoetter, 9-27-49, "The Central Intelligence Agency and National Organization for Intelligence," by Dulles, William H. Jackson, and Mathias Correa, 1-1-49, Darling, notes of interview with Hillenkoetter, 10-24-52, all in Boxes 6, 7, 12, CIA/HSC. Darling, *Central Intelligence Agency,* p. 327.

10. CIA, "Comments on the Dulles Report," 2-28-49, *FRUS: Emergence,* pp. 936–42.

11. Howe to Armstrong, 9-8-49, *FRUS: Emergence,* p. 1011. Houston and Pforzheimer to Hillenkoetter, 9-27-49, Box 7, CIA/HSC. Emphasis in the original.

THE SOVIET A-BOMB: "WE APPARENTLY DON'T HAVE THE REMOTEST IDEA"

1. *CR,* 9-22-49, pp. 13140–42. David E. Lilienthal, *The Atomic Energy Years, 1945–1950,* vol. 2 of *The Journals of David E. Lilienthal* (New York: Harper and Row, 1964), pp. 472, 592–93. On McMahon and JCAE, see Stephen Schwartz, ed., *Atomic Audit: The Costs and Consequences of U.S. Nuclear Weapons since 1940* (Washington, DC: Brookings, 1998), pp. 502–4.

2. *Time,* 10-3-49, p. 8. Topics are listed for six secret JCAE hearings (not the only ones that occurred) in the *CIS Index to Unpublished House of Representatives*

Committee Hearings, 1947–1954 (Washington, DC: Congressional Information Service, 1980).

3. *CR*, 9-23-49, p. 13191. *Time*, 10-3-49, p. 7. McMahon to Johnson, 7-14-49, *FRUS: National Security Affairs, 1949* (Washington, DC: GPO, 1976), pp. 482–84. *Philadelphia Inquirer*, 9-24-49, p. 2.

4. Richard J. Aldrich, *The Hidden Hand: Britain, America, and Cold War Secret Intelligence* (New York: Overlook Press, 2002), p. 228. Machle to Hillenkoetter, 10-29-49, *FRUS: Emergence*, pp. 1012–16. *Times*, 9-24-49, p. 1. *U.S. News and World Report*, 10-7-49, p. 18. *Newsweek*, 10-3-49, p. 21, 10-10-49, p. 29.

5. *Times*, 9-26-49, p. 3, 9-25-49, p. E6. *CR*, 9-28-49, p. 13472. *Philadelphia Inquirer*, 9-25-49, p. 2.

6. *Newsweek*, 10-3-49, p. 26. John Ranelagh, *The Agency: The Rise and Decline of the CIA* (New York: Simon and Schuster, 1986), pp. 171–72. Lilienthal, *Atomic Energy Years*, p. 335. Without naming the CIA, Lilienthal is obviously talking about it in the Hoover conversation. Hillenkoetter, office diary, 7-10-47, CREST.

7. JCAE, "Summary of Executive Meeting," 3-21-49, and "Notes on Closed Meeting," 10-14-49, *CIS Unpublished U.S. House of Representatives Hearings on Microfiche* (Washington, DC: Congressional Information Service) (hereafter, *CIS Unpublished House Hearings*); "Record of the Meeting of the Joint Committee," 7-20-49, and memorandum of McMahon-Acheson telephone conversation, 7-18-49, *FRUS: National Security Affairs, 1949*, pp. 485, 490–99. "Intelligence Memorandum No. 225," 9-20-49, Warner, *CIA under Harry Truman*, pp. 319–20. Pforzheimer, author interview.

8. *CR*, 9-26-49, p. 13261. Aldrich, *Hidden Hand*, pp. 225, 378. Darling, *Central Intelligence Agency*, p. 295. JCAE hearing, 10-17-49, *CIS Unpublished House Hearings*.

9. McMahon to Truman, 11-21-49, *FRUS: National Security Affairs, 1949*, vol. 1, pp. 588–95. Schwartz, *Atomic Audit*, p. 452. Harry S. Truman, *Years of Trial and Hope*, vol. 2 of *Memoirs* (Garden City, NY: Doubleday, 1956), p. 307. Lilienthal, *Atomic Energy Years*, pp. 580, 584–85. Pforzheimer and Houston to Hillenkoetter, 9-27-49, Box 7, CIA/HSC. Pforzheimer to Hillenkoetter, 2-7-50, CREST.

COMMUNISTS AND "PERVERTS" IN THE CIA

1. Lilienthal, *Atomic Energy Years*, p. 634. Pforzheimer, diary, 2-3-50 (the CIA had no "material in connection with Dr. Fuchs"), and to DCI, 2-7-50, CREST. *Times*, 2-21-50, p. 13. *Post*, 2-21-50, p. 1. *Time*, 3-6-50, p. 17.

2. *Time*, 3-6-50, p. 17. Caroline H. Keith, *"For Hell and a Brown Mule": The Biography of Senator Millard E. Tydings* (Lanham, MD: Madison Books, 1991), pp. 3–5.

3. Pforzheimer, author interview, and diary, 2-21-50, 2-22-50, 2-23-50, and 3-2-50, CREST. Hillenkoetter to McCarthy, 3-2-50, Series 5, Box 4, Millard Tydings Papers. The DCI refers to a previous letter to McCarthy, in which Hillenkoetter promised the thorough investigation.

4. *CR*, 2-20-50, p. 1961. Pearson, *Diaries*, pp. 113–16. Gallup poll, cited in William Ewald, *Who Killed Joe McCarthy?* (New York: Simon and Schuster, 1984), p. 24.

5. Undated 1950 hearing transcript, ONI memo attached, "Sex Perverts in Government" folder, Box 039073, Styles Bridges Papers. *CR*, 2-20-50, p. 1961.

6. Drew Pearson, *Post*, 7-11-53, p. B27; Hank Greenspun, *Sun*, 3-30-53. "Homosexual Investigations," undated (1950s), CREST. Correspondence re McCarthy, Series V, Box 4, Tydings Papers.

7. *CR*, 4-24-50, pp. 5572–77, 4-25-50, pp. 5703–4, 12-15-50, p. 16587.

8. *CR*, 3-31-50, p. 4527, 4-4-50, pp. 4669–70, 4-19-50, pp. 5401–3.

9. William N. Eskridge, "Privacy Jurisprudence and the Apartheid of the Closet, 1946–1961," *Florida State University Law Review* 24, no. 4 (Summer 1997). Neil Miller, *Out of the Past: Gay and Lesbian History from 1869 to the Present* (New York: Vintage Books, 1995), chap. 18.

10. Seymour Hersh, *The Old Boys: The American Elite and the Origins of the CIA* (New York: Scribner's, 1992), pp. 42, 61, 67, 154, 252, 255, 259, 269. Peter Grose, *Operation Rollback: America's Secret War behind the Iron Curtain* (Boston: Houghton Mifflin, 2000), p. 113. Evan Thomas, *The Very Best Men: Four Who Dared: The Early Years of the CIA* (New York: Simon and Schuster, 1995), p. 34. Pforzheimer, author interview.

11. Hearing transcript, undated, 1950, in file "Sex Perverts," Box 039073, Bridges Papers. Pforzheimer, author interview.

12. Pforzheimer, author interview, and diary, CREST. *Post*, 3-15-50, p. 1. Hersh, *The Old Boys*, p. 443.

13. Pforzheimer, office diary, 4-3-50, 4-4-50, and 4-14-50, CREST. *Times*, 4-19-50, p. 25. President's Diary, 4-18-50, HST Library.

14. *CR*, 4-24-50, pp. 5572–77, 4-25-50, pp. 5699–712. *Times*, 4-25-50, p. 1. Hersh, *The Old Boys*, pp. 150–52.

15. Pforzheimer, diary, CREST. *CR*, 4-25-50, pp. 5699–712.

16. *CR*, 2-20-50, p. 1961. *Times*, 3-9-50, p. 1, 3-15-50, p. 1, 4-19-50, p. 25, 4-26-50, p. 1. *Post*, 4-26-50, p. 1. Hersh, *The Old Boys*, pp. 295, 327, 447–48.

17. *Times*, 6-15-50, p. 6. Hillenkoetter testimony, 7-14-50, *CIS Unpublished U.S. Senate Committee Hearings on Microfiche* (Washington, DC: Congressional Information Service). The DCI referred briefly to a recently dismissed homosexual (possibly the other one referred to by Pforzheimer) whose characteristics did not match Offie's.

18. Pforzheimer, diary, 11-6-50 and 11-28-50, with attachment, CREST. *CR*, 12-18-50 (*Times-Herald* report), p. A7755.

19. Robert Griffith, *The Politics of Fear: Joseph R. McCarthy and the Senate*, 2nd ed. (Amherst: University of Massachusetts Press, 1987), pp. 100–101. Keith, *"For Hell and a Brown Mule,"* pp. 103–4. *Newsweek*, 7-31-50, pp. 25–26. *CR*, 12-15-50, p. 16588. Hersh, *The Old Boys*, pp. 443–46.

KOREA: "NO BETTER TODAY THAN ON DECEMBER 7, 1941"

1. *Post*, 6-26-50, p. 1.

2. *CR*, 7-13-50, p. 10086. On June 29, 1950, Drew Pearson reported that "two days before the Korean attack," the CIA reported that "not since V-J Day had the world seemed more peaceful." See *Post*, p. 13B.

3. Gallup, *Gallup Poll,* vol. 2, pp. 759, 906, 964. Bruce Cummings, *The Roaring of the Cataract, 1947–1950,* vol. 2 of *The Origins of the Korean War* (Princeton: Princeton University Press, 1990), pp. 603–15. *Times,* 6-26-50, p. 1. Using first names only, a 2001 *Times* story on a history conference at Princeton reported, "Bill rose to say he had predicted the outbreak of the Korean War, but that his later attempt to get his own paper using the Freedom of Information Act came up empty. Eight seats over, Herb leaped up to announce that he had handled the request and apologized that the document could not be located." *Times,* 3-17-01, p. B1.

4. Styles Bridges, *Post,* 6-27-50, p. 1, *Times,* 6-27-50, p. 3, and Box 073034, Bridges Papers. Drew Pearson (testimony), *Post,* 7-1-50, p. 15B. Pforzheimer, author interview. "Synopsis of significant comments" (Truman on CIA reports), undated, CREST.

5. Drew Pearson (testimony), *Post,* 7-1-50, p. 15B. The columnist and his wife were friends of Senator and Mrs. Bridges. Pforzheimer considered Bridges a rare legislative overseer of the CIA who leaked. Richard L. Riedel, *Halls of the Mighty: My 47 Years at the Senate* (Washington, DC: Robert Luce, 1969), pp. 206, 211. *CR,* 7-5-50, p. 9641.

6. Pforzheimer, author interview. Knowland (Smith confirmation hearing), 8-24-50, Box 3, Walter Bedell Smith Papers. *CR,* 7-27-50, p. A5431. *Times,* 6-27-50, p. 3.

7. Pforzheimer, diary, 7-31-50, CREST. *Post,* 6-26-50, p. 3, and 7-29-50, p. 1. Gallup, *Gallup Poll,* vol. 2, pp. 903, 939. H. Alexander Smith, diary, 6-28-50, H. Alexander Smith Papers.

8. CIA, "Intelligence Memorandum No. 300," 6-28-50, NSC Records, HST Library. Bridges, 7-11-50, Box 071134, Bridges Papers.

9. *CR,* 6-30-50, p. 9526, 7-10-50, p. 6788, 7-11-50, p. A5026, 7-13-50, p. 10086.

10. *CR* (Patterson), 7-27-50, p. A5431. JCAE, 7-12-50, *CIS Unpublished House Hearings,* pp. 60–65.

11. *CR* (*Herald-Tribune*), 8-2-50, pp. A5623–24.

12. Hillenkoetter to Truman, 8-3-50, NSC Records, HST Library. Appropriations hearing: Pforzheimer, diary, 8-28-50, CREST. Short broadcast, 10-9-50, Box 564, Dewey Short Papers. Marvin Stromer, *Kenneth S. Wherry and the U.S. Senate* (Lincoln: University of Nebraska Press, 1969), pp. 41–42. *Times,* 8-19-50, p. 1. *U.S. News and World Report,* 7-21-50, pp. 26–27. Darling, *Central Intelligence Agency,* p. 384. *CR,* 8-22-50, p. 13062.

A NEW DCI

1. Smith correspondence (including Benton to HST, 8-22-50), Boxes 3, 13, and confirmation hearing, 8-24-50, Box 3, Walter Bedell Smith Papers. Friends spelled Smith's nickname in diverse ways. *Times,* 8-19-50, p. 1. Pforzheimer, author interview.

2. Confirmation hearing, 8-24-50, Box 3, and Coffin to Smith, Box 13, Walter Bedell Smith Papers. Houston to Smith, 8-29-50, in Warner, *CIA under Harry Truman,* pp. 341–46. *CR* (Hickenlooper), 8-25-50, pp. 13420–1.

3. ADD/A (L. K. White) diary, 6-26-52, Box 4, CIA Declassified Reference Materials (hereafter, CIA/DRM). Pforzheimer, diary, 12-4-50, CREST. Church Commit-

tee, *Final Report*, Book Four, p. 40. Ironically, the quote comes from an unnamed former legislative counsel for the CIA. Pforzheimer, author interview.

4. Pforzheimer, author interview.

5. Gurney to Tydings, 11-28-50, Box 164, Saltonstall Papers. Short, telephone transcript, 12-1-50, Box 564, and letter to Mr. and Mrs. Joe Mason, 12-9-51, Box 542, Short Papers. Truman, *Years of Trial and Hope*, pp. 390–91.

THE "DIRTY BUSINESS"

1. Smith, 10-22-51 and 4-23-52, Warner, *CIA under Harry Truman*, pp. 436, 457–64. Telephone conversation transcript, Short and unidentified friend, 12-1-50, Box DS 542, Short Papers.

2. Bridges, cited in Memo for the President, 5-20-48, *FRUS: Emergence*, pp. 686–87. "Highlights of Armed Forces Hearing," 1-19-50, created by or for Taber, in "Miscellaneous notes," Taber Papers. Acheson, memo re: Richards, 1-9-50, *FRUS: Memoranda of Conversations of the Secretary of State, 1947–1952*, Microfiche Supplement.

3. JCAE hearing, 7-12-50, *CIS Unpublished House Hearings*.

4. Smith confirmation hearing, 8-24-50, Box 3, Walter Bedell Smith Papers. H. A. Smith, memo of conference with J. F. Dulles (Flanders), 8-7-50, Box 107, H. Alexander Smith Papers, and R. Flanders to A. Dulles, 8-10-49, Allen Dulles Papers, obtained under the Freedom of Information Act (hereafter Dulles FOIA Papers).

5. Acheson, memo of conversation, 12-27-50, *FRUS: Memoranda of Conversations of the Secretary of State, 1947–1952*, Microfiche Supplement. Hickenlooper is belatedly answered by Frank Holober's *Raiders of the China Coast: CIA Covert Operations during the Korean War* (Annapolis, MD: Naval Institute Press, 1999).

6. McMahon to Smith, 1-17-51, excerpted in JCAE hearing transcript, 4-27-51, *CIS Unpublished House Hearings*. Dulles to H. C. Lodge, 3-12-51, and Donovan to H. A. Smith, 3-23-50 and 4-5-50, Box 14, and Smith to J. F. Dulles letters, 8-7-50 and 8-17-50, Box 107, all in H. Alexander Smith Papers; and Donovan to Smith, 4-2-51 (found in Dulles's file; quotation from attachment by Jun Ke Choy), both in Dulles FOIA Papers. *CR* (J. D. Lodge), 3-25-48, pp. 3525–26. Dulles to H. A. Smith, 3-8-52, Series I, Box 52, Allen Dulles Papers.

7. Pearson, *Diaries*, pp. 111–12.

8. Pforzheimer, author interview. C. Norberg, memo of conversation, 1-4-52, PSB 032, Box 2, HST Library.

9. Hillenkoetter to Byrd, 11-15-47 and 3-1-48, CREST. Byrd insisted in 1948 on receiving the agency's "vouchered strength figures" in writing for his "personal information only." The DCI agreed.

10. Materials for planned 7-12-51 hearing; Pforzheimer memo, 7-12-51, CREST. O'Mahoney informed the CIA that he had another event scheduled for July 12, and that he would reschedule. His office treated the CIA patronizingly; Pforzheimer noted that an aide said "it may be that 24 hours will be as much notice as they will be able to furnish us."

11. Lyman Kirkpatrick, *The Real CIA* (New York: Macmillan, 1968), pp. 268–69.

12. Pforzheimer, author interview. "Magnitude Conference" notes, 3-29-51, Box 30, CIA/DRM. "Foreign Intelligence and Related Activities," by CIA, 4-17-52, *FRUS: National Security Affairs, 1952–1954,* vol. 2 (Washington, DC: GPO, 1984), pp. 50–53.

13. "Magnitude Conference," notes, 3-29-51, Box 30, CIA/DRM. Pforzheimer, author interview. "Central Intelligence Agency: Location of Budgeted Funds," 2-15-52, George Mahon Papers. ADD/A diary (Senate budget cut), 6-30-52 and 7-1-52, CREST.

14. Darling, notes on 12-9-52 interview, Box 13, CIA/HSC.

15. *Current Biography, 1952,* pp. 301–2.

16. Wallace Carroll, quoted in Grose, *Operation Rollback,* pp. 149–50. Linebarger, "Hotfoot for Stalin," *Life,* August 1951, reprinted in *CR,* 8-13-51, pp. A5121–22.

17. *CR,* 3-21-51, pp. A1607–8, 4-17-51, p. 4022, 7-17-51, pp. A4444–46, 8-14-51 (Acheson, etc.), pp. A5116–19.

18. *CR,* 8-17-51, pp. 10261–63, 10-11-51, p. 12996, 10-16-51, pp. A6444–45, 10-5-51, p. 12713. *CQ Almanac, 1951,* pp. 204–11.

19. Kersten to Vishinsky, 12-1-53, Comm. on Communist Aggression, Box 12, NA. *CR,* 8-13-51 (Linebarger), pp. A5121–22, 2-21-52 (Considine), p. A1101, 3-26-52, pp. A2052–54.

20. *Times,* 8-18-51, p. 1, 11-4-51, p. 1, 11-24-51 (Vishinsky), p. 4. *CR,* 10-20-51, pp. A6642–43.

21. *Selected Executive Session Hearings of the Committee on Foreign Affairs, 1951–1956,* vol. 14 (Washington, DC: GPO, 1980), pp. 327–49, 453. The transcript has Richards saying "disassemble," but it is likelier that he said "dissemble." Jeffery C. Livingston, *Ohio Congressman John L. Vorys,* Ph.D. diss. (Ann Arbor: University Microfilms, 1989), pp. 252, 260. Pforzheimer, diary (Bolton), 1-31-51, CREST.

22. L. Becker to Wisner, Box 187, CIA/DRM. R. Cutler to DDE, 1-27-53, Central/Official Files, Box 673, Dwight D. Eisenhower (hereafter DDE) Library. CIA "staff draft" ("Probable communist reactions"), 3-30-53, "Creation of foreign military units," fall 1953, CREST. Kersten to Wiley, 4-15-54, Series 6, Box 1, Charles Kersten Papers. J. McTigue to Kersten, 5-29-54, and Radio Prague transcript, 6-19-54, Comm. on Communist Aggression, Boxes 6, 47, NA.

PORTRAITS

1. Gilbert Fite, *Richard B. Russell, Senator from Georgia* (Chapel Hill: University of North Carolina Press, 1991), pp. 256–57, 327–28.

2. Russell arranged with Foreign Relations Committee chair Tom Connally that their two committees should explore the event through closed joint hearings, with Russell in charge. Russell to Marshall, 3-30-51, and related memoranda, Senate Armed Services Committee (hereafter SAS), Box 193, NA. Fite, *Richard B. Russell,* pp. 255–64.

3. Russell to Bridges, 6-21-51, Box 187, and to Sen. Cain, 5-24-51, Box 188, SAS. Gen. Bradley to Russell, 5-2-51, Box 077104, Bridges Papers. Director's staff meeting notes, 5-9-51, Pforzheimer, diary, 5-24-51, CREST. Defense Secretary Marshall handled the committee's requests for documents, including those from the CIA. A week before

Truman was to announce politically sensitive new aid toward the communist Yugoslavian government (facing Soviet military pressures), he sent Russell an outline of the program. Although U.S. negotiations continued on the issue with Britain and France, Truman trusted Russell's discretion. Box 185, SAS.

4. Gallup, *Gallup Poll*, vol. 2, p. 994. John E. Wiltz, "The MacArthur Inquiry, 1951," in *Congress Investigates: A Documented History, 1792–1974*, vol. 5, ed. Arthur Schlesinger Jr. and Roger Bruns (New York: Chelsea House, 1975), pp. 3626, 3631. Pforzheimer, "Intelligence References in MacArthur Hearings," 12-14-51, Box 239, CIA/DRM.

5. *Time* on Saltonstall, quoted in *Current Biography, 1944*, pp. 582–85. Russell-Knowland correspondence, 1-22-51, 2-3-51, 3-19-51, and Verne Mudge to "Herb," undated, Box 190, SAS. Pforzheimer, author interview.

6. Pforzheimer, memo for record (O'Mahoney and Ferguson), 10-25-51, and author interview. Warner, *CIA under Harry Truman*, pp. 441–43. Ferguson, O'Mahoney, and Bridges: *Current Biography, 1943*, pp. 202–4, *1945*, pp. 436–38, and *1948*, pp. 63–66. David E. Lilienthal, *Venturesome Years, 1950–1955*, vol. 3 of *The Journals of David E. Lilienthal* (New York: Harper and Row, 1964), p. 417. C. Norberg, memo of conversation, 1-4-52, PSB 032, Box 2, HST Library.

7. James F. Cook's *Carl Vinson: Patriarch of the Armed Forces* (Macon, GA: Mercer University Press, 2004) is useful, but does not mention the CIA. Pforzheimer, author interview. Short, in *Current Biography, 1951*, pp. 580–82. Pearson, *Diaries*, p. 87. Kirkpatrick, *Real CIA*, p. 269 (Cannon and history).

8. Paul Healy, "Nobody Loves Clarence," *Saturday Evening Post*, March 25, 1950, p. 133. Everett Dirksen, *The Education of a Senator* (Urbana: University of Illinois Press, 1998), pp. 128–29. See Taber article in *Political Profiles: The Truman Years* (New York: Facts on File, 1978), pp. 531–32. See Cannon article in *Political Profiles: The Kennedy Years*, pp. 70–71.

CIA SUBCOMMITTEES, INTELLIGENCE ROLES, AND BUDGETS

1. Houston to Hillenkoetter, 4-7-48, *FRUS: Emergence*, pp. 597–99. Cabell to Mansfield, 9-4-53, in Harry Howe Ransom, *Central Intelligence and National Security* (Cambridge: Harvard University Press, 1959), pp. 226–27. Only the calendars of the two DCIs who served before the CIA's creation were declassified by 2004. Pforzheimer, author interview.

2. Kirkpatrick, *Real CIA*, pp. 116–17.

3. Dulles to Russell, 3-3-56, Box 291, SAS. *FRUS: Emergence*, p. 701. Financial Division to OPC and SRI, 3-21-52, Box 37, CIA/DRM.

4. NIA meeting minutes, 10-16-46, pp. 427–32, and Armstrong to Acheson, 2-9-49, p. 952, *FRUS: Emergence*. Conflicting estimates of past CIA budgets show up in reputable publications. Kai Bird's *The Chairman: John J. McCloy, the Making of the American Establishment* (New York: Simon and Schuster, 1992), claims on p. 304 that the agency budget in 1948 was $70 million. Possibly this includes subsequent emergency appropriations.

5. Pforzheimer, interview, 10-14-98, and memo for record, 10-25-51, Warner, *CIA under Harry Truman,* pp. 441–43.

6. "Joint Statement of Departments of Defense and State on CIA Budget for Fiscal 1951," 2-23-50, and Wisner, memo for record, 11-16-58, *FRUS: Emergence,* pp. 732, 1073. Grose, *Operation Rollback,* p. 117. Smith to NSC, 4-23-52, Warner, *CIA under Harry Truman,* pp. 459–60. Church Committee, *Final Report,* Book Four, pp. 31, 32, 41. Chief, Organization and Methods Service, to DD/A, 5-5-52, Box 28, CIA/DRM. CIA Appropriations subcommittee members' probable knowledge of "counterpart" funds' usage has not been documented.

7. "Central Intelligence Agency: Location of Budgeted Funds, Fiscal Year 1953," 2-15-52, Mahon Papers, shows where CIA funds were hidden in the Defense Department's budget. Roughly equal amounts were hidden in the accounts of the three major military services. $92 million, the amount for that year's Reserve Contingency Fund, was hidden in the air force budget as "Project 120, Aircraft component spares and spare parts." The Senate may have cut this House-approved budget somewhat.

8. Houston to Hillenkoetter, 4-7-48, *FRUS: Emergence,* pp. 597–99. Mahon, Staff conference minutes, 4-7-52, Box 8, CIA/HSC. Pforzheimer, memo for the record, 10-25-51, Warner, *CIA under Harry Truman,* pp. 441–43.

9. DCI's staff conference, 4-7-52, Box 8, CIA/HSC. Smith to NSC, 4-23-52, Warner, *CIA under Harry Truman,* pp. 457–62. E. R. Saunders to G. Nease, Senate Appropriations Committee staff, 5-11-54, Bridges to Dulles, 5-12-54, and Taber to R. Hughes, 4-27-54 (all re FY 1953), Box 57, Bridges Papers. Ranelagh, *Agency,* p. 202. The fiscal year now begins on October 1 and ends on September 30.

10. Pforzheimer, author interview. FY 1953 budget, Mahon to McNeil and Mahon to Pforzheimer, 10-9-51, McNeil to Mahon, 10-22-51, Mahon to Smith, 10-23-51 and 4-15-52, Smith to Mahon, 10-26-51, all in Mahon Papers; and staff conference minutes, 4-7-52, Box 8, CIA/HSC. CIA History Staff, *Planning and Construction of the Agency Headquarters Building* (1973), p. 32, CREST. Ludwell L. Montague, *General Walter Bedell Smith as Director of Central Intelligence* (University Park: Pennsylvania State University Press, 1992), pp. 200–201.

11. Darling, *Central Intelligence Agency,* p. 192. Jack Plano and Milton Greenberg, *The American Political Dictionary,* 10th ed. (Fort Worth: Harcourt Brace, 1997), p. 392. GAO's power over the CIA would be drastically reduced in the early 1960s.

12. "Historical Study of the Use of Confidential Funds, Compiled by the Office of General Counsel," undated (from 1952–1954), L. K. White, "CIA Notice No. 103-52," 8-6-52, Warren to Smith, 11-21-51, Darling, Houston interview notes, 11-28-51, Boxes 7, 12, 13, CIA/HSC. Darling, *Central Intelligence Agency,* pp. 192, 323, 413.

"WE DON'T LET JUST ANYBODY LOOK AT OUR FILES"

1. Mahon-Truman (limiting access of a non-CIA subcommittee), 11-24-50 and 11-27-50, Official File, Box 1656, HST Library. JCAE hearings, 7-12-50, 4-27-51, *CIS Unpublished House Hearings.* Most hearings were not transcribed or declassified.

The agency prepared two estimates annually on Soviet atomic capabilities and related topics, then testified on them before the JCAE. In 1960, Hillenkoetter would publicly advise the government to explore the likelihood that UFOs were real and dangerous. See *CR*, 8-31-60, pp. 18955–56.

2. Montague, *General Walter Bedell Smith*, pp. 256–57. Hillenkoetter to Truman, quoted in Ranelagh, *Agency*, p. 752n14. Pforzheimer, interview (COMINT). Indications of U.S. progress in monitoring Soviet nuclear capabilities, and some congressional knowledge of this, in "Report of the National Security Council," with attachments, 6-5-52, *FRUS: National Security Affairs, 1952–1954*, vol. 2, pp. 21–53. Pforzheimer to Borden, 4-12-51, CREST.

3. JCAE hearing transcripts, 4-27-51 and 6-27-52, *CIS Unpublished House Hearings*. Montague, *General Walter Bedell Smith*, pp. 246–47.

4. McCarran-Hillenkoetter correspondence, 6-30-49 and 7-13-49, in *CR*, 6-14-51, pp. 6567–68. Joseph McCarthy later used Hillenkoetter's letter and the CIA investigation to attack the Truman administration. The House Committee on Expenditures in the Executive Branch was not prominent on CIA matters after its 1948 investigation of the Colombian affair. When Carl Vinson regained the Armed Services Committee chairmanship in 1949, he was of no mind to let any other House body — except Appropriations, which was beyond his control — have much say over the CIA. House Expenditures had gained a new chairman, William Dawson (D-IL), who was black. Had he tried to monitor CIA significantly, it would have produced interesting social and political history, but he did not. Senate Expenditures infrequently examined agency matters during the Smith era. In a few years, it would adopt a different name (Government Operations) and be energized by a new chair, Joseph McCarthy. In 1948, Congress sponsored the Hoover Commission on the Organization of the Executive Branch, which investigated and reported on the CIA. That report, mostly favorable toward the agency, apparently had little impact. See Darling, *Central Intelligence Agency*, chap. 8, and *CR*, 8-12-49, pp. 11324–25.

5. Untitled CIA report on budgetary/security issues, 5-5-52, Box 28, CIA/DRM.

6. Peter Grose, *Gentleman Spy: The Life of Allen Dulles* (Boston: Houghton Mifflin, 1994), pp. 315–18. Ranelagh, *Agency*, pp. 156–57.

7. Ben Bagdikian, "Unsecretive Report on the CIA," *New York Times Magazine*, October 27, 1963, p. 108.

8. *Times* (Smith-Davies), 9-30-52, p. 4. Griffith, *The Politics of Fear*, pp. 200–201. Kirkpatrick, *Real CIA*, pp. 119–20. "Director's meeting" notes, 2-18-52, CREST.

9. *Post*, 10-2-52 (Smith-DDE), p. 1, (Lippmann), p. 15. Smith to HST, 9-30-52 and 10-2-52, and Benton to Smith, 10-2-52, Box 5, Walter Bedell Smith Papers.

10. "Official diary," 10-1-52, and Grogan to DCI, 10-10-52, CREST. *Testimony of Gen. Walter Bedell Smith*, 10-13-52 (Washington, DC: GPO, 1952). I have found two somewhat different versions of this published hearing transcript. *Times* and *Philadelphia Inquirer*, 10-14-52, p. 1. Kim Philby, *My Silent War* (New York: Grove Press, 1968), p. 228. *CR*, 2-20-51, pp. A953–A955. Walter article in *Current Biography, 1952*, pp. 616–18. Les Whitten, undated handwritten notes of interview years later, Box 70, Les Whitten Papers.

11. Smith remarks, 11-21-52, in "Training Bulletin," 2-11-53, Box 3, CIA/HSC, and 11-21-51, 10-27-52, Warner, *CIA under Harry Truman*, pp. 449, 470. McCarthy later dropped his lawsuit.

"THERE WILL BE NO CHANGES"

1. Troy, *Donovan*, p. 411. For citations of such articles, see the bibliography of Ransom's *Central Intelligence and National Security*. Kent to Hansen, 6-6-52, and Hansen to Deputy DCI, 6-26-52, Box 25, CIA/HSC. John Gunther, "Inside CIA," *Look*, August 12, 1952, pp. 25–29. Pforzheimer, diary, 3-5-51, CREST.

2. Truman, 11-21-52, Smith to NSC, 4-23-52, Warner, *CIA under Harry Truman*, pp. 457–62, 471–73. On the likelihood of war, see Amory, Official Diary, 12-1-52, CREST.

3. Pforzheimer, author interview. "Remarks of General Smith," 11-21-52, Box 217, CIA/DRM.

4. "Remarks of General Smith," 11-21-52, Box 217, CIA/DRM. Grose, *Gentleman Spy*, pp. 334–35. Montague, *General Walter Bedell Smith*, pp. 264–65. John Helgerson offers a somewhat different account in *Getting to Know the President: CIA Briefings of Presidential Candidates, 1952–1992* (Washington, DC: Center for the Study of Intelligence, 1996), chap. 2. Smith had mixed feelings, but wrote Gen. Robert Schow on January 27, 1953, that "I do dislike leaving my present organization — of which I have become very proud" (Box 5, Walter Bedell Smith Papers). Pforzheimer, author interview. Les Whitten notes, undated, Box 70, Whitten Papers.

MEDDLING?

1. Nelson Polsby, *How Congress Evolves: Social Bases of Institutional Change* (New York: Oxford University Press, 2004), p. 147. Lewis Dexter, "Congressmen and the Making of Military Policy," in *New Perspectives on the House of Representatives*, ed. Robert Peabody and Nelson Polsby (Chicago: Rand McNally, 1963), pp. 306, 312. Donald Matthews, *U.S. Senators and Their World* (Chapel Hill: University of North Carolina Press, 1960), p. 140.

2. Eisenhower to agency heads, 3-6-53, Whitman File, Box 3, and NSC notes, 3-4-53, DDE Library. DCI briefing notes, 1-29-53, CREST.

3. JCAE: ADD/A (L. K. White), "Official Diary," 2-26-53 and 2-27-53, Box 24, CIA/DRM. The response to the JCAE demand seems to have been a briefing of the committee chair only.

4. Notes on Dulles's talk, 4-3-53, R. Amory, memo for record ("intelligence use"), 9-3-53, Boxes 18, 187, CIA/DRM. *U.S. News and World Report*, 3-19-54, p. 62. Saltonstall, papers on Sprague Report, March 1954, Box 240, SAS.

5. Russell to Morris Abram, 11-13-52, Gen. Correspondence, Saltonstall, draft remarks, January 1953, Box 182, SAS. Joseph Martin, *My First Fifty Years in Politics* (New York: McGraw-Hill, 1960) p. 232.

6. ADD/A diary, 1-8-53, Pforzheimer, diary, 2-20-53, CREST.

7. Bridges: Baird to Inspector General, 3-1-54, CREST. Pearson, *Diaries,* pp. 321–25, 504–5. Harlow, quoted in Whitman Diary, 7-18-58, DDE Library.

8. McCarran: A-DD/A diary, 7-9-53. L. K. White, DD/A by the 6-2-54 session, wrote that it had little "discussion of the budget, itself, but rather a discussion of the world situation and the substantive aspects of CIA's work" (DD/A diary, 6-17-54, CREST).

9. Dulles to Saltonstall, 4-14-54, CREST. Russell Baker, *The Good Times* (New York: Morrow, 1989), p. 281. Leverett Saltonstall, *Salty: Recollections of a Yankee in Politics* (Boston: Boston Globe, 1976). Church Committee, *Final Report,* Book Four, p. 52. Smith, diary, 6-29-50, Box 282, H. Alexander Smith Papers. Dulles's home: Richard Harkness and Gladys Harkness, "The Mysterious Doings of CIA," pt. 3, *Saturday Evening Post,* November 13, 1954, p. 133.

10. *Current Biography, 1951,* pp. 580–82.

11. Taber form letter, November 1953, Box 117, Taber Papers. Taber to Dulles, 3-18-53, CREST.

12. A-DD/A diary, 2-3, 2-4, 7-9-53, DD/A diary, 6-2-54, Pforzheimer, diary, 6-12-53, CREST. The Senate restored part of what Eisenhower wanted.

13. *Post,* 1-9-53, p. A20.

14. Daily Log, 2-6-53, A-DD/A diary 1-5 and 1-22-54, CREST. *Post,* 7-11-53, p. 1. SAS executive session notes, 2-19-53, Box 18, CIA/HSC. *CR,* 4-1-53, pp. 2644–51. Charles P. Cabell, *A Man of Intelligence: Memoirs of War, Peace, and the CIA* (Colorado Springs: Impavide, 1997), pp. 292–93.

GETTING "TABERIZED"

1. "Staff conference" notes, 2-9-53, Dulles to CIA employees, 2-26-53, Boxes 8, 13, CIA/HSC. Church Committee, *Covert Action,* vol. 7 (Washington, DC: GPO, 1976), p. 8.

2. Nixon, to 9th Agency Orientation Course, 2-20-53, CREST.

3. *Newsweek,* 3-2-53, pp. 21–22. Pearson, *Post,* 2-27-53, p. 39. At another White House session on 2-19-53, Dulles told two dozen legislators, "In Korea, the communists are capable of launching a large-scale offensive virtually without warning," and "By mid-1955, the USSR may have several hundred atomic bombs, together with improved methods for delivering those bombs against the U.S. and its allies." However, it was unlikely that the Kremlin would "initiate general war." CREST. Records are unclear if Dulles made these remarks on Capitol Hill and at the White House; he met legislators at both locations that day.

4. Pforzheimer, diary, 4-23-53, CREST.

5. Wisner notes, 4-25-53, Dulles FOIA Papers.

6. "Staff Conference" minutes, 5-4-53, Box 8, CIA/HSC. A-DD/A diary, 5-5-53, and memo to Inspector General, 9-18-53, Pforzheimer, diary, 4-27 and 4-29-53, CREST.

7. Dulles to Taber, 5-13, with undated clipping, and 5-15-53, Taber Papers. A-DD/A diary, 6-9 and 6-10-53, CREST.

8. [Name deleted] to Dulles, 7-1-53, Amory to Dulles, 7-2-53, CREST. Ass't. to DD/I diary entries, 7-1 and 7-3-53 and undated; Pforzheimer, diary, 7-28-53, and White, memo for record, 7-30 and 8-3-53, all CREST, and Boxes 24 and 153, CIA/DRM. [Unsigned] to DD/I, 2-24-56, CREST, suggests that 1953 "personnel ceilings" created "pressing" problems of firing mediocre employees. Attendance at 1954 hearings: Pforzheimer to DCI, 2-21-55, CREST. In 1952, House Appropriations approved a $587 million Fiscal Year 1953 CIA budget, but Senate Appropriations may have reduced it somewhat. 1952 files, Mahon Papers.

9. Taber budget notes, special 1954 file, Taber Papers. CIA FY 1953 budget, 1952 files, Mahon Papers. FY 1955 CIA budgets and letters, Box 57, Bridges Papers. DD/A to Dulles (air conditioning), 5-11-53, CREST.

10. Taber budget notes, ibid.

11. CIA budgets, Box 57, Bridges Papers. End-of-year accounting for Fiscal Year 1954 shows nonusage of unvouchered funds. However, agency heads apparently sometimes used moneys from the fund then reimbursed it from "normal" accounts.

12. *Post*, 3-23-54, p. 1. DD/A, two memos for record, 3-23-54, CREST.

13. "Notes for briefing of Appropriations Committee: Clandestine Services," 3-11-54, Box 4, CIA/DRM. The notes survived censorship in 1998, apparently because no specific operations or countries are mentioned, and the chart of successes and failures is not included.

14. Ass't to DD/I diary, 3-8-54, and DD/A diary, 6-17 and 9-23-54, Boxes 4 and 24, CIA/DRM. Pforzheimer, diary, 3-11-54 (Bridges), A-DD/A diary, 1-26, 2-17, 4-26, 5-20, and 6-2-54, DD/A memo for record, 4-27-54, and Pforzheimer to Dulles (1954 subcommittee hearing) 2-21-55, and [name deleted] to Dulles (reduction pledge) 4-8-54, and Kirkpatrick (drinkers) 4-15-54, all CREST. Since (1) CIA leaders remembered Taber's suspicion in 1953 that they might hold back on him, (2) the DCI specifically requested "high level" briefing notes and color charts from Plans and other directorates, (3) CIA's Budget Division Chief's subsequent memo (3-30-54, CREST) to the Reproduction Division's Chief, says "the five color charts," which illustrated points in Dulles's notes, "were used very successfully," and (4) the notes are free of the details that the DCI wished to share only with the CIA subcommittee, I assume Dulles used the notes at the March hearings rather than the subsequent smaller hearing. Dulles to Wisner (expenditures), 4-15-53, Box 5, CIA/DRM.

GUATEMALA: STERILIZING A "RED INFECTION"

1. ADD/I diary, 12-12-52; Harold Bull to Dulles, 4-22-54, Box 185, CIA/DRM.

2. Richard Immerman, *The CIA in Guatemala: The Foreign Policy of Intervention* (Austin: University of Texas Press, 1982). Piero Gleijeses, *Shattered Hope: The Guatemalan Revolution and the United States, 1944–1954* (Princeton: Princeton Uni-

versity Press, 1991). *Foreign Relations of the United States: Guatemala, 1952–54* (Washington, DC: GPO, 2003).

3. S. Kent to Dulles, 2-23-55, Box 185, CIA/DRM. Even "the relevant branch" of the Plans Directorate, which carried out the operation, agreed with the analysis. "Secrets Congressmen Can't Get," *U.S. News and World Report,* 7-16-54, pp. 38–39. "Product of CIA Expenses Queried on Capitol Hill," *Washington Evening Star,* 2-21-56, reprinted in *CR,* 4-9-56, pp. 5932–33. See also Harkness and Harkness, "Mysterious Doings," *Saturday Evening Post,* October 30, November 6, and November 13, 1954. Christopher M. Andrew, *For the President's Eyes Only: Secret Intelligence and the American Presidency from Washington to Bush* (New York: Harper Collins, 1995), pp. 209–10. Clinton, quoted in *Times,* 3-11-99.

4. Wiley, quoted in Immerman, *Guatemala,* pp. 102, 115, 156.

5. Hillings, quoted in *New York Herald Tribune,* 5-21-54, and *Post,* 6-6-54, Box 111, CIA/DRM. Pforzheimer, diary, 6-5-54, Dulles on Kersten, "Official Diary," 2-20-53, CREST. Nixon to Hillings, 6-25-54, Box 342, Nixon Vice-Presidential Papers. Smathers, *CR,* 5-28-54, pp. 7336–38. Kersten, quoted in Immerman, *Guatemala,* p. 153. Hillings would continue travels with a staffer to Guatemala; they and Kersten would cooperate with the CIA after the coup in gathering and publicizing evidence of the Arbenz government's communist connections. In August, Dulles would cable a CIA officer in Guatemala about his hope that "providing this and additional documentary material" would "minimize chances that their continuing investigation of communism in Central America may run afoul of or cross wires" with CIA activities. In September, Dulles cabled, "Committee is completely unwitting of PBSuccess and should remain unwitting." Two Guatemalans who worked for the CIA in 1954 were murdered subsequent to being identified publicly by the Hillings subcommittee, but it is unclear if the publicity in any way caused the murders. See Max Holland, "Operation PBHISTORY: The Aftermath of SUCCESS," *International Journal of Intelligence and Counterintelligence* 17, no. 2 (Summer 2004): 300–332. CD: *CIA Historical Documents on 1954 Guatemala Coup* (Washington, DC: Central Intelligence Agency, 2003).

6. Johnson and Republican leader William Knowland, *CR,* 6-25-54, pp. 8922–26.

7. *CR,* 6-29-54, pp. 9176–79.

8. *CR,* 6-28-54, pp. 9065–66. Smathers: *Herald-Tribune,* 6-24-54, CREST.

9. Bernard C. Cohen, *The Press and Foreign Policy* (Princeton: Princeton University Press, 1963), pp. 40–41, 134–35, cited in Immerman, *Guatemala,* p. 115.

10. *Times,* 6-20-54, pp. 1 and 8E, 6-24-54, p. 26. *Inquirer,* 6-22-54, p. 20. I examined every *Times* and *Post* issue of May–June 1954. Dulles to Eisenhower, 6-20-54, Whitman File, Admin. Series, Box 13, DDE Library. On Gruson, see his *Times* obituary, 3-9-98, p. B8.

11. Pforzheimer, author interview.

12. The two documents are cryptic CIA cables referring to PBSuccess and noting that the congressional staffers had some information on some type of "infiltration." CIA Guatemala records, 1952–54, Box 1, NA. Immerman, *Guatemala,* p. 152. Cutler to Elmer Staats, Dulles, and others, 5-20-54, WH Office, NSC Staff Papers, Box 34, DDE Library.

13. W. Saltonstall to Saltonstall, 6-1-66, Box 43, Saltonstall Papers. Darden to Saltonstall, 3-19-54, Box 230, SAS.

14. "Weekly *PBSUCCESS* meeting with [word(s) deleted]," 3-9-54, CIA-Guatemala records, 1952-43, Box 1, NA. Smith and Eisenhower-Knowland: Immerman, *Guatemala*, pp. 151–53.

15. Wisner memo, 4-15-54, *FRUS: Guatemala, 1952–1954* (Washington, DC: GPO, 2003), p. 237. See also the 1995 paper: Gerald K. Haines, "CIA and Guatemala Assassination Proposals, 1952–1954," CIA Records, NA. Nick Cullather, *Secret History: The CIA's Classified Account of Its Operation in Guatemala, 1952–1954* (Stanford: Stanford University Press, 1999). *CR*, 6-30-54, p. 9267.

MR. MANSFIELD GOES TO THE SENATE

1. Dulles speech, 1953, Dulles FOIA Papers. Don Oberdorfer, *Senator Mansfield: The Extraordinary Life of a Great American Statesman and Diplomat* (Washington, DC: Smithsonian Books, 2003). *CR*, 3-10-54, p. 2986.

2. Exec. Officer (Admin.) to DD/I, Official Diary, 4-3-53, Special Assistant (Admin.) to DD/I, Official Diary, 4-10-53, and Associated Press report on JCAE, 4-27-53, Boxes 18, 24, CIA/DRM. *Post*, 8-22-53, p. A1.

3. Dulles speech, 1953, Dulles FOIA Papers. Kirkpatrick to Dulles, 7-21-53, Pforzheimer, diary, 10-16-53, and A-DD/A to Inspector General, 9-18-53, and diary, 11-21-53, CREST. Saltonstall to Mansfield, 7-28-53, Box 230, SAS.

4. Pforzheimer, author interview. Clement Zablocki (D-WI), *CR*, 7-24-53, p. 9798.

5. *Post*, 3-11-54, p. 1. Harkness and Harkness, "Mysterious Doings," pt. 1, 10-30-54, p. 165. Mansfield cited the *News-Leader*, 3-30-53, 7-17-53, and 7-24-53, an unidentified 12-30-52 *Washington Star* column, a 7-19-53 *Times* story, and the 1-9-53 *Post* editorial (*CR*, 3-10-54, pp. 2986–90).

6. Darden to Saltonstall, 3-19-54, Box 230, SAS. Pforzheimer, diary, 3-18-54, CREST.

7. *Times*, 6-3-54, p. 13. Darden, author interview, and Pforzheimer, author interview. "Opening Statement," 3-22-54, Box 230, SAS.

8. *Times*, 6-3-54 (Baldwin), p. 13, 6-7-54, pp. 1, 16 (assassination), 6-20-54, p. 10E.

9. Dulles to Baldwin, 6-28-54, Box 61, Dulles Papers. Dulles's one public response to Mansfield: *U.S. News and World Report*, 3-19-54, pp. 62–68.

JOSEPH MCCARTHY: THE CIA'S OTHER WOULD-BE OVERSEER

1. McCarthy to Dulles, 8-3-53, Series I, Box 39, Dulles Papers. On McCarthy's papers, see Thomas C. Reeves, *The Life and Times of Joe McCarthy* (Lanham, MD: Madison Books, 1997), p. 787. Except for an interview with Don Surine (p. 746n28), Reeves does not substantiate his questionable claim that Beetle Smith, then undersecretary of state, gave McCarthy information damaging to the CIA. Pforzheimer

told me in 1999 that Smith "would have just as soon dealt with the Nazi general staff." Telephone Conversations, 12-9-53, Box 2, J. F. Dulles Papers.

2. Roy Cohn, *McCarthy* (New York: New American Library, 1968), pp. 48–49.

3. Richard Nixon, *RN: The Memoirs of Richard Nixon* (New York: Grosset and Dunlap, 1978), p. 139. Reeves, *McCarthy*, pp. 438–39, 507.

4. On the dangers of Soviet espionage in the United States, see Herbert Romerstein and Eric Breindel, *The Venona Secrets: Exposing Soviet Espionage and America's Traitors* (Washington, DC: Regnery, 2000). Kirkpatrick, *Real CIA*, p. 135. *CR*, 4-1-53, p. 2649. Pforzheimer, author interview.

5. Reeves, *McCarthy*, pp. 287–90, 502. Pforzheimer to Dulles, 4-6-53, CREST, and described in L. K. White's diary, 4-3-53, Box 16, CIA/DRM. On McCarthy's "standard," see Cohn, *McCarthy*, p. 50; on "extensive" CIA data, see p. 63. Bridges: Richard L. Riedel, *Halls of the Mighty: My 47 Years at the Senate* (Washington, DC: Robert B. Luce, 1969), pp. 148–49.

6. Dulles-Ford, Series I, Box 39, Dulles Papers. *Times,* 3-18-53, p. 19. Kirkpatrick, *Real CIA*, pp. 133–34, 151–52.

7. Pforzheimer to Dulles, 4-6-53 and 5-5-53, CREST; and Overseas Writers' speech notes, 4-3-53, Box 18, CIA/DRM. Dulles-Ford correspondence, Series I, Box 39, Dulles Papers. Kirkpatrick, *Real CIA*, p. 138. Kirkpatrick returned to the CIA in March 1953, after treatment for polio. Alsop, *Post,* 7-13-53, p. 6.

8. Symington: Cohn, *McCarthy,* p. 63, *Army-McCarthy Hearings,* 6-2-54, and Linda McFarland, *Cold War Strategist: Stuart Symington and the Search for National Security* (Westport, CT: Praeger, 2001), chap. 5. Eisenhower to H. Bullis, 5-18-53, in Louis Galambos and Daun Van Ee, eds., *The Papers of Dwight D. Eisenhower,* vol. 14 (Baltimore: Johns Hopkins University Press, 1996), pp. 233–34. *Post,* 7-10-53, p. 1. Reeves, *McCarthy,* p. 501.

9. David M. Oshinsky, *A Conspiracy So Immense: The World of Joe McCarthy* (New York: Free Press, 1983), p. 324. Leonard Mosley, *Dulles: A Biography of Eleanor, Allen, and John Foster Dulles and Their Family Network* (New York: Dial Press, 1978), p. 319. *CR*, 7-9-53, pp. 8277–78.

10. Dulles to Lippmann, 8-7-53, Series I, Box 38, Dulles Papers. Pforzheimer, author interview. Amory: Grose, *Gentleman Spy,* p. 345.

11. Telephone Conversation Series, 7-10-53, Box 1, J. F. Dulles Papers. Kai Bird, *The Color of Truth: McGeorge Bundy and William Bundy, Brothers in Arms* (New York: Simon and Schuster, 1998), pp. 162–65. *Post,* 7-11-53, pp. 1, 3. Robert Cutler, *No Time for Rest* (Boston: Little, Brown, 1966), pp. 150, 330. President's appointment calendar, 7-13-53, DDE Library.

12. Pforzheimer, Wisner, and Hillenkoetter had already been subpoenaed and had testified for two days before Senator Pat McCarran's Internal Security Subcommittee, just before the Truman administration ended. The case of foreign service officer John Paton Davies, alleged cause of the "loss" of China, was the topic. Pforzheimer, daily log, 1-14-53, CREST. Kirkpatrick, *Real CIA*, p. 133. Nixon, *RN,* pp. 139–40. Alsop, *Post,* 7-13-53, p. 6. *Times* (Rogers), 6-3-54, p. 13. Mosley, *Dulles,* p. 322. Cohn, *McCarthy,* p. 64. Oshinsky, *Conspiracy,* p. 325.

13. *Times,* 7-15-53, p. 16. Alsop, *Herald-Tribune,* 7-17-53, Series I, Box 39, Dulles Papers. C. D. Jackson, diary, 11-27-53, DDE Library.

14. Dulles brothers, 7-17-53, Telephone Conversation Series, Box 1, J. F. Dulles Papers. Unsigned CIA office diary, 7-15-53, CREST. On 6-27-53, Saltonstall attended "dinner @ 8" arranged by Mrs. Dulles; 1953 pocket calendar, Box 347, Saltonstall Papers. Saltonstall, *Salty,* p. 164. Bird, *Color,* p. 167.

15. Dulles-McCarthy letters, Series I, Box 39, Dulles Papers.

16. Telephone notes, 7-17-53, J. F. Dulles Papers. Adolf Berle, *Navigating the Rapids* (New York: Harcourt, Brace, 1973), p. 628. Bird, *Color,* p. 169. Grose, *Gentleman Spy,* pp. 343–46. *Post,* 7-11-53.

17. U.S. Senate, *Executive Sessions of the Senate Permanent Subcommittee on Investigations of the Committee on Government Operations,* vol. 5 (Washington, DC: GPO, 2003), pp. 165–76. Kent to Dulles, 7-15-53, Series I, Box 39, Dulles Papers. Grose, *Gentleman Spy,* pp. 343–45. Kirkpatrick, *Real CIA,* p. 139.

18. *CR,* 7-13-53, pp. 8619–20, 7-16-53, p. 8940. *Post,* 7-14-53, p. 10. *Times* (Monroney-McCarthy), 7-30-53, p. 15.

19. Dulles to Davis, 7-22-53, *Times,* 7-30-53, Dulles to Lippmann, 8-7-53, all Series I, Boxes 38, 39, Dulles Papers.

20. Bird, *Color,* p. 169. Grose, *Gentleman Spy,* pp. 346–47. Ewald, *Who Killed Joe McCarthy?* p. 89.

21. Cohn, *McCarthy,* pp. 69–70. Sherman Adams, *Firsthand Report: The Story of the Eisenhower Administration* (New York: Harper, 1961), pp. 140–41. Diary, Exec. Officer (Admin.), DD/I, 2-24-53, Guthe to DD/I, 7-28-53, Boxes 24, 178, CIA/DRM. Dulles brothers, 12-3-53, Telephone Series, Box 2, J. F. Dulles Papers.

22. Unsigned, undated DD/I memo, following Stalin's death, Box 13, CIA/DRM. Dulles brothers, 9-20-53, Telephone Series, Box 1, J. F. Dulles Papers. The *San Diego Union* had the fullest account (especially on 10-11-53) of the "Beria" affair; a *Union* reporter was an intermediary. See Box 4, CIA/DRM.

23. Bird, *Color,* pp. 169–70.

24. Dulles to McCarthy, 10-22-53, Office of Staff Secretary (hereafter OSS)/Subject/Alpha, Box 13, DDE Library. Army-McCarthy hearings, 6-2-54, pp. 1903–4, 6-16-54, p. 2872, Government Operations Committee, Box 1, NA. *Times,* 6-24-54, p. 1, 5-14-54, p. 14, 6-3-54, pp. 1, 14, and 6-7-54, pp. 1, 16. Dulles response, 6-2-54, Dulles FOIA Papers. V. Mudge to Saltonstall, 6-7-54, Box 239, SAS.

25. Hagerty, diary, 6-8-54, Cutler to Adams, 6-6-54, White House Office (hereafter, WHO) /Alpha/Sub, Box 7, DDE Library.

26. *Times,* 6-27-54, p. 27. Eisenhower to Adams, 6-18-54, Whitman File, DDE diary, Box 7, DDE Library. A. Smith to Dulles, 7-21-54, Box 114, H. Alexander Smith Papers. Pforzheimer, diary (Smith and covert action), 10-28-53, CREST. Bird, *Color,* pp. 169–70.

27. Adams, *Firsthand Report,* p. 140. Dwight D. Eisenhower, *Mandate for Change: 1953–1956* (Garden City, NY: Doubleday, 1963), p. 331. Dulles notes, 1962, Series I, Box 39, Dulles Papers.

"YOU, WHO CHAMPIONED OUR CAUSE"

1. Shortly before this book went to press, former CIA analyst Mark Stout wrote that "by 1946, 'The Pond' became the name generally used by the few who knew anything at all about the group." See "The Pond: Running Agents for State, War, and the CIA," *Studies in Intelligence* 48, no. 3 (2004): 69–82. The "voluminous records" of the group, discovered in 2001, are to be made available at NA. Robert H. Ferrell, ed., *The Eisenhower Diaries* (New York: Norton, 1981), p. 270.

2. Grombach, House Expenditures Committee hearing, 6-27-47, Box 399, NA. Kirkpatrick, *Real CIA,* pp. 149–53.

3. Organization memoranda and letters, Box 07408, also personal 1954 calendar, Bridges Papers. Dulles-Bridges-Grombach: Pforzheimer, diary, 6-12-53, CREST.

4. Organization memoranda and letters, Box 07408, also personal 1954 calendar, Bridges Papers. Hayden: Pforzheimer to DD/A, 3-23-51, and *Daily News,* 1-7-54, CREST. Grose, *Gentleman Spy,* pp. 349, 407. Clements was editor of the publication *American Mercury.*

5. Memos to Dulles (congressional contacts), December 1953, *New York Mirror,* 8-14-53, Pforzheimer, diary, 1-29-54, all CREST. Grogan to Dulles, 11-9-55, Box 15, CIA/HSC. Soon Drury would join the *Times,* taking along what Grogan called his "CIA bias." Harkness and Harkness, "Mysterious Doings," pt. 2, 11-6-54, p. 68. Subcommittee to Investigate . . . Internal Security Laws, *Hearings* (Washington, DC: GPO, 1954), pt. 5, p. 294.

BARONS RESTORED

1. Martin, *My First Fifty Years in Politics,* p. 228. "Memorandum of appointment" (DDE/LBJ), 8-26-57, Whitman Diary, DDE Library. William S. White, *Citadel: The Story of the U.S. Senate* (New York: Harper, 1957), pp. 88–89.

2. Hayden's CIA subcommittee would function without Homer Ferguson, who was defeated. Riedel, *Halls of the Mighty,* pp. 212–13.

3. [Unsigned] to D. Short (Vinson), 11-3-54, Box DS 2112, Short Papers. Harlow notes, undated, Harlow Papers, Box 12, DDE Library. *Times,* 1-5-55, p. 12, and 12-26-64, p. 18. *Times* magazine, 5-4-58, pp. 13, 78. White, *Home Place,* pp. 121–24.

4. Appropriations: Polsby, *Congress and the Presidency,* p. 92. Mahon: *Times,* 5-22-57, p. 13; White, *Home Place,* pp. 65–66, 121. Transcript, Dulles-Kersten aide, 7-19-54, Dulles FOIA Papers. Pforzheimer to Kirkpatrick, 11-9-54, CREST.

5. Scoville, memo for record, 10-27-55, provided by CIA, Center for the Study of Intelligence. Dulles to Russell, 11-13-55, Box 78, Dulles Papers. Pforzheimer to Dulles, 12-29-55, CREST. Gerald Haines, "CIA's Role in the Study of UFOs, 1947–1990," *Studies in Intelligence* 1 (1977): 67–84. Fite, *Richard B. Russell,* pp. 360–61.

6. Amory to Dulles, 12-19-55, and S. Kent to Assistant Director for Operations, 9-21-55, Box 188, CIA/DRM.

7. Dulles to Mahon, 11-19-58, Box 78, Dulles Papers. "Report on Congressional Briefings," 10-26-55, and Warner to Dulles, 3-17-58, CREST.

8. "Debriefing of Sen. Ellender," 1-10-57, and "Some Points Made by Justice Douglas," 11-18-55, Boxes 81, 2, CIA/DRM. "Debriefing . . . Whitten," 1-31-57, and Deputies meeting notes, 7-27-53 (accompanying a senator abroad), CREST. Whitten was not on a CIA subcommittee. Samuel Halpern, author interview.

"DODGING DEAD CATS"

1. Lecture to new CIA officers, undated (from mid-1950s), CREST.

2. United Press article, 3-20-56, lecture to new CIA officers, undated (from mid-1950s), CREST. *Times,* 3-17-56, p. 38.

3. Carey, memo for record, 11-18-54, CIA Records (Doolittle, etc.), Box 1, NA. Whitman Diary, 5-24-55, Box 5, DDE Library. Dulles, notes for 1-27-55 speech, Box 68, Dulles Papers.

4. At a luncheon Dulles hosted, though, Senate minority leader William Knowland predicted that Mansfield had no chance in 1955. DD/S diary, 2-28-55, CREST. *Times,* 1-15-55, p. 7, 2-4-55, p. 7, 2-7-55, p. 15. Harlow to J. Martin, Martin Papers, Box 1, DDE Library. Russell-Dulles correspondence, 2-23-55 and 3-7-55, Box 291, SAS.

5. Eisenhower to Doolittle and to Dulles, 7-26-54, Whitman/Admin., Box 13, DDE Library. *Times,* 10-14-54, p. 1, and 10-20-54, p. 16.

6. Unsigned notes, Eisenhower-Doolittle Committee meeting, 10-19-54, and Eisenhower memo, 10-22-54, Whitman/Admin., Box 13, DDE Library. A heavily censored copy of the Report is in CIA, Doolittle-Hoover (Clark), Box 1, NA. R. Cutler, memo (conflicting intelligence), 3-11-55, CREST.

7. J. Andrew to G. Carey (regarding Miller), 11-19-54, and partially censored memo to Carey, 12-1-54, CIA Records, Doolittle-Hoover (Clark), Box 1, NA. *Post,* 1-15-55, p. 2. *Times,* 6-29-55, p. 1. *U.S. News and World Report,* 7-8-55, pp. 34–36. "Man-hours and Cost for Clark Committee," 3-29-55, Box 170, CIA/DRM, and "Report of Survey," by Miller and John McGruder, 5-10-55, Box 6, CIA/HSC. Task Force report with CIA comments, undated (from May 1955), WHO/Sp. Asst./Subject, Box 3, Whitman File, DDE diary, Box 11; A. Minnich, journal notation, 6-21-55, Minnich Series, Box 1; both DDE Library. DD/S diary (McCarthy-Eastland), 5-15-56, CREST. Mansfield, testimony to the Rules Committee (Bridges), 1-25-56, Series 22, Box 16, Mansfield Papers.

8. Mudge to Russell, 6-29-55, Box 291, SAS. On Wisner, see Thomas's *The Very Best Men.* Wisner may have been unaware that the Doolittle group criticized his work; he judged them as having "called their shots as they saw them." Helms circulated Wisner's analysis on 7-20-55; Doolittle-Hoover (Clark), Box 1, NA.

"THEY HAVE TO HAVE A BUILDING"

1. CIA budgetary records, Box 57, Bridges Papers. "Agency staff personnel strength" of 13,306 as of 6-30-55: CIA Records, Box 23; the censored Doolittle Report,

presented to Eisenhower on 10-19-54, mentions the 20,000 figure; see CIA Records, Doolittle/Hoover (Clark), Box 1; on 1954 budget, see Dulles's "Notes for Briefing of Appropriations Committee," 3-11-54, Box 4, CIA/DRM; all NA. L. K. White, memo: Dulles-M. Stans meeting (minimal personnel decline), 11-25-58, CREST.

2. Miller and McGruder, report to Clark, 5-10-55, Doolittle-Hoover (Clark), Box 6, NA. DD/S diary, 3-7-5 through 3-11-55 (House Appropriations), 6-15-55 (Dworshak; no hearing), CREST.

3. Exec. Ass't. to the Dir. to Comptroller (cables), 9-2-55, CREST. The "free ride" quote is attributed, remarkably, to "a former CIA Legislative Counsel" in the Church Committee's *Final Report,* Book Four, p. 40.

4. CIA History Staff, *Planning and Construction of the Agency Headquarters Building* (1973), CREST. Senate Armed Services hearing, 6-17-55, CIS *Unpublished Senate Hearings* microfiche. The *Times* claimed (on 3-13-55, p. 82) that the agency failed at another attempt in 1953 to extract $38 million from Congress for a building. No available records support that claim.

5. James Hanrahan's "Soldier, Manager, Leader: An Interview with Former CIA Executive Director Lawrence K. "Red" White," *Studies in Intelligence* (Winter 1999–2000): 29–41, romanticizes the process and misidentifies legislators. Senate Armed Services hearing, 6-17-55, CIS *Unpublished Senate Hearings* microfiche. CIA History Staff, *Planning and Construction,* pp. 35–36, 71, 94, 187–88, CREST.

6. DD/S diary, 9-23-55, CREST. Smith to George, 1-26-56, Box 124, Smith Papers.

7. *Washington Star,* 2-20-56, CREST. *CR,* 6-25-56, p. 10870. Cannon to Dulles, 8-9-55, Folder 8, Cannon Papers. CIA History Staff, *Planning and Construction,* pp. 35–36, 71, 94, 187–88, CREST.

8. Deputies Meetings, 1-9-57 and 2-2-57, CREST. CIA History Staff, *Planning and Construction,* pp. 35–36, 71, 94, 187–88, CREST. Dulles to Russell, 7-17-56, with attachments, Series IX, Box 106, Richard B. Russell Library. Claussen memos (with testimony excerpts), 5-4-56 and 5-21-56, Box 25, CIA/DRM. Grose ("highballs"), *Gentleman Spy,* p. 418.

9. Miller-McGruder to Clark, 5-10-55, CIA Records, Doolittle-Hoover (Clark), Box 6. Church Committee, *Final Report,* Book Four, p. 45. Dulles, "Notes for briefing," 3-11-54, L. Houston, on behalf of Dulles, "Budget Policy for Fiscal Year 1956," 8-19-54, minutes of the Geographic Area staff meeting, 8-8-55, Amory to Assistant Directors, DD/I, 11-18-55, Amory to Kirkpatrick, 11-29-55 (emphasis added), Amory to Dulles, 8-5-55 and 12-5-55, Boxes 4, 206, 188, all CIA/DRM. In the latter document, Amory refers to the congressional initiative coming from the Chairman of the House Committee on Post Office and Civil Service. DD/S diary, 11-10-55, CIA notes on House Armed Services CIA subcommittee, 1-28-56, and CIA Historical Staff, *CIA Support Functions, 1953–56,* pp. 81–84, CREST.

10. *CR,* 5-27-57, p. 7739. *Times,* 5-28-57, p. 1.

11. *CIA Support Functions,* pp. 2, 4, CREST. R. Macy to Cassidy, "Trends in Intelligence Costs, FY 1956–58," 6-4-57, and James Lay, "Discussion at Special Meeting in the President's Office," 1-18-57, both Special Assistant for National Security Affairs (hereafter SANSA)/NSC/ Subject, Box 7, DDE Library. Memorandum of NSC discussion

(CIA budget), 4-11-57, *FRUS: National Security Policy, 1955–1957,* vol. 19 (Washington, DC: GPO, 1990), p. 475. James Lay, "Trends in National Security Programs," 8-6-56, provided to the author by William Burr, from State Department Records, NA.

12. *Times,* 5-28-57, p. 23. *CR,* 5-27-57, p. 7724. *Washington Star* (McCarthy), 2-21-56, Box 18, CIA/DRM.

THE NEW MANSFIELD RESOLUTION: TWO SURPRISES

1. Russell to Hayden, 1-17-56, and to Mansfield, 1-6-56, Boxes 291, 326, SAS. Smith notation, undated, Box 161, H. Alexander Smith Papers. *Times,* 2-7-55, p. 15, 10-17-55, p. 13. Smathers, oral history, U.S. Senate Historical Office, 1991, p. 61. Riedel, *Halls of the Mighty,* p. 153.

2. Dulles to DDE, 11-15-55, Dulles FOIA Papers. *Times,* 2-7-55, p. 15, 10-17-55, p. 130. Editorials are reprinted in *CR,* 4-9-46, pp. 5931–35. Drury, *Waterloo* (IA) *Courier,* 7-14-53, *Palo Alto* (CA) *Times,* 7-9-54, excerpts of Dulles-Drury correspondence, 8-12-53 and 9-14-53, Grogan to Dulles, 11-9-55, all Box 15, CIA/HSC. Grogan to Dulles, 11-19-56, 11-20-56, and undated (1955), CREST. *Wall Street Journal* editorial, 1-27-56, Box 18, CIA/DRM.

3. Green to Russell/Hayden, 1-11-56, with Hayden attachment, Box 669, Rules Committee, NA. Russell to Green, 1-16-56, and to Saltonstall, 1-17-56, Box 291, SAS. Mansfield, Rules testimony, 1-25-56, Series 22, Box 16, Mansfield Papers. Dulles, memo for files (Saltonstall), 1-28-56, CREST. *Times,* 1-26-56, p. 20.

4. *Times,* 2-24-56, p. 1. Anderson to Nixon, 1-31-56, SANSA/Subject, Box 2, DDE Library. Dulles to F. L. Belin, 2-22-56, Dulles FOIA Papers. CIA testimony frequency: "CIA Congressional Relations," undated (1956), CREST, and other assorted documents. Pforzheimer, author interview. In anticipation of debate over Mansfield's resolution, Russell had Dulles summarize, in writing, how the process worked. Dulles to Russell, 3-3-56, Box 291, SAS.

5. Philip K. Edwards, "The President's Board: 1956–60," *Studies in Intelligence* 13 (Summer 1969): 113–14. Dulles-DDE: Whitman Diary, 11-15-55, Box 11, and Dulles to S. Adams, Central/Official Files, Box 929, DDE Library; and Dulles to DDE, 11-15-55, Dulles FOIA Papers. Eisenhower, 1-24-56, DDE diary, DDE Library. *Times,* 2-22-56, p. 20.

6. Notes by A. Minnich, Eisenhower with legislators, 1-31-56, WH/OSS/Legislative Meetings, Box 3; 2-28-56 session, summary version in G. Morgan Files, Box 18; D. Anderson to Eisenhower (Rayburn), 2-2-56, WHO/Central/Subject, Box 14; all DDE Library. Vinson to Hayden, 2-29-56, Box 291, Hayden Papers. "Memo, CIA Subcommittee, House Armed Services Subcommittee," 1-28-56, CREST.

7. Dulles to Cannon (field trip), 3-24-56, Box 18, CIA/DRM. *Times,* 1-15-56 (Baldwin), p. 24, 4-6-56 (White), p. 9.

8. *CR,* 4-9-56 and 4-11-56, pp. 5891–939, 6048–68. Emphasis added. CIA Director of Training Matt Baird thanked "Club" member Hayden for seeing the agency through a "rough time." Baird to Hayden, 8-10-56, Box 186, Carl Hayden Papers.

Times, 4-9-56 and 4-11-56, p. 1, 4-10-56, p. 26, and 4-12-56, p. 1 (Drury). *Post,* 4-9-56 and 4-11-56, p. 1. McCarthy: Riedel, *Halls of the Mighty,* p. 229. Frank Madison, *A View from the Floor: The Journal of a U.S. Senate Page Boy* (Englewood Cliffs, NJ: Prentice-Hall, 1967), pp. 89–90. Grose, *Gentleman Spy,* p. 416.

9. White, *Citadel,* pp. 86–87. *CR,* 5-15-58 (Mansfield), p. 8898. After the vote, Dulles wrote a friend, "I expect that proposals of this kind will be presented from time to time." Dulles–George Gordon correspondence, 4-13-56 and 6-12-56, Box 69, Dulles Papers. Dulles probably read the comments of Francis Case (R-SD), a resolution cosponsor who turned against it, warning Russell and other CIA subcommittee members to exert "closer supervision" of the agency. Months later, at Hayden's CIA subcommittee hearing, Russell urged Dulles to cut the agency's personnel and budget, even minimally, thereby banishing the joint committee concept for years. DD/S diary, 6-13-56, CREST.

"WE HAVE A HISTORY OF UNDERESTIMATION"

1. Eisenhower: *U.S. News and World Report,* 2-15-57, p. 96. *CR,* 1-24-50 (Bridges), p. 813, 2-7-56 (Cannon), p. 2243, 4-14-48 (Vinson), p. 4453. Symington, 12-5-56, reprinted in *CR,* 1-17-57, p. 797. Russell, 12-8-59, reprinted in Calvin Logue and Dwight Freshley, eds., *Voice of Georgia: Speeches of Richard B. Russell, 1928–1969* (Macon, GA: Mercer University Press, 1997), p. 265.

2. *CR,* 2-7-56, pp. 2243–45. *CQ Almanac, 1956,* pp. 609, 716–20.

3. Alsop's column is reprinted in their *The Reporter's Trade* (New York: Reynal, 1958), p. 283. Eisenhower to R. Simon, 4-4-56, Galambos and Van Ee, eds., *Papers of Dwight D. Eisenhower,* pp. 2113–14.

4. DDE-Wilson: *FRUS: National Security Policy, 1955–1957,* vol. 19, pp. 279. Russell, quoted in *Post,* 2-24-56, p. 2. Estimates: John Prados, *The Soviet Estimate: U.S. Intelligence Analysis and Russian Military Strength* (New York: Dial Press, 1982), p. 44. N. Paul to Dulles, 3-16-56, CREST.

5. Dulles to Clinton Anderson, 6-1-55, Dulles FOIA Papers.

6. Eisenhower-Dulles discussions, 1-12-56 and 2-9-56, and JCAE preparation, 1-18-56: *FRUS: National Security Policy, 1955–1957,* p. 192. Eisenhower-Dulles and others, 1-18-56, Office of SS Records, "Atomic Energy," Box 5, DDE Library. JCAE subcommittee transcript, 1-12-56, *CIS Unpublished Senate Hearings* microfiche.

7. Notes of Armed Services CIA subcommittee hearing, 1-28-56, DD/S diary, 1-16-56, CREST. Dulles also "gave a run down of the CIA budget, both as to magnitude and composition, during the past five years," and discussed personnel, using "a chart to illustrate the rapid rise in strength in the early years and leveling off from 1952 onward."

8. Eisenhower-Dulles, 2-9-56, *FRUS: National Security Policy, 1955–1957,* p. 192.

9. Grogan to Dulles, 2-21-56, 2-28-56, Box 18, CIA/DRM.

10. "Questions discussed [on 2-27-56] . . . House Committee on Appropriations," 3-1-56, CREST.

11. "DCI Presentation for Symington Committee, 18 April 1956," with handwritten

notations for usage in the hearing; Kent to Dulles, "Testimony on ICBM . . . 18 April 1956," 6-25-56, and [name deleted] to Dulles ("absurd response"), 3-5-56, Boxes 16 and 183, CIA/DRM and CREST. Air power hearing transcript, 4-18-56, CREST. NIE 11-56, in Donald P. Steury, ed., *Intentions and Capabilities: Estimates on Soviet Strategic Forces, 1950–1983* (Washington, DC: CIA, 1996), pp. 9–37. Air Force intelligence: Prados, *Soviet Estimate*, pp. 45–47. "Bear" was the U.S. nickname for the Soviets' Tupolev TU-20, while the Myasishchev M-6 was referred to as the "Bison." *CQ Almanac, 1956,* pp. 716–20, also lists Allen Dulles as testifying in closed session on May 9.

12. Air power hearing transcripts, 4-23-56 and 4-24-56, CREST.

13. Dulles to Symington, 5-8-56, and to Goodpaster, 5-11-56, OSS/ Subject/Alpha, Box 7, DDE Library.

14. Air power hearing transcripts, 4-23-56 and 4-24-56, CREST. [Name deleted] to DDI, "Admiral Radford's testimony," 8-3-56, Box 16, CIA/DRM. LeMay quotes, CIA news clipping file, CREST. Saltonstall: memo, W. Persons, 4-4-56, CIA website, www.foia.cia.gov/; *Post,* 4-19-56, p. A8; and E. McCabe to Persons, 4-25-56, McCabe Records, Box 1, DDE Library.

15. Symington-Wilson: *CQ Almanac, 1956,* p. 719. *CR,* 6-21-56, 6-25-56, and 6-26-56, pp. 10488–99, 10775, 10883–86, and 10971–78.

16. *CR,* 6-18-56, pp. 10488–89. Dulles-Ostertag: Cabell to Dulles, undated cables, Wisner to Dulles, 6-22-56 (emphasis in the original), and related memos, Dulles FOIA Papers.

17. *Times,* 6-26-56, p. 1, and *Post,* 6-18-56, p. A4. *CQ Almanac, 1956,* p. 609. Symington, quoted by Associated Press, 4-18-56, Box 18, CIA/DRM.

18. S. Kent to Dulles, 7-2-56; ONE to N. Paul, 10-12-56 and 11-2-56, Box 16, CIA/DRM. Twining: Prados, *Soviet Estimate,* p. 44.

19. ONE to DD/I, 7-27-56, Box 16, CIA/DRM.

20. S. Kent to Dulles, "Downward Revisions of Estimates on Soviet Bison Strength," 3-11-57, Box 183, CIA/DRM.

21. Symington-Dulles, 3-18-57 and 4-4-57, Box 36, and unsigned memo to Symington, 3-9-57, Folder 3514, Stuart Symington Papers. S. Kent to Dulles, "Downward Revisions of Estimates on Soviet Bison Strength," 3-11-57, Box 183, CIA/DRM. [Name deleted] to DD/I, 7-27-56, Boxes 183, 16, CIA/DRM. Goodpaster: Prados, *Soviet Estimate,* p. 47. "Air Power" report, 1-30-57, excerpted, 2-8-57, pp. 106–9, and "A 900 Million Dollar Bobble," 3-8-57, pp. 56–59, *U.S. News and World Report.* The air force actually used the bulk of its additional funding to accelerate its missile programs. Robert A. Divine, *The Sputnik Challenge* (New York: Oxford University Press, 1993), pp. 30–31. Soviet concentration: Steury, *Intentions and Capabilities,* p. 6.

HUNGARY AND THE SUEZ: "WE HAD A VERY
GOOD IDEA, SENATOR"

1. "Stenographic notes of conversation between DCI [words censored]," 7-21-56, CREST. Czechoslovakia's unrest is treated in Christian F. Ostermann, ed., *Upris-*

ing in East Germany, 1953 (Budapest: Central European University Press, 2001), pp. 113–32.

2. Wrightsman to Dulles, 8-1-56, Dulles FOIA Papers. Grose, *Gentleman Spy*, pp. 436–43.

3. DCI remarks, 11-9-56, Bipartisan Legislative Meeting Series, Box 2, DDE Library. Dulles tried to exonerate RFE in a memo to Eisenhower, 11-20-56, *FRUS: Eastern Europe, 1955–1957* (Washington, DC: GPO, 1990), pp. 473–75. Eisenhower–J. F. Dulles remarks, 10-29-56 and 10-30-56, *FRUS: Suez Canal Crisis, 1955–1957* (Washington, DC: GPO, 1990), pp. 833–39, 874.

4. Goodpaster, memo for record, 11-12-56, OSS/Subject/Alpha, Box 7, DDE Library.

5. U.S. Senate, *Executive Sessions of Foreign Relations Committee,* vol. 8, 11-12-56, pp. 605–60. *FRUS: Eastern Europe, 1955–1957,* pp. 16–23, 115–18.

6. U.S. Senate, *Executive Sessions of Foreign Relations Committee,* vol. 8, 11-12-56, pp. 605–60. *FRUS: Eastern Europe, 1955–1957,* Dulles-NSC: pp. 358–59, 418–21, Murphy/Hoover: p. 364, and Wailes: pp. 520–23.

7. U.S. Senate, *Executive Sessions of Foreign Relations Committee,* vol. 8, 11-12-56, pp. 605–60. DDE diary, 10-15-56, Eisenhower to L. Douglas, 11-30-56, and to E. Hazlett, 11-2-56, Galambos and Van Ee, eds., *Papers of Dwight D. Eisenhower,* pp. 2330, 2352, 2413–14, 2424.

8. U.S. Senate, *Executive Sessions of Foreign Relations Committee,* vol. 8, 11-12-56, pp. 605–60. *FRUS: Suez Canal Crisis, 1955–1957,* pp. 833–39, 862. Mosley, *Dulles,* p. 417. Grose's *Gentleman Spy* (pp. 436–43) and Ranelagh's *Agency* (pp. 296–302) credit Dulles and CIA with predictive success.

9. Mansfield: *Times,* 11-19-56, p. 23, and 11-28-56, p. 6. Grogan to Dulles, 1-31-57, Box 30, CIA/DRM. Dulles also discussed Soviet defector Nikolai Khokhlov with the reporters. He had claimed to have been on an assassination mission before his 1954 defection and was a public figure by 1956. He is a "queer bird," said Dulles. Khokhlov had been "checked by our people," and some believed him trustworthy, but the DCI "had cautioned our people to be careful" in dealing with him. Grogan, memo for record, 11-20-56 (Dulles on Khokhlov, etc.), CREST. *U.S. News and World Report,* 12-7-57, pp. 98–100.

10. Grogan to Dulles, 3-1-57 (over 100 news articles attached, categorized according to questions that might be asked), Box 14, CIA/HSC. The hearing may not have happened until the end of March or later. Senator Byrd, at the confidential Russell-Dulles meeting, aggressively questioned the DCI about personnel issues, which probably dominated the eventual hearing. See N. Paul, memo of Dulles-Russell, etc., 2-1-57, CREST; and Russell to Dulles, 3-21-57, Box 401, SAS. On Dulles speeches and Hungary before the uprising: Grogan to J. Tilton, 3-21-57, Box 20, CIA/DRM. Dulles-Yale: *Times,* 11-28-56, p. 6.

11. N. Paul, notes of Appropriations hearing, 1-11-57, "Deputies" meetings, 6-29-53, DD/S diary, 5-1 and 7-1-57, (all regarding Appropriations subcommittee), CREST.

12. "Stenographic notes" (DCI-Blatnik), 10-22-57, CREST. Grogan to Dulles, 1-31-57, Box 30, CIA/DRM.

13. James Pfiffner, *The Modern Presidency*, 4th ed. (Belmont, CA: Thomas Wadsworth, 2005), p. 185. C. Marcy to Mansfield, 12-31-58, Series 22, Box 16, Mansfield Papers.

14. N. Paul, memo of Vinson-Dulles meeting, 1-9-57, and House Armed Services subcommittee hearing, 1-16-57, CREST. "CIA Career Council" transcript, 2-7-57, Box 226, CIA/DRM.

15. Dulles to Mahon, 11-20-5, Dulles FOIA Papers. "Stenographic notes" (DCI-Fairbanks), 12-2-57, CREST.

SPUTNIK

1. Divine, *Sputnik*, Introduction, p. 83. *Newsweek*, 10-14-57, pp. 37–40, 10-21-57, pp. 23–33. *Time*, 10-21-57, pp. 27–28, 50.

2. CBS and NBC transcripts: *CR*, 1-13-58, pp. 263–73.

3. Jackson speech, reprinted in *CR*, 1-9-58, p. 213; Vinson speech, 1-5-58, reprinted in *CR*, 1-8-58, pp. 127–28. Symington: *St. Louis Post-Dispatch*, 10-11-57, Harlow Records, Box 2, DDE Library. Divine, *Sputnik*, p. xv.

4. *Aviation Week* (Wilson/Adams/Mesta), 10-21-57, pp. 27–28. "Deputies Meeting," 10-16-57, CREST.

5. R. McGrath and colleagues to Dulles (emphasis in the original), 10-23-57, and Dulles to Goodpaster, 10-28-57, Office of Sp. Asst. for Science-Technology, Box 1, DDE Library. Dwight D. Eisenhower, *Waging Peace: The White House Years, 1956–1961* (Garden City, NY: Doubleday, 1965), pp. 224–25, 229.

6. *CR*, 2-1-56, p. 1765. Goodpaster to Dulles, 2-12-59, Dulles FOIA Papers. "Mid-1955 Correspondence on Ballistic Missiles," 2-13-59, Box 25, CIA/DRM.

7. Prados, *Soviet Estimate*, p. 59. [Name deleted] to DDI (Mahon), 1-13-58, "Guided Missile Intelligence Presented by the DCI to Congressional Committees," 1-6-58, both in Box 25, CIA/DRM. NIE 11-5-57, 3-12-57, in Steury, *Intentions and Capabilities*, pp. 59–64.

8. Vinson: *CR*, 1-8-58, pp. 127–28. Deputies Meeting, 11-1-57, CREST. Fite's *Richard B. Russell*, pp. 361–64, says the Soviet launches "surprised" the senator, but this seems highly unlikely. *Newsweek*, 10-21-57, p. 23. Saltonstall to Charles Wilson, 11-14-57, Box 203, Saltonstall Papers. Divine, *Sputnik* (Russell-LBJ-Symington), p. 62. Prados, *Soviet Estimate*, p. 59.

9. Goodpaster, memo for record, 11-15-57, WHO/OSS, DDE Library. G. Siegel to E. Weisl, 11-20-57, Box 086142, Bridges Papers. J. Warner memoranda (staffers), 11-19-57 and 12-2-57, CREST.

10. Dulles-Scoville prepared remarks, 11-26/27-57, Box 25, CIA/DRM. Emphasis in the original.

11. *Aviation Week*, 10-21-57, pp. 21, 26–29.

12. Bridges: *Times*, 11-28-57, p. 1. Edited and unedited summaries of Dulles's testimony, with his handwritten markings and notation, "OK, AWD": Lyndon B. Johnson (hereafter LBJ) Senate papers, Box 355, LBJ Library. Emphasis in the original.

13. Prados, *Soviet Estimate*, p. 62. Stephen Ambrose writes (in *Nixon: The Educa-*

tion of a Politician, 1913–1962 [New York: Simon and Schuster, 1987], p. 442) that Eisenhower encountered a "distinct surprise" with Sputnik's launch; if so, he had forgotten Dulles's warning.

14. Lewis commentary, 11-27-57, CREST. Harry McPherson, *A Political Education* (Boston: Little, Brown, 1974), p. 59. LBJ's and Symington's public reactions: Senate papers, Box 355, LBJ Library. Cannon on Symington, 12-3-57, *CQ Weekly,* 6-10-60. Divine, *Sputnik,* pp. 41, 67.

15. *Herald-Tribune* article, 12-1-57, Grogan to Dulles (O'Mahoney-Morse), 12-5-57, CREST. *Newsweek,* 12-9-57, pp. 51–52. By this time, the USSR had launched Sputnik II.

16. Preparedness, "Excerpt from . . . Inquiry into Satellite and Missile Programs," 12-13-57, DDE Library. Prados, *Soviet Estimate,* p. 77.

17. Dulles to Johnson, undated (December 1957), OSS/Subject/Alpha, Box 15, DDE Library. Eisenhower, *Waging Peace,* p. 240.

18. Gaither-Dulles, 1-3-58, NSC meeting, 1-6-58, *FRUS: National Security Policy, 1958–1960,* pp. 2–9. Eisenhower, *Waging Peace,* p. 226. Divine, *Sputnik,* pp. 35–41, 77–78. "Stenographic notes" (DCI–D. Fairbanks), 12-2-57, CREST.

AN EARLY "YEAR OF INTELLIGENCE"?

1. "Year of Intelligence": Loch Johnson, *Secret Agencies: U.S. Intelligence in a Hostile World* (New Haven: Yale University Press, 1996), p. x. Mathew D. McCubbins and Thomas Schwartz, "Congressional Oversight Overlooked: Police Patrols versus Fire Alarms," *American Journal of Political Science* 28 (1984): 165–79. Memo to Dulles (by L. K. White or L. Houston), 9-24-58, CREST.

2. Grose, *Gentleman Spy,* p. 454. Bridges-Cutler letters, 3-25-58, 3-28-58, Boxes 075062, 086142, Bridges Papers. J. Eisenhower memo, 12-22-58, Whitman File, DDE diary, Box 58; Gray memoranda, 10-25-58, 11-3-58, 12-30-58, 6-26-59, WHO/SANSA/ Subject, Boxes 3, 15, DDE Library.

3. From late March to early May, CIA leaders testified before the House Committee on Aeronautics and Space Exploration, and before House Appropriations' Commerce and CIA Subcommittees. List of CIA congressional appearances: attachment, Dulles to Harlow, 12-6-58, Goodpaster's SANSA files, DDE Library. Also, Dulles to Exec. Sec., NSC (regarding 5412 Group), 10-17-59, SANSA/NSC/Subject, Box 7. *CQ Weekly Report,* 10-16-59, p. 1421. In 1958, 47 of 106 Senate Armed Services Committee meetings were closed; its House counterpart closed 93 of 195 meetings.

4. Mahon to D. Ferris, 1-13-58 and 1-14-58, Mahon to Kelly, 1-27-58, Mahon Papers. Kilday to Kelly, 11-23-57, Box 2E418, Paul Kilday Papers. Dulles to Kelly, 12-11-57, CREST. Serge L. Levitsky, "Red Part in IGY," *America,* 5-18-57, p. 220. *U.S. News and World Report,* 12-13-57, pp. 31–33, 54–58. *Times,* 11-21-57, pp. 1, 18. Amory to Dulles, 1-13-58, Box 25, CIA/DRM. Pforzheimer, author interview, and Warner, author interview.

5. Green to Dulles, 1-29-58, with J. Earman to Goodpaster attachment, 1-30-58, WHO/OSS/Subject/Alpha, Box 7, DDE Library. Houston to Dulles, 1-28-58, Dulles FOIA Papers.

6. U.S. Senate, *Executive Sessions,* vol. 10, 2-7-58, pp. 77–124. Smith to Dulles, 2-10-58, Box 124, H. Alexander Smith Papers. No records suggest another CIA appearance before the full Committee in the following weeks; its disarmament subcommittee heard CIA testimony for some days in mid-March. *Times,* 8-23-58 (appropriation), p. 5. Gallup, *Gallup Poll,* vol. 2, p. 1552.

"I CANNOT ALWAYS PREDICT WHEN THERE IS GOING TO BE A RIOT"

1. Nixon, *Six Crises,* chap. 4. Ambrose, *Nixon: Education of a Politician,* pp. 462–79. *FRUS: National Security Policy, 1958–1960,* vol. 5: *American Republics,* pp. 222–48. For a different account of warnings reaching Nixon, see Grose, *Gentleman Spy,* pp. 454–55.
   2. *CR,* 5-15-58, pp. 8889–901 (debate and Unna article). *Times,* 5-16-58, p. 14.
   3. *CR,* 5-13-58, pp. 8554–57, 5-14-58, pp. 8652–54. *Times,* 5-18-58 (Bridges), p. 24.
   4. CR, 5-15-58 (Lippmann), pp. 8797–98. Grogan to Dulles, 5-19-58, 5-22-58, 5-26-58, and 6-2-58, Box 13, CIA/HSC. Chamberlain to Dulles, 5-19-58, CREST. Nixon, *Six Crises,* pp. 210–28.
   5. U.S. Senate, *Executive Sessions,* 5-19-58, pp. 232–55. [Name deleted] to Dulles (in preparation for the hearing), 5-18-58, Dulles FOIA Papers.
   6. Houston, "CIA subcommittees," 5-26-58, CREST. Dulles statement to Inter-American Affairs Subcommittee, 6-18-58, Dulles FOIA Papers. Russell: *CR,* 1-13-58, pp. 255–62. Other quotations: Grogan to Dulles, undated and 6-2-58, Box 13, CIA/HSC.
   7. *Times,* 6-18-58, p. 1. Goodpaster, "Conference with the President, June 17," 6-18-58, OSS/Subject/Alpha, Box 3; CIA, "Appearances Before Congressional Committees," attached to DCI to Harlow, 12-6-58; both DDE Library.

IRAQ: "OUR INTELLIGENCE WAS JUST PLAIN LOUSY"

1. Eisenhower, *Waging Peace,* pp. 182–83, 263–82.
   2. *FRUS: Lebanon and Jordan, 1958–1960,* p. 208; *FRUS: Near East Region, 1958–1960,* p. 303; Abdul-Salaam Yousif, "The Struggle for Cultural Hegemony during Iraqi Revolution," and William Louis, "The British and the Origins of the Revolution," in Robert Fernea and William Louis, eds., *The Iraqi Revolution of 1958* (New York: I. B. Tauris, 1991), pp. 58, 172.
   3. Meeting notes, 7-14-58: Goodpaster, *FRUS: Lebanon and Jordan, 1958–1960,* pp. 218–27; Harlow, Harlow Records, Box 6, DDE Library. Adams, *Firsthand Report,* pp. 290–93. *Post,* 7-15-58, p. 1.
   4. Smith diary, 7-15-58, Box 282, H. Alexander Smith Papers. *Post,* 7-14-58 and 7-15-58, p. 1. Meeting notes, 7-14-58: Goodpaster and Harlow. *FRUS: Lebanon and Jordan, 1958–1960,* pp. 167, 171–75, 226–27 (leaks); *FRUS: Near East Region, 1958–1960,* pp. 304–6 (Wisner), 308–11, 321 (Nixon).

5. DDE-Twining: *FRUS: Lebanon and Jordan, 1958–1960*, pp. 244–45. *CR*, 7-16-58, pp. 13912, 13944, 7-17-58, pp. 14163–65; other quotations are from Grogan memos to Dulles, Box 12, CIA/HSC.

6. Warner, memo (Cabell-Mahon), 10-16-58, and White (Cannon), diary, 8-1-58, CREST. Grogan to Dulles (Hays), 8-6-58, Box 12, CIA/HSC.

7. Pearson, *Post*, 7-17-58, p. C23, 7-22-58, p. B19, 7-31-58, p. D11. *Times*, 7-29-58, p. 6. Mosley, *Dulles*, p. 435. *FRUS: Near East Region, 1958–1960*, pp. 333–34.

8. U.S. Senate, *Executive Sessions*, vol. 10, pp. 643–77. *Times*, 7-30-58, p. 6. Langer: Grogan to Dulles, 8-3-58, Box 12, CIA/HSC.

9. Grogan reports (analysis of Baldwin, etc., 8-12-58), with attachments, Box 12, CIA/HSC. [Name deleted] to DCI, 8-14-58, and Warner, memo (Smart), 12-10-58, CREST. Eisenhower, *Waging Peace*, p. 289. Thomas Powers, *The Man Who Kept the Secrets: Richard Helms and the CIA* (New York: Knopf, 1979), pp. 129–30.

RETURN TO MISSILE GAP

1. Edward P. Morgan, "The Missouri Compromise," in Eric Sevareid, ed., *Candidates 1960* (New York: Basic Books, 1959), pp. 245–79. Robert W. Merry, *Taking on the World: Joseph and Stewart Alsop, Guardians of the American Century* (New York: Viking, 1996), p. 343. Drew Pearson, *Diaries*, pp. 328, 540, 544. Reedy, *The U.S. Senate* (New York: Crown Publishers, 1986), pp. 98–162. Biographers of Symington barely mention his interactions with CIA in the 1957–1961 period.

2. "Ballistic Missiles" and "Soviet Long Range Bomber Force," both 7-21-58, Symington-Johnson folders, Box 25, CIA/DRM. "Summer night": DCI testimony, Preparedness Subcommittee, 3-18-59, Harlow Records, DDE Library.

3. Grose, *Gentleman Spy* (Dulles's office), p. 387. For an overview, see Edgar Bottome, *The Missile Gap: A Study of the Formulation of Military and Political Policy* (Rutherford, NJ: Fairleigh Dickinson University Press, 1971).

4. Bottome, *Gap*, pp. 69–71.

5. Eisenhower, 12-6-58 and 1-12-59, *FRUS: National Security Policy, 1958–1960*, pp. 162–63, 172–73. Eisenhower, *Waging Peace*, pp. 367–68.

6. Stoertz, memo for record, 8-18-58, OSS/Alpha, Box 21, DDE Library.

7. Goodpaster, DDE-Symington meeting notes, *FRUS: National Security Policy, 1958–1960*, pp. 137–38. DDE diary, 8-29-58, Box 35, DDE Library.

8. Symington to Eisenhower, 8-29-58, Harlow to Symington, 9-4-58, and Dulles to Eisenhower, 10-10-58, all Harlow Records, Boxes 2, 7, DDE Library. [Name deleted], "Discussions with Senator Symington," 2-8-59, Box 25, CIA/DRM.

9. Prados, *Soviet Estimate*, pp. 61, 77. Dulles to GMIC, 10-9-58, Harlow Records, Box 2, DDE Library. CIA "Appearances before Congressional Committees," on 1-8-59 and 6-5-59, touched on possible Soviet deceptions; see M. Feldman File, WH staff files, John F. Kennedy (hereafter JFK) Library. Lloyd Mallan, "The Big Red Lie," *True*, May 1959, pp. 38–43, 102–7. Follow-up articles were published in June and July. H. Lloyd to Dulles (Cannon), 4-30-59, CREST. Lunik (Luna I): T. A. Heppenheimer,

Countdown: A History of Space Flight (New York: Wiley, 1997), p. 155. Ed Welsh to Symington (CIA-Mallan), 6-15-59, Folder 3521, Symington Papers.

10. Harlow-Symington correspondence, 12-10-58 and 12-15-58, Harlow Records, Box 2, Goodpaster memo (Dulles/Salstonstall/Russell), 1-13-59, OSS/Subject/Alpha, Box 7, all DDE Library. "DCI Briefing Notes . . . for 16 December 1958," and Stoertz, memo of conversation, 12-16-58, Box 25, CIA/DRM. Dulles, memo (Saltonstall/Russell), 1-13-59, Dulles FOIA Papers.

FROM THE PFORZHEIMER ERA TO THE WARNER ERA

1. Hull to Eisenhower, 10-30-58 (obtained under "Mandatory Review" process); J. Eisenhower, memoranda of conference [on 12-16-58], 12-22-58, OSS/Subject/Alpha and Whitman File, DDE diary, Boxes 15, 38, DDE Library.

2. *CR*, 2-13-58 and 4-16-58, pp. 2181, 6605–6. Dulles's indifference: Grose, *Gentleman Spy*, pp. 453–54.

3. J. F. Dulles to NSC, 2-20-58, *FRUS: National Security Policy, 1958–1960*, p. 54. Board critique of Indonesian operation: Arthur Schlesinger, *Robert Kennedy and His Times* (Boston: Houghton Mifflin, 1978), pp. 454–58. David Wise, *The Politics of Lying: Government Deception, Secrecy, and Power* (New York: Random House, 1973), p. 36. Schlesinger asserts, wrongly, that Allen Dulles "ignored" the Board and that Eisenhower "gave it no support."

4. J. Warner, memo of White House meeting, 11-10-58, CREST. Dulles to Harlow, 12-6-58, with attachments; Gray, "Memo of Meeting with the President . . . December 26, 1958," 1-29-59, plus attachments; Goodpaster to Harlow, 1-2-59, and memo for record, 1-13-59; OSS/ Subject/Alpha, Boxes 7, 15, DDE Library. Ike showed "some interest" in the old idea of creating a joint intelligence committee, but the thought would lead nowhere.

5. Dulles to Goodpaster (Cannon), 10-22-58, and Dulles to Goodpaster (Symington), 12-23-58, WHO/OSS/Alpha, Boxes 7, 21, DDE Library. On Goodpaster, see John Prados, *Keepers of the Keys: A History of the National Security Council from Truman to Bush* (New York: Morrow, 1991), pp. 67–68. Undated, "Appearances before Congressional Committees [in 1959]," undated, M. Feldman File, WH Staff Files, Box 5, JFK Library. Dulles to [name deleted], 1-17-59, Dulles FOIA Papers.

6. John Warner, author interview, and diary, 12-16-59, CREST. Dulles to Goodpaster, 10-22-58, WHO/OSS/Alpha, Box 7, DDE Library. DD/S diary, 1-16-59 (Mahon), 6-19-59 (Cannon), CREST. Dulles memo (White House/Goodpaster meeting), 6-18-59, Dulles FOIA Papers. In handwritten notes for hearings on 2-2-59 and 2-3-59, Mahon reminded himself, "Caution committee that this is not hearing on CIA budget," Mahon Papers, 1959. Hearings before the Appropriations CIA subcommittee (in addition to budget sessions) may have been instituted as early as 1958, in which case Dulles was seeking protection from Mahon and Cannon for an already established practice.

7. Macy presentation to IAC, 11-17-53; H. G. Lloyd to "Deputy Director," 4-30-59,

and Saunders to Dulles, 6-3-59 (Cannon subcommittee); DD/S diary, 3-31-60 (DCI home); IAC Working Group minutes, 9-18-58; all CREST.

8. Dulles to Goodpaster, 10-22-58, OSS/Subject/Alpha, Box 7, DDE Library. DD/S diary, 3-31-60 (Cannon); Saunders to Dulles, undated (1960); Cabell to Cannon, 4-6-60; Cost Estimates Committee minutes and notes, 5-3-60 and undated (August 1960, regarding "demanded"); DD/S diary, 2-21-63; all CREST.

9. Warner, author interview. While liaison, Warner remained deputy counsel for the agency. He later told how Lawrence Houston, CIA's legal counsel, characterized his and Warner's roles: "Warner was Houston's deputy for legal affairs, and Houston was Warner's deputy for congressional matters." Warner memo (Hewitt) 8-15-58; [name deleted] to T. Karamessines, 3-5-59 (staff knowledge); Cannon-Dulles, 10-3-60 and 10-21-60 (Crosby); all CREST. Unsigned note (Crosby), 10-14-59, Mahon Papers.

10. Darden, author interview, and Warner, author interview. BeLieu married Warner's secretary, and the CIA liaison became a periodic guest at the BeLieus' home. Houston to BeLieu, 11-12-59, CREST.

11. Short to M. Kronheim, 9-8-47, folder 442, Short Papers. Smart: Warner memo, 3-23-59, and notes of deputies' meetings, 10-3-58 and 10-6-58, CREST. Smart may have settled for an oral presentation on NIE dissents.

12. Warner, Darden, Pforzheimer, author interviews. Chief, Budget Division to Comptroller, 8-24-59, CREST.

13. J. Warner to Dulles (personnel cases), 10-17-58, with appendices; Pforzheimer, diary, 8-12-54, N. Paul to Dulles, 2-29-56, CREST; and Warner to Dulles (all regarding Walter), 7-10-58, Dulles FOIA Papers.

14. Pforzheimer and Warner, author interviews. J. Warner to Dulles, 10-17-58, with appendices; L. K. White to L. Kirkpatrick (President's Board), 9-26-58; L. Houston to Dulles (drafted by Warner), 9-24-58; OCG to President's Board (undated, February 1958); CREST. Emphasis in the original. "Appearance before congressional committees," attached to Dulles to Harlow, 12-6-58, DDE Library. Dulles, memo (Goodpaster, regularized briefings), 6-18-59, Dulles FOIA Papers. Unsigned and DD/S (L. K. White), diary notes, 6-16-58, 10-3-58, 10-6-58, 10-13-58, and 11-21-58, and 2-4-59; and Warner to "SA/PD/DCI" (U-2), 11-26-58; CREST.

15. Goodpaster, memo of conversation, 1-20-59, OSS/Subject/Alpha, Box 3, DDE Library. DD/S diary, 2-4-59, and "Briefing Paper, Legislative Counsel," undated (1960), CREST.

SUBORDINATING INTELLIGENCE?

1. The Alsops, quoted in Prados, *Soviet Estimate*, p. 80. *Times*, 1-24-59, p. 1, 1-30-59, p. 1. *CR*, 1-23-59, pp. 1101–2.

2. J. Eisenhower, memo of conference with President, 2-9-59, *FRUS: National Security Policy, 1958–1960*, pp. 181–83. Goodpaster, memo of conversation, 2-10-59, OSS/Subject/Alpha, Box 15, DDE Library.

3. J. Eisenhower, memos of meetings, 12-16-58 and 2-12-59, OSS/Subject/Alpha, Box 15, DDE Library.

4. Goodpaster, memo of conversation, 4-7-59, OSS/Subject/Alpha, Box 15, DDE Library.

5. Ibid. Grogan, memos to Dulles, Box 12, CIA/HSC. Mahon, handwritten notes of Dulles hearings, 2-2-59 and 2-3-59, with attachment, Mahon Papers. *Times*, 2-16-59, p. 1.

6. *Times*, 2-4-59, p. 1. "DCI briefing" (Russell subcommittee), 1-16-59, CREST. U.S. Senate Foreign Relations Committee, *Executive Sessions*, 1-26-59, pp. 85–130.

7. Wayne G. Jackson, *Allen Welsh Dulles as Director of Central Intelligence*, unpublished manuscript, vol. 4, pp. 76–80, NA.

8. DCI briefing notes, 2-4-59 and 3-13-59, and memo to Dulles, 2-6-59, on revised estimates, Box 25, CIA/DRM.

9. "Excerpts from DCI testimony . . . 18 March 1959," Symington to Dulles, 3-21-59, and Dulles to Goodpaster, 4-3-59, Harlow Records, Box 7, DDE Library. Dulles memo (Symington call), 7-9-59, CREST.

IN AND OUT OF HEARING ROOMS

1. "[CIA, 1959] Appearances before Congressional Committees," undated, M. Feldman File, W. H. Staff, Box 5, JFK Library. Two other hearings are mentioned in Russell's handwritten notes, 1-14-59, Intra-Office, Box 20, Russell Library, and in *CR: Daily Digest*, 2-4-59, and possibly another one in Mahon's papers from 1959. Warner, author interview.

2. Dulles memos (Cannon), 1-11-58, CREST; 12-23-58 and 1-10-59, Dulles FOIA Papers. On June 16, 1958, a Dulles associate wrote that the agency "had received a copy of Mr. Cannon's letter . . . approving the amount of money we requested for Fiscal Year 1959, but denying our request for 'no year' funds." CIA had asked that the unused portions of its contingency reserve be carried over automatically from one year to the next, a recurring point of contention. Unsigned "Diary notes," 6-16-58, CREST. *Time*, 2-2-59, pp. 12, 14.

3. White, memo (Dulles-Stans), 11-25-58, Stans to Dulles (DDE budget approval), CREST. Dulles memo (Cannon), 12-23-58, Dulles FOIA Papers.

4. "Tire Production in the USSR," 4-3-58, Box 196, CIA/DRM. Dulles to Goodpaster (Capehart), 3-14-58, J. Z. Anderson to S. Adams (Becker), 5-15-58, OSS/Subject/Alpha, Box 7, DDE Library.

5. Vinson to Kilday, 9-21-50, Box 2E421, Kilday Papers. *Current Biography, 1958* (Defense reorganization, Krock), pp. 227–29.

6. DD/S diary, 2-4-59; Office of General Counsel, "Semi-annual Report," 10-14-59; Warner, memo (Rayburn, "prior"), 2-20-59; all CREST. Allen-Scott article, 10-14-59, Box 9S/10, Kilday Papers.

7. Kilday to P. Tillett, 3-18-59, Box 9S/10, Kilday Papers. [Name deleted], memo

(hearings' frequency), 2-20-59, DD/S diary, 6-30-59, CREST. A. Smith–W. Castle, 1955 correspondence (ore), Box 124, H. Alexander Smith Papers.

8. GAO, related Kilday subcommittee inquiries: Dulles to DDE, 6-30-59, OSS/Subject/Alpha, Box 8, DDE Library. R. Smart to H. H. Ransom, 10-7-60, constituent to Kilday, 10-14-59, Kilday to Dulles (GAO), 6-18-59 and 7-28-59, Campbell to Kilday, 5-29-59, Boxes 9S/10, 2E420, and 2E421, Kilday Papers. E. Chappell, "Memorandum" (Smart), 3-17-59, and DD/S diary, 6-22-59, 7-8-59, 9-9-59, all CREST. GAO could audit less sensitive projects and accounts; 45 to 50 percent of the agency's budget was thus scrutinized, wrote Joseph Pois in *Watchdog on the Potomac: A Study of the Comptroller General of the United States* (Washington, DC: University Press of America, 1979), pp. 132–34. Frederick Mosher, *The GAO: The Quest for Accountability in American Government* (Boulder, CO: Westview Press, 1979), pp. 104, 137–38, 259, 274, 301. Though not comprehensive, such audits were more systematic than prior types. Vinson put Charles Bennett, of middling seniority, on the subcommittee in 1958 (Bennett-Kilday correspondence, Box 9S/10). Eisenhower-Russell-Vinson, 3-6-59, Whitman File, DDE Diary Series, Box 40, DDE Library.

9. Victor Marchetti and John Marks, *The CIA and the Cult of Intelligence* (New York: Knopf, 1974), pp. 133–42.

10. Holifield to Carter, 6-19-59, with attachments, Box 9S/10, Kilday Papers. Warner, "Congressional Action" (Carter), December 1960, and DD/S diary, 6-24-59, CREST. *Post*, 11-5-59, p. B2. Prouty, interviewed by David Ratcliffe, http://www.ratical.org/ratville/JFK/USP/.

11. *Time*, 9-28-59, pp. 9–16. Fulbright to Dulles (Khrushchev transcript), 9-18-59, CREST.

12. Henry Cabot Lodge Jr., *The Storm Has Many Eyes: A Personal Narrative* (New York: Norton, 1973), pp. 165–66. Hahn to S. Rayburn, 10-2-59, Box 9S/10, Kilday Papers.

13. Bennett to Kilday, 11-3-59, and related correspondence, Box 9S/10, Kilday Papers. Mahon memo, 10-14-59, Mahon Papers. *Time* (Dulles-Khrushchev), 9-28-59, p. 13. *Times*, 10-4-59, p. 6.

14. Dulles to Kilday, 11-7-59, Box 9S/10, Kilday Papers. *Times*, 9-17-59, p. 1. *Post*, 9-17-59, p. 1. Grose, *Gentleman Spy*, pp. 467–68. James Bamford, *The Puzzle Palace: A Report on America's Most Secret Agency* (Boston: Houghton Mifflin, 1982), p. 154.

15. Dulles memos: (Russell/Saltonstall/ Hayden), 1-13-59, Dulles FOIA Papers; and 7-7-59, 7-8-59, and 7-11-59, and DD/S diary, 7-14-59, CREST.

16. In June, Dulles fumed at the CIA, upon being warned that the Budget Bureau would probably not permit the agency to use its contingency reserve to finance "Walnut." A Dulles aide wrote, "I told him that it was my understanding that the Bureau and the Congress did not approve of using the Contingency Reserve for items which we could foresee and budget for in the normal way" (DD/S diary, 6-24-59, CREST). The undated "Heathcotte" transcript has a typewritten cover note, plus a handwritten notation about Dulles and Angleton dated "9-59," in Mahon's 1959 papers. The name "Heathcotte" is not on CIA documents listing 1959 hearings. In retirement,

Mahon did not have all sensitive documents removed from his papers, as happened with Cannon's. As of 1997, Mahon's papers were only roughly processed, but there is a finding aid. Samuel Halpern, author interview.

"WHO ARE OUR LIQUIDATORS?"

1. U.S. Senate, *Executive Sessions,* vol. 11, 4-28-59, pp. 309–30. Marchetti and Marks, *CIA and the Cult of Intelligence,* pp. 115–17, suggests that the non-Tibetans on the ground there were "Agency contract mercenaries." In an interview with the author, former CIA officer John K. Knaus expressed certainty that Americans were not "on the ground" with Tibetans. See his *Orphans of the Cold War: America and the Tibetan Struggle for Survival* (New York: Public Affairs, 1999), especially chaps. 8–10; see also, Roger McCarthy, *Tears of the Lotus: Accounts of Tibetan Resistance to the Chinese Invasion, 1950–1962* (Jefferson, NC: McFarland, 1997), and Dalai Lama, *Freedom in Exile: The Autobiography of the Dalai Lama* (San Freancisco: HarperCollins, 1990), pp. 127, 140, 192. Dulles to Goodpaster (Dalai Lama letter to DDE and Herter), 6-17-59, Dulles FOIA Papers. K. Harr to DDE (OCB), 9-1-59, WHO/SANSA, Box 2, DDE Library. ADD/I diary (Fulbright), 12-1-52, Box 185, CIA/DRM.
2. U.S. Senate, *Executive Sessions,* pp. 318–29.
3. Dulles remarks, Box 197, CIA/DRM. *Times,* 11-14-59, p. 1.

"I'D LIKE TO TELL HIM TO HIS FACE WHAT I THINK ABOUT HIM"

1. An untitled list of the CIA's 1960 congressional appearances (in CREST) shows eighteen days; other sources indicate an additional two. Goodpaster, 4-9-60, Whitman/DDE Diary, Box 49, DDE Library.
2. Alsop, *Post,* 1-28-60, p. A23. NIE, 11-8-59, and NSC discussion, 1-7-60, *FRUS: National Security Policy, 1958–1960,* pp. 353–59, 375–80.
3. Jackson, *Allen Welsh Dulles,* vol. 5, pp. 85–86.
4. NSC discussion, p. 356. Prados, *Soviet Estimate,* pp. 88–89.
5. "Procedures for Briefing," undated, from 1960, CREST.
6. Mahon, handwritten notes of 1-11-60 and 1-12-60 hearings, 1960 files, Mahon Papers.
7. U.S. Senate, *Executive Sessions,* 1-18-60, pp. 7–51. Kaznacheev authored *Inside a Soviet Embassy: Experiences of a Russian Diplomat in Burma* (Philadelphia: Lippincott, 1962).
8. *CR,* 1-27-60, pp. 1372–73. *Times,* 1-28-60, p. 1. Gates: *Post,* 1-20-60, 1-21-60, and 1-27-60, all p. A1, and 1-22-60, pp. A6, A14.
9. *Post,* 1-27-60, p. A1.
10. *CR,* 1-27-60, pp. 1372–73. Eisenhower, *Waging Peace,* pp. 389–90, 547. Defense spending: Polsby, *Congress and the Presidency,* p. 86.
11. *Times,* 1-28-60, p. 13.

12. *CR*, 1-28-60, 1544–48. *Times*, 2-10-60, p. 1. *Post*, 1-29-60, p. A10. Grose, *Gentleman Spy*, p. 474. *CQ Weekly*, 1-22-60. Bottome, *Gap*, pp. 121, 131.

13. *Newsweek*, 2-1-60, p. 17. Power: *Post*, 1-29-60, p. A10; *Times*, 1-29-60, p. 6. Eisenhower: *CQ Weekly*, 2-5-60, p. 212.

14. *Post*, 1-22-60 ("furor"), p. A6; 1-29-60 ("no record"), p. A10.

15. U.S. Senate, Armed Services and Aeronautical and Space Sciences Committees, *Missiles, Space, and Other Major Defense Matters* (Washington, DC: GPO, 1960), pp. 402, 415, 435.

16. Dulles to Goodpaster and to L. Johnson, 2-8-60, OSS/ Subject/Alpha, Box 8, DDE Library. Pearson, reprinted in *CR*, 2-8-60, pp. 2164–65. *CQ Weekly*, 2-5-60, p. 3.

17. *Time*, 2-1-60, p. 9. DDE-Gates: Michael R. Beschloss, *May-Day: Eisenhower, Khrushchev, and the U-2 Affair* (New York: Harper, 1986), p. 237; Goodpaster, memo, 2-2-60, Whitman/DDE Diary, Box 47, DDE Library.

18. *Post*, 2-5-60, p. A15. Merry, *Taking on the World*, p. 363. Dulles to L. Johnson, 2-8-60, and Goodpaster, memo of conversation (Alsop), 3-11-60, both OSS/Subject/Alpha, Boxes 8 and 3, DDE Library.

19. Dulles on Alsop, 3-4-60, handwritten note, related correspondence, Dulles FOIA Papers. Alsop to W. Jackson, 1-22-51, CREST. Foy Kohler, notes (Eisenhower-MacMillan), 3-28-60, *FRUS: National Security Policy, 1958–1960*, p. 259. Jackson, *Allen Welsh Dulles*, vol. 5, pp. 104–5.

20. Gallup, *Gallup Poll*, vol. 3, pp. 1651, 1654. *Times*, 2-12-60, 2-18-60, both p. 1. *CQ Weekly*, 2-12-60, p. 240.

21. Jackson, *Allen Welsh Dulles*, vol. 5, p. 108. Mahon to "Walter," undated, 1960 files, Mahon Papers. *Times*, 2-20-60, p. 1. *CQ Weekly*, 2-12-60, p. 240.

22. Prados, *Soviet Estimate*, pp. 92–95. Jackson, *Allen Welsh Dulles*, vol. 5, pp. 108–10. *Times*, 2-10-60, p. 1.

23. *Times*, 2-18-60, pp. 1, 12. Prados, *Soviet Estimate*, pp. 92–95. Jackson, *Allen Welsh Dulles*, vol. 5, pp. 82–108.

24. Jackson, *Allen Welsh Dulles*, vol. 5, pp. 107–9. "Mistake": Prados, *Soviet Estimate*, p. 94. "Outline of Statement for the Johnson Committee," Box 16, CIA/DRM.

25. *Times*, 3-1-60, p. 4. *CR*, pp. 3012–42, includes the 2-19-60 debate and many newspaper articles. Gregory Pedlow and Donald Welzenbach, *The CIA and the U-2 Program, 1954–1974* (Washington, DC: Center for the Study of Intelligence, 1998), pp. 165, 170. J. Eisenhower, memo for record, 2-12-59, WHO/OSS/Subject/Alpha, Box 15, DDE Library.

U-2: "WE HAVE FELT THESE OPERATIONS WERE APPROPRIATE"

1. Saltonstall, *Salty*, p. 164.

2. "Questions discussed [on 2-27-56] . . . House Committee on Appropriations," 3-1-56, CREST. *Post* and *Times*, 2-24-56, both p. 1. Pedlow and Welzenbach, *CIA and the U-2 Program*, p. 88.

3. Dulles, interview excerpts, Box 108, Dulles Papers. Darden and Warner, author interviews.

4. Kefauver: William S. White, *The Making of a Journalist* (Lexington: University Press of Kentucky, 1986), pp. 167–68. Dino A. Brugioni, *Eyeball to Eyeball: The Inside Story of the Cuban Missile Crisis,* ed. Robert F. McCort (New York: Random House, 1991), p. 36.

5. J. Cunningham to F. Wisner, 1-6-60, CREST. David Wise and Thomas Ross, *The U-2 Affair* (New York: Random House, 1962), pp. 58–59.

6. Beschloss, *May-Day,* pp. 89–90 (funding), 108 (Nixon). U.S. Senate, Committee on Foreign Relations, *Events Relating to the Summit Conference* (Washington, DC: GPO, 1960), p. 5. U-2 funding: DD/S diary notes, 11-20-57, and "Briefing Memorandum," 3-16-55, Boxes 4, 42, CIA/DRM; suggestive of conflicting accounts, Richard Bissell, *Reflections of a Cold Warrior: From Yalta to the Bay of Pigs* (New Haven: Yale University Press, 1996), pp. 96, 254n3. Warner to Dulles ("special briefing"), 12-6-57, CREST. Pedlow and Welzenbach, *CIA and the U-2 Program,* pp. 39–45, 108.

7. Bissell, *Reflections of a Cold Warrior,* pp. 130–31.

8. J. Eisenhower memo, 2-12-59, and Goodpaster memo, 4-7-59 meeting, both OSS/Subject/Alpha, Box 15, DDE Library. Goodpaster memo, 10-30-59, DDE Library website, www:eisenhower.utexas.edu.

9. Beschloss, *May-Day,* pp. 216–17. "Gen. Power's testimony," 3-31-60, CREST. Pedlow and Welzenbach, *CIA and the U-2 Program,* pp. 167–73.

10. Whitman Diary, 5-5-60, DDE Library. Beschloss, *May-Day,* pp. 43–44, 48–49. Pedlow and Welzenbach, *CIA and the U-2 Program,* p. 176. Andrew, *President's Eyes,* pp. 244–46. Wise and Ross, *U-2 Affair,* p. 29.

POURING OIL ON FIRE

1. Beschloss, *May-Day,* pp. 39–54.

2. *CR,* 5-5-60, pp. 9493–94.

3. *CR,* 5-6-60, p. 9716. *Post,* 5-6-60, p. A1. *Times,* 5-6-60, p. 7, 5-8-60, p. 30. "Memorandum . . . Senator Saltonstall," 5-6-60, CREST. *CQ Weekly,* 5-13-60, p. 859.

4. George Kistiakowsky, *Scientist at the White House* (Cambridge: Harvard University Press, 1976), pp. 318–19.

5. Beschloss, *May-Day,* pp. 234, 242–52. *Times,* 5-6-60, p. 9.

6. *CR,* 5-9-60, p. A3941, 5-11-60, p. A4046. Andrew, *President's Eyes,* p. 246. *Times,* 5-8-60, p. 1.

7. *Post,* 5-8-60, pp. A1, A4. Eisenhower, *Waging Peace,* pp. 549–50. "That lie": Wise, *Politics of Lying,* p. 35.

8. *CR,* 5-9-60, pp. 9803–5, A3961–62. *Times,* 5-9-60, p. 1.

9. Thompson to State Department, 5-9-60, *FRUS: Eastern Europe, 1955–1957, Soviet Union,* vol. 10, pp. 519–21. E. McCabe to A. Whitman (Case), Whitman File, DDE diary, Box 5, and Whitman Diary, both 5-9-60, DDE Library.

10. J. F. terHorst and Ralph Albertazzie, *The Flying White House: The Story of Air*

Force One (New York: Coward, McCann, and Geoghegan, 1979), pp. 194–98. Beschloss's *May-Day* (pp. 228–29) claims that Eisenhower knew something of Project Lida Rose. It was later abandoned.

11. *Times*, 5-9-60, p. 1. Staffer to Bridges (Amory), 1-8-60, Box 075164, Bridges Papers.

12. *CR*, 5-9-60, pp. 9779–87, A3941. "Briefing of Congressional Leadership . . . 9 May 1960," Dulles FOIA Papers. Beschloss, *May-Day*, p. 255. Grose, *Gentleman Spy*, pp. 486–87. Brugioni, *Eyeball to Eyeball*, p. 32. Gray, notes of 5-16-60 OCB meeting, OSS/Sp. Asst./ Pres., Box 5, DDE Library. Prados, *Keepers*, pp. 77–79. Wise and Ross, *U-2 Affair*, pp. 115–16. *Post*, 5-11-60, pp. A8, A13. Lippmann, reprinted in *CR*, 5-12-60, p. 10113. *CQ Weekly*, 5-13-60, pp. 859–60.

13. Saltonstall, 5-10-60, Box 155, Saltonstall Papers. *CR*, 5-9-60, pp. 9779–87, 9809–12, 9900–9901, A4021, 5-11-60, p. 9968. Memo, Kilday-Dulles telephone conversation, 5-10-60, CREST. *Post*, 5-10-60, p. A1. *Times*, 5-10 and 5-11-60, p. 1.

14. Rayburn: Pforzheimer to DD/I, 1-10-55, CREST; also, Harlow, memo for record, 5-10-60, WHO/OSS/Subject, Box 1, DDE Library; also D. B. Hardeman and Donald Bacon, *Rayburn: A Biography* (Austin: Texas Monthly Press, 1987), pp. 290–91. Frederic Cowart, "Mahon and Manhattan: Sharing the Secret," unpublished article (with Mahon's memo attached), Reference File, Mahon Papers. Wanda Evans, *One Honest Man: George Mahon* (Canyon, TX: Staked Plains Press, 1978), p. 5.

15. *Post*, 5-11-60, p. A11, and 5-12-60, p. A19. *Times*, 3-9-57, p. 10.

"THEIR ANSWER TO THAT DEMAND": CONGRESSIONAL PATERNITY?

1. Paul Healy, *Saturday Evening Post*, 3-25-50, pp. 38–39, 133, 137. *Political Profiles: The Truman Years*, vol. 1 (New York: Facts on File, 1978), pp. 80–81. Memo, Mahon-Dulles telephone conversation, 3-24-60, CREST. White to Dulles (compensation plan), 9-19-60, CREST. The aide told the CIA's Red White that "there was no possibility of accomplishing this prior to January 1961."

2. *CR*, 5-10-60, pp. 9854–55. *Post*, 5-11-60, p. A1. *Times*, 5-11-60, p. 1. World War II leak: Andrew, *President's Eyes*, p. 138.

3. *Post*, 5-11-60, p. A11.

4. G. Koski to Cannon, 5-11-60, Folder 3010, Dulles to Cannon, 5-16-60, Folder 599, Cannon Papers. Saltonstall to J. Lawrence, 5-10-60, Box 153, Saltonstall Papers. Jones to Dulles, 5-12-60, Folder 3338, Jones Papers. Pearson, *Post*, 5-11-60, p. D13.

5. DDE to Cannon, 5-12-60, Folder 3111, Cannon Papers. Goodpaster, memos for record, 7-19-56 and 11-5-56, quoted in Pedlow and Welzenbach, *CIA and the U-2 Program*, pp. 110, 124. J. Eisenhower, memo for record, 2-12-59, OSS/Subject/Alpha, Box 15, DDE Library.

6. *Public Papers of the Presidents, 1960*, pp. 403–9, 414–15. *Post*, 5-12-60, pp. A1, A19, A26. *Times*, 5-12-60, p. 1. Beschloss, *May-Day*, pp. 240, 252. *CR*, 5-12-60, p. 10114 (*Times* editorial), and p. 10214 ("ashes").

7. Pforzheimer, author interview. Hanrahan, *Soldier,* pp. 29–41. Beschloss, *May-Day,* p. 129. David Wise and Thomas Ross, *The Invisible Government* (New York: Random House, 1964), p. 266.

8. Kirkpatrick, *Real CIA,* p. 269. Cabell, *Man of Intelligence,* p. 344. Hearst story, 5-12-60, Folder 3011, Cannon Papers. Untitled, undated, Agency 1960 appearances list, CREST.

9. Pedlow and Welzenbach, *CIA and the U-2 Program,* pp. 29–34. Beschloss, *May-Day,* pp. 81–84. Dulles memo (Cannon), 5-17-60, Dulles FOIA Papers.

"MY OPINION OF THE CIA WENT SKYROCKETING"

1. An unsigned December 1960 memo, "Congressional Action Relating to a Joint Committee" says "Vinson was disturbed that the Kilday Subcommittee had not been briefed on this project." See also Kilday-Dulles, 5-10-60, and Warner to Dulles, 12-6-57 (Vinson/Arends briefing), all CREST. Kilday to Johnson, 9-26-60, Box 2E420, Kilday Papers.

2. *CR,* 5-16-60, p. 10344. Beschloss, *May-Day,* pp. 283–84.

3. *Times,* 5-17-60, p. 1. *CR,* 5-16-60, pp. 10312–14, 5-18-60, p. 10497. Beschloss, *May-Day,* pp. 284–90, 300. Goodpaster, memo of 5-15-60 meeting, and unsigned memo for record ("bombs"), 5-15-60, *FRUS: National Security Policy, 1958–1960,* vol. 9, pp. 423, 425. Kent, "Conversation with Livingston Merchant," 10-18-71, Box 9, CIA/HSC, and "The Summit Conference of 1960: An Intelligence Officer's View," *Studies in Intelligence,* Special Edition, 1972, available at www.cia.gov/csi/. *Times* editorial quoted in *Time* magazine, 5-23-60, p. 35.

4. Beschloss, *May-Day,* p. 304. *CR,* 5-17-60, pp. 10392–93, 5-18-60, p. 10627, 5-24-60 (Young), p. 10886.

5. Goodpaster, "Memo of Conference," 5-20-60, WHO/OSS, DDE Library.

6. *CR,* 5-23-60, pp. 10756–10852, 5-24-60, p. 10886. Carroll voices his suspicion on p. 10813. LBJ: Theodore White, *The Making of the President, 1960* (New York: Atheneum, 1961), pp. 143–48. *Public Papers of the Presidents: Eisenhower,* pp. 435–45. *Times,* 5-24-60, p. 1. *Post,* 5-24-60, p. A1, 5-25-60, pp. A1, A22.

7. *Post,* 6-1-60, pp. 11527–30. *Time,* 6-13-60, pp. 22–23. White, *Making of the President,* pp. 143–48.

8. *Post,* 5-25-60, p. A1. *Times,* 5-25-60, p. 1. Gray, Memo, meeting with President, 5-24-60, DDE Library.

9. *Post,* 5-26-60, p. B8. Goodpaster, memo of conference with President, 3-11-60, OSS/Subject/Alpha, Box 3, J. Lay, memo for NSC Planning Board, 5-24-60, DDE Library. Memo of NSC Meeting, 5-24-60, *FRUS: Eastern Europe, 1955–1957, Soviet Union,* vol. 10, pp. 522–28. *CR,* 5-24-60, p. 10822. "Senate Foreign Relations," undated, Dulles FOIA Papers.

10. Houston to Dulles (regarding House committee), 5-25-60, CREST. "House Foreign Affairs Committee," undated, Dulles FOIA Papers. Hagerty, "Memo of conversation, Bipartisan leaders," 5-26-60, Whitman File, DDE diary, Box 50, DDE Library.

Haynes Johnson and Bernard Gwertzman, *Fulbright the Dissenter* (New York: Double-day, 1968), pp. 7, 157.

11. "Appearances before congressional committees," Feldman File, WH staff, Box 5, JFK Library. DD/S diary, 5-26-60 and 5-27-60, CREST. Appropriations staffers were to visit a CIA site as a result of the hearing. Mahon to J. Frazier, 5-13-60, CIA file, 1960, Mahon Papers. *CR*, 5-24-60 (Ford), pp. 11015–16.

12. *Times*, 5-28-60, pp. 1–3. *Time*, 5-30-60, p. 10. Helms to Dulles, 5-28-60, Dulles FOIA Papers.

13. U.S. Senate, *Executive Sessions*, vol. 12, pp. 279–359. Edited Dulles presentation drafts, OSS/Subject/Alpha, Box 25; L. A. Minnich, "Minutes of Cabinet Meeting," 5-26-60, Whitman File, DDE Diary Series, Box 50; both DDE Library. *Newsweek*, 6-6-60, pp. 30–31. BeLieu to Johnson, 7-27-60, Famous Names: A. Dulles, Box 3, LBJ Library. Wise and Ross, *U-2 Affair*, pp. 171–72.

14. *Times*, 6-1-60, p. 1. Gray, conversation with J. Hoghland, 6-21-60, WHO/SANSA/NSC, Box 18, DDE Library. House Committee on Foreign Affairs hearing transcript, 6-1-60, Dulles FOIA Papers.

15. U.S. Senate, Committee on Foreign Relations, *Events Relating to the Summit Conference* (Washington, DC: GPO, 1960). *Times*, 6-26-60, pp. 1, 13.

16. *CR*, 6-28-60, pp. 14733–38, 6-1-60 (Wiley), pp. 11522–24, 7-1-60, pp. 15336–48.

17. *Times*, 6-26-60, p. 1, 6-1-60, p. 1, 7-2-60, p. 1. *CR*, 5-23-60 (letters), p. 10794, 5-25-60 (Wiley/satellites), p. 11026, 7-2-60 (Lausche), p. 15657. *Post*, 6-1-60, p. A8. Gallup, *Gallup Poll*, vol. 3, p. 1672. Dulles (letters), 5-23-60, DD/S diary, CREST.

18. *Philadelphia Inquirer*, 5-25-60, p. 1 (Russell). Russell to Fulbright, 7-18-60, and Russell-Engle, 5-18-60, Box 495, SAS. Cabell, *Man of Intelligence*, p. 344. Conceivably, Cabell misidentified the Foreign Relations hearing as Armed Services. No August hearing before Russell's subcommittee is listed in available documents, but they are typically incomplete. Calendar entry, 8-30-60, Box 347, Saltonstall Papers. Hayden to J. Mulcahey, 6-10-60, Box 379, Hayden Papers.

19. CIA, memo of conversation (Church), 8-30-60, CREST. Walter to Dulles, 9-2-60, and Dulles to Walter, 9-9-60, Subject Files, Box 12; Dulles-Walter correspondence, 1-8-58 and 3-4-58, Chairman's correspondence, Box 8, all HUAC Papers. Memo of Dulles-Walter conversation, 9-2-60, CREST.

20. *CQ Weekly*, 6-3-60, p. 979. Dulles to Gray, 6-3-60, SANSA/NSC/Briefing, Box 4, DDE Library. *Times*, 5-27-60, p. 4. *CR*, 5-26-60 (Symington), p. 11226, 6-1-60 (Goldwater), p. 11529. *CR*'s index misses most May–June CIA commentary. *American*, quoted in *Time*, 5-23-60, p. 34. Houston to J. McCone, 2-7-63, Box 30, CIA/DRM. Dulles to Symington, 5-16-60, Series I, Box 54, Dulles Papers. *Newsweek*, 5-16-60, p. 30. Twining: Beschloss, *May-Day*, p. 260. *Aviation Week*, 5-16-60, p. 21.

CASTRO: "THIS FELLOW IS BAD AND OUGHT TO GO"

1. *Newsweek*, 4-27-59, p. 35. *Post*, 4-16-59, pp. A1, A12. *Time*, 4-27-59, pp. 9, 27.
2. Kirkpatrick, *Real CIA*, chap. 7. *FRUS: Cuba, 1958–1960*, p. 90.

3. *FRUS: Cuba, 1958–1960,* pp. 286 (Ellender), 311 (Eisenhower).

4. U.S. Senate, *Executive Sessions,* 1-26-59, pp. 124–26. Hays, 1-21-59, quoted in *The Guardian* (UK), 3-1-00.

5. *Times,* 4-18-59, p. 1. Nixon-Castro: Peter Wyden, *Bay of Pigs: The Untold Story* (New York: Touchstone, 1979), pp. 27–28; Nixon, *Six Crises,* pp. 351–52. Nixon, memo of conversation with Castro, 4-25-59, obtained from www.gwu.edu/~nsarchiv/.

6. *Times,* 4-18-59, p. 1. *Post,* 4-17-59, p. A1, 4-18-59, p. A10.

7. *Post,* 4-16-59, p. A2, 4-18-59, p. A10. Smathers, oral history interview, U.S. Senate Historical Office. Brian Crispell, *Testing the Limits: George Armistead Smathers and Cold War America* (Athens: University of Georgia Press, 1999), pp. 153, 191. *Time,* 4-27-59, p. 27. Raul Castro: Aleksandr Fursenko and Timothy Naftali, *"One Hell of a Gamble": Khrushchev, Castro, and Kennedy, 1958–1964* (New York: Norton, 1997), p. 17.

8. Randall Woods, *J. William Fulbright, Vietnam, and the Search for a Cold War Foreign Policy* (New York: Cambridge University Press, 1998), p. 26. *FRUS: Cuba, 1958–1960,* pp. 642–46.

9. Dulles, unpublished manuscript, Series II, Box 61, Dulles Papers.

10. Houston, "CIA subcommittees" (Bridges/Saltonstall), 5-26-58, and "Luncheon," 6-24-59, CREST.

11. U.S. Senate, *Executive Sessions,* 1-18-60, pp. 33, 37. *Public Papers of the Presidents: Eisenhower,* 1-26-60, pp. 134–36.

12. Harlow, memo for record, 3-4-60 (2-18-60 conversation), Whitman File, DDE Diary Series, Box 47, Goodpaster, memo of 3-17-60 meeting, OSS/Subject/Alpha, Box 15, both DDE Library.

13. *CR,* 2-25-60, pp. 3416–45, 3-2-60, p. A1813.

14. Gray, memo of 3-12-60 meeting with DDE, SANSA/Sp. Asst./Presidential, Box 4, DDE Library. *CR,* 3-18-60, pp. 5962–73.

15. *CR,* 6-18-60, pp. 13209–11, 6-24-60, pp. 14174–80. J. Hughes to Nixon, 5-27-60, Nixon pre-presidential, Box 582, NA (Pacific Region). *Philadelphia Inquirer,* 6-25-60, p. 1.

16. *CR,* 6-25-60, pp. 14340, 14381–93; Pforzheimer, diary, 2-15-50, CREST. Pearson, *Diaries,* p. 545. Cuba and sugar came up in a CIA subcommittee hearing that Bow attended. See Mahon, handwritten notes, 1-11-60, 1960 files, Mahon Papers.

17. *CR,* 6-30-60, pp. 15228–47.

18. *CR,* 8-9-60, p. 16053. Goodpaster, memo of conversation with President, 4-25-60, OSS/Subject/Alpha, Box 15, Gray, memoranda, meetings with President, 8-18-60 and 11-29-60, SANSA/Presidential, Box 5, all DDE Library.

19. *CR,* 8-31-60, pp. 18551–61.

20. *CR,* 2-25-60, p. 3452, 3-18-60, p. 5964, 5-2-60 (with 4-19-60 letter), p. 9111, 6-15-60, p. 12742, 6-16-60, p. 12940, 6-27-60, p. 14649, 8-29-60, p. 18160, 9-1-60, p. 18995. Dillon to DDE, 5-12-60, Whitman/Dulles-Herter, Box 13, DDE Library. Hayden to constituent, 6-10-60, Box 379, Hayden Papers. Constituent correspondence, 1960, Mahon Papers. Dulles would always deny that he informed the Democratic candidates about Cuba plans.

"WHAT IS THE RATIONALE BEHIND THAT?"

1. Gray, memo of meeting with President, 11-29-60, OSS/SANSA/Presidential, Box 5, DDE Library. Wyden, *Bay of Pigs*, p. 69. Kennedy's knowledge in 1959 and 1960 of CIA plans against Cuba were admitted by McGeorge Bundy to John McCone on 3-19-62. See untitled notes of McCone telephone conversations, CREST.

2. *FRUS: Cuba, 1961–1962*, p. 44. Grose, *Gentleman Spy*, p. 516. Dillon to Eisenhower (Smathers), 5-12-60, Whitman/Dulles-Herter, Box 13, DDE Library. Max Holland, "A Luce Connection: Senator Keating, William Pawley, and the Cuban Missile Crisis," *Journal of Cold War Studies* 1, no. 3 (1999): 159.

3. Crispell, *Testing*, pp. 149, 168. J. McCone–Dulles telephone conversation notes (Nixon-Smathers), 3-20-62, CREST.

4. Crispell, *Testing*, p. 140. Joan Blair and Clay Blair, *The Search for JFK* (New York: Berkley, 1976), pp. 523–25.

5. Saltonstall, 1961 calendar, and letter to constituent, 1-21-61, Box 51, Saltonstall Papers. *FRUS: Cuba, 1961–1962*, pp. 61–62, 108–12.

6. *Post*, 3-10-61, p. A1.

7. Warner, author interview.

8. Ibid. Kelly: *Times*, 3-10-61, p. 1, 3-5-61, p. 56, and 3-6-61, p. 22.

9. "Excerpts from verbatim transcript . . . CIA subcommittee of House Armed Services Committee," 3-10-61, Dulles FOIA Papers. Dulles, *The Craft of Intelligence* (New York: Harper and Row, 1963), p. 169. Smart's title had been committee clerk, but by 1961, with three other lawyers serving the committee, he was "chief counsel."

10. Russell: J. Warner, "Defense Posture Hearings," 4-6-61, CREST. Dulles to Cannon, 1-20-61, Folder 599, Cannon Papers. Powers, *Man Who Kept the Secrets*, p. 103.

11. Memo, Smathers-Dulles conversation, 1-24-61, CREST.

12. Smathers, oral history, JFK Library, and quoted in Church Committee, *Alleged Assassination Plots Involving Foreign Leaders* (New York: Norton, 1976), pp. 91, 123–24. Crispell, *Testing*, p. 168. Blair and Blair, *Search for JFK*, pp. 523–25. Andrew, *President's Eyes*, p. 263. Thomas Reeves, *A Question of Character: A Life of John F. Kennedy* (New York: Free Press, 1991), p. 262. Seymour Hersh, *The Dark Side of Camelot* (Boston: Little, Brown, 1997), p. 200. Possible assassination attempts against Castro (and responsibility for them) remain shrouded, as "plausible deniability" intended. Hersh charges Kennedy with culpability for them. Christopher Matthews, *Kennedy and Nixon* (New York: Simon and Schuster, 1996), p. 57. Smathers publicly defended the Cuban intervention afterwards: *CR*, 4-18-61, pp. 6064–65. Warner, "Defense Posture Hearings" ("irrefutable"), 4-6-61, CREST.

13. *FRUS: Cuba, 1961–1962*, p. 25 (DDE/Fulbright committee).

14. Fulbright: Wyden, *Bay of Pigs*, pp. 122–23, 146–51. *FRUS: Cuba, 1961–1962*, pp. 85 (military intervention pressure), 185 (Fulbright attendance), 196–202 (Schlesinger memo), 210–12 (Congress).

"I AGREE THAT YOU HAD TO REPLACE DULLES"

1. Wyden, *Bay of Pigs*, p. 269. Crispell, *Testing*, p. 170–71. *Times*, 4-21-61, p. 4.

2. *CR*, 4-25-61, pp. 6648–77. *Post*, 4-26-61, p. A14, and 5-5-61 (Gallup), p. A15.

3. *CR*, 4-24-61 (Morse), pp. 6566–96. *Post*, 4-27-61, p. A11.

4. Fursenko and Naftali, *"One Hell of a Gamble,"* pp. 99–100.

5. Taylor Cuba Study Group to JFK, 6-13-61, *FRUS: Cuba, 1961–1962*, pp. 576–600. Kirkpatrick report, downloaded from website www.gwu.edu/~nsarchiv/.

6. *Times*, 5-2-61, p. 1. Foreign Relations hearing excerpts, 5-2-61, Dulles FOIA Papers.

7. *Post*, 5-3-61, p. A19. *Times*, 5-3-61, p. 1; 6-5-61, p. 3. Lippmann, reprinted in *CR*, 5-3-61, pp. 7111–12.

8. Correspondence and press clippings about hearing, Box 9S/10, Kilday Papers. Memo, 4-24-61, scheduled briefing of Kilday, and DD/S diary, 6-11-61 and 7-17-61, all CREST.

9. Mahon to constituent, 6-8-61, Mahon to Kennedy, 4-27-61 and 4-28-61, all 1961 files, Mahon Papers. DD/S diary, 5-12-61, CREST.

10. Bridges to Louis Johnson, Box 080151, Bridges Papers. *Times*, 1-29-61, p. 1. Hayden to constituent, 5-22-61, Box 399, Hayden Papers. Hayden's, Kilday's and Bridges's surviving papers include dozens of angry constituent letters. Russell-Gore, 5-5-61 and 5-8-61, Armed Services Correspondence, IX, Legislation, Box 130, Russell Library. JFK-Dulles: name change, *FRUS: Cuba, 1961–1962*, p. 526.

11. Russell-Kennedy transcript, 11-9-61, Special Pres. File, 1941–1967, Russell Library. Russell to Kennedy and Johnson, 4-24-61, VP Security, Box 4, LBJ Library. Cannon to Dulles, 10-16-61, Folder 599, Cannon Papers. Cannon and colleagues to Kennedy, 5-15-61, Box 93, Dulles Papers. Mahon to Dulles, 11-11-61, 1961 files, Mahon Papers.

12. *Times*, 5-9-61, p. 38. Undated note ("Mr. M"), 1961 files, Mahon Papers.

13. *CR*, 4-27-61, pp. 6799–6800. *Times*, 5-3-61, p. 1; 5-4-61, p. 11; 5-9-61, p. 38. *Post*, 4-25-61, p. A8. R. Hilsman memo, 7-10-61, Hilsman Papers, Box 7; Clifford to Kennedy, 10-25-61, Pres. Office Files, Box 72; both JFK Library.

14. *Times* Index, 1961. *Post*, 4-20-61 (Pearson), p. B15; 4-24-61 (Alsop), p. A15; 4-26-61 (Roberts), p. A12. Smathers, oral history, JFK Library.

15. Taylor to JFK, 6-23-61, *FRUS: Cuba, 1961–1962*, pp. 612–14. *CR*, 7-12-61, p. 12320. DD/S diary, 7-17-61, CREST. *Army Times* story, related memos, 12-12-61, Folder 3321, Symington Papers.

AFTERWORD: ALARMS

1. A whole subfield of political science is devoted to the development of American political practices, laws, and institutions. See Karen Orren and Stephen Skowronek, *The Search for American Political Development* (New York: Cambridge University Press, 2004). House: Polsby, *Congress and the Presidency*, p. 49.

2. Matthew McCubbins and Thomas Schwartz, "Congressional Oversight Over-

looked: Police Patrols versus Fire Alarms," *American Journal of Political Science* 28 (1984): 165–79.

3. Grose's *Operation Rollback* is an exception. See pp. 202–4, 208, 212.

4. One example from a multitude: "The Spy Agency That Lost $2 Billion," *Times*, 2-1-96, p. A20, which criticized the Senate intelligence committee's "failure to detect gross mismanagement" at the National Reconnaissance Office. The "need for just such essential work was a primary reason the Senate and House established intelligence committees two decades ago." In 2004, the September 11th Commission would conclude that "the unglamorous but essential work of oversight has been neglected."

Selected Bibliography

NOTE ON SOURCES

I have often felt frustrated by government policies that withhold early CIA budgets and innumerable other Cold War–era documents from public inspection and dismayed that certain congressional leaders did not ensure the survival of their own records. Still, I have relished taking on this project's research challenges.

The bibliography lists every archive that I (or, on a couple of occasions, an assistant) visited in the creation of this book. Of those holding papers of deceased Congress members, the collections with the most on the CIA were those of George Mahon, John Taber, Stuart Symington, and Styles Bridges. Even at those archives, the research process was akin to searching for needles in haystacks. Somewhat less useful were the papers of Richard Russell, Leverett Saltonstall, Millard Tydings, Paul Kilday, Charles Kersten, and Mike Mansfield. A few other collections were of very minimal use, and the papers of Clarence Cannon, Francis Walter, and Les Arends were of no value for this project.

None of this is meant to reflect on the archives holding those papers. I feel tremendous gratitude to their archivists and other professionals. The generally poor quality of CIA materials results, I believe, from those legislators' choices about what to put (and not put) on paper and what to preserve.

Records of congressional committees are held at the National Archives in Washington, DC. However, there are essentially no records of the House Appropriations Committee that come from the time frame of this book. Records of the House Armed Services Committee have nothing on the CIA. On the Senate side, the Armed Services Committee (whose CIA subcommittee took on the responsibilities of Appropriations as well) retained records that are modestly useful. So did the House Committee on Un-American Activities and the Senate Permanent Subcommittee on Investigations.

The National Archives II in College Park, Maryland, has the Central Intelligence Agency's declassified records. The boxes of materials are substantial, though not abundant. No collection is devoted specifically to the agency's congressional relations. More helpful are records available under the CIA Records Search Tool (CREST), by which researchers access documents at a computer terminal. There I obtained documents that included work diary entries by Walter Pforzheimer, L. K. White, and John Warner.

The Dwight D. Eisenhower and Harry S. Truman libraries were essential to my research. At the former, the work diaries of the president and his secretary, Ann Whitman, were valuable. So were the records of the Office of Staff Secretary (OSS) and Special Assistants for National Security Affairs (SANSA). The papers of Beetle Smith and legislative liaison Bryce Harlow are also there. "CIA Holdings at the Truman

Library" served as a valuable guide at that archive, as did an untitled list of collections relating to intelligence.

Among published collections of documents, the *Foreign Relations of the United States (FRUS)* volumes, compiled by the State Department's history office, are essential. So are the Senate Foreign Relations Committee's *Executive Sessions* series and the Congressional Information Service's microfiches of congressional hearings. Some of CIS's previously "unpublished" hearings seem never to have been used by scholars.

While the *Congressional Record* is imperfect since legislators could "edit" their remarks, it remains a valuable guide to congressional sentiment toward the CIA in its early years. I routinely checked major newspapers, especially the *New York Times* and the *Washington Post* (themselves, valuable resources) to get a second account of what occurred in congressional debates.

Regrettably, many a significant legislator has not been the subject of even one biography. A skillfully researched and written account of Styles Bridges's life and career would be a valuable and good read, for example. Some have been described in biographies that are deficient. Even in substantial biographies of legislators such as Richard Russell, Stuart Symington, and Mike Mansfield though, the CIA of 1947–1961 is hardly mentioned.

There are no full-scale biographies of Roscoe Hillenkoetter or Beetle Smith. Fortunately, CIA in-house histories of their directorships have been published. Allen Dulles's life and career is much better covered, in an unpublished CIA history (available at the National Archives) and, notably, in Peter Grose's *Gentleman Spy*, which pays some shrewd attention to Congress. Though most ignore Congress beyond its passage of the National Security Act and the CIA Act, there are many good histories of the agency's early days.

I plan to donate my collection of documents to the Richard Russell Library at the University of Georgia after completing further writings about the agency and Congress. An in-house CIA historian suggested to me that my documents are probably better than those that the agency itself has kept regarding its early legislative relations. I hope not.

BOOKS, ARTICLES, AND PUBLISHED DOCUMENTS

Adams, Sherman. *Firsthand Report: The Story of the Eisenhower Administration.* New York: Harper and Brothers, 1961.

Aldrich, Richard J. *The Hidden Hand: Britain, America, and Cold War Secret Intelligence.* New York: Overlook Press, 2002.

Alsop, Joseph, and Stewart Alsop. *The Reporter's Trade.* New York: Reynal, 1958.

Ambrose, Stephen. *Nixon: The Education of a Politician, 1913–1962.* New York: Simon and Schuster, 1987.

Andrew, Christopher M. *For the President's Eyes Only: Secret Intelligence and the American Presidency from Washington to Bush.* New York: Harper Collins, 1995.

Bagdikian, Ben. "Unsecretive Report on the CIA." *New York Times Magazine,* October 27, 1963.

Baker, Russell James. *The Good Times.* New York: Morrow, 1989.

Beschloss, Michael, R. *May-Day: Eisenhower, Khrushchev, and the U-2 Affair.* New York: Harper and Row, 1986.

Bird, Kai. *The Chairman: John J. McCloy, The Making of the American Establishment.* New York: Simon and Schuster, 1992.

———. *The Color of Truth: McGeorge Bundy and William Bundy, Brothers in Arms.* New York: Simon and Schuster, 1998.

Bottome, Edgar. *The Missile Gap: A Study of the Formulation of Military and Political Policy.* Rutherford, NJ: Fairleigh Dickinson University Press, 1971.

Brugioni, Dino A. *Eyeball to Eyeball: The Inside Story of the Cuban Missile Crisis.* Edited by Robert F. McCort. New York: Random House, 1991.

Byrne, Malcolm. *Uprising in East Germany 1953.* Budapest, Hungary: Central European University Press, 2001.

Cabell, Charles P. *A Man of Intelligence.* Colorado Springs: Impavide, 1997.

Chandler, Alfred D., Stephen E. Ambrose, et al., eds. *The Papers of Dwight David Eisenhower.* Baltimore: Johns Hopkins University Press, 1970–2001.

CIA History Staff. *Planning and Construction of the Agency Headquarters Building.* 1973. CIA Records Search Tool (CREST).

Cohn, Roy. *McCarthy.* New York: New American Library, 1968.

Congressional Information Service. *CIS Unpublished U.S. House of Representatives Hearings on Microfiche.* Washington, DC: CIS.

———. *CIS Unpublished U.S. Senate Committee Hearings on Microfiche.* Washington, DC: CIS.

Congressional Quarterly Almanac, 1947–1961.

Congressional Record, 79th Congress–87th Congress, 1946–1961.

Cook, James F. *Carl Vinson: Patriarch of the Armed Forces.* Macon, GA: Mercer University Press, 2004.

Crispell, Brian. *Testing the Limits: George Armistead Smathers and Cold War America.* Athens: University of Georgia Press, 1999.

Cullather, Nick. *Secret History: The CIA's Account of Its Operation in Guatemala, 1952–1954.* Stanford: Stanford University Press, 1999.

Cummings, Bruce. *The Origins of the Korean War, Volume II: The Roaring of the Cataract, 1947–1950.* Princeton: Princeton University Press, 1990.

Cutler, Robert. *No Time for Rest.* Boston: Little, Brown, 1966.

Dalai Lama. *Freedom in Exile: The Autobiography of the Dalai Lama.* San Francisco: Harper Perennial, 1991.

Darling, Arthur. *Central Intelligence Agency: An Instrument of Government, to 1950.* University Park: Pennsylvania State University Press, 1990.

Dirksen, Everett. *The Education of a Senator.* Urbana: University of Illinois Press, 1998.

Divine, Robert. *The Sputnik Challenge.* New York: Oxford University Press, 1993.

Dulles, Allen. *The Craft of Intelligence.* New York: Harper and Row, 1963.
Edwards, Philip K. "The President's Board: 1956–60." *Studies in Intelligence* 13 (Summer 1969): 113–28.
Eisenhower, Dwight D. *Mandate for Change, 1953–1956: The White House Years.* Garden City, NY: Doubleday, 1963.
———. *Waging Peace: The White House Years, 1956–1961.* Garden City, NY: Doubleday, 1965.
Evans, Wanda. *One Honest Man: George Mahon.* Canyon, TX: Staked Plains Press, 1978.
Ewald, William. *Who Killed Joe McCarthy?* New York: Simon and Schuster, 1984.
Fenno, Richard. *The Power of the Purse: Appropriations Politics in Congress.* Boston: Little, Brown, 1966.
Ferrell, Robert H., ed. *The Eisenhower Diaries.* New York: Norton, 1981.
Fite, Gilbert. *Richard B. Russell, Senator from Georgia.* Chapel Hill: University of North Carolina Press, 1991.
Fursenko, Aleksandr, and Timothy Naftali. *"One Hell of a Gamble": Khrushchev, Castro, and Kennedy, 1958–1964.* New York: Norton, 1997.
Galambos, Louis, and Daun Van Ee, eds. *The Papers of Dwight D. Eisenhower.* Baltimore: Johns Hopkins University Press, 1996.
Galloway, George, and Sidney Wise. *History of the House of Representatives.* 2nd ed. New York: Crowell, 1976.
Gallup, George. *The Gallup Poll: Public Opinion, 1935–1971.* 3 vols. New York: Random House, 1972.
Griffith, Robert. *The Politics of Fear: Joseph R. McCarthy and the Senate.* 2nd ed. Amherst: University of Massachusetts Press, 1987.
Grose, Peter. *Gentleman Spy: The Life of Allen Dulles.* Boston: Houghton Mifflin, 1994.
———. *Operation Rollback: America's Secret War behind the Iron Curtain.* Boston: Houghton Mifflin, 2000.
Gunther, John. "Inside CIA." *Look,* August 1952.
Haines, Gerald. "CIA's Role in the Study of UFOs, 1947–1990." *Studies in Intelligence* (1977): 67–84.
Hanrahan, James. "Soldier, Manager, Leader: An Interview with Former CIA Executive Director Lawrence K. 'Red' White." *Studies in Intelligence* (Winter 1999–2000): 29–41.
Hardeman, D. B., and Donald Bacon. *Rayburn: A Biography.* Austin: Texas Monthly Press, 1987.
Harkness, Richard, and Gladys Harkness. "The Mysterious Doings of CIA," Pt. 1. *Saturday Evening Post,* October 30, 1954, pp. 19–21, 162, 165.
———. "The Mysterious Doings of CIA," Pt. 3. *Saturday Evening Post, November 13, 1954,* pp. 30, 132–34.
Healy, Paul. "Nobody Loves Clarence." *Saturday Evening Post,* March 25, 1950, pp. 38–39, 132–37.
Hersh, Burton. *The Old Boys: The American Elite and the Origins of the CIA.* New York: Scribner's, 1992.
Hersh, Seymour. *The Dark Side of Camelot.* Boston: Little, Brown, 1997.

Holland, Max. "A Luce Connection: Senator Keating, William Pawley, and the Cuban Missile Crisis." *Journal of Cold War Studies* 1, no. 3 (1999): 139–67.

———. "Operation PBHISTORY: The Aftermath of SUCCESS." *International Journal of Intelligence and Counterintelligence* 17, no. 2 (Summer 2004): 300–332.

Horn, Stephen. *Unused Power: The Work of the Senate Committee on Appropriations.* Washington, DC: Brookings, 1970.

Horst, J. F., and Ralph Albertazzie. *The Flying White House: The Story of Air Force One.* New York: Coward, McCann, and Geoghegan, 1979.

Immerman, Richard. *The CIA in Guatemala: The Foreign Policy of Intervention.* Austin: University of Texas Press, 1982.

Inspector General's Survey of the Cuban Operation, (The Kirkpatrick Report). Downloaded from www.gwu.edu/~nsarchiv/ (accessed February 2, 2005).

Jackson, Wayne. *Allen Dulles as Director of Central Intelligence.* Unpublished manuscript at National Archives, 1973.

Johnson, Haynes, and Bernard Gwertzman. *Fulbright the Dissenter.* New York: Doubleday, 1968.

Johnson, Loch. *Secret Agencies: U.S. Intelligence in a Hostile World.* New Haven: Yale University Press, 1996.

Keith, Caroline H. *"For Hell and a Brown Mule": The Biography of Senator Millard E. Tydings.* Lanham, MD: Madison Books, 1991.

Kirkpatrick, Lyman. *The Real CIA.* New York: MacMillan, 1968.

Kistiakowsky, George. *Scientist at the White House.* Cambridge: Harvard University Press, 1976.

Knaus, John K. *Orphans of the Cold War: America and the Tibetan Struggle for Survival.* New York: Public Affairs, 1999.

Leary, William, ed. *The Central Intelligence Agency: History and Documents.* Tuscaloosa: University of Alabama Press, 1984.

Lilienthal, David E. *The Atomic Energy Years, 1945–1950. Vol. 2 of The Journals of David E. Lilienthal.* New York: Harper and Row, 1964.

———. *Venturesome Years, 1950–1955. Vol. 3 of The Journals of David E. Lilienthal.* New York: Harper and Row, 1964.

Livingston, Jeffery C. *Ohio Congressman John L. Vorys.* Ph.D. diss. Ann Arbor: University Microfilms, 1989.

Lodge, Henry Cabot, Jr. *The Storm Has Many Eyes: A Personal Narrative.* New York: Norton, 1973.

Logue, Calvin, and Dwight Freshley, eds. *Voice of Georgia: Speeches of Richard B. Russell, 1928–1969.* Macon, GA: Mercer University Press, 1997.

Marchetti, Victor, and John Marks. *The CIA and the Cult of Intelligence.* New York: Knopf, 1974.

Martin, Joseph. *My First Fifty Years in Politics.* New York: McGraw-Hill, 1960.

Matthews, Donald. *U.S. Senators and Their World.* Chapel Hill: University of North Carolina Press, 1960.

McFarland, Linda. *Stuart Symington and the Search for National Security.* Westport, CT: Praeger, 2001.

McPherson, Harry. *A Political Education*. Boston: Little, Brown, 1974.

Merry, Robert W. *Taking on the World: Joseph and Stewart Alsop, Guardians of the American Century*. New York: Viking, 1996.

Miller, Neil. *Out of the Past: Gay and Lesbian History from 1869 to the Present*. New York: Vintage Books, 1995.

Montague, Ludwell L. *General Walter Bedell Smith as Director of Central Intelligence*. University Park: Pennsylvania State University Press, 1992.

Mosher, Frederick. *The GAO: The Quest for Accountability in American Government*. Boulder: Westview Press, 1979.

Mosley, Leonard. *Dulles: A Biography of Eleanor, Allen, and John Foster Dulles and Their Family Network*. New York: Dial Press, 1978.

Nixon, Richard. *RN: The Memoirs of Richard Nixon*. New York: Grosset and Dunlap, 1978.

———. *Six Crises*. Garden City, NY: Doubleday, 1962.

Oberdorfer, Don. *Senator Mansfield: The Extraordinary Life of a Great American Statesman and Diplomat*. Washington, DC: Smithsonian Books, 2003.

Oshinsky, David M. *A Conspiracy So Immense: The World of Joe McCarthy*. New York: Free Press, 1983.

Peabody, Robert, and Nelson Polsby. *New Perspectives on the House of Representatives*. Chicago: Rand McNally, 1963.

Pearson, Drew. *Diaries: 1949–1959*. Edited by Tyler Abell. New York: Holt, Rinehart, and Winston, 1974.

Pedlow, Gregory, and Donald Welzenbach. *The CIA and the U-2 Program, 1954–1974*. Washington, DC: Center for the Study of Intelligence, 1998.

Philby, Kim. *My Silent War*. New York: Grove Press, 1968.

Pois, Joseph. *Watchdog on the Potomac: A Study of the Comptroller General of the United States*. Washington, DC: University Press of America, 1979.

Polsby, Nelson. *Congress and the Presidency*. Englewood Cliffs, NJ: Prentice-Hall, 1964.

———. *How Congress Evolves: Social Bases of Institutional Change*. New York: Oxford University Press, 2004.

Powers, Thomas. *The Man Who Kept the Secrets: Richard Helms and the CIA*. New York: Knopf, 1979.

Prados, John. *Keepers of the Keys: A History of the National Security Council from Truman to Bush*. New York: Morrow, 1991.

———. *The Soviet Estimate: U.S. Intelligence Analysis and Russian Military Strength*. New York: Dial Press, 1982.

Public Papers of the Presidents: Harry S. Truman, Dwight D. Eisenhower, and John F. Kennedy. Washington, DC: GPO, 1947–1961.

Ranelagh, John. *The Agency: The Rise and Decline of the CIA*. New York: Simon and Schuster, 1986.

Ransom, Harry Howe. *Central Intelligence and National Security*. Cambridge: Harvard University Press, 1959.

Reedy, George. *The U.S. Senate*. New York: Crown Publishers, 1986.

Reeves, Thomas C. *The Life and Times of Joe McCarthy*. Lanham, MD: Madison Books, 1997.

————. *A Question of Character: A Life of John F. Kennedy*. New York: Free Press, 1991.

Riedel, Richard L. *Halls of the Mighty: My 47 Years at the Senate*. Washington, DC: Robert B. Luce, 1969.

Rudgers, David F. *Creating the Secret State: The Origins of the Central Intelligence Agency*. Lawrence: University Press of Kansas, 2000.

Saltonstall, Leverett. *Salty: Recollections of a Yankee in Politics*. Boston: Boston Globe, 1976.

Schlesinger, Arthur. *Robert Kennedy and His Times*. Boston: Houghton Mifflin, 1978.

Schwartz, Stephen. *Atomic Audit: The Costs and Consequences of U.S. Nuclear Weapons since 1940*. Washington, DC: Brookings, 1998.

Steury, Donald P., ed. *Intentions and Capabilities: Estimates on Soviet Strategic Forces, 1950–1983*. Washington, DC: CIA, 1996.

Stromer, Marvin. *Kenneth S. Wherry and the U.S. Senate*. Lincoln: University of Nebraska Press, 1969.

Thomas, Evan. *The Very Best Men: Four Who Dared: The Early Years of the CIA*. New York: Simon and Schuster, 1995.

Troy, Thomas. *Donovan and the CIA: A History of the Establishment of the Central Intelligence Agency*. Frederick, MD: University Publications of America, 1981.

Truman, Harry S. *Memoirs, Vol. II: Years of Trial and Hope*. Garden City, NY: Doubleday, 1956.

U.S. Congress. Joint Committee on Atomic Energy. *Report of the Central Intelligence Agency*. Congressional Information Service: Microfiche, 1949.

U.S. Department of State. *Foreign Relations of the United States (hereafter FRUS). Berlin Crisis, 1959–1960*. Washington, DC: GPO, 1993.

————. *FRUS. Cuba, 1958–1960*. Washington, DC: GPO, 1991.

————. *FRUS. Cuba, 1961–1962*. Washington, DC: GPO, 1997.

————. *FRUS. Eastern Europe, 1955–1957*. Washington, DC: GPO, 1990.

————. *FRUS. Emergence of the Intelligence Establishment, 1945–1950*. Microfiche Supplement. Washington, DC: GPO, 1996.

————. *FRUS. Guatemala, 1952–54*. Washington, DC: GPO, 2003.

————. *FRUS. Korea, 1950*. Washington, DC: GPO, 1976.

————. *FRUS. Lebanon and Jordan, 1958–1960*. Washington, DC: GPO, 1992.

————. *FRUS. Memoranda of Conversations of the Secretary of State, 1947–1952*. Microfiche Supplement. Washington, DC: GPO, 1988.

————. *FRUS. National Security Affairs, 1949*. Washington, DC: GPO, 1976.

————. *FRUS. National Security Affairs, 1952–1954*. Washington, DC: GPO, 1984.

————. *FRUS. National Security Policy, 1955–1957*. Washington, DC: GPO, 1990.

————. *FRUS. National Security Policy, 1958–1960*. Washington, DC: GPO, 1996.

————. *FRUS. Near East Region, 1958–1960*. Washington, DC: GPO, 1993.

————. *FRUS. Secretary of State's Memoranda of Conversation, 1952–1954*. Microfiche Supplement. Washington, DC: GPO, 1992.

————. *FRUS. Suez Canal Crisis, 1956*. Washington, DC: GPO, 1990.

———. *FRUS. The Western Hemisphere, 1948.* Washington, DC: GPO, 1972.

U.S. House of Representatives. Committee on Un-American Activities. *Testimony of General Walter Bedell Smith.* Washington, DC: GPO, 1952.

———. *Selected Executive Session Hearings of the Committee on Foreign Affairs, 1951–1956,* vol. 14. Washington, DC: GPO, 1980.

U.S. Senate. Armed Services and Aeronautical and Space Science Committees. *Missiles, Space, and Other Major Defense Matters.* Washington, DC: GPO, 1960.

———. Committee on Foreign Relations. *Events Relating to the Summit.* Washington, DC: GPO, 1960.

———. Committee on Foreign Relations. *Foreign Relief Act: 1947.* Washington, DC: GPO, 1973.

———. *Executive Sessions of the Senate Permanent Subcommittee on Investigations of the Committee on Government Operations,* vol. 5. Washington, DC: GPO, 2003.

———. Select Committee to Study Governmental Operations with Respect to Intelligence Activities. *Interim Report: Alleged Assassination Plots Involving Foreign Leaders.* Washington, DC: GPO, 1975.

———. Select Committee to Study Governmental Operations with Respect to Intelligence Activities. *Covert Action.* Washington, DC: GPO, 1976.

———. Select Committee to Study Governmental Operations with Respect to Intelligence Activities. *Final Report.* Washington, DC: GPO, 1976.

Warner, Michael, ed. *The CIA under Harry Truman.* Washington, DC: Center for Study of Intelligence, 1994.

White, William S. *Citadel: The Story of the U.S. Senate.* New York: Harper, 1957.

———. *Home Place: The Story of the U.S. House of Representatives.* Boston: Houghton Mifflin, 1965.

———. *The Making of a Journalist.* Lexington: University Press of Kentucky, 1986.

White, Theodore. *The Making of the President, 1960.* New York: Atheneum, 1961.

Wiltz, John E. "The MacArthur Inquiry, 1951." In *Congress Investigates: A Documented History, 1792–1974,* vol. 5, edited by Arthur Schlesinger Jr. and Roger Bruns. New York: Chelsea House, 1975.

Wise, David. *The Politics of Lying: Government Deception, Secrecy, and Power.* New York: Random House, 1973.

Wise, David, and Thomas Ross. *The Invisible Government.* New York: Random House, 1964.

———. *The U-2 Affair.* New York: Random House, 1962.

Woods, Randall. *J. William Fulbright, Vietnam and the Search for a Cold War Foreign Policy.* New York: Cambridge University Press, 1998.

Wyden, Peter. *Bay of Pigs: The Untold Story.* New York: Touchstone, 1979.

ARCHIVAL MATERIALS

Allen Dulles Papers, Mudd Library, Princeton University
Allen Dulles Papers, obtained under the Freedom of Information Act

Bryce Harlow Papers, Dwight D. Eisenhower Library, Abilene, Kansas
Carl Hayden Papers, Hayden Library, Arizona State University
Central Intelligence Agency Records, National Archives, College Park, Maryland
Charles Kersten Papers, Raynor Memorial Libraries, Marquette University
Clarence Cannon Papers, Western Historical Manuscript Collection, University of Missouri–Columbia
Dewey Short Papers, Lyons Library, College of the Ozarks (Missouri)
Dwight D. Eisenhower Library, Abilene, Kansas
George Mahon Papers, Southwest Collection, Texas Tech University
H. Alexander Smith Papers, Mudd Library, Princeton University
Harry S. Truman Library, Independence, Missouri
John F. Kennedy Library, Boston, Massachusetts
John Foster Dulles Papers, Mudd Library, Princeton University
John Taber Papers, Kroch Library, Cornell University
Joseph O'Mahoney Papers, American Heritage Center, University of Wyoming
Les Arends Papers, Sheean Library, Illinois Wesleyan University
Les Whitten Papers and Francis Walter Papers, Linderman Library, Lehigh University
Leverett Saltonstall Papers, Massachusetts Historical Society
Lyndon B. Johnson Library, University of Texas at Austin
Mike Mansfield Papers, Mansfield Library, University of Montana–Missoula
Millard Tydings Papers, University of Maryland at College Park Libraries
Paul Jones Papers, Western Historical Manuscript Collection, University of Missouri–Columbia
Paul Kilday Papers, Center for American History, University of Texas at Austin
Richard B. Russell Papers, Richard B. Russell Library, University of Georgia
Richard Nixon Vice-Presidential Papers. National Archives–Pacific Southwest Region, Laguna Niguel, California
Stuart Symington Papers, Western Historical Manuscript Collection, University of Missouri–Columbia
Styles Bridges Papers, New Hampshire State Archives
United States Congress Records, National Archives, Washington, DC
Walter Bedell Smith Papers, Dwight D. Eisenhower Library, Abilene, Kansas

ORAL HISTORY INTERVIEWS CONDUCTED BY THE AUTHOR

Elias Demetracopoulos
John Warner
Samuel Halpern
Walter Pforzheimer
William Darden

Index

CPSIA information can be obtained
at www.ICGtesting.com
Printed in the USA
BVHW040040051221
623262BV00017B/269